PUBLIC TRANSPORTATION

Second Edition

GEORGE E. GRAY   LESTER A. HOEL

Editors

PRENTICE HALL, Englewood Cliffs, New Jersey 07632

Library of Congress Cataloging-in-Publication Data

Public transportation / editors, George E. Gray, Lester A. Hoel. —
2nd ed.

      p. cm.
Includes bibliographical references and index.
ISBN 0-13-726381-3
1. Urban transportation. 2. Local transit. 3. Transportation-
-Planning. I. Gray, George E. II. Hoel, Lester A.
HE305.P8 1992   91-2063
388.4—dc20   CIP

Editorial/production supervision: **BARBARA MARTTINE**
Cover designer: **LUNDGREN GRAPHICS, LTD.**
Manufacturing buyer: **SUSAN BRUNKE**
Prepress buyer: **MARY MCCARTNEY**
Acquisitions editor: **MICHAEL HAYS**

 ©1992, 1979 by Prentice-Hall, Inc.
A Simon & Schuster Company
Englewood Cliffs, New Jersey 07632

The publisher offers discounts on this book when ordered
in bulk quantities. For more information, write:

    Special Sales/College Marketing
    Prentice-Hall, Inc.
    College Technical and Reference Division
    Englewood Cliffs, New Jersey 07632

Printed in the United States of America

10 9 8 7 6 5 4 3

ISBN   0-13-726381-3

PRENTICE-HALL INTERNATIONAL (UK) LIMITED, *London*
PRENTICE-HALL OF AUSTRALIA PTY. LIMITED, *Sydney*
PRENTICE-HALL CANADA INC., *Toronto*
PRENTICE-HALL HISPANOAMERICANA, S.A., *Mexico*
PRENTICE-HALL OF INDIA PRIVATE LIMITED, *New Delhi*
PRENTICE-HALL OF JAPAN, INC., *Tokyo*
SIMON & SCHUSTER ASIA PTE. LTD., *Singapore*
EDITORA PRENTICE-HALL DO BRASIL, LTDA., *Rio de Janeiro*

This book is dedicated to the parents of
George and Benita Gray and of Lester and Unni Hoel

Mary T. and Sabin V.   Julie and Johannes
Mary and Les   Sonja and Rolf

CONTENTS

PREFACE

It has been over a decade since the first edition of *Public Transportation: Planning, Operations and Management* was published. The book was well received and has served as both a reference work for practitioners and a textbook for students. Public transportation is a dynamic subject with newly published material appearing frequently and issues constantly changing as they reflect new societal values and priorities. Accordingly, we have revised the book so that it will continue to serve practitioners and students into the twenty-first century, as the first edition did for readers through the 1980s. The reader should be aware that the book is basically oriented to the United States, although reference is made to public transportation in other areas of the world.

In revising the book the editors have endeavored to recognize new and emerging areas as well as to update and modernize continuing ones. Because of the book's broad coverage, the subtitle used in the first edition has been dropped. We use the term *Public Transportation* as defined in the *Urban Public Transportation Glossary* published by the Transportation Research Board (1989) to include both public transit service and paratransit services that are available to the general public. The glossary has been used as the standard reference for terminology and definitions for the book and is recommended as a supplemental resource for our readers.

The book is divided into seven parts, I: Historical Development, II: Systems and Technologies, III: Comparing Alternatives, IV: Planning, V: Management and Operations, VI: Policy Considerations, and VII: The Future. We have changed the format of the individual chapters to include examples and case studies that serve to illustrate major points and have added discussion questions and references to supplement classroom lectures.

Public transportation has played a major role in the development and viability of urban areas. Issues such as street and highway congestion, conservation of space and energy, air pollution, travel for the carless and disabled, and sources of funding assure it will remain a significant factor in our society. Its exact form and use and the extent of society's investment will depend on conditions at any given time and location. Planners, operators, managers, public officials, and concerned citizens must be informed about how public transportation can serve to meet their transportation needs as they enter a new century. We hope that this revision of *Public Transportation* will contribute to the need for knowledge and understanding of this vital component of modern society.

Many transportation issues have received renewed study since the first edition of this book, but most of them have not been a focus of consistent actual decision making because all levels of government tend to concentrate on short-term problems. As we view the future, the following questions call for more enduring attention:

- Should transportation reinforce existing life-styles, or should it encourage or force change in life-styles?
- How should land-use patterns be coordinated to enhance providing for needed mobility?
- Should we focus on short- or long-range solutions to transportation problems? Or can we do both?
- How should we pay for transit service? Who should pay—the user, the local taxpayer, or the national taxpayer? In what proportion?
- Who should make decisions relative to providing service? The federal, state, regional, or local government?
- How much mobility is necessary? We have a tremendous capacity in this country now—with about three seats available for our use at any particular moment—but is this capacity efficiently used? This leads to a similar question.
- How do we optimize air quality improvements, energy use, land use, and transportation modes to provide needed mobility at least cost?
- How do we coordinate services and transportation system management (TSM) elements to make them more effective and efficient?

The readers should keep these questions in mind as they progress through the book.

We wish to thank each contributor and his or her support staff for working closely with us to complete this book. They were both responsible and timely in submitting drafts and making revisions. The production of the book was under the direction of Benita Gray, who prepared camera-ready copy from computer disks submitted by authors. This process significantly reduced the total time required to produce a final product, and her efforts and dedication were essential to the book's completion. We wish to thank the staff at the Institute of Transportation Studies, University of California, Irvine, for its support of the project while one of the editors was a visitor on sabbatical leave from the University of Virginia. We also wish to thank the many organizations and individuals that furnished photographs and illustrations used in the book.

GEORGE E. GRAY

LESTER A. HOEL

THE EDITORS

GEORGE E. GRAY is Deputy Director of Planning and Public Transportation for District IV of the California Department of Transportation (Caltrans). He has 40 years experience in highways and public transportation with Caltrans, the private sector, and as an adviser on public transportation to the Kingdom of Saudi Arabia for the Office of the Secretary of Transportation, U.S. Department of Transportation. He was responsible for the Division of Mass Transportation in Caltrans from its inception to 1980. Gray, a registered professional engineer, has authored papers on various aspects of public transportation and developed training and educational programs in transportation, including the Bay Area Urban Transportation Institute. He is active in the APWA, ASCE, and TRB, where he has served on many committees. He holds a B.S.C.E. from Stanford University, an M.P.A. from California State University, San Diego, and an M.S. in transportation planning from the University of California, Davis. His present responsibilities include management of the Caltrain regional rail service between San Jose and San Francisco.

LESTER A. HOEL is Hamilton Professor of Civil Engineering, University of Virginia, and was Department Chair from 1974-1989. He taught at Carnegie–Mellon and San Diego State University, and was Principal Engineer with Wilbur Smith and Associates. He was a Fulbright Research Scholar and Visiting Professor at the Norwegian Institute of Technology. Hoel is a registered professional engineer and holds a B.C.E. from the City College of N.Y. (cum Laude), an M.C.E. from Polytechnic University of N.Y., and a D.Eng. from the University of California, Berkeley. His research interests include both highway and urban transportation systems. He is the author of over 100 publications in these fields and is co-author of the textbook *Traffic and Highway Engineering*. He has served on ASCE and TRB committees and task forces and on the TRB Executive Committee from 1982–1988, and as Chairman in 1986. Hoel is a recipient of the ASCE Huber Research Prize and Frank Master's Transportation Engineering Award, the TRB Pyke Johnson Award, and the HUF Stanley Gustafson Leadership Award. He was elected to the National Academy of Engineering in 1989.

THE CONTRIBUTORS

WAYNE BERMAN is with the Office of Traffic Operations, Federal Highway Administration, from which he provides technical assistance and training to state and local agencies on transportation system management (TSM), specializing in travel demand management. Berman has prepared numerous technical studies on the effectiveness of programs that make better use of the existing transportation system and has conducted research in various related areas, including the application of new technologies to transportation system management. He is active in the ITE and TRB. He holds a B.S.C.E. from the University of Pittsburgh and an M.S.C.E. from the University of Maryland.

CLIFFORD A. CHAMBERS is a principal with Crain & Associates, Inc., Menlo Park, California. As such, he specializes in transportation system management, paratransit, and strategic transit planning. Chambers founded one of the nation's first transportation management associations (TMA) and has conducted a series of statewide TMA workshops. He provides planning and research consulting services to an array of private and public sector clients, including Caltrans and the Metropolitan Transportation Commission. Chambers is active in the ACT. He holds a B.A. from the University of California, Los Angeles, and an M.C.P. from the University of California, Berkeley.

A. FRANK W. DAVIS, JR. is a professor of marketing, logistics, and transportation, College of Business Administration, University of Tennessee and formerly served as Associate Director of the Transportation Research Center. He has 20 years of experience in industry, teaching, and research and as a consultant to government agencies, including the U.S. Department of Transportation and the White House. Davis has authored numerous articles on transportation and marketing. He is active in the TRB and the American Marketing Association. He holds a B.S.M.E. (Virginia Polytechnic Institute), an M.B.A. (Brigham Young University), and a Ph.D. in transportation and logistics (Michigan State University).

ELIZABETH DEAKIN is an assistant professor of city and regional planning at the University of California, Berkeley. She has been a transportation researcher since the early 1970s and has taught graduate courses in transportation and land-use planning at Stanford University and the University of California, Berkeley. Deakin also has an active consulting practice specializing in transportation planning and policy. She has published numerous articles, papers, book chapters, and research reports and is the co-author of *Residential Street Design and Traffic Control*. She is active in the TRB and the APA. She holds an S.B. and S.M. from the Massachusetts Institute of Technology and a J.D. from Boston College Law School.

THOMAS B. DEEN is Executive Director of the Transportation Research Board. He was formerly a partner with Alan M. Voorhees and Associates where he served as vice-president for international operations and for transit planning, president, and chairman of the board. He has lectured at research institutes throughout the world. Deen has published numerous papers and books and serves on three editorial boards for research journals. He is active with ITE and APWA. A registered professional engineer in seven states, he holds a B.S. from the University of Kentucky and did graduate work at the University of Chicago and graduated from Yale University's Bureau of Highway Traffic.

MICHAEL G. FERRERI is a senior vice-president of Booz, Allen & Hamilton, Inc. He is a nationally recognized expert in transit management, operations, and finance with over 30 years of experience consulting for public agencies and private enterprise in the United States, Canada, Australia, and Europe. Ferreri is an industry leader in the development, testing, and refinement of costing techniques. He has lectured at several universities and published extensively on mass transit and related isssues. A registered professional engineer, he is active in the ITE, APTA, and ASCE. He holds a B.C.E. from Villanova University and completed graduate studies at Yale University's Bureau of Highway Traffic.

JOHN J. FRUIN is a specialist in pedestrian traffic analysis. He has over 30 years diversified experience in project management, research, and the planning, design, and operation of transportation facilities for the Port Authority of New York & New Jersey and as a consultant to government agencies and others. Fruin is the author of *Pedestrian Planning and Design*. In 1983, he received the ASCE Transportation Engineering Award for contributions to pedestrian traffic research. He is active in the ASCE, ITE, and TRB. A licensed professional engineer, he holds a B.C.E. (Manhattan College) and an M.S. and Ph.D. in transportation planning (Polytechnic University of Brooklyn).

W. L. GARRISON is a professor of civil engineering and research engineer, Institute of Transportation Studies, University of California, Berkeley. He has served as a consultant or contributor to programs for foreign, local, and federal agencies, including the U.S. Departments of Transportation, Energy, and Commerce. Garrison has also consulted for private industry and research institutes. He has authored numerous articles on transportation and is active in several professional organizations including the TRB and, in the past, the National Research Council Committee on Transportation. He holds a B.S. and M.A. from Peabody College and a Ph.D. from Northwestern University.

CLARK HENDERSON is an independent consultant. He was a staff scientist and director of the transportation department with SRI International. Henderson has consulted for the U.S. Departments of Transportation and Energy and NASA, local public agencies, and private industry on urban transportation systems, specializing in conceptual designs, operations and economic analysis, planning, evaluation, market analysis, and energy studies. His publications include *Future Urban Transportation Systems* and *Automated Guideway Transit*. He taught in the School of Engineering, Stanford University. He holds a B.S. from the University of Kentucky and an M.B.A. from Stanford University.

DAVID W. JONES, JR., is a consultant specializing in strategic planning for metropolitan transportation. He has entered private practice after more than a decade on the research staff of the Institute for Transportation Studies at the University of California, Berkeley. While at Berkeley he taught transportation policy, management, and economics. Jones has published numerous articles, papers, and reports in his fields of expertise. He is the author of a history of freeway development in California and another text in Prentice-Hall's transit series, *Urban Transit Policy: An Economic and Political History*. He holds a B.A. (Yale University), an M.S. (Northwestern University), and a Ph.D. (Stanford University).

DENNIS C. JUDYCKI is Associate Administrator for Safety and System Applications, Federal Highway Administration. He has over 20 years of professional transportation engineering and management experience with the FHWA and has served as Director of the Office of Traffic Operations, Chief of Urban Planning and Transportation Management Division, and Special Assistant to the Executive Director. Judycki is active in several professional organizations including the AASHTO, TRB, ITE, and APWA. He holds a B.S.C.E. from New England College, Henniker, New Hampshire, and an M.S.C.E. in urban transportation planning and traffic operations from West Virginia University.

RONALD F. KIRBY is Director of the Department of Transportation Planning, Metropolitan Washington Council of Governments. Formerly, he was Director of Transportation Studies and a research associate with the Urban Institute and conducted studies for both national and international agencies, including the U.S. Department of Transportation and the World Bank. Kirby has authored many publications, book sections, reports, and articles on various aspects of public transportation. He is active in the TRB and the ORSA. He has served as editor or on the editorial advisory board for three transportation journals. Kirby holds a B.Sc., B.Sc. (Honors), and Ph.D. from the University of Adelaide.

ROBERT L. KNIGHT is a founder and Vice-President of Bevilacqua-Knight, Inc., an energy and transportation consulting firm headquartered in Oakland, California, since 1980. His professional emphasis is on the process of introducing new technologies, ranging from electric vehicles to energy storage and control systems. He served as technical director for the BART Impact Program's environmental studies and authored the study *Land Use Impacts of Rapid Transit* for the U.S. Department of Transportation. Knight holds degrees in engineering, industrial administration, and planning from the University of California, Berkeley, and Northwestern University in Chicago.

ROBERT W. KOSKI, retired, was the Director of Planning and Marketing for the Sacramento Regional Transit District in California. He also served as Director of Transportation Planning for the Sacramento Regional Area Planning Commission and Director of Planning for the City of Wenatchee and Chelan County, Washington, joint planning program. Koski was an assistant professor of urban planning at the University of Washington, where he also held the position of campus planning officer. He holds a bachelor's degree in business administration and a master's degree in urban planning from the University of Washington. He is a member of the board of directors, Modern Transit Society, Sacramento.

HERBERT S. LEVINSON is a principal of Herbert S. Levinson Transportation Consultant. He is a recognized authority on transportation planning and engineering and has consulted for the United Nations, World Bank, Singapore government, and many public agencies in the United States. Formerly, he taught at several universities and was senior vice-president of Wilbur Smith and Associates. Levinson has authored several major books and research reports and more than 100 papers. He is active in the APA, ASCE, ITE, and TRB. A registered engineer in several states, he holds a B.S.C.E. from Illinois Institute of Technology and graduated from Yale University's Bureau of Highway Traffic.

MICHAEL D. MEYER is a professor in the school of civil engineering at the Georgia Institute of Technology. Previously he was Director of Transportation Planning and Development for the state of Massachusetts and a professor in the civil engineering department at the Massachusetts Institute of Technology. Meyer has written over 80 technical articles and co-authored a textbook on transportation planning, *Urban Transportation Planning: A Decision-Oriented Approach.* A registered professional engineer, he has been an active member of numerous professional organizations. He holds a B.S.C.E. (University of Wisconsin) and an M.S.C.E. (Northwestern University). His doctorate in civil engineering is from M.I.T.

PATRICIA LYON MOKHTARIAN is an assistant professor in the Department of Civil Engineering at the University of California, Davis. Her research interests include applying econometric methods to transportation forecasting and evaluations, and analyzing the impact of telecommunications technology on transportation and the environment. As technical vice-president of Schimpeler—Corradino, she did transportation planning work for the Los Angeles Metrorail. Mokhtarian spent 9 years in consulting and regional planning before joining the University of California, Davis. She holds a B.A. from Florida State University and an M.S. and Ph.D in operations research from Northwestern University.

RAY A. MUNDY is a professor of marketing and transportation, College of Business Administration, University of Tennessee, and Director of the department's Transportation Management and Policy Studies Program. He is active as a consultant to industry and government (including the World Bank, International Monetary Fund, Airport Ground Transportation Association, and U.S. Department of Transportation) in the areas of management, marketing, and contracting. Mundy has authored numerous articles in the fields of transportation and distribution. He holds B.S. and M.B.A. degrees from Bowling Green State University and a Ph.D from Pennsylvania State University.

WILFRED OWEN is a former senior fellow and now guest scholar at the Brookings Institution in Washington, D.C. He has been a consultant to the governments of Japan, Korea, India, Pakistan, and Brazil and has worked for the World Bank, the Asian Development Bank, the United Nations, and other international organizations on projects in Asia, Europe, and Latin America. Owen is the author of *The Accessible City, Transportation and World Development, The Metropolitan Problem, Distance and Development, Strategy for Mobility*, and numerous articles on the relation of mobility to the economy. He is a graduate of Harvard University in economics.

RICHARD H. PRATT consults to public and private clients through Richard H. Pratt, Consultant, Inc. Previously he was Vice-President (systems analysis) of Barton-Aschman Associates and was earlier associated with other consulting firms including Alan M. Voorhees & Associates. His many planning projects include transit, multimodal, and highway studies in the metropolitan areas of Washington—Baltimore, Minneapolis—St. Paul, Dallas, Los Angeles, Buenos Aires, and Mexico City. Pratt has authored several U.S. federal research reports and handbooks. He is a registered engineer and holds a B.S. from the the California Institute of Technology and an M.S.C.E. from Northwestern University.

SANDRA ROSENBLOOM is Executive Director of the Drachman Institute of Land Use & Regional Development, University of Arizona, Tucson. Previously, she served as David Bruton Centennial Professor of Urban Design, University of Texas, Austin. Rosenbloom is an internationally known authority on the travel patterns and needs of disadvantaged groups (including single mothers, the elderly, and the handicapped) and has consulted for seven national governments and a variety of American state and local public agencies. A recognized expert on the development and operation of paratransit modes, she chairs the TRB Paratransit Committee. Her doctorate is from the University of California, Los Angeles.

ARTHUR SALTZMAN is a professor of marketing at California State University, San Bernardino. Previously, he was the Director of the Transportation Institute at North Carolina A&T State University, Greensboro, where he developed a research and training program focusing on small-city transportation and paratransit. Saltzman's interest and research in transit history have extended over more than 15 years. He has published in many marketing and transportation journals and testified on public transportation before several congressional committees. He holds a B.S. from Brooklyn College, a masters in management from the Massachusetts Institute of Technology, and a Ph.D. from the University of California, Irvine.

PETER SCHAUER has consulted for local, state, and federal agencies (including the U.S. Department of Transportation) and private companies in transportation management for 11 years. He has provided management services, feasibility and coordination studies, and cross-cultural planning in 46 states. Schauer has 6 years' experience as General Manager of a rural elderly and handicapped transportation system, which received UMTA's Administrator's Award for excellence in 1985. He is active in the TRB, National Council on Transportation Disadvantaged, and National Association of Transportation Alternatives. He holds a B.S. (University of Missouri) and an M.A. and M.R.P. (Pennsylvania State University).

GEORGE M. SMERK has been Director of the Institute for Urban Transportation since 1969. He is a professor of transportation at Indiana University and has been the Governor's Trustee on the Board of the Northern Indiana Commuter Transportation District since 1977. Smerk has written extensively on federal transportation policy, including *The Federal Role in Urban Mass Transportation*. He also co-authored *Mass Transit Management: A Handbook for Small Cities* and *Mass Transit Management Peformance Audits*. He has been active for many years in the Indiana Transportation Association, APTA, and TRB. He holds a B.S. and M.B.A. from Bradley University and a Ph.D. from Indiana University.

J. WILLIAM VIGRASS, transportation economist, is a project manager for Hill International, Inc., providing management oversight services for SEPTA's Norristown High Speed Line Modernization Program. From 1968 to 1988 he was with the Port Authority Transit Corporation as Superintendent of Traffic and Planning, Superintendent of Equipment, and Assistant General Manager, Administration. Vigrass previously worked for the Battelle Memorial Institute, the Union Pacific Railroad Company; and the Erie Railroad Company Traffic Department. He is active in both the APTA and TRB. He holds a B.A. from Allegheny College and an M.B.A. from Western Reserve University.

VUKAN R. VUCHIC is UPS Foundation professor of transportation engineering at the University of Pennsylvania, where he initiated the graduate program in that field. An internationally known consultant, he has presented major seminars to several ministries of transport. Vuchic has lectured at universities, conferences, and scientific institutions throughout the world. He has published about 100 reports, book sections, and articles and is the author of *Urban Public Transportation Systems and Technology*. He is active in the ASCE, ITE, TRB, and UITP. A graduate of the University of Belgrade, he holds M.Eng. and Ph.D. degrees in civil engineering—transportation from the University of California, Berkeley.

EDWARD WEINER has been a senior policy analyst in the Office of the Secretary of the U.S. Department of Transportation since 1970 and is responsible for urban transportation and highway policy, planning, and legislative issues. He formerly was with the Federal Highway Administration. Weiner has authored papers on national transportation policy, travel demand forecasting, transportation evaluation, transit needs, financing, and urban transportation planning. He is a registered professional engineer. He is active on several TRB committees. He holds a B.A. and B.C.E. from New York University, an M.S.C.E. (urban planning) from Purdue University, and an M.P.A. from the University of Southern California.

PART I

HISTORICAL DEVELOPMENT

Chapter 1

PUBLIC TRANSPORTATION AND THE CITY

GEORGE M. SMERK

The city is the hallmark of a civilization. History is full of exploits of battle, discovery, endurance, and victory over the hostility of nature that took place away from cities and urban places. Yet the true progress of humankind is measured by the felicity of the good life; the excitement of great adventures of the mind; the glow of creativity as expressed in music, poetry, and the graphic arts; the formulation of law to protect people from one another and from overly rapacious government; the fellowship of society; and the greater productivity possible from the sharing of talents and skills—such progress is apparently possible only in an urban place.

IN THE BEGINNING: THE CITY

Cities as permanent places of habitation are a product of the first great turning point reached by humankind: the agricultural revolution. Early human beings hunted and gathered locally available foodstuffs and other materials necessary for survival. Even a rich area was soon depleted of animals fit for food or of berries or other wild edibles, which meant that the human residents were forced to move on to other places not yet fully exploited in order to survive. When we learned how to plant crops and domesticate certain animals, we could exchange the role of nomads for that of urban dwellers.

The agricultural revolution by itself was not sufficient to cause the development of major urban centers. The growth, development, and shaping of cities in their modern form is closely related to the availability of transportation. To begin with, in order to grow to any great size, an urban place requires an external transportation system to bring in necessary food and materials, because urban dwellers tend to be specialists in tasks other than raising food and gathering supplies. Since the beginning of larger-scale urbanization, urban residents necessarily have traded the fruits of their specialization for the surpluses of foodstuffs and supplies brought in from other areas. How large a population of specialists a city may support is, therefore, directly related to the size of the hinterland that an urban place may tap for its food and supplies.

In ancient times, before mechanical means of transportation or engineered transportation improvements were possible, land travel was difficult and slow. The capacity to move goods over land was limited by lack of carrying capacity. The use of pack animals bearing only small loads was common. Wheeled vehicles were scarce because they were expensive and troublesome to make; roads were rough and difficult to use if they existed at all. With capital always scarce, primitive societies simply could not afford to take the time and effort—nor were the skills available—to provide good land transportation. On the other hand, rivers, lakes, streams, and the oceans provided natural means of transportation that enabled large quantities of goods to be moved, in early times on simple rafts and later by means of more sophisticated vessels. Urban places located on waterways thus had the potential to grow because their available hinterland was larger than that of an urban location away from water. For example, a budding community located in a river basin, especially if it was downstream, was in an excellent position to grow; the closer to the mouth of a river, the larger the hinterland that might be tapped for food and other supplies necessary to support life. In an age without mechanical transportation, heavy materials could be moved easily downstream with only the current. Cities located at the mouth of a river at the sea had the potential of supporting a large population; they not only had access to the surplus of the entire river basin upstream, but could also trade with other seashore cities.

Because of the importance of water transportation to help supply cities with sustenance, even today most of the major cities of the world are located on waterways or on large lakes. With the advent of mechanization, nonwaterside locations also became attractive for modern urban locations, because railroads, highways, pipelines, and airplanes can move the supplies and foodstuffs necessary to support a large population. Water transportation is no longer a prerequisite for the growth of a large city, although the momentum of an early start has allowed water-oriented cities to continue growing, and most major U.S. cities are located on water.

THE GENESIS OF URBAN MASS TRANSPORTATION: THE AGE OF THE OMNIBUS

As long as an urban area was small in size, residents could make their way about on foot and goods could be carried or moved with relative ease by simple and even crude means of transport. With increased city size, however, getting about on foot became a different proposition, greatly limiting the size of internal markets for goods and services, and making difficult the process of gathering a labor force from throughout the whole of the community. If a city grows large enough, limitations on the means of internal circulation of people, as well as goods, can have a decided dampening effect on urban growth and development. On the other hand, given good external and internal transportation, growth is affected not only by transportation, but by other economic, social, cultural, and geographic factors. Furthermore, over time, the means of internal transportation can actually help to shape the growth of an urban area.

The idea of providing a land-based public conveyance for passengers within an urban area can be dated back at least 300 years. In 1662, as a reflection of urban growth in the city, the eminent and practical French mathematician Pascal began to operate a horse-drawn wagon line carrying passengers in Paris. In the beginning the service was free of charge. Pascal's brainchild became popular and it was quite the rage for people of quality, as well as others of less elegant status, to utilize the new means of urban transportation. When a fare was finally charged, after the period of free operation, the public rebelled and patronage fell off so sharply that Pascal was forced to quit the transportation business.

With the industrial revolution of the eighteenth century came both the rapid growth of cities and the separation of home and workplace. Workers no longer possessed the tools of a trade that could be plied at home; they worked at machines in factories, both of which belonged to someone else. The need to travel regularly between home and factory made the now familiar peak-hour trip a common feature of urban life. As the leader in industrialization, London, by the early 1800s, was awash with a tidal wave of humanity at the beginning and end of each working day as tens of thousands of working people, from the highest position to the lowest, crowded the streets, walking back and forth to work.

The lure of the suburbs began to attract upper-middle-class London merchants by 1750. Business had to be conducted in the center of the city where the exchange of information was not only crucial but possible in the face-to-face contact that was mandatory in an age innocent of modern communication. You did not have to live in the city, however, if you could afford horses and a carriage. A religious revival in the Anglican church preached the need to take the children out and away from the noise and dirt of the city. With ample means to pay for the necessary transportation, the London upper middle class began to leave the city for the quiet, hearty, and fresh air of the areas lying 4 or 5 mi outside of it. The trend caught on, as more common people aped their wealthier fellow citizens. During the nineteenth century, as transport improved, the trickle of persons moving to the suburbs became a strong flow.

Mass transportation finally came to the British capital in 1829, when an enterprising coach builder named George Shillibeer introduced the first modern *omnibus*. The omnibus was a high-wheeled wagonlike vehicle, with the entrance at the rear. Seats inside, for perhaps as many as 18 to 20 passengers, were arranged longitudinally along the walls so that the passengers sat facing one another. The rear entrance, with a step down to the ground level, made it possible to enter and exit with relative ease compared to a stagecoach. Regular pickup and drop-off of passengers was provided and the vehicle was operated along a regular route from Paddington Green to the Bank. Although Shillibeer's company did not stay in business very long, the idea of the omnibus caught on; soon these vehicles crowded the streets of the great cities of the world, beginning with London and gaining popularity in Paris, New York, and elsewhere during the 1830s.

Omnibuses had few amenities for the passengers apart from what was usually a fancy and brightly painted exterior. There was, of course, no heat in cold weather and passengers had to be content with straw piled on the floor in which to snuggle their feet. If the vehicles lacked amenities, there was no lack of color and vigor in their operation. Omnibus drivers were known for their large vocabulary of profanity as they questioned the heritage and other habits of fellow drivers in mad dashes to the curb to pick up potential passengers. Accidents were common as the number of omnibuses grew along with the rise of other street traffic. Crowding was soon so bad in London that, to provide greater mass transportation capacity, the double-decked omnibus became a common feature, as a forerunner of the present-day, double-decker bus of London.

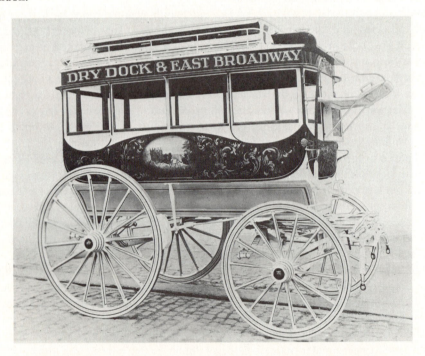

Figure 1-1 *Early omnibus. Used in New York City. (courtesy of American Public Transit Association)*

In several cities—particularly in Europe—the omnibus allowed people of modest income to live beyond walking distance from work. The possibilities of better climate and better housing on the outskirts of the city opened up for a great mass of population. At the same time, omnibuses were usually more expensive to ride than the streetcar that appeared on the scene a bit later. Because of the slow pace of urban population growth, omnibuses were not heavily used in the United States except in a few of the largest cities, but they were especially popular and long-lived in New York City. New York saw its first omnibus in 1831, when Abraham Brower began to operate a line along Broadway between the Battery and Bond Street.

Where it was utilized, the omnibus strengthened the central business district (CBD) of cities, helping to make the central area a focal point for internal travel. Because of their limited speed of about 3 mi/h (5 km/h), however, they could not be extended for long distances into relatively undeveloped areas and consequently had little influence on expanding city boundaries. The horse-drawn omnibus was in use in many cities throughout the world until the early 1900s; in those places where they were used so long, it was usually because of local restrictions against laying rail for horsecars in certain streets. As a result, omnibuses were often directly replaced by motor buses, as was the case on Fifth Avenue in New York.

The omnibus had the virtues of relatively low capital cost and inherent flexibility. Balanced against the advantages were the discomfort of operations on poor road surfaces, low speed, and very limited passenger capacity. As useful as it was, the omnibus was a mode of mass transportation with considerable limitations. It is small wonder, then, that its use was never as extensive—at least in the United States—as was its successor in time, the horsecar.

THE MASS TRANSIT REVOLUTION:
THE AGE OF THE STREET RAILWAY, 1830–1920

HORSE-DRAWN STREETCARS

The streetcar as a mode of public transportation was introduced in New York City in November 1832 almost as an afterthought. A line of track had been laid along Fourth Avenue to bring the cars of the New York and Harlem Railroad into the heart of the city. Because city restrictions prohibited the use of steam locomotives in the streets of lower Manhattan, passenger cars were pulled by horses from Harlem into the downtown area. The enterprising promoters of the Harlem Railroad saw the potential for hauling local passengers in regular urban transit service, in addition to pulling the steam railroad coaches downtown. Lightweight cars were built to save money and to lighten the horses' loads, and the Fourth Avenue line became the world's first streetcar service.

Figure 1-2 *Horsecar used in Philadelphia in 1880. Note "No Smoking" sign.*
(courtesy of American Public Transit Association)

The horse-drawn streetcar had a number of advantages over the omnibus. Cars with metal wheels rolling on iron rails were easier to pull than the omnibuses on rough roads. Thus, horsecars could be larger than omnibuses and so carry higher payloads with the same number of horses. A horsecar could maintain a speed of about 4 mi/h (6.4 km/h), which is about 1 mi/h faster than was possible by the omnibus.

By the late 1840s, after a slow start outside New York City, the horse-drawn streetcar appeared in a number of other American cities. By the time of the Civil War and immediately thereafter, almost all American cities and towns of any size, or those with even a modest delusion of metropolitan grandeur, had horse- or mule-powered street railway companies. As with the omnibuses, there were many competitors in a business—urban public transit—which was later usually thought of as a natural monopoly. Typically, in a community of any size at all there was no single city transit company operating all the omnibuses or streetcars; in a large city, service on each street was usually offered by a separate firm having a franchise granting monopoly power to operate. The possibility of a multiplicity of transit operations in a town was often a fact. Philadelphia had 39 streetcar companies all operating at virtually the same time. The public was not generally well served in the broad civic sense by competition among several local horsecar companies. Each firm served only a limited area; longer trips required changing vehicles and paying separate fares each time a different company was used. Multiple companies with multiple fares discouraged long trips.

Figure 1-3 *Fifty-fifty. On this archaic line, in the outskirts of Denver, a horse pulled the car up hill and then rode down on the rear platform. He was on the job so long that his shoes wore grooves in the flooring. (courtesy of American Public Transit Association)*

Mergers between street railway companies began to take place during horsecar days. Later, as the transit industry moved toward mechanical means of transportation, the increased need for capital accelerated the merger process because larger, more stable companies fared better in the capital market.

Horsecars required a larger capital investment than did omnibuses because track had to be laid. Horsecars, depending on size, ranged in cost from about $600 to $1000. Over time the horses, as with the omnibus, were the most expensive part of the investment. Horses cost about $200 each and were kept in service for about 5 years. Because one or two horses per car could be worked for only about 5 h/day, three to six horses were required to provide 15 h of service. On steep grades, additional horses were often required.

Because tracks were constructed in public streets, franchises were usually necessary so that the public thoroughfare could be used for private enterprise. The franchise bore with it certain responsibilities, such as payment of an annual franchise tax. It was common to demand that the street railway pave the area around its tracks and clear snow from the paved track area in winter. If that were the only cleared portion of the street, as was commonly the case, wagons and buggies soon cluttered up the streetcar right-of-way. In some cases, the street railway company was required to pave the entire street from curb to curb, which could be a substantial financial burden and, in later years, this requirement aided and abetted the buses and automobiles that competed with the street railways. Another requirement was that, in the summer, the unpaved part of the street be sprayed with water in order to control dust. Later, when electric railways were used, streetcar companies were often required to maintain the public bridges they used. Under most franchises in the United States, the fare imposed on the public could be no more than 5 cents. The nickel fare proved to be lucrative in most places during the last 30 years of the nineteenth century, when prices were relatively stable, but became a problem later.

At the horsecar's operating speed, one could travel 2 mi in a half-hour commute. Therefore, it was possible for the nineteenth-century horsecar commuter to find a pleasant area to live, several miles from his downtown work location, where the benefits of better or cheaper housing could be enjoyed without the burden of inordinately long walks or travel time. Thus, the horsecar helped to stimulate the outward growth of the city. Although the growth tended to be relatively compact, often there were a few long fingers of growth along major streets out into underdeveloped areas. The street railways added to the importance of the established downtown area by helping to make it the most accessible place in the city and, therefore, the prime location for most economic, social, and cultural activities.

CABLE CARS

Despite its many advantages over the omnibus, street railway managers kept seeking improvements to the horse-drawn streetcar. Many attempts were made to find a means of mechanical power that could replace the horse. A major breakthrough in motive power was the successful operation of cable cars in San Francisco in 1873. Invented by Andrew Hallidie in 1869, the ingenious part of the cable car was a grip that allowed a cable, running continuously in a slot between the tracks and beneath the street, to be grasped and released so that cars could start and stop. The cable was powered by giant steam engines and the cable car, therefore, had great potential for mass movement.

The cable railway was first used to climb San Francisco's formidable hills; the areas on Nob Hill, Russian Hill, and to the north and west of Market Street were immediately opened for urban development. But the cable car was not merely a street railway vehicle for a city with steep hills. The passenger-carrying capacity of a cable railway system was substantial because of the power available, and cities without the problems of hill-climbing soon adopted the new type of urban transportation. Indeed, Chicago, a city not known for hills, had the largest cable car operation in the United States. Grip cars pulling up to three trailers, and traveling at close headways, provided the capacity to move thousands of people into a central location. The importance of downtown Chicago as a great and vibrant business district and major place of employment was actually made possible by the cable car, long before the familiar elevated railway loop (the Loop) was built in the central business district.

What made the cable car attractive, particularly in large cities, was that it had a much lower operating cost than the horse-powered railway. If the cable railway provided relief from operating cost, nevertheless, the formidable (for that day) capital

Figure 1-4 *Cable car. California Street, San Francisco cable car in 1974 and still going strong. (courtesy of Harre W. Demoro Collection)*

investment required—probably a minimum of $100,000 per route-mile and perhaps much more—meant that the cable car was practical only where there were large numbers of people to move.

Because of its relatively high speed, the cable car helped draw city development out along its routes. Of course, the need for a dense traffic level meant that most cable lines were located in well-built-up sections of a city, usually as a replacement for busy horsecar lines. The development attributable to cable traction would have been even greater had the cable car not so soon been superseded by another and better form of mass transportation.

ELECTRIC STREETCARS

For many years, people fascinated with electricity had been attempting to devise some method of electrically propelling a vehicle along rails. Early experiments using battery-powered cars had not been particularly successful. It was not until dynamo-generated current was perfected in the late 1860s and the transmission of power over a relatively great distance through wires became possible that electrically propelled transportation was at all practical.

A number of pioneers experimented with electric locomotives or electric railway cars with more or less success during the early 1880s. In 1883, Charles Van Depoele operated an experimental electric line in Chicago, and on the heels of that success operated a service at the Toronto Exposition in 1885. The spring-loaded pole pressing on the bottom of the wire, with the return circuit made through the running rails, was perfected by Van Depoele. The early electric cars were crude and undependable. Most were nothing more than converted horsecars, with the motor placed on the platform next to the driver, now dubbed a motorman. The rheostatic control was rough, and a chain drive was used to power the wheels of the car. Vibration was a major problem, and the weight of the motor often caused the platform of the car to buckle.

In 1888, however, the state of the art was greatly improved when Frank J. Sprague electrified a portion of the horsecar lines in Richmond, Virginia, and brought together all the elements, which he and others had devised, that were necessary for the successful operation of electrically powered streetcars. Sprague used Van DePoele's idea of overhead wire with a bottom-contact, spring-loaded trolley pole to collect the current, the return circuit through the rails. Sprague also devised an improved control system so that the cars were easier to operate. He also developed a means of suspending the electric motors so that there would be a minimum of wear and tear on the motors and gears from vibration, and the operation of the cars would be relatively smooth and trouble free. After a few more years of development, the electric streetcar was ready to take its place as the preeminent means of urban transportation for the next 30 years.

The electric streetcar precipitated a revolution in urban public transportation. Within 2 years of the completion of Sprague's electrification project in Richmond, better than 1200 mi (1900 km) of electric street railways were in operation in the United States. From a cost viewpoint, the electric railway car was far superior to both the cable car and the horse-powered street railway. It cost a great deal less to install track and the overhead wire and power distribution system for an electric railway than it did to put in the costly and complex cable system. Capital costs were lower than for the cable railway and operating costs lower than for the horse railway.

The electric railway car could operate at an average speed of at least 10 mi/h (16 km/h). This permitted street railways to be extended even farther from the central business districts than either horsecar or cable car lines. Within a few years, the electric streetcar played an important role in shaping the city it served as the population oriented itself to the location of the expanding street railway system. Many streetcar companies were also in the real estate business, and city development was often by design of the companies. Electric traction promoters would buy large tracts of land in promising outlying territory and then extend the streetcar line to the land that they owned. The transit company stood to profit from people buying its land, building or buying houses, and becoming regular streetcar customers.

The coming of the electric streetcar also had an impact on the structure of the transit industry. The multiplicity of street railway operations that were common during the horsecar days were no longer practical. Generally, there were wholesale mergers as dispersed companies pulled together to form a "Union Traction Company." The larger company was better able to attract capital for the purposes of electrification than were separate, small, independent horse-railway companies. Unfortunately, many small companies not only were overcapitalized, but much of the capital was in the form of debt. When mergers were consummated, the surviving company had embraced the capital structure of the absorbed firms and was usually burdened by capitalization that often greatly exceeded the value of the assets.

Figure 1-5 *CBD in transportation transition. Los Angeles at the turn of the century. Horse, electric, and gasoline vehicles vie for the right-of-way. (courtesy of Southern California Rapid Transit District)*

The shaky financial situation in the transit industry was widespread, although it did not include the entire industry. Nevertheless, as long as prices and costs were stable—as they were for most of the last 30 years of the nineteenth century—and patronage continued to grow, the transit industry could function as a safe, stable, and seemingly profitable institution. At the same time, overcapitalized transit firms were on the edge of financial disaster if prices in general should rise or if patronage should fall.

By the time of World War I, the electric streetcar had had a major impact on the growth and structure of cities and had opened up the outlying suburban areas to the middle and upper middle classes as well as to less affluent Americans. The huge influx of immigrants from abroad and from rural areas of the nation into U.S. cities had helped swell urban growth, and the development of the urban area was often channeled along the streetcar lines. Like the arms of a starfish, streetcar lines projected from the central business district out as much as 5 mi (8 km) or more. The electric streetcar provided the basic transportation for American cities before the coming of the auto age. Typically, service was good, fares were relatively cheap, and the streetcar was a part of everyday life for citizens of all classes, occupations, ages, and economic levels. It is fair to say that the streetcar was the most decisive factor in shaping U.S. cities until the automobile.

Figure 1-6 *Early streetcar (California type). Oakland, California, about 1895. (courtesy of Harre W. Demoro Collection)*

For the first two decades of the twentieth century, all large U.S. cities depended on streetcars. The central focal point was, of course, the bustling downtown. Strip shopping streets developed along the streetcar's radial arteries, and often local shopping centers formed where several streetcar lines intersected. Housing, to be convenient and marketable, had to be within no more than two or three blocks of the streetcar line. Large factories or major employment centers of any kind had to locate where there was either the existence or potential of streetcar service. The public-transit-oriented city was relatively compact and population was relatively concentrated. Lesser densities were possible out along the suburban and interurban electric lines or the commuter railroads, but even there homes tended to cluster. The classic suburb had developed.

THE MASS TRANSPORTATION AGE: FERRIES, COMMUTER RAILROADS, INTERURBANS, AND RAPID TRANSIT

FERRIES

In discussing transportation by omnibus and by rail in the early days of the development of modern cities, one must not forget the ferryboat and its role in urbanization. A number of American cities were faced with water barriers; urbanization across those barriers would have been impossible without the ferry. Early nineteenth century engineering knowledge and available structural materials were so limited that it was not possible to construct bridges across, for instance, the Hudson and the East rivers in New York, the Delaware River in Philadelphia, or Boston Bay and San Francisco Bay. The ferry provided a means of crossing water barriers quickly and at relatively low cost. Thus, the ferry made possible the expansion of urbanization from an original core city to many other adjacent areas. Like the street railway, it permitted persons of ordinary means the opportunity to find good housing at reasonable cost and, perhaps, a more favorable environment than were available in the major city center. The ferry, along with the other modes of public transportation, allowed cities to develop horizontally at a time when engineering skill and the quality of materials precluded vertical development of high-rise housing.

COMMUTER RAILROADS

Commuter rail service had its inception when enterprising nineteenth-century railroad management noted that it was possible to pick up additional passengers on trains already being operated if those trains entered the city in the morning hours coinciding with the beginning of work and departed at the end of the workday. Obviously, if a railroad was already operating a long-distance passenger train into the city, the extra cost of stopping at the outskirts was virtually nil; the revenue collected from the passengers was almost all profit. In the nineteenth century, railroads encouraged this kind of traffic. Some involved themselves in land development schemes, much like the early street railway companies, in order to encourage suburban development. In any event, to be attractive to the would-be suburban passenger, the railroads typically cut, or commuted, a part of the fare. Thus developed the name *commuter* for the regular, shuttling passenger on the railways and, indeed, for all who traveled back and forth regularly.

Eventually, in some places, the commuter or suburban railroad operations became very large in scope as cities expanded. The development of Long Island beyond Queens and Brooklyn is an example; its growth was due to the substantial commuter operations of the Long Island Rail Road. Across the Hudson in New Jersey, a large number of suburbs and cities formed along the lines of railroads aimed at the great metropolis and joined to it by ferries. The commuter railroad was like the ferry in that middle-class people had access to better housing and a better family environment than were available in the major city center. In Boston, Philadelphia, Chicago, and along the peninsula in San Francisco, commuter rail service fostered a great outward spread of population. It should be noted, however, that the pattern of development was different from that influenced by the streetcar. Because of the economics and operating nature of the steam locomotives originally used as the motive power in commuter rail operations, growth was not along a solid corridor adjacent to the railroad, but, rather, resembled beads spaced on a string. It was uneconomical to start and stop steam locomotives much more often than about every 2 or 3 mi; the stops therefore tended to be so spaced. Housing would develop around the railway stations. In many cases, these communities along the railway remained enclaves of suburbanization in otherwise rural areas and did not grow together until well after the coming of the automobile age.

INTERURBANS

In the Midwest, in particular, there was another variation of the growth pattern caused by the commuter railroad. In the late 1890s, interurban electric railway lines were developed linking smaller cities, often 50 mi (80 km) or more distant, with a larger regional city. The interurban cars, while closely related in technology to the local streetcar, were larger and more comfortable and capable of relatively high speeds. The economics and technology of the interurban were such that stops could be efficiently spaced at intervals as short as a quarter of a mile apart where necessary. A beads-on-a-string type of development, similar to the commuter railroads, took place in the outskirts of many cities served by interurbans; but because the separate clusters of housing were closer together, the process of growing together into a long suburban arm of development was more likely to take place. Los Angeles was greatly affected by the building of interurban electric railways as an integral part of real estate development. The spread-out nature of Los Angeles was largely caused by the Pacific Electric Railway and its thousand-plus miles of track.

RAIL RAPID TRANSIT

In some places the growth of a city and its population was so great that it became evident more than a century ago that some means of fast transportation utilizing other than the street surface was necessary. Street traffic had reached such formidable proportions in London by the 1850s that mobility was seriously threatened, and it was obvious that some new form of fast transportation had to be developed on a grade-separated right-of-way. The British response was the 1863 opening of the Metropolitan Railway's steam-powered underground line in London from Farringdon Street in the city to Bishop's Road, Paddington. Shortly thereafter, in 1868, the first elevated railway was opened in New York City. As with the earlier London subway, the New York elevated trains were propelled by steam locomotives.

With the coming of electrification after 1888, and Frank Sprague's invention of multiple-unit train control in the 1890s, rail rapid transit became even more popular for handling large crowds with a swiftness denied the surface modes. With electrification, unlucky pedestrians need not worry about hot ashes falling on them from an elevated railway, and Londoners traveling on their underground railway system did not have to worry about suffocating or bearing on their clothes and faces the environmental pollution of steam locomotives. By the first decade of the twentieth century, a network of electric elevated railways covered parts of Brooklyn and Manhattan. Chicago enjoyed the services of several steam-powered elevated railways in the 1890s; with the coming of electrification, the systems were greatly extended and linked together in the famous downtown Loop. The first American subway was a streetcar subway in Boston, opened in 1898, and soon followed by a subway built for trains. New York's first subway was opened in 1904, and construction of additional subways proceeded rapidly for the next 35 years. Philadelphia's first subway opened in 1907, and Chicago began using its first underground railway not long before World War II. Cleveland started construction of a rail rapid transit system in the 1920s; delayed by the Great Depression and World War II, it was finally opened in the 1950s. Toronto opened its first line in 1954, Montreal in 1966. The San Francisco Bay area built its system in the 1960s and 1970s as an antidote to the automobile. In the 1970s, Washington, Baltimore, Atlanta, Miami, and Buffalo joined the ranks of cities with subways and rail rapid transit. The 1980s saw Los Angeles begin the long process of subway construction.

Rail rapid transit was feasible only where the population was very large and dense and where street crowding was so overwhelming that there was no choice but to move to some high-capacity, rapid means of public transportation. Generally, rail rapid transit systems were built only in the developed parts of a city and, therefore, their impact on spreading growth was relatively modest. On the other hand, some of the earliest of New York's elevated railways were built out from the most highly developed parts of the city into almost farmlike lands well in advance of housing and commercial construction, and thus strongly influenced growth in the Bronx, Brooklyn, and Queens. Locations around the rapid transit stations were often choice spots for high-density development of apartment buildings, factories, or mercantile establishments. In the London area, however, beginning in the teens and especially the twenties of the century, the underground rapid transit railway system was extended far into the suburbs on the north side of the Thames. Today people may travel as far as 35 mi (56 km) by "underground"—mostly running on the surface, however—to find their way eventually into downtown London. The Bay Area Rapid Transit District system in the San Francisco area resembles the London system in its ability to shape and stimulate growth well out into the suburbs, as well as serving as a backbone of public transportation in the more densely populated parts of Oakland, Berkeley, and San

Francisco. Likewise, the Washington Metropolitan Area Transit Authority rapid transit lines extend for many miles out into the suburbs of Maryland and Virginia. These far-ranging rapid transit systems resemble the interurban electric railways of an earlier era and function much like commuter railroads.

MASS TRANSPORTATION IN THE HIGHWAY AGE: THE MOTOR BUS AND TROLLEYBUS, 1920 TO THE PRESENT

With the construction of subways in many parts of the world in the 1920s, the first great age of public transportation came to an end. Insofar as urban growth and development were concerned, the major transportation force of the next 70 years—especially in the United States—was the private automobile. The rapidly rising costs of the World War I period forced the overcapitalized transit systems to the wall. Even though patronage broke all records, the franchise-regulated fare of a nickel limited revenues while debt capital still demanded payment of bond interest. There was not enough revenue in many places to pay operating costs and capital obligations. By 1918 half of the street railway mileage in the United States was in bankruptcy. Even with financial reorganization, many of the nation's transit firms were unable to meet the challenge of the automobile age. This does not, of course, mean that development of new forms of transit was at an end.

In the 1930s, members of the transit industry allied to produce a new type of streetcar. The PCC (Electric Railway Presidents' Conference Committee) car was the superb result, the end product of the first systems engineering effort in U.S. history (see Chap. 5). As good as it was, the PCC car could not turn the tide in the United States against the move away from fixed-facility surface transportation with its burden of track and overhead wire maintenance cost.

MOTOR BUSES

The motor bus and the trolleybus are the major transit innovations of the mid-twentieth-century move away from the street railway. The motor bus is an obvious offshoot of the development of the automobile and the truck. The first regular use of buses by an existing transit firm took place in New York in 1905 when the Fifth Avenue Coach Company replaced some of its omnibuses with imported motor buses. In 1912, Cleveland Railways began to use buses as feeders to its streetcar lines. These vehicles were often crude and uncomfortable and suffered from the same uncertainties as the early automobile. Other cities began to see early, crude buses—often nothing more than a passenger body fastened to a truck chassis—offer service in less densely populated areas.

What was needed for the real development of the motor bus was a conveyance that was easy to get into and use. The Fageol brothers provided such a vehicle in the early 1920s with the construction of front-engine buses that were designed from the ground up to be motor carriers of passengers. These buses had relatively low entrance steps, doors that could be operated by the driver, and—except for the engine location—were very much like smaller versions of the buses of today.

Figure 1-7 *Early buses—the streetcar killers. (courtesy of California Department of Transportation)*

Over the years, bus design and reliability improved greatly, and by the late 1930s all the elements of the modern motor bus, with the exception of air conditioning and air suspension systems, were brought together in a single vehicle. By 1939, the motor bus that was to become typical was powered by a large, powerful diesel engine mounted at the rear and driving the vehicle through an automatic transmission. Buses by that time were produced up to a length of 40 ft (12 m) with a capacity of more than 50 seated passengers. Some gasoline-powered—and, later, propane-powered buses—continued to be produced into the 1950s, but the diesel soon became the standard.

The great advantage of the motor bus is, of course, its flexibility, since it can go anywhere there is a decently paved street. Happily, the motor bus does not require any sort of overhead power distribution or the installation and maintenance of rails in the street as did the streetcar, and is thus a truly independent vehicle. Better yet, the cost of the street surface that the motor bus uses is shared with all the other vehicles that operate on that street. The advantage of not having to pay the entire cost of the streets they use is marred for the transit bus by having to share that surface with all other motor vehicles; the bus wallowing in automobile traffic is a typical modern sight. As a result, service is often slow and undependable.

Small buses began to make inroads on streetcar operations in the 1920s. The street railway companies, sometimes burdened with motor bus competition, but often going into the motor bus business themselves when they recognized its advantages for service on lightly traveled lines, soon adopted the bus as a regular part of their operations. Starting in the 1920s, shuttle streetcar lines and light-traffic suburban lines began to be converted into bus operations. With the advent of the large diesel-powered buses in the late 1930s, even major streetcar lines with heavy patronage soon fell to the conquering modern relative of the omnibus.

TROLLEYBUSES

Another twentieth-century innovation is the trolleybus, a combination of both the electric streetcar and the bus. Equipped with twin trolley poles to gather electricity from overhead wires, the trolleybus enjoys the quiet power of electric traction. At the same time, because it travels on rubber tires like a bus, there is no need for the expensive business of laying track in the street. Moreover, the trolleybus, because it is free to move at some distance from under the center line of its wires, can easily get around obstacles in the street that would block conventional rail-bound streetcars. Many conversions from streetcar to bus operations in the United States enjoyed an interim period of a switchover to the trolleybus. The reason behind this intermediate move was the advantage to the transit property of being able to continue to utilize its major investment in power stations and power distribution equipment for several more years after the abandonment of the street railway. When the necessity for repairs or modernization of the power distribution system became substantial enough, the trolleybuses were typically replaced with motor buses.

It is very difficult to find evidence that either the motor bus or electric trolleybus had any part in shaping the growth of modern American cities because recent urban growth came at the same time as the whirlwind upsurge in use of the private automobile. It is the automobile that has been the prime factor in shaping and developing recent urban growth, so whatever impact the bus or trolleybus may have had is virtually invisible. Coupled with the allure of government-insured mortgages, subsidized highway travel, and employer subsidized parking for employees, the automobile was formidable competition. It was no contest in the scattered, thinly developed suburbs, where transit foundered in a feckless effort to serve places with insufficient density to support conventional transit services.

Figure 1-8 *Downtown Chicago, Dearborn and Randolph Streets, 1910—congestion! (courtesy of Federal Highway Administration)*

Figure 1-9 *Downtown congestion. Same location 56 years later. (courtesy of Federal Highway Administration)*

SUMMARY

There is much being written about the possible virtues and growth-shaping possibilities of new and exotic forms of urban mass transportation. Regardless of what may actually happen, it is unlikely that in the foreseeable future any of the new means of public transportation now under development will have any greater impact on urban growth than did the streetcar in the United States.

The story of public transportation in the twentieth century will be covered in the next chapter, land use and transportation are addressed in Chap. 12, and prospects for the future are discussed in Part VI. As we will see, all over the world increased attention has been directed to upgrading and improving mass transportation. As a result of environmental pollution often caused by automobile exhausts and stunning levels of automotive congestion, it is likely that over the next half-century mass transit will once again become a potent force for shaping cities as well as serving them.

REFERENCES

A previously published article on this subject is: GEORGE M. SMERK, "200 Years in Transit," *MASS TRANSIT*, 3, no. 7 (July-August 1976), 4-9.

FURTHER READING

CORLISS, CARLTON, JR., *Main Line of Mid-America*. New York: Creative Age Press, 1950.

DAY, JOHN R., *The Story of London's Underground*. London: London Transport, 1963.

FISHMAN, ROBERT, *Bourgeois Utopias: The Rise and Fall of Suburbia*. New York: Basic Books, Inc., 1987.

GILMORE, HARLAN W., *Transportation and the Growth of Cities*. Glencoe, Ill.: The Free Press, 1953.

GLAAB, CHARLES N., AND A. THEODORE BROWN, *A History of Urban America* (3rd ed.). New York: Macmillan Publishing Co., Inc., 1983.

GRAS, NORMAN S. B., *Introduction to Economic History*. New York: Harper & Brothers, Publishers, 1922.

HILTON, GEORGE W., *The Cable Car in America*. Berkeley, Calif.: Howell-North Books, 1971.

——, AND JOHN F. DUE, *The Electric Interurban Railways in America*. Stanford, Calif.: Stanford University Press, 1960.

JACKSON, KENNETH T., *Crabgrass Frontier: The Suburbanization of America*. New York: Oxford University Press, Inc., 1985.

MIDDLETON, WILLIAM D., *The Interurban Era*. Milwaukee, Wis.: Kalmbach Publishing Co., 1961.

——, *The Time of the Trolley*. Milwaukee, Wis.: Kalmbach Publishing Co., 1967.

MILLER, JOHN ANDERSON, *Fares, Please!* New York: Dover Publications, Inc., 1960. (Published originally in 1940.)

MUMFORD, LEWIS, *The Culture of Cities*. New York: Harcourt, Brace and Company, 1938.

———, *The City in History: Its Origins, Its Transformations, and Its Prospects*. New York: Harcourt Brace & World, 1961.

PFEIFFER, JOHN, "Man's First Revolution," *Horizon*, 5 (September 1962), 6.

ROWSOME, FRANK, JR., *Trolley Car Treasury*. New York: Bonanza Books, 1956.

SCHAEFFER, K. H., AND ELLIOTT SCLAR, *Access for All: Transportation and Urban Growth*. New York: Columbia University Press, 1980.

SEBREE, MAC, *The Trolley Coach in North America*, Interurban Special. Cerritos, Calif.: I. L. Swett, 1974.

———' AND PAUL WARD, *Transit's Stepchild: The Trolley Coach*. Cerritos, Calif.: Interurbans, 1973.

YAGO, GLENN, *The Decline of Transit: Urban Transportation in German and U.S. Cities 1900–1970*. New York: Cambridge University Press, 1984.

EXERCISES

1-1   Why are urban places or cities important in economic, social, and cultural life?

1-2   Why was the agricultural revolution critical in the development of urban places?

1-3   What role did water transportation play in the growth of urban places?

1-4   What role did the horse-drawn omnibus play in urban development in the nineteenth century?

1-5   What part was played by the horse railway in urban growth? Why were franchises required and what was required of the franchise holder?

1-6   What was the impact of the cable car on American cities?

1-7   How did the electric street railway revolutionize urban growth patterns in the late nineteenth and early twentieth centuries?

1-8   How did ferry boats, commuter railways, and electric interurban railways affect American cities?

1-9   Where was rapid transit first introduced in the United States? What job does it do that other modes cannot perform?

1-10   Why were the motor bus and trolleybus developed? What is their unique contribution?

Chapter 2

PUBLIC TRANSPORTATION IN THE 20TH CENTURY

ARTHUR SALTZMAN

It is difficult for younger persons living in the auto-oriented society of the 1990s to conceive of the important role that transit once played in urban America. To the urban dweller of the first quarter of the twentieth century, transit was as pervasive a travel mode and sociological phenomenon as the automobile is today.

America's urbanization in the early part of the twentieth century was shaped to a great degree by the electric street railway. The patterns of land use and population dispersion that took place followed the spokelike patterns of new street railway lines, which allowed workers not only to commute in and out of the city but also to provide the benefits of open spaces for their families. Transit, in some cities, captured the imagination of the most prestigious citizens, who recognized that commercial and residential development would follow the transit tracks. Elevated railways and subways in the larger cities were among the largest public works of their time. They commanded the attention of financiers, who saw transit as a public utility that would yield a reasonable return on their investment. Those who needed stable investments were advised to invest in the "transit trusts" because they were such a reliable source of income.

The street railway system not only provided access to downtown areas for urban residents during their 6-day workweek, but also allowed the family a Sunday visit to amusement parks located at the end of the transit line. Cemeteries were also often at the end of the street railway lines, and many family outings would include a visit to the grave of a deceased relative, followed by a picnic, and then a visit to the amusement park. A true transit habit was ingrained in urban dwellers of all ages. There were few safety or security problems, and, by the time they were ready to go to school, many urban children had already been taught how to use the local transit system. Many youngsters, who developed the transit habit going to and from school, maintained it for going to work after their school years were over.

But even as the majority of travelers were making virtually all their trips by transit, wealthier urban residents were testing the new mode that eventually would be the aspiration of all Americans and become the symbol of mobility and a suburbanized life-style. At first the automobile was considered a rich man's toy, but a general increase in affluence and the reduction in auto purchase prices resulting from mass production soon made auto ownership affordable for an increasing portion of the population.

Figure 2-1   *Transportation in transition—stages to automobiles. San Francisco at foot of Market Street (courtesy of California Department of Transportation)*

Transit simultaneously lost its glamour and pervasiveness as it lost its patronage. Instead of serving all types of trips, transit became the preferred mode only for the journey to work, and then gradually it lost predominance even in this area, being largely replaced by the private automobile for every type of trip. Transit rapidly became the conveyance for those who had no other choice.

While competition from the automobile is the reason most cited for the decline of transit, institutional, regulatory, and financial factors also affected the transit industry's performance. The transit industry lacked innovative management and was preoccupied with operational problems to the exclusion of marketing efforts.[1] Much of this criticism is justified, but, as subsequent sections of this chapter will show, external forces over which the industry had little control were far more important in determining the destiny of transit.

The industry at times tried to respond to changing travel demands, but new ways of doing things came primarily from outside sources. Attempts at innovation from within the industry were infrequent and, generally, not widely adopted. For instance, between 1916 and 1921 many street railway operators tried to raise their service level by using a smaller, lighter streetcar called the Birney Safety Car, which was equipped to operate with one man instead of two. The savings in labor were then used to increase the frequency of service. Several experiments showed that ridership increased between 34% and 59% after the headways were decreased from 15 to 8 min.[2] After 1921, however, it became obvious that the Birney car was not large enough to cope with the demands of heavy peak-hour traffic, and its lighter weight made it more susceptible to being stopped by snow or ice conditions. Thus, this industry-developed innovation lost its popularity almost as rapidly as it had been gained.

Motor buses were a major innovation in the transit industry, but the street railway industry was slow to take advantage of this new technology because it was not a rail component. However, by 1930, many operators had accepted the motor bus, at least for service into new territory. Experimentation with motor buses was widespread, including many different vehicle configurations, such as double-decker and articulated buses. Even luxury routes at first-class fares were tried. Unfortunately, few new ideas took hold. In the late 1930s, most transit companies exhibited little incentive to do very much more in the way of innovation than to continue to convert their street railway routes to almost identical bus routes. The transit picture was one of a large number of operators each having a monopoly within their own area. Like most utilities, the structure of the transit industry ruled out direct competition, and operators were not prone to adopt successful innovations that were developed in other cities. The major exception was the Electric Railway Presidents' Conference Committee (PCC) car, which was developed by the industry in the mid-1930s. Unfortunately, this standardized trolley was introduced just as motor buses were replacing most street railway systems.

There was little innovation between the end of World War II and the early 1960s. The industry began a downward cycle of decreasing ridership, which led to reduced revenue, causing reductions in service in order to reduce cost. Lower service levels inevitably led more passengers to seek another mode (usually the auto) and, thus, the cycle would begin again. The declining ridership experienced by public transportation started in 1945 and continued until the mid-1970s, when massive infusions of public funds, used to expand service, reversed the trend. It is difficult to say that widespread adoption of innovations during this period would have reversed the decline in ridership, but perhaps it might have slowed it somewhat.

The remainder of this chapter reviews the various forces that have influenced the transit industry. Ridership trends and the change of emphasis from streetcars to motor buses is discussed. The financial and ownership problems of the transit industry are reviewed. The final section concerns the effect of government activities on the decline of transit.

TRANSIT RIDERSHIP TRENDS

Accurate historical data on transit ridership are difficult to find. Although the industry was criticized for the lack of complete and accurate data as early as 1917, there was no generally accepted standard for collecting data on ridership until 1980. In that year, the industry started to use procedures defined by Section 15 of the Urban Mass Transportation Act (see Chap. 3).

Figure 2-2 depicts ridership trends for selected years from 1900 to 1990. Data covering the period before 1921 were obtained from the Electrical Industry Censuses of 1902, 1907, 1912, and 1917. For other years in that period, the data are speculative. The U.S. Census did not distinguish between interurban and urban electric railway passengers until 1937, and did not account for non-street-railway-company-operated buses until 1932. Estimates of motor bus patronage before 1932 are low enough so that they do not skew the data noticeably. However, the effect of intercity patronage and the lack of standardized accounting for transfer passengers (the definition apparently changed every 5 years) can make as much as a 10 to 20% difference in urban revenue passenger estimates. Other data used to prepare Fig. 2-2 come from Barger[3] (who corrected for interurban passengers) and various corporate entries in Moody's *Public Utility Manual*[4] and Moody's *Transportation Manual*.[5] Passenger data are usually reported as *revenue passengers*, which refers to initial boarding passengers only, and *total passengers*, which includes all transfer, charter, and nonrevenue rides. Thus, the peak ridership in 1945 as reported by the American Public Transit Association[6] was 23,254 million total passengers or 18,982 million revenue passengers.

Despite these problems with the data, the numbers are still useful in depicting ridership trends of the transit industry. To review these trends, it is useful to distinguish among five time segments. These are the initial rapid growth from 1900 to 1919; a period of fluctuation from 1920 to 1939; the war-induced growth from 1940 to 1945; the lengthy decline covering the period 1946 to 1972; and finally the modest growth from 1973 to 1990.

INITIAL RAPID GROWTH (1900-1919)

During the period 1900 to 1919, per capita ridership rose faster than the urban population. The introduction of electricity to the horse railways has been offered as the primary explanation for this.[7] The higher average speeds and capacity of line-haul electric railways permitted cities to greatly expand their urbanized areas. This dispersion necessitated more transit travel than the compact nineteenth-century city required.

FLUCTUATION (1920-1939)

At the end of the World War I, ridership growth continued but at a slower rate than previously. Because of the increasing urban population, this slower growth in passengers actually represents a decreasing share of the urban transportation market.[8]

Between 1929 and 1933 the lower income and loss of employment related to the Great Depression caused about a 20% decline in revenue passengers. Much of this loss was regained by the industry as the country started to climb out of its financial depression in the late 1930s.

WAR-INDUCED GROWTH (1940-1945)

A war-induced spurt of ridership started in 1939 because of gas rationing, wartime industrial production, and automobile tire and parts shortages. By 1945, ridership had climbed to almost twice its prewar level.

LENGTHY DECLINE (1946-1972)

The enormous demand for automobile ownership had been suppressed by the war. When automobile manufacturing facilities resumed production in 1946, the public demanded more autos than were available. The establishment of the auto as the dominant urban transportation mode was spurred on by changing land-use patterns and higher incomes, and the transit industry was virtually decimated. The 5-day workweek was also a factor. Except in the large, congested urban areas, transit became the mode only for those who had no other choice. "Transit dependents" and peak-hour commuters were the principal markets for public transportation.

MODEST GROWTH (1973-1990)

The reversal in the decline of public transportation patronage coincided with the gasoline shortages of the early 1970s and the availability of public funds for transit support. For a variety of social and political reasons, federal, state, and local governments provided capital assistance and then operating assistance during these years. (See Chap. 3.) In the 1980s and early 1990s, patronage continued to increase slowly as services improved and the effects of energy cost and environmental concerns affected the public.

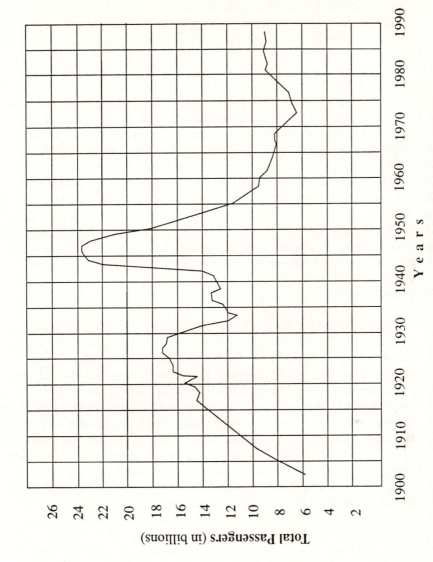

Figure 2-2 *Trends in transit patronage in the United States, 1900-1990. [See text for sources.]*

29

While the decline in transit ridership has been pervasive, it has not been uniform. Until recently, virtually every urban area lost transit ridership, but in the smaller cities, both the increase in World War II and the subsequent loss of patronage were more severe than in the larger ones.

The increased percentage of transit patronage during the war was the greatest in the smaller cities. Ridership in cities of 50,000 to 100,000 almost doubled between 1940 and 1950, while in cities of less than 50,000 population, the increase was a phenomenal 150%.[9] In smaller cities, less transit service had been offered, and the per capita transit ridership had been comparatively low before the war. Consequently, gasoline rationing and other shortages during the war spurred transit ridership to a greater degree in the smaller urban areas.

The decline in ridership which started in 1945 was, predictably, most severe in the smaller cities. Not only did riders opt for the auto, but decreased ridership resulted in the demise of many small transit systems. The attractive travel times of rail rapid transit and high parking costs in congested larger cities were major factors in retaining patronage. Patronage in the dispersed smaller cities, where congestion and parking fees were not as onerous to the auto driver, dropped more precipitously.

PEAK-HOUR DOMINANCE

Since a high percentage of its ridership is associated with work trips, transit suffers from a demand profile that is severely peaked. It is difficult to utilize vehicles and drivers efficiently where the transit traveling public takes up to five times as many rides per hour during morning and evening peak hours than during the off-peak hours. Unfortunately, this peaking phenomenon was exacerbated during the period of transit decline. Proportionately, more off-peak riders stopped using transit than peak-hour patrons. Transit operators attempted to recoup some of this loss of off-peak riders by offering reduced fares to non-peak-hour riders, but usually to no avail. The journey-to-work trip, which causes the peak in transit demand, maintained its patronage, while nonwork trips, which tend to be more evenly distributed throughout the day, decreased markedly. So, while ridership and revenue dropped, there was not a corresponding opportunity for reductions in cost. This worsening peaking problem is further complicated by labor work rules, which often give little opportunity for the operator to reduce the work force during the middle of the day.

FROM STREETCARS TO BUSES

Accompanying the decline in patronage was a shift in modes. Table 2-1 shows that streetcars, now included in light rail transit, were used for 94% of urban passenger trips in 1907. Rail rapid transit accounted for virtually all the other riders in that year. It was not until the 1920s that bus ridership became a discernible portion of the total.

TABLE 2-1
Trends in Methods of Transit in the United States
Selected Years 1907-1988
(billions of total passengers)[a]

Year	Streetcar/ Light Rail		Rail Rapid Transit		Trolley Coach		Bus		Total Passengers
	Psgrs.	% of Total	Psgrs.	% of Total	Psgrs.	% of Total	Psgrs.	% of Total	
1907	8.9	94	0.7	7	—		—		9.5
1912	11.2	93	1.0	8	—		—		12.1
1920	13.7	88	1.8	12	—		—		15.5
1925	12.9	77	2.3	14	—		1.5	9	16.7
1930	10.5	67	2.6	17	—		2.5	16	15.6
1935	7.3	60	2.2	18	0.1	1	2.6	21	12.2
1940	5.9	45	2.4	18	0.5	4	4.2	32	13.1
1945	9.4	40	2.7	16	1.2	5	9.9	42	23.3
1950	3.9	23	2.3	13	1.7	10	9.4	55	17.2
1955	1.2	10	1.9	16	1.2	10	7.2	63	11.5
1960	0.6	5	1.8	19	0.7	11	6.4	68	9.4
1965	0.3	4	1.9	23	0.3	4	5.8	70	8.3
1970	0.2	3	1.9	26	0.2	3	5.0	68	7.3
1975	0.1	1	1.7	24	0.1	1	5.1	72	7.3
1980	0.1	1	2.1	24	0.1	1	5.8	67	8.6
1985	0.1	1	2.3	26	0.1	1	5.7	66	8.9
1988	0.2	2	2.3	3	0.1	1	5.8	65	8.9

[a]Total passengers include transfer, nonrevenue, and charter passengers as well as revenue passengers.
    Sources: American Public Transit Association, *Transit Fact Book*, 1975-76 ed. and 1989 ed. (Washington, D.C.: American Public Transit Association, 1976 and 1989). Data for 1907-1940 from Wilfred Owen, *The Metropolitan Transportation Problem*, rev. ed. (Washington, D.C.: The Brookings Institution, 1966), Appendix Table 16. Because of rounding, figures may not add to totals.

The first application of the internal combustion engine to public transport occurred soon after the introduction of the gasoline-powered automobile in both Europe and the United States near the turn of the century. By 1905, motor buses, not too dissimilar from contemporary streetcar physical designs albeit somewhat smaller, were running on regular routes in London and New York. A 34-passenger double-decker bus had been imported to the United States in 1905 for a trial, and in 1907, the Fifth Avenue Coach Company in Manhattan had 14 more in service.[10]

Early buses were noisy and uncomfortable and more expensive than later versions (to both the operator and the passenger, who often paid a double fare on a bus), but their use in New York, London, and many other European cities indicated that satisfactory equipment for innovation was available. In fact, by 1914, the London horse-drawn omnibuses had been entirely supplanted by more than 3000 motor buses designed, built, and operated by the London General Omnibus Company.

In contrast, horse-drawn streetcars remained in service on some crosstown routes in Manhattan until 1923 because the operator could not afford to electrify, nor was the service especially amenable to the motor bus. The horsecars were later replaced with battery-powered streetcars. In Europe the motor bus was very competitive with the streetcar, a condition that was not entirely unnoticed in the United States. In a paper read at the Sixth National Conference on City Planning in May 1914, John A. McCollum stated that:

> The operating efficiency of the motor bus in London . . . probably exceeds the efficiency of many street railway systems. In Paris there are more than 1,000 vehicles of a type unlike those in London, operating under different conditions, but performing nevertheless an efficient passenger service. New motor bus routes are being established daily in European cities. Some are being added to street railway systems and are designed to supplement the railway services by extension into districts where the traffic does not warrant the permanent investments of the large sums necessary for the operation of a railway.[11]

Probably the main reason that motor buses did not take immediate hold was that the "transit trusts" had vast sums invested in their streetcar lines and were not willing to make their investment obsolete or to take a chance on new technology. These operators, with some exceptions, seemed to take the attitude that they were in the electric railway industry as opposed to being in the business of providing urban transportation.[12]

A member of the motor bus industry attended an American Electric Railway Association Convention in 1922 as the representative of a bus manufacturer in Chicago. He reported that there was enough ill feeling toward the motor bus industry at the convention that he was "testing the hardness of some red apples being comforted in their possibilities as weapons of defense, if necessary in covering our retreat from the convention."[13] However, a few years later in 1925, the same representative was to praise the progress made by the street railway industry in changing its attitude toward the motor bus.[14]

Figure 2-3 *New York's Fifth Avenue double-deck buses—1930s. (courtesy of American Public Transit Association)*

Although consistent and accurate statistics are not readily available on independent lines, the use of motor buses by electric railway companies accelerated from 370 buses on 700 rte.-mi (1130 rte.-km) in 1922 to 8277 buses on 14,300 rte.-mi (23,000 rte.-km) in 1927.[15] In 1925, as indicated in Table 2-1, buses carried 1.5 billion total passengers, which was only about 9% of the total of 16.7 billion urban passengers for the entire industry. The urban transit industry hit its peak ridership in 1927, with about 17.2 billion total passengers (12 to 13 billion revenue passengers); buses accounted for 2.3 billion; streetcars and rail rapid transit carried the remainder.

Streetcar companies were eventually forced to make the change to the motor bus. By the 1930s, streetcar equipment was badly in need of replacement, but investment money had been difficult to attract because the industry's growth had been stemmed after World War I and, even more so, during the Great Depression. Buses were generally cheaper to purchase than streetcars; so with the restricted capital available, the wisdom of changing over to the motor bus became clearer. However, most of the impetus for change came from outside the established industry. This was caused primarily by the lack of financial and management resources within the transit companies, exacerbated, perhaps, by the vacuum created during the forced divestures of operating properties from the power trusts, which will be discussed in a subsequent section of this chapter.

In some colorful reporting in 1936 by *Fortune* magazine, the virtues of the bus are contrasted with the streetcar.

> Over the past fifteen years or so, the city bus has clawed, butted, and fought its way through traffic-glutted streets, through spongier and more perilous politic-glutted operating franchises, until it is, today, a phenomenon of mass transportation. You see city buses everywhere—mastodonic metal hulks gliding in and out of traffic with a soft hissing of air brakes, a rich sound of balloon tires on asphalt, a resonant hum of engines concealed within their structures. And the main reason this almost brand new vehicle became a phenomenon is because the faithful electric trolley had sunk into such a state of obsolescence as to be scarcely tolerable. During the fifteen years the bus was growing, the trolley, as an invention, virtually stood still. It just grew older and the street it was still suffered to haunt grew noisier with its clanking decrepitude. Half the trolleys now in use are twenty years old or older: the average age is around sixteen.[16]

The streetcar industry did band together, beginning in the early 1930s, to build an ideal trolley. As previously indicated, this industry group, called the Electric Railway President's Conference Committee (PCC), did an extremely good job in producing the PCC car. By the late 1930s, PCC cars were in wide use, and they proved to be capable performers. Drivers, operators, and the public all liked the PCCs, but their introduction did not greatly avert the steady abandonment of streetcar lines.

The replacement of trolleys by buses ("bustitution" as it is acrimoniously described by trolley fans) was almost complete in the United States, although there are still trolley operations in a few cities. In addition to the places where streetcars have been in continuous service since the first part of this century, several cities have recently introduced light rail systems. Table 2-1 indicates streetcar/light rail systems currently account for a small, but growing, fraction of total annual passenger volume.

Rail rapid transit has been the most stable of the transit modes. Its ridership peak during World War II and its subsequent decline have been moderate compared with total transit passenger counts. This stability can be ascribed to the same forces that caused ridership in larger urban areas to fluctuate less than those in smaller cities. Rail rapid transit primarily serves the journey-to-work trip in the largest, densest, and oldest cities, where congestion and high parking fees act as a deterrent to automobile usage. It also has maintained a high level of service, despite increased auto traffic, because the right-of-way is grade separated. Table 2-1 clearly shows that rapid transit ridership has always fluctuated less than that of the industry totals.

FINANCIAL PROBLEMS AND FORCED PUBLIC OWNERSHIP

Early street railway operators went to great lengths to secure exclusive franchise rights. Their resulting monopoly positions encouraged them to be inflexible. Given the absence of competition, transit operators counted on their rapidly increasing ridership to pay for the conversion from horsecars to electric street railways. This conversion often resulted in an excessive valuation of equipment, land, and franchises. Further overcapitalization occurred when local street railways merged to provide a unified system in each urban area. Behling, for example, noted that "mountainous capitalization created in the more severe days of strong monopoly, have resulted in inflexibility and have made the traction companies loath to adjust fares to changed conditions of demand."[17]

Heavily watered stock and other abuses led much of the public, and their political leaders, to mistrust the "transit trusts." Much of the lack of public empathy with the industry's problems could be traced to the commonly held image of the companies—that they were socially and financially irresponsible. This was often true, unfortunately, and was constantly reiterated by local politicians and newspapers.[18, 19]

Another problem faced by the transit industry in those days was that it was not possible to raise fares rapidly enough to keep pace with rising costs. The concept of a fixed fare was often written into the franchise at the request of the street railway companies as a hedge against future political pressures to reduce fares.[20, 21] The public accepted this concept and later believed that the early 5-cent fare was their right. Ex-President Taft once testified that "if you inquired of a great many [of the public] you would find some such idea . . . that [the 5-cent fare] was guaranteed to them in the Constitution; that anything above five cents would indicate a return to investors that was outrageous. So strong is the question of fares that few politicians today would enthusiastically endorse a fare raise."[22]

Early street railway operators wanted profits and thought a fixed fare could guarantee them. However, by World War I the industry was "caught between the upper millstone of the customary and franchise-fixed fare of five cents and the nether millstone of rapidly rising wartime costs."[23] While ridership and revenue remained relatively consistent, operating costs were increased by severe inflation during the war. By 1919, one-third of the operating companies were bankrupt. So serious was the plight of the industry that in 1919 President Wilson appointed the Federal Electric Railways Commission to publicize and investigate the problem.[24]

It is not surprising that average fares were still only 6.9 cents in 1945. However, post-World War II inflation finally caused transit fares to start rising rapidly. By 1954, the average fare was almost 20 cents and the industry was still barely able to cover operating expenses from the fareboxes. In 1968, the first year the industry reported a net operating loss, average fares had risen to almost 23 cents. In 1988, average fares were 62 cents, but the revenue generated by passengers only covered 36% of operating expenses.[25] The remainder of the funds needed to operate came mainly from federal, state, and local government sources.

A massive restructuring of the transit industry occurred during the 1920s. What emerged were large utility holding companies that controlled the transit operating organization, in addition to holding majority stock of other utilities, such as electric power and gas. The street railways were able to use the credit of the holding companies for capital requirements and, as a result, continued to offer a reasonably high level of transit service. As will be indicated later, federal antitrust regulations interceded and stopped this cross-subsidization in the late 1930s.

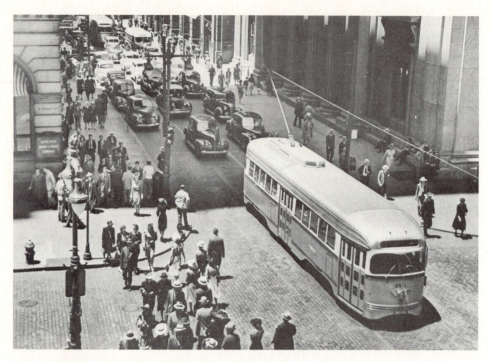

Figure 2-4 *PCC car—Philadelphia. (courtesy of American Public Transit Association)*

Public ownership of transit was thus unusual during the first half of the twentieth century. While there were still private operators willing to provide service, there was little incentive for municipal governments to own or operate transit. However, by midcentury, private companies, faced with increasing deficits, petitioned local officials to either provide an annual subsidy or purchase the operation.

Transit properties in the larger cities were the first to be publicly owned. By the 1970s, virtually all the larger city operations had passed from private to public ownership. The properties that remained under private control were found in the smaller cities and carried a relatively small proportion of the industry's total patrons. For example, in 1985, although only 29% of the 1435 transit companies in the United States were publicly owned, this segment carried 96% of the annual revenue passengers.[26] Even in most of the remaining private systems, public funds were used to provide the difference between farebox receipts and operating costs. Whether publicly or privately owned, transit properties had become dependent on government financial support.

GOVERNMENT ACTIVITIES

A number of public policies that were not directed toward public transit have directly influenced the industry's performance. Not until the 1960s was federal policy intentionally directed to the industry. This period began when Congress passed the Housing Act of 1961, which will be discussed later in this chapter.

Although 1961 was the first time there was direct congressional activity in mass transit, there have been other federal activities which either involved other institutions than Congress or were not primarily directed at mass transit, but nonetheless had an impact on that industry. An example of nonlegislative activities was the antitrust prosecution of General Motors, National City Lines, and others initiated by the Department of Justice in 1947. Legislative actions not specifically directed at the transit industry are exemplified by the Public Utility Holding Company Act of 1935 and federal policies toward housing and highways. The effects of each of these will be explored. Clearly, antitrust prosecutions and the Public Utility Holding Act had less influence on the industry than the investment-oriented policies that encouraged highway building and home ownership. However, no analytical framework has yet been developed that would allow a precise assessment of these government activities.

PUBLIC UTILITY HOLDING COMPANY ACT OF 1935

Utility holding companies played a key role in the provision of capital for electrification of the street railways. By acquiring utilities, holding companies would control power, gas, water, and transit in many cities. Often a large holding company had control over utilities in several dispersed urban areas. A Federal Trade Commission (FTC) study of the power, gas, and oil industry estimated that power holding companies directly controlled transit operations serving 878.9 million revenue passengers in 1931, about 10% of the nationwide total.[27] The study also identified 171 transit companies, representing one-fourth of the total, that were indirectly controlled by interlocking directorates among some dozen power trusts.

Congressional hearings and an FTC investigation did not adequately consider the potential effect the Public Utility Holding Company Act of 1935 would have on the transit industry and the act was passed. The act's key provision stated that "after Jan. 1, 1938 . . . each registered holding company . . . [must] limit [its] operations to a single integrated public utility system."[28] The Securities and Exchange Commission (SEC) could modify this provision where economies of scale were demonstrated, but few holding companies requested an exemption from the act.

Because the transit operations of the power companies were showing consistent losses, the power trusts seemed pleased to find an excuse to dispose of transit companies without incurring the wrath of local communities. They were able to eliminate the need for cross-subsidizing transit and, therefore, improve the profit of their basic operation.

Removal of the support of the power trusts was a severe blow to transit. Within a few years after the act took effect in 1938, only a few transit companies were left in the hands of power trusts. In New Orleans, for example, long after most public utility companies had divested their transit properties, the power company subsidized the transit operation as part of New Orleans Public Service's utility franchise agreement with the locality. The high per capita ridership that this property recorded for many years—second only to New York—is one indication of the effect of the 1935 act on public transit.[29] One can only speculate on what would have happened if Congress and the SEC had better anticipated the effect of this legislation.

ANTITRUST PROSECUTIONS

Moving into the vacuum created by the divestment of the power trusts, General Motors Corporation (GMC) and several other motor bus, parts, and gasoline suppliers entered the transit business. They acquired stock in operating companies in exchange for capital and management services. This was similar to the techniques power companies had used to electrify, and eventually control, the street railway companies. For example, Yellow Bus and Coach, the bus-building subsidiary of GMC, had been the leader in sales since buses came on the scene in the 1920s. Its primary customers were the fleets controlled by its own subsidiary, the Hertz Omnibus Company.

Hertz, originally in the taxi business, extended its control of transit operations to many different cities and converted all of them from streetcars to buses. Hertz also was linked to the National City Lines (NCL), which, by 1946, had acquired some 46 transit systems. The acquisitions were financed almost entirely by stock shares sold to GMC and Firestone Tire and Rubber and, through the NCL subsidiary Pacific (later American) City Lines, to Phillips Petroleum, Standard Oil of California, and Mack Manufacturing Corporation.

In 1947, the Department of Justice sought an injunction against NCL and its suppliers, accusing them of being in violation of antitrust laws. The case was ultimately settled 19 years later when GMC signed a consent decree that severely curtailed its involvement in transit operations.

At a time when large injections of capital were needed to replace the worn-out fleet of transit vehicles that had limped through the peak ridership of World War II, an application of federal statutes had once again deprived transit of a source of funds. It appears, in retrospect, that the Justice Department did not consider the plight of the transit industry. One could conjecture what would have happened if a strong federal Department of Transportation had been available to argue the case of the transit industry or to supply alternative solutions to the court mandate. Again, although no analysis is available, it is doubtful that the current ridership or profit picture would be significantly different if NCL, GMC, and the others involved in the case had been allowed to continue their involvement in transit. The basic forces of affluence and suburbanization that caused the decline of transit probably would have dominated any potential capital improvements they may have made; and most of the firms involved could have obtained better returns on their funds by investing in automobile-related industries.

The attention paid to the role of GMC as the villain in a plot to decimate transit continued when, during the spring of 1974, much publicity was generated by the hearings held on this issue by the Senate Subcommittee on Antitrust and Monopoly. A report by Bradford Snell, a Senate staff member, suggested that GMC, Ford, and Chrysler had purposefully suppressed the bus and rail transit industry.[30] He reported that the social consequences of the monopoly position of GMC had been very costly. "The motorization of Los Angeles and the dieselization of the New Haven Railroad are two of the most appalling episodes in the history of American transportation. These and other shocking incidents, however, were the inevitable outgrowth of concentrated economic power."[31]

Snell was dramatic and premature in his 1974 observation that "we are witnessing today the collapse of a society based on the automobile" and his depicting of General Motors as "a sovereign economic state."[32]

General Motors' response to this attack pointed out that the demise of the streetcars started long before GMC was involved in the operation of transit companies.[33] It is probable that GMC did not act in an underhanded way to cause the demise of street railways. On the other hand, there is little indication that they attempted to preserve rail systems. GMC was simply ready to supply transit operators with motor buses, which were both cheaper to buy and operate than streetcars and which also allowed the transit operators more flexibility in their routing of vehicles.

FEDERAL POLICIES TOWARD HOUSING AND HIGHWAYS

Transportation analysts usually point to auto competition as the primary cause of transit decline. They suggest that the affluent American demanded and received more and better roads, which were then clogged by an increasing number of vehicles. Thus, an induced demand for roads was perpetuated by patterns of increased auto ownership, the demand itself being primed by the addition of new roads.

It is doubtful that anyone in the Veterans Administration or the Federal Housing Administration thought that they were going to create increased suburbanization and urban sprawl by their federally insured home mortgage programs. Yet, it is clear that these programs were a major force in the establishment and growth of low-density areas around dense urban centers. Mortgage guarantees and government purchases of mortgages were some of the instruments used between 1945 and 1960 to induce housing construction and, more specifically, allow as many Americans as possible to own homes.

As a way of maximizing the security of these loans, the lenders looked for safe investments. Conventional wisdom holds that security is found in single-family homes in areas of social and racial homogeneity.[34] In short, lenders preferred to invest in homes that were in the suburbs, which are difficult areas to serve with conventional transit. As a result, a policy aimed at providing better housing had the effect of placing more persons in areas that were relatively expensive and inefficient to serve by public transit.

The rapid growth of highways further enhanced the auto in comparison to transit. This growth was clearly spurred on by federal policies, starting with Works Progress Administration (WPA) and Public Works Administration (PWA) efforts during the 1930s, which were begun primarily as relief from the Great Depression. But it was not until the late 1950s that federal highway funding became a major factor.

Administered by the Bureau of Public Roads (and subsequently by the Federal Highway Administration), the National System of Interstate and Defense Highways was to become the largest public works project in the history of the world. Federal legislation provided for a gas tax, which secured a dedicated source of revenue for the Highway Trust Fund. Funds were made available to the states to build their portion of the Interstate Highway System on a 90% federal, 10% state matching basis. State legislatures lost little time in voting for their own highway user taxes, which were used to provide the matching funds. The interstate program and more highway building in general had overwhelming support among virtually every sector of American society, and the highway lobby became a powerful force at every level of government. Thus, in the 1950s and early 1960s the public purchased more and more automobiles and responsive governments built more and better roads.

FEDERAL POLICIES TOWARD TRANSIT

There was no malice toward transit in these highway programs. In the period right after World War II, it was accepted policy that the federal government had no role in public transit. Each transit property was expected to be self-supporting, and transit was considered by most to be a local problem for municipal governments to handle. Several factors were to change this prevailing attitude. First, under Presidents Kennedy and Johnson, there was an increased attention to urban problems. Even though the Nixon and Ford administrations de-emphasized the urban programs of the previous administrations, they still embraced transit problems in an attempt to accommodate all perspectives on the urban problem. Transit was being asked to solve a variety of societal goals, including restoring the economic vitality of cities, protecting the environment, conserving energy, easing the mobility of transit-dependent persons, and providing inner-city residents with better access to jobs.[35] Meanwhile, the highway builders were facing citizens' revolts against more road building.

In this decision-making environment the Congress passed more and more powerful transit legislation (see also Chapter 3), starting with the Housing Act of 1961, which contained three provisions affecting mass transportation: (1) a demonstration program, (2) requirements for including mass transportation as an integral part of comprehensive urban planning, and (3) a loan program for mass transportation agencies.[36] The first federal capital assistance was included in the Urban Mass Transportation Act of 1964, while funds to defray operating expenses were authorized by Congress in 1974. Initially administered by the Department of Housing and Urban Development (HUD), these urban transportation programs were transferred in 1968 to the Department of Transportation's Urban Mass Transportation Administration (UMTA).

Unfortunately, the transit industry was being asked to solve too many problems simultaneously. For transit programs to be successful, the automobile rider had to be diverted to public transit. This expectation has not been realized. Even though transit service has improved in many cities, most passengers are still those who do not have easy access to an automobile and are thus "captive" to the transit system. Almost all American citizens, except those in very dense urban areas, have ready access to an automobile. Even among groups who are generally considered transportation disadvantaged—elderly, physically handicapped, and economically disadvantaged persons—the automobile mode dominates.

Although the transit decline has been halted, the industry has not increased its share of the market. The infusion of public funds to cover capital and operating expenses appears to have had three major impacts. Equipment has been upgraded, the cost of production has increased, and the fare has been stabilized and, in some cases, lowered.[37] However, transit programs have been very resistant to attempts to eliminate them. Although Republican administrations in the 1980s wanted to do away with the operating subsidies, they were not able to do so. Congress continued to appropriate funds for transit properties to purchase equipment and to cover operating expenses.

SUMMARY

This chapter has reviewed the many events that occurred in the twentieth century that led to the decline of transit as the dominant mode of travel. During this century, as automobile ownership became available to almost every citizen, a demand was also generated for more and better roads. A more mobile life-style, which included single-family homes, suburban shopping centers, and industrial parks, resulted in dispersed trip-making patterns that were best served by the automobile operating on high-speed roads and that, on the other hand were difficult for transit to serve. Government policies in housing and highway development also contributed to this dispersion.

Unfortunately, the transit industry was not able to respond to changing public transportation needs. This was partly due to the industry's conservative approach to innovation, which was more acceptable when the industry was in a monopoly situation. Before the mass production of automobiles, transit did not have to compete for its share of the urban transportation market, and urban dwellers had a well-developed "transit habit." Once mass-produced automobiles became available, the transit industry started to lose its share of the travel market and did little to attract new passengers or to keep its old ones.

With restrictions on automobile travel caused by World War II, transit ridership started to grow again. The transit industry almost doubled its patronage during the war years, but this induced ridership was an aberration.

Exacerbating the problems of the transit industry were the 1935 Public Utility Holding Company Act and antitrust prosecution against major bus suppliers. These actions, initiated by the government, tended to restrict the flow of investment capital into the transit industry at a time when the increased patronage of the war years had left transit equipment in a severely deteriorated state.

As soon as wartime shortages ended, a wave of suburbanization and automobile buying began. Reduced employment had its effect on ridership, and the change from a 6-day to a 5-day workweek cut into weekend transit trip making.

Public ownership and government subsidies were the remedies for transit. The results have been limited. Transit ridership appeared to level off in the early 1970s, and then, aided by gasoline shortages, patronage has increased slowly, starting in the mid-1970s. But along with this success in stopping the decline in patronage was a dramatic increase in operating expenses. It remains to be seen whether the industry can continue to attract more passengers while abating escalating costs. Public funds are not limitless and the industry cannot expect to continue to increase its share of public resources while providing only a small portion of total urban trips.

REFERENCES

1   LEWIS M. SCHNEIDER, *Marketing Urban Mass Transit: A Comparative Study of Management Strategies* (Boston: Harvard University, Graduate School of Business Administration, Division of Research, 1965).

2   WILLIAM D. MIDDLETON, *The Time of the Trolley* (Milwaukee, Wis.: Kalmbach Publishing Co., 1967), p. 125.

3   HAROLD BARGER, *The Transportation Industries, 1889-1946: A Study of Output, Employment, and Productivity* (New York: National Bureau of Economic Research, 1951).

4   MOODY'S INVESTORS SERVICE, INC., *Moody's Public Utility Manual*, ed. Frank J. St. Clair (New York: Moody's Investors Service, Inc., 1969).

5   MOODY'S INVESTORS SERVICE, INC., *Moody's Transportation Manual*, ed. Frank J. St. Clair (New York: Moody's Investors Service, Inc., 1969).

6   AMERICAN PUBLIC TRANSIT ASSOCIATION, *Transit Fact Book*, 1975-76 ed. (Washington, D.C.: American Public Transit Association, 1976), pp. 30-32.

7   *Proceedings of the Federal Electric Railways Commission*, 3 vols. (Washington, D.C.: U.S. Government Printing Office, 1920), pp. 2163-78.

8   DAVID W. JONES, JR., *Urban Transit Policy: An Economic and Political History* (Englewood Cliffs, N.J.: Prentice-Hall, Inc., 1985), p. 22.

9   WILFRED OWEN, *The Metropolitan Transportation Problem*, rev. ed. (Washington, D.C.: The Brookings Institution, 1966), pp. 70-73.

10   FRANK HOMER MOSSMAN, ed., *Principles of Urban Transportation* (Cleveland, Ohio: Press of Western Reserve University, 1967).

11   JOHN A. McCOLLUM, "Utility of the Motor Bus and Municipal Problems Pertaining to Its Operation" (unpublished paper read before the Sixth National Conference on City Planning, Toronto, May 1914), p. 5. This paper was transmitted to the Board of Estimate and Apportionment, and the Mayor of the City of New York by the Bureau of Franchises where its author was Assistant Engineer.

12   MARTIN G. GLAESER, *Public Utilities in American Capitalism* (New York: The Macmillan Company, 1957). © The Macmillan Company, 1957.

13   T. R. DAHL, "The Field of the Motor Bus in the Trolley Industry," pamphlet from *American Electric Railway Association Magazine*, March 1925.

14   Ibid., pp. 3-5.

15   MOODY'S INVESTORS SERVICE, INC., *Moody's Manual of Investments American and Foreign: Public Utility Securities,* ed. John Sherman Porter (New York: Moody's Investors Service, Inc., 1937).

16   "Yellow Truck and Coach," *Fortune Magazine*, 14, no. 1 (July 1936), 63-65.

17   BURTON N. BEHLING, *Competition and Monopoly in Public Utility Industries*, Illinois Studies in the Social Sciences, vol. 23, nos. 1-2 (Urbana, Ill.: University of Illinois Press, 1938).

18   EDWARD S. MASON, *The Street Railway in Massachusetts: The Rise and Decline of an Industry*, Harvard Economic Studies, vol. 37 (Cambridge, Mass.: Harvard University Press, 1932).

19   DALLAS M. YOUNG, *Twentieth-Century Experience in Urban Transit: A Study of the Cleveland System and Its Development* (Cleveland, Ohio: Press of Western Reserve University, 1960).

20   MASON, *The Street Railway*, p. 119.

21   YOUNG, *Twentieth-Century Experience*, pp. 12-20.

22   *Proceedings Electric Railways Commission*, p. 4

23   GLAESER, *Public Utilities in American Capitalism*, p. 86.

24   MOSSMAN, *Principles of Urban Transportation*, p. 6.

25   AMERICAN PUBLIC TRANSIT ASSOCIATION, *Transit Fact Book*, 1989 ed. (Washington, D.C.: American Public Transit Fact Book, 1989), pp. 27, 56.

26   Ibid, p. 14.

27   FEDERAL TRADE COMMISSION, *Utility Corporations*, issued in parts from 1928 to 1937 and published as Senate Document no. 92, 70th Congress, 1st Session, 95 vols. *Index*, vol. 84-D, index to Parts 21 to 84-C (Washington, D.C.: U.S. Government Printing Office, 1937).

28   CHARLES W. THOMPSON AND W. R. SMITH, *Public Utility Economics* (New York: McGraw-Hill Book Company, 1941), p. 494.

29   FRED A. TARPLEY, "The Economics of Combined Utility and Transit Operations" (unpublished Ph.D. dissertation, Tulane University, 1967), particularly pp. 292-360.

30   "American Ground Transport," pp. A-1 to A-103, and "The Truth About 'American Ground Transport'—A Reply by General Motors," pp. A-107 to A-144, in *The Industrial Reorganization Act Hearing Before the Subcommittee on Antitrust and Monopoly*, United States Senate, Part 4A—Appendix to Part 4, 93rd Congress, 2nd Session (Washington, D.C.: U.S. Government Printing Office, 1974). The study, "American Ground Transport," by Bradford C. Snell was financed by the Stern Foundation.

31   Ibid., p. A-3.

32   Ibid., p. A-7.

33   Ibid., pp. A-107 to A-127.

34   ALAN ALTSHULER, WITH JAMES P. WOMACK, AND JOHN R. PUCHER, *The Urban Transportation System: Politics and Policy Innovation* (Cambridge, Mass.: The MIT Press, 1979).

35   CHARLES A. LAVE, ed., *Urban Transit: The Private Challenge to Public Transportation*, Pacific Studies in Public Policy (Cambridge, Mass.: Ballinger Publishing Company, 1985).

36   GEORGE M. SMERK, *Urban Mass Transportation: A Dozen Years of Federal Policy* (Bloomington, Ind.: Indiana University Press, 1974).

37   LAVE, *Urban Transit*.

FURTHER READING

SALTZMAN, ARTHUR, AND RICHARD J. SOLOMON, "Historical Overview of the Decline of the Transit Industry," in *Public Transportation and Passenger Characteristics*, Highway Research Record 417, pp. 1-11. Washington, D.C.: Highway Research Board, 1972.

URBAN MASS TRANSPORTATION ADMINISTRATION, *The Status of the Nations Local Mass Transportation: Performance and Conditions*, Report of the Secretary of Transportation to the United States Congress, Pursuant to 49 USC 308, prepared by UMTA. Washington, D.C.: U.S. Government Printing Office, June 1988.

EXERCISES

2-1   Why did many more urban residents have a "transit habit" in the early twentieth century than is the case in the late twentieth century?

2-2   The transit industry had severe financial problems during the early twentieth century because operating costs began to exceed operating revenues. Why did this occur?

2-3   After World War I, many transit companies became part of public utility holding companies. Describe these companies and indicate how this restructuring of the industry affected transit.

2-4   In the early twentieth century, why was transit considered to be a good financial investment? Why did this change?

2-5   In what ways did transit shape cities?

2-6   As transit patronage declined, why did small-city and off-peak ridership decrease much more rapidly than large-city and peak-hour ridership?

2-7   Describe why the definition of those who are transit dependent has changed from 1900 to 1990.

2-8   Why were transit companies reluctant to replace electric streetcars with buses?

2-9   Which government programs directly assisted transit?

2-10   Several government activities were not directed at transit yet had major impacts on the industry. Describe the activities and the impacts.

2-11   How has the ownership of transit changed? Why has this change occurred?

Chapter 3

HISTORY OF URBAN TRANSPORTATION PLANNING

Edward Weiner

Urban transportation planning in the United States has always been conducted by state and local agencies. This is entirely appropriate since highway and transit facilities and services are owned and operated largely by the states and local agencies. The role of the federal government has been to set national policy, provide financial aid, supply technical assistance and training, and conduct research. Over the years, the federal government has attached requirements to its financial assistance. From a planning perspective, the most important has been the requirement that transportation projects in urbanized areas of 50,000 or more in population be based on an urban transportation planning process. This requirement was first incorporated into the Federal-Aid Highway Act of 1962.

The Federal-Aid Highway Act of 1962 created the federal mandate for urban transportation planning in the United States. The act was the capstone of two decades of experimentation and development of urban transportation procedures and institutions. It was passed at a time when urban areas were beginning to plan interstate highway routes through and around their areas. The 1962 act combined with the incentive of 90% federal funding for interstate highway projects caused urban transportation planning to spread quickly throughout the United States. It also had a significant influence on urban transportation planning in other parts of the world.

In some ways, the urban transportation planning process and planning techniques have changed little since then. Yet, in other ways, urban transportation has evolved over these years in response to changing issues, conditions, and values and a greater understanding of urban transportation phenomena. Urban transportation planning practice in the 1990s is considerably more sophisticated, complex, and costly than its highway planning predecessor.

Modifications in the planning process took many years to evolve. As new concerns and issues arose, changes in planning techniques and processes were introduced. These modifications sought to make the planning process more responsive and sensitive to those areas of concern. Urban areas that had the resources and technical ability were the first to develop and adopt new concepts and techniques. These new ideas were diffused by various means throughout the nation, usually with the assistance of the federal government. The rate at which the new concepts were accepted varied from area to area. Consequently, the quality and depth of planning are highly variable at any point in time.

Other requirements have been incorporated into federal legislation and regulations over the years. At times these requirements were very exacting in their detail. At other times, greater flexibility was allowed. Many of these requirements are chronicled in this chapter. The chapter focuses on key events in the evolution of urban transportation planning, including developments in technical procedures, philosophy, processes, and institutions. Furthermore, it includes changes in legislation, policy, regulations, and technology to provide a more complete picture of the forces that have affected and often continue to affect public transportation planning. The chapter concentrates on the key events of national significance and thereby tries to capture the overall evolution of public transportation planning.

BEGINNINGS OF URBAN TRANSPORTATION PLANNING

PIONEERING URBAN TRANSPORTATION STUDIES

Analytical methodology began to be applied in pioneering urban transportation studies in the late 1940s and during the 1950s. Before these studies, urban transportation planning, when accomplished, was based on existing travel demands or on travel forecasts using uniform growth factors applied on an areawide basis.

In 1955 the Chicago Area Transportation Study (CATS) began, and it set the standard for future urban transportation studies. CATS used a basic six-step procedure pioneered in Detroit: data collection, forecasts, goal formulation, preparation of network proposals, testing of proposals, and evaluation of proposals. Transportation networks were developed to serve travel generated by projected land-use patterns. They were tested using systems analysis that considered the effect of each facility on other facilities in the network. Networks were evaluated based on economic efficiency—the maximum amount of travel carried at the least cost. CATS used trip generation, trip distribution, modal split, and traffic assignment models for travel forecasting. A simple land-use forecasting procedure was employed to forecast future land-use and activity patterns. The CATS staff made major advances in the use of the computer in travel forecasting.[1, 2, 3]

The plans resulting from early studies were heavily oriented to regional highway networks based primarily on the criteria of economic costs and benefits. Transit was given secondary consideration. New facilities were evaluated against traffic engineering improvements. Little consideration was given to regulatory or pricing approaches or new technologies. The pioneering urban transportation studies set the content and tone for future studies. They also provided the basis for later federal guidelines.

FEDERAL-AID HIGHWAY ACT OF 1956

The Federal-Aid Highway Act of 1956 was passed during this early period in the development of urban transportation planning. The act launched the largest public works program yet undertaken: construction of the *National System of Interstate and Defense Highways*. The act was the culmination of two decades of studies and negotiation. The act authorized a 41,000-mi (66,000-km) system to link 90% of the cities with populations of 50,000 or greater and many smaller cities and towns as well. The act also authorized the expenditure of $24.8 billion in 13 fiscal years from 1957 to 1969 at a 90% federal share. The act provided construction standards and maximum sizes and weights of vehicles that could operate on the system. The system was to be completed by 1972.[4]

The companion Highway Revenue Act of 1956 increased federal taxes on gasoline and other motor fuels and excise taxes on tires and established new taxes on retreaded tires and a weight tax on heavy trucks and buses. It created a *highway trust fund* to receive the tax revenue, which was dedicated solely for highway purposes. This provision broke with a long-standing congressional precedent not to earmark taxes for specific authorized purposes.[5]

These provisions dominated urban transportation planning for years to come and eventually caused the development of countervailing forces to balance the urban highway program.

SAGAMORE CONFERENCE ON HIGHWAYS AND URBAN DEVELOPMENT

A conference[6] held in 1958 in the Sagamore Center at Syracuse University focused on the need to conduct the planning of urban transportation, including public transportation, on a regionwide, comprehensive basis in a manner that supported the orderly development of urban areas. The conference report recognized that urban transportation plans should be evaluated through a grand accounting of benefits and costs that included both user and nonuser impacts.

HOUSING ACT OF 1961

The first piece of federal legislation to deal explicitly with urban mass transportation was the Housing Act of 1961, passed largely as a result of the growing financial difficulties with commuter rail services. The act inaugurated a demonstration program and a small, low-interest loan program for acquisitions and capital improvements for mass transit systems.

The act also contained a provision for making federal planning assistance available for "preparation of comprehensive urban transportation surveys, studies, and plans to aid in solving problems of traffic congestion, facilitating the circulation of people and goods in metropolitan and other urban areas and reducing transportation needs." The act permitted federal aid to "facilitate comprehensive planning for urban development, including coordinated transportation systems, on a continuing basis." [7]

URBAN TRANSPORTATION PLANNING COMES OF AGE

JOINT REPORT ON URBAN MASS TRANSPORTATION

In March 1962 a joint report on urban mass transportation was submitted to President Kennedy, at his request. This report integrated the objectives for highways and mass transit, which were comparatively independent up to that point but had been growing closer through cooperative activities. The general thrust of the congressional report, as it related to planning, can be summarized by the following excerpt from the transmittal letter:

> federal aid for urban transportation should be made available only when urban communities have prepared or are actively preparing up-to-date general plans for the entire urban area which relate transportation plans to land-use and development plans.

> The major objectives of urban transportation policy are the achievement of sound land-use patterns, the assurance of transportation facilities for all segments of the population, the improvement of overall traffic flow, and the meeting of total transportation needs at minimum cost. Only a balanced transportation system can attain these goals—and in many urban areas this means an extensive mass transportation network fully integrated with the highway and street system. . . . We therefore recommend a new program of grants and loans for urban mass transportation.[8]

PRESIDENT KENNEDY'S TRANSPORTATION MESSAGE

In April 1962, President Kennedy delivered his first message to Congress on the subject of transportation. Many of the ideas related to urban transportation in the message drew upon the previously mentioned joint report. The president's message recognized the close relationship between community development and the need to properly balance the use of private automobiles and mass transportation to help shape and serve urban areas.[9]

FEDERAL-AID HIGHWAY ACT OF 1962

The Federal-Aid Highway Act of 1962 was the first piece of federal legislation to mandate urban transportation planning as a condition for receiving federal funds in urbanized areas. It asserted that federal concern in urban transportation was to be integrated with land development and provided a major stimulus to urban transportation planning.[10]

Two features of the act were particularly significant with respect to the organizational arrangements for carrying out the planning process. First, it called for a planning process in urban areas rather than cities, which set the scale at the metropolitan or regional level. Second, it called for the process to be carried on cooperatively by the states and local communities. Because qualified planning agencies to mount such a transportation planning process were lacking in many urban areas, the Bureau of Public Roads (BPR) required the creation of planning agencies or organizational arrangements that would be capable of carrying out the required planning process. These planning organizations quickly came into being because of the growing momentum of the highway program and the cooperative financing of the planning process by the Housing and Home Finance Administration (HHFA) and the BPR.[11]

IMPLEMENTATION OF THE 1962 FEDERAL-AID HIGHWAY ACT

The BPR moved quickly to implement the planning requirements of the 1962 Federal-Aid Highway Act. Instructional Memorandum 50-2-63, published in March 1963[12] and later superseded by Policy and Procedure Memorandum 50-9,[12] interpreted the act's provisions related to a "continuing, comprehensive, and cooperative" (3C) planning process. *Cooperative* was defined to include not only cooperation between the federal, state, and local levels of government but also among the various agencies within the same level of government. *Continuing* referred to the need to periodically reevaluate and update a transportation plan. *Comprehensive* was defined to include the basic 10 elements of a 3C planning process for which inventories and analyses were required:

1. Economic factors affecting development.
2. Population.
3. Land use.
4. Transportation facilities including those for mass transportation.
5. Travel patterns.
6. Terminal and transfer facilities.
7. Traffic control features.
8. Zoning ordinances, subdivision regulations, building codes, and the like.
9. Financial resources.
10. Social and community-value factors, such as preservation of open space, parks, and recreational facilities; preservation of historical sites and buildings; environmental amenities; and aesthetics.

URBAN MASS TRANSPORTATION ACT OF 1964

The first real effort to provide federal assistance for urban mass transportation development was the passage of the Urban Mass Transportation Act of 1964. The objective of the act, still in the spirit of President Kennedy's Transportation Message, was "to encourage the planning and establishment of areawide urban mass transportation systems needed for economical and desirable urban development."[13]

The act authorized federal capital grants for up to two-thirds of the net project cost of construction, reconstruction, or acquisition of mass transportation facilities and equipment. *Net project cost* was defined as that portion of the total project cost that could not be financed readily from transit revenues. Furthermore, the federal share was to be held to 50% in those areas that had not completed their comprehensive planning process, that is, had not produced a plan. All federal funds had to be channeled through public agencies. Transit projects were to be initiated locally.

WILLIAMSBURG CONFERENCE ON HIGHWAYS AND URBAN DEVELOPMENT

By 1965, there was concern that planning processes were not adequately evaluating social and community values. Few planning studies had developed goal-based evaluation methodologies. A second conference on Highways and Urban Development was held in Williamsburg, Virginia, to discuss this problem.[14] The conference concluded that transportation must be directed toward raising urban standards and enhancing aggregate community values. Transportation values such as safety, economy, and comfort are part of the total set of community values and should be weighted appropriately.

IMPROVED INTERGOVERNMENTAL COORDINATION

HOUSING AND URBAN DEVELOPMENT ACT OF 1965

The Housing and Urban Development Act of 1965 created the Department of Housing and Urban Development (HUD) to better coordinate urban programs at the federal level. In addition, the act amended the Section 701 urban planning assistance program established under the Housing Act of 1954 by authorizing grants to be made to "organizations composed of public officials whom he (the Secretary of HUD) finds to be representative of the political jurisdictions within a metropolitan area or urban region" for the purposes of comprehensive planning.[15]

1966 AMENDMENTS TO THE URBAN MASS TRANSPORTATION ACT

To fill several gaps in the 1964 Urban Mass Transportation Act, a number of amendments were passed in 1966. One created the technical studies program, which provided federal assistance up to a two-thirds federal matching share for planning, engineering, and designing of urban mass transportation projects or other similar technical activities leading to application for a capital grant.

Another section authorized grants to be made for management training. A third authorized a project to study and prepare a program of research for developing new systems of urban transportation. This section resulted in a report to Congress in 1968, *Tomorrow's Transportation: New Systems for the Urban Future*, which recommended a long-range balanced program for research on hardware, planning, and operational improvements.[16] It was this study that first brought to public attention many new systems such as dial-a-bus, personal rapid transit, dual mode, pallet systems, and tracked air-cushioned vehicle systems. This study was the basis for numerous research efforts to develop and refine new urban transportation technologies that would improve on existing ones. (See Chap. 4 and 24 for definitions of these systems.)

DEPARTMENT OF TRANSPORTATION ACT OF 1966

In 1966 the Department of Transportation (DOT) was created to coordinate transportation programs and to facilitate development and improvement of coordinated transportation service utilizing private enterprise to the maximum extent feasible. The Department of Transportation Act declared that the nation required fast, safe, efficient, and convenient transportation at the lowest cost consistent with other national objectives, including the conservation of natural resources. DOT was directed to provide leadership in the identification of transportation problems and solutions, stimulate new technological advances, encourage cooperation among all interested parties, and recommend national policies and programs to accomplish these objectives.

DEMONSTRATION CITIES AND METROPOLITAN DEVELOPMENT ACT OF 1966

With the growth in federal grant programs for urban renewal, highways, transit, and other construction projects, there was a need for a mechanism to coordinate these projects. The Demonstration Cities and Metropolitan Development Act of 1966 was enacted to ensure that federal grants were not working at cross purposes. Section 204 of that act was significant in asserting federal interest in improving the coordination of public facility construction projects to obtain maximum effectiveness of federal spending and to relate such projects to areawide development plans.

Section 204 required that all applications for the planning and construction of facilities be submitted to an areawide planning agency for review and comment. The areawide agency was required to be composed of local elected officials. The objective was to encourage the coordination of planning and construction of physical facilities in urban areas. In response to these review requirements, many urban areas established new planning agencies or reorganized existing agencies to include elected officials on their policy boards. By the end of 1969, only six metropolitan areas lacked an areawide review agency.[17]

FEDERAL-AID HIGHWAY ACT OF 1968

The Federal-Aid Highway Act of 1968 established the Traffic Operations Program to Improve Capacity and Safety (TOPICS). The program was designed to reduce traffic congestion and facilitate the flow of traffic in urban areas. Prior to the act, the Bureau of Public Roads had initiated TOPICS as an experimental program.

In addition to launching the TOPICS program, the Federal-Aid Highway Act of 1968 incorporated several provisions designed to protect the environment and reduce the negative effects of highway construction. The act repeated the requirement in Section 4(f) of the Department of Transportation Act of 1966 on the preservation of public park and recreation lands, wildlife and waterfowl refuges, and historic sites to clarify that the provision also applied to highways. Moreover, the act required public hearings on the economic, social, and environmental effects of proposed highway projects and their consistency with local urban goals and objectives. The act also established the highway beautification program. In addition, a highway relocation assistance program was authorized to provide payments to households and businesses displaced by construction projects.

BUREAU OF THE BUDGET'S CIRCULAR NO. A-95

The 1968 Intergovernmental Cooperation Act required that the areawide planning agency be established under state enabling legislation. To implement the act, the Bureau of the Budget issued Circular No. A-95 in July 1969. This circular required that the governor of each state designate a *clearinghouse* at the state level and for each metropolitan area. The function of these clearinghouses was to review and comment on projects proposed for federal aid in terms of their compatibility with comprehensive plans and to coordinate among agencies having plans and programs that might be affected by the projects. The clearinghouses had to be empowered under state or local laws to perform comprehensive planning in an area.

Circular No. A-95 provided the most definitive federal statement of the process through which planning for urban areas should be accomplished. Its emphasis was not on substance but on process and on the intergovernmental linkages required to carry out the process.

The various acts and regulations to improve intergovernmental program coordination accelerated the creation of broader multifunctional agencies. At the state level, 39 departments of transportation had been created by 1977. Most of the departments had multimodal planning, programming, and coordinating functions. At the local level, there was a growing trend for transportation planning to be performed by comprehensive planning agencies, generally those designated as the A-95 clearinghouses.[18]

THE ENVIRONMENT AND CITIZEN INVOLVEMENT

NATIONAL ENVIRONMENTAL POLICY ACT OF 1969

The federal government's concern for environmental issues dated back to the passage of the Air Quality Control Act of 1955, which directed the U.S. Surgeon General to conduct research to abate air pollution. Through a series of acts since that time, the federal government's involvement in environmental matters has broadened and deepened.

In 1969 a singularly important piece of environmental legislation was passed, the National Environmental Policy Act of 1969 (NEPA). This act presented a significant departure from prior legislation in that it enunciated for the first time a broad national policy to prevent or eliminate damage to the environment. The act stated that it was national policy to "encourage productive and enjoyable harmony between man and his environment."[19]

Federal agencies were required under the act to use a systematic interdisciplinary approach to the planning and decision making that affected the environment. It also required that an *environmental impact statement* (EIS) be prepared for all legislation and major federal actions that would affect the environment significantly. The EIS was to contain information on the environmental impacts of the proposed action, unavoidable impacts, alternatives to the action, the relationship between short-term and long-term impacts, and irretrievable commitments of resources. The federal agency was to seek comments on the action and its impacts from affected jurisdictions and make all information public.

ENVIRONMENTAL QUALITY IMPROVEMENT ACT OF 1970

The Environmental Quality Improvement Act of 1970 was passed as a companion to the NEPA. It established the Office of Environmental Quality under the Council on Environmental Quality. The office was charged with assisting federal agencies in evaluating present and proposed programs and with promoting research on the environment.

These two acts marked the first reversal in over a decade of the trend to decentralize decision making to the state and local levels of government. It required the federal government to make the final determination on the trade-off between facility improvements and environmental quality. Furthermore, it created a complicated and expensive process by requiring the preparation of an EIS and the seeking of comments from all concerned agencies. In this manner, the acts actually created a new planning process in parallel with the existing urban transportation planning process.

CLEAN AIR ACT AMENDMENTS OF 1970

The Clean Air Act Amendments of 1970 reinforced the central position of the federal government to make final decisions affecting the environment. This act created the Environmental Protection Agency (EPA) and empowered it to set ambient air quality standards. In 1971, the EPA promulgated national ambient air quality standards and proposed regulations on *state implementation plans* (SIPs) to meet these standards.

The preparation, submission, and review of the SIPs occurred outside the traditional urban transportation planning process and, in many instances, did not involve the planning agencies developing transportation plans. This problem became particularly difficult for urban areas that could not meet the air quality standards even with new automobiles that met the air pollution emission standards. In these instances, *transportation control plans* (TCPs) were required that contained changes in urban transportation systems and their operation to effect the reduction in emissions. Rarely were these TCPs developed jointly with those agencies developing urban transportation plans. It took several years of dialogue between these air pollution and transportation planning agencies to mediate joint plans and policies for urban transportation and air quality.

BEGINNINGS OF MULTIMODAL URBAN TRANSPORTATION PLANNING

URBAN MASS TRANSPORTATION ASSISTANCE ACT OF 1970

The Urban Mass Transportation Assistance Act of 1970 was another landmark in federal financing for mass transportation. It provided the first long-term commitment of federal funds. Until the passage of this act, federal funds for mass transportation had been limited. It was difficult to plan and implement a program of mass transportation projects over several years because of the uncertainty of future funding.

This act also established a strong federal policy on transportation for elderly and handicapped persons:

> elderly and handicapped persons have the same right as other persons to utilize mass transportation facilities and services; that special efforts shall be made in the planning and design of mass transportation facilities and services so that the availability to elderly and handicapped persons to mass transportation which they can effectively utilize will be assured. . . .[20]

FEDERAL-AID HIGHWAY ACT OF 1970

The Federal-Aid Highway Act of 1970 established the *federal-aid urban highway system*. The system in each urban area was to be designed to serve major centers of activity and to serve local goals and objectives. Routes on the system were to be selected by local officials and state departments cooperatively. This provision significantly increased the influence of local jurisdictions in urban highway decisions. The influence of local officials in urban areas was further strengthened by an amendment to Section 134 on urban transportation planning:

> No highway project may be constructed in any urban area of 50,000 population or more unless the responsible local officials of such urban area . . . have been consulted and their views considered with respect to the corridor, the location and the design of the project.[21]

This act also incorporated a number of requirements related to the environment.

One required the issuance of guidelines for full consideration of economic, social, and environmental impacts of highway projects. A second related to the promulgation of guidelines for assuring that highway projects were consistent with SIPs developed under the Clean Air Act.

As a result of the 1970 highway and transit acts, projects for both modes would have to meet similar criteria related to impact assessment and public hearings.

MT. POCONO CONFERENCE ON URBAN TRANSPORTATION PLANNING

In recognition of the widespread awareness that urban transportation planning had not kept pace with changing conditions, a conference on Organization for Continuing Urban Transportation Planning was held at Mt. Pocono, Pennsylvania, in 1971. The focus of this conference was on multimodal transportation planning, evolving from the earlier conferences that had focused on highway planning, and the separation between planning and implementation.[22]

The conference recommended close of planning efforts as a means of achieving orderly development of urban areas and relating the planning process more closely to decision-making processes at all levels of government. It urged that urban planning be strengthened through state enabling legislation and bolstered by equitable local representation. Furthermore, citizen participation should occur continually throughout the planning process but should not be considered as a substitute for decision making by elected officials.[23]

WILLIAMSBURG CONFERENCE ON URBAN TRAVEL DEMAND FORECASTING

By the latter part of the 1960s, policy issues and options had changed, but travel demand forecasting techniques had not. This was addressed at a conference on Urban Travel Demand Forecasting held at Williamsburg, Virginia, in December 1972. The conference concluded that there was a need for travel forecasting procedures that were sensitive to the wide range of policy issues and alternatives to be considered, quicker and less costly than conventional methods, more informative and useful to decision makers, and in a form that nontechnical people could understand.[24]

FEDERAL-AID HIGHWAY ACT OF 1973

The Federal-Aid Highway Act of 1973 contained two provisions that increased the flexibility in the use of highway funds for urban mass transportation in the spirit of the Mt. Pocono conference. First, federal-aid urban system funds were to be used for capital expenditures on urban mass transportation projects. This provision took effect gradually, but was unrestricted starting in fiscal year 1976. Second, funds for interstate highway projects could be relinquished and replaced by an equivalent amount from the general fund and spent on mass transportation projects in a particular state. The relinquished funds reverted back to the highway trust fund.

This opening up of the highway trust fund for urban mass transportation was a significant breakthrough sought for many years by transit supporters. These changes provided completely new avenues of federal assistance for funding urban mass transportation.

The 1973 Federal-Aid Highway Act took a significant step toward integrating and balancing the highway and mass transportation programs. It also increased the role of local officials in the selection of urban highway projects and broadened the scope of transportation planning by metropolitan planning organizations (MPOs), which were to be designated by the states to perform this planning function.

NATIONAL MASS TRANSPORTATION ASSISTANCE ACT OF 1974

The National Mass Transportation Assistance Act of 1974 authorized for the first time the use of federal funds for transit operating assistance. It thereby continued the trend to broaden the use of federal urban transportation funds and provide state and local officials more flexibility. This act was the culmination of a major lobbying effort by the transit industry and urban interests to secure federal operating assistance for transit.

Section 105(g) of the act required applicants for transit projects to meet the same planning statute as Section 134 of the highway act. Finally, highway and transit projects were subject to the same long-range planning requirement. Although many urbanized areas already had a joint highway–transit planning process, this section formalized the requirement for multimodal transportation planning.

The act also required transit systems to charge elderly and handicapped persons fares that were half regular fares when they traveled in off-peak hours. This was a further condition to receiving federal funds.

The act created a new Section 15 that required the U.S. Department of Transportation to establish a data-reporting system for financial and operating information and a uniform system of accounts and records. After July 1978 no grant could be made to any applicant unless it was reporting data under both systems.

TRANSITION TO SHORT-TERM PLANNING

EMERGENCY ENERGY LEGISLATION

In October 1973 the Organization of Petroleum Exporting Countries (OPEC) embargoed oil shipments to the United States and, in doing so, began a new era in transportation planning. The importance of oil was so paramount to the economy and, in particular, the transportation sector that oil shortages and price increases gradually became one of the major issues in transportation planning.

The Emergency Highway Energy Conservation Act, signed on January 2, 1974, established a national 55 mi/h speed limit to reduce gasoline consumption. It was extended indefinitely on January 4, 1975[25] (and rescinded in 1988, allowing 65 mi/h in rural areas). It also provided that federal-aid highway funds could be used for ridesharing demonstration programs. As the immediate crisis abated, the focus shifted to long-term actions and policies to reduce the nation's dependence on oil, especially imported oil.

JOINT HIGHWAY–TRANSIT PLANNING REGULATIONS

The Urban Mass Transportation Administration (UMTA) and the Federal Highway Administration (FHWA) had worked for several years on joint regulations to guide urban transportation planning. Final regulations were issued to take effect in October 1975.[26] They superseded all previous guidelines, policies, and regulations issued on urban transportation planning by UMTA and the FHWA.

The regulations provided for the joint designation of MPOs to carry out urban transportation planning and required agreements on the division of responsibility where the MPOs and A-95 agencies were different. The MPO was intended to be the forum for cooperative decision making by principal elected officials of general-purpose local government. A *multiyear prospectus* and *annual unified work program* had to be submitted specifying all transportation-related planning activities for an urban area as a condition for receiving federal planning funds.

The urban transportation planning process was required to produce a long-range transportation plan, which had to be reviewed annually to confirm its validity. The transportation plan had to contain a *long-range element* and a shorter-range *transportation systems management element* (TSME) for improving the operation of existing transportation systems without new facilities.

A multiyear *transportation improvement program* (TIP) also had to be developed consistent with the transportation plan. The TIP had to include all highway and transit projects to be implemented within the coming 5 years. It thereby became the linkage between the planning and programming of urban transportation projects. It also brought together all highway and transit projects into a single document that could be reviewed and approved by decision makers. The TIP had to contain an *annual element* that would be the basis for the federal funding decisions on projects for the coming year.

These joint regulations applied to all urban highway and transit programs, including those for transit operating assistance. They represented the most important action up to that time to bring about multimodal urban transportation planning and programming of projects and change the emphasis from long-term planning to shorter-range transportation system management, thus providing a stronger linkage between planning and programming. These regulations were another turning point in the evolution of urban transportation planning that set the tone for the next several years.

POLICY ON MAJOR URBAN MASS TRANSPORTATION INVESTMENTS

The level of federal funds for urban mass transportation increased dramatically after 1970. However, the requests for federal funds from urban areas outpaced that increase. In particular, there was a resurgence of interest in rail transit systems, which many argued could help solve the problems of congestion and petroleum dependence while promoting efficient development patterns. (See Chap. 5.) Consequently, the need to assure that these funds were used effectively and productively became apparent.

UMTA set forth its views on this issue in the document, *Preliminary Guidelines and Background Analysis.*[27] The guidelines embodied a number of principles. First, areawide transportation improvement plans should be multimodal and include regionwide and community-level transit services. Second, major mass transportation investment projects should be planned and implemented in stages to avoid premature investment in costly fixed facilities and to preserve maximum flexibility to respond to future unknowns. Third, full consideration should be given to improving the management and operation of existing transportation systems. Fourth, the analysis of alternatives should include a determination of which alternative meets the local area's social, environmental, and transportation goals in a cost-effective manner. And fifth, full opportunity should be provided for involvement of the public and local officials in all phases of the planning and evaluation process.[28]

UMTA stated that the level of federal funding would be based on a cost-effective alternative that would meet urban area needs and goals in a 5- to 15-year time frame and that was consistent with the long-range transportation plan.

In February 1978, UMTA provided further elaboration in its "Policy Toward Rail Transit."[29] The policy stated that new rail transit lines or extensions would be funded in areas where population densities, travel volumes, and growth patterns indicated the need. Preference would be given to corridors serving densely populated urban centers. It reaffirmed the principles of analysis of alternatives, including transportation system management (TSM) measures, incremental implementation, and cost-effectiveness analysis. The policy added the requirement that the local area had to commit itself to a program of supportive actions designed to improve the cost effectiveness, patronage, and prospect for economic viability of the investment. This requirement included automobile management policies; feeder service; plans, policies, and incentives to stimulate high-density private development near stations; and other measures to revitalize nearby older neighborhoods and the central business district. With this policy supplement, rail transit was to become a tool for urban redevelopment.

CLEAN AIR ACT AMENDMENTS OF 1977

The Clean Air Act Amendments of 1977 increased the flexibility and local responsibility in the administration of the Clean Air Act. The amendments required state and local governments to develop revisions to state implementation plans (SIPs) for all areas where the national ambient air quality standards had not been attained. The revised SIPs were to be submitted to the EPA by January 1, 1979, and approved by May 1, 1979.

The revised plans had to provide for attainment of national ambient air quality standards by 1982 or, in the case of areas with severe photochemical oxidant or carbon monoxide problems, no later than 1987. In the latter case, a state had to demonstrate that the standards could not be met with all reasonable stationary and transportation control measures. The plans also had to provide for incremental reductions in emissions ("reasonable further progress") between the time the plans were submitted and the attainment deadline. If a state failed to submit a SIP or if the EPA disapproved the SIP and the state failed to revise it in a satisfactory manner, the EPA was required to promulgate regulations establishing a SIP by July 1, 1979. If, after July 1, 1979, the EPA determined that a state was not fulfilling the requirements under the act, it was to impose sanctions.[30]

In many major urbanized areas the revised SIPs required the development of *transportation control plans* (TCPs) that included strategies to reduce emissions from transportation-related sources by means of structural or operational changes in the transportation system. Since state and local governments implement changes in the transportation system, the act strongly encouraged the preparation of transportation elements of the SIP by MPOs. These local planning organizations were responsible for developing the transportation control measure element of the SIP.

From 1978 to 1980, DOT and the EPA, after long negotiations, jointly issued several policy documents to implement the Clean Air Act's transportation requirements. One of these, signed in June 1978, was a "Memorandum of Understanding" that established the means by which DOT and the EPA would assure the integration of transportation and air quality planning. A second document issued also in June 1978, "Transportation Air Quality Planning Guidelines," described the acceptable planning process to satisfy the requirements.

In January 1981, DOT issued regulations on air quality conformance and priority procedures for use in federal highway and transit programs. The regulations required that transportation plans, programs, and projects conform with the approved SIPs in areas that had not met ambient air quality standards, termed *nonattainment areas*. In those areas, priority for transportation funds was to be given to *transportation control measures* (TCMs) that contributed to reducing air pollution emissions from transportation sources. Where an area's transportation plan or program was not in conformance with the TCP, "sanctions" were to be applied that prohibited the use of federal funds on major transportation projects.[31]

URBAN ECONOMIC REVITALIZATION

Surface Transportation Assistance Act of 1978

The Surface Transportation Assistance Act of 1978 was the first act that combined highway, public transportation, and highway safety authorizations in one piece of legislation. Title III of the act expanded the Section 5 formula grant program. The basic program of operating and capital assistance was retained with the same population and population density formula at higher authorization levels. A "second tier" program was authorized with the same project eligibility and apportionment formula. A third tier was established for routine purchases of buses and related facilities and equipment. A new fourth tier replaced the Section 17 and 18 commuter rail programs. The funds could be used for commuter rail or rail transit capital or operating expenses. The act changed the availability of funds for transit from 2 to 4 years. It formalized the "letter of intent" process whereby the federal government committed funds for a transit project in the Section 3 discretionary grant program. Public hearings were required for all general increases in fares or substantial changes in service. A small formula grant program for nonurbanized areas (Section 18) was established for capital and operating assistance. Apportioned on nonurbanized area population, it authorized an 80% federal share for capital projects and 50% for operating assistance. The act also established an intercity bus terminal development program, intercity bus service operating subsidy program, and human resources program for urban transit systems.

NATIONAL ENERGY ACT OF 1978

In October 1978 the Congress passed the National Energy Act, which was composed of five bills. The National Energy Conservation Policy Act of 1978 extended two state energy conservation programs that required states to undertake specific conservation actions, including the promotion of carpools and vanpools. Further legislation and an executive order extended energy conservation efforts. In August 1980, DOT issued regulations requiring that all phases of transportation projects be conducted in a manner that conserved fuel. It also incorporated energy conservation as a goal into the urban transportation planning process and required an analysis of alternative TSM improvements to reduce energy consumption.

COUNCIL ON ENVIRONMENTAL QUALITY'S REGULATIONS

The Council on Environmental Quality (CEQ) issued final regulations on November 29, 1978, establishing uniform procedures for implementing the procedural provisions of the National Environmental Policy Act of 1969. They applied to all federal agencies and took effect on July 30, 1979. They were issued because the 1973 CEQ guidelines for preparing environmental impact statements (EISs) were not viewed consistently by all agencies, leading to differences in interpretations.[32]

The regulations embodied several new concepts designed to make the EIS more useful to decision makers and the public and to reduce paper work and delays. First, the regulations created a *scoping* process to provide for the early identification of significant impacts and issues. It also provided for allocating responsibility for the EIS among the lead agency and cooperating agencies. The scoping process was to be integrated with other planning activities.

Second, the regulations permitted *tiering* of the EIS process. This provided that environmental analyses completed at a broad scale (for example, regional) need not be duplicated for site-specific projects; the broader analyses could be summarized and incorporated by reference. The purpose of tiering was to eliminate repetition and allow discussion of issues at the appropriate level of detail.

Third, in addition to the previously required EIS, which discussed the alternatives being considered, a *record of decision* document was required. It had to identify the "environmentally preferable" alternative, the other alternatives considered, and the factors used in reaching the decision. Until this document was issued, no action could be taken on an alternative that would adversely effect the environment or limit the choice of alternatives.

In October 1980 the FHWA and UMTA published supplemental implementing procedures. They established a single set of environmental procedures for highway and urban transit projects. They also integrated UMTA's procedures for alternatives analysis under its major investment policy with the new EIS procedures. This permitted the preparation of a single draft EIS/alternatives analysis document. These regulations were an important step toward integrating highway and transit planning and reducing duplicative documentation.[33]

DECENTRALIZATION OF DECISION MAKING

AIRLIE HOUSE CONFERENCE ON URBAN TRANSPORTATION PLANNING IN THE 1980S

Concern had been growing in the planning community about the future of urban transportation planning. On the one hand, planning requirements had become more complex, new planning techniques had not found their way into practice, and future changes in social, demographic, energy, environmental, and technological factors were unclear. On the other hand, fiscal constraints were tight and the federal government was shifting the burden of decision making to state and local governments and the private sector. The future of planning was in doubt.

To address these concerns, a conference was held at Airlie House, in Virginia, November 1981, on Urban Transportation Planning in the 1980s. The conference reaffirmed the need for systematic urban transportation planning, especially to maximize the effectiveness of limited public funds. But the planning process needed to be adjusted to the nature and scope of an area's problems.[34]

The conferees also concluded that the federal government had been overly restrictive in its regulations, making the planning process costly, time consuming, and difficult to administer. It was concluded that the regulations should be streamlined, specifying goals to be achieved and leaving the decisions on how to meet them to the states and local governments. The conference recommendations reflected the new mood that the federal government had overregulated and was too specific in its requirements. The planning process was straining under this burden and finding it difficult to plan to meet local needs.

EXECUTIVE ORDER 12372

Office of Management and Budget's Circular A-95 (which replaced Bureau of the Budget Circular A-95) had governed the consultation process on federal grant programs with state and local governments since its issuance in July 1969. Although the A-95 process had served a useful function in assuring intergovernmental cooperation on federal grant programs, there were concerns that the process had become too rigid and cumbersome and caused unnecessary paper work. To respond to these concerns and to delegate more responsibility and authority to state and local governments, the president signed Executive Order 12372, "Intergovernmental Review of Federal Programs," on July 14, 1982.[35]

The objectives of the executive order were to foster an intergovernmental partnership and strengthen federalism by relying on state and local processes for intergovernmental coordination and review of federal financial assistance and direct federal development. The executive order had several purposes. First, it allowed states, after consultation with local officials, to establish their own process for review and comment on proposed federal financial assistance and direct federal development. Second, it increased federal responsiveness to state and local officials by requiring federal agencies to "accommodate" or "explain" when considering certain state and local views. Third, it allowed states to simplify, consolidate, or substitute state plans for federal planning requirements. The order also revoked OMB Circular A-95, although regulations implementing this circular remained in effect until September 30, 1983.

WOODS HOLE CONFERENCE ON FUTURE DIRECTIONS

A diverse group of conferees met at the Woods Hole Study Center in Massachusetts in September 1982 to discuss future directions of urban public transportation.[36] The conference addressed the role of public transportation, present and future, the context within which public transportation functioned, and strategies for the future.

The conferees agreed that "strategic planning for public transportation should be conducted at both the local and national levels." The transit industry should be more aggressive in working with developers and local governments in growing parts of metropolitan areas to capitalize on opportunities to integrate transit facilities into major new developments. The industry needed to improve its relationship with highway and public works agencies as well as state and local decision makers. Financing transit had become more complex and difficult but had created new opportunities.

EASTON CONFERENCE ON TRAVEL ANALYSIS METHODS FOR THE 1980s

A conference was held at Easton, Maryland, in November 1982 to discuss how well travel analysis methods were adapted to the issues and problems of the 1980s. This conference on Travel Analysis Methods for the 1980s focused on defining the state of the art versus the state of practice, describing how the methods have been and can be applied, and identifying gaps between art and practice that needed more dissemination of current knowledge, research, or development.[37]

The new mathematical techniques and theoretical bases from econometrics and psychometrics had been difficult for practitioners to learn. Moreover, the new techniques were not easily integrated into conventional planning practices. The conferees concluded that the travel demand community should concentrate on transferring the new travel analysis methods into practice. A wide range of technology transfer approaches was suggested.

SURFACE TRANSPORTATION ASSISTANCE ACT OF 1982

Through the decade of the 1970s there was mounting evidence of deterioration in the nation's highway and transit infrastructure. Money during that period had been concentrated on building new capacity, and the transition to funding rehabilitation of the infrastructure had been slow. By the time the problem had been faced, the cost estimate to refurbish the highways, bridges, and transit systems had reached hundreds of billions of dollars.[38]

The Surface Transportation Assistance Act of 1982 was passed to address this infrastructure problem. The act extended authorizations for the highway, safety, and transit programs. In addition, the act raised the highway user charges by 5 cents (to 9 cents) a gallon on fuel. Other taxes were changed, including a substantial increase in the truck user fees. Of the revenues raised from the 5-cent increase (about $5.5 billion annually), the equivalent of a 4-cent raise in fuel user charges was to increase highway programs, and the remaining 1 cent was for transit programs.

The act authorized the administration of highway planning and research (HP&R) funds as a single fund. As a result of the large expansion in the construction program, the level of funding increased substantially for the HP&R program and urban transportation planning purposes.

The act restructured federal urban transit programs. No new authorizations were made for the Section 5 formula grant program. Instead, a new Section 9 formula grant program was created that allowed expenditures on planning, capital, and operating items. Substantial discretion was given to state and local governments in selecting projects to be funded using formula grants with minimal federal interference. There were limitations, however, on the use of the funds for operating expenses.

The revenue from the 1-cent increase in highway user charges was to be placed into a mass transit account of the highway trust fund. The funds could only be used for capital projects. They were to be allocated by a formula in fiscal year 1983, but were discretionary in later years. The definition of capital was changed to include associated capital maintenance items. The act also provided that a substantial number of federal requirements be self-certified by the applicants and that other requirements be consolidated to reduce paper work.

A requirement was also included for a biennial report on transit performance and needs, with the first report due in January 1984. In addition, the act provided that regulations be published that set minimum criteria on transportation services for the handicapped and elderly.

The Surface Transportation Assistance Act of 1982 was passed under considerable controversy about the future federal role in transportation, particularly the administration's position to phase out of federal transit operating subsidies. Debates on later appropriations bills demonstrated that the issue remained controversial.

NEW URBAN TRANSPORTATION PLANNING REGULATIONS

The joint FHWA–UMTA urban transportation planning regulations had served as the key federal guidance since 1975. During 1980, there was an intensive effort to amend these regulations to ensure more citizen involvement, to increase the emphasis on urban revitalization, and to integrate corridor planning into the urban transportation planning process.[39]

The result of this effort was reviewed under the criteria set forth in Executive Order 12291. The revised regulations, issued on June 30, 1983, had been rewritten to remove items that were not actually required. The regulations contained new statutory requirements and retained the requirements for a transportation plan, a transportation improvement program (TIP) including an annual element (or biennial element), and a *unified planning work program* (UPWP), the latter only for areas of 200,000 or more in population. The planning process was to be self-certified by the states and MPOs as to its conformance with all requirements when submitting the TIP.[40]

The regulations drew a distinction between federal requirements and good planning practice. They stated the product was required but left the details of the process to the state and local agencies, so the regulations no longer contained the elements of the process nor factors to consider in conducting the process.

The revised regulations marked a major shift in the evolution of urban transportation planning. Up to that time, the response to new issues and problems was to create additional federal requirements. These regulations changed the focus of responsibility and control to the state and local governments. The federal government remained committed to urban planning by requiring that projects be based on a 3C planning process and by continuing to provide funding for planning activities. But it would no longer specify how the process was to be performed.

PRIVATE SECTOR PARTICIPATION

REVISED MAJOR TRANSIT CAPITAL INVESTMENT POLICY

By the early 1980s there had been a huge upsurge of interest in building new urban rail transit systems and extensions to existing ones. Beginning in 1972, new urban rail systems had begun revenue service in the United States in San Francisco, Washington, D.C., Atlanta, Baltimore, San Diego, Miami, and Buffalo. Construction was underway for new systems in Portland (Oregon), Detroit (Michigan), and

Sacramento and San Jose (California). A total of 32 urban areas were conducting studies for major new transit investments in 46 corridors. It was estimated by UMTA that if all of those projects were carried out, the cost to the federal government would be at least $19 billion.

The federal funds for rail projects came, for the most part, from the Section 3 discretionary grant program. This program was funded by the revenue from 1 cent of the 5-cent increase in the user charge on motor fuels that was included in the Surface Transportation Assistance Act of 1982 and amounted to $1.1 billion annually. UMTA, however, was giving priority to projects for rehabilitation of existing rail and bus systems. Only $400 million annually was targeted for use on new urban rail projects. The resulting gap between the demand for federal funds for major transit projects and the available funds was, therefore, very large.

In an attempt to manage the demand for federal funds, UMTA issued a revised "Urban Mass Transportation Major Capital Investment Policy" on May 18, 1984.[41] It was a further refinement of the evaluation process for major transit projects that had been evolving over a number of years. (See Chap. 11.) Under the policy, UMTA would use the results of local planning studies to calculate the cost effectiveness and local financial support for each project. These criteria would be used to rate the projects. UMTA would fund only those projects that ranked high on both criteria to the extent that they did not exceed the available funds. The lower-ranked projects were still eligible for funding if additional money became available.

The project development process involved a number of stages. After each completed stage, UMTA would make a decision on whether or not to proceed to the next stage. The most critical decision occurred after the alternatives analysis and draft environmental impact statement (AA/DEIS) were completed. During this stage, the cost effectiveness of new fixed-guideway projects was compared to a base system called the "transportation system management" alternative. Projects were rated on cost effectiveness and local fiscal effort after the AA/DEIS was completed.

The pressure for federal funds for new urban rail projects was so great, however, that the matter was often settled politically. Starting in fiscal year 1981, Congress began to earmark Section 3 discretionary grant funds for specific projects, thereby preempting UMTA from making the selection. UMTA continued to rate the projects and make the information available to congressional committees.

In 1987, the Surface Transportation and Uniform Relocation Assistance Act established grant criteria for new fixed-guideway projects along the lines that UMTA had been using. The projects had to be based on alternatives analysis and preliminary engineering, be cost effective, and be supported by an acceptable degree of local financial commitment.

PRIVATE PARTICIPATION IN THE TRANSIT PROGRAM

The Reagan administration (1981-1989) was committed to a greater private sector role in addressing the needs of communities. Consequently, the Department of Transportation sought to remove barriers to greater involvement of the private sector in the provision of urban transportation services and in the financing of these services. To promote increased involvement of the private sector in the provision of public transportation services, UMTA issued a "Policy on Private Participation in the Urban Mass Transportation Program."[42] It provided guidance for achieving compliance with several sections of the Urban Mass Transportation Act. Section 8(e) required maximum participation of the private sector in the planning of public transportation services. Section 9(f), which was added by the Surface Transportation Assistance Act of 1982, established procedures for involving the private sector in the development of the transportation improvement program as a condition for federal funding.

This policy represented a major departure from past federal policy toward public transportation operators. Previously, public operators had had a virtual monopoly on federal funds for transit facilities, equipment, and service; now they needed to consider private sector operators as competitors for providing those services.

SURFACE TRANSPORTATION AND UNIFORM RELOCATION ASSISTANCE ACT OF 1987

With five titles and 149 sections, the Surface Transportation and Uniform Relocation Assistance Act of 1987 (STURAA) was the most complicated piece of legislation up to that time on surface transportation matters. It was passed on April 2, 1987, over President Reagan's veto. The STURAA authorized $87.6 billion for the 5-year period from fiscal year 1987 to fiscal year 1991 for the federal-aid highway, safety, and mass transportation programs. It also updated the rules for compensating persons and businesses displaced by federal development and extended the highway trust fund through June 30, 1994.[43]

Title I, the Federal-Aid Highway Act of 1987, authorized $67.1 billion for highway and bridge programs over a 5-year period. The act permitted states to raise the speed limit on interstate routes outside urbanized areas from 55 to 65 mi/h. With regard to bridge tolls, the act required that they be "just and reasonable" and removed any federal review and regulation.

An allocation of 0.25% of highway authorizations was set aside for a new cooperative research program directed at highway construction materials and pavements and construction and maintenance procedures. This Strategic Highway Research Program (SHRP) was to be carried out with the cooperation of the National Academy of Sciences and the American Association of State Highway and Transportation Officials.

Title II, the Highway Safety Act of 1987, authorized $795 million over 5 years for safety programs in addition to the $1.75 billion for safety construction programs in the Federal-Aid Highway Act of 1987. It required the identification of those programs that are most effective in reducing accidents, injuries, and deaths. Only those programs would be eligible for federal-aid funds under the Section 402 state and community grant program. Safety "standards" that states must meet to comply with this program were redefined as "guidelines."

Title III, the Federal Mass Transportation Act of 1987, authorized $17.8 billion for federal mass transit assistance for fiscal years 1987 through 1991. The act continued the Section 3 discretionary grant program at graduated authorization levels of $1.097 billion in FY 1987, rising to $1.2 billion in FY 1991 funded from the mass transit account of the highway trust fund. The program was to be split: 40% for new rail starts and extensions, 40% for rail modernization grants, 10% for major bus projects, and 10% on a discretionary basis.

Grant criteria were established for new fixed-guideway systems and extensions. The project selection would be based on alternatives analysis, preliminary engineering, and cost-effectiveness analysis and supported by an acceptable degree of local financial commitment. A plan for the expenditure of Section 3 funds was required to be submitted to Congress annually.

With regard to planning, the act required development of long-term financial plans for regional urban mass transit improvements and the revenue available from current and potential sources to implement such improvements.

Title IV, the Uniform Relocation Act Amendments of 1987, revised and updated some of the provisions of the Uniform Relocation Assistance and Real Property Act of 1970. The act generally increased payments for residences and businesses displaced by construction of transportation projects and broadened eligibility for payments under the program. The FHWA was designated as the lead federal agency to develop regulations to implement the act.

Title V, the Highway Revenue Act of 1987, extended the highway trust fund to June 30, 1993, and extended taxes and exemptions to September 30, 1993.

NATIONAL CONFERENCE ON TRANSPORTATION PLANNING APPLICATIONS

By the mid-1980s, there was a broader range of issues than ever for urban transportation planners to deal with. State and local planning agencies had to be resourceful in adapting existing planning procedures to fit individual needs. Often planning methods or data had not been available when needed to adequately support planning and project decisions. Compromises between accuracy, practicality, simplifying assumptions, quicker responses, and judgment often resulted in innovative analysis methods and applications.

To share experiences and highlight new and effective applications of planning techniques, a National Conference on Transportation Planning Applications was held in Orlando, Florida, in April 1987. The conference was attended mainly by practicing planners from state and local agencies and the consulting community who described the application of planning techniques to actual transportation problems and issues.[44]

Several important issues surfaced at the conference. First, the realm of urban transportation planning was no longer solely long term at the regional scale. The conference gave equal emphasis to both the corridor- and site-level scale of planning in addition to the regional level. Many issues at the local level occurred at finer scales, and planners were spending considerably more effort at these scales than at the regional scale. The time horizon too had shifted to short term, with many planning agencies concentrating on rehabilitating infrastructure and managing traffic on the existing system.

Second, the microcomputer revolution had arrived. Microcomputers were no longer curiosities but essential tools used by planners. There were many presentations about microcomputer applications of planning techniques.

Third, with tighter budgets and the increasing demands being placed on them, transportation planning agencies found it increasingly difficult to collect large-scale regional data sets such as home-interview, origin–destination surveys. Consequently, there was considerable discussion about approaches to obtain new data at minimal cost. Approaches ranged from expanded use of secondary data sources such as census data, to small stratified sample surveys, to extended use of traffic counts. Low-cost techniques for updating land-use data bases were not available.

Fourth, there was concern about the quality of demographic and economic forecasts and their effects on travel demand forecasts. It was observed that errors in demographic and economic forecasts could be more significant than errors in the specification and calibration of the travel demand models. With this observation in mind, there was discussion about appropriate techniques for demographic forecasting during periods of economic uncertainty.

Fifth, a clear need was identified to develop integrated analysis tools that could bridge between planning and project development. The outputs for regional-scale forecasting procedures could not be used directly as inputs for project development, yet there were no standard procedures or rationales for performing the necessary adjustments. Without standard procedures, each agency had to develop their own approaches to this problem.

NATIONAL COUNCIL ON PUBLIC WORKS IMPROVEMENT

Concern for the nation's deteriorating infrastructure prompted Congress to enact the Public Works Improvement Act of 1984. The act created the National Council on Public Works Improvement to provide an objective and comprehensive overview of the state of the nation's infrastructure. The council carried out a broad research program.

The council's first report provided an overview of available knowledge, explored the definition of needs, and reviewed key issues, including the importance of transportation to the economy, management and decision-making practices, technological innovation, government roles, and finance and expenditure trends.[45] The second report was a series of study papers assessing the main issues in nine categories of public works facilities and services, including highways and bridges[46] and mass transit.[47]

The final report of the council concluded that most categories of public works were performing at only passable levels and that U.S. infrastructure was inadequate to meet the demands of future economic growth and development. Highways were given a grade of C+, with the council concluding that, although the decline of pavement conditions had been halted, overall service continued to decline. Spending for system expansion had fallen short of need in high-growth suburban and urban areas, and many highways and bridges still needed to be replaced. Mass transit was graded at C-. The council concluded that transit productivity had declined significantly and that it was overcapitalized in many smaller cities and inadequate in large older cities. Mass transit faced increasing difficulty in diverting persons from automobiles and was rarely linked to land-use planning and broader transportation goals.[48]

Part of the problem was found to be financial, with investment in public works having declined as a percentage of the gross national product from 1960 to 1985. The council recommended that all levels of government increase their expenditures by as much as 100%. It endorsed the principle that users and other beneficiaries should pay a greater share of the cost of infrastructure service. The council also recommended clarification of government roles to focus on responsibility, improvement in system performance, capital budgeting at all levels of government, incentives to improve maintenance, and more widespread use of low-capital techniques such as demand management and land-use planning. The council called for additional support for research and development to accelerate technological innovation and for training of public works professionals.

SUMMARY

Urban transportation planning evolved from highway and transit planning activities in the 1930s and 1940s. These efforts were primarily intended to improve the design and operation of individual transportation facilities. The focus was on upgrading and expanding facilities.

Early urban transportation planning studies were primarily systems oriented with a 20-year horizon and regionwide in scope. This perspective was largely the result of legislation for the National System of Interstate and Defense Highways, which required that these major highways be designed for traffic projected 20 years into the future. As a result, the focus of the planning process through the decade of the 1960s was on this long-range time horizon and broad regional scale. Gradually, starting in the early 1970s, planning processes turned to shorter-term time horizons and the corridor-level scale. This change came about as the result of a realization that long-range planning had been dominated by concern for major regional highway and transit facilities, and little attention had been paid to facility modifications that offered opportunity to improve the efficiency of the existing system. This shift was reinforced by the increasing difficulties and cost in constructing new facilities, growing environmental concerns, and the Arab oil embargo.

Early efforts with programs such as TOPICS and express bus priorities eventually broadened into the strategy of transportation system management. A period of learning and adaptation was necessary to redirect planning processes so that they could perform this new type of planning. As the 1980s dawned, urban transportation planning had become primarily short-term oriented in most urbanized areas.

Major new issues began affecting urban transportation planning in the latter half of the 1960s and on through the 1970s. The list of issues included safety, citizen involvement, preservation of park land and natural areas, equal opportunity for disadvantaged persons, environmental concerns (particularly air quality), transportation for the elderly and handicapped, energy conservation, and revitalization of urban centers. Most recently, these have been joined by concerns for deterioration of the highway and transit infrastructure. By 1980 the federal requirements to address all these matters had become extensive, complex, and sometimes conflicting.

During this same period, various transportation options were advocated as solutions to this vast array of problems and concerns. The solutions included new highways, express buses, rail transit systems, pricing, automated guideway transit, paratransit, brokerage, and dual-mode transit. It was difficult at times to determine whether these options were advanced as the answer to all the problems or for just some of them. Transportation system management was an attempt to integrate the short-term, low-capital options into reinforcing strategies to accomplish one or more objectives. Alternatives analysis was designed to evaluate trade-offs among various major investments options as well as transportation system management techniques.

Transportation planning techniques also evolved during this time. Procedures for specific purposes were integrated into an urban travel forecasting process in the early urban transportation studies in the 1950s. Through the 1960s, improvements in planning techniques were made primarily by practitioners, and these new approaches were integrated into practice fairly easily. The FHWA and UMTA carried out extensive activities to develop and disseminate analytical techniques and computer programs for use by state and local governments. The Urban Transportation Planning System (UTPS) became the standard computer battery for urban transportation analysis by the mid-1970s.

During the 1970s, new travel forecasting techniques were developed for the most part by the research community, largely in universities. These disaggregate travel forecasting approaches differed from the aggregate approaches being used in practice at the time. They used new mathematical techniques and theoretical bases from econometrics and psychometrics that were difficult for practitioners to learn. Moreover, the new techniques were not easily integrated into conventional planning practices. Communication between researchers and practitioners was fitful. While researchers were developing more appropriate ways to analyze this complex array of issues and options, practitioners stayed wedded to the older techniques. The gap between research and practice was only gradually being closed.

The 1980s brought a new challenge to urban transportation planning, the decentralization of authority and responsibility. The national mood shifted, and centralized approaches were no longer considered to be the appropriate means for dealing with national problems. The federal government reduced its involvement, leaving the states and local governments more flexibility to respond in whatever manner they chose. The federal statutes remained in force, but additional federal guidance or elaboration was reduced and eliminated.

Reduction in federal regulation and prescription offered expanded opportunities to fashion planning procedures and institutions to local problems and needs. More time and effort could be used to produce information for local decisions rather than to meet federal requirements. Urban areas experiencing growth in population and employment, for example, could focus on long-range development plans to expand their transportation systems. Stable or declining urban areas could deal with redevelopment issues and infrastructure rehabilitation. Less regulation resulted in more flexibility in the elements of the planning process and in the division of responsibilities to perform them.

On the other hand, planning had to be more responsive to the needs of local decision makers and citizens and adjust to the realities of long-term budget constraints in many urban areas. The urban transportation planning processes had been attuned to federal requirements. It was, therefore, difficult to realign procedures and institutional arrangements to address local issues and needs.

Many of the issues that were debated in the 1970s are being revisited in the 1990s. One issue is the appropriate balance between long-range and short-term planning. A second is the level of effort devoted to system expansion, infrastructure rehabilitation, system management, and possibly even system retrenchment (for example, removal of certain facilities or routes) to match declining population, travel demand, and financial resources. The issues of changing institutional arrangements and locus of decision-making are being raised in a number of urban areas.

Some urban areas are struggling with using transportation to foster economic development while still providing mobility. The use of innovative financing techniques such as joint development and increased participation by the private sector has increased to offset shortfalls in public sector funds. The matters of environmental quality, transportation for special groups, and energy conservation are being revalued differently across the spectrum of urban areas and are affecting planning processes in these areas in different ways.

The level of detail and complexity of planning procedures is being reassessed. Smaller urban areas are opting for a simpler planning process that is commensurate with their fewer problems and less complex planning context. The larger areas have many more problems to address, options to evaluate, and organizational arrangements and procedures to use. Greater emphasis in transportation planning is being placed on both the corridor- and site-level scale of planning, in addition to the regional scale. Transportation analysis is beginning to become better integrated with land-use planning, at least at the site level.

The planning community is being challenged to further adapt its technical procedures, and it is responding. State and local planning agencies have become more resourceful in tailoring planning procedures and techniques to fit local requirements. Often, planning methods have not been available when needed to adequately support planning and project decisions. Compromises between accuracy, practicality, simplifying assumptions, quicker responses, and judgment are resulting in innovative analysis methods and applications. New transportation options and travel analysis methods that were researched in the past are being applied in at least a limited fashion.

With tighter budgets and the increasing demands being placed on them, transportation planning agencies are finding it increasingly difficult to collect large-scale regional data sets such as home-interview, origin–destination surveys.

Planning agencies are seeking alternative data sources to fill this gap.

Clearly, the microcomputer revolution has arrived. The microcomputer is no longer a revolutionary tool. It has become firmly entrenched in the planning process, and is now an essential tool without which planning could not be done.

All of this demonstrates that urban transportation planning is going through another evolutionary stage to reshape planning processes to changing needs.

REFERENCES

This chapter is taken from *Urban Transportation Planning in the United States: An Historical Overview*, by Edward Weiner (Praeger Publishers, New York, an imprint of Greenwood Publishing Group, Inc., 1987). Copyright © by Edward Weiner. Abridged and revised with permission of the publisher.

Some citations are no longer available from their original source. These citations are often available from the National Technical Information Service, U.S. Department of Commerce, 5285 Port Royal Road, Springfield, VA 22161. We have verified the order numbers for many of these citations, and they are found at the end of the citation. Prices are available through NTIS at the address above.

1   *Chicago Area Transportation Study, Final Report in Three Parts, Volume I: Study Findings, December 1959; Volume II: Data Projections, July 1960; Volume III: Transportation Plan, April 1962* (Chicago: Harrison Lithographing, 1959-1962).

2   CARL N. SWERDLOFF AND JOSEPH R. STOWERS, "A Test of Some First Generation Residential Land Use Models," in *Land Use Forecasting Concepts*, Highway Research Record 126 (Washington, D.C.: Highway Research Board, 1966), pp. 38-59.

3   JOHN D. WELLS AND OTHERS, *An Analysis of the Financial and Institutional Framework for Urban Transportation Planning and Investment* (Arlington, Va.: Institute for Defense Analyses, June 1970).

4   THOMAS J. KUEHN, *The Development of National Highway Policy* (Seattle, Wash.: University of Washington, August 1976).

5   U.S. DEPARTMENT OF COMMERCE, BUREAU OF PUBLIC ROADS, *The Administration of Federal-Aid for Highways and Other Activities of the Bureau of Public Roads* (Washington, D.C.: U.S. Department of Commerce, January 1957).

6   *Sagamore Conference on Highways and Urban Development, Guidelines for Action,* October 5-9, 1958, sponsored by American Municipal Association, AASHO, HRB, and Syracuse University (n.p.:n.d.).

7   WASHINGTON CENTER FOR METROPOLITAN STUDIES, *Comprehensive Planning for Metropolitan Development*, prepared for UMTA (Washington, D.C.: U.S. Department of Transportation, 1970). Now available as PB 200 135.

8   U.S. CONGRESS, SENATE, "Urban Transportation—Joint Report to the President by the Secretary of Commerce and the Housing and Home Finance Administration," *Urban Mass Transportation—1962*, 87th Congress, 2nd Session (Washington, D.C.: U.S. Government Printing Office), pp. 71-81.

9   WASHINGTON CENTER, *Comprehensive Planning*.

10   FEDERAL HIGHWAY ADMINISTRATION, *Federal Laws and Material Relating to the Federal Highway Administration* (Washington, D.C.: U.S. Government Printing Office, 1980).

11   GARLAND E. MARPLE, "Urban Areas Make Transportation Plans" (unpublished paper presented at the 1969 American Society of Civil Engineers Meeting on Transportation Engineering).

12   FEDERAL HIGHWAY ADMINISTRATION, Policy and Procedure Memorandum 50-9, "Urban Transportation Planning" (Washington, D.C.: Federal Highway Administration and the Bureau of Public Roads, June 21, 1967).

13   URBAN MASS TRANSPORTATION ADMINISTRATION, *Urban Mass Transportation Act of 1964, as amended through February 1988, and Related Laws* (Washington, D.C.: U.S. Government Printing Office, 1988).

14   *Highways and Urban Development*, report on the Second National Conference, Williamsburg, Virginia, December 12-16, 1965, sponsored by AASHO, National Association of Counties, and National League of Cities (n.p.: n.d.).

15   WASHINGTON CENTER, *Comprehensive Planning*.

16   LEON MONROE COLE, ed., *Tomorrow's Transportation: New Systems for the Urban Future*, prepared by U.S. Department of Housing and Urban Development (Washington, D.C.: U.S. Government Printing Office, 1968).

17   WASHINGTON CENTER, *Comprehensive Planning*.

18   ADVISORY COMMISSION ON INTERGOVERNMENTAL RELATIONS, *Toward More Balanced Transportation: New Intergovernmental Proposals*, Report A-49 (Washington, D.C.: U.S. Government Printing Office, 1974).

19   National Environmental Policy Act of 1969, 83 Stat. 852, P.L. 91-190, 91st congress, S. 1075, January 1, 1970.

20   UMTA, *Urban Mass Transportation Act*, p. 54.

21   FHWA, *Federal Laws and Material*.

22   HIGHWAY RESEARCH BOARD, *Organization for Continuing Urban Transportation Planning*, Special Report 139 (Washington, D.C.: Highway Research Board, 1973).

23   ADVISORY COMMISSION, *Toward More*.

24   HIGHWAY RESEARCH BOARD, *Urban Travel Demand Forecasting*, eds. Daniel Brand and Marvin L. Manheim, Special Report 143, proceedings of a conference held at Williamsburg, Virginia, December 3-7, 1972 (Washington, D.C.: Highway Research Board, 1973).

25   U.S. DEPARTMENT OF TRANSPORTATION, *Energy Conservation in Transportation*, Technology Sharing Program (n.p.: U.S. Department of Transportation, January 1979).

26   FEDERAL HIGHWAY ADMINISTRATION AND URBAN MASS TRANSPORTATION ADMINISTRATION, "Planning Assistance and Standards," *Federal Register*, 40, no. 181 (September 17, 1975), pp. 42976-84.

27   TRANSPORTATION RESEARCH BOARD, *A Review of Urban Mass Transportation Guidelines for Evaluation of Urban Transportation Alternatives*, a report of conferences held February 23-26, 1975, at Airlie House, Virginia, and March 29-April 1, 1976, at Hunt Valley, Maryland, sponsored by UMTA (Washington, D.C.: Transportation Research Board, February 23-26, 1975).

28   TRANSPORTATION RESEARCH BOARD, *Urban Transportation Alternatives: Evolution of Federal Policy*, Special Report 177 (Washington, D.C.: Transportation Research Board, 1977).

29   URBAN MASS TRANSPORTATION ADMINISTRATION, "Policy Toward Rail Transit," *Federal Register*, 43, no. 45 (March 7, 1978), pp. 9428-30.

30   NORMAN L. COOPER AND JOHN O. HIDINGER, "Integration of Air Quality and Transportation Planning," in *Proceedings of a Conference on Transportation and the 1977 Clean Air Act Amendments*, Jack Tar Hotel, San Francisco, Calif. (New York: American Society of Civil Engineers, 1980).

31   FEDERAL HIGHWAY ADMINISTRATION AND URBAN MASS TRANSPORTATION ADMINISTRATION, Air Quality Conformity and Priority Procedures for Use in Federal-Aid Highway and Federally-Funded Transit Programs," *Federal Register*, 46, no. 16 (January 26, 1981), pp. 8426-32.

32   COUNCIL ON ENVIRONMENTAL QUALITY, "National Environmental Policy Act - Regulations," *Federal Register*, 43, no. 230 (November 29, 1978), pp. 55978-56007.

33   FEDERAL HIGHWAY ADMINISTRATION AND URBAN MASS TRANSPORTATION ADMINISTRATION, "Environmental Impact and Related Procedures," *Federal Register*, 45, no. 212 (October 30, 1980), pp. 71968-87.

34   TRANSPORTATION RESEARCH BOARD, *Urban Transportation Planning in the 1980s*, Special Report 196, proceedings of a conference held November 9-12, 1981, in Warrenton, Virginia (Washington, D.C.: Transportation Research Board, 1982).

35   RONALD REAGAN, "Intergovernmental Review of Federal Programs," Executive Order 12372, *Federal Register*, 47, no. 137 (July 16, 1982), pp. 30959-60.

36   TRANSPORTATION RESEARCH BOARD, *Future Directions of Urban Public Transportation*, Special Report 199, proceedings of a conference held September 26-29, 1982, at Woods Hole, Massachusetts (Washington, D.C.: Transportation Research Board, 1983).

37   TRANSPORTATION RESEARCH BOARD, *Travel Analysis Methods for the 1980s*, Special Report 201, proceedings of a conference held October 3-7, 1982, at Easton, Maryland (Washington, D.C.: Transportation Research Board, 1983).

38   EDWARD WEINER, "Redefinition of Roles and Responsibilities in U.S. Transportation," *Transportation*, vol. 11 (1983), pp. 211-24.

39   VINCENT F. PAPARELLA, *An Administrative History of the Development of the FHWA/UMTA Joint Urban Transportation Planning Regulations* (Washington, D.C.: Urban Mass Transportation Administration, February 1982).

40   FEDERAL HIGHWAY ADMINISTRATION AND URBAN MASS TRANSPORTATION ADMINISTRATION, "Urban Transportation Planning," *Federal Register*, 48, no. 127 (June 30, 1983), pp. 30332-43.

41   URBAN MASS TRANSPORTATION ADMINISTRATION, "Urban Mass Transportation Major Capital Investment Policy," *Federal Register*, 49, no. 98 (May 18, 1984), pp. 21284-91.

42   URBAN MASS TRANSPORTATION ADMINISTRATION, "Private Enterprise Participation in the Urban Mass Transportation Program," *Federal Register*, 49, no. 205 (October 22, 1984), pp. 41310-12.

43   U.S. DEPARTMENT OF TRANSPORTATION, "Surface Transportation and Uniform Relocation Assistance Act of 1987," *Fact Sheet* (Washington, D.C.: U.S. Department of Transportation, April 10, 1987), P.L. 100-17.

44   WILLIAM F. BROWN AND EDWARD WEINER, eds., *Transportation Planning Applications: A Compendium of Papers Based on a Conference Held in Orlando, Florida*, held in April 1987 (Washington, D.C.: U.S. Department of Transportation, December 1987).

45   NATIONAL COUNCIL ON PUBLIC WORKS IMPROVEMENT, *The Nation's Public Works: Defining the Issues*, report to the President and the Congress (Washington, D.C.: National Council on Public Works Improvement, September 1986).

46   ALAN E. PISARSKI, *The Nation's Public Works: Report on Highways Streets, Roads and Bridges* (Washington, D.C.: National Council on Public Works Improvement, May 1987). Title also appears as "A Study of Policy Issues in Highways, Streets, and Bridges."

47   RONALD F. KIRBY AND ARLEE T. RENO, *Study of Policy Issues in the Public Works Category of Mass Transit*, [cover title] *The Nation's Public Works: Report on Mass Transit*, prepared for the National Council on Public Works Improvement by The Urban Institute, Categories of Public Works Series (Washington, D.C.: National Council on Public Works Improvement, May 1987).

48   NATIONAL COUNCIL ON PUBLIC WORKS IMPROVEMENT, *Fragile Foundations: A Report on America's Public Works*, Final Report to the President and Congress (Washington, D.C.: U.S. Government Printing Office, February 1988).

EXERCISES

3-1   In the conventional urban transportation planning process, discuss the meaning of the 3Cs, and name the ten elements in the process.

3-2   Discuss the developments that lead up to the federal government requiring urban transportation planning as a condition for federal-aid highway funds in the Federal-Aid Highway Act of 1962.

3-3   Discuss the shift in urban transportation planning emphasis from long-term planning to shorter-term planning during the 1970s. Identify the causes of this change and the responses by the federal government and state and local agencies.

3-4   How has urban transportation policy evolved over the last 25 years? What have been the primary forces causing these changes and what has been their effects on urban transportation?

3-5   What historically has been the role of the private sector in urban transportation? How has this role changed since 1970?

3-6   What are the current legislative proposals at the federal level affecting urban transportation? Discuss their advantages and disadvantages.

3-7   What are the current legislative proposals in your state affecting urban transportation? Discuss their advantages and disadvantages.

3-8   What are the major forces affecting urban transportation today and into the foreseeable future? What has been the response to these forces? Has this response been adequate and, if not, what further needs to be done?

PART II

SYSTEMS

AND TECHNOLOGIES

Chapter 4

URBAN PASSENGER TRANSPORTATION MODES

Vukan R. Vuchic

This chapter presents a systematic classification of concepts and definitions of terms in urban public transport, focusing mainly on transit. Features of the basic mode characteristics, such as guided versus steered technologies and small versus large vehicles, are also presented and then applied to a comparison of different transit modes.

TRANSIT CLASSIFICATIONS AND DEFINITIONS

Modes and concepts can be classified on several different bases. Some of the classifications are interdependent. For example, mode, often identified only with system technology, actually also incorporates characteristics of rights-of-way and operations. All major classifications are given here, from the basic classification of all urban travel to the definitions of physical system components and performance concepts.

CLASSIFICATION BY TYPE OF USAGE

There are three basic categories of transportation by type of operation and usage: private, for-hire, and public or common carrier. The main characteristics, typical modes, and optimal operating domains of these categories are given in Table 4-1.

TABLE 4-1
Classification of Urban Passenger Transportation by Type of Usage

Characteristic / Usage Type	Private	For-hire	Public or Common Carrier
Common designation	Private transportation	Paratransit	Transit
Service availability	Owner	Public	Public
Service supplier	User	Carrier	Carrier
Route determination	User (flexible)	User / User (carrier)	Carrier (fixed)
Time-schedule determination	User (flexible)	User / User (carrier)	Carrier (fixed)
Cost-price	User absorbs	Fixed rate	Fixed fare

	Private		For-hire		Public or Common Carrier
	Individual		Individual		Group
Carrier type — Modes	Automobile	Carpools	Taxi	Dial-a-ride	Street transit (bus, trolleybus, streetcar)
	Motorcycle	Vanpools	Rented car	Jitney	Semirapid transit (semirapid bus, light rail transit)
	Bicycle			Charter bus	Rapid transit (rail, rubber-tired, regional rail)
	Walking				Special and proposed modes

Optimum (but not exclusive) domain of operation:	Private		For-hire	Public or Common Carrier
Area density	Low-medium		Low	High-medium
Routing	Dispersed	Origin: low / Destination: high	Dispersed	Concentrated (radial)
		Radial		
Time	Off-peak	Peak only	All times	Peak
Trip purposes	Recreation, shopping, business	Work only	Business	Work, school, business

Private transportation consists of privately owned vehicles operated by owners for their own use, usually on publicly provided and operated streets. Private auto is the most common mode, but motorcycle, bicycle, and, of course, walking also belong in this category.

For-hire urban passenger transportation is commonly designated as *paratransit*. It is transportation service provided by an operator and available to all parties who meet the conditions of a contract for carriage [that is, pay prescribed prices (rates)], but which is adjustable in various degrees to individual users' desires. Most paratransit modes do not have fixed routes and schedules. Taxi, dial-a-bus, and jitney are major modes.

Common-carrier urban passenger transportation is known as *transit, mass transit*, or *mass transportation*. These are transportation systems with fixed routes and schedules, available for use by all persons who pay the established fare. Most common representatives are bus, light rail, and rapid transit, but there exist a number of other modes.

Paratransit modes with routes and schedules that change with the desires of individual users are referred to as *demand responsive*; when the difference is pointed out, transit is described as *fixed-route, fixed-schedule service*.

Urban public transportation, strictly defined, includes both transit and paratransit categories, since both are available for public use. However, since public transportation is frequently identified with transit only, inclusion of paratransit is often specifically emphasized.

A secondary classification of travel categorizes transportation as individual or group. *Individual transportation* refers to systems in which each vehicle serves a separate party (person or organized group); *group transportation* carries unrelated persons in the same vehicles. As Table 4-1 shows, the former is predominantly private transportation and the latter is transit, while paratransit encompasses modes from both categories.

TRANSIT MODES

A transit mode is defined by three characteristics:

- Right-of-way (ROW) category.
- Technology.
- Type of service.

Modes vary with each of these characteristics. Contrary to the common belief that technologies mostly determine modal characteristics, the ROW category has the strongest influence on both performance and costs of modes. For example, streetcar service is more similar to surface bus than to rail rapid transit service.

Right-of-Way

Transit ROW is the strip of land on which the transit vehicles operate. There are three basic ROW categories, distinguished by the degree of their separation from other traffic.

1. *Category C* represents surface streets with *mixed traffic*. Transit may have preferential treatment, such as reserved lanes separated by lines or special signals, or may be mixed with other traffic.
2. *Category B* includes ROW types that are *longitudinally physically separated* by curbs, barriers, grade separation, and the like from other traffic, but with grade crossings for vehicles and pedestrians, including regular street intersections. High-occupancy vehicle (HOV) lanes or roadways represent a lower-quality ROW category B: they provide better traffic flow than other lanes, but they do not separate public from private vehicles, the most important element for giving transit the favored role on the basis of its type of service and higher efficiency than private transportation.
3. *Category A* is a *fully controlled* ROW without grade crossings or any legal access by other vehicles or persons. It is also referred to as "grade-separated" or "exclusive" ROW. In exceptional cases the ROW may have widely spaced grade crossings with signal override and gate protection of the tracks, and yet be considered as category A, since such crossings have little effect on line performance, although they may adversely affect safety.

Technology

Technology of transit modes refers to the mechanical features of their vehicles and ways. The four most important features are defined here.

1. *Support* is the vertical contact between vehicle and riding surface that transfers the vehicle weight. The most common types are rubber tire on concrete, asphalt, or other surface and steel wheel on steel rail. Other types of support are vehicle body on water (boats and hydrofoils), air cushion (hovercraft), and magnetic levitation. Technologies with support under the vehicle body are *supported*; those with the body around the guideway are *straddled*; those with support above the vehicle body are *suspended*. The supported type is by far the most common.
2. *Guidance* refers to the means of lateral vehicle guidance. Highway vehicles are *steered* (by the driver) and their lateral stability is provided by wheel/support adhesion. Rail vehicles are *guided* by flanges and the conical form of the wheel surfaces. A distinct feature of rail technology is that its wheel/rail assembly combines both support and guidance. Externally guided rubber-tired vehicles in all forms must have additional horizontal wheels and vertical surfaces for guidance.

3. *Propulsion* refers to the type of propulsion unit and method of transferring acceleration/deceleration forces. Its major components are:

   a. *Type of propulsion unit*—the most common are the diesel internal combustion engine (ICE), used on buses and some regional rail, and electric motors, used on trolleybuses and most rail modes. Gasoline ICEs dominate small highway vehicles, while the gas turbine, steam engine, and others are still under development. Several rail systems built in the 1980s are propelled by linear induction motors (LIM).

   b. *Methods of transferring tractive force* include friction/adhesion (dominant), magnetic, cable, and propeller, among others.

4. *Control* is the means of regulating travel of one or all vehicles in a system. The most important control is for longitudinal spacing of the vehicles, which may be manual/visual, manual/signal, fully automatic, or various combinations of these.

Conventionally, transit technologies were defined only by the techniques of support and guidance. Such definitions are not precise enough to distinguish bus from trolleybus or light rail from rapid transit. With support, guidance, propulsion, and control, all technologies can be defined to any desired degree of precision.

Type of Service

There are many different types of transit services. They can be classified into groups by three characteristics. The first classification is by the *types of routes and trips served*:

- *Short-haul transit* is defined as low-speed service within small areas with high travel density, such as central business districts (CBDs), campuses, airports, and exhibition grounds.
- *City transit*, the most common type, includes transit routes serving the entire city. They may operate on any ROW category (A, B, or C).
- *Regional transit* consists of long, high-speed routes with few stops, serving long trips within the metropolitan region. Regional rail and some express bus routes exemplify this category.

The second classification is by *stopping schedule*:

- *Local service* is with all vehicles stopping at all stops (or as required by passengers).
- *Accelerated service* is when successive vehicles skip different sets of stations on a predetermined schedule (for example, skip-stop and zonal service).
- *Express service* is with all vehicles on a route stopping only at widely spaced stops. These routes often parallel local service but serve fewer stops/stations, making express/local service.

The third classification is by *time of operation*:

- *All-day service* is transit operated during most daily hours. This is the basic transit service, and it includes a great majority of transit lines.
- *Peak-hour service* or *commuter transit* refers to routes operated during peak hours only. They are usually radial from suburbs, focusing on the CBD, and designed mostly to serve work trips (for example, buses on the Shirley HOV Express Roadway in the Washington, D.C., area). Commuter transit service is a supplement to, but not a substitute for, all-day regular transit.
- *Irregular service* is transit operated only during special events, such as sport events, exhibitions, or public celebrations.

Generic Classes of Transit Modes

There is no rigorous definition of what differences in ROW category, technology, or service make a separate mode, but it is common to consider systems as different modes if they differ substantially in one or more of the three characteristics. Thus, bus and trolleybus operating the same type of service on the same ROW are different modes because of their substantial technological and performance differences; but standard and articulated buses operating under the same conditions would not be considered different modes. An express bus line is a different mode than a shopper shuttle, even if the vehicles are identical, because of the drastically different services; but skip-stop transit service during peak hours is not considered a different mode than the same line operating locally at other times because the two services are quite similar.

The best known classification of transit modes is into three generic classes, based mostly, but not entirely, on ROW category. They are defined here.

1. *Street transit* (also known as *surface transit*) designates modes operated on streets with mixed traffic (ROW category C); its reliability is often low because of various interferences, and its speed is lower than the speed of traffic flow, owing to the time lost at passenger stops: buses, trolleybuses, and streetcars are in this class.
2. *Semirapid transit* consists of modes utilizing mostly ROW category B, but C or A may also be used for some sections. This class includes a wide range of modes, from those with B and C categories, such as buses and light rail transit (LRT) operating on separated ROW and streets on the low side, to largely grade separated LRT (B and A) on the high side. The performance of these modes depends greatly on the degree and locations of ROW separation; it is particularly important that transit be separated from other vehicular traffic in central, congested urban areas. Another factor is technology; rail modes can operate in short trains and have higher safety through automatic signalization than buses. Higher types of semirapid transit (with little or no C category ROW) can match or exceed the speed and reliability of auto travel.

3. *Rapid transit* modes operate exclusively on category A ROW and have high speed, capacity, reliability, and safety. All existing rapid transit systems utilize guided technologies (rail or rubber tire), which permit the operation of trains (high capacity) and automatic signal control (high safety). Strictly, "bus rapid transit" does not exist since a bus line operating entirely on ROW category A would have much lower capacity, higher operating costs (single vehicles), and lower safety (steering instead of guidance, no automatic signals) than rail modes.

Most transit modes belong to one of the three generic classes. The exceptions are such modes as ferryboats, aerial tramways, and inclines. The latter two do have exclusive ROW, but they have no other features of rapid transit. These modes are therefore classified as *special transit*.

A matrix of mode classification by ROW category and major technological features (mainly support and guidance) is given in Table 4-2. Other technological and some service variations are given in individual matrix boxes. In addition to all street transit modes, category C contains also water- and airborne modes. Semirapid transit modes are in category B, while all rapid transit modes belong, by definition, in category A. This category also includes, however, all guided nonrail modes, since they cannot tolerate grade crossings. Inclines and aerials are also included. Thus, the three generic classes correspond closely, but not exactly, to the three ROW categories.

An overview of the preceding mode definitions, classifications, and characteristics is presented in Fig. 4-1.

TRANSIT SYSTEM COMPONENTS

The physical components of the transit systems are generally classified into the following items:

Vehicles or *cars* are referred to collectively as *fleet* for buses and *rolling stock* for rail vehicles. A *transit unit* (*TU*) is a set of vehicles traveling together; it may be a *single vehicle* unit or a *train* with several vehicles.

Ways, travel ways, or rights-of-way may be common streets and highways, reserved lanes (designated only), exclusive lanes (physically separated), transit streets, busways (grade-separated roadways for buses only), tracks in roadways, on partially or fully controlled ROW at grade, above grade (embankments and aerials), or below grade (cuts and tunnels).

Locations and facilities at which vehicles stop to pick up and drop off passengers can be of several types. *Stops* are locations along streets with simple facilities (signs, shelters, and so on); *stations* are usually buildings below, on, or above ground with facilities for passengers and system operation. *Terminals* are end stations of major transit lines. *Transfer stations* serve more than one line and provide for passenger interchange among them. *Multimodal transfer stations* are served by several modes. *Interface* is another term for a transfer station.

TABLE 4-2
Classification of Urban Public Transportation Modes[a]

ROW Category	Technology	Highway— Driver-Steered	Rubber-Tired— Guided, Partially Guided	Rail	Special
C		*Paratransit* *Shuttle bus* *Regular bus* *Express bus (on streets)*	*Trolleybus*	*Streetcar* Cable car	*Ferryboat* Hydrofoil Helicopter
B		Semirapid bus	O-Bahn	*Light rail transit*	
A		Bus on busway only*	*Rubber-tired RT* Rubber-tired monorails Automated guided transit GRT PRT*	Light rapid transit Schwebebahn *Rail rapid transit* *Regional rail* Commuter rail	*Incline* Aerial tramway Continuous short-haul systems

[a]Modes extensively used are in italic type. Modes that are not operational are designated by asterisks.

Figure 4-1 An overview of transit mode definition, classification, and characteristics

Determinant Factors	Categories /Types	Basic Characteristics	Individual Modes*	Generic Classes
Separation from other traffic	C B A	Right-of-way Categories	(Paratransit modes) Shuttle bus Regular bus Express bus/street Trolleybus Streetcar Cable car	Street transit
			Semirapid bus O-Bahn Light rail transit	Semirapid transit
Support Guidance Propulsion - Motor/Engine - Traction Control	Highway—driver-steered Rubber-tired—guided, semiguided Rail Special	Technology	Schwebebahn Rubber-tired monorails Light rail rapid transit RT (rail and rubber-tired) Regional rail	Rapid transit
Line length Type of operation Trips served	Short-haul Regular Regional Local Accelerated Express	Type of Service	Automated guided transit (rubber-tired, rail, magnetic) Ferryboat Helicopter Inclines Belt systems	Special transit

*The list is not exhaustive.

Bus garages or *depots* and *rail yards* are buildings or areas for vehicle storage. *Shops* are facilities for vehicle maintenance and repair.

Control systems include vehicle detection, communication and signal equipment, as well as any central control facility. *Power supply systems* on electrically powered modes consist of substations, distribution wiring, catenary or third-rail structures, and related equipment. Except for the vehicles, all these items constitute *fixed facilities* of transit systems, or their *infrastructure*.

Transit route or *transit line* is a designated set of streets or separated rights-of-way that transit vehicles regularly traverse. The term route is commonly used for buses and line for rail modes and for sections on which several routes overlap, but the two terms are sometimes used interchangeably. The collection of all routes/lines in a city is its *transit network*.

TRANSIT SYSTEM OPERATIONS, SERVICE, AND CHARACTERISTICS

Transit operations include such activities as scheduling, crew rostering, running and supervision of TUs, fare collection, and system maintenance. Together they produce transportation that is offered to potential users.

Transit service is the transit system operation as seen by its actual and potential users.

Transit system characteristics are classified in four categories.

1. *System performance* refers to the entire set of *performance elements*, the most important ones being:
   a. *Service frequency* (f), number of TU departures per hour.
   b. *Operating speed* (V_o), speed of travel on the line that passengers experience.
   c. *Reliability*, expressed as a percentage of TU arrivals with less than a fixed time deviation from schedule (for example, 4 min).
   d. *Safety*, measured by the number of fatalities, injuries, and property damage per 100 million passenger-km (passenger-mi), or a similar unit.
   e. *Line capacity* (C), the maximum number of spaces (offered capacity) or persons (utilized capacity) transit vehicles can carry past a point along the line during 1 hour.
   f. *Productive capacity* (P_c), the product of operating speed and line capacity ($V_o \times C$). As a composite indicator incorporating one basic element affecting passengers (speed) and one affecting operator (capacity), productive capacity is a very convenient performance indicator for mode comparisons.
   g. *Productivity*, the quantity of output per unit of resource [for example, vehicle-km, space-km, or person-km per unit of labor, operating cost, fuel, ROW width, and so on].
   h. *Utilization*, also the ratio of output to input, but of the same or similar units, for example, person-mi/space-mi (person-km/space-km) offered.

2. *Level of service* (LOS) is the overall measure of all service characteristics that affect users. LOS is a basic element in attracting potential users to the system. Major factors comprising LOS can be divided into three groups:
   a. *Performance elements that affect users*, such as operating speed, reliability, and safety.
   b. *Service quality* (SQ), consisting of qualitative elements of service, such as convenience and simplicity of using the system, riding comfort, aesthetics, cleanliness, and behavior of passengers.
   c. *Price* the user must pay for the service (that is, its fare or rate).
3. *Impacts* are the effects transit service has on its surroundings and the entire area it serves. They may be *positive* or *negative*. *Short-term impacts* include reduced street congestion, changes in air pollution, noise, and aesthetics along a new line. *Long-term impacts* consist of changes in land values, economic activities, physical form, and the social/human environment of the city.
4. *Costs* are usually divided into two major categories: *investment costs* (or capital costs) are those required to construct or later make permanent changes in the physical plant of the transit system. *Operating costs* are those costs incurred by regular operation of the system.

The *evaluation and comparative analysis* of transit systems must include all four categories: performance, LOS, impacts, and costs of each system. The preferred mode is usually not the one with the highest performance or lowest costs, but the one with the most advantageous "package" or combination of the four.

THE FAMILY OF TRANSIT MODES: DEFINITIONS AND COMPARISONS

Transit modes can be ordered into a family, ranging from taxis to regional rail systems. Brief definitions and characteristics of the commonly used modes are presented here. Several pairs of modes "adjacent" to each other in the family of modes are compared. Detailed methodology for their comparison is presented in Chap. 10.

LOW-CAPACITY MODES: PARATRANSIT

Taxis are automobiles operated by a driver and hired by users for individual trips. The service they offer is tailored entirely to the user's desire. Users may find a taxi at a number of locations in the city; they may hail it on the street; or they may telephone a central dispatching office. The use of a taxi may involve longer waiting than with a private car, but there is no parking problem. The user avoids the financial responsibility of owning a car, but the out-of-pocket cost of taxi travel is the highest of all modes. Since most of the cost covers the driver's time, a high price is inherent in this mode.

Dial-a-ride or *dial-a-bus* consists of minibuses or vans directed from a central dispatching office. Passengers call the office and give their origin, destination, and desired time of travel. The office plans the bus routings so that as many passengers as possible are served on a single trip.

Dial-a-bus usually operates within geographically delineated low-density areas. It serves trips that have one common end ("one-to-many" or "many-to-one") or both ends dispersed ("many-to-many"). Thus, this mode provides a service between those of taxi and regular bus.

Compared with *taxi, dial-a-ride* offers:
+   Lower-cost service.
+   More comfortable ride (larger vehicles).
−   Slower, less direct travel.
−   Less personalized service.
−   Service within a limited area only.

Experience has shown that in most cases dial-a-rides have low average vehicle occupancies, which result in high cost per passenger. Where moderate fares are required to attract a substantial number of riders, dial-a-ride may require a considerably higher public assistance per rider than conventional transit services.

Jitneys are privately owned large passenger cars or vans (6- to 15-seat vehicles) that operate on a fixed route (in some cases with minor deviations), without fixed schedules. They pick up and drop off passengers along their route by request at designated stops or, in some cities, practically anywhere, contributing to traffic congestion. Because of their small capacity, jitneys operate in large numbers and offer high-frequency service on major routes; on lightly traveled routes their service is often unreliable. Since each individual jitney stops less frequently than a bus, jitneys' travel speeds are higher than those of buses on the same facilities.

Consequently, jitneys typically offer more frequent and faster service, but with lower reliability, safety, and comfort than regular transit. They are used extensively in many developing countries with very low labor wages, particularly in cities with inadequate transit services.

MEDIUM-CAPACITY MODES: STREET TRANSIT

Regular bus (RB) service consists of buses operating along fixed routes on fixed schedules. Buses comprise by far the most widely used transit mode. With vehicles varying in capacity from minibuses (20 to 35 spaces) to articulated buses (up to 130 spaces) and the ability to operate on nearly all streets, arterials, and freeways, buses provide services covering a wide range of LOS, performance, costs, and impacts.

At the lower end of their application range, regular buses serve low-volume suburban routes, overlapping somewhat with the domain of dial-a-ride applications. In marginal cases it is possible to operate regular buses as dial-a-bus service during hours of low demand. The more the travel demand is concentrated along corridors, the more advantageous the regular bus becomes.

Compared with *dial-a-ride,* the *regular bus* offers:
+   Higher reliability (fixed schedule, predictable waiting times).
+   Lower cost per passenger (lower fares and/or lower public assistance).
−   Less personalized service (not door-to-door).
−   Less frequent (not by request) service.

The most typical bus services are street transit routes, which may represent the entire transit network (small and most medium-size cities) or supplementary and feeder services to rail networks. At the upper end of their application range, regular buses overlap with the LRT domain: they can serve lines with 3000 to 5000 pr/h, exceptionally with even higher volumes. Their largest overlap, however, is with the domains of trolleybuses and streetcars.

Express bus service is provided by fast, comfortable buses on long routes with widely spaced stops. It is characterized by higher speed and more comfortable travel, but serves fewer points. It sometimes has a higher fare than regular buses. Its reliability of service is dependent on traffic conditions along the route.

Trolleybuses (TB) are the same vehicles as buses except that they are propelled by an electric motor and obtain power from two overhead wires along their route. The trolleybus can basically be used for the same services as the regular bus. It involves a higher investment cost and more complex operations, which some operators do not like. The advantages the trolleybus offers include higher riding quality (smooth vehicle motion), ability to operate on steep grades, and excellent environmental features (extremely low noise and no exhaust). Since these factors are not directly reflected in the operator's revenues, financial problems of transit agencies have often led to substitution of buses for trolleybuses, even where this change was not in the interest of either transit users or the general public.

Streetcars (SCR), also known as *tramways* or *trolleys*, are electrically powered rail transit vehicles operating in 1- to 3-car TUs, mostly on streets. Their tracks and distinct vehicles give streetcar service a strong identity. Spacious vehicles and comfortable ride are also popular with passengers. Operation on the streets with congested traffic, however, causes considerable friction with other vehicles, impeding both the streetcars and the auto traffic.

A number of street design and regulatory traffic engineering techniques exist that can alleviate these problems and even provide a better flow for streetcars than for buses. But without such measures, buses usually offer superior speed and reliability in street operation. For this and several other reasons, streetcars, which used to be the basic transit mode, have been either replaced by buses or gradually upgraded into higher-performance rail modes in most cities.

Streetcars compared with *buses* have:
+ More comfortable ride.
+ Quieter, pollution-free operation.
+ Better vehicle performance.
+ Higher labor productivity (larger vehicles).
+ Higher line capacity.
− Higher investment cost.
− Less reliable street operation unless transit enjoys priority treatment.
− Less flexible operation (detours, use for charters, and so on).
− Higher maintenance of way and power supply system costs.
− Greater impedance of other traffic.

HIGH-PERFORMANCE MODES: SEMIRAPID TRANSIT AND RAPID TRANSIT

Transit modes in the upper range of the "mode family" are better characterized by high overall performance than specifically by high capacity. They all offer high speed and reliability, but their capacity and productivity vary greatly between the two extremes, semirapid buses and rail rapid transit. Semirapid transit includes only semirapid bus and light rail transit. Rapid transit includes light rail rapid transit, rubber-tired rapid transit, rail rapid transit, regional rail and, in a broader sense, automated guided transit.

Semirapid Transit

Semirapid buses (SRB) are regular or high-performance buses operating on routes that include substantial sections of ROW categories B or A. The performance of such systems depends greatly on the following factors:

1. Proportion and locations of separated ROW sections: their provision in congested areas is more important than in suburban, low-density areas.
2. ROW types: HOV- or bus-only lanes, streets, or roadways.
3. Types of operation: routings, transfers, stop spacings, speed, frequency, safety, and reliability of service.

The concept of *buses on busway* was exemplified by the initial operation of Shirley Busway in the Washington, D.C., area. In spite of its successful operation, this and most other busways in the United States have been converted under pressures of highway interests into HOV facilities. This conversion represents a degradation (decreased reliability, diminished identity) of transit services and upgrading of their competition, certain classes of private vehicles, which often "steal" transit passengers. This results in further decrease in the level of transit services.

In either case, busway or HOV roadway, this mode consists of a facility usually in a freeway median that is utilized by a great number of bus routes converging during the commuting hours from suburban areas. Buses travel on the high-speed facility with few or without any stops to the CBD, where they use streets for distribution. Routes are usually radial, terminating in the CBD, and have few coordinated transfers with other routes. During the afternoon peak the same operation occurs in reverse. The exclusive facility may be used for travel in one or both directions.

In most cases these services exist only during peaks; sometimes a few routes operate throughout the day. Thus, *buses on busways* or *HOV roadways* typically represent commuter rather than regular transit. They are an efficient mode for peak-hour travel, but offer a lower type of service, if any, in the off-peak hours. The main reason for this deficiency is that, since they follow freeway alignments, busways are not optimally located with respect to transit demand. Moreover, they provide high-speed travel in outlying, low-density areas, but the service drastically deteriorates in slow distribution and frequent congestion in the CBD.

Oriented to CBD commuters, the SRB mode does not serve the increasing volumes of "reverse commuters" (from central city into suburbs) as well as many rapid transit or regional rail systems do with their much more frequent and regular services.

These deficiencies of buses are not necessarily inherent in the SRB mode. If properly designed, SRB can utilize different types of reserved or exclusive ROW, including busways that follow alignments of major passenger travel. Its routes can be simpler (similar to rail lines), have stop spacings of 400 to 800 m (1250 to 2500 ft), have transfers with other routes, and operate with reasonable frequencies throughout the day. This type of system exists in Ottawa, Canada, where extensive facilities in suburbs and the CBD are provided strictly for transit buses, and the entire network is operated as an all-day, regular transit system serving many suburban and center-city stops with satisfactory frequency.

Adelaide, Australia, has a semirapid bus system utilizing O-Bahn (that is, guided buses on a radial facility, which technically precludes all other vehicles and thus guarantees bus exclusivity). By concept, however—a long busway with very few stations and street operation in the CBD—this system is similar to its counterparts in several U.S. cities and inferior to the much more extensive Ottawa SRB network with its many stations.

Because of the separated ROW, the SRB mode requires a considerably higher investment than regular buses for its infrastructure, but it offers a higher LOS and system performance.

Light rail transit (LRT) is a mode utilizing predominantly reserved, but not necessarily grade-separated ROW. Its electrically propelled rail vehicles operate singly or in trains. LRT provides a wide range of LOS and performance characteristics.

LRT takes advantage of a feature of rail technology that is unique among guided systems: the ability to operate not only on ROW category A, but also on B and C. Unlike virtually all other guided technologies, rail technology can have crossings of its tracks and crossings of tracks with streets, as well as running along streets. This gives LRT the ability to utilize all types of ROW on the same line, and yet offer the advantages of guided technology: high capacity, high labor productivity (train operation), very high riding comfort, and so on. Street running is least desirable because of the disadvantages described before for streetcar operation; fully controlled ROW is the most desirable, but the most capital-intensive type of facility.

Consequently, a typical LRT network, such as those found in Cologne and Stuttgart, Germany, or San Francisco may have tunnels under the most congested central area, while its degree of separation decreases toward outlying areas where congestion is not a problem. LRT can also operate in pedestrian malls (as in Zurich, Switzerland, Mannheim, Germany, and San Diego). The lower noise, absence of exhaust fumes, and better safety record make LRT more compatible with pedestrian environments than buses. Because of the limited speed, however, mall running can be used only on short sections, usually up to 1 to 2 km (one mile).

LRT is a higher-investment, higher-performance mode than streetcars. Its relationship with regular buses is similar to that with streetcars: their comparison would show that LRT is superior in nearly all LOS and performance items, but that it requires a much higher investment and, therefore, has a more limited network. Consequently, it has a smaller area coverage for walking access, but a much stronger ability than buses to attract park-and-ride users from large areas. Hence, the most important comparison is between LRT and SRB: both utilize similar ROW categories and require similar investments, but have different technologies.

This comparison shows that, as the extent of B and A ROW on a transit line increases, LRT becomes more advantageous than SRB. Since most of the infrastructure construction costs depend on ROW type, investments required for bus or rail on the same alignment are rather similar. The relatively small additional investment for LRT as compared to buses brings the very significant advantages of rail mode over buses in LOS, performance, operating costs, and impacts.

Another factor to consider in comparing bus and rail modes is the type of network. Buses have the greatest ability to operate on interconnected and overlapping routes; rail rapid transit (metro) is least capable of that. Metro networks typically consist of independent lines that may have a few (usually two) branches. They rely on easy transfers or even simultaneous passenger exchange across platforms among frequent services on different lines. Thus the trade-off is between fewer transfers in overlapping bus networks and higher frequency and greater simplicity and reliability of service in rail networks. The selection of either type of service and mode depends on local conditions. In some cases no-transfer service, which buses offer, prevails; in others, regimes on branches and trunk lines are so different that the use of different modes (bus feeder with rail on trunk) or different vehicles (minibus feeders and regular or articulated buses on the trunk) offers a much more reliable and economical network service. LRT is between these two modes and it often represents a good compromise of these features: LRT can have more branches than metro, and it offers considerably more reliable and comfortable service than buses. Due to their higher LOS and stronger image, rail modes attract considerably greater ridership than buses under comparable conditions.

Light rail transit compared with *semirapid buses* on the corresponding alignments is characterized by:

+ Easier securing of B or A ROW (less pressure to mix with other traffic).
+ Stronger image and identity of lines (rail technology).
+ More spacious, comfortable vehicles.
+ Higher passenger attraction (result of the preceding two).
+ Lower noise, no exhausts.
+ Better vehicle performance due to electric traction.
+ Higher system performance (capacity, productivity, reliability, etc.).
+ Lower operating cost per space-km.
+ Ability to operate in tunnels.
+ Ability to upgrade into rapid transit.
− Lower service frequency for a given demand due to larger vehicles.
− Somewhat higher investment for the same alignment.
− For new applications, a need to introduce new facilities for a different technology.
− Lower ability to branch out, requiring more transfers.
− A longer implementation period.

The LRT mode was developed in an evolutionary manner from streetcars in several European countries, particularly West Germany, since the late 1950s. A number of systems with LRT characteristics that had existed in U.S. cities several decades earlier had disappeared with the serious neglect of transit on this continent. With the revival of transit during the late 1960s and 1970s, LRT finally became a recognized transit mode. It has had a significant development worldwide since that time.

Since the late 1970s, new LRT systems have been built in a number of U.S. cities (four in California alone), in Canada (Edmonton and Calgary), and Mexico (Guadalajara). Many cities in other developed countries (France, Great Britain, the Netherlands, and Switzerland) have been joined by some cities in developing countries (Tunisia, Brazil, Hong Kong, and the Philippines) in building new LRT systems.

Rapid Transit (RT)

Light rail rapid transit (LRRT) or *light rapid transit* represents small-scale rapid transit: it consists of light rail vehicles (LRVs) operating only on ROW category A. There are very few conventional systems of this mode in operation (the Norristown line in Philadelphia and line 8 in Göteborg, Sweden, are the best known). The significance of this mode is increasing rapidly with the recent introduction of fully automated rail transit lines. During the 1980s, Vancouver, British Columbia, and London, England, opened automated LRT lines, and a number of cities began to plan constructing such systems.

Rubber-tired rapid transit (RTRT) consists of moderately large vehicles (gross floor areas between 36 and 53 m^2 or 380 and 570 ft^2) supported and guided by rubber tires, running on wooden, concrete, or steel surfaces in trains of 5 to 9 cars. The cars also have steel wheels for switching and for support in the case of a tire failure.

Rail rapid transit (RRT), increasingly known in most countries as *metro*, typically consists of large four-axle rail vehicles (area up to 70 m^2 or 750 ft^2) that operate in trains of 2 to 10 cars on fully controlled category A ROW, which allows high speed, high reliability, high capacity, rapid boarding, and fail-safe operation (in the case of driver's error or disability, the train is stopped automatically). Some RRT systems are further characterized by a high degree of automated operation.

Although the main representatives of semirapid transit (LRT) and of rapid transit (RRT or metro) are extremely similar in their technologies and can have compatible operations, the full ROW control gives RRT several significant distinctions, as the following summary comparison of the two modes shows.

Rail rapid transit compared with *light rail transit* has:
+ Higher LOS (speed, reliability, comfort, and so on).
+ Higher system performance (capacity due to long trains, productivity, efficiency).
+ Higher safety (signalized, fail-safe).
+ Stronger image (separate ROW *and* rail technology).
+ Higher passenger attraction and land-use impact (result of the above).
− Higher investment.
− Lower ability to fit into urban environment.
− Less conducive to stage construction.
− Longer implementation.

Rail rapid transit represents the ultimate mode for line-haul transportation (that is, for serving a number of points along a line). Trains of spacious vehicles with several doors on each side board passengers from high-level platforms without fare collection delays at rates of up to 40 persons/sec, many times higher than any other mode; with train capacities, where required, often exceeding 2000 spaces and up to 40 trains/h passing a point, the capacity of RRT greatly exceeds that of any other transportation mode; full ROW control allows the most reliable and safe travel at the maximum speeds that station spacings and passenger comfort permit. In all these features there is no physical way that a major further improvement in performance can be achieved for line-haul service. This highest performance is achieved, however, at an investment cost higher than for any other mode; provision of its major item, a fully controlled ROW (A) through urban areas, requires a considerably higher cost than any other ROW type.

Regional rail (RGR) is a transit mode usually operated by railroad companies. It has high standards of alignment geometry and utilizes the largest vehicles of all rail transit systems (up to 80 m^2 or 860 ft^2, or more in bilevel cars) that operate in trains of 1-12 cars, on longer routes, with fewer stations, at higher speeds than typical for RRT. Thus, RGR functionally represents a "large-scale RRT" which serves most efficiently regional and longer urban trips.

Electric rail transit represents the oldest group of mechanically powered transit modes. Yet, the development of the technology and operation of these modes continues to be very dynamic. Since 1970, the diversity of rail modes has increased significantly. In addition to numerous technical inventions, a number of systems have been built that represent combinations of features of two or more different modes. For example, many cities have lines that represent a transition between streetcars and LRT; Rotterdam, the Netherlands, has a line that is a combination between LRT and metro; the BART system in San Francisco and the Washington, D.C., Metro represent systems between metro and regional rail modes, while Manchester, England, has developed a set of regional rail lines served by light rail vehicles, so that they have been extended through the center city and operate there as typical LRT lines.

Consequently, the family of rail transit modes now represents a nearly continuous spectrum of characteristics; yet, systems typical of the four rail transit modes (SCR, LRT, RT, and RGR) have distinctly different features, as the above discussion and their comparisons show.

Automated guided transit (AGT) is the group of modes that operates in a fully automated manner (their TUs have no crews). "Automated *guideway* transit," although often used, is conceptually incorrect: systems are automated, not guideways. During the period of development of many new concepts for transit systems (1960 through the 1970s), AGT modes, also known as *people-mover systems* (PMS), referred to rubber-tired guided systems with vehicles of small to medium size. It should be noted that the term people-mover system has been used liberally for all short-haul modes except conventional bus and rail. AGTs were originally classified into the following two categories. (See Chap. 24 for a more detailed discussion of AGT classifications and operating systems.)

Personal rapid transit (PRT) systems consist of small (3-6 seat) vehicles operating automatically on a complex network of guideways and serving only individuals or parties traveling together. This theoretical system concept is infeasible for applications because it combines an investment-intensive system (extensive infrastructure and sophisticated automation) with the very low transporting capacity of small vehicles. This low capacity is physically incompatible with high-density urban development. Consequently, in spite of numerous theoretical papers, no PRT has been built for real-world application.

Group rapid transit (GRT) systems consist of medium-capacity (15 to 100 spaces) vehicles operating singly or in short trains on exclusive guideways without crews. Following a number of applications of these systems as shuttle and short-line services in airports, campuses, and amusement parks, they have now been developed and built as regular transit lines in various cities, including Kobe and Osaka, Japan; Lille, France; Miami; Detroit (see also Chap. 5); and several others. The term *downtown people mover* (DPM) is identified with GRT modes used for local service within city centers.

In recent years, several developments with automated transit systems have occurred. First, while the PRT mode has remained without any applications, automated systems that have been built are larger in size than initial concepts indicated; these systems matured into actual transit applications. Present automated transit systems, which are, strictly, GRT by initial definition, have become better known under the term *AGT*.

An additional development has been the introduction of fully automated conventional rail systems (LRRT) in several cities (Vancouver, London), so AGT modes are no longer limited to unconventional, rubber-tired systems. AGT is therefore defined as medium-capacity guided transit modes operating on category A ROW in a fully automated manner. Line capacities of AGTs are typically in the range from 8000 to 15,000 sp/h, although some systems (primarily rail) can have capacities considerably above this range. For example, the Vancouver Advanced Light Rail Transit (ALRT) has been designed for some 28,000 sp/h (see also Chap. 5).

Table 4-3 classifies guided modes by guidance and support technology and vehicle size. It encompasses all guided transit modes except special ones, such as funiculars and aerial tramways.

Fully automated operation (driverless TUs) is technically feasible for all guided modes on category A ROW. For some AGT systems, however, such operation is a sine qua non for their economic feasibility, since the small size of their TUs would make labor costs prohibitively high; for metro systems, full automation is desirable but not crucial, because of their inherently high labor productivity.

Referring to Table 4-3, it can be seen that the large-vehicle modes (third column) are by far the most common. Applications of medium-vehicle modes will increase further as automation improves and becomes more common. Small-vehicle modes are entirely experimental, and there are no realistic prospects that they will become technically and economically feasible in the near future.

TABLE 4-3
Classification of Guided Modes with ROW Category
A by Vehicle Size and Guidance Technology[a]

Guidance Technology \ Vehicle Size	Small	Medium	Large
Rubber-tired	Rubber-tired PRT* (Aramis, CVS, Kabinentaxi, Monocab)	GRT or people mover systems (Skybus, Airtrans, VAL, Transurban*)	Monorails (Alweg, Safege*) *Rubber-tired RT* (Paris, Montreal, Mexico City)
Rail	Rail PRT* (Palomino, Minitram)	ALRT (Vancouver) Light rail rapid transit	*Rail rapid transit* *Regional rail*
	Automated guided transit	Rapid transit	

[a]Modes extensively used are in italic type. Modes that are not operational are designated by asterisks.

REVIEW OF THE FAMILY OF REGULAR TRANSIT MODES

A systematic overview of the categories and types of characteristics for all major modes defined here is presented in Table 4-4. The characteristics of the factors determining modes (see Classification by Type of Usage and Fig. 4-1) are ordered in the sequence of increasing performance; modes are also ordered ascending from the lowest performance up; the correlation between the two shows in the table as the diagonal set of × marks. The two frames designate the lowest and the highest performance sets in the family of modes. It is emphasized, however, that performance refers to absolute values of system capacity, productivity, and efficiency and does not imply evaluation of modes; the lowest and highest performance modes are by no means "the worst" and "the best" in the family; they are only best suited to the minimum and maximum demand conditions, respectively.

Several other comparisons of modes and their generic classes are given in the next six tables and figures. The ranges given encompass all existing systems, with the exception of some extreme values found in very special cases. Since individual systems seldom have several extreme values (for example, maximum TU capacity and maximum frequency), the maximum values of derived performance measures (capacity and productive capacity) are less than the products of the maximum values of their components. Thus, the boundaries of modal characteristics depicted in the diagrams are neither absolute nor precise limits, but the ranges of values derived from existing systems.

Table 4-5 gives the ranges of the basic technical, operational, and system characteristics of the most important modes, classified into the three generic classes: street, semirapid, and rapid transit. Private auto is included for comparison. Several modes that are similar in the given characteristics to the selected ones are not included (for example, taxi is similar to auto, trolleybus to bus, RTRT to RRT, and commuter to regional rail).

Table 4-6 summarizes the values from Table 4-5 by generic classes and presents several numerical examples of systems typical for each class. This table is the basis for Figs. 4-2, 4-3, and 4-4, which graphically show such basic characteristics as capacity, speed, cost, and productive capacity. Both representative systems and ranges of values for each class are plotted. Other important aspects, including LOS and impacts, cannot be shown graphically. They are discussed in Chap. 10.

Figure 4-2 shows the relationship between TU capacity, maximum line frequency, and line capacity (as area) for different modes. The diagram shows that, starting from the auto (taxi) toward higher-performance modes, maximum frequencies decrease while TU capacities increase. The most common values form a hyperbolic set of points (dashed lines) with rapidly increasing line capacities.

Since a comparison of capacities is incomplete without consideration of speed, Fig. 4-3 shows mode capacities, speeds, and productive capacities (as areas). The diagram clearly shows the large differences in all these performance elements among the classes; street transit has far lower capacity and operating speed than semirapid and rapid transit. This last mode has by far the best performance and the broadest range of performance values.

The most important factor for mode evaluation, relationship of performance and investment costs, is presented in Fig. 4-4. Productive capacity is plotted as the best representative of performance: it is the product of speed, affecting primarily passengers, and capacity, important for the operator. Similar to Fig. 4-3, the differences among classes of modes are major. There is a jump in investment cost between street and semirapid transit, and then a continuous investment range through rapid transit, with a rapid increase in productive capacity. Maximum productive capacity increases from street to semirapid transit by a factor of 4, and to rapid transit by about 13. The low performance of the auto/highway mode is conspicuous.

Figure 4-4 shows that although RRT can be designed for 70,000 sp/h, 50 km/h, and involve an investment cost of 50×10^6/km, it can also have much lower values of all these items. Its particularly broad range stretches from high-performance systems such as San Francisco's BART (by its yet to be achieved design specifications it would have 2.16×10^6 space-km/h^2, at the upper boundary) to low-performance systems such as some lines on the Chicago rapid transit, which overlap with high-performance LRTs (for example, Boston's Green Line).

Another important modal characteristic is passenger attraction, which is a function of LOS. Since LOS is generally strongly correlated with system performance, the passenger attraction of transit modes increases significantly from street to rapid transit, as the conceptual dashed lines in Fig. 4-4 indicate. Street transit, always inferior in LOS to that of auto, mostly serves captive riders. Rapid transit, usually superior to auto in the same corridor, attracts most of the trips and generates additional travel.

TABLE 4-4
Review of Basic Features of Urban Public Transit Modes

The table cross-classifies Categories-Types against Determinant Factors (marked with *) and against Modes (marked with X). "(X)" indicates less common applications.

Modes: Paratransit; Regular bus (RB); Trolleybus (TB); Streetcar (SCR); Semirapid bus (SRB); Light rail transit (LRT); Rubber-tired RT (RTR); Rail rapid transit (RRT); Region rail (RGR).

Determinant Factors: R/W category; Support; Guidance; Propulsion; Control; Transit unit.

Categories-Types	Determinant Factor	Paratransit	RB	TB	SCR	SRB	LRT	RTR	RRT	RGR
Streets (C)	R/W category	X	X	X	X					
Rubber tires	Support	X	X	X		X		X		
Steered	Guidance	X	X	X		X				
ICE	Propulsion	X	X			X				
Manual	Control	X	X	X	X	X				
Small vehicle (<30 pers.)	Transit unit	X								
Medium vehicle (30–100 pers.)	Transit unit		(X)	(X)	X	(X)	X			
Part. control (B)	R/W category					X	X			(X) a
Large vehicle (>100 pers.)	Transit unit			X			X	(X)	X	X
Electric	Propulsion			X	X		X	X	X	X
Guided	Guidance				X		X	X	X	X
Steel wheels	Support				X		X	(X)	X	X
Short trains (1–3 cars)	Transit unit				(X)		X			
Semiautomatic	Control						X	X	X	X
Full control (A)	R/W category						X	X	X	X
Long trains (>3 cars)	Transit unit							X	X	X
Fully automatic	Control							(X)	(X)	(X)

Annotations on the Modes matrix: the lower-left group of entries is labeled "Minimum performance"; the upper-right group of entries is labeled "Maximum performance".

a (X) indicates less common applications.

101

TABLE 4-5
Technical, Operational, and System Characteristics of Urban Transportation Modes[a]

Characteristic	Generic Class → Mode	Private		Street transit		Semirapid Transit		Rapid Transit	
	Unit	Auto on Street	Auto on Freeway	RB	SCR	SRB	LRT	RRT	RGR
1. Vehicle capacity, C_v	sp/veh	4-6 total,	1.2-2.0 usable	40-120	100-180	40-120	110-250	140-280	140-210
2. Vehicles/transit unit	veh/TU	1	1	1	1-3	1	1-4	1-10	1-10
3. Transit unit capacity	sp/TU	4-6 total,	1.2-2.0 usable	40-120	100-300	40-120	110-600[b]	140-2400	140-1800
4. Maximum technical speed, V	km/h	40-80	80-90	40-80	60-70	70-90	60-100	80-100	80-130
5. Maximum frequency, f_{max}[c]	TU/h	600-800	1500-2200	60-180	60-120	60-90	40-90	20-40	10-30
6. Line capacity, C	sp/h	720-1050[b, d]	1800-2600[d]	2400-12,000	4000-20,000	4000-12,000	6000-20,000	10,000-72,000	8000-60,000
7. Normal operating speed, V^o	km/h	20-50	60-120	15-25	12-20	20-40	20-45	25-60	40-70
8. Operating speed at capacity, V_C	km/h	10-30	20-60	6-15	5-13	15-30	15-40	24-55	38-65
9. Productive capacity, P_c	(sp-km/h²) x 10⁻³	10-25[b]	50-120	20-90	30-150	75-200	120-260	400-1800	500-2000
10. Lane width (one-way)	m	3.00-3.65	3.65-3.75	3.00-3.65	3.00-3.50	3.65-3.75	3.40-3.75	3.70-4.30	4.00-4.75
11. Vehicle control[e]		Man./vis.	Man./vis.	Man./vis.	Man./vis.	Man./vis.	Man./vis.-sig.	Man.-aut./sig.	Man.-aut./sig.
12. Reliability		Low-med.	Med.-high	Low-med.	Low-med.	High	High	Very high	Very high
13. Safety		Low	Low-med.	Med.	Med.	High	High	Very high	Very high
14. Station spacing	m	—	—	200-500	250-500	350-800	350-800	500-2000	1200-4500
15. Investment cost per pair of lanes	($/km) x 10⁻⁶	0.4-4.0	5.0-40.0	0.2-0.8	2.0-4.0	5.0-15.0	5.0-20.0	15.0-50.0	10.0-60.0

[a] Metric conversion: 1 km = 0.62 mi. Abbreviations: sp, spaces; veh, vehicles; TU, transit unit.

[b] Values for C and P_c are not necessarily products of the extreme values of their components because these seldom coincide.

[c] For auto, lane capacity; for transit, line (station) capacity; single lane, but 2-lane stops for buses; single track for rail.

[d] For private auto, capacity is product of average occupancy (1.2-1.3) and f_{max} since all spaces cannot be utilized.

[e] Abbreviations are for: manual, visual, signal, and automatic.

TABLE 4-6
Performance Values for Generic Classes of Modes
(Based on Table 4-5) and for Several Typical Systems[a]

Generic class — Characteristic	Unit[b]	Private auto on — Street	Private auto on — Freeway	Street transit	Semirapid transit	Rapid transit
1. Transit unit capacity	sp/TU	1.2-	2.0[c]	40-300	40-600	140-2200
2. Maximum frequency, f_{max}	TU/h	600-800	1500-2200	60-180	40-90	10-40
3. Line capacity, C	sp/h	720-1050	1800-2600	2400-20,000	4000-20,000	10,000-72,000
4. Operating speed, V^o	(km/h)	20-50	60-120	5-20	15-45	24-70
5. Productive capacity, P_c	$(\text{sp-km/h}^2) \times 10^{-3}$	10-25	50-120	20-150	75-600	400-2000
6. Investment cost per pair of lanes	$(\$/\text{km}) \times 10^{-6}$	0.4-4.0	0.5-40.0	0.2-4.0	3.0-20.0	15.0-60.0

Typical systems[d] — Characteristic	Unit	System "s"	System "f"	RB-1	RB-2	SCR	SRB	LRT-1	LRT-2	RRT-1	RRT-2	RGR
1. Transit unit capacity	sp/Tu	1.3	1.3	65	75	140	100[e]	180	430	800	1100	1000
2. Maximum frequency, f_{max}	TU/h	700	1800	120	90	90	100	90	40	30	35	28
3. Line capacity, C	sp/h	910	2340	7800	6750	12,600	10,000	16,200	17,200	24,000	38,500	28,000
4. Normal operating speed, V_o	km/h	35	80	20	18	16	26	30	33	38	36	50
5. Operating speed at capacity, V_o^C		20	40	10	12	11	18	23	25	38	34	48
6. Productive capacity, P_c	$(\text{sp-km/h}^2) \times 10^{-3}$	18.2	93.6	78	81	138.6	180	372.6	430	912	1309	1394
7. Investment cost per pair of lanes	$(\$/\text{km}) \times 10^{-6}$	0.6	8.0	0.2	0.3	1.6	7.0	8.0	9.0	12.0	20.0	18.0

[a]The systems shown are assumed to be heavily loaded, but somewhat below capacity of respective mode.
[b]Metric conversion: 1 km = 0.62 mi.
[c]Maximum number of spaces that can be utilized.
[d]Designation used in Figs. 4-2, 4-3, and 4-4.
[e]Articulated buses.

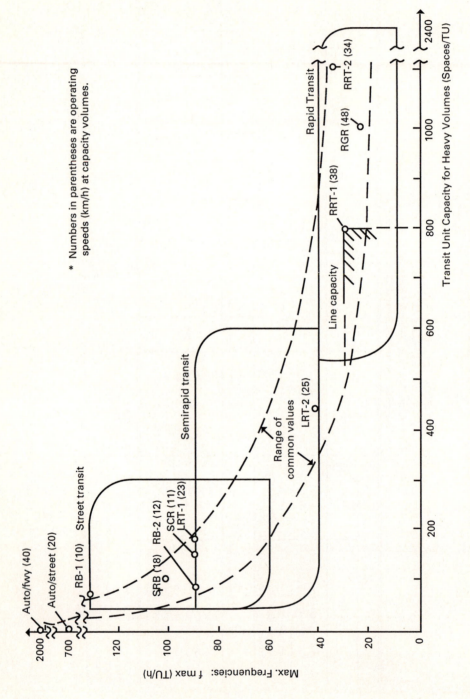

Figure 4-2 *Vehicle capacities, maximum frequencies, and line capacities of different modes.*

104

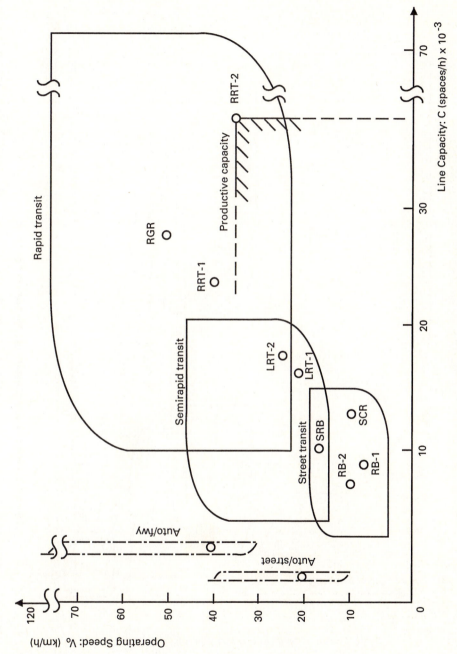

Figure 4-3 *Line capacities, operating speeds, and productive capacities of different modes.*

105

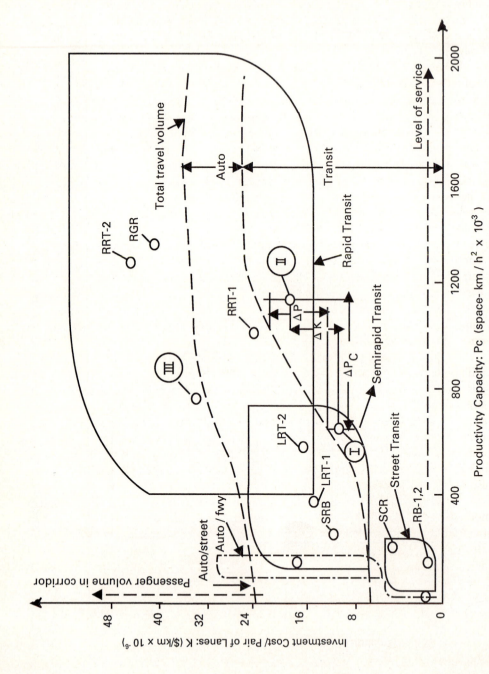

Figure 4-4 *Relationship between productive capacity, investment cost, and passenger attraction of different generic classes of transit modes.*

It is clear from Fig. 4-4 that comparisons of modes based on costs only can be highly deceptive; they compare ordinates of modes, disregarding their abscissa values. For modes with similar performance, the error caused by disregarding abscissa values may not be great, but for modes as diverse as street and rapid transit, the error is always very large.

Although the mode comparison must include many different factors, the basic relationship of performance/cost characteristics of different modes is illustrated in Fig. 4-4 by hypothetical systems I, II, and III. System III can be easily eliminated as inferior to system II: it has a higher cost, has much lower productivity, and attracts fewer passengers. A comparison between I and II must evaluate the trade-off between the higher productive capacity (ΔP_c) and passenger attraction (ΔP) of system II against the lower cost (ΔK) of system I.

Observing modal characteristics in the three diagrams (Figs. 4-2, 4-3, and 4-4), it is interesting to note that the relative positions of the 11 plotted systems vary considerably; LRT-1 and LRT-2 are remote in the first, but close in the second and third diagrams. However, they all fall in the ranges plotted for their generic classes. The overlaps between classes also vary among the diagrams, but in all three they clearly show the same sequence from low to high performance. Most modes fall in the central zone of the class areas (for example, the dashed lines in Fig. 4-2), forming a nearly continuous family of transit modes. The extreme corners have been rounded off on the diagrams since they represent either extremes impractical to operate (for example, smallest transit unit and lowest maximum frequency) or a nonoptimal combination (highest investment and lowest performance).

Another way of illustrating differences in modal capacities is by a sketch of the facilities required for transporting 15,000 pr/h by different modes, shown in Fig. 4-5. This volume is found in many cities since even facilities carrying only 5000 to 7000 pr/h obtain rates of flow of 15,000 to 20,000 pr/h for a 15- to 20-min period, making the latter the design volume. Line capacity reserves are also given since they influence LOS (comfort). Terminal areas are quoted as a significant component of the space efficiency of modes. The figure clearly shows the superiority of high-capacity modes in serving high-density areas, particularly when their much lower terminal area requirements are also taken into account.

In conclusion, this review of the family of modes shows that all major transit modes have optimal domains of application; adjacent modes overlap their domains to some extent (dial-a-ride and RB, or LRT and RRT), but modes as remote from each other as taxi and bus or bus and RRT should never be competitive, but complementary. For example, there is no way in which it can be more efficient and economical to transport 40 persons from point A to point B at one time in 20 taxis than in one bus, or 750 people in 15 buses than in one train, unless the lower-capacity mode is operated by underpaid drivers, has low comfort and safety standards, and is indirectly subsidized, while the higher-capacity mode is excessively luxurious, inefficiently operated, and driven by overpaid drivers. Similarly, it can never be more efficient to transport a single passenger from one suburb to another by a bus than by a taxi. As a matter of fact, when such remote modes are competitive, it is a clear sign that the

Mode	Schematic of R/W	Line Capacity Reserve	Terminal Area Requirements
Private autos on street (Persons/vehicle: 1.3; maximum freq.: 700)	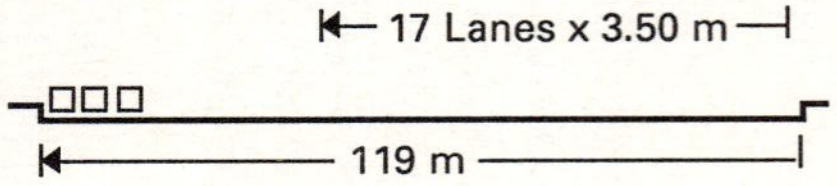 17 Lanes x 3.50 m; 119 m	None	Parking: 23 m²/person For 15,000 people, 34.5 ha (85 acres)
Private autos on freeway (1.3 : 1800)	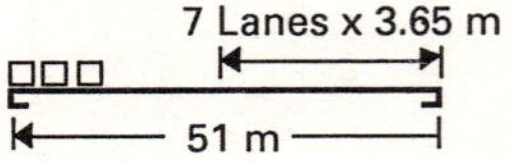 7 Lanes x 3.65 m; 51 m	None	Same as above, plus interchanges
Regular buses (R/W C) (75 : 100)	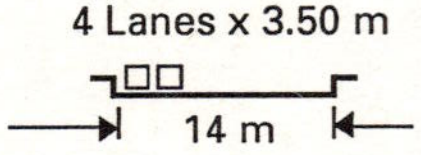 4 Lanes x 3.50 m; 14 m	None (station and way capacities reached)	Each station 20 x 80 m on the surface
Semirapid buses (artic., R/W B) (100 : 90)	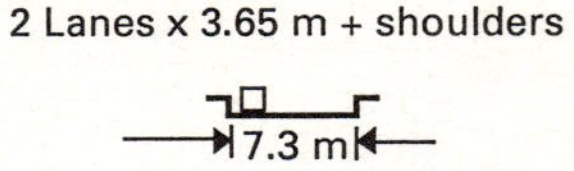 2 Lanes x 3.65 m + shoulders; 17.3 m	None (station capacity reached, way capacity not)	Each station from 25 x 100 m
Light rail transit (400 : 50)	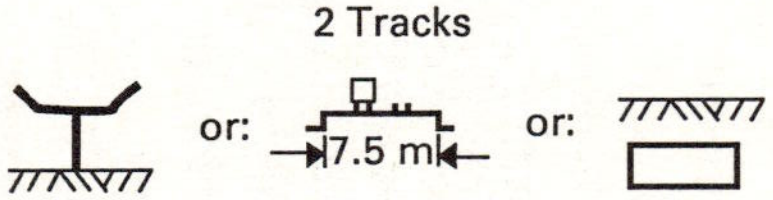 2 Tracks; 7.5 m or:	33%	Each station from 12 x 50 m on the surface to 20 x 90 m grade separated
Rail rapid transit (1000 : 25 RGR; 1000 : 40 RRT)	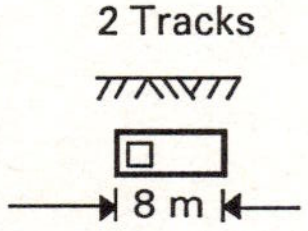 2 Tracks; 8 m	67–167%	Each station from 20 x 100 to 25 x 210 m grade separated. No surface occupancy.

Figure 4-5 *Areas required for transporting 15,000 persons per hour by different modes.*

conditions (policies, financing, planning, regulation, design, and the like) are greatly distorted against the mode that should be optimal in that application. This is clearly the case in cities where auto travel into the CBD during peak hours is not only competitive, but superior to bus or even to rail services.

This analysis also shows that there can never be a single optimal mode for all urban transportation. Conditions and requirements for urban travel vary so much that *in most cities*, except very small ones, *the optimal (sometimes referred to as balanced) transportation system should consist of several complementary modes coordinated into a single integrated multimodal system.*

COMMUTER TRANSIT

In addition to the regular public transportation services operated by the modes previously defined, some cities have separate commuter services that use standard transit technologies as well as other modes. In medium-size cities, commuter transit may represent the dominant share of public transportation; many bus routes operate during the peaks only. As city size increases, the relative role of these services decreases. In large cities, if regular transit provides adequate services throughout the city at all times of the day, commuter transit should only be a minor supplement to these services. The great attention given to commuter transit in U.S. cities is a consequence of the unsatisfactory condition of regular transit and highway congestion in most cities.

The following modes are used for commuter transit:

Carpooling is travel of different parties (two to six persons) together in a private car on a regular basis. Since carpooling is private transportation, it cannot be organized, scheduled, or regulated by an agency, but its use can be encouraged by such measures as assistance in establishing contacts among potential users, reduced or eliminated toll and parking charges, provision of special lanes, and so on.

Carpools are socially more desirable than individual travel by car because they take less space and cause fewer negative side effects per person-km of travel. Their use is limited, however, to commuting because they require that travel of the participants in each pool coincides in origin, destination, time of departure, and time of return. Moreover, carpooling is often a greater deprivation of privacy than transit travel; it involves precise travel coordination, cost sharing, and joint ride in private cars of persons who may have nothing else in common but travel pattern.

Vanpools are privately or publicly provided vans (8 to 18 seats) transporting groups of persons to and from work on a regular basis. Owing to their lower unit transportation cost and space occupancy, vanpools are even more socially desirable than carpools. They require, however, a more formal organization for vehicle purchase, maintenance, driving, insurance, and so on.

Subscription bus is bus service provided for persons who subscribe for a time period (week or month) to travel every working day at the same time on the same route (commuting).

Express commuter bus, express bus service operated during peak hours only, is a common mode of commuter transit. Usually, express commuter bus routes operate locally in suburbs and then use arterials and freeways for fast travel into the CBD.

Commuter rail is regional rail operating during peak hours only. This term is often incorrectly used for all regional rail systems.

Commuter buses that utilize busways and commuter rail have fixed facilities used for transit during peak hours only. This represents a poor utilization of facilities, which can often be greatly improved by the introduction of properly marketed and efficiently operated regular transit services.

Figure 4-6 shows schematically corridor service by regular transit and by commuter bus transit and lists their characteristics. The figure shows that regular transit offers service between any two stops on feeder routes or stations on the trunk line, while commuter bus transit serves only the trips between the suburban collection area and CBD, the many-to-one travel pattern. Moreover, each of the m collector routes offers service to only one of the n CBD distributors. Transfer to the other distributors can be organized if all routes use the same freeway exit, but this is seldom the case. Direct, no-transfer connections among all feeders and all distributors would require $m \times n$ routes (33 in the example), resulting in much lower frequencies on each of them than on regular transit lines. A schematic of the network in Fig. 4-7 shows that commuter transit serves an even smaller fraction of all urban trips than corridor trips: it cannot serve any suburb-to-suburb trips. Consequently, the more decentralized the city is, the more important is the role of regular transit relative to commuter transit. Equally important is the advantage that regular transit operates at all hours, whereas commuter transit operates only during the peaks.

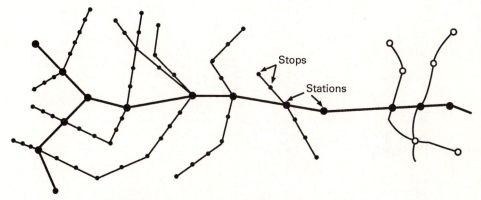

(a) Regular bus transit: high-frequency, trunk-line service, transfers to feeders; all-day service

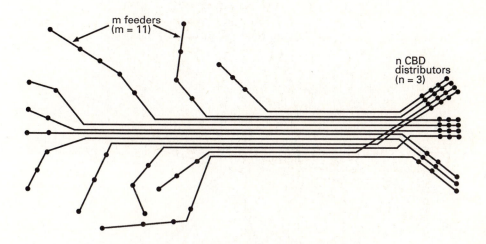

(b) Commuter bus transit: feeders travel directly to CBD: no transfers; low frequency, no service along trunk section; peak-hour service only

Figure 4-6 *Corridor services by regular bus transit and by commuter bus transit.*

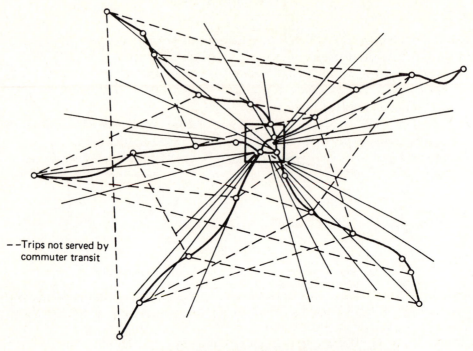

– –Trips not served by
commuter transit

(a) Regular transit network and trips it can serve

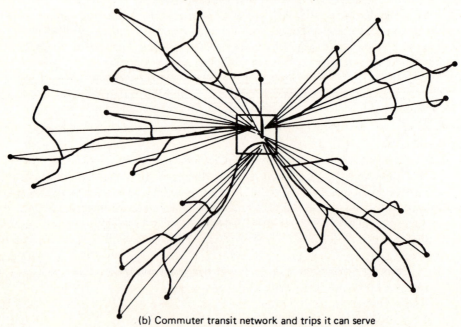

(b) Commuter transit network and trips it can serve

Figure 4-7 *Urban trips served by regular transit and by commuter transit.*

FURTHER READING

INSTITUTE OF TRANSPORTATION ENGINEERS, *Transportation and Traffic Engineering Handbook* (2nd ed.), ed. Wolfgang S. Homburger. Englewood Cliffs, N.J.: Prentice-Hall, Inc., 1982.

LEIBBRAND, KURT, *Transportation and Town Planning*. Cambridge, Mass.: The MIT Press, 1970.

PUSHKAREV, BORIS S., AND JEFFREY M. ZUPAN, *Public Transportation and Land Use Policy*, a Regional Plan Association Book. Bloomington, Ind.: Indiana University Press, 1977.

———, WITH JEFFREY M. ZUPAN AND ROBERT S. CUMELLA, *Urban Rail in America: An Exploration of Criteria for Fixed-Guideway Transit*. Bloomington, Ind.: Indiana University Press, 1982.

VUCHIC, VUKAN R., *Urban Public Transportation Systems and Technology*. Englewood Cliffs, N.J.: Prentice-Hall, Inc., 1981.

EXERCISES

4-1   Which characteristics of a transportation system determine whether it is private or public? If a private bus operator operates a transit line, is that private or public transportation?

4-2   Which basic characteristics make the following systems different modes: dial-a-ride and regular bus; bus and streetcar; light rail transit and metro?

4-3   What are the basic differences between steered and guided technology systems with respect to their investment costs, operating costs, and performance?

4-4   If passenger volume on a transit line steadily increases, how should vehicle size, method of guidance, ROW category, and degree of automation change?

4-5   Give definitions, dimensions, and common units in both the SI and English system for service frequency, offered capacity, utilized capacity, and operating speed.

4-6   Which modes frequently use two or all three ROW categories, even along the same line?

4-7   In a corridor that needs improved transit service, the main alternative systems are semirapid bus (SRB) with exclusive busways, rather than HOV lanes, on trunk sections and light rail transit (LRT). Explain how the following factors would influence the mode choice (i.e., which of the following conditions or changes would favor SRB, which LRT?): the outlying network has many branches and the common trunk section is rather short; street congestion is so bad that a tunnel has to be built in the CBD; labor wages are very high; in several suburban areas, operation ROW C (street running) is unavoidable; there is considerable potential for future development in the corridor.

4-8   Define productive capacity and explain for what purposes it can be used in evaluating and comparing transit systems or modes.

4-9   What are the differences between commuter transit and regular transit?

Chapter 5

RAIL TRANSIT

J. William Vigrass

This chapter will provide an overview of rail modes as they are applied to urban public transportation. Included is fully grade separated rail rapid transit with various degrees of automation. Second is light rail transit and its highest refinement, light rail rapid transit, which have received renewed interest in the United States. Third and last is regional rail or commuter service, best exemplified in the Chicago, Philadelphia, Boston, and New York areas of the United States and in Toronto in Canada.

The general physical and operational characteristics of these modes will be briefly explained and a few examples of each cited and described. The intent is for students, planners, engineers, and other interested individuals to obtain an overall picture of what each submode can do in the urban and suburban environment.

First, let us look at the components of rail transit. Whether conventional rail rapid transit, light rail transit, or a regional rail system, they have certain common features. First, there is the track and, second, the flanged wheel. The steel rail and flanged steel wheel were devised in the early nineteenth century for intercity railroad use. They were well developed by the latter part of that century, and during its last three decades, steam-powered urban railways were built in a few cities. The elevated railways in New York and Chicago were built during this period. They used 25-ton steam locomotives that could pull six light coaches at about 25 mi/h. This speed merited the term rapid transit when compared to the horse-drawn traffic below.

Beginning in the 1830s and 1840s, horse-drawn street railway systems were built in many cities. By the late nineteenth century, thousands of horse-drawn cars were in use. Practical application of electricity as motive power to replace the costly horses developed quickly after pioneer installations proved workable. By 1900, many street and elevated railways had been converted to electric power, and by 1910, this conversion was essentially complete. New routes followed rapidly until a peak was reached in the early 1920s. The street railway then moved into the suburbs—and far beyond—in the form of the interurban electric railway. The latter is best exemplified by the once-great Pacific Electric Railway of the Los Angeles region, then the world's largest interurban railway under one management with over 1000 mi of routes. During this period, the flanged steel wheel on steel rails was refined to a highly reliable system with many special devices to meet specific needs.

From 1930 to the mid-1950s, a rapid decline in urban surface street railways took place, owing to the greatly increased use of private automobiles in urban areas, with motor buses often taking over the ridership of the replaced street railways. Nevertheless, rail rapid transit held up relatively well. Streetcar lines having private rights-of-way also held up well because they had a competitive advantage over private automobiles or street-bound buses. The resurgence of interest in transit has focused attention on the modes and submodes that did hold up well during the decline of transit, that is, the grade separated or semiseparated rail modes.

THE GUIDEWAY

The rail guideway is the only form of guideway in general use throughout the world. The railway track is formed of T-rails that weigh, for modern applications, 85 to 132 lb/yd (42 to 65 kg/m). Track gauge is generally 4 ft 8.5 in (1.44 m), a dimension inherited from England, which, in turn, inherited it from the Romans. Light rail and rapid transit, however, have various gauges from 1 m (3.3 ft) in Europe to 5 ft 4.5 in (1.63 m), Baltimore's former streetcar gauge; San Francisco Bay Area Rapid Transit (BART) uses 5 ft 6 in for stability, but Los Angeles Railways streetcar lines used 3 ft 6 in for economy of construction. Pittsburgh and Philadelphia light rail lines use 5 ft 2.5 in, as does New Orleans' one remaining street railway line. Anything reasonable will work, but, generally, standard gauge (4 ft 8.5 in) has been used because of the easy availability of railroad hardware.

For many years, railroads and most existing urban railways have used wood ties, with rails spiked to the ties. Construction in the 1970s began to favor concrete ties with various kinds of pads with spring clips to hold the rail. Concrete promised to last longer, and because of their weight, such ties hold the rails down more firmly. Concrete slabs under track have been used in Europe and in some subway installations in the United States.

Use of the flanged steel wheel on the rail has provided a positive guidance system for over 150 years. Switches and crossings are fully designed and have proved reliable. Railroad track may be ordered from catalogs and is suitable for most rapid transit and many light rail applications. Older street and interurban railway geometric designs may still be quite suitable for proposed new light rail installations. Some innovation in trackwork has appeared in Europe and has been duplicated in the United States in a few places where it was desired to emulate the smoothness of European trackage.

The metallurgy of the rail and wheel has been thoroughly studied, particularly for railroad use, and both items are fully engineered and available. Their service life is known, so costs and operational ability can be forecast with confidence. Railway track can be, and has been, installed (1) on private right-of-way on the surface, as ordinary railroad track; (2) on elevated or aerial structure; (3) in subways; (4) in median strips on boulevards or freeways; and (5) in paved streets as streetcar track or light rail track.

PUEBLO TEST TRACK

In 1971, the U.S. Department of Transportation dedicated a test facility near Pueblo, Colorado, for railroad and rail transit research and development. Several types of track were installed, arranged as several test loops, and a stub-end impact track was provided. Included is a small loop of 4.8-mi (7.7-km) circumference with curves of up to 5° and grades up to 2%. It is labeled the FAST track, for Facility for Accelerated Service Testing. A "typical" freight train operates 16 h/day to produce 1 million ton-miles per day on this track to life-test both track and rolling stock. Another objective is to learn more about train/track dynamics. Roughly, 1-year testing at FAST is equal to 10 years of real-world service.

The Pueblo facility also includes a 9.1-mi (14.6-km) oval to test urban and suburban rapid transit and light rail vehicles. It is electrified with a conventional 600-V third rail, and part of it is equipped with catenary at the same voltage to test light rail vehicles. A specially built substation can provide several voltages and can simulate certain electrical faults.

The outcome of the railroad and light rail transit testing at Pueblo should be improved life and reliability for a mode that already typically has long service life and high reliability for its components.

RUBBER-TIRED SYSTEMS

Automated rubber-tired guideway systems have been developed since the mid-1950s. A moderate number are in use in major activity centers such as airports, resort complexes, and academic campuses. One, Miami's Metromover (Florida), performs a downtown people-mover function. Chapter 24, on new technology, delves deeper into automated people movers. In this chapter, only the rubber-tired rapid transit vehicles developed in Paris and used, for example, in Montreal, Mexico City, and Sapporo (Japan) will be discussed. These systems use a conventional railway track for switching and return current, plus vertical third and fourth rails for positive current and guidance. The rubber-tired main carrying and traction wheels run on a concrete (or other material) runway immediately outboard of the standard-gauge railway track. Proponents of this mode point out that the rubber tires allow use of grades of up to 6%, whereas conventional heavy rapid transit is limited to 4%. While generally true, grades of up to 5% are found on heavy rail elsewhere, an example being the transition from subway to the Benjamin Franklin Bridge on PATCO's Lindenwold Hi-Speed Line. Light rail has examples of even greater grades, with several 7% grades on the Sacramento light rail line.

The rubber-tired system was dramatically more quiet than older conventional heavy rail systems in use when the Paris and Montreal systems were inaugurated. Later improvements in conventional rail systems, however, have reduced the difference to the point that there is little noise difference to the passenger.

It has been found that the rubber-tired systems use more power than do steel wheel systems because of the flexing of the tires. One result is that the subway tunnels used by rubber-tired trains are noticeably warmer. The cars are narrower and shorter than those used on contemporary heavy rail lines; the narrow cars allow narrower tunnels which are somewhat less expensive to build. One reason for the smaller cars is that the weight-carrying capacity of rubber tires is less than that for steel wheels. On the other hand, more cars and more trains are needed to provide the same capacity. A classic trade-off analysis will reveal which alternative is preferable for a given site-specific application. The rubber-tired rail-guided submode remains relatively uncommon.

MONORAIL

Every generation or so, various forms of monorail are rediscovered and promoted, and each time their inherent drawbacks are learned anew by those who have neglected to study the history of technology as applied to urban transportation. It has been said that monorail is the mode of the future, and, except for limited installations, it always has been and probably always will be!

The Wuppertal Schwebebahn or Suspended Railway in Germany has often been cited by monorail enthusiasts. It has been in successful operation since the very early twentieth century. From time to time, it has been provided with new rolling stock. But it has not been extended. Increased transit provided in the area has been by surface light rail or by suburban railroad. If the suspended monorail had all the merit many of its proponents claim, it would seem that its originators in Germany would have expanded the mode. See Table 5-1 on page 95 for comparative information on this mode.

SOURCE OF ENERGY

Urban railways have almost always been electrically operated, usually employing 600 volts direct current (V dc) or some variation of it, such as 700 or 750 V dc. In a very few cases, self-propelled equipment using internal combustion engines has been used (for example, the diesel-electric streetcars of Sapporo). Such arrangements are possible but are seldom used in actual practice. An unusual, interesting, and successful example of nonelectrified rail transit is found in the northern suburbs of Hamburg, Germany. There, three different light rail lines feed the Hamburg transit system, one using large articulated light rail vehicles with diesel-electric drive while two use four-wheel rail cars with diesel-mechanical drive.

The use of a moderately low voltage direct current has distinct advantages. Only one current collector is needed on the vehicle and the rails act as the ground return. The simplicity of this single collector should not be ignored. Some of the more novel modes that have been promoted use three-phase alternating current, typically 480 V. These need at least three collectors, and in one case five (two more for ground and signaling), all of which adds to complexity and, in turn, unreliability. A considerable amount of equipment is already developed and available for the usual 600- to 750-V dc system.

Regional railroad service most commonly uses diesel-electric locomotives to haul trains, but in New York City, Philadelphia, and Chicago electric power is used. Some rail diesel cars are self-propelled.

Regional railroad service can be defined as having routes approximately 15 to 50 mi in length, with frequent stops, typically 1 to 3 mi apart. It is distinctly different from intercity high-speed railroad passenger service, such as is provided by the Metroliners in the Northeast Corridor of the United States, the TGV (Train of Great Speed) of France, or the Shinkansen lines in Japan. The latter routes are several hundred miles long with stops 50 to 100 mi apart.

RAIL RAPID TRANSIT

OLDER SYSTEMS

In the United States, the form of urban rail transit that presently carries the most people per year is rail rapid transit. This mode is characterized by full grade separation, electric propulsion, multiple-unit trains, and speeds of 45 to 80 mi/h (72 to 130 km/h) maximum, and 20 to 50 mi/h (32 to 80 km/h) overall schedule. The very extensive New York City Transit Authority (NYCTA) subway system has nearly 7000 cars and represents, by itself, the majority of rail rapid transit in the United States. Its use of four-track subway routes with local and express trains is unique (except for Philadelphia's Broad Street Subway), as is its common use of 10-car trains. Crowding in NYCTA trains is legendary, and official standards call for 255 passengers per 60-ft (18-m) car, at 2.3 ft² (0.2 m²) of floor area per passenger. Thus, a 10-car train will handle 2550 persons, and on some routes such trains operate every 2 min in the peak, carrying passengers at the rate of 76,500/h past a given point. This rate is seldom achieved for more than 15 to 30 min, however.

Such volumes are not found elsewhere in the United States, and the student of urban transportation should recognize that there are unique New York problems. Other cities, such as Boston, Philadelphia, and Chicago, have rail transit systems dating from the same period as New York's, about 1905–1940, with some more recent extensions. Routes in these cities typically handle from 50,000 to 300,000 passengers/day, with perhaps 15 to 20% of the day's travel during each peak hour.

In older intraurban systems, stations are typically a quarter- to a half-mile apart. Chicago's average spacing is 3700 ft (1100 m). In more modern systems, center-city stations are similarly spaced, but in the suburbs, spacings of 1 to 2 mi are more common. In past years, planning was based on walk-on patrons or transfer riders from surface streetcar lines. Emphasis in the suburbs now is on highway access by park-and-ride and kiss-and-ride or feeder bus service. Boston had a highly developed streetcar feeder system with streetcars operating down into subway stations or up onto elevated stations. Several such stations have been converted for trolleybus and motor bus access to provide what is often considered the most convenient transferring on any U.S. system.

Fare collection on these older systems is mostly by cashiers in booths, assisted by coin- or token-operated turnstiles. In Chicago, during the off-peak on lightly used routes, conductors hand-collect fares on two-car trains in a manner not seen elsewhere for many decades. Conductors collect fares on board trains at certain unattended stations in Philadelphia during "owl" (midnight to 5 a.m.) hours.

Operating costs of traditional, labor-intensive rail rapid transit systems tend to be high because of two-person (operator and conductor) train crews and the attended stations necessary for fare collection. On the other hand, with very high volumes (found in only a few places), cost per passenger is sometimes quite low.

MODERN SYSTEMS

Modern rail rapid transit is an evolutionary development of traditional rapid transit. It is fully grade separated and uses railway track and direct-current electrification at moderate voltages, 650 to 1000 (up from the older 600 V dc). It stresses high-performance trains with running speeds of 70 to 80 mi/h (112 to 130 km/h), averaging 35 to 50 mi/h (56 to 80 km/h), and employs some forms of automation. The first generation of these systems opened in 1969–1972 and is exemplified by the Bay Area Rapid Transit (BART) in the San Francisco area of California and the Port Authority Transit Corporation (PATCO) connecting Philadelphia to southern New Jersey. Both systems were designed specifically to compete with the private automobile. They feature fast, frequent service and convenient highway access, with large park-and-ride lots at outlying stations.

Trains are one-person-operated to reduce operating expenses, this being made feasible by various forms of automatic train operation (ATO). Automatic fare collection in the stations keeps all money under lock and key and minimizes station staff.

Modern rapid transit is expensive to build, but the modern operating properties have proved that the American motorist can be attracted to transit if the service is fast, frequent, and reliable. (For example, over 90% of PATCO's daily riders start their trip by getting into a private automobile and driving, or being driven, to a station, then getting out of the automobile and into a train for the remaining journey to center city.)

Major corridors carrying large volumes of passengers between a relatively small number of points are the best places for modern rail rapid transit. Good highway access is essential, as is good downtown distribution from relatively closely spaced stations to provide convenient pedestrian egress. Environmental impacts are usually favorable as compared to the automobile. The ride can be pleasant as well as fast. It can be a very positive asset to a metropolitan region.

BART

The BART system as completed in 1970–1972 has 71 mi (115 km) of route of which 19 mi (31 km) is in tunnel and 23 mi (37 km) is elevated on dual-track concrete structure. There are four lines with 34 stations. BART's designers chose a broader-than-standard track gauge at 5 ft 6 in (1.7 m) to achieve better lateral stability in high winds. They selected 1000 V dc for electrical engineering reasons: the higher voltage delivers more power with less loss and requires fewer substations. It is a nonstandard voltage, however, and requires custom-built equipment on board the trains. BART also chose a newly developed form of signaling and train control, the reliability of which is still not completely demonstrated. To attain the very high frequency (short headways) of a train every 90 s, BART's designers opted for a central computer so that trains from the three-branch system could funnel into the Transbay Tube from Oakland to San Francisco with a minimum of delay. It should be noted that BART's signaling and control system has not attained 90-s headways even after substantial investment in modifications.

Stations feature automatic fare collection with change-making ticket vendors that accept coins and bills. A heavy paper ticket with a magnetic data stripe is vended for whatever sum (up to $40) is inserted by the passenger. The passenger then inserts the ticket into a gate's ticket slot and the stored-value ticket is read, encoded for the station of entry, and returned to the passenger passing through the gate. At the destination, the passenger inserts the ticket into the exit side of a gate and the gate reads the ticket, deducts the value of the trip from the value on the ticket, and returns the ticket to the passenger. An "add fare" machine allows a ticket with insufficient value to be upgraded for exit at that station. Stations have attendants at all times to provide information to passengers and to deal with minor problems with the AFC system.

BART has 440 cars from its original 450-car 1970–1972 fleet, composed of A cab cars that must be at the end of a train and B blind motorized cars used between A cars. In 1987–1990, 150 C cars were delivered that have one cab and end door that can be coupled within trains. All trains are operated by one person.

Figure 5-1 *BART—the first post-World War II U.S. rail system. Lake Merritt Station, Oakland. (courtesy of Harre W. Demoro Collection)*

Figure 5-2 *BART—Rohr rapid transit cars. (courtesy of Rohr Industries, Inc.)*

A program to increase capacity is underway to permit operation of 57 trains rather than 43 as in the past. An extension of the tail tracks (track extending beyond a terminal station that is used for turning back or storing trains) at Daly City terminal allows more capacity to reverse and to store trains. Major extensions to Warm Springs, Dublin, San Bruno, and Pittsburg are under study.

Although BART has had highly publicized problems in its train control equipment and in the cars themselves, it nonetheless has proved to be automobile-competitive and has captured many new riders for transit in its region. Its trains average about 50 mi/h (80 km/h); they have operated at 77 to 80 mi/h (124 to 129 km/h) running speed, passing vehicular traffic on nearby freeway lanes; and its filled parking lots, crowded trains, and plans for extensive extensions attest to its popularity. Its technical problems have been ameliorated if not completely solved.

BART especially proved its value to the San Francisco Bay region after the October 17, 1989, earthquake when it was the only intact crossing between San Francisco and Oakland. It carried nearly double its usual volume of passengers and retained many of them after the San Francisco–Oakland Bay Bridge was restored to service.

PATCO

In contrast to the vast BART undertaking of providing a regional system in essentially one overall effort, the Delaware River Port Authority (DRPA) developed a single line to connect the suburban borough of Lindenwold, New Jersey, with center-city Philadelphia, a distance of 14.2 mi (22.9 km). The DRPA had little choice; that was all it could afford using its own resources in 1962. A three-branch system had been proposed and is still an objective, but so far only the central line has been built. The designers chose evolutionary development of conventional technology, partly because the new line was to use the existing 3.8-mi (6.1-km) Philadelphia–Camden Hi-Speed Line over the Benjamin Franklin Bridge, a route opened in 1936 using a heavyweight, deluxe subway-type car. Standard-gauge track with a conventional third rail was already in place. There was little reason to change the conventional technology since it could easily provide the performance desired: a 75-mi/h (121-km/h) running speed, 3.0-mi/h/s (1.3-m/s^2) acceleration, with an average speed of about 34 mi/h (54 km/h), the latter influenced by sharp curvature and steep grades on the older part of the line.

The new construction, from Camden to Lindenwold, used the right-of-way of the Pennsylvania–Reading Seashore Lines, a jointly owned subsidiary of the Pennsylvania Railroad and the Reading Company. This line had been very much underutilized and was finally abandoned and the land sold to the Delaware River Port Authority. Much of the original railroad track was at grade, but DRPA converted it to a fully grade separated facility. The inner part is on embankment or concrete aerial structure, a short segment through Haddonfield is in a walled cut, and the outer 6 mi is at grade, passing over a few streets, with one road passing over the line. A shop and yard at the outer terminus complete the physical plant.

Stations feature fully automatic fare collection, with no employees permanently assigned to any given station. Roving supervisors check each station frequently, and part-time employees manually sell tickets during the morning peak hours at suburban stations, but, generally, stations are unattended. They are under closed-circuit TV surveillance from Center Tower, PATCO's control center in Camden, New Jersey. The passenger service representatives observe the TV screens and can communicate with passengers by using a public address system or through a call-for-aid telephone in each station. Unattended stations allow PATCO to have one of the highest ratios of passengers to employees of any transit facility in the United States, about 130 passengers per day per employee. During most of its first years (1969–1975) of operation, PATCO earned its operating expenses from the farebox. More recently (1984–1989), it recovered about 76% of its expenses from fares, the highest recovery rate of any United States heavy rail system.

PATCO's cars have four series-wound dc motors and use a cam controller with resistors. A General Electric ATO (automatic train operation) system working in conjunction with a 100-Hz (hertz) Westinghouse Air Brake Company (WABCO) cab signal system controls the trains. The 100-Hz system has been in use since 1925, having been pioneered by the Pennsylvania Railroad. While PATCO's version had improvements, the principles were already well proved.

The original 75 cars were built by the Budd Company in 1968 and are almost completely stainless steel. They have proved to be extremely strong and have stood up remarkably well. As a result, when more cars were required, 46 nearly identical cars were acquired in 1980 from Vickers Canada, Inc., under license from the Budd Company. Improvements to enhance reliability were incorporated into these cars which operate in trains at the same performance level of the still used 1968 Budd cars.

Since it opened, PATCO has operated 24 h/day, 7 days/week, continuously. Trains run every 10 to 12 min in midday, every 2 to 8 min in the peak hours, every 12 min in late evening, and every 40 min all night. On Sundays, a 20-min headway is provided. One of PATCO's purposes is to provide an around-the-clock service that people can count on. There is no "last train" to catch. Patrons can always get back to their automobiles parked in one of PATCO's lots. Meanwhile, PATCO's own police will look in on the cars from time to time to minimize theft or vandalism.

PATCO takes pride in the fact that it has operated 99% of its trains on time (within 4 min of timetable) on a yearly basis. From 1969 to 1980, it ran 70 of its 75 cars in each peak hour, 5 days a week. Only five cars were not needed for scheduled service, and of these, three or four were in scheduled maintenance; thus, only one or two cars were available as spares most days. PATCO cars are designed for quick changeout of defective components; that was the key to running 70 of the available 75 cars twice a day. And that is why the DRPA and its subsidiary, PATCO, plan on continuing with evolutionary improvements of the conventional. It has worked well in practice.

Expansion to three routes was planned, to be funded by state and federal governmental agencies; preliminary feasibility and engineering were completed in 1975, but funding has not yet been found.

Other U.S. Systems

Modern rapid transit systems have been built in Washington, D.C., Miami, Baltimore, and Atlanta, and a new line is under construction in Los Angeles. These systems share major concepts with BART or PATCO or both: high performance with automation to varying degrees.

Washington Metro (WMATA) began operation of a short segment of its projected 103-mi (165-km) regional system in 1976. Ridership on this initial portion exceeded preliminary estimates. Metro's consultants selected standard-gauge, conventional third rail, and a 750-V dc power supply, along with a conventional resistance controller used in conjunction with automatic train operation. Later cars have dc chopper control that permits regenerative braking, smoother acceleration and deceleration, less energy losses when accelerating, and lowered periodic and corrective maintenance. The system has been relatively free of significant technical failures such as those that affected BART.

Metro uses an automatic fare collection (AFC) system of the stored-value type that permits fares to be related to distance and that, in addition, provides data necessary to determine subsidies from the several political entities that constitute WMATA. Metro features bus-to-train transfers, park-and-ride lots, and fast, frequent service.

Figure 5-3 *Washington, D.C., Metro—Rhode Island Avenue Station. Note convenient feeder-bus access. (photo by Phil Portlock, courtesy of Washington Metropolitan Area Transit Authority)*

Figure 5-4 *Washington, D.C. Metro—Metro Center Station. (photo by Paul Myatt, courtesy of Washington Metropolitan Area Transit Authority)*

Metro has experienced very high construction costs, so consideration was given to truncating the planned system, but Congressional support has been strong and construction has continued, with added segments of the system opened throughout the 1980s. Completion of the full 103-mi system is scheduled for the mid-1990s. While it has been expensive to build, it has yielded significant benefits, the primary one being that it has made it easy for persons to travel by transit throughout the District of Columbia and its suburbs in Virginia and Maryland.

The *Metropolitan Atlanta Rapid Transit Authority* (MARTA) is another relatively new system. Its construction began in 1975 and the first line opened in 1979. It is a cross-shaped system with a north-south line and an east-west line. The south terminal serves Hartsfield International Airport, one of the busiest airports in the United States. As of 1989, MARTA had 32 mi (52 km) of route, 29 stations, and 200 cars. The latter are 75 ft (22 m) long and slightly over 10 ft (3 m) wide and operate on standard-gauge track using 750-V dc third rail at up to 70 mi/h (112 km/h). Stations are generally unattended and employ automatic fare collection.

Long-term plans call for a 53-mi (85-km) rapid transit system with 39 stations. MARTA is a completely coordinated regional transit system (unlike BART and PATCO which are rail only) that includes a 750-bus fleet, which provides feeder and connecting services.

Baltimore Metro is operated by the Maryland Mass Transit Administration, a state agency. It has a single line, 13.9 mi (22.4 km) long, of which almost a third is tunnel.

The outer segment to Owings Mills, which opened in 1987, is in the median of an interstate highway. A 2-mi subway extension to Johns Hopkins Hospital from the present center-city terminus at Charles Center is under construction.

A 100-car fleet of stainless steel cars was delivered in 1983–1986. The cars are 75 ft long and 10 ft wide and operate at up to 70 mi/h on standard-gauge track with a 750-V third rail.

Baltimore Metro is part of an integrated regional transit system that has an 800-bus fleet. A light rail line is under construction with 35 light rail vehicles on order.

Dade County Metrorail, serving Miami, Florida, is a contemporary of Baltimore Metro and shares the same car design. The single 21.4-mi (34.5-km) line runs generally north-south and is entirely elevated except for a few short segments passing under elevated highways. The system has 136 cars and 20 stations with both AFC and attendants. Most outlying stations have park-and-ride lots. An additional station in the central business district (CBD) has been proposed at the river bend, where Metrorail crosses the Miami River on a high bridge.

Metrorail is part of an integrated regional system that includes Metrobus (544 vehicles) and Metromover, a downtown people mover using Westinghouse Electric rubber-tired technology. Metromover is fully automated with unattended stations and serves to distribute Metrorail passengers locally throughout the CBD. Extensions to Metromover are in progress.

The systems built in Atlanta, Baltimore, and Miami are generally similar in that the cars are about the same size, have about the same performance, operate on standard-gauge track, employ 750 V dc with automatic train operation, and use automatic fare collection of various technologies.

Los Angeles Metro Rail will follow the same basic technology for its Wilshire Boulevard subway, of which 4.4 mi (7 km) is under construction, with much more planned. Cars will be similar to those of Baltimore and Miami, but will be constructed in Italy rather than in the United States.

LIGHT RAIL TRANSIT

A speaker at the first light rail conference in Philadelphia in 1975 said that "Light rail is a state of mind" that does not have a precise technical definition. By 1989, the state of mind had become concrete enough for the TRB Subcommittee on Light Rail Transit to define a light rail transit (LRT) system as "a metropolitan electric railway system characterized by its ability to operate single cars or short trains along exclusive rights-of-way at ground level, on aerial structures, in subways, or, occasionally, in streets, and to board and discharge passengers at track or car floor level."[1]

LRT is an evolutionary development of the street railway toward modern rapid transit. It usually uses overhead electric power distribution and employs cars much like streetcars, but possessing higher performance. Its track is usually segregated from traffic, but not necessarily grade separated throughout. Often median strips of boulevards or freeways are used. If vehicular traffic is light, track can be in the street. In congested city centers, subway or aerial structure often provides full grade separation. In some European and North American cities, the track area in center city is reserved solely for light rail vehicles or as a paved mall for pedestrians and light rail vehicles.

The light rail vehicle (LRV) often operates as its own feeder. Access is very convenient, so that even though the lack of grade separation enforces lower speeds than for modern rail rapid transit, overall door-to-door speeds may be quite attractive. In 1960, Frankfurt, Germany, studied three alternative systems for providing improved transportation. The three alternatives were supported monorail (Alweg), light rail transit, and conventional rapid transit, mostly in subway. Table 5-1 gives information on the salient features of the three systems studied. It is interesting to note that in this study it was determined that the total peak passenger travel time is less for the light rail transit alternative. This is a result of the self-feeding feature.

Light rail, having evolved from the streetcar, can accommodate very sharp curvature, steep grades, and a variety of station configurations, from the simplest to the most grandiose. Grades of up to 9% and horizontal curvature of 42 ft (13 m) can be taken by the articulated Boeing-Vertol light rail vehicle (LRV) built for Muni and Boston in the 1970s. Older streetcar equipment, such as PCC streetcars, can take a 36-ft (11-m) radius, at low speed, of course. Such curves and grades are found in paved street trackage.

Figure 5-5 *Boeing-Vertol light rail vehicles. A two-car train at Longwood Station on Boston's Riverside line on a test run in 1976. These cars entered revenue service during January 1977. (courtesy of Boeing-Vertol)*

TABLE 5-1
Comparison of Monorailway, Light Rail Transit, and Conventional
Rapid Transit Systems Designed for Frankfurt[a]

Item	Monorailway	Light Rail Transit	Conventional Rapid Transit
Route length of railway (mi)			
In tunnels	2.83[b]	13.15	23.76
On elevated way	36.30[c]	4.42	15.42
On separate roadbed	—	46.48	—
Total	39.18	64.03	39.18
Year of completion	1968	1974	1981
Number of rail stations	82	192	91
Average distance between stations (ft)	2,387	1,686	2,099
Total number of stations and stops	307	349	316
Average speed for rail system (mi/h)	17.76	16.02	17.53
Number of peak-hour passengers	95,600	95,600	95,600
Percentage of peak-hour passengers			
Not transferring	21.0	36.7	24.6
Making 1 transfer	44.3	47.8	45.3
Making 2 transfers	29.3	14.1	24.3
Making 3 transfers	5.4	1.4	5.6
Total peak transfer movements	113,500	76,519	106,812
Total peak passenger travel time (h)	52,200	49,300	50,300
Adjusted annual cost of system for first 10 years (no interest)	$22,900,000	$16,100,000	$22,700,000
Annual cost as percentage of present street railway costs	95	47	93

[a]Metric conversion: 1 mi = 1.6 km; 1 ft = 0.305 m.
[b]With alternative plan: 4.3 mi (6.9 km).
[c]With alternative plan: 34.7 mi (55.8 km).

Source: Adapted from Gordon J. Thompson, "Light Rail Transit Social Costs and Benefits," in *Light Rail Transit*, Special Report 161 (Washington, D.C.: Transportation Research Board, 1975), p. 149. From translation by Charles J. Lietwiler of K. Leibbrand, "Stadtbehn Frankfurt-am-Main—Planerische Gesamtubersicht," City of Frankfurt-am-Main, Germany, 1960.

Light rail trackage, electrification, and structures are generally much lighter and less costly than for rail rapid transit. Since the LRVs are not notably lighter or cheaper than rapid transit cars, the big savings in LRT are in the civil engineering features. Because it requires less investment, light rail is often justified in corridors having less traffic than is required to justify investment in full-scale rapid transit. Furthermore, light rail can be upgraded one segment at a time to provide performance nearly equal to grade-separated rapid transit. The investment need not be made all at once.

PCC CARS

Until the 1970s nearly all existing light rail lines in the United States and Canada were operated with PCC streetcars. The initials PCC stand for the Presidents' Conference Committee of electric railway company presidents that was formed in the late 1920s and operated in the early 1930s to supervise the creation of a radically new street railway vehicle to stem the decline in ridership then afflicting the transit industry. A sum of about $700,000 (eventually to reach about $1,000,000) was raised from member street railway companies and from suppliers, nearly all of whom were in difficult financial straits. (Consider that inflation by a factor of 15 to 20 has taken place since that time.) C. F. Hirschfeld of the Detroit Edison Company was chosen to head the project team.

Hirschfeld's team attacked the problem using one of the first applications of systems analysis. First, the physics of motion were studied, including what changes in the rate of acceleration and deceleration a standing passenger could tolerate. Next, sources of noise were studied. Then the duties of the motorman were analyzed. Other factors were studied intensively. A truly integrated design resulted. The car body, trucks, and propulsion were designed as a "system," not merely a collection of different manufacturers' parts, as had been the industry practice.

It was recognized that one car size could not meet the needs of every operator; therefore, a limited number of variations was made available. While the standard car was single ended, a few were built for double-end operation, and while most PCC cars were single-unit streetcars, some were built for multiple-unit (MU) operation, with couplers. Three lengths, 43, 46, and 50 ft, and three widths, 8 ft 4 in, 8 ft 8 in, and 9 ft, were offered. The 43-ft car, 8 ft 4 in wide, was unique to Capital Transit Company of Washington, D.C. All the 50-ft cars were 9 ft wide, while the popular 46-ft car was built in all three widths.

The two major electrical suppliers, General Electric and Westinghouse Electric, designed control and propulsion equipment to meet Hirschfeld's specifications. While the designs of the controllers were different, they were compatible in performance and could run together in multiple-unit trains. Over 6000 such cars were built for use in the United States and Canada between 1936 and the mid-1950s. Some of these PCC cars are still in operation. In 1990, Toronto opened its Harbourfront line, which uses rebuilt PCC cars along with Canadian LRVs. Several builders in Europe were licensed to build them, and construction has continued in Belgium and Czechoslovakia.

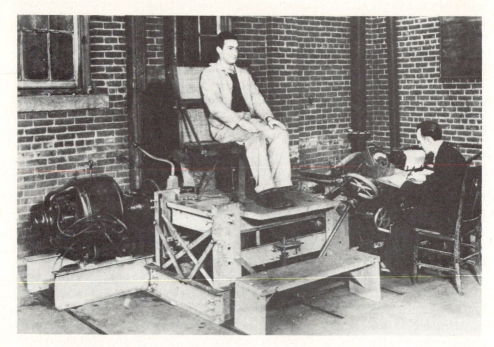

Figure 5-6 *PCC testing. Engineers are shown making tests to obtain data to improve riding comfort for the PCC car. (courtesy of American Public Transit Association)*

LRT VERSATILITY

Muni

San Francisco Municipal Railway (Muni) has implemented a true light rail system, the Muni Metro, with subway under Market Street in center city, using car-floor-height platforms, and at-grade track in the outlying residential areas. Although the track is at grade in these outlying areas, some is on private right-of-way, some is in a highway median strip, while some is in a paved street but separated from vehicular lanes by roughened paving. Automotive vehicles can drive on this rough paving in emergency, but normally the area is reserved for the light rail vehicles. In still other places, the light rail vehicles run as ordinary streetcars. The cars are trainable and have convertible steps to allow loading from both floor-height platforms and street level. There are five lines in the system, which merge into a single line that runs under Market Street. Up to four-car trains are possible, and the highest planned volume is 9000 passengers/h. Speeds of up to 55 mi/h (88 km/h) are attainable in the subway, but only 25 to 40 mi/h (40 to 64 km/h) are allowed on the surface portion. The train operator needs a positive signal indicated by the "green light" (using the 100-Hz cab signal system, the rails carrying the signal) to be able to achieve that higher speed in the subway. In the absence of that signal, the vehicle cannot go over a set speed, say 40 or 35 mi/h. Muni's full use of the light rail concept merits careful study and observation by rail system planners.

M & O Subway

Light rail is versatile and flexible and can be designed to meet a very wide demand. At one end of the spectrum is San Francisco Muni's major semimetro system, at the other end is the M & O Subway. Tandy Center (Radio Shack) in Fort Worth, Texas, has its own light rail line named after Marvin and Obediah Leonard, the founders and previous owners. In 1963, Obie Leonard bought five ex-Washington, D.C., PCC streetcars, laid about 1.5 mi (2.4 km) of track, reworked the cars to make them appear new, added air conditioning, built a huge parking lot along the flood plain of a river, dug a very short subway to the basement of the store, and happily hauled thousands of people into the store every day. The ride is free.

The track is about on a par with a railroad industrial siding. Speeds are low, 15 to 25 mi/h (24 to 40 km/h). The power supply is said to be ex-United States Navy submarine generators, war surplus. The trolley poles are short mine type, so they will fit in the subway. The whole system is a triumph of ingenuity, but the subway is especially so. The street was opened (various buildings of the Tandy complex front on both sides) and war-surplus Quonset huts were installed end to end. Then the street was backfilled—an instant subway with arched roof. It leaks a bit, but it works.

No Urban Mass Transportation Administration (UMTA) funds were involved, nor were local government funds. No large-scale professional consulting engineer reports were made. The work was largely done in-house by company maintenance forces who converted the old District of Columbia trolleys from single-end streetcars to double-end, air-conditioned, high-platform light rail vehicles. It is a marvel of practical engineering. The Tandy Subway was modernized in the 1980s by building a three-track terminal at Tandy Center and totally rebuilding the cars with the boxy bodies of contemporary LRVs. The parking-lot-shuttle type of operation could be quite useful in a variety of situations in smaller communities where a planner might not normally consider rail transit of any kind.

Pittsburgh

Pittsburgh's LRT line to the South Hills combines several features to yield a unique line. Because it is a rebuilt street railway line, it retained the 5-ft 2.5-in gauge of the Pittsburgh Railways Company. New sections of private right-of-way, including a downtown subway, feature high-platform stations with attendants and conventional fare collection. Segments of paved-street track use low-platform loading through a single-stream door adjacent to the train operator.

The right-of-way includes a new subway, a recycled massive railroad bridge across the Monongahela River, a reused streetcar tunnel through Mt. Washington, rebuilt street railway on private right-of-way, some rebuilt street track, a new tunnel in Mt. Lebanon (with no station), and some new right-of-way. It is an excellent illustration of the versatility of light rail transit.

Skokie Swift

Another rail variation is the Skokie Swift line of the Chicago Transit Authority (CTA), a 5-mi (8-km) shuttle line using one-car one-person-crew trains. It feeds the northern terminal of the Chicago mainline subway/elevated line from the suburban village of Skokie. The line has only two stations, a park-and-ride station in Skokie and the Howard Street terminus of the El. It is popular, economical to operate, and a worthwhile addition to Chicago's rapid transit system. While it uses high-platform rapid-transit-type cars, the CTA considers it light rail because of the one-car trains and at-grade construction of much of the line—an abandoned interurban electric railway taken over by the CTA for this purpose.

Figure 5-7 *Skokie Swift. Chicago's articulated "Paul Revere" in Bicentennial livery is used as a one-man operated unit on the suburban line. Skokie trains are equipped with both third rail and catenary current collection. (courtesy of Chicago Transit Authority)*

Newark

The Newark (New Jersey) City Subway, which opened in 1935, should not be overlooked. It is at the light end of the LRT spectrum. The shortest of publicly owned light rail lines at 4.2 mi (6.7 km), it provides very frequent service with 22 PCC streetcars (single unit, single end, fare collection on board, 600-V current collected by trolley pole). There are 11 stations of which 4 are in the 1.2-mi (1.9-km) subway portion. The line was built in the bed of the abandoned Morris Canal in order to remove some streetcar lines from the congested streets of New Jersey's largest city. This location provided full grade separation except for one grade crossing. Newark's other streetcar lines were converted to motor bus in the 1940–1950s, leaving Route 7, City Subway, as the sole surviving light rail line in New Jersey. The second-hand PCC cars were acquired after a proposal to convert the line to a dual-mode trolleybus line was rejected.

New Jersey Transit Corporation (NJT) rehabilitated Route 7 in the late 1980s. The PCC cars were overhauled in-house and are meticulously maintained. Procurement of new LRVs was considered, but it was concluded that the rehabilitated PCCs could do the job.

Route 7, City Subway, is merely one route in the vast bus system operated by NJT Bus Operations, Inc. At its Franklin Avenue outer terminal, connection is made with several bus lines. Along its route, a number of bus lines are intersected. At Penn Station, Newark City Subway reaches NJT's major hub, where connections are made with the commuter rail lines of NJT Rail Operations, Inc., with numerous bus lines, and with Amtrak's Northeast Corridor. The heaviest and lightest of rail modes meet in this location.

These illustrations are a sampling of the versatility of LRT systems. Older services in such diverse cities as Boston, Philadelphia, New Orleans, and Toronto are also good examples of the ability of LRT to be molded to the needs of the cities it serves.

MODERN U.S. AND CANADIAN SYSTEMS

Edmonton

Edmonton, Alberta, Canada, brought the new generation of light rail to North America on April 22, 1978, when its 4.5-mi (7.2-km) route opened. It featured all high-platform stations, U-2 cars built by Siemens-Duewag in Germany, a downtown subway, with the line then rising to grade, to share a railroad right-of-way. Because of grade crossings, speed was a modest 30 mi/h (48 km/h). Work on a southern extension to the University of Alberta is under construction (1989–1992) and will include a bridge over the North Saskatchewan River. Further extensions are planned.

Two- and three-car trains are operated in the peak hours. There were 37 cars in the fleet as of 1989. Self-service proof-of-payment fare collection is employed. The line is an integral part of the Edmonton Transit System and is the furthest north of any North American rail transit line.

Calgary

Calgary, Alberta, some 185 mi (296 km) south of Edmonton, has built an all at-grade LRT system. The initial southern line opened in 1981, a northeast line in 1985, and a northwest line in 1987. It is high-platform, proof-of-payment fare collection, and operates through a downtown pedestrian and transit mall (with buses). As of 1990, it had 17 rte.-mi (27 rte.-km) of double track, with more under construction, and had a fleet of 83 U-2 cars. There are two routes, both sharing the center-city mall.

The more extensive at-grade Calgary C-Train system contrasts with the short subway and surface line in Edmonton and illustrates how rapidly a system can be expanded at grade.

San Diego

The initiator of the modern generation of light rail line in the United States is operated by San Diego Trolley, Inc. It was built by the Metropolitan Transit Development Board, opening for service on July 26, 1981, between the Santa Fe Railroad station in downtown San Diego, and extending south 15.9 mi (25.4 km) to San Ysidro, California, on the Mexican border adjacent to Tijuana. Fourteen Siemens-Duewag low-platform U-2 articulated LRVs provided service over what had been the San Diego & Arizona Eastern Railroad. Initially, the line was single track, with sidings or short sections of double track spaced to allow a 15-min headway.

Nicknamed the "Tijuana Trolley," the line was instantly popular, resulting in pressure to add more cars and double track. These improvements were carried out over several years. Trains grew from two to three and eventually four cars. The fourth car is uncoupled to operate separately in the street in central San Diego because a four-car train blocks cross streets. An eastern extension to Euclid Avenue opened in 1986; it was continued to La Mesa and El Cajon in 1989 to total 32 mi (51 km) of route. A short 2-mi route along the waterfront in San Diego creates a triangular loop between the end of street trackage and the Santa Fe station. Additional extensions are under study.

The MTDB continues freight train operation using a private contractor, the San Diego & Imperial Valley Railroad. Most freight train activity is at night.

Portland

Portland, Oregon, opened MAX (Metropolitan Area Express) between center-city Portland and Gresham City on September 8, 1986. The line operates in paved streets in center city. From there it is located in a freeway median, in the median of Banfield Boulevard, and thence in a former electric railway right-of-way to Gresham, 15.1 mi (24.2 km) to the east. The last 2.5 mi is single track. The 26 articulated low-platform LRVs can attain 55 mi/h (88 km/h). Maximum train length is two cars in deference to cross streets in downtown Portland. MAX is unusual in U.S. practice in that a magnetic inductive train stop system is used to enforce red block signals.

Historic-appearing new single-unit streetcars have been acquired to provide a local service within the downtown area. Portland's MAX has enjoyed unusually heavy weekend traffic, with Saturdays often being busier than weekdays as a result of a festival market and other CBD attractions. The Portland line has been very well accepted by the area residents, is well used, and can be an example to transit planners elsewhere. A western extension is under study.

Sacramento

Sacramento, California, opened its LRT line, RT Metro, in 1987, using 26 Siemens-Duewag U-2 articulated low-platform LRVs. The U-shaped route consists of the 9-mi (14-km) North Line and the 9.3-mi (14.9-km) East or Folsom Line. About 60% of the line is single track, with sidings spaced to allow a 15-min headway. Trains of up to four LRVs are operated.

The North Line uses a segment of what was intended to be an Interstate-80 bypass. Ballasted track rests on top of never used concrete pavement near the Watt/I-80 station and on a graded but never-used right-of-way east of the car shop near the Marconi–Arcade station. The line was constructed using interstate transfer funds from the abandoned I-80 project. Its designers used some of the most innovative approaches applied in the United States to LRT and achieved one of the lowest costs per route-mile of any new system at about $10 million/mi. In the downtown area, track is in a pedestrian mall, in the rest of center city it is in paved streets. Extensions are planned.

San Jose

The 20-mi (32-km) Guadalupe light rail project being built by the Santa Clara County Transportation Agency opened its first section of line on December 11, 1987. It was followed by the section to downtown San Jose, California, which opened June 17, 1988, to total 9 rte.-mi (14 rte.-km). The next unit opened on August 17, 1990 (11 weeks ahead of schedule). This section extends the service about 2 mi south of center city to a station that will be shared with the extended Caltrain commute rail service in late 1991 when the last section of the initial system will also open. The system is all double tracked and has 33 stations.

Fifty LRVs were obtained from the Urban Transportation Development Corporation of Canada. They have air suspension and are air conditioned. Their top speed is about 65 mi/h, but they will operate at 55 mi/h. Additional local service within the CBD of San Jose is provided by a small fleet of restored historic trolleys, some of which actually operated in the region.

Service extensions for areas north of San Jose (Milpitas, Santa Clara, Mountain View, and Sunnyvale) are being studied.

Los Angeles–Long Beach

The 21.5-mi (34.4-km) Los Angeles–Long Beach light rail line, built by the Los Angeles County Transportation Commission, opened on July 14, 1990. It restores service along 16 mi (26 km) of a route that had been operated by the Pacific Electric Railway Company (PE) from 1902 to 1961. There are 33 grade crossings (all with warning devices and gates), but five major grade separations eliminated a number of at-grade PE crossings of streets and railroads. The 54 articulated LRVs are high platform, have a top speed of 55 mi/h, and were built in Japan. The line uses cab signals, which, with the high-platform stations, places this line at the heavier end of the light rail spectrum.

The LRT line is part of the regional transit system operated by Southern California Rapid Transit District that will later include Los Angeles Metro Rail and the 16.5-mi (26.4-km) Century Freeway automated light rail line. The Long Beach line will share the 7th & Flower Street subway station of Metro Rail in downtown Los Angles when it is completed in 1991.

All the West Coast LRT lines except San Francisco Muni Metro use the proof-of-payment fare collection system with off-train vending of tickets in conjunction with periodic inspection on board. This method is reported to work well.

St. Louis

Bi-State Metro Link, 18 mi (29 km) long, will connect East St. Louis, Illinois, with St. Louis, Missouri, its western suburbs, and Lambert International Airport by 1993. It will use the historic (1854) Eads Bridge, a 4500-ft railroad tunnel, and underutilized railroad rights-of-way. It will employ high platforms and a few grade crossings (all with warning devices). Thirty-one LRVs were ordered from Siemens in 1990. They are very similar to those used in Pittsburgh.

Baltimore

In 1989, Baltimore ordered 35 very large LRVs, 95 ft (28.5 m) long and 9.5 ft (2.9 m) wide, for its 28-mi (45-km) north-south LRT line. It will operate at grade in a pedestrian mall in downtown Baltimore, and hence can be considered classic LRT.

Buffalo

Buffalo's LRT line opened October 10, 1984, featuring a double-tracked line 1.2 mi (1.9 km) long in a paved pedestrian mall on Main Street. The remainder of the line, in subway, opened in September 1986 to provide a 6.2-mi (9.9-km) route. The subway portion employs high-platform stations; the street trackage employs low-level loading with retractable steps on board the cars. Conceptually, it is somewhat like SF Muni, only reversed—on street downtown and in subway elsewhere. This is a legacy of its initial planning as a true rapid transit subway system throughout; however, its potential ridership did not meet federal requirements for full rapid transit. Consequently, the plan was altered to become generally light rail rapid transit with some surface operation LRT downtown.

The 27 cars are single-unit (nonarticulated), double-truck, double-end cars built in Japan, equipped with a U.S. propulsion system, and assembled in the United States.

Several extensions have been proposed and provision was made in the subway structure for a junction as well as an extension.

Niagara Frontier Transportation Authority, operator of the line, had a difficult financial situation that culminated in a system shutdown (including the extensive bus system) in early 1990. After a few days, new funding was agreed upon by city and county authorities, and the system resumed operation.

LIGHT RAIL RAPID TRANSIT

Light rail rapid transit (LRRT) is a composite of rail rapid transit and light rail. The one characteristic that differentiates LRRT from LRT is an exclusive, grade-separated right-of-way for the entire system, which qualifies the system as true rapid transit. LRRT systems may have low- or high-level platforms or both. They may be run with either visual or signal control. Many LRT systems have sections that qualify as LRRT and, in a few cases such as Buffalo, the whole system is referred to, although inaccurately, as light rail rapid transit.

CLEVELAND

The composite of light rail and rapid transit is exemplified by the Greater Cleveland Regional Transit Authority (GCRTA) Red Line route from Windermere in East Cleveland to Cleveland Hopkins Airport on the far-southwest side of that industrial city. The GCRTA 19-mi (30-km) rapid is fully grade separated, uses overhead electrification and high platforms, and runs one-car one-person-operated trains in off-peak hours, with fare collection on board. During peak hours, two- or three-car trains are operated with two-person crews (operator and conductor) and station collection of fares. Speeds are moderate, 55 mi/h (88 km/h), and headways relatively frequent. The GCRTA rapid hauls about 20,000 persons per day.

About 2.6 mi (4.2 km) of its track is shared with the Shaker Heights (Blue and Green) line, which operates articulated Breda light rail vehicles utilizing low-platform loading. The Shaker Heights line is also owned and operated by the GCRTA, but it was originally constructed in 1919 as a transportation link between downtown Cleveland and a new land development.

Cleveland was a pioneer in large-scale park-and-ride lots, along with extensive and well-coordinated feeder bus lines. It has shown that rapid transit can be successfully provided in areas of moderate population density and high auto ownership. Most of the areas served by the GCRTA rapid and the Shaker Heights light rail are single homes, with a modest sprinkling of apartments.

An interesting facet of the Cleveland rail system is the use of the word rapid as a noun. This word, usually an adjective, is used to describe the system as "The Rapid" or a car or train as "a rapid." This use evolved among the local population.

INTERMEDIATE CAPACITY TRANSIT SYSTEMS

A variation of light rapid transit is the Intermediate Capacity Transit System (ICTS) developed by the Urban Transit Development Corporation of Ontario, Canada. It is based on a standard-gauge railway track as a guideway, with 600-V dc, third-rail power distribution. There its similarity to conventional technology ends.

The ICTS features a small bus-size car powered by a linear induction motor (LIM) controlled by an on-board V dc-ac inverter. A variable block system is used to enforce train separation, with block length proportional to speed. The lower the speed is, the shorter the block, allowing closer train spacing and more throughput. Full automation is designed into the system; no on-board train operator is required. Speeds of up to 50 mi/h (80 km/h) are attained along with acceleration of 3.0 mi/h/s (1.3 m/s^2), as fast a rate as is customary for either light or heavy rail.

Radial axle trucks are used along with flanged wheels that are smaller in diameter than those customarily used on rapid transit or light rail cars. These wheels are not used for propulsion or braking, those functions are provided by the LIM. A friction parking brake is provided. The radial truck is intended to reduce flange wear.

The ICTS inherently requires full grade separation. Most existing mileage is on elevated structure, with some surface and a very small amount of tunnel mileage. The small profile provided by the small car body on small wheels allows a small tunnel.

By 1989, ICTSs had been installed in three locations in North America. The first was in Vancouver, British Columbia, where it is called SkyTrain and first operated in 1986 for Expo '86. It performs a line-haul function and is over 13 mi (21 km) long, plus a recently opened 2-mi (3-km) extension with more extensions planned. It is the backbone of Vancouver's transit system and provides a high level of exceptionally frequent service with two-, four-, and six-car trains.

In Toronto, Canada, an ICTS line 4-mi (6.4-km) long provides a feeder service to the east terminal of the Bloor-Danforth subway line. Toronto initially opted to employ train operators on its trains. The change was made to automatic operation during 1989–1990, although an on-board attendant was retained.

In Detroit, the ICTS is used as a downtown people mover under an UMTA-funded demonstration project. One- and two-car trains are operated on a single-track continuous loop 2.9 mi (4.6 km) long.

While all three installations encountered some "teething" problems, such as are usually encountered in new technology, all provide a high level of service that is attractive to users. The ICTS has demonstrated that full automatic operation is workable in the North American environment.

COMMUTER RAILROAD

Commuter railroad service has existed on a major scale continuously for many years in New York, Philadelphia, Boston, Chicago, and San Francisco. Typically, railroad commuter services have very heavy peak-hour service with little, or even no, off-peak service. Regular interval service of a train every 30 to 60 min in off-peak periods is generally considered good, with peak-hour trains every 4 to 30 min. It is not uncommon for a certain corridor in major cities to have only three inbound trains in the morning and three outbound at night. A number of medium-size cities had or have one train each way daily on certain routes. This all means that most, indeed all, railroad commuter services are heavy losers financially if evaluated of and by themselves. They often handle "the peak of the peak," however, and so reduce the need for investment in plant and equipment to handle a peak load by some other mode, whether highway or transit.

If freight train conflicts can be reduced or eliminated, commuter service can begin to approach rail rapid transit in frequency and convenience. As long as trains are operated by railroad employees represented by railroad unions, traditional labor practices ensure high operating expenses and a high probability of significant deficits. Nonetheless, at times it is still an attractive alternative financially and is nearly always popular with passengers. Some public transit agencies operate commuter trains directly with their own employees at transit pay rates and work rules with resulting lower costs. Because underutilized railroad track exists in many places, it is often possible to run a few peak-hour trains by providing only added locomotives, cars, and labor. The expensive fixed plant, a right-of-way through an urban area, is already there. Therefore, to a public transit agency, contracting for railroad commuter services may at times be an attractive alternative to massive investment in other modes.

EASTERN UNITED STATES

In the New York and Philadelphia metropolitan areas, most commuter trains consist of electrically powered multiple-unit cars. Many of these are relatively new and have performance approaching that of modern rail rapid transit. Single-level commuter rail cars are typically 85 ft (26 m) long, 10 ft (3 m) wide, and 14 ft (4 m) high and seat from 90 (in 2-2 seating) to 130 (in 3-2 seating). Some use 600 to 650-V dc third rail; others use catenary overhead at 11,000 V ac, 25 Hz; and one, the New Haven, uses both. New York area stations have floor-level platforms since the New York systems use high-platform cars. Philadelphia favors ground-level loading at most stations.

For the newer equipment, acceleration is in the range of 1.5 to 2.2 mi/h/s (0.67 to 0.98 m/s^2). Top speed is generally 85 mi/h (137 km/h), but certain cars were designed to reach 100 mi/h (160 km/h). But only the Jersey Arrow cars running the 58 mi (93 km) between Trenton, New Jersey, and New York City (Penn Station) regularly reach that speed. For longer suburban journeys of about 50 mi, such high speeds could reduce trip times substantially, but only if the number of stops is strictly limited.

Figure 5-8 *SEPTA—Silverliner II at DeKalb Street, Norristown, Pennsylvania. These suburban commuter cars are used in the Philadelphia area. (courtesy of J. William Vigrass)*

In the Boston area, an extensive and moderately intensive service is operated by Amtrak for the Massachusetts Bay Transportation Authority (MBTA). Service is provided by diesel-electric-powered, push-pull equipment using ground-level low platforms. Two distinctly separate services are operated: from North Station over Boston & Maine trackage and from South Station over former New Haven Railroad line trackage as well as ConRail (formerly Boston & Albany).

CHICAGO AREA

In Chicago, most suburban railroad service is with bilevel coaches seating 140 to 160, pulled or pushed by medium-horsepower diesel-electric locomotives. These trains load from ground-level platforms. A driving cab is located in the rearmost car of the train to remotely control the locomotive in the push mode. This type of operation minimizes switching and fosters fast turnaround. The bilevel cars are some 16 ft (5 m) high, a height that cannot be accommodated in the below-ground terminals in eastern cities.

All Chicago suburban rail services are operated by railroad owners under contract to METRA (Metropolitan Rail), an agency of the Chicago Regional Transportation

Authority. Operators include the Burlington Northern, Chicago & North Western, and the former Rock Island line, which has had a succession of owners.

Two Chicago railroad lines are electrified. The Illinois Central Gulf(ICG) uses a 1500-V dc catenary system. The line runs south from the Chicago Loop, along Lake Michigan's shoreline. There are two branches. A fleet of bilevel high-platform cars was acquired in the 1970s, partly with public funds.

The Chicago South Shore & South Bend Railroad has a single route from South Bend through Michigan City and Gary, Indiana, to downtown Chicago, using ICG rails within Chicago. The South Shore line is largely in Indiana yet received no financial aid from Indiana sources until 1978. Public funds were made available in the late 1970s through the Northern Indiana Commuter Transportation District (NICTD). The NICTD's funds are severely limited but were adequate to obtain 44 new electric multiple-unit cars built in 1981–1982 by Sumitomo (of Japan) with General Electric (U.S.) propulsion equipment similar to that provided for the ICG cars. The South Shore cars are single deck and thus somewhat lighter than ICG's bilevels. The South Shore cars attain speeds of 70 to 75 mi/h (112 to 120 km/h). Low-level loading is used at South Shore's own stations.

SAN FRANCISCO BAY AREA

In the West, only one area, San Francisco, presently has extensive commuter railroad service. It is provided by Caltrain, an agency of the California Department of Transportation (Caltrans) with the service operated under contract to the Southern Pacific Transportation Company. It operates over 60 trains a weekday between San Francisco and San Jose, a distance of 47 mi (75 km). Relatively new bilevel coaches are operated in the push-pull mode with diesel-electric locomotives. The line is entirely low platform. Over 23,000 riders per day use the service, which is unique in that it also serves as an intercity rail passenger service between the third and fourth largest California cities. Construction started in 1990 on a 2-mi (3-km) extension of the service to connect to the new light rail system in south San Jose. Extensions at both ends of the present service are under study.

Unique aspects of the service are the use of a Peninsula Pass, which allows commuters to also travel on connecting transit services in Santa Clara, San Mateo, and San Francisco counties, and some free shuttle bus services.

TORONTO AREA

Toronto, Canada, has one of the most efficient and effective rail commuter systems. It is operated by the Canadian National Railways (CN) for the Province of Ontario, and hence is known as GO Transit (for Government of Ontario). Like many North American cities, Toronto grew in area greatly following World War II. Although it always possessed a very effective urban transit system, it depended largely on buses for outer suburban service, with a few scheduled local passenger trains operated at an out-of-pocket loss by the two railways, the CN and CP (Canadian Pacific Rail).

Figure 5-9 *Caltrain commuter push-pull train at historic Menlo Park Station. (courtesy of California Department of Transportation)*

Figure 5-10 *GO Transit train. Leaving Toronto Union Station, it is headed by an auxiliary power unit cab, an ex F-97 locomotive (freight/passenger). (courtesy of Toronto Area Transit Operating Authority)*

By the early 1960s, it was evident that an outer suburban service on private right-of-way was highly desirable. The high cost of urban freeways caused further pressure to seek an alternative to more freeways. In 1965, GO Transit was authorized, and service was inaugurated in May 1967.

GO Transit provides regular interval service between Whitby 31.3 mi (50.2 km) to the east and Oakville 25.8 mi (41.2 km) to the west, via Toronto's Union Station. A few trains are extended beyond Oakville to Hamilton, 39.3 mi (63.3 km) from Toronto. A basic hourly service is provided, with trains every 20 min during peak hours. Trains have a locomotive at one end with either a driving cab or a former locomotive used as an auxiliary power car with controls at the other end.

Ridership has risen steadily to about 90,000 riders per day in 1989, with additional rolling stock being added periodically. Trains of up to 10 cars are operated, their length being limited by station platforms. To accommodate increasing ridership, a number of double-deck cars were ordered for delivery in 1977–1978, with several additional orders received subsequently. These are true two-floor cars and are not "gallery cars" such as those used in Chicago and San Francisco. Expansion of GO's system to the northwest came in the 1970s, beginning with three round trips per day. Routes to the north and northeast were added during the 1980s. A total of 152 rte.-mi (243 rte.-km) was operated in 1989.

GO Transit is a composite of railroad and transit practices. Fare collection is at stations, allowing a minimum-size train crew. Proof-of-payment was first inaugurated on certain lightly serviced branches to the north. It was successful, as anticipated, so GO changed their entire system to proof-of-payment with tickets vended in stations and roving fare inspectors such as are used on light rail lines in San Diego, Sacramento, and San Jose in California and Calgary and Edmonton in Canada. Fares are distance related. Doors are power operated by one conductor, as on rapid transit.

Also included in GO Transit are express buses furnishing direct connections from Oakville to Hamilton on the west and from Whitby to Oshawa on the east. These are not merely feeder buses, but are a continuation of a specific train schedule and stop at stations having park-and-ride lots and enclosed waiting rooms. It is, perhaps, the most effective bus–train service anywhere. These buses are operated by Gray Coach Lines (a subsidiary of Toronto Transit Commission) under contract to GO Transit. The combination provides excellent regional coverage at reasonable cost.

New Systems

Recently, new services have been established in a number of areas. For instance, a moderately extensive and intensive commuter railroad service is provided by MARC (Maryland Rail Commuter of the Maryland Department of Transportation) in the Washington, D.C., area. MARC connects Washington and Baltimore via the electrified Northeast Corridor, as well as the diesel-powered CSX (ex-B&O) line. It also provides diesel-powered trains to Brunswick, Maryland, and Martinsburg, West Virginia, on former B&O mainline to the west.

In 1989, Tri-Rail inaugurated commuter service on CSX trackage for communities on Florida's east coast. It connects Miami with West Palm Beach, 67 mi (107 km) to the north. Other new services are planned to operate from Washington, D.C., to points in northern Virginia, from Oceanside to San Diego in California, and from San Juan Capistrano to Los Angeles, also in California.

SUMMARY

The rail mode is versatile. It has provided a 1.5-mi parking lot-to-department store shuttle, the 71-mi Bay Area Rapid Transit system, urban systems covering major metropolitan areas, light rail systems serving busy center-city commercial districts and exclusive suburban residential areas, and far-flung suburban railroad commuter operations.

The versatility of the rail mode can be seen in the examples cited. Track can be single, double, or multiple; it can be at grade, depressed, in subway, or elevated. Signaling can be advanced cab signals with speed control or wayside block signals with or without stop enforcement, or operation can be "on sight" at moderate speeds. Stations can be high or low platform, with or without controlled access. Fare collection can be proof-of-payment (sometimes called the honor system), controlled access (with turnstiles or gates), or conventional fare collection on board. Stations can be elaborate or simple. Track gauge is usually 4 ft 8.5 in standard but can be wide (5 ft 2.5 in as in Pittsburgh or Philadelphia) or narrow (as meter gauge overseas). Power supply is generally 750 V dc, although 600 V dc has been used for some new systems. It all works.

Off-the-shelf applications have been proved and can be implemented with minimal research and development. If evolutionary development of what has been successful is adopted by the planner and engineer, there is a very high probability of successful operation. Construction and operating costs are known and can be projected.

Rail transit has also been proved, and it can do many jobs in the urban and suburban environment. It can use electric power effectively, thus reducing pollution and improving the general quality of life. The opportunities to use rail transit effectively should be kept constantly in mind by the transit planner and engineer because it can be a useful tool.

REFERENCES

1   TRANSPORTATION RESEARCH BOARD, *Urban Public Transportation Glossary*, ed. Benita H. Gray (Washington, D.C.: Transportation Research Board, 1989), p. 65.

FURTHER READING

Some citations are no longer available from their original source. These citations are often available from the National Technical Information Service, U.S. Department of Commerce, 5285 Port Royal Road, Springfield, VA 22161. We have verified the order numbers for many of these citations, and they are found at the end of the citation. Prices are available through NTIS at the address above.

BEI, RINO, "San Francisco's Muni Metro, A Light-Rail Transit System," in *Light-Rail Transit: Planning and Technology*, Special Report 182, pp. 18-23. Washington, D.C.: Transportation Research Board, 1978.

DEMORO, HARRE W., *California's Electric Railways: An Illustrated Review*, Interurban Special 100. Glendale, Calif.: Interurban Press, 1986.

DIAMANT, E. S., AND OTHERS, *Light Rail Transit: (A) State of the Art Review*, Final Report, prepared for UMTA, Report no. DOT-UT-50009. Chicago: De Leuw, Cather & Company, Spring 1976. Now available as PB 256 821.

DOVER, A. T., *Electric Traction* (4th ed.). London: Sir Isaac Pitman & Sons Ltd., 1963.

GOVERNMENT OF ONTARIO TRANSIT, *(The) GO Transit (Story)*. n.p.: Toronto Area Transit Operating Authority, November 1974.

HATCHER, COLIN K., AND TOM SCHWARZKOPF, *Edmonton's Electric Transit: The Story of Edmonton's Streetcars and Trolley Buses*. Toronto, Canada: Railfare Enterprise Ltd., 1983.

Jane's Urban Transport Systems 1990 (9th ed.), ed. Chris Bushell. New York: Jane's Publishing Inc., 1990.

KASHIN, SEYMOUR, AND HARRE [W.] DEMORO, *An American Original, The PCC Car*. Glendale, Calif.: Interurban Press, 1986.

LIGHT RAIL TRANSIT ASSOCIATION, *Light Rail '87*, A Light Rail Special Publication by the Light Rail Transit Association, September 1987 and *Light Rail Review 1*, 1989. Additional copies of Light Rail obtainable from LRTA Publications, 13A The Precinct, Broxbourne, Herts EN 10 7HY, Great Britain.

MADIGAN, RONALD J., *Urban Rail Supporting Technology Program Fiscal Year 1975, Year End Summary*, prepared for UMTA by Transportation Systems Center. Washington, D.C.: U.S. Department of Transportation, December 1975. Now available as PB 250 447.

MCKANE, JOHN, AND ANTHONY PERLES, *Inside Muni: The Properties and Operations of the Municipal Railway of San Francisco*. Glendale, Calif.: Interurban Press, 1982.

MIDDLETON, WILLIAM D., *The Time of the Trolley*. Milwaukee, Wis.: Kalmbach Publishing Co., 1967. Being reissued as three volumes by Golden West Books.

MILLER, JOHN ANDERSON, *Fares, Please!* New York: Dover Publications, Inc., 1960. (Published originally in 1940.)

MUEHLBERGER, R. F., *Standard Light Rail Vehicle*, presented at Intersociety Conference on Transportation, Denver, Colorado, September 23-27, 1973, Report no. 73-ICT-80. New York: American Society of Mechanical Engineers, June 5, 1973.

SAN FRANCISCO BAY AREA RAPID TRANSIT DISTRICT, *The Composite Report, Bay Area Rapid Transit, May 1962*. n.p.: San Francisco Bay Area Rapid Transit District, May, 1962.

SCHUMANN, JOHN W., "Evaluations of Operating Light-Rail Transit and Streetcar Systems in the United States," in *Light-Rail Transit: Planning and Technology*, Special Report 182, pp. 94-103. Washington, D.C.: Transportation Research Board, 1978.

SILIEN, JOSEPH S., AND JEFFREY G. MORA, "North American Light Rail Vehicles," in *Light Rail Transit*, Special Report 161, pp. 93-98. Washington, D.C.: Transportation Research Board, 1975.

TRANSPORTATION RESEARCH BOARD, *Light Rail Transit: New System Success at Affordable Prices*, Special Report 221, papers presented at the National Conference on Light Rail Transit, May 8-11, 1988, at San Jose, Calif. Washington, D.C.: Transportation Research Board, 1989.

——, *Light Rail Transit: Planning, Design, and Implementation,* papers presented at the Conference on Light Rail Transit, March 28-30, 1982, San Diego, California, Special Report 195. Washington, D.C.: Transportation Research Board, 1982.

TRANSPORTATION SYSTEMS CENTER, *Urban Rail Supporting Technology: A Five Year Progress Summary, 1971-1976*, prepared for UMTA. Washington, D.C.: U.S. Department of Transportation, June 1976. Now available as PB 259 090.

VON ROHR, JOACHIM, "Foreign Light Rail Vehicle Development," in *Light Rail Transit*, Special Report 161, pp. 99-110. Washington, D.C.: Transportation Research Board, 1975.

PERIODICALS

The following periodicals are suggested for those interested in rail mode. They offer both historical information and current activities.

Electric Traction, The Urban Transit Magazine for Australia. Australian Electric Traction Association, G.P.O. Box 1017, Sydney, NSW, 2001 Australia (monthly).

Headlights. The Electric Railroaders Association Inc., 145 Greenwich Street, New York, N.Y. 10006 (monthly, actually irregular).

Mass Transit. Mass Transit, 210 Crossways Park Drive, Woodbury, NY 11797 (monthly).

Modern Railroads. Modern Railroads, P.O. Box 653, Holmes, PA 19043 (monthly).

Modern Tramway and Light Rail Transit. Ian Allen Ltd., Coombelands House, Addlestone, Weybridge, KT15 1HY, England (monthly).

Railway Age. Railway Age, Subscription Department, 345 Hudson Street, New York, NY 10014 (semimonthly).

Railway Gazette International. Reed Business Publishing Ltd., Quadrant Subscription Services, Oakfield House, Perrymount Road, Haywards Heath, Sussex RH163DH, England (monthly).

EXERCISES

5-1   What are the two essential features of the rail guideway that make it unique and without which it would not work? Why are these features essential?

5-2 Urban transit does not always employ a standard-gauge rail guideway. Cite examples of the use of nonstandard gauges and the reasons they were used.

5-3 Monorails are a popular mode that is being widely installed throughout the world. True or false? Explain your answer.

5-4 Light rail is always electrified, using trolley wire with pantographs. True or false? Explain your answer.

5-5 Cite some examples of high-speed (in excess of 100 mi/h) rail systems. Discuss when is the use of high-speed rail appropriate? Inappropriate?

5-6 Some critics of public investment in urban/suburban rail transit strongly contend that such systems have attracted few, if any, new riders to public transit. Is this true? Cite examples.

5-7 What is light rail transit?

5-8 What is light rail rapid transit?

5-9 Since commuter railroads usually operate at a substantial deficit, why should a public agency consider this mode?

5-10 The railway, as a mode, is over 200 years old; therefore, it must be obsolete. True or false? Explain your answer.

Chapter 6

BUS TRANSIT

ROBERT W. KOSKI

This chapter presents elements of planning and operations for urban fixed-route bus transit systems. Although rail and paratransit modes have been receiving increased attention, conventional fixed-route bus systems are the most prevalent form of public transportation in the United States. The relative importance of fixed-route bus systems in terms of equipment and ridership for American Public Transit Association (APTA) member transit systems is shown in Table 6-1.

COMPARISON BETWEEN RAIL AND BUS SYSTEMS

The advantages of fixed-route bus systems compared with rail systems include:

- Relative ease of adjustment to meet changing travel patterns.
- Comparatively low capital costs.
- Relatively short time required to inaugurate or expand systems.
- A proven, relatively trouble free technology.
- Ease of bypassing barriers (accidents, fires, and the like) to the normal route.

TABLE 6-1
Transit Equipment and Ridership
(APTA Members)

Mode	Active Vehicles 1988	Passenger-Miles (millions) 1988
Motor bus (fixed route)	60,388	21,322
Demand responsive	18,190	601
Heavy rail	10,539	11,365
Commuter railroad	4,649	6,941
Vanpool	940	a
Light rail	831	471
Trolleybus	710	211
Automated guideway	99	a
Ferryboat	88	274
Cable car	44	a
Inclined plane	10	a
Aerial tramway	2	a
Total	96,490	41,377

[a]The total combined passenger-miles for vanpool, automated guideway, cable car, inclined plane, and aerial tramway is 182 million.

Source: American Public Transit Association, *Transit Fact Book*, 1989 ed. (Washington, D.C.: American Public Transit Association, 1989), pp. 10-12.

Disadvantages of bus transit compared with rail, which become increasingly important in larger urban areas, include:

- Lower capacity in high-volume travel corridors.
- Limited ability to reduce labor cost in high-volume corridors.
- Susceptibility to delays from other vehicles, except where exclusive bus or HOV facilities are provided.
- Less visibility of the route network (compared with rail), frequently resulting in less public awareness and understanding of available service and coverage.

In larger cities with dense and heavily used rail networks, buses are necessary to supplement rail routes and to feed into rail terminals. In 1989, for example, the New York City Transit Authority operated 6469 heavy rail cars and 4540 buses and the

Chicago Transit Authority operated 1217 heavy rail cars and 2218 buses.[1]

Even with the resurgence of interest in rail systems in many U.S. cities (see Chaps. 5 and 11) and the expanded emphasis on paratransit operations (see Chaps. 7 and 21), fixed-route bus networks will continue to provide an essential role within the family of available transit technologies.

TYPES OF BUSES

Transit buses are classified into three types: standard, minibuses, and high capacity. Most transit buses purchased prior to 1980 in the United States were manufactured in this country. More recently the production of buses (as with rail cars and automobiles) has become multinational. United States law requires that any vehicle purchase that entails even the partial use of federal funds must contain a certain minimum percentage of domestic wages and materials. Accordingly, to meet this requirement, non-U.S. manufacturers have established U.S. assembly plants and use U.S.-made components. As of 1989, the inventory of active transit buses in the United States included the following top five manufacturers, by percentage of the active fleet: General Motors Corporation (35.7%), Flxible (24.1%), Neoplan U.S.A. Corporation (6.9%), AM General Corporation (4.4%), and M.A.N. Truck and Bus Corporation (4.1%).[2]

STANDARD BUSES

The manufacturers of standard-size buses generally produce 35- and 40-ft (11- and 12-m)-long vehicles. Depending on seating arrangements, a 35-ft-long bus typically seats 40 to 45 passengers, whereas a 40-ft-long vehicle typically seats 47 to 53 passengers. The buses may be either 96 in (2.4 m) or 102 in (2.6 m) wide. The wider buses provide for either wider, more comfortable seats or wider aisles. Recently, more attention has been devoted to upgrading standard bus design by providing lower floors, wider doors, wheelchair lifts or ramps, and other features designed to make them more accessible to the elderly and handicapped.

MINIBUSES

Minibuses are produced by a large number of American and foreign manufacturers. The configurations vary widely, and there continues to be a considerable degree of experimentation. Proliferation of models, mostly produced in small quantities, has been influenced by the interest and concern over service to the elderly and handicapped, demand-responsive services, and service to rural and low-density areas. (See also Chaps. 14 and 21.)

A common misconception is that minibuses are cheaper to operate than standard-size buses in fixed-route service. The largest single item of expense in bus operations is the driver's wage, which usually does not vary regardless of bus size. There is very little difference in fuel costs. Although the initial cost of a minibus may be lower, this is offset by a shorter life span. Thus, the operating costs of standard-size and minibuses are nearly the same. If only one trip per day requires standard-size seating capacities, it would be cheaper to operate a larger bus all day with many empty seats during most of the day than to operate a second minibus for the peak trip. Nevertheless, minibuses play important roles where volumes are always low and where maneuverability is paramount, as in many dial-a-ride or rural operations.

HIGH-CAPACITY BUSES

The United States has turned increasingly to the use of high-capacity buses, long used in Europe and elsewhere. The high-capacity bus, despite its higher initial cost, is frequently attractive economically on high-density routes because of savings in labor costs. The two basic types are the double-decker bus and the articulated (bending) bus.

Figure 6-1 *Double-decker, gas-powered tourist bus in Yosemite National Park. Such buses are used in areas not open to autos. (courtesy of California Department of Transportation)*

The double-decker bus, although still popular in a number of European cities, particularly in Britain and the British Commonwealth countries, is actually less prevalent now in the United States than it was many years ago when they were used in New York City and elsewhere. The Southern California Rapid Transit District still has 18 Neoplan double-deckers (each seating 82 passengers) in its active fleet, and the University Transport System of Davis, California, uses seven antique double-deckers imported from London. In addition, the San Francisco Muni has been conducting a small-scale experiment with double-deckers prompted by the difficulties they have had with articulated buses in crowded traffic. Nevertheless, it appears that the use of double-decker buses in regular transit service in the United States is near extinction. One of the main disadvantages of double-decker buses is the slower loading and unloading of passengers because of the awkward and slow access to the upper deck.

On the other hand, many U.S. transit operators have been ordering articulated buses. Typically, they are 50 to 60 ft (15 to 18 m) long and seat 66 to 72 passengers. With at least two, frequently three, and sometimes four extra-wide doors, loading and unloading is much faster than with double-decker buses. Of course, greater street space is required than for a double-decker bus accommodating the same or a larger number of passengers.

Figure 6-2 *AM General/MAN articulated bus. (courtesy of California Department of Transportation)*

SPECIALIZED CATEGORIES

In addition to classifying transit buses according to size, some specialized categories should also be mentioned.

Trolleybuses. Early trolleybuses are discussed in Chap. 1. Modern trolleybuses are manufactured by several of the same companies that make motor buses and are available in standard-size and articulated versions. They should usually be considered as an alternative to buses powered by fossil fuels only on routes with high passenger volumes supporting frequent service that can justify the added capital expense of the electric power-distribution system. An added incentive for their use in cities such as Seattle and San Francisco has been their superior performance in climbing steep hills.

Dual-powered buses. In 1990, Seattle completed and opened a 1.3-mile transit tunnel under the central business district to provide added transit capacity to a severely constrained street system. Originally, it was planned for this tunnel to be used by diesel buses. Further study revealed that it would be extremely difficult to provide an adequate ventilation system to remove the exhaust fumes, so it was decided that the tunnel would require the use of electric-powered vehicles. Many long suburban transit routes, most operating for considerable distances on freeways, feed into the downtown tunnel. It is not feasible to electrify the outer portion of all these routes. Therefore, Seattle chose to place an order with Breda of Italy for more than 200 specially designed dual-powered buses, which operate by diesel power for the major portion of each trip and then switch to electric power for the trip through the tunnel.

Figure 6-3 *Seattle dual-powered bus—trolleybus in tunnel and diesel electric on surface. (courtesy of Harre W. Demoro Collection)*

Trolley replicas. Buses designed to resemble trolleys or trams are appearing in a growing number of tourist areas, central business districts, and specialized shopping areas. Since they operate on rubber tires and have no trolley pole, the use of the word trolley is really a misnomer. They are usually built with wood exteriors to resemble antique streetcars to give them a nostalgic appeal.

FIXED FACILITIES

DIVISION FACILITIES

All bus systems require an administrative office and one or more storage, servicing, and maintenance bases. The administrative offices may or may not be in conjunction with a maintenance facility. Routine servicing includes fueling, removal of farebox receipts, interior cleaning, and exterior washing. Other maintenance functions include engine overhauls, repair of malfunctioning equipment, body painting, and repair of damaged seats and other interior furnishings. The dispatching function at each storage and servicing base (often called a *division* by transit operators) involves assigning buses and drivers to the schedules on each route assigned to that base.

A typical division in a medium-size transit system may support 200 to 300 buses. Above that number of buses, the savings from centralization of functions and avoidance of duplication should be measured against the potential operating savings of an additional division through reduction of *deadhead* bus mileage between the storage area and the start of in-service trips. There is, of course, no magic formula; each geographical and scheduling situation is unique. In any event, all service facilities should be carefully placed in relationship to the transit route network so as to minimize deadheading. A middle ground between centralization and decentralization would be to provide routine servicing at all divisions, but to concentrate the other maintenance functions requiring specialized equipment, personnel, and parts inventories at only certain division locations.

PARK AND RIDE

Park-and-ride lots are becoming an increasingly important aspect of bus transit systems in a number of cities. They provide convenient access to transit via auto or bicycle for those persons who do not live within convenient walking distance of a bus line. By concentrating boardings at a single point, a more frequent level of service can be supported. Most park-and-ride lots are used primarily by commuters headed for central business districts or other major employment centers. By far the most successful lots are the ones that are large enough to support frequent bus departures during the peak hours. Usually, the best locations are near freeways where fast peak-period express service can be provided to employment centers.

In many cases, buses may perform normal residential neighborhood pickup, making their last stop at a park-and-ride lot, and then operate in the express mode. In this style of operation, several pickup routes could converge at one park-and-ride lot and support very frequent and attractive service at that location. It is desirable to locate park-and-ride lots on an all-day bus route (not necessarily express) in order that commuters not be isolated from their autos during noncommuting hours.

BUSWAYS

Some cities, such as Pittsburgh and Ottawa (Canada), have constructed and continue to operate busways for the exclusive use of express bus service. In other cases, such as the El Monte busway in Los Angeles and Shirley busway in suburban Washington, D.C., facilities originally constructed as exclusive busways have been downgraded to high-occupancy vehicle (HOV) lanes by allowing joint use of the facility by carpools. Numerous other cities, such as Houston, are constructing new HOV lanes to speed express bus service, but since carpools are also allowed on these facilities, technically they should not be called busways.[3, 4]

COMMUNICATIONS

There has been rapid growth in the capabilities and reliability of bus communications systems since 1970. Initially, only supervisor's cars had two-way voice radio contact with the central dispatcher; now almost all buses have two-way voice radios of increasing sophistication. Drivers can quickly report traffic delays, accidents, ill passengers, and other incidents, and dispatchers can quickly reach drivers to issue instructions in cases of emergency or service disruption. Most systems also have "silent alarms" so that the driver can alert the dispatcher who can in turn contact police in case such assistance is needed. Voice communication will probably be gradually supplemented and in some cases replaced by automatic data communication. Data communication reduces transmission time and can deal with more information. Examples of newly developing data communication include automatic vehicle location systems (useful in conjunction with the silent alarm system and for more complete and continuous monitoring of schedule adherence) and automatic passenger counting. The availability of more data concerning passenger boardings and alightings at each bus stop and the number of persons on board each bus between each stop will enable planning and scheduling departments to do their jobs much more effectively.[5]

USER AMENITIES

Other facilities in an all-bus system frequently include passenger waiting shelters or stations and bus-stop signs. An attractive marketing image should be conveyed by user amenities. In addition, signs should be accurate, useful, easy to read, and consistent in format.

Figure 6-4 *Reversible bus- and carpool lanes on Shirley Highway in Virginia. (courtesy of Federal Highway Administration)*

Figure 6-5 *San Bernardino Busway—El Monte Station. Present eastern terminal of busway, showing station and parking. (courtesy of California Department of Transportation)*

TYPES OF BUS NETWORKS

Perhaps the most important factor in the quality and adequacy of service provided by a fixed-route bus system is the design of the network of routes. This section describes the major types of bus networks; in actual practice, most urban bus systems will employ some attributes of several network types.

RADIAL PATTERNS

In older cities, where most major activities were concentrated in the downtown area, streetcar lines typically fanned out in a radial pattern from the central business district (CBD) into the suburbs (Fig. 6-6). Often, when streetcars were phased out, buses followed the same routes although usually with some adjustments. As new suburbs were added, the routes were extended. Although crosstown lines were often added, some local transit systems still follow a basic radial pattern.

Radial patterns can continue to serve work trips to downtown effectively as long as there is a reasonable concentration of employment there. But if downtown commercial activities, such as shopping, are relocated to the suburbs, this type of transit network may not have convenient access to the new locations. Instead of being able, for example, to go shopping downtown from every neighborhood, access to a new shopping center by transit is possible only if you happen to live in the same transit corridor.

Many urban activities have become decentralized, including employment, medical facilities, college campuses, and entertainment. These profound changes in land use in the typical American city have made it difficult for a radially oriented bus network to provide adequate service for most urban trips. Clearly, other approaches must be considered.

GRID-TYPE NETWORKS

Grid-type bus route networks (Fig. 6-7) feature relatively straight, parallel routes spaced at regular intervals and crossed by a second group of routes with similar characteristics. They generally require a minimum of geographic or topographic barriers and an evenly spaced network of arterial streets suitable for bus operations.

An example of a grid-type network can be found in Chicago, where surface bus operations of the Chicago Transit Authority follow a grid pattern but interconnect with rail rapid transit and commuter railroad lines that follow a radial pattern. Other examples of a grid bus network are those operated by the Southern California Rapid Transit District in Los Angeles and by the Toronto Transit Commission in Canada.

A major advantage of a grid-type system for an area that has widely scattered activity centers is that riders can get from almost anyplace to almost anyplace else with one transfer, without having to travel back through a central point such as the CBD.

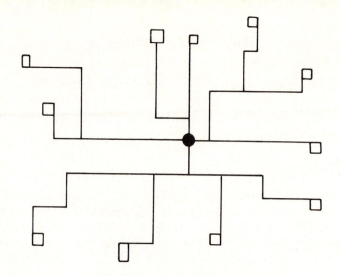

Figure 6-6 *Radial bus route network.*

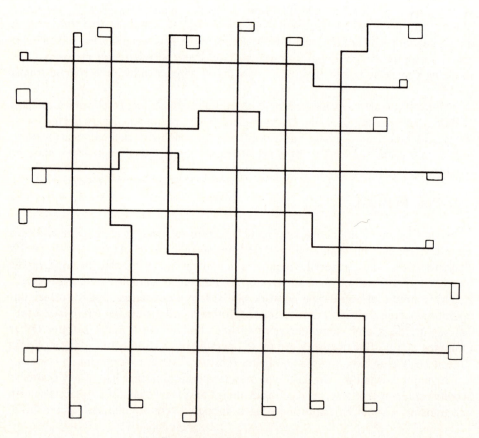

Figure 6-7 *Grid bus route network.*

Another advantage is the relative simplicity of the system. The major disadvantage of the grid system is that in order to get from anyplace to almost anyplace else, a transfer is usually necessary. For example, for a high volume of trips between two points diagonal to the grid, all passengers would be required to make a transfer. In another kind of network, the high volume of trips between two points might be accommodated by more direct routing.

For a grid system to work well, frequent service should be furnished on almost every line: headways should be every 15 or 20 min, or even less. A grid system will not work well with half-hour headways because it is mathematically impossible to schedule more than a few key locations for convenient transfer connections. The remaining locations will involve long waits for transfers. (The theoretical average wait on a grid system is half the headway.) A successful grid system depends on random connections and frequent headways. If population density or ridership is low and will not support frequent headways, it is doubtful that a grid system will be very successful.

RADIAL CRISSCROSS

One way to obtain certain characteristics of a grid system and still maintain the benefits of a radial system is to crisscross the lines and provide additional points where lines converge, such as at shopping centers or colleges. In Fig. 6-8, all four lines operate directly from the central business district to an outlying regional shopping center. By crisscrossing, the lines also provide grid-type transfer opportunities to intermediate locations. Under a pure grid system, there would be no direct service from the CBD to the shopping center.

TRUNK LINE WITH FEEDERS

The trunk line with feeders system (Fig. 6-9) is based on a strong major transit artery, either bus or rail, serving a major travel corridor. Because of topography, geographical barriers, street patterns, or other reasons, it is preferable to provide feeder service to the major trunk line rather than to run bus lines all the way to the ultimate major destination. A major disadvantage of this system is the necessity for most passengers to change vehicles. An advantage is that a system of feeders can support a higher level of service on the trunk line than if it were supported only by passengers walking to stops.

Examples of trunk lines with feeders include certain bus–rail connections of the transit systems in Edmonton (Canada), Atlanta (Georgia), and Sacramento (California); connections between Alameda–Contra Costa Transit buses and Bay Area Rapid Transit (BART) in the San Francisco Bay area; low-density neighborhood shuttle-bus connections to main bus lines in many cities; and the Postal bus system in Switzerland, which feeds into, but is prohibited by law from paralleling, the Swiss National Railways.

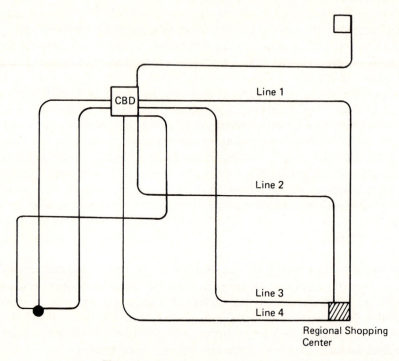

Figure 6-8 *Radial crisscross bus route network.*

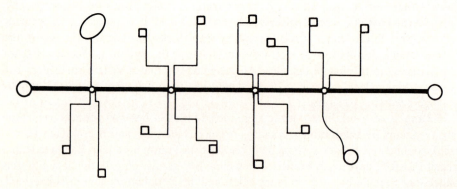

Figure 6-9 *Trunk line with feeders.*

TIMED TRANSFER NETWORKS

Timed transfer networks require an unusually high degree of coordination between route planning and scheduling. Most transportation networks have certain locations where vehicles are scheduled to meet, or at least intersect in timed sequence, to allow interchange of passengers. In a timed transfer network, entire systems or major segments of systems are laid out to facilitate such transfers. At a limited number of locations, bus lines may converge at passenger interchange points or *timed transfer focal points*, which are frequently located at regional shopping centers or other major activity centers. All lines serving a given interchange point operate at the same frequency and are scheduled to arrive at about the same time and to leave at the same time, following a layover period that allows passengers to change buses. The advantages to the passenger include not having to go downtown for transfers, as in a radial system, or having to rely on random transfers, perhaps with long waits at inhospitable street corners, as in the grid system. With the timed transfer network, most transfers can be made within a short period of time and under favorable conditions.

Edmonton was one of the first cities in North America to establish a timed transfer network on a large scale. Other North American cities that are establishing or expanding timed transfer service include Portland, Oregon, and Sacramento, California.

A timed transfer network can be extremely complicated to design and requires very careful planning. Among the problems that must be resolved are:

1. Possible differences in running time between several routes operating between the same pair of focal points.
2. Scheduling conflicts between the demands of focal points and those of intermediate points, such as class-break times at school and colleges.
3. Differences in running times by time of day due to traffic congestion.
4. Differences in passenger volumes by time of day on some routes serving timed transfer focal points, making evenly spaced headways unsuitable.
5. Unsuitable relationships between running times and frequency of service, causing wasted vehicle and operator hours.
6. One or more lines serving a focal point being subject to fluctuating and unpredictable traffic delays, resulting in either missed connections or, if it is the policy for buses to wait for connections, one delayed bus causing an entire group of buses to be delayed.

BRANCHES AND LOOPS

As the service area of any transit system expands, it becomes difficult to provide adequate route coverage to remote areas. One approach to serving the outermost fringes of a radial network is to branch the lines. For example, a route may have a 15-min frequency on the trunk portion, a 30-min frequency on each of two branches, and an hourly frequency on each of four subbranches.

One way to cover more territory without reducing frequency is to add a loop. The basic trade-off to passengers is the increased frequency of service made possible by the loop as compared with the increased riding time. A rider living near the beginning of a loop has a longer ride inbound, and one living near the end of a loop has a longer ride outbound. If layover or recovery time is included in the schedule for the loop, the situation becomes even more undesirable in terms of passenger service. Therefore, if possible, all or most recovery time should be scheduled at the end of the line opposite from the loop, and lines with loops at both ends should be avoided. As a general rule, loops are more desirable with longer headways; branches, with shorter headways.

THROUGH ROUTING

Some bus systems bring all buses from all neighborhoods to downtown, loop them around, and send them back. This policy results in a lot of turning movements downtown, but each line can be operated as an individual entity. Combined routing or *through routing* can reduce mileage, turning movements, congestion, and transferring.

In order to through-route, it is necessary to balance the characteristics of the combined lines so that the frequency and hours of service needed on each are the same. Obviously, it is not feasible to through-route a line on a 10-min headway with one on a 15-min headway. It is possible (although not ideal) to through-route a line on a 30-min headway with another on a 15-min headway and have alternate buses turn back.

Another consideration in through routing is the relationship between headways and the lengths of the lines and running times. For example, consider a hypothetical single line that would take 62 min to run a round trip without recovery time, with passenger loadings justifying about a half-hour headway. Allowing for layover, it is not desirable to run two buses at 35- or 37-min headways, for reasons that will be outlined later. Running three buses at a 30-min headway would result in excessive and wasteful layover. One solution to the problem would be to through-route with another line that takes somewhat less than 1 h for a round trip so that four buses could maintain an even 30-min headway on the through-route combination.

DETAILED FACTORS IN BUS ROUTE PLANNING

The following sections are intended to serve as a checklist and brief description of details that should be considered when route planning.

GOALS AND OBJECTIVES

The goals and objectives, including service standards and level-of-service criteria, adopted by the transit agency should be the starting point for route planning. For example, what policy has been adopted with regard to the degree of effort that should be directed toward serving the needs of the transit-dependent population versus the degree of effort devoted to serving the needs of commuters, who are apt to be choice riders? An emphasis on the former will be more directed toward meeting the social needs of the community, whereas an emphasis on the latter would undoubtedly mean greater concern for goals such as energy conservation and reduction of congestion and air pollution.

DEMOGRAPHIC DATA

Maps of key demographic factors by census tract or other convenient subarea should be prepared for the transit service area as a basic reference in laying out the route network. Examples would include the percentage of population without cars, percentage of population over age 65, average income, and residence location of college students. These data give useful insight into the "home" end of home-based trips.

LAND USE

Major activity centers in the community should be mapped, including major shopping centers, major employers, schools and colleges, and hospitals and clinics. A convenient way to accomplish this is to indicate a precise location for each activity center, with the size of the symbol proportional to the number of person-trips generated per day. This precise mapping is far more useful in transit-route planning than a generalized level of activity by zones. Precise mapping is necessary because bus routes must travel within a short distance of the entrance to these activity centers if the bus system is to be used for access.

Close liaison must be maintained with local and regional planning agencies to ascertain land-use planning policies as they relate to the layout of future transit routes. Increasingly, planning agencies will be called on to pursue such policies as the clustering of activities that facilitate transit use.

Residential density must be carefully noted. The higher the density is, the more closely spaced and/or more frequent the level of transit service that can be supported. It is useful to arrange with local planning commissions to obtain copies of proposed subdivision plats in order to influence possible transit amenities and to learn in advance of areas where route extensions may be needed in the near future.

STREET STANDARDS AND SAFETY CONSIDERATIONS

If existing streets do not meet minimum standards of continuity, width, and load-carrying capacity, routing compromises will be required. The transit operating agency should have a role in the decision-making process regarding street layout and design when new areas are developed or older areas renovated.

Safety factors include the avoidance of potentially hazardous turns and the availability of traffic signals and stop-sign protection. For example, left-turn entries into busy arterials should be made only at intersections with traffic signals.

PEDESTRIAN ACCESS

A commonly used rule of thumb is that transit patrons should not be required to walk more than 0.25 mi (0.4 km) to reach the nearest bus stop. This would result in parallel routes being spaced about 0.5 mi apart. In low-density suburbs, this goal might have to be compromised if there is an insufficient density of housing to support a close network of lines.

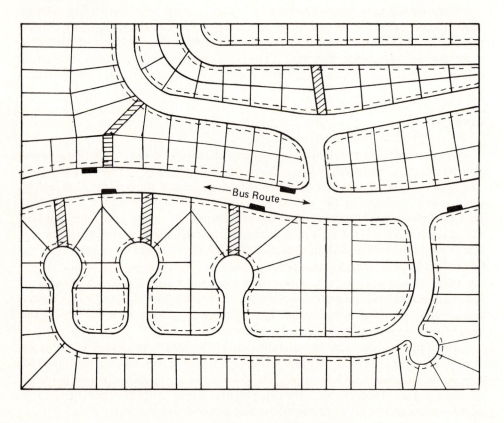

▬■▬	Bus Stops
⧄⧄⧄⧄	Walkway Needed
- - - - -	Sidewalks Needed

Figure 6-10 *Subdivision plan showing pedestrian access.*

Pedestrian access is becoming an increasingly important factor, particularly in newer subdivisions designed with curvilinear streets to discourage through traffic (Fig. 6-10). Increasingly, transit-route planners are faced with situations where routes might be within the standard 0.25 mi of each residence "as the crow flies." The shortest path from some houses to the nearest bus stop, however, might actually be much longer through the maze of streets that must be followed. The transit operating agency should be sure local planning agencies are constantly aware of the need for convenient and direct pedestrian access to the streets where bus routes are located.

FINANCING CONSTRAINTS

Route planning must be done not only under the constraint of the total budget, but also within the limits of alternative routings that would produce the greatest revenue per mile. In some cases, regional operators may also have formula restrictions regarding allocation of levels of service among various jurisdictions served. (See also Chap. 15.)

MARKETING STRATEGY

Included are considerations as to which market or neighborhood or line would be easiest to sell. Depending upon the circumstances in a particular community, it might be an important factor to concentrate initially on lines most likely to quickly succeed in terms of increased patronage in order to be able to point to success as a catalyst for future success.

TRAVEL PATTERNS

Overall travel patterns within the community, most of which are undoubtedly by auto, are important. However, methods of analyzing these patterns for purposes of designing street and highway networks, frequently using computer modeling as a tool, are not always helpful for bus route planning. Travel patterns are typically aggregated by analysis zones, which may be too large to help in the detailed planning necessary in laying out bus routes. The broad travel patterns should, of course, be analyzed and understood in determining general corridors and major travel flows, but they are only one factor. As for computer modeling of bus networks, one must first lay out a network or series of networks to be tested by the model in order to lay out a service network with some chance of success. In this process, the other factors listed take on prime importance.

Care should be taken in tinkering with long-established lines with entrenched transit ridership patterns. In the hope of gaining 100 passengers by rerouting a line, you could lose 500 already riding the existing service.

CONVENIENCE, SIMPLICITY, AND CLARITY

The various lines of a transit-route network cannot be analyzed independently. Each must be thought of in terms of how it relates to others in the network. Provision of safe, convenient, and pleasant locations for transfers is an especially important factor.

The objectives of simplicity and clarity to the user should not be overlooked in an effort to consider all the other factors. An intricate, sophisticated network that works on paper will be a failure if it attracts few riders because it is too complex for the public to understand.

SCHEDULING CONSIDERATIONS

Factors such as headways, running times, number of vehicles, loops, and short turns should be taken into consideration. If the route planner has an option of extending either of two routes into a new subdivision, scheduling considerations might be the deciding factor regarding which of the routes should be extended.

POLITICAL CONSIDERATIONS

The degree of public support for alternative proposals and the level of requests and petitions for alternative transit improvements must always be considered. Transit needs usually do not match up closely with city and county boundary lines. It is not unusual for a single transit line to pass through several political jurisdictions. Depending on financing arrangements and decision-making authority and procedures, reaching agreement among all the concerned parties may be time consuming and difficult.

SCHEDULING

POLICY HEADWAYS

The frequency of service on a given route is usually based either on *policy headway,* a formally adopted or unstated policy regarding the minimum level of service to be provided, or on the frequency of service necessary to handle the passenger loads, or on some combination of the two. Policy headway (typically every 60, 30, 20, or 15 min) is more apt to be used during nonpeak hours, and passenger loads are used during peak hours. Since there may be considerable unused midday capacity on lines operating policy headways, one could argue that costs could be cut by reducing service. During peak hours and on more heavily traveled lines, however, the frequency of service is more apt to be a function of passenger volume. Since additional drivers and buses are usually required to handle peak-hour loadings, the out-of-pocket costs of providing a higher level of partially used midday service are less than they would otherwise be.

It is desirable to have headways longer than 10 min to be evenly divisible into 60 (60, 30, 20, 15, 12, 10). Similar headways are necessary to facilitate transfer connections, with or without a full-scale timed transfer network. Departure times of any headway divisible into 60 repeat themselves each hour, and riders can more easily remember them. It is much easier for a telephone information clerk to tell a caller that a bus "leaves at 10 and 40 minutes past each hour" (30-min headway) than to have to say the bus "leaves at 9:10, 9:37, 10:04, 10:31, and 10:58" (27-min headway). Also, it is important to coordinate schedules with class starting and ending times at local colleges, and the like, which are usually on a 1-h cycle.

For headways shorter than 10 min, these factors are relatively unimportant, since riders no longer tend to rely on timetables and are more likely to arrive at bus stops randomly.

LAYOVER OR RECOVERY TIME

There are several reasons why layover time is scheduled at one or both ends of each line:

1. To give the driver a rest.
2. To maintain schedule reliability. Traffic conditions vary from day to day because of accidents, unusual congestion, and so on. For any number of other reasons, the running time from one end of the line to the other may be different from one day to the next. It is necessary to have a time cushion to allow the bus to leave on time on the next trip.
3. To maintain reasonable headways. It is better practice to run a bus every 30 min than every 27 min, even if it means the driver has 3 additional minutes of layover time each trip.

PEAK-TO-BASE RATIO

The peak-to-base ratio of a transit system is the ratio between the number of vehicles operated during the peak hour compared to the number scheduled during the midday or base period. Some systems with a high proportion of transit-dependent riders, who may use the system primarily for shopping or medical or social purposes, can accommodate passenger volumes without adding additional buses during the rush hour. The peak-to-base ratio in such a case would be 1 : 1 .

As a system becomes successful in capturing home-to-work trips, additional buses must be added to handle the higher peak-hour volumes. These buses are less productive since they operate fewer hours per day. Even more important, it becomes increasingly difficult, even with split shifts, to arrange a full day of productive work for all drivers. Many transit systems help fill part of the midday gap in demand for buses and drivers by scheduling service to schools (usually just after the morning commuter rush and just before the evening commuter rush), special midday shopper shuttles, and other services targeted to off-peak ridership markets.

STAGGERED WORK HOURS

One partial solution to the problem of equipment and driver utilization during peak travel hours is the encouragement of staggered work hours. To the degree that staggered work hours reduce traffic congestion and thereby increase speeds and schedule reliability, they, of course, benefit transit. For the staggered hours to have significant impact on equipment utilization, however, the spread between the first and last starting and ending work shifts must be great enough for *tripper* buses (buses used during peak hours only) to travel to the end of the line and return for second trips. As cities sprawl and bus lines get longer, this becomes increasingly difficult. More second trips can be produced by deadheading some buses back nonstop in the low-volume direction, or by short-turning alternate buses before the end of the line on high-frequency lines.

Surprisingly, staggered work hours even work to the detriment of transit in some circumstances. First, if the spread between work hours is great enough to allow a large number of second trips by tripper buses, then it becomes increasingly difficult to meet restrictions contained in most bus-driver labor contracts, which limit the spread between the start of the first piece of work and the end of the last piece of work of split shifts.

Second, in some isolated low-density suburbs, there may be only one or two bus loads of commuters destined for a given employment center. With standardized work hours, direct express bus service might be provided. With staggered work hours, either the bus schedules will not match work times, or extra half-empty buses would have to be operated to meet the additional shift-change times. (See also Chap. 12.)

FARE COLLECTION

FLAT FARES

Flat, or uniform, fares for the entire system have the advantages of simplicity, understandability, marketability, and ease of collection. The major disadvantages of flat fares are equity and forfeiture of potential revenues, particularly on longer trips. Fares differ by class of passenger: one of the requirements for U.S. transit systems to be eligible for federal subsidies is that they charge not more than half the regular fare to elderly and handicapped persons during nonpeak hours. Most systems also provide reduced rates for youth or school riders. Some systems charge higher fares during peak hours in recognition of the higher costs incurred in providing peak-hour service and as an incentive to those having the option to ride during nonpeak hours, thus tending to level demand.

Prior to 1970, 25 cents was a common flat fare. It had the advantage of being a single-coin fare that could also be paid by multiple coins. This factor became of increased importance when most transit systems, for security reasons, adopted an exact fare policy so drivers would no longer have to carry change. As inflation caused the 25-cent fare to be a thing of the past, tokens or tickets worth odd amounts, such as 35 cents or 65 cents, took on added importance for customer convenience, and additional transit system energies had to be devoted to providing convenient sales outlets for them. As single flat fares approached or exceeded a dollar, an added complication has been that fareboxes were not designed to accept paper money, and major changes in the design of fareboxes and methods of handling fare receipts were required. Many transit systems had to go to the considerable expense of replacing all their fareboxes, and handling, counting, and providing security for paper money has proved to be more expensive than dealing only with coins.

ZONE FARES

Newer rail systems, such as BART and the Washington, D.C., Metro, have established fare-collection hardware to make it possible to charge by the length of the ride, which is more equitable than a flat fare. Lacking, thus far, the necessary automated equipment, the closest that bus operators can come to charging according to the length of the ride is through use of a zone system, which is difficult to administer.

Traditionally, a zone system has consisted of one large central zone surrounded by several concentric outer zones. A basic fare (for example, 75 cents) is charged upon boarding, and additional zone charges (for example, 15 or 25 cents) are collected for each zone line crossed.

There are two basic methods of collecting the extra zone charges. The first relies on driver memory and works best in radial-type networks. It assumes that most inbound passengers have a destination in the central zone. Most passengers on boarding inbound pay the full fare, including zone charges to the central zone. Any passenger intending to get off before crossing one or more zone lines would so inform the driver, who would collect the lesser fare and then be expected to see that the passenger gets off within the proper zone.

Outbound, the basic fare is collected upon boarding in the central zone, and once the first zone line is crossed, zone surcharges are collected as passengers leave the bus. Passengers boarding in outer zones are issued receipts noting their boarding point so that they are not charged for zone lines not crossed. Obviously, this system is cumbersome to drivers and passengers alike and very confusing.

Outbound in outer zones it is not possible to use the rear door for exit, as all leaving passengers must file past the farebox to deposit their zone surcharges. This slows down operating speeds. Having to pay twice on the same trip (with multiple coins) is also very inconvenient to passengers.

The other method of collecting zone charges is for passengers to pay the full fare upon boarding, with the driver issuing a receipt for any zone fares paid. The bus is stopped at each zone crossing, and the driver then passes through the bus to collect zone receipts. This method is more workable in grid-type bus networks and eliminates the need for the driver to remember which inbound passengers promised to get off before crossing zone lines. The rear door may also be used for exit at all times. But the delays at zone crossings can be extensive.

Zone systems can be inequitable, too. Short trips crossing zone lines cost more than longer trips that may be entirely within one zone. Obviously, some technological breakthroughs are needed in bus fare-collection systems.

FARE-FREE ZONES

Several cities, including Pittsburgh (Pennsylvania), Seattle (Washington), and Portland (Oregon), have established fare-free zones within their central business districts. These zones were installed to facilitate circulation within the CBD and to reduce traffic congestion and have generally been considered successful. Operationally, they are made possible by paying on entering the bus inbound and paying on exiting outbound. Loading and unloading is expedited in the CBD, since both front and rear doors may be used to either enter or leave the bus. But time is lost on the outbound trip, since after leaving the CBD, only the front door may be used and fare transactions may be involved.

TRANSFERS

Most bus systems issue transfers to passengers so that they may continue their journeys when a single bus line does not serve both trip origin and destination. Usually, transfers are free, although some systems may charge a small amount for them. Traditionally, transfers have had both a time limit and complex rules regarding acceptance designed to reduce opportunities for riders to make a round trip on a single fare. Complex transfer acceptance rules tend to foster confrontations between drivers and passengers regarding their interpretation. Such rules are a legacy from the years when public transportation was a profit-making enterprise and cheating with transfers was considered a drain on revenues.

With increased emphasis on transit as a public service, assuming increased public benefits with increased usage, cheating with transfers has become less of an issue, and there is a trend toward liberalizing transfer rules. Another influence has undoubtedly been a desire to reduce the potential for unpleasant conflict between drivers and passengers over the interpretation of complex rules. In many systems, the use of transfers is now limited only by time, and passengers are permitted to make round trips if they can do so before the time limit expires.

FARE PREPAYMENT

In recent years, transit operators have given increased emphasis to fare prepayment plans, generally involving passes good for unlimited riding during a given period, usually a month. Daily, weekly, and annual passes are also used. Several systems offer a youth pass good for the summer school/vacation season. From a marketing standpoint, these passes encourage additional riding, eliminate the inconvenience of having to carry a pocketful of coins and the need for transfers, and emphasize the low monthly cost of transit riding compared with driving an automobile.

More systems, especially in tourist areas, are now offering day passes, good for one day of unlimited riding. Sometimes these are available only for weekend riding; in other systems they are valid 7 days a week. In some cases, day passes are available from the bus driver, in others they must be prepurchased at special limited locations. Vancouver, B.C., sells a particularly innovative day pass in the form of a "scratch-off" cardboard ticket. They are sold at all SkyTrain stations and at other retail locations. Users may purchase these tickets in advance, and the day of use need not be determined until the user scratches off the appropriate date on the ticket before the first use.

Such prepayment schemes also offer possibilities of payroll deduction and/or subsidization by employers who desire to encourage transit use and thereby reduce parking needs. To the transit operator, they offer benefits such as reduced money-handling expenses and slightly improved cash flow by providing payment in advance. Balanced against these advantages must be the costs of the pass-distribution system.

As transit systems strive to compete with the private automobile in whatever manner possible, the convenience of fare prepayment systems compared to having to deposit multiple coins in the farebox and having to worry about restrictive transfer rules takes on considerable importance.

SELF-SERVICE BARRIER-FREE FARE COLLECTION

Self-service fare collection systems have sometimes been called "honor" systems, but this is a misnomer, because such systems rely on spot-checks by inspectors and the levying of fines for attempted fare evasion. They have been used in both rail and bus applications in numerous European cities and, more recently, have been installed very successfully in several newer North American light rail systems (Edmonton and Calgary, Canada; Portland, Oregon; and Sacramento, San Jose, San Diego, and Los Angeles–Long Beach, California). (See Chap. 5).

One large-scale North American experiment applied self-service fare methods to an entire bus network. In 1982, the Tri-County Metropolitan Transportation District (Tri-Met) in the Portland, Oregon, area converted its entire bus network to self-service fare collection, with the financial assistance of an UMTA demonstration grant.[6, 7, 8] Numerous unexpected difficulties were encountered. There were some problems with the fare collection equipment on the buses, but the major problem was an unacceptably high fare-evasion rate. In 1984 the experiment was terminated and fare collection on buses reverted to the previous more traditional system. On the other hand, self-service fare collection methods were successfully introduced and continue to be used on the Portland light rail system.

It appears that on high-density transit routes, such as on the Portland light rail line, it is financially feasible to employ enough fare inspectors to keep the fare evasion rate to an acceptably low level. On a far-flung bus system, with many low-frequency, low-volume bus trips, it apparently is not feasible to do so.

Nevertheless, this experiment undoubtedly produced much useful information, and any bus operator contemplating innovations involving self-service fare collection techniques would be well advised to study the Portland experience carefully.

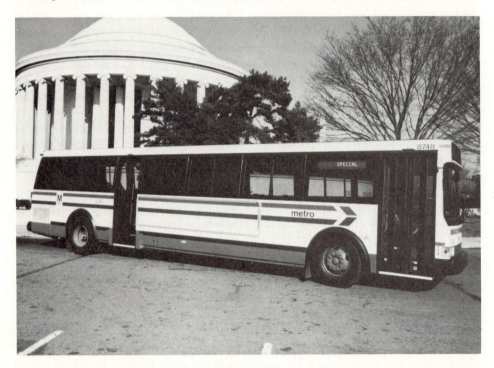

Figure 6-11 *WMATA Flxible bus at the Jefferson Memorial, Washington, D.C. (courtesy of Washington Metropolitan Area Transit Authority)*

SUMMARY

Conventional fixed-route bus systems are the most prevalent form of urban transit in the United States in terms of number of vehicles, number of passengers carried, and route-miles. Despite continued interest and research in other operational methods, such as dial-a-ride, and in improved rail technologies and rail service expansion, conventional bus routes play a major role in moving people in cities. Opportunities exist for improving service and efficiency in such systems. Buses may lack glamour compared with other transit modes, but they nevertheless deserve further development and improvement as a vital aspect of public transportation.

REFERENCES

Some citations are no longer available from their original source. These citations are often available from the National Technical Information Service, U.S. Department of Commerce, 5285 Port Royal Road, Springfield, VA 22161. We have verified the order numbers for many of these citations, and they are found at the end of the citation. Prices are available through NTIS at the address above.

1   AMERICAN PUBLIC TRANSIT ASSOCIATION, *Transit Passenger Vehicle Fleet Inventory as of January 1, 1989*, [cover] *1989 Transit Passenger Vehicle Fleet Inventory* (Washington, D.C.: American Public Transit Association, 1989).

2   Ibid.

3   VUKAN R. VUCHIC, *Urban Public Transportation Systems and Technology* (Englewood Cliffs, N.J.: Prentice-Hall, Inc., 1981), pp. 264-66.

4   V. R. VUCHIC AND R. M. STANGER, "Lindenwold Rail Line and Shirley Busway: A Comparison," in *Evaluation of Bus Transit Strategies*, Highway Research Record 459 (Washington, D.C.: Highway Research Board, 1973), pp. 13-28.

5   REX C. KLOPFENSTEIN, *Bus Communication Systems*, Synthesis of Transit Practice 8 (Washington, D.C.: Transportation Research Board, September 1986).

6   LAWRENCE DEIBEL AND OTHERS, *Self-Service Fare Collection, Volume I: Review and Summary*, prepared by The Mitre Corporation for UMTA, Report no. UMTA-VA-06-0049-79-2 (Washington, D.C.: Urban Mass Transportation Administration, August 1979). Now available as PB 80 132 251.

7   TRANSPORTATION SYSTEMS CENTER, *Bus Transit Fare Collection Equipment Overview*, Technology Sharing Program, Report no. DOT-TSC-UMTA-82-9 (Washington, D.C.: Urban Mass Transportation Administration, April 1982), pp. 19-26.

8   DANIEL W. WAGNER, WESLEY HARPER, AND OLIVER SCHUEFTAN, *Self-Service Fare Collection on Buses in Portland, Or.*, Final Report, prepared by Peat, Marwick, Mitchell & Co. for UMTA, Report no. UMTA-OR-06-0008-86-1 (Washington, D.C.: U.S. Department of Transportation, 1986 [June 1985]). Now available as through NTIS.

FURTHER READING

FIELDING, GORDON J., AND LEE HANSON, *Determinants of Superior Performance in Public Transit*, Final Report, prepared by the Institute of Transportation Studies and School of Social Science for UMTA, Report no. UMTA-CA-11-0029-1. Irvine, Calif.: University of California, August 1987.

INSTITUTE OF TRANSPORTATION ENGINEERS, *Transportation and Traffic Engineering Handbook* (2nd ed.), ed. Wolfgang S. Homburger. Englewood Cliffs, N.J.: Prentice-Hall, Inc., 1982.

LEVINSON, HERBERT S., CROSBY L. ADAMS, AND WILLIAM F. HOEY, *Bus Use of Highways: Planning and Design Guidelines*, NCHRP Report 155. Washington, D.C.: Transportation Research Board, 1975.

——, AND OTHERS, *Bus Use of Highways: State of the Art*, NCHRP Report 143. Washington, D.C.: Highway Research Board, 1973.

METROPOLITAN TRANSIT AUTHORITY OF HARRIS COUNTY (METRO), *Bus Service Evaluation Methods: A Review*, prepared for UMTA, Technology Sharing Program, Report no. DOT-I-84-49. Washington, D.C.: U.S. Department of Transportation, November 1984.

ROSENBLOOM, SANDRA, *Bus Transit Accessibility for the Handicapped in Urban Areas*, NCHRP Synthesis of Highway Practice 83. Washington, D.C.: Transportation Research Board, October 1981.

THOMPSON, GREGORY LEE, "Planning Considerations for Alternative Transit Route Structures," *Journal of the American Institute of Planners*, 43, no. 2 (April 1977), 158-68.

THURLOW, VIRGIL S., JOHN A. BACHMAN, AND C. DENVER LOVETT, *Bus Maintenance Facilities: A Transit Management Handbook*, prepared for UMTA by The Mitre Corporation. Washington, D.C.: U.S. Government Printing Office, November 1975. Now available as PB 250 475.

TRANSPORTATION RESEARCH BOARD, *Advances in Bus Service Planning Practices*, Transportation Research Record 1011. Washington, D.C.: Transportation Research Board, 1985.

——, *Bus Route and Schedule Planning Guidelines*, NCHRP Synthesis of Highway Practice 69. Washington, D.C.: Transportation Research Board, May 1980.

——, *Bus Transit Service Strategies*, Transportation Research Record 1051. Washington, D.C.: Transportation Research Board, 1986.

——, *Bus Transportation Strategies*, Transportation Research Record 606. Washington, D.C.: Transportation Research Board, 1977.

——, *Recent Advances in Bus Transit Operations Planning*, Transportation Research Record 994. Washington, D.C.: Transportation Research Board, 1984.

——, *Transit Bus Maintenance Management*, Transportation Research Record 1066. Washington, D.C.: Transportation Research Board, 1986.

U.S. DEPARTMENT OF TRANSPORTATION, *Priority Techniques for High Occupancy Vehicles: State-of-the-Art Overview*, Technology Sharing Program. Washington, D.C.: U.S. Government Printing Office, 1975.

VUCHIC, VUKAN R., *Timed Transfer System Planning, Design and Operation*, Final Report, prepared for UMTA University Research and Training Program, Report no. PA-11-0021. Philadelphia, Pa.: University of Pennsylvania, Department of Civil and Urban Engineering, October 1981.

PERIODICALS

The following periodicals are suggested for those interested in the bus mode. They offer both historical information and current activities.

Bus Ride. Friendship Publications, Inc., Box 1472, Spokane, WA 99210 (eight issues per year).

Bus World. Magazine of Buses and Bus Systems, P.O. Box 39, Woodland Hills, CA (quarterly).

Mass Transit. Mass Transit, P.O. Box 1478, Riverton, NJ 08077 (nine issues per year).

Passenger Transport. American Public Transit Association, 1201 New York Ave., N.W., Washington, DC 20005 (weekly).

EXERCISES

6-1   Name five different types of bus route networks. Describe the circumstances under which each type would be most successful; least successful.

6-2   Obtain systemwide bus route maps for three different urban transit systems. Analyze the type or types of networks used by each system. It is possible that different network types may be used by different portions of the same system.

6-3   Discuss the advantages and disadvantages of using branches versus loops in bus routes.

6-4   Name three reasons for including layover or recovery time in bus schedules.

6-5   Obtain public timetables for six different bus routes. Indicate examples of (a) policy headways, (b) headways based on ridership demand, and (c) possible examples of branching or short-turning. Discuss whether the timetable is relatively easy to understand and whether some routing or scheduling changes might make this portion of the system more convenient or user friendly. What would be the cost or other trade-offs in making such changes?

6-6   What are the advantages and disadvantages of a flat-fare system versus a zone-fare system?

6-7   Review your city's subdivision or lot-platting regulations. Make suggestions for revisions that would make the design of future neighborhoods more convenient for laying out bus routes and for pedestrians to gain access to bus stops.

6-8   Determine the location of bus maintenance bases serving your local transit system. Suppose that an increase in the size of the bus fleet of 50% will need to be accommodated within 5 years to serve projected ridership increases. Prepare an outline of the steps to be included in a technical study of whether it would be better to enlarge one or more existing maintenance bases or to establish one or more new ones and, if new ones, where?

6-9   You are at a public meeting representing your local transit system. During the question-and-answer session following your short talk, one person asks why your system does not purchase smaller, cheaper buses to run at midday, since he or she notices so many buses around town that are only half full. What is your reply to this question?

6-10   It has been determined to start a program of establishing park-and-ride lots to serve a fictitious bus-only transit system. Discuss the factors that should be considered in establishing the locations for these lots.

Chapter 7

PARATRANSIT AND RIDESHARING

DAVID W. JONES, JR., AND CLIFFORD A. CHAMBERS

Travel in privately owned vehicles accounts for the lion's share of trip making in metropolitan America—81.3% of all local trips.[1] Walking accounts for another 8.8% of local trip making, while public transportation accounts for only 2.9%. These are nationwide aggregate statistics, but they demonstrate that it is the automobile, van, and pickup truck that provide mass transportation for urban America.

Such data are a striking reminder that the United States is overwhelmingly dependent on the automobile for urban mobility. But examined more closely, the same travel data reveal how frequently Americans put private transportation to collective use through ridesharing. Passengers riding in cars, vans, and trucks account for almost 32% of the mileage traveled in metropolitan America.[2] In other words, the collective use of private vehicles provides Americans with a source of mass mobility that other nations have sought from public transportation.

"Going together" is an apt description of most ridesharing: informal and unorganized—a husband and wife driving together, teenagers on a date, friends going shopping together. In a motorized society, going together by car is not perceived as ridesharing, much less carpooling. But no matter how informal such arrangements may be, ridesharing makes an enormous contribution to urban mobility. This is shown in Table 7-1, which provides an aggregate, nationwide profile of metropolitan trip making.

While informal ridesharing has been with us since the earliest days of motoring, organized ridesharing is a more recent phenomenon. Carpooling was first promoted during World War II as a petroleum and rubber conservation measure and was promoted again during the energy crisis of the 1990s and 1980s. Carpooling has also been advanced as a strategy for reducing automotive pollution and managing traffic congestion.

TABLE 7-1
Aggregate Profile of Trip Making in Metropolitan America

Mode of Trip Making	Share of All Trips	Share of Home-to-Work Trips
By auto and van drivers	54.3%	74.5%
By auto and van passengers	27.0%	11.7%
By public transportation	2.9%	6.2%
By walking, motorcycle, bicycle, other means	15.8%	7.6%

Source: Adapted from Dieter Klinger and J. Richard Kuzmyak, *Personal Travel in the United States; Vol. I and II, Nationwide Personal Transportation Study*, prepared by COMSIS Corporation for FHWA (Washington, D.C.: U.S. Department of Transportation, August 1986).

Paratransit consists of public and semipublic transportation services that are more flexible and personalized than conventional fixed-route, fixed-schedule service. It utilizes low- and medium-capacity highway vehicles. Public paratransit is available to anyone who pays a predetermined fare (for example, taxis, jitneys, and dial-a-ride). Semipublic paratransit is available only to people of a certain group, such as the elderly, employees of a company, or residents of a neighborhood (as in, vanpools and subscription buses).

Some forms of paratransit and ridesharing have been advanced as a response to the special transportation needs of the elderly and handicapped. Still other forms have been introduced in suburban and rural communities where travel patterns are inimical to the efficient operation of conventional transit service. Recent efforts to organize and facilitate paratransit and ridesharing entail three distinguishable thrusts: (1) efforts to promote carpooling, vanpooling, and club-bus arrangements to serve commute trips; (2) efforts to field transitlike services with the routing and scheduling flexibility necessary to serve small towns and outlying suburbs; and (3) efforts to provide specialized transportation services for the elderly and handicapped. Table 7-2 profiles the three primary methods and markets of these types of transportation. It must be emphasized that each type has its own history, its own political constituency, and its own niche in the transportation marketplace.

What these services have in common is the use of freewheeling vehicles in combination with organizational effort to provide what might be called personalized transit services. The result is a family of services that lies intermediate between personal and mass transportation. We have coined the phrase "plural transportation" to describe these travel arrangements. By *plural transportation* we mean a diverse set of market-specialized transportation services and organized travel arrangements that make collective use of private transportation. We have coined this terminology and will use it in the pages that follow because prevailing nomenclature does not communicate the diversity of ways that freewheeling transportation can be organized for shared or collective use.

TABLE 7-2
Three Primary Types of Paratransit and Ridesharing

	Basic Service Concept	Typical Methods	Primary Market	Key Policy Objectives
On-demand transportation services	Service is provided on telephone request; vehicle tours are determined by trips to be served.	• Dial-a-ride • Shared-ride taxi • Route deviation bus service	General travel in small cities and low-density suburbs.	Basic transit services for transit dependent.
Commuter ridesharing	A third party recruits potential riders and matches them with prospective drivers or commercial providers.	• Organized carpooling • Vanpooling • Club or subscription bus service	Commute trips longer than 15 miles for carpools; over 25 miles for vanpools and buspools.	Congestion management. Improved air quality. Episodic energy conservation.
Client transportation for special need groups	Client transportation is arranged, sponsored, provided, or subsidized by a social service agency or public paratransit program.	• Volunteer drivers • Social service agency provides • Private operator provides	The elderly and handicapped.	Basic mobility for transportation disadvantaged.

Figure 7-1 begins to illuminate this diversity by showing common arrangements for commuting and for getting to the doctor's. As the figure illustrates, plural transportation is a diverse set of travel arrangements that enable urban residents to ride together in pairs, threes, groups, or series. As it also shows, plural transportation is *organized* transportation that lies intermediate between personal use of the private car and mass public transportation. This is its significance: Efficiently organized plural transportation can retain much of the flexibility of personal transportation, while offering most of the price advantage of mass transportation.

THE CHARACTERISTICS OF PLURAL TRANSPORTATION

Organization is the hallmark of plural transportation. By organization we mean some arrangement for aggregating demand, sharing costs, and then providing transportation. Such arrangements can range from simple understandings between friends to elaborate arrangements that involve multiple parties and complex financial agreements. Five examples will illustrate the range of possible arrangements.[3]

- John X asks friend and co-worker Frank Y if he would like to share a ride to work. Frank agrees to pay for gas, and John drives.
- The XYZ Corporation administers an aggressive ridesharing program designed to allay community concern about traffic congestion near the suburban office park where the company is headquartered. Employees who carpool are guaranteed close-in parking and reserved spaces. A registry of carpools is maintained with cross-filing by employee home zip codes. The carpool registry

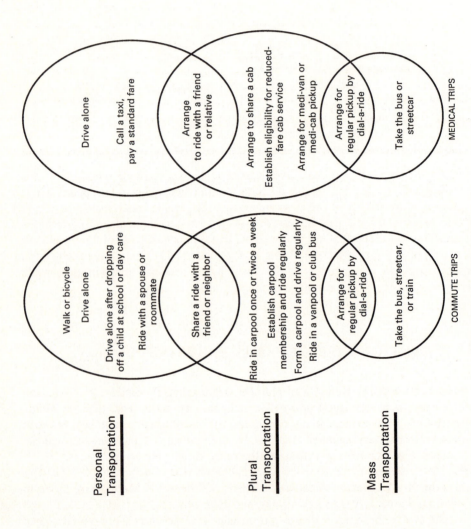

Personal Transportation

Walk or bicycle

Drive alone

Drive alone after dropping off a child at school or day care

Ride with a spouse or roommate

Share a ride with a friend or neighbor

Plural Transportation

Ride in carpool once or twice a week

Establish carpool membership and ride regularly

Form a carpool and drive regularly

Ride in a vanpool or club bus

Arrange for regular pickup by dial-a-ride

Mass Transportation

Take the bus, streetcar, or train

COMMUTE TRIPS

Drive alone

Call a taxi, pay a standard fare

Arrange to ride with a friend or relative

Arrange to share a cab

Establish eligibility for reduced-fare cab service

Arrange for medi-van or medi-cab pickup

Arrange for regular pickup by dial-a-ride

Take the bus or streetcar

MEDICAL TRIPS

Figure 7-1 *Common travel arrangements.*

allows the company's commute coordinator to keep track of empty seats in some 200 carpools. New employees are urged to join established carpools when they sign on with the company.[4]

- Regional Rideshare operates a vanpooling program that screens and qualifies van drivers, recruits vanpool riders, and brokers lease agreements for 12 to 15 passenger vans. It recruits riders through direct advertising and a workplace outreach program. Potential riders are paired together on computer match lists, with personalized attention to geographic clusters large enough to form a vanpool. After a driver is recruited and a van is placed in service, it continues to recruit riders to fill empty seats. Regional Rideshare is a nonprofit organization; its operations are financed by a highway department.[5]

- The city of New Z manages a program that enables senior citizens to obtain taxi service at below-market rates. The program is built around a state subsidy for paratransit and a formal agreement with the city's taxicab operators. Taxi operators have agreed to accept redeemable script from senior citizens in lieu of cash payment. Seniors purchase the script from the city at 50% of its face value. It is redeemed at full value, with state funds used to make up the difference. At the outset of the program, taxi operators agreed to roll back fares because additional ridership by seniors allows the companies to do a brisk business during otherwise slack periods of the day.[6]

- The state highway department has built an additional freeway lane in a congested urban corridor. This high-occupancy vehicle (HOV) lane is reserved for exclusive use by buses, carpools, and vanpools. The HOV lane enables buses and carpools to bypass congestion and provides an incentive for ridesharing. The installation of park-and-ride facilities in the same corridor provides a convenient place for carpool riders and drivers to meet. Additional use of the HOV lane is encouraged by means of an aggressive ride-matching program that provides transit information and carpool matching assistance to commuters at their place of work. The ride-matching program is sponsored by a consortium of private employers and public agencies called a transportation management association (TMA). The board of directors of the TMA includes representatives of local business, local government, the transit agency, and the state highway department.[7]

As these examples suggest, the essential characteristic of plural transportation is some arrangement for aggregating demand so as to exploit the economies of scale latent in the joint use of freewheeling transportation. The most common form of joint use is ridesharing—multiple riders using the same vehicle at the same time. But joint use can also be accomplished by organizing and scheduling trips in productive series. As the taxicab example suggests, *serial* use can produce economies similar to those realized through *shared* use. Dial-a-ride systems, it should be noted, embody both forms of joint use—shared and serial.

THE RECENT HISTORY OF PLURAL TRANSPORTATION

The recent history of plural transportation evidences two countervailing dynamics. The first of these dynamics is social and demographic: on a percentage basis, fewer Americans are ridesharing this generation than last.[8] The second dynamic is policy driven—the effort of governmental agencies to promote ridesharing and provide special transportation services. These are countervailing dynamics, but the first is far more powerful than the second. Governmental efforts to encourage carpooling and other forms of plural transportation have been nowhere near sufficient to offset social and demographic trends that are eroding the contribution that informal ridesharing once made to urban mobility. In other words, the effort to promote and institutionalize ridesharing and paratransit is losing ground due to the changing travel patterns and demography of metropolitan America. In this sense, plural transportation is much like public transportation: its market share is declining in the face of social and geographic changes that have reduced the percentage of trips for which any form of collective transportation offers a compelling alternative.

Table 7-3, based on nationwide aggregate data, shows three ways of quantifying plural transportation's shrinking presence in the transportation marketplace. As it shows, average vehicle occupancy is declining, as are the share of trips and VMT logged as riders rather than drivers.

TABLE 7-3
Aggregate Trend of Metropolitan Travel

Year	Work-Trip Vehicle Occupancy (persons per vehicle)	Share of Work Trips by Riders Not Drivers	Share of Work-Related VMT by Multi-Occupancy Vehicles
1969	1.4	—	—
1977	1.3	17.3%	21.2%
1983	1.2	11.7%	19.2%

Source: Adapted from Dieter Klinger and J. Richard Kuzmyak, *Personal Travel in the United States; Vol. I and II, Nationwide Personal Transportation Study*, prepared by COMSIS Corporation for FHWA (Washington, D.C.: U.S. Department of Transportation, August 1986).

The principal dynamics underlying these trends are geographic and demographic:

- Differential growth rates that have diminished the share of the nation's population that lives in the older and denser cities of the Northeast.[9]
- The rapid growth of sunbelt employment and sunbelt cities with auto-oriented travel and settlement patterns.
- The rapid growth of suburban population and employment, and the increasing prevalence of intra- and intersuburban commuting.[10]
- The increasing prevalence of intrasuburban commutes that end at a workplace that provides free parking.

- Sharp increases in the rate of women's labor force participation, and corresponding increases in the proportion of two-income, two-car households.[11]
- The coming of age of a generation of senior citizens that is accustomed to driving and expects to do so well into retirement.[12]

Table 7-4 profiles some of the outcomes associated with these trends. As the table suggests, changes in the geography and demography of employment have had significant impacts in the aggregate—on auto ownership, on urban population density, and on the share of trips for which plural and public transportation offers a compelling alternative.

TABLE 7-4
Evidence of America's Increasing Reliance on the Automobile and Individual Transportation

Year	Suburban Share of the Nation's Metropolitan Population	Average Number of Vehicles per Household	Average Vehicle Occupancy for Trips to Work
1950	42%	—	—
1969	54%	1.2	1.4
1977	—	1.6	1.3
1983	58%	1.7	1.2

Source: Adapted from Dieter Klinger and J. Richard Kuzmyak, *Personal Travel in the United States; Vol. I and II, Nationwide Personal Transportation Study*, prepared by COMSIS Corporation for FHWA (Washington, D.C.: U.S. Department of Transportation, August 1986) and U.S. Department of Commerce, U.S. Bureau of the Census, *State and Metropolitan Area Book* (Washington, D.C.: U.S. Government Printing Office, 1989).

The secular erosion of plural transportation would not matter much if policy makers were not relying on it to achieve congestion relief, pollution control, and the mobility of the elderly and the handicapped. But policy makers are relying on the *expansion* of plural transportation, while metropolitan development trends are *diminishing* its presence in the transportation marketplace.[13] In other words, these are trends with significant policy implications. They explain why the nation has made no progress in diminishing its dependence on imported oil; why improvements in metropolitan air quality have proved so hard to achieve; why suburban congestion has become, almost overnight, a salient political concern; and why both plural and mass transportation systems have continued to surrender market share despite government subsidy and promotion. These trends provide the backdrop against which to understand and evaluate governmental efforts to promote ridesharing and other forms of plural transportation.

GOVERNMENTAL EFFORTS TO PROMOTE PLURAL TRANSPORTATION

Although *informal* ridesharing arrangements have been eroded by social and geographic change, *formal* and *organized* ridesharing has been encouraged by governmental promotion. Government funding and regulation have both played an important role in the development of commuter ridesharing programs, demand-responsive transit service, and paratransit services for the elderly and handicapped. Federal funding played an important role in the initial development and diffusion of these services; state and local funding and local regulations have made the difference between programs that are vigorous and programs that are not.

The development of dial-a-ride and other forms of demand-responsive transit service is most advanced in Michigan and California, where state funding is earmarked for such services.[14] Paratransit development is also well advanced in California counties that have reserved sales tax funds for creating user-side subsidy programs and modifying taxi ordinances to enable shared-ride operation.[15]

The creation of regional ridesharing agencies was financed by the federal government, and federal funds play an important role in sustaining these operations. But ridesharing promotion efforts are most vigorous in communities where local governments have used their regulatory powers to engage employers in ride matching. In turn, regional air quality districts have required employers to meet more strenuous standards designed to reduce automotive pollution.

As these examples suggest, the institutionalization of plural transportation is reasonably well advanced. Service concepts developed in the 1960s and demonstrated in the 1970s have taken local root in the 1980s.[16] The organization, regulation, and funding necessary to support and sustain ridesharing and paratransit services remain fragile and limited, but permanent institutional commitments have been made.

With permanent commitments has come a burden of social expectations, as relatively small programs were asked to achieve large social purposes. Dial-a-ride systems were touted as an opportunity for transit to capture urban market shares in suburban communities.[17] Ridesharing programs were advertised for their contribution to energy conservation and air quality.[18] Paratransit was asked to compensate for the mobility disadvantage of the carless elderly and handicapped. And, most recently, commuter ridesharing has been advanced as a cornerstone of suburban plans for congestion management.[19] In the pages that follow, we will examine how well plural transportation has acquitted itself in the face of these lofty policy expectations.

COMMUTER RIDESHARING AND CONGESTION MANAGEMENT

The events of the 1960s and 1970s produced a profound change in the premises with which urban planners approached metropolitan transportation. This change was shaped by the conflict and controversy over the urban routes of the Interstate Highway

System, the energy crisis, the growth of environmentalism, increasing awareness of the health effects of air pollution, and growing awareness of the costs of sprawl. Transportation planners emerged from the 1960s and 1970s doubting the efficacy of plans premised on the unconstrained growth of automobile traffic and the endless attenuation of metropolitan boundaries. As an alternative, they proposed a planning strategy with two complementary elements: *urban containment* and *traffic management*.[20] This new metropolitan strategy was designed to constrain the sprawling growth of outlying suburbs and to provide incentive for commuters to use collective transportation.

This new strategy has been widely endorsed but only partially implemented. Traffic management has been widely accepted as the appropriate strategy of transportation planning, but metropolitan planners have had virtually no success in obtaining decisive commitments to constrain and redirect suburban growth. In other words, a policy commitment has been made to traffic management, but not to urban containment.

The policy commitment to traffic management is the context in which commuter ridesharing and other strategies to increase vehicle occupancy have been vested with significant social expectations.[21] In turn, the 1970s and 1980s witnessed increasing linkage between ridesharing programs and congestion management. As a result, ridesharing agencies that were first established as a response to the 1973 oil embargo and the energy crisis were reemployed as agents of congestion management.

The linkage between ridesharing and congestion management created a flurry of organizational effort to engage employers in ride brokering, to create multicity ridesharing programs, and to coordinate ridesharing campaigns with the development of HOV lanes and park-and-ride facilities. Thus, the 1980s saw the creation of the organizational infrastructure necessary to harness ridesharing as a strategy of congestion management. These institutional arrangements are shown in Fig. 7-2. As the figure shows, mandatory legal requirements that oblige employers and developers to participate in ride-brokering programs were a prominent feature of many plans developed in the 1980s and early 1990s. In the pages that follow, we will reprise the most important developments in commuter ridesharing.

EMPLOYER-BASED RIDE BROKERING

Work-site ridesharing campaigns have a long history, but the creation of *permanent* employer-based ridesharing programs is a comparatively new phenomenon. Historically, employers have avoided commitments that would burden companies with the responsibility for employee transportation. The exception was wartime emergencies when commerce and industry played an active role in carpooling campaigns. But the developments of the 1970s and 1980s have engaged employers in ridesharing on a permanent basis. Initial engagement occurred with the energy crisis and has become virtually permanent for employers located in metropolitan areas where air quality and suburban congestion are a continuing problem.

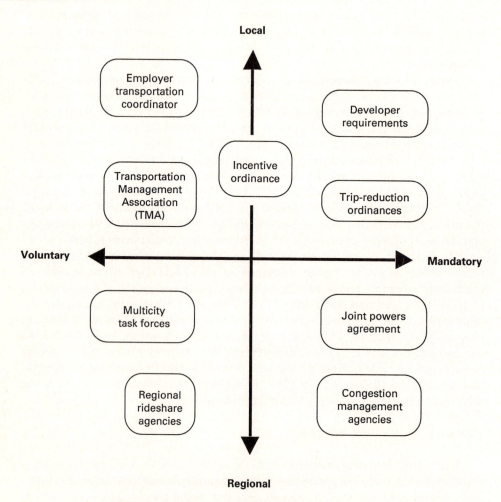

Figure 7-2 *Institutional response to congestion management.*

The permanent involvement of employers in ride brokering is an important development for obvious reasons. Fellow employees share a common destination and are thus "presorted" prospects for ridesharing. The communication channels of the workplace provide an opportunity to recruit ridesharing candidates. New employees are prime candidates for ridesharing. Data routinely collected by personnel departments provide the information base necessary to plan and target ridesharing programs. Corporate staffing of ridesharing programs increases the effectiveness of regional ridesharing agencies. As important, company staffing—even part-time staffing—provides the personnel necessary to provide personalized ridesharing assistance. And the coordination of ridesharing programs with changes in parking policy can provide a proven incentive for carpool formation.

The involvement of many companies in ridesharing has been reluctant—an ambivalent commitment prodded by governmental request or regulation. But some companies have actively embraced ridesharing as an expression of a high-profile corporation's commitment to good citizenship and community service. For example, the 3M Company in Minneapolis, Minnesota, launched the nation's first vanpool program in 1973. The program was motivated by conventional business logic: vanpooling offered a way for the company to expand its headquarters staff without devoting precious land to additional parking space. The program was a phenomenal success, and 3M built good will by assisting other corporations in developing their own vanpooling programs. Indeed, a list of the corporations most active in ridesharing reads like the Dow Jones Industrials—ARCO, ATT, Conoco, Hewlett-Packard, Lockheed, the Travelers, and State Farm, to name a few.

The cornerstone of employer-based ridesharing efforts is transportation brokerage—a concept borrowed from the trucking industry. A workplace broker or transportation coordinator finds the best commute alternative for individual employees—supplying the managerial effort needed to organize carpools or vanpools, arrange charter bus service, procure shuttle bus services, or sell transit passes. Employer-based transportation brokerage has historically been market oriented, matching employee needs with a full mix of commute options. It should be noted that most brokerage efforts have been small scale, with time commitment ranging from a few hours a week to a full-time position for the largest firms. In a recent study of 252 Los Angeles firms, it was found that the average firm spent 0.31 h and $5.07 per employee per year on employee ridesharing programs.[22]

Even part-time staffing permits the personalization of ridesharing programs. The key to the personalized approach is the one-to-one interaction between a trained transportation coordinator and a prospective ridesharer. Instead of relying solely on an impersonal lobby locator list or a computer printout, the employer coordinator makes the introductions necessary for ridesharing candidates to feel comfortable about joining a carpool or vanpool, or at least committing to trial membership. The theory of personalized assistance was bolstered by a major survey of carpooling behavior conducted by Margolin and Misch.[23] These researchers found that 85% of the commuters they surveyed insisted on meeting the other members of a carpool before making a commitment to join. Employer-based programs provide a ready framework for personal introductions. Indeed, personalized placement is the defining characteristic of the most successful ride-brokering programs.

How successful have such programs been? Evidence from recent studies indicates that companies that make a sustained, full-time commitment to transportation brokerage are able to achieve significant results. Table 7-5 shows the performance of leading employer-based programs. Reported trip reductions range from 5.5% to 48%. The common feature of these exemplary programs is the provision of a wide range of commute alternatives, including carpooling, vanpooling, and improved transit service.[24]

TABLE 7-5
Results from 11 of the Nation's Leading Brokerage Programs

Location	Company	Travel Base	Vehicle[a] Trip Rate	Percent Reduction
Hartford, CT	Travelers	10,000	42.8	25.4%
Hartford, CT	Hartford Steam Boiler	1100	49.6	13.6%
St. Paul, MN	3M Company	12,000	82.7	9.7%
Bellevue, WA	US WEST	1150	45.2	47.6%
Bellevue, WA	CH$_2$M Hill	400	59.4	31.2%
Bishop Ranch, San Ramon, CA	Pacific Bell	6900	72.8	27.8%
Hacienda Business Park, Pleasanton, CA	AT&T	3890	80.5	13.4%
Los Angeles, CA	UCLA	18,000	79.0	5.5%
Los Angeles, CA	ARCO	2000	55.3	19.1%
Orange County, CA	State Farm	980	64.3	30.4%
Montgomery County, MD	Nuclear Regulatory Commission	1400	53.7	41.6%

[a]The vehicle trip generation rate, expressed as the number of vehicle trips/100 travelers. The rate assumes 2.5 persons/carpool, 12 persons/vanpool, and 30 persons/transit trip.
    Source: Adapted from J. Richard Kuzmyak and Eric N. Schreffler, *Evaluation of Travel Demand Management (TDM) Measures to Relieve Congestion*, prepared by COMSIS Corporation in association with Harold Katz & Associates (Washington, D.C.: Federal Highway Administration, 1990), p. 26.

A study of Los Angeles programs points to the importance of full-service transportation brokerage. The average mode split for a firm with 1000 employees and no personalized matching assistance was approximately 89% drive alone, 8% ridesharing, and 2% public transit use. The average mode split for a firm with 1000 employees that provides a typical level of personalized matching assistance was 78% drive alone, 19% ridesharing, and 2% public transit use.[25]

Can these results be sustained over time? A 10-year evaluation of San Francisco-based programs found that only a handful of the region's largest employers and developers have made the long-term commitment necessary to institutionalize and sustain full-service brokerage. Scores of other companies have started programs and achieved initial success, only to see performance wane as commitment lapsed.[26]

MULTIEMPLOYER RIDE BROKERING

If permanent employer programs were the most important ridesharing innovation of the 1980s, multiemployer programs promise to be the most important organizational innovation of the 1990s. Multiemployer programs can take many forms, ranging from adjacent companies sharing an employee transportation coordinator, to formal arrangements called transportation management associations (TMA). A TMA is an organization through which employers, developers, and local government can cooperate in providing brokerage and marketing services jointly or cooperatively. There was significant growth in the number of TMAs during the late 1980s. In 1987, there were approximately 20 TMAs nationwide. But by 1989 there were 55 established and emerging TMAs and that number is expected to increase rapidly in the future.[27] In California alone, the state Department of Transportation has awarded some $2.2 million in seed grant funds to 44 emerging TMAs.

The motivation for starting a TMA can vary widely. In some cases, the catalyst has been a business concern that congestion will lead to stifling limits on future growth. In other cases, the need for a TMA has sprung from a local trip-reduction ordinance or air quality ruling.

A TMA typically provides at least some of the following services:[28]

- *Information on commute options* including buses, vanpools, and carpools.
- *Ridesharing assistance* tailored to localized needs.
- *Promotional materials* designed to promote the benefits of commute alternatives.
- *Procurement of services*, including club buses, shuttles, or emergency rides home.
- *Advocacy planning*, including efforts to implement improved transit services or municipal bikeways.
- *Management consulting* on alternative work-hour programs, telecommuting, and parking pricing policies.

The genesis of a TMA is normally attributed to a prime advocate, who mobilizes support for cooperative effort—often a "public-private partnership." For example, the Bishop Ranch Transportation Association, one of the most successful TMAs in the San Francisco Bay area, was formed at the instigation of a major developer, who saw ridesharing and a shuttle service as a way to alleviate environmental concerns and to enhance the marketability of a 20,000-employee office-park development project.[29]

Many TMAs are satellites of an existing organization, such as a chamber of commerce or industrial association, and share staff with the parent organization. For example, the Century City TMA in Los Angeles is part of the chamber of commerce and operates on a fee-for-service basis. The service area for a TMA is typically a few square miles. An example of a citywide TMA is the Joint Institutional Transportation Brokers Association in San Francisco, which includes all the city's major hospitals and universities.

The formation of TMAs to implement multiemployer ride brokering is a fairly recent phenomenon, and there has been no opportunity to evaluate their long-term effectiveness. The best available evidence indicates that a well-run TMA can have a significant impact on ridesharing rates. In Bellevue, Washington, carpool and vanpool participation rates for the area served by an effective TMA are 19% compared to control site rates of 12%.[30] At the Hacienda Business Park in Pleasanton, California, ridesharing rates are 18% compared to 12% in Pleasanton at large.[31] And, at Bishop Ranch in nearby San Ramon, the ridesharing rate is 28% compared to an ambient rate of 24%.[32] Such results indicate the promise of multiemployer programs, but it should also be noted that these results are from leading TMAs, not necessarily typical ones.

LOCAL GOVERNMENT REGULATION

An increasing number of sunbelt cities and counties are using their regulatory powers to mandate employer and developer involvement in ridesharing and other traffic mitigation efforts. Mandatory programs are gradually displacing voluntary ones as localities seek antidotes to employer and developer commitments that are halfhearted or short-lived. The trend is toward binding contractual requirements for developers and mandatory employer programs based on explicit performance requirements.

Conditions on Development Approvals

Since new development generates traffic, local governments can place conditions on developer permit approvals to mitigate traffic as long as the requirements are reasonably necessary to the protection of the public health, safety, and general welfare. Although most conditions on development approvals relate to supply-side improvements, such as improved signalization or additional access road capacity, many local jurisdictions negotiate traffic mitigation requirements with development sponsors. Probably the most extensive set of mitigation requirements are in the city of San Francisco, where approvals of all major mixed-use commercial development projects over the past decade have included transportation brokerage as a condition on development approval.[33] Requirements include sale of public transit tickets, distribution of ridesharing information, provision of priority parking for carpool vehicles, establishing parking rates that encourage ridesharing, and conducting surveys to monitor program performance.

Incentive Ordinances

A growing number of municipalities have adopted ordinances to create a legal obligation for employers and developers to alleviate local traffic. Two different types of ordinances have emerged: (1) incentive ordinances and (2) trip-reduction ordinances.

Incentive ordinances typically offer developers reduced on-site parking requirements. In return, the developer agrees to implement specified traffic mitigation measures. Some jurisdictions such as Sacramento, California, have established a schedule of permitted parking reductions based on specific actions. Ridesharing programs enable developers to reduce parking allowances 10 to 20%.[34] Other cities negotiate agreements on a case by case basis. In Orlando Florida, under a 1982 ordinance, a developer could avoid the construction of up to 20% of required parking in exchange for contributions to a transportation management trust fund.[35]

To date, there has been little diffusion of incentive ordinances. Developers have been reluctant to provide less than "adequate" parking and are fearful that lenders would balk at financing such projects.

Trip-Reduction Ordinances

The most common type of ridesharing ordinance is a trip-reduction ordinance. The first such ordinance was adopted in Placer County, California, in 1981. But it was a 1984 ordinance adopted in Pleasanton, California, that has been most imitated. Developers and the city of Pleasanton worked together to design an ordinance to reduce drive-alone commuting during peak hours.[36] The ordinance embodies two standards: a required level of peak-hour trip reduction and an operating standard for the community's arterial street system. The basic standard is a 55% limit on the percentage of the work force that drives to and from work alone in the peak hour. Compliance requires employers and developers to either stagger work hours or induce their employees to share a ride. Most companies employ both approaches.

Following Pleasanton's example, most trip-reduction ordinances apply to both new and existing development. Ordinance goals are typically expressed as a performance standard: a participation rate for ridesharing, a target vehicle-occupancy rate for the peak period, or a level-of-service standard for local intersections. Some ordinances require implementation of specific TSM measures, but most leave the specifics of implementation to employers or developers. When specific actions are required, less stringent requirements are typically placed on smaller employers than larger ones. No known ordinance requires attainment of trip-reduction goals; rather, evidence of good faith effort is normally sufficient. Most ordinances assign oversight authority to either an advisory committee or task force.[37]

The adoption of multicity trip-reduction ordinances seems to be the likely next stage in the regulation of generated traffic. Five California cities—Belmont, Foster City, Redwood City, San Carlos, and San Mateo—have adopted the same trip-reduction ordinance.[38] Unique features of this subregional ordinance include (1) uniform requirements on all employers in the five-city area, (2) a per-employee fee designed to finance program implementation, and (3) multicity administration by a TSM coordinator. Similar subregional approaches are being considered in two other California counties, Marin and Santa Clara.

Corridor Planning for Buses, Carpools, and Congestion Management

Since the 1970s, state highway departments have made increasing efforts to incorporate special facilities for buses and carpools in their plans for highway development. Measures that have been implemented include reserved lanes for buses and carpools (high-occupancy vehicle lanes); ramp metering with preferential entry (the reconstruction of freeway ramps to enable buses and carpools to bypass the queue at metered ramps); park-and-ride facilities; and the incorporation of transit transfer centers and park-and-ride facilities within the geometric envelope of freeway projects. The objective, of course, is to transform freeways into multimodal transportation facilities with increased peak-hour people-carrying capacity. These efforts have been stimulated by changes in federal funding arrangements that have made auxiliary facilities eligible for federal reimbursement. Further stimulus has come from a new federal program that allows state highway departments to use federal highway funds for transit operations and ridesharing programs *during highway reconstruction.*

Many observers believe that this program could represent a first step toward active state and federal involvement in *ongoing* traffic management programs that provide long-term funding for bus-on-freeway rapid transit and corridor-scale ride-brokering campaigns. Table 7-6 outlines the elements of a comprehensive congestion management program—an idealized program that could be implemented if funding were more flexibly available for ongoing traffic management programs and localities were actively engaged in the process of corridor planning.

As the table shows, a large number of organizational innovations would be necessary to implement a comprehensive congestion management program. And, to date, most metropolitan areas lack the organizational infrastructure—the consensus, financing, and institutional arrangements—to implement comprehensive traffic management programs. Thus, no corridor planning effort has embodied the thorough integration of infrastructure design, transit operation, ridesharing, and land-use controls that are outlined in the table.[39] Existing plans typically emphasize the facilities element of a comprehensive program, leaving integration and the implementation of complementary elements to chance.

HOV Lanes and Ramp Metering

HOV lanes and ramp metering are the most commonly implemented elements of present plans. HOV lanes enhance freeway operation by (1) adding capacity and (2) enabling buses and carpools to bypass congestion.[40] In turn, time savings realized by buses and carpools provide an incentive for transit use and carpool formation. Ramp

TABLE 7-6
Elements of a Comprehensive Traffic Management
Program for a Congested Urban Corridor

Element	Innovation Required
Infrastructure	
• HOV lane.	• None
• Integration of transit stations in freeway design.	• State funding for transit stations and transfer centers.
• Integration of park-and-ride facilities in interchange design.	• Dedicated funding for park-and-ride facilities within the state highway program.
• Reconstruction of ramps to increase storage capacity.	• None
Highway operations	
• Ramp metering with priority entry for buses and carpools.	• None
• Geometric metering to keep mainline and ramp inputs in equitable balance.	• Modification of planning and design guidelines to recognize the constructive role that bottlenecks can play in the operation of the highway system.
Transit operations	
• Expansion of bus operations to provide bus-on-freeway rapid transit.	• State financing for transit operations with participation based on a share of direct operating expenses.
• Operation of shuttle-service connections to major employment centers.	• Coordination of mainline services with community-level transit, paratransit, and shuttle services.
Land use	
• Adoption by localities of a common or universal mitigation ordinance establishing limits on work-site traffic generation.	• Joint agreement by multiple local governments, including joint limits on work-site parking.
• Agreement by localities on a multijurisdictional growth budget that establishes ceiling allowances for commercial and industrial development.	• Joint agreement on growth limits and allowances.
Ridesharing	
• Creation of a TMA with a corridor-scale scope of operation.	• Tripartite state, local, and private financing for TMA operations.

metering enhances freeway operation by (1) giving mainline movement priority over merging vehicles, (2) breaking up platoons of merging traffic, and (3) limiting the density of freeway traffic so as to sustain stable flow. The appropriateness of ramp metering or HOV lanes is situational. Ramp metering is unlikely to be appropriate where ramps are cramped and provide limited storage capacity. HOV lanes are unlikely to be appropriate where initial vehicle occupancy is low and short trips are prevalent. In other words, the effectiveness of ramp metering is contingent on the availability of ramp capacity; the effectiveness of HOV lanes is contingent on significant time savings for HOVs and relatively high levels of ridesharing and transit use prior to implementation.[41]

Table 7-7 shows the productivity of HOV lanes implemented during the 1970s and 1980s. As the table indicates, the productivity of HOV lanes is highly variable. At the high end of the range is the Shirley Highway HOV lane, which serves 7100 passengers per hour, including 5530 bus passengers. At the low end of the range are a number of facilities that serve passenger volumes only marginally greater than a freeway lane that is used for mixed traffic. HOV lanes with high levels of productivity share a common

TABLE 7-7
Productivity of Transitways and HOV Lanes in the United States and Canada
(a.m. peak-hour vehicles and passenger volumes)

Facilities	Buses	Bus Passengers	Van/Carpool Vehicles	Van/Carpool Passengers
HOV lanes sharing freeway ROW				
Exclusive facilities				
1. Houston, Texas				
I-10 (Katy)	35	1235	115	620
I-45 (North)	70	2490	180	1470
2. Los Angeles, I-10 (El Monte)	75	3450	905	2860
3. Washington, D.C.				
I-395 (Shirley)	150	5320	1890	8880
I-66	70	2450	2365	8810
Concurrent flow				
1. Honolulu, Moanalua Fwy.	—	—	—	—
2. Los Angeles, Rte. 91	NA	NA	NA	NA
3. Miami, I-95	9	350	1300	2460
4. Orange County, Calif., Rte. 55	2	50	1100	2310
5. Orlando, Fla., I-4 North/South	—	—	—	—
6. San Francisco, Calif.				
S.F.-Oakland Bay Bridge	200	6320	3000	10,850
U.S. 101	70	2590	360	1100
7. Seattle, Wash.				
I-5	55	2160	404	1130
SR 520	55	2300	255	1060
Contraflow				
1. Honolulu, Kalanianole Hwy.	10	510	205	810
2. New York City, NJ Rte. 495	725	34,685	NA	NA
3. San Francisco, Calif., U.S. 101	NA	NA	NA	NA
Transitways with separate ROW				
1. Ottawa, Canada				
Southeast Transitway	156	8100	NA	NA
West Transitway	132	6900	NA	NA
Southwest Transitway	92	4200	NA	NA
2. Pittsburgh, Pa.				
East PatWay	105	5590	NA	NA
South PatWay	75	2950	NA	NA

Source: Adapted from Institute of Transportation Engineers, *The Effectiveness of High-Occupancy Vehicle Facilities: An Informational Report* (Washington, D.C.: Institute of Transportation Engineers, 1988).

characteristic: all carry significant numbers of buses and bus passengers. HOV systems to cover an entire urban area are now emerging. They offer the opportunity to encourage urban ridesharing with diverse trip ends.

REGIONAL RIDESHARING AGENCIES

There is a surprising diversity of organizational and funding arrangements for regional ridesharing agencies. There are successful examples of regional ridesharing agencies sponsored by state departments of transportation, metropolitan planning organizations, councils of government, public transit operators, private nonprofit corporations, counties, and even universities.

Most ridesharing agencies are actively engaged in the employer-based ridesharing, transportation management associations, and corridor-level strategies discussed previously. Basic functions include:

- Ride information for both existing and potential carpoolers and vanpoolers. Most matching systems are computerized, with the trend toward interactive systems that allow a full array of searches, for example, along a corridor. Some agencies provide more personalized assistance and make follow-up calls to see if the match list was useful.
- Marketing activities through one of three traditional channels: through employers to employees, via mass media to the public directly, or to workers at their place of residence. The "selling" of commute alternatives is a major emphasis of most ridesharing agencies.
- Assisting vanpool formation by meeting with prospective vanpoolers, monitoring vanpool vendors to make sure vanpool groups get what they need, and providing information on laws affecting vanpools.
- Contracting for more specialized services, such as managing a TMA.

Regional ridesharing agencies can play an important facilitation role in promoting an increase in vehicle occupancy. However, several factors beyond the authority of regional ridesharing agencies influence their effectiveness.

FACTORS INFLUENCING THE EFFECTIVENESS OF CONGESTION MANAGEMENT

In a growing number of suburban communities across the United States, state and local authorities are relying on increased vehicle occupancy to accommodate future traffic growth. For this strategy to succeed, traffic mitigation programs must produce results that are both significant and sustainable, and such results are difficult to achieve. Recent research indicates that the performance of ridesharing programs is "highly variable, subject to change over time, and influenced by variables outside manager control."[42] Results are "contingent rather than certain"[43] and "can reduce traffic on highways by small amounts, and on local streets by more significant amounts."[44] In other words, caution is indicated. Ride brokering and other traffic mitigation measures can dampen the growth of congestion, but cannot offer an alternative to capital investment for communities that are experiencing rapid growth in employment and population. Exemplary programs have demonstrated the potential of employer-based ride brokering, but the success of such programs depends on a "chain of ifs." The most significant "ifs" that affect performance are itemized in Table 7-8.

TABLE 7-8
Factors Influencing the Effectiveness of Employer-Based Ridesharing Programs

	Factors That Enhance Effectiveness	Factors That Limit Effectiveness
Program management	Appointment of a permanent transportation coordinator.	No permanent assignment of administrative responsibility.
	Training for the coordinator.	Ambivalent support from top management.
	Long-term support from top management.	
Program style	Work-site program provides personalized, one-to-one services and offers a full menu of commuting alternatives.	Work-site program relies on regional ridesharing agency to provide most services, including employee contact.
	Work-site program relies on the regional ridesharing agency for technical services, but not employee contact.	
Parking policies	Close-in parking is reserved for carpools.	Parking is free and space is made available to all comers.
	Carpools are registered and new employees are encouraged to join existing carpools.	Existing carpools not sustained.
Employer size	More than 2000 employees (the scale threshold necessary to justify employment of a full-time commute coordinator).	Fewer than 500 employees at the work site or employment cluster.
Travel patterns	A sizable proportion of work force lives more than 15 miles from the work site.	Most employees are drawn from communities in the immediate vicinity of the work site.
Mix of land uses in the immediate vicinity of the work site	Mixed land use satisfies midday needs and creates a pleasant environment for walking.	Midday needs cannot be satisfied without driving during the lunch hour.

The implications of Table 7-8 are important. The first is that the effectiveness of ride-brokering programs is contingent on a host of factors beyond administrative control. The second is that large companies that develop professionalized programs with a personal touch can offer their employees compelling alternatives to driving alone. And the third is that most companies are not large enough to develop fully professionalized programs or a full menu of alternatives. The third point is crucially important, because only about a quarter of the metropolitan work force is employed by companies large enough to develop full-service brokerage programs. In turn, this means that the ability of most employers to participate in ride brokering effectively depends on the future development of multiemployer ridesharing associations and the implementation of comprehensive corridor plans. In other words, the opportunity for more employers to participate effectively in ridesharing programs hinges on an organization-building process that is underway, but far from complete.

DIVERSIFYING THE SOURCES OF SUBURBAN MOBILITY

A generation ago urban geographers could speak of the prototypical American city—a nuclear city with a predominant core and central industrial areas surrounded by an inner ring of multistory, multifamily apartment buildings and row houses, encircled in turn by successive generations of suburban housing. The suburbs of this prototypical American city were dependent on the central city for employment and, in turn, housed a growing share of its work force.[45]

The imagery of the nuclear city continues to inform our thinking about urban geography, but such imagery bears less and less resemblance to urban reality. This is because the growth of the service and information industries has transformed suburbs from bedroom precincts into commercial and industrial districts of metropolitan significance. Suburbs have become cities—in function, if not density—and the result is a profound change in metropolitan employment and travel patterns.[46]

Table 7-9 shows the travel patterns that prevailed in 1980 in the nation's 25 largest urbanized areas. As it shows, 52% of all metropolitan workers were employed in the suburbs. By comparison, only 8% of the work force commuted to jobs in the central business district (CBD). As these data indicate, the imagery of the nuclear city no longer describes the geography of employment or commuting in most American cities. The nuclear city has evolved into a loosely clustered metropolitan complex.

With the growth of suburban employment has come (1) an increase in crosstown and suburb-to-suburb commuting; (2) an increase in trip making from outer suburbs to inner suburbs, that is, an increase in trips to intermediate suburban destinations along radial corridors that lead to the central city and the CBD; (3) an increase in the proportion of trips that end at suburban work sites where parking is free and plentiful; (4) an increase in the proportion of trips for which mass transit is noncompetitive; (5) an increase in the share of urban commute trips made by workers driving alone; and (6) an increase in suburban congestion.

Increased congestion in the suburbs and in radial corridors has given impetus to the congestion management efforts discussed in the previous section. Such plans are an apt but partial response to suburban transportation problems. These plans respond to commute period congestion by enhancing the availability and attractiveness of commute alternatives that serve trips considerably longer than the average. But congestion management plans typically fail to diversify the travel options available for

TABLE 7-9
Metropolitan Commuting Patterns in 1980:
Work-Trip Travel in the Nation's 25 Largest Metropolitan Areas

Commute Pattern	Share of All Commute Trips
Trips that begin and end in the suburbs.	45.7%
Trips that begin in the suburbs and end in the CBD.	3.7%
Trips that begin in the central city and end in the CBD.	4.7%
Trips that begin in the central city and end in the suburbs.	6.8%
Trips that end in the central city, but not in the CBD.	39.0%

Source: Adapted from William O'Hare and Milton Morris, *Demographic Change and Recent Worktrip Travel Trends*, prepared by the Joint Center for Political Studies for UMTA, Technical Assistance Program, Report no. UMTA-DC-09-7009 (Washington, D.C.: U.S. Department of Transportation, February 1985).

short commutes and off-peak travel. In central cities, this is the segment of the travel market served by street transit—buses, streetcars, and trolley buses. But in the suburbs, low-density land use and the pattern of the street network prevent transit agencies from operating services that provide comparable suburban coverage. Instead, most suburban transit systems are designed to provide feeder service to trunk-line rail or bus systems that serve the CBD. In other words, suburban bus systems are typically designed to serve the travel patterns of the nuclear city. Such services are a chance fit with short, intrasuburban commutes and the dispersed travel patterns characteristic of off-peak suburban travel. As a result, bus systems designed to provide trunk-line feeder service offer a noncompetitive alternative for most suburban trips. A 1985 UMTA study showed that the transit share of suburb-to-CBD commute trips in 1980 was 55%, while the suburb-to-suburb share was only 2.7%.[47]

Dial-a-ride systems were developed to serve suburban areas, and this is the form of transit service best matched to the largest number of suburban trips. But the deployment of demand-responsive services has been preempted by the operation of conventional bus systems designed to provide feeder service. This has left most suburban residents without service that is attractive for intrasuburban travel.

Considering the high levels of automobile ownership found in the suburbs, transit planners are not inclined to view this outcome as a critical problem—and for the majority of the suburban population it is not. But it can be a problem for some segments of the population. These include:

- Teenagers who experience enforced isolation.
- First-time workers who would prefer to defer the cost of automobile ownership, but have no acceptable alternative.
- The stay-at-home member of two-adult, one-car households.

- First-time home buyers who would prefer to defer the purchase of a second car, but have no acceptable alternative.
- Older residents who are no longer confident of their driving skills.

In many suburbs, descriptors such as these characterize one-quarter to one-third of the population.[48] In other words, enforced isolation and involuntary reliance on the automobile are much more pervasive than most planners recognize. In turn, this argues for reconsideration of the mix of transit services offered in suburban communities. Specifically, it argues for the consideration of hybrid systems that provide fixed-route feeder service during the peak period and demand-responsive services during off-peak hours. Such a radical service innovation may be inappropriate for many communities. It is presented here not as a sure thing, but as an invitation and challenge to design transit services that match the travel patterns of the nonnuclear metropolis.

PLURAL TRANSPORTATION AND AIR QUALITY

The Clean Air Act and subsequent amendments call for the planning and implementation of transportation control measures (TCMs). Transportation control measures are synonymous with "transportation controls" and "transportation air quality measures." Table 7-10 lists the control measures that the U.S. Environmental Protection Agency (EPA) has endorsed as "reasonably available" for metropolitan implementation. Carpooling programs and other efforts to increase vehicle occupancy are prominently featured on the EPA list and are prominently represented in the control plans developed for metropolitan areas that violate air quality standards. In the pages that follow, we will examine the effort to harness plural transportation as a pollution control measure.

INSTITUTIONAL CONTEXT[49]

The Clean Air Act of 1970 required the development of state implementation plans (SIPs) for bringing air quality up to national standards through controls on both stationary and mobile pollution sources. Control of stationary sources such as factories and power plants has proved relatively easy to accomplish using a conventional regulatory approach: set standards and exact compliance. But mobile sources of pollution—autos and trucks—are difficult to control using conventional regulatory methods. This is because mobile-source controls imply changes in individual travel behavior. In turn, their implementation requires the cooperation or compliance of individual travelers and truckers in large numbers.

TABLE 7-10
EPA's List of Reasonably Available Control Measures

Voluntary No-Drive Days
Trip Reduction Ordinances
Employer-Based Transportation Management
Work-Schedule Changes
Rideshare Incentives
Improved Public Transit
Traffic Flow Improvements
Road Pricing/Tolls
Parking Management Programs
Park & Ride/Fringe Parking
Control of Extended Vehicle Idling
Reduction of Cold-Start Emissions
Gasoline Fuel Additives
Conversion of Fleet Vehicles to Cleaner Fuels or Engines

The first generation of transportation control plans—developed with the U.S. Environmental Protection Agency in a lead role—can be described most accurately as a learning experience. Planners accustomed to the command-and-control methods of regulatory rule making had to learn through trial and error how to devise plans appropriate to the atomistic environment of personal transportation.[50]

Many first-generation plans included measures that the public perceived as draconian or punitive—measures such as gas rationing and parking surcharges. These measures galvanized almost instant opposition and forced the EPA to postpone its original 1977 deadline for implementation of TCMs. But the first generation of plans was not wholly fruitless. Some TCMs—the creation of regional ridesharing programs and the involvement of employers in ridesharing—proved widely acceptable and have been incorporated in second-generation plans. More important, air quality planners learned that control plans could not be implemented either hastily or unilaterally: effective air quality planning requires a long-term commitment to the creation of a broad-based social partnership.

This orientation influenced the 1977 Clean Air Act Amendments, which placed new emphasis on the establishment of a participatory, continuing process for air quality planning and decision making. The 1977 legislation also articulated detailed expectations for transportation controls, making regional controls a key strategy of the Clean Air Act.

IMPLEMENTATION EXPERIENCE

By the early 1980s, most major metropolitan areas had implemented the voluntary carpool and vanpool programs proposed in the first generation of control plans. Implementation responsibility was typically assigned to a regional ridesharing agency, and the control orientation of the initial plan was replaced by the service orientation typical of ridesharing agencies. This softening of orientation has produced extensive implementation of ridesharing programs, but the air quality impact of these programs has been limited.

Four factors limit the potential for voluntary, employer-oriented programs to achieve significant reductions in pollutant emissions:

1. Such programs target work trips that account for only 20 to 25% of all urban trip making.
2. Carpooling is an uncompetitive alternative for most work trips—because most work trips are short and end with free parking. (Due to "cold starts" and "hot soaks" it is *trip* reduction, not *VMT* reduction that makes the primary contribution to emissions reduction.)
3. Large employers—those with 100 or more employees—employ less than half of the metropolitan work force.[51]
4. Employer commitment to voluntary programs tends to erode with time.

Because of these limiting factors, a vigorous but voluntary ridesharing effort cannot be expected to reduce automotive emissions by even 1% in most metropolitan areas.[52] A vigorous program paired with incentives such as HOV lanes and preferential parking could achieve emission reductions somewhat greater. But pairing with forceful incentives (a financial bonus for carpooling) or with aggressive disincentives (such as parking charges) is necessary to obtain truly significant reductions in automotive emissions. Ridesharing programs paired with aggressive pricing and regulatory policies that impinge on both work and nonwork travel could reduce automotive emissions by 5% or more.[53] To date, metropolitan policy makers have been understandably reluctant to endorse policies that are sufficiently aggressive to achieve such results.

But it is just such issues that policy makers have been forced to confront as voluntary efforts failed to meet the compliance requirements of the Clean Air Act. Failure to comply with federal standards has forced a second round of control planning in some 15 metropolitan areas. All of California's major metropolitan areas violate Clean Air Act standards, and it is in California that the question of stringent disincentives is receiving the most earnest debate. Thus it is instructive to examine the progress of control planning in Los Angeles and the San Francisco Bay area. In Los Angeles, regional authorities have adopted a stringent regulatory approach to the implementation of employer carpooling programs. In San Francisco, regional authorities are debating a dramatically different approach—one that emphasizes the use of price incentives.

Mandatory Ridesharing in Los Angeles

Los Angeles is the nation's most heavily polluted air basin, and its plan for pollution abatement entails the nation's most aggressive use of regulatory powers to influence commute behavior. The regulatory approach adopted in Los Angeles requires *employers* to adopt and implement plans that will induce their *employees* to carpool and vanpool.[54] Employer compliance is mandatory, and the standard of compliance is the attainment of a specified level of vehicle occupancy: 1.75 persons per vehicle in central Los Angeles, and 1.3 persons per vehicle in suburban Los Angeles. These attainment targets reflect the vehicle-occupancy rate necessary to increase aggregate vehicle occupancy from its present level—1.13 persons per vehicle—to a regional standard of 1.5 persons per vehicle.

The mandatory standard—called Regulation XV—has been adopted by the South Coast Air Quality Management District and presently applies to all employers of 100 or more employees in a four-county area. Regulation XV requires employers to adopt a plan for meeting the average vehicle ridership (AVR) standard, provide whatever incentives are necessary to implement the plan, and employ a professional transportation coordinator to implement the plan. Employers are not penalized if they fail to meet the average vehicle ridership target (1.3 or 1.75), but they can be fined if they fail to submit a trip-reduction plan or fail to offer reasonable incentives as part of the plan. The incentives provided must be sufficient to achieve the AVR target within 12 months—a requirement that has motivated many employers to provide financial bonuses for employees who pool. These carpooling bonuses seem to be the new element that distinguishes Regulation XV plans from employer-based ridesharing efforts in other areas.

The implementation of Regulation XV is still in progress, and thus it is too early to determine whether employers will be willing and able to muster incentives sufficient to induce the changes in travel behavior that the regulation contemplates. If the Air District's targets are met, it is estimated that Regulation XV will reduce carbon monoxide by 100 to 216 tons per day, hydrocarbon emissions by 11 to 24 tons per day, and nitrogen oxide emissions by 16 to 34 tons per day.[55]

Air Quality Planning in the San Francisco Bay Area

The San Francisco Bay area has relatively clean air compared to Los Angeles, but nonetheless fails to meet federal air quality standards. Moreover, it is expected that the growth of population and urban activity will degrade air quality faster than automotive emission controls can reduce tailpipe emissions. Thus, regional authorities are obliged to implement transportation control measures.

In 1982, the region obtained federal approval for a control plan that emphasized mandatory vehicle inspection and maintenance and voluntary increases in ridesharing and transit use. But by 1988 it was clear that the region would not achieve timely compliance with federal air quality standards because vehicle inspection was contributing lower-than-projected emission reductions, while the growth of suburban employment was obsoleting projected increases in carpooling and transit use. Clean Air Act compliance required the adoption and implementation of additional TCMs, and the Bay Area initiated a new round of air quality planning in 1988.[56] Its compliance efforts were augmented under court order in 1989.

This new planning effort has been informed by a conscious decision to follow a path different from that pursued in Los Angeles. Public officials in the Bay Area are debating pricing policies that would discipline automobile use while providing a stream of revenues sufficient to improve transit service significantly. This approach emphasizes pricing policies that would impinge on travelers directly, rather than regulatory policies that would impinge on travelers indirectly.[57] Their approach was first proposed by a business-oriented group hopeful of using a market-oriented strategy that employees *congestion tolls* and *pollution pricing*. Their approach has been endorsed by an array of business leaders who hope to avoid the direct involvement and regulatory entanglement of the Regulation XV approach in Los Angeles. It has also been endorsed by the environmental groups that obtained the court order forcing timely adoption of new TCMs.

The theoretical argument for congestion tolls and pollution pricing is well known, as are the practical difficulties associated with the implementation of full-costing pricing. Those practical difficulties have led regional planners to emphasize look-alike measures that are proxies for pricing: increased bridge tolls, increased vehicle registration fees (keyed to emissions performance), and, perhaps, parking fees and surcharges.[58]

Regional approval for a pricing-oriented plan remains uncertain, as does the passage of state implementing legislation. Nonetheless, the Bay Area's nascent commitment to pricing provides an instructive example of a market-oriented strategy with the potential for impacts as significant as those expected from Regulation XV.

In the Bay Area, Los Angeles, and elsewhere, the process of control planning has forced policy makers to grapple with issues that are inherently difficult and controversial: for the short term, how to induce willing change in travel behavior; for the mid-term, how to induce significant further improvement in the technology of emissions control; and for the long term, how to grow cities that are less exclusively reliant on the individual use of private transportation. The California experience suggests that we are close to answering the first and second questions, but far from answering the third.

PLURAL TRANSPORTATION AND ENERGY CONSERVATION

Energy conservation has been an intermittent priority of U.S transportation policy. During wartime, the United States behaves like an oil-importing nation and gives priority to conservation. During peacetime, the United States behaves like an oil-producing nation and allows conservation efforts to lapse. The United States is, of course, both an oil-importing and an oil-producing nation, and this duality explains the ambivalence of U.S. policy toward conservation.

The ambivalence of U.S. conservation efforts can also be explained by the relative recency of the nation's heavy dependence on imported oil. As late as 1970, imported petroleum accounted for only 23% of U.S. fuel consumption—an acceptable level of international risk exposure.[59] But by 1973, the first year of the Arab oil embargo, imports accounted for 36% of U.S. consumption, and by 1990 imports accounted for half of U.S. consumption—a patently unacceptable level of risk exposure. The 1990 "Oil War" indicates both the level of risk and the importance of oil to the nation's economy.

Most of the world's industrial nations have imposed a vanity or vice tax on motor fuels to provide a persistent incentive for conservation.[60] The United States has not, relying instead on emergency rationing, an emergency oil reserve, and the public's responsiveness to emergency conservation campaigns. In other words, most elements of U.S. transportation energy policy involve standby measures that can be implemented if and when crises occur. Regulatory standards for motor-vehicle fuel economy are a notable exception. They are the nation's only significant long-term commitment to transportation energy conservation.

As we have noted, carpooling campaigns were instigated during World War II, the Korean conflict, and the energy crisis of the 1970s. Ridesharing campaigns square with the crisis orientation of U.S. transportation energy policy: they can be implemented on a contingency basis, and their implementation does not entail long lead times or major start-up costs. As important, carpooling campaigns take aim at a big target—the 34% of vehicle-miles traveled for work-related purposes. But the size of the target should not lead to exaggerated expectations that carpooling programs can have significant impacts on national energy accounts. Table 7-11 shows that it would take a 17% nationwide increase in carpooling to achieve a 1% reduction in VMT, and that a "realistic" 5% increase in work-related ridesharing would reduce daily oil consumption only two-tenths of 1%. Carpooling programs obviously have extremely limited leverage on the nation's aggregate oil requirements. Such programs enable individual commuters to realize significant savings in the cost of commuting, but the potential for translating individual monetary savings into national energy savings is inherently limited.

TABLE 7-11
Commuter Carpooling in the Context of National Energy Accounts

Share of U.S. oil consumption used for transportation.	63%
Personal transportation's share of transportation energy consumption.	69%
Work-related VMT as a share of total daily VMT.	34%
Share of work-related VMT logged by carpools and vanpools.	19%
Carpool/vanpool share of total VMT.	7%
Increase in carpooling and vanpooling necessary to reduce automotive VMT by 1%.	17%
Reduction in nationwide energy consumption attributable to a 5% increase in organized carpooling.	0.2%

Source: Calculated from data supplied by the American Petroleum Institute and the *Nationwide Personal Transportation Study*, 1983-84.

The prospect for using carpool programs to achieve long-term energy conservation goals is even more discouraging. The typical ridesharing program provides services, not incentives. And in the absence of crisis conditions, powerful incentives would be necessary to overcome the erosion of informal ridesharing arrangements that is occurring with the suburbanization of employment and the continuing growth of automobile ownership. Background trends are eroding informal ridesharing arrangements faster than ridesharing programs can field formal carpools and vanpools. Indeed, the mismatch is overwhelming. Ridesharing's contribution to metropolitan mobility declined sharply from 48.0% of the total VMT in 1977 to 42.6% in 1983.[61] There is no doubt that the work of ridesharing agencies retarded these trends—for example, the share of VMT logged by vanpools increased fourfold—but these efforts were overwhelmed by countervailing social and economic trends.[62]

SUMMARY

Plural transportation is a family of transportation services that lies intermediate between personal and mass transportation. It is a diverse set of market-specialized transportation services and organized travel arrangements that make collective use of private transportation. Plural transportation plays an important role in America's mix of transportation modes. Passengers riding in cars, vans, and trucks account for almost 32% of the mileage traveled in metropolitan America. The collective use of private vehicles provides Americans with a source of mass mobility that other nations have sought from public transportation.

Recent efforts to organize and facilitate ridesharing and paratransit entail three distinguishable thrusts: (1) efforts to promote carpooling and vanpooling to serve commute trips, (2) efforts to field transitlike services with the routing and scheduling flexibility necessary to serve small towns and outlying suburbs, and (3) efforts to provide specialized transportation services for the elderly and handicapped.

Public policy has placed high expectations on plural transportation. Dial-a-ride systems were touted as an opportunity for transit to capture urban market shares in suburban communities. Ridesharing programs were first advertised for their contribution to energy conservation and have become a cornerstone of suburban plans for congestion management and air quality improvement. Paratransit has been asked to provide a mobility lifeline for the elderly and handicapped. Thus, small programs have been assigned large missions. At the same time, the results that could be expected from such programs were being overwhelmed by countervailing forces—the growth of suburban employment centers, the growth of sunbelt cities, and the growth of women's labor-force participation.

The rapid growth of suburban population and employment has resulted in the increasing prevalence of suburb-to-suburb trips that end at a workplace that provides abundant free parking. Sharp increases in the rate of women's labor-force participation have produced corresponding increases in the proportion of two-income, two-car households, with the average number of vehicles per household increasing from 1.2 to 1.7 between 1969 and 1983. These geographic and demographic trends have countermanded recent efforts to increase auto occupancy through ridesharing. Between 1969 and 1983, work-trip auto occupancy in metropolitan America dropped from 1.4

to 1.2. Consequently, ridesharing's aggregate contribution to energy conservation, air quality, and metropolitan mobility has declined—despite the best efforts of carpooling programs.

Although efforts to increase vehicle occupancy were losing ground, ridesharing was still able to make a significant contribution to the solution of small-scale problems. Carpools and vanpools provide economical transportation for large numbers of individual commuters, and employer-based ridesharing programs have made a measurable contribution to congestion relief in urban and suburban employment centers. Large employers who have provided their employees with intensive and personalized commute assistance report a significant increase in the use of collective transportation. It is to be hoped that the emergence of multiemployer transportation management associations will provide the organizational infrastructure necessary for ridesharing to make a similar contribution at the corridor scale.

But the future contribution of plural transportation to metropolitan mobility at large will depend on the relative strength of countervailing forces. Continuing deconcentration of the metropolitan population will diminish both plural and mass transportation's contribution to urban mobility. A concerted effort to manage traffic *and contain urban growth* would enhance collective transportation's contribution to urban mobility. In turn, land-use trends and land-use policy will determine the extent to which plural transportation can contribute—over the long term—to energy conservation, air quality improvement, and other large social purposes.

In the 1970s and 1980s, policy makers asked plural transportation to solve problems that are, in fact, deeply imbedded in the land-use patterns and disorderly development processes characteristic of metropolitan America. These problems must be confronted directly—with policies designed to manage and contain urban growth. Then plural transportation can make a lasting contribution to urban mobility, environmental quality, and energy security.

REFERENCES

1 Dieter Klinger and J. Richard Kuzmyak, *Personal Travel in the United States; Vol. I and II, Nationwide Personal Transportation Study*, prepared by COMSIS Corporation for the FHWA (Washington, D.C.: U.S. Department of Transportation, August 1986), p. 6-13.

2 Ibid., p. E-117.

3 Each of these examples is drawn from programs that are operational. In some cases, elements from two or more programs are described as if they were part and parcel of one program.

4 Such programs operate at Bishop Ranch in San Ramon, California, and Lawrence Livermore Laboratories, Livermore, California.

5 The referent here is San Francisco's RIDES for Bay Area Commuters.

6 So-called user-side subsidy programs operate in 12 cities of Alameda County, California, including Oakland, Berkeley, Hayward, and Fremont.

7   An aggressive plan for coordinating HOV-lane development with employer-based ride marketing has been adopted in Santa Clara County, California.

8   KLINGER, *Personal Travel*, pp. 7-9 and 8-4.

9   U.S. DEPARTMENT OF COMMERCE, BUREAU OF THE CENSUS, *Statistical Abstract of the United States*, and *State and Metropolitan Area Data Book* (Washington, D.C.: U.S. Government Printing Office, 1989).

10 WILLIAM O'HARE AND MILTON MORRIS, *Demographic Change and Recent Worktrip Travel Trends*, prepared by the Joint Center for Political Studies for UMTA, Technical Assistance Program, Report no. UMTA-DC-09-7009 (Washington, D.C.: U.S. Department of Transportation, February 1985), Tables M-70 and M-80.

11 KLINGER, *Personal Travel*, p. 4-19.

12 See Chap. 22.

13 KLINGER, *Personal Travel*, p. 8-8.

14 CALIFORNIA DEPARTMENT OF TRANSPORTATION, DIVISION OF MASS TRANSPORTATION, *Transportation Development Act: Statutes and Administrative Code for 1989* (Sacramento, Calif.: Caltrans, January 1990).

15 See CRAIN & ASSOCIATES, INC., AND JLM CONSULTING, *Alameda County Five-Year Paratransit Plan*, Final Report, prepared for Metropolitan Transportation Commission. (Menlo Park, Calif.: Crain & Associates, 1989).

16 SYSTAN, *Paratransit Integration: State-of-the-Art Report* (Cambridge, Mass: Transportation Systems Center, December 1978), p. 4.

17 TRANSPORTATION RESEARCH BOARD, *Demand Responsive Transportation Systems*, Special Report 136 (Washington, D.C.: Transportation Research Board, 1973).

18 U.S. DEPARTMENT OF TRANSPORTATION, *Carpool Incentives and Opportunities*, Report of the Secretary of Transportation to the United States Congress, Pursuant to Section 3(e), Public Law 93-239, Emergency Highway Energy Conservation Act (Washington, D.C.: U.S. Department of Transportation, February 1975).

19 See, for example, Santa Clara County, California, 1987.

20 The "new strategy" was given early articulation by WILFRED OWEN WITH INAI BRADFELD, *The Accessible City* (Washington, D.C.: The Brookings Institution, 1972), and *Traffic in Towns: A Study of the Long Term Problems of Traffic in Urban Areas*, Reports of the Steering Group and Working Group appointed by the Minister of Transport (London: Her Majesty's Stationery Office, 1963).

21 See "Transportation Improvement Program," *Federal Register*, 40, no. 181 (September 17, 1975), p. 42979.

22 ERIK FERGUSON, "An Evaluation of Employer Ridesharing Programs in Southern California," paper presented to Transportation Research Board 69th Annual Meeting, January 1990, p. 3.

23 JOSEPH B. MARGOLIN AND MARION RUTH MISCH, *Incentives and Disincentives for Ridesharing: A Behavioral Study*, prepared for the FHWA (Washington, D.C.: U.S. Government Printing Office, 1978).

24 J. RICHARD KUZMYAK AND ERIC N. SCHREFFLER, *Evaluation of Travel Demand Management Measures (TDM) to Relieve Congestion*, prepared by COMSIS Corporation in association with Harold Katz & Associates (Washington, D.C.: Federal Highway Administration, 1990), pp. 12-29.

25 FERGUSON, "An Evaluation of Ridesharing Programs."

26   DAVID W. JONES, DAVID CURRY, AND CLIFF CHAMBERS, *A New Gameplan for Traffic Mitigation*, prepared by Crain & Associates for Metropolitan Transportation Commission (Oakland, Calif.: Metropolitan Transportation Commission, December 1988), p. 114.

27   ASSOCIATION FOR COMMUTER TRANSPORTATION, *Transportation Management Association Directory*, 1989 ed. (Washington, D.C.: Association for Commuter Transportation, 1989), p. iii.

28   JESSE GLAZER AND CLIFF CHAMBERS, *Project Summary: TMA Workshops and Vanpool Guide*, prepared by Crain & Associates in cooperation with Ekistic Mobility Consultants for Caltrans (Menlo Park, Calif.: Crain and Associates, June 1990), pp. B-17 to B-22.

29   Ibid, p. A-1.

30   KUZMYAK, *Evaluation of Travel Demand Measures*, p. 81.

31   JONES, *New Gameplan*, p. 59, and more recent data from RIDES for Bay Area Commuters, San Francisco, Calif.

32   JONES, *New Gameplan*, p. 74.

33   SAN FRANCISCO DEPARTMENT OF CITY PLANNING, *Transportation Management Programs in Greater Downtown: Developer's Manual for Procedures and Performance Criteria*, 3rd ed. (San Francisco: San Francisco Department of City Planning, January 1988), p. 2.

34   ELIZABETH A. DEAKIN AND WILLIAM L. GARRISON, Private Sector Funding for Urban Transportation: Some Comments on Public-Private Partnerships, paper presented at the American Society of Civil Engineers Specialty Conference, "Shaping the Future of America's Highways," San Diego, Calif., April 15-17, 1985, Working Paper UCB-ITS-WP-85-9 (Berkeley, Calif.: Institute of Transportation Studies, University of California, 1985), p. 15.

35   CAROLYN P. FLYNN AND LAWRENCE JESSE GLAZER, "Ten Cities' Strategies for Transportation Demand Management," in *Ridesharing—Transportation Demand Management*, Transportation Research Record 1212 (Washington D.C.: Transportation Research Board), p. 17.

36   JONES, *New Gameplan*, p. 67-77.

37   Based on the review of CALIFORNIA DEPARTMENT OF TRANSPORTATION, DIVISION OF TRANSPORTATION PLANNING, *Transportation System Management Ordinance Guide* (Sacramento, Calif.: Caltrans, n.d.).

38   CLIFF CHAMBERS AND A. J. ZISSLER, *Inter-City TSM Authority Marketing Plan* (Menlo Park, Calif.: Crain & Associates, August 1990), pp. 1-3.

39   The work of the Golden Triangle Task Force, a committee of the Santa Clara County Transportation Agency, Santa Clara County, California, provides the closest approximation of a traffic management plan that includes land-use controls. See JONES, *New Gameplan*, p. 91-111.

40   INSTITUTE OF TRANSPORTATION ENGINEERS, *The Effectiveness of High-Occupancy Vehicle Facilities: An Informational Report* (Washington, D.C.: Institute of Transportation Engineers, 1988).

41   JONES, *New Gameplan*, p. 112-15.

42   KIRAN BHATT AND THOMAS HIGGINS, *An Assessment of Travel Demand Approaches at Suburban Activity Centers*, Final Report, prepared by K. T. Analytics, Inc., for TSC and UMTA (Cambridge, Mass.: Transportation Systems Center, July 1989), p. 30.

43   JONES, *New Gameplan*, p. 112.

44   SUSAN PULTZ, "Key Considerations for Developing Local Government Transportation System Management Programs," in *Ridesharing—Transportation Demand Management*, Transportation Research Record 1212 (Washington D.C.: Transportation Research Board, 1989), p. 33.

45 JAMES E. VANCE, JR., *Geography and Urban Evolution in the San Francisco Bay Area*, Institute of Governmental Studies (Berkeley, Calif.: University of California, Berkeley, 1964), p. 4.

46 JOINT CENTER FOR POLITICAL STUDIES, *Demographic Change*.

47 Ibid., Table M-80.

48 DONALD M. FOLEY, "The Components of Transportation Disadvantage," Department of City and Regional Planning, University of California at Berkeley, unpublished manuscript, 1977.

49 Much of this section was adopted from ELIZABETH DEAKIN AND OTHERS, *A Study of Transportation System, Facilities and Control Measures That Contribute to Achieving Air Quality Goals*, Research Report UCB-ITS-RR-31-3 (Berkeley, Calif.: Institute of Transportation Studies, University of California, Berkeley, January 1981), pp. 13-15.

50 EUGENE Y. LEONG, "Air Quality Planning in the San Francisco Bay Area," unpublished paper no. 89-39.z, presented at the 82nd Air Pollution Control Association Annual Meeting, Anaheim, Calif., June, 1989.

51 U.S. DEPARTMENT OF COMMERCE, BUREAU OF THE CENSUS, *County Business Patterns: 1985*, CBP-85 (Washington, D.C.: U.S. Government Printing Office, 1987).

52 DEAKIN, *A Study of Transportation System Facilities*, pp. 13-15.

53 Ibid.

54 SOUTH COAST AIR QUALITY MANAGEMENT DISTRICT, *A Guide for Chief Executives: Answers to Questions about the Commuter Program (Regulation XV)* (Los Angeles, Calif.: South Coast Air Quality Management District, 1989).

55 ROBERT E. PAASWELL, "Air Quality and the Transportation Community," *TR News*, no. 148 (May-June 1990), p. 9.

56 METROPOLITAN TRANSPORTATION COMMISSION, *Proposed Transportation Control Measures for the Contingency Plan* (January 12, 1990), p. 1-3, and *Transportation Control Measures for State Clean Air Plan*, Draft (Oakland, Calif.: Metropolitan Transportation Commission, June 8, 1990).

57 RANDALL JOHNSTON POZDENA, *Market-Based Solutions to the Transportation Crisis: The Concept* (San Francisco: Bay Area Economic Forum, May 1990), p. 2.

58 GREIG HARVEY, *Detailed Strategies for Packages E and F*, memorandum prepared by TCM Task Force (Oakland, Calif.: Metropolitan Transportation Commission, April 1990).

59 CRAUFURD D. GOODWIN, ed., *Energy Policy in Perspective: Today's Problems, Yesterday's Solutions* (Washington, D.C., The Brookings Institution, 1981), p. 694.

60 R. WHITFORD AND OTHERS, *Transportation Energy Futures: Paths of Transition*, prepared by Purdue University, Automotive Transportation Center for U.S. DOT (West Lafayette, Ind.: Automotive Transportation Center, 1981).

61 KLINGER, *Personal Travel*, p. 8-6.

62 Ibid., p. 8-5.

FURTHER READING

CERVERO, ROBERT, *Suburban Gridlock*. New Brunswick, N.J.: Center for Urban Policy Research, 1986.

———, *America's Suburban Centers: A Study of the Land Use—Transportation Link*, Final Report, prepared for UMTA and Rice Center, Joint Center for Urban Mobility Research, Technology Sharing Program, Report no. DOT-T-88-14. Washington, D.C.: U.S. Government Printing Office, January 1988.

COMSIS CORPORATION AND LOUIS E. KEEFER ASSOCIATES, *Public-Private Partnerships in Transportation: A Casebook for Local Elected Officials,* Final Report, prepared for Office of the Secretary of Transportation, Report no. DOT-I-86-15. Washington, D.C.: U.S. Department of Transportation, February 1986.

DUNPHY, ROBERT T., AND BEN C. LIN, *Transportation Management through Partnerships*. Washington, D.C.: Urban Land Institute, 1990.

FEDERAL HIGHWAY ADMINISTRATION, OFFICE OF PLANNING, *Transportation Management for Corridors and Activity Centers: Opportunities and Experiences*, Final Report, Technology Sharing Program, Report no. DOT-I-86-21. Washington, D.C.: U.S. Department of Transportation, 1986.

KIRBY, RONALD F., AND OTHERS, *Para-Transit: Neglected Options for Urban Mobility*. Washington, D.C.: The Urban Institute, 1974.

LEVINSON, HERBERT S., AND ROBERT A. WEANT, eds., *Urban Transportation: Perspectives and Prospects*. Westport, Conn.: Eno Foundation, 1982.

BARTON-ASCHMAN ASSOCIATES, INC., R. H. PRATT & CO. DIVISION, *Traveler Response to Transportation System Changes* (2nd ed.), prepared for the FHWA. Washington, D.C.: U.S. Government Printing Office, July 1981.

TEAL, ROGER F., "Carpooling: Who, How and Why," *Transportation Research*, Part A: General, 21A, no. 3 (1987), pp. 203-14.

WAGNER, FREDERICK A., *Energy Impacts of Urban Transportation Improvements*. Washington, D.C.: Institute of Transportation Engineers, 1980.

EXERCISES

7-1   What are realistic expectations for ridesharing and paratransit programs?

7-2   Develop a taxonomy for classifying commute trips that are most and least likely to be made by carpool (as opposed to mass transit or by automobile alone).

7-3   Conduct interviews in your community to determine the extent to which local employers are involved in congestion management programs. If employers are actively involved, is that involvement reluctant or energetic?

7-4   Develop an implementation plan for a transit system that provides fixed-route service during the peak period and on-demand service during the off-peak. What operating policies would be needed to implement the plan?

7-5   Select a metropolitan area and investigate the trend of trip making in the region you have selected. Using market share as your primary indicator, examine whether ridesharing and transit use are increasing or decreasing. What variables explain the trend in your area?

Chapter 8

DESIGNING FOR PEDESTRIANS

Walking is not usually considered a transportation mode. Perhaps this is because it does not employ vehicles or because it is such a fundamental means of movement. But walking is actually the most vital mode of transportation upon which all societal activities depend. Upright human locomotion has been recognized as our most significant evolutionary accomplishment—a unique physical skill that eventually led to the technological triumph of the "walk" on the moon. Walking has been interwoven into all aspects of human development. The first cities were organized to concentrate the means of survival within a convenient walking distance. Even in the mechanized society of today, walking is the primary means of internal movement within cities. It is the only means of attaining the necessary face-to-face interaction involved in all the commercial and cultural activities that comprise the urban milieu. With the exception of cycling, walking is the only means of human movement by which we can dramatically experience the sensory gradients of sight, sound, and smell that define a place.

As a means of transportation, walking has many important attributes directly related to the quality of life. Walking provides a versatile linkage between other transportation modes that would be impossible to duplicate. The practical range of human walking distances determines the effective service area, convenience, and utility of transit systems. As a transportation mode, walking offers predictable travel times; continuous availability; ubiquitous and easily maintainable routes; reliable, free, nonpolluting, non-energy-consuming service; and, for many, healthful, relaxing exercise. The pedestrian mode is gaining recognition as a basic building block in urban system design. Increasing attention is being given to developing vehicle-free zones to reduce urban pollution and return the inner city to its former role as a place for personal interaction. Attempts are being made to improve the walking experience, to make it more safe, convenient, and attractive.

Transit station effectiveness is determined by the ability of the modal interface to accommodate pedestrian movement. Station planners and operators must understand pedestrian traffic characteristics to provide a convenient and safe passenger environment. This understanding requires knowledge of pedestrian speeds, traffic flow relationships of corridors and stairs, escalators, platforms, and fare processing rates. Analytical techniques available to evaluate pedestrian facilities include *level-of-service (LOS) standards*, a series of measures that defines relative degrees of convenience for different pedestrian traffic volumes and densities, and the *time–space (TS)* analysis method, used to evaluate complex spaces such as platforms and fare-control areas where both waiting and walking can occur simultaneously. The technique compares a TS supply, consisting of the product of the analysis period and the functional area available, and the TS demand created by passengers walking and waiting in the area during this period.

HUMAN FACTORS AND BEHAVIORAL ASPECTS

Human body dimensions, locomotion characteristics (both walking and using stairs), and behavioral preferences help to establish the requirements for accommodating pedestrians safely and conveniently. Human locomotion involves many complex skills of balance, timing (gait, perception, and reaction), and vision that are often taken for granted except by the physically impaired. Natural unimpeded walking requires a uniform, nonslip walking surface and sufficient space both laterally and longitudinally to avoid conflicts with others. The width of the human body plus allowance for body sway determine lateral spacing, and individual pacing distance combined with perception and reaction times, the longitudinal spacing. Vision plays an important role in locomotion to perceive and react to variances in the walking surface and to avoid conflicts with others.

WALKING CYCLE

The human walking cycle begins by leaning forward and swinging the leading foot into a heel strike. At about the same time the rear foot begins a rolling push-off and is swung forward for a new heel strike and a repeat of the cycle. Walking speed is determined by stride length, pacing rate, and shifts in the body center of gravity. Sufficient surface friction is necessary at the heel strike of the forward foot and rear foot push-off to avoid slipping, and a uniform surface is needed on the follow-through to avoid tripping. Surface friction values of 0.5 or better are desirable for flooring materials in public transit facilities.

MOVEMENT ON STAIRS

Stair climbing and descent are quite different from walking. When climbing stairs, the body center of gravity is shifted forward, the leading foot is placed on the tread above, and both the leading and rear legs combine for the push-off to lift the rear foot to the next tread above. In descent the body center of gravity is shifted backward, the lead foot is placed on the step below, and the rear foot lifted, swung forward and placed on the next step below. Most accidents on stairs occur in the down direction, and these accidents are usually more severe because of the greater energy and impact of the fall.

People using stairs cannot select their natural pace because the tread width dictates the same pace length for all persons. The stair riser changes patterns of leg and body movement, requiring greater bending of the knee and more careful balance. These differences, combined with increased energy demands, inconvenience many who otherwise have little difficulty walking.

RAMPS

Sometimes used as an alternative to stairs, ramps have a higher traffic capacity as the same width stair, but occupy much greater area because of their more gradual slope. Ramps up to a slope of approximately 3% are perceived to be almost level by most pedestrians, and slopes of up to 10% for short distances are considered acceptable, except for wheelchair use, for which slopes are limited to 8.33% by most authorities. Sidewalk slopes exceeding 20% occur in cities such as San Francisco and Seattle. Surface friction values are reduced on sloped surfaces and may require special treatment to avoid slipping hazards.

PERSONAL SPACE PREFERENCES

Human behavioral factors, including personal space preferences and interactions with others, are important in understanding pedestrian requirements. People prefer to avoid contact with others except where such crowding is unavoidable. At poorly managed public events, excessive crowding at extreme densities equaling the area of the human body, has resulted in mass fatalities. Crowd management may be necessary in transit facilities when unusual demands occur, for example, after a sporting event or parade.

The plan view of the human body can be viewed approximately as an ellipse defined by the body depth and shoulder breadth measurements. Human factors studies have shown that the fully clothed dimensions of the 95th percentile of the population (95% are less than this) are 13 in (330 mm) body depth and 23 in (580 mm) shoulder breadth. The plan view of the average male human body occupies an area of approximately 1.5 ft^2 (0.14 m^2). A 18 × 24 in body ellipse equivalent to a standing area of 2.3 ft^2/pr has been used by the New York City Transit Authority to determine the standee capacity of its subway cars. This level of crowding results in unavoidable physical contact by passengers, which can be psychologically disturbing for some persons. Observations of crowding in elevators has shown that unavoidable contact with others begins at personal space occupancies of 2.75 ft²/pr.

Behavioral experiments involving personal space preferences have shown minimum desirable occupancies ranging between 5 and 10 ft²/pr, where physical contact with others is avoidable. As a point of reference, an opened 30-in (760-mm)-diameter umbrella covers an area of about 5 ft² (0.5 m²). The larger personal space preferences are observed in crowded queues, whereas occupancies involving physical contact occur only in the most crowded elevators and transit vehicles.

SPACE FOR MOVEMENT

The characteristics of human movement, body dimensions, and personal space preferences are useful for understanding pedestrian traffic relationships. Considering the width of the human shoulders, body sway, and avoidance of contact with others, people require a lateral space of 28 to 30 in (710 to 760 mm) for comfortable movement. The longitudinal spacing for walking, including space for pacing and avoiding conflicts, would be 8 to 10 ft (2.5 to 3 m). This results in a minimum personal area of 20 to 30 ft²/pr (2 to 3 m²/pr) for relatively unimpeded walking in groups on level surfaces. Much smaller personal areas are observed in queues and other crowded situations where movement is restricted. The personal space required for comfortable movement on stairs is less than walking because of the limitations imposed by the treads and concerns for safety. People need to attend to only about 2 to 3 treads ahead when using stairs; this equates to a minimum personal area of about 10 to 20 ft²/pr for stair movement. The personal spaces required for comfortable movement help us understand the traffic relationships and design standards that are presented later in this chapter.

PEDESTRIAN CHARACTERISTICS

The primary characteristics needed to evaluate pedestrian facilities are walking speeds, walking distances, demand patterns, and traffic-flow relationships. The ability of pedestrians to select their own individual walking pace and speed is a qualitative measure of convenience. Walking distances define the effective service area of transit stations, with shorter distances improving passenger perceptions of service and convenience. The patterns of passenger demand affect the methods used to analyze pedestrian facilities and the applications of service standards.

WALKING SPEEDS

Pedestrian speeds, in addition to being directly related to traffic density, have been found to vary for a wide range of conditions, including individual age, sex, personal disabilities, environmental factors, and trip purpose. Normal walking speeds unimpeded by pedestrian crowding have been found to vary between 150 and 350 ft/min (0.76 and 1.76 m/s), with the average at about 270 ft/min. As a point of comparison, running the 4-min mile is equivalent to a speed of 1320 ft/min or almost 5 times normal walking speed. Walking speeds decline with age, particularly after age 65, but healthy older adults are capable of increasing their walking speed by 40% for short distances. Dense pedestrian traffic has the effect of reducing walking speed for all persons. The smaller personal space limits pacing distances and the ability to pass slower moving pedestrians or to cross the traffic stream.

Photographic studies of pedestrian traffic flow on walkways have shown that individual area occupancies of at least 35 ft^2/pr (3 m^2/pr) are required for pedestrians to attain normal walking speeds and to avoid conflicts with others. Interestingly, the maximum pedestrian traffic-flow volume is not obtained when people can walk the fastest, but when average area occupancies are at about 5 ft^2/pr, and pedestrians are limited to an uncomfortable shuffling gait less than half normal walking speed. At individual space occupancies below 2 ft^2/pr, approaching the plan area of the human body, virtually all movement is stopped. When there is a large crowd in a confined space, this density can result in shock waves and potentially fatal crowd pressures.

SPEEDS ON STAIRWAYS

Movement on stairways is restrained by tread and riser dimensions, added exertion, and greater concerns for safety. These restraints result in lower speeds and lower traffic capacity on stairways than on walkways. Ascending stair speeds vary from 50 to 300 ft/min, with the average at about 100 ft/min, or one-third level walking speed. Descending speeds are about 10% faster than ascent because of the assist of gravity. A much wider variation of individual speeds exists on stairways because even minor vision or joint disabilities can significantly affect climbing or descending movements. For this reason greater attention to human factors and safety requirements is required in stairway design. Most building codes use a 22-in (560-mm) lane width as an egress standard, and multiples of this width are often used in designing stairs. This arbitrary selection can result in inconveniently narrow stairs, particularly in transit facilities where there is heavy two-way movement and people with hand-carried articles. Based on human factors considerations, lane widths on stairs in transit facilities should be in multiples of 28 to 30 in (711 to 760 mm), with a minimum width of 60 in needed for fluid two-way movement.

STAIRWAY DESIGN

Other design details that are frequently misunderstood are the dimensions of stair risers, treads, and handrails. Excessively steep stairs are sometimes specified to simplify structural framing and reduce construction costs. This false economy penalizes all users of the stairway for the life of the building and can be unsafe. Recognizing user safety and convenience issues, designers are typically using lower risers and wider treads than in the past. Risers as low as 5 in (130 mm) and treads as wide as 14 in (360 mm) are being specified to provide more convenient leg movement and added space for foot placement. The serviceability of more gently sloped stairs has been amply proved by a 6-in riser and 14-in tread-width stair in constant heavy use for more than 50 years in New York's Pennsylvania Railroad Station.

Stairway handrails are an important safety consideration because the handrail may be the only means of stopping a serious descending fall. Handrails should be *reachable* to anyone on the stair and *graspable*, with an ideal gripping circumference. These considerations translate to a maximum width of 60 in (1520 mm) between handrails and a handrail circumference of 4.4 to 5.2 in (112 to 132 mm), which is equal to a cylindrical handrail 1.4 to 1.7 in (36 to 42 mm) in diameter or the rounded shape equivalent. Handrails should also be at the greatest height allowable by code, extended past landings to aid the disabled and where there is an exposure to a fall to a lower level, supplemented by guardrails at least 42 in (1070 mm) in height. Lighting on stairs should be of good quality to avoid shadows and glare and, preferably, should be at least 270 lux (25 foot-candles).

WALKING DISTANCE

As with many other aspects of pedestrian behavior, human walking distances vary significantly according to trip purposes and the environmental setting. Numerous surveys of automobile drivers show preferred parking locations within 500 ft (152 m) of their destination, about a 2-min walk, but the auto provides the means of getting even closer to that destination. Interestingly, drivers will go to great lengths to obtain a parking spot close to the entrance of a shopping mall, but have no problems walking 1 or 2 mi within the mall itself. Walking distances within major museums can often exceed 3 mi (5 km).

Transportation planners generally use about 0.25 mi (0.4 km), approximately a 5-min walk, as the acceptable walking distance to transit stops, beyond which another connecting mode is required or public transit will not be used for the trip. There is evidence, however, that much longer walking distances are accepted in larger cities. A study conducted in downtown Boston indicated that 60% of walking trips were greater than 0.25 mi and 18% beyond 0.5 mi. Average walking distances in Manhattan were found to be 1720 ft (524 m), with a median at 1070 ft. Higher average walking distances were found for passengers at the New York Port Authority Bus Terminal. About one-third of all departing passengers walk to this terminal, and the remainder use other connecting modes. Virtually all passengers within 1000 ft of the Port

Authority Terminal walk to it, within 1 mi about half walked and half used another connecting mode, and at 1.5 mi, 10% walked.

These data show that the limits of human walking distance are more situation related than energy related. Nevertheless, in specific situations such as modal transfer facilities where the passenger places a magnified value on *time*, walking distances should be kept as short and direct as possible. This policy has the added benefit of reducing signing and other information requirements.

DEMAND CHARACTERISTICS

It is important for the transportation analyst to thoroughly understand the traffic patterns associated with any pedestrian facility. For example, traffic flow is intermittent on sidewalks because of interruptions by traffic signals or in transit terminals due to the intermittent arrivals of trains. Also, there are differences between arriving and departing peaks in transit terminals. In the arriving peak, large volumes of passengers are discharged from trains in a short period, typically placing maximum demand on pedestrian facilities. In the departing peak, passenger arrivals at the platform are more gradual, making the available platform space for queuing the important consideration.

PEDESTRIAN TRAFFIC-FLOW EQUATION

The volume of pedestrians that can be accommodated on walkways and stairs is related to traffic density and the average speed attainable at that density. *Pedestrian density*, typically expressed in pedestrians per unit of area (ft^2 or m^2) is an unwieldy unit and difficult to visualize, so the reciprocal, area per pedestrian (ft^2/pr or m^2/pr) is preferred for analysis. The fundamental pedestrian traffic flow equation for walkways and stairs is expressed in Eq. (8-1).

$$f = \frac{s}{a} \qquad (8\text{-}1)$$

where f =   volume in pedestrians per foot- or meter-width of traffic
way per minute (pr/ft-min or pr/m-min)
  s =   average pedestrian speed (ft/min or m/min)
  a =   average area per pedestrian within the traffic stream
(ft^2/pr or m^2/pr)

Example: At the near average normal walking speed of 250 ft/min (1.26 m/s), average pedestrian space is 25 ft^2/pr (2.32 m^2/pr), and the flow per foot of effective corridor width is 10 pr/min (0.54 pr/s-m).

Equation (8-1) is based on an analogy to hydraulic flow in channels and therefore is only applicable where there is continuous and reasonably uniform pedestrian movement. In spaces where uniform flow does not exist and where there are other activities such as queuing, alternative analytical techniques such as the time–space (TS) method must be used.

Time–Space Analysis

The pedestrian traffic equation and the LOS standards presented in the following sections are applicable to corridors where pedestrian traffic flow is moving uniformly. There are many other types of pedestrian spaces, however, where flow is not strictly uniform, people may combine other activities with walking, such as queuing, or traffic flow is multidirectional. In these situations some pedestrians may spend only a brief time in the space by directly walking through it, whereas others may spend longer times both walking in it and performing other functions. The space necessary to perform these functions may also vary.

Time–space (TS) analysis can provide a better understanding of the dynamics of these more complicated spaces by combining the knowledge of personal area occupancies developed in the LOS standards with a more discrete analysis of pedestrian activities. With the TS method, the product of the time of the analysis period, for example, the peak 15 min, and the area of the analysis space in ft^2 or m^2 establishes a TS *supply*. The *demand* for this TS supply is determined by the product of the total number of pedestrians using the analysis space and their time of occupancy.

The typical application of the TS method is the evaluation of the adequacy of a space where there is a forecasted peak-period pedestrian demand, the configuration and area of the space are known, and occupancy times for pedestrian functions such as walking or waiting can be predicted. The average area per pedestrian and LOS under these conditions can be obtained by dividing the TS demand into the TS supply. This is expressed in Eq. (8-2).

$$a = \frac{TS\ supply}{TS\ demand} = \frac{TS}{nt} \qquad (8\text{-}2)$$

where a = average area per pedestrian (ft^2/pr or m^2/pr) within the analysis space, during the analysis period
   T = time of the analysis period (min)
   S = net effective area of the analysis space (ft^2 or m^2)
   n = number of pedestrians occupying the space or performing discrete functions in the space such as walking, waiting, or ticket purchase
   t = predicted occupancy times of pedestrians for functions performed during the analysis period

Example: During a 15-min peak, 1500 passengers pass through a 2500-ft^2 area fare-control space. Average walk time through the space is 15 s. One-quarter of these passengers spend an additional 10 s waiting in line to purchase transit tokens. What is the average area per person during the peak 15-min period?

$$\text{TS supply} = TS = (15 \text{ min})(2500 \text{ ft}^2) = 37{,}500 \text{ ft}^2\text{--min}$$

$$\text{TS demand} = nt = \frac{\{(1500)(15 \text{ s})\} + \{(1500)(0.25)(10 \text{ s})\}}{60 \text{ s/min}} = 437.5 \text{ pr--min}$$

$$a = \frac{\text{TS supply}}{\text{TS demand}} = \frac{37{,}500 \text{ ft}^2\text{--min}}{437.5 \text{ pr--min}} = 85.7 \text{ ft}^2/\text{pr}$$

This relationship can also be used to determine corridor widths where desired LOS and area per person are specified, the length of the corridor section is known, and where the times for walking through the corridor section, waiting in lines, obtaining information, or other functions can be predicted. Equation (8-2) would have the following form when the TS method is used to determine corridor widths:

$$w = \frac{ant}{Tl} \tag{8-3}$$

where w =   corridor width (ft or m)
$\quad\quad\quad l$ =   corridor length (ft or m)

Example: Determine the width (w) of a 100-ft (30.5-m)-long (l) corridor with a predicted flow of 200 (n) people per minute where the walking speed is estimated at 4 ft/s (1.2 m/s), and it is desired that the average area per person (a) be 25 ft^2/pr (2.3 m^2/pr). Note that t is 25 s or 0.42 min; T = 1 min.

$$w = \frac{(25)(200)(0.42)}{(1)(100)} = 21 \text{ ft } (6.4 \text{ m})$$

APPLICATIONS TO TRANSIT STATION DESIGN

The LOS standards and TS analysis procedures presented in this chapter can be used to design new transit stations or to evaluate the relative convenience of existing stations. The New York City Planning Commission requires this type of analysis as part of the environmental impact statement (EIS) procedure for the approval of new building projects. As previously noted, it is important to have a thorough understanding of pedestrian traffic demand characteristics so that the LOS standards are not misapplied or misinterpreted. For example, in the arrival mode at heavily used transit platforms, stairs and escalators will be used to maximum capacity until all arriving passengers are accommodated. It is important in this condition to evaluate average passenger waiting times, queue lengths and queuing areas, and the overall platform clearance time. Minimum standards for these conditions could consist of clearance of the platform before the next train arrival and average pedestrian waiting times not to exceed the escalator trip time or stair-use time.

Analysts and students are encouraged to make their own observations of the use of pedestrian facilities, potentially to modify analytical techniques to provide a better model of observed conditions or service standards for levels of crowding and convenience appropriate to local norms.

CORRIDORS

Walkways have significant pedestrian traffic capacity, but the provision of too narrow walkways should be avoided because of human factors and user convenience considerations. Two persons walking abreast require a width of 5 ft (1.5 m) to walk comfortably. Considering that transit facilities can experience heavy two-way traffic movement, minimum corridor widths of 10 ft are indicated. Also, LOS standards are based on the net effective width of the walkway, requiring that 6 in (150 mm) be added to each edge to account for the avoidance of walls. Consideration also must be given to reductions in effective corridor width where doors open into the corridor, where there are columns, or where there are other conflicts such as the extension of queue lines into the traffic stream.

STAIRWAYS

The traffic capacity of a stairway is less than the equivalent-width walkway, frequently resulting in pedestrian queuing at stair approaches. For this reason, the approach configuration should be given careful consideration. The minimum-width stair in transit applications should be 5 ft to provide for convenient two-way, single-file movement. Wherever possible, wider stairs should be provided. The net effective width of stairways is clear distance between handrails. Stairways in transit applications are subjected to two different types of demands. In the departure peak, demands are more nearly uniform throughout the peak period. In the arrival peak, however, large numbers of passengers can be unloaded from trains in very short periods, causing stairs to be overloaded and queuing to develop. During these periods stairways will operate at full capacity, or LOS E. In the arrival situation, pedestrian delay times, queue size, and platform clearance times become convenience measures rather than crowding density.

FARE-CONTROL AREAS

Time–space analysis of fare-control areas, for example, to determine the average pedestrian LOS during the 15-min peak period, requires a determination of the effective usable area in the fare-control section; the total numbers of people passing through the section; the proportion of those purchasing tickets, requesting information, or waiting at turnstiles; and the predicted times for performing these activities. Average area per person and LOS for the peak period are determined by adding all the various demands in pedestrian minutes and dividing it into the TS supply.

TRANSIT PLATFORMS

Passengers using transit platforms in the departure mode distribute themselves on the platform by walking from a connecting stairway or escalator to a position where they stand and wait for the train. Passenger distribution on the platform may not be uniform, and this might have to be taken into consideration. Some platforms may also need to accommodate passengers transferring across the platform from other trains. Platforms can be analyzed for a peak period or for the headway in minutes between trains. Passenger time–space demand consists of the product of the number of passengers using the platform and their average walk and wait times. It should be emphasized that the area per pedestrian and LOS for the platform is an average for the analysis period. It is advisable, particularly where platforms are heavily used, to examine the maximum occupancy of the platform that occurs just before train doors open to accept passengers. If this maximum occupancy is below queuing LOS C, it is desirable to add train service and reduce headways to avoid potentially dangerous crowding.

PEDESTRIAN LEVEL-OF-SERVICE STANDARDS

Traffic standards have been developed for both walkways and stairways based on photographic studies of pedestrian movement on these facilities. The standards define flow relationships for various volume levels and average personal areas and related qualitative attributes such as the ability to bypass slower moving pedestrians and to avoid conflicts with others. These standards have been classified into various levels of service (LOS) ranging from A to F, with LOS A representing the threshold of unimpeded free flow and with LOS F at critical density or breakdown of movement continuity. LOS standards have also been developed for waiting areas, such as transit platforms, based on pedestrian densities and relative degrees of mobility within the waiting area. Care must be taken when applying these standards to facilities where the demand is such that capacity will invariably be exceeded for short periods. An example is a transit platform where potentially more than 1000 passengers could be discharged onto the platform in less than a minute. In such facilities, platform clearance times or average pedestrian delay may provide a more realistic standard of service, since typically all facilities would be operating at maximum capacity. It should be noted that all the LOS walkway and stairway standards represent heavy pedestrian traffic flow conditions, which in other nontransit environments may be considered to be too crowded.

WALKWAY LOS

Relationships for walkway volumes and density at LOSs A to F are illustrated graphically in Fig. 8-1. Standards for walkway traffic volumes, area per person, speed

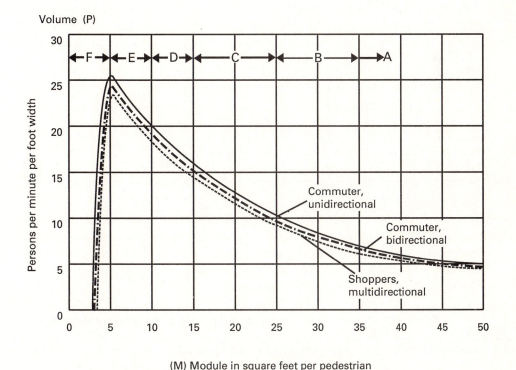

(M) Module in square feet per pedestrian

Figure 8-1 *Level-of-service standards for walkways—volume versus module.*

data, and qualitative descriptions of related traffic conditions for walkway LOSs A to F are also summarized in Table 8-1. Traffic-flow standards are applicable only to the net effective width of the walkway, deducting any obstructions in the walkway space and taking into account that pedestrians do not walk close to corridor walls. Typically, pedestrians will keep about 6 in (150 mm) away from walls and columns in indoor environments and up to 18 in from walls and curbs in outdoor locations. Where there are doors opening into corridors, persons accessing change machines, or other functions that would reduce the net effective width available for movement, added reductions may be necessary.

TABLE 8-1
Walkway Level of Service Descriptions

LOS	Ped. Volume (f) min		Average Area (a)		Description
	pr/ft	pr/m	ft²/pr	m²/pr	
A	7 or less	23 or less	35 or more	3.3 or more	Threshold of of free flow, convenient passing, conflicts avoidable.
B	7-10	23-33	25-35	2.3-3.3	Minor conflicts, passing and speed restrictions.
C	10-15	33-49	15-25	1.4-2.3	Crowded but fluid movement, passing restricted, cross and reverse flows difficult.
D	15-20	49-66	10-15	0.9-1.4	Significant conflicts, passing and speed restrictions, intermittent shuffling.
E	20-25	66-82	5-10	0.5-0.9	Shuffling walk; reverse, passing and cross flows very difficult; intermittent stopping.
F	Flow variable up to maximum		5 or less	0.5 or less	Critical density, flow sporadic, frequent stops, contacts with others.

Example: Determine the recommended width of a 200-ft (61-m)-long corridor connection to a transit station with a forecasted two-way, peak-hour pedestrian traffic of 10,000 pr/h under the following conditions:

Alternative 1: commuters only, no doors entering the corridor, no columns, no other services.
Alternative 2: same volume, but with retail development along the corridor edges in a shopping mall configuration.

Solution for Alternative 1: This requires the selection of a design LOS and appropriate design peak. Unless there are significant restraints, the approximate mid-range of LOS C, or 12.5 pr/ft min, is an appropriate standard. The 15-min peak, typically about 40% of peak-hour volume, is an appropriate design period.

$$\text{Net effective width} = \frac{(10{,}000 \text{ pr})(0.40)}{(15 \text{ min})(12.5 \text{ pr/ft}-\text{min})} = 21.3 \text{ ft}$$

$$\text{Add edge effect} = (2)(6 \text{ in}) = \underline{1.0 \text{ ft}}$$

$$\text{Total} = 22.3 \text{ ft}$$

Recommended corridor width = 22.3 ft (6.8 m)

Solution for Alternative 2: The shopping mall alternative can be analyzed as (a) a corridor with additions at the edges to allow window-shopping and door-opening "lanes" or (b) on a time–space basis, assuming some percentage of the commuters will spend additional time in the corridor. For illustrative purposes, it will be assumed that 100% of the commuters walk through the corridor, but that 30% of this total stop to window-shop for an additional 1 min each. It is desired to provide a density of 20 ft^2/p average within the corridor during the 15-min peak.

(a)

$$\text{Net effective width} = \frac{(10{,}000 \text{ pr})(0.40)}{(15 \text{ min})(12.5 \text{ pr/ft}-\text{min})} = 21.3 \text{ ft}$$

$$\text{Add edge effect doors} = (2)(3 \text{ ft}) = \underline{6.0 \text{ ft}}$$

$$\text{Total} = 27.3 \text{ ft}$$

Recommended corridor width = 27.3 ft (8.3 m)

(b) The *TS supply* is the product of the 15-min time of the analysis period, the corridor width (w), and the length (l) of 200 ft. Refer to Eq. (8-3).

$$\text{TS supply} = (w)(200 \text{ ft})(15 \text{ min}) = 3000w \text{ (area}-\text{min)}$$

The *TS demand* is the time required to walk through the corridor at an assumed walking speed of 250 ft-min (0.8 min), plus the time spent window-shopping.

$$\text{Walk time} = (10{,}000)(0.4)(0.8 \text{ min}) = 3200 \text{ pr}-\text{min}$$

$$\text{Shop time} = (10{,}000)(0.4)(0.30)(1 \text{ min}) = \underline{1200 \text{ pr}-\text{min}}$$

$$\text{Total} = 4400 \text{ pr}-\text{min}$$

$$\text{TS demand} = (4400 \text{ pr--min})(20 \text{ ft}^2/\text{pr}) = 88{,}000 \text{ ft}^2\text{--min}$$

$$\text{TS supply} = \text{TS demand}$$
$$3000w = 88{,}000 \text{ ft}^2\text{--min}$$
$$w = \frac{88{,}000}{3000}$$
$$w = 29.3 \text{ ft } (8.9 \text{ m})$$

$$\text{Recommended corridor width} = 29.3 \text{ ft } (8.9 \text{ m})$$

You will note that the two different methods give roughly similar results under rather different assumptions. However, the TS method provides greater flexibility to input more variations in pedestrian behavior and to do sensitivity analyses of the impact of these variations on proposed designs.

STAIRWAY LOS

Flow relationships for stairway volumes and densities at LOSs A to F are illustrated graphically in Fig. 8-2. A summary of volume, area per person, speed, and a qualitative description of flow conditions at these various levels of service are shown in Table 8-2. Stairway volume data must also be applied to the effective width of the stairway, not the overall width. The net effective width of the stairway is the clear distance between handrails. The adequacy of queuing space at stair approaches, particularly at upper landings, should be examined in relation to expected volumes of traffic to avoid excessive and potentially dangerous crowding.

Example: Determine the width of stairs required on a 600-ft (183-m)-long, 20-ft (6.1-m)-wide, side-loading transit platform to accommodate a departure volume of 10,000 peak-hour passengers and an arrival volume of 1500 passengers on the most crowded peak train. The peak-period headway between train arrivals is 5 min.

Solution for the departure peak: The departing peak-hour passengers arrive on a more gradual basis, typically 40% in the peak 15 min. The appropriate LOS for this condition is stairway LOS C, with a midrange design flow of about 8.5 pr/ft-min (28 pr/m- min). Note that the effective width equals the clearance between handrails.

$$\text{Total effective stair width} = \frac{(10{,}000)(0.4)}{(8.5 \text{ pr/ft--min})(15 \text{ min})} = 31.4 \text{ ft}$$

Alternatives: Two 16-ft end stairs or three 10.5-ft stairs

VOLUME (P)

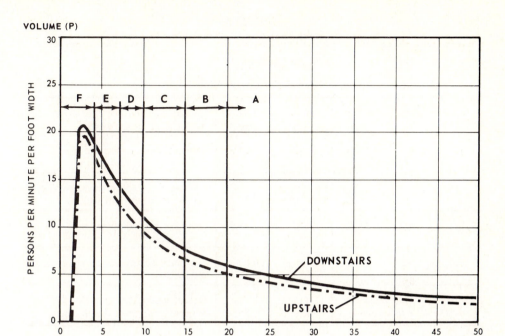

metric conversion : 1 ft = .3m, 1 ft² = .0 9 m².

Figure 8-2 *Level-of-service standards for stairways—volume versus module.*

Solution for the arriving peak: The typical transit car configuration, with up to three sets of wide double-doors per car opening simultaneously, has the capability of discharging 1500 passengers in a minute. All stairways are almost immediately subjected to LOS E capacity conditions or a flow of 17 pr/ft-min (56 pr/m-min). The desirable standard is that the platform be cleared before the next peak-train arrival or sooner. The trial design width selected for the departure peak will be tested for its ability to accommodate the arriving peak train.

$$\text{Capacity of stairs} = (31.4 \text{ ft})(17 \text{ pr/ft–min}) = 534 \text{ pr/min}$$

$$\text{Platform clearance time} = \frac{1500 \text{ pr}}{534 \text{ pr/min}} = 2.8 \text{ min}$$

The clearance time is less than the train headway of 5 min, and therefore the design is satisfactory for both arriving and departing peaks.

TABLE 8-2
Stairway Level of Service Descriptions

LOS	Ped. Volume (f) min		Average Area (a)		Description
	pr/ft	pr/m	ft²/pr	m²/pr	
A	5 or less	16 or less	20 or more	1.9 or more	Threshold of free flow, convenient passing, conflicts avoidable.
B	5-7	16-23	15-20	1.4-1.9	Minor conflicts, passing and speed restrictions.
C	7-10	23-33	10-15	0.9-1.4	Crowded but fluid movement, passing and reverse flows restricted.
D	10-13	33-43	7-10	0.7-0.9	Severely restricted passing and reverse flow.
E	13-17	43-56	4-7	0.4-70.	Maximum capacity, no passing or reverse flow.
F	Flow variable up to maximum		4 or less	0.4 or less	Critical density, flow sporadic, frequent stops, contacts with others.

QUEUING LOS

The provision of inadequate space where pedestrian waiting occurs can cause problems ranging from temporary inconvenience and discomfort to crowd-induced falls and other hazards. Queuing often occurs in transit stations on platforms; at escalators, stairs, turnstiles, doors, and ticket dispensing machines; and at any location where passengers may be delayed, even momentarily. Queues may be classified into two general types, the *linear* or *ordered queue*, in which pedestrians line up and are served in their order of arrival, and the *undisciplined* or *bulk queue,* where there is more general, less ordered crowding. The spacing between persons in linear queues is surprisingly uniform and consistent with behavioral studies of personal space preferences. In disciplined linear queues the interpersonal spacing is 19 to 20 in (480 to 500 mm), and the recommended lateral single-file width for railings or other dividers is 30 in (760 mm).

Interpersonal spacing and area occupancies in undisciplined bulk queues are naturally more variable and are therefore rated according to the degree of mobility within the queuing space at different pedestrian densities. For example, on transit platforms it is necessary to provide sufficient space not only for passengers to stand and wait, but also for others to move through these standees and distribute themselves along the platform. Queuing LOSs based on pedestrian area occupancies and relative degrees of mobility within the waiting space are summarized in Table 8-3.

TABLE 8-3
Queuing Level of Service Descriptions

LOS	Average Area ft²/pr	m²/pr	Interpersonal Spacing ft	m	Description
A	13 or more	1.2 or more	4 or more	1.2 or more	Standing, circulation within queuing area possible without disturbing others.
B	10-13	0.9-1.2	3.5-4	1.1-1.2	Standing, partially restricted circulation.
C	7-10	0.7-0.9	3-3.5	0.9-1.1	Standing, restricted circulation by disturbing others, "excuse me" zone.
D	3-7	0.3-0.7	2-3	0.6-0.9	Standing without contact possible, but movement is severely restricted and disturbing to others. Long-term waiting discomforting.
E	2-3	0.2-0.3	1-2	0.3-0.6	Standing without contact, movement within queue not possible. Threshold potentially dangerous crowd pressure.
F	2 or less	0.2 or less	1 or less	0.3 or less	Close contact with all. Uncomfortable and psychologically disturbing. Potential for shock waves in mass crowds, falls, other hazards.

PLATFORM LOS

Like stairs, platforms have different functions and characteristics during departing and arriving peak conditions. For the arriving peak, the platform must have sufficient area and vertical access facilities for passengers to quickly move through it. During the departing peak, the platform acts as a storage area for passengers waiting for a train and as a movement space for passengers distributing themselves along the platform. TS analysis is useful for determining the average per person area available for these purposes, for comparison with the LOS standards. The net effective platform width is determined by deducting a 1.5-ft (0.45-m)-safety edge along the length of the platform and the footprint area of any stairs, columns, or other space-consuming features on the platform. There are a number of alternatives for the placement of stairs on platforms. Uniform spacing of stairs on the platform provides for a more even distribution of passengers, but the stairs take up more platform space. End locations allow wider stairs with no footprint on the platform, but walking distances are longer and uneven distribution of passengers occurs. TS analysis provides the means of analyzing various placement alternatives for stairs and the potential impact on pedestrian LOS. It also allows a section-by-section analysis of the platform where there are irregularly spaced stairs or variations in platform conditions, such as differences in occupancy.

Example: Determine the pedestrian LOS of a 600-ft (183-m)-long, 20-ft (6.1-m)-wide, side-loading transit platform for average and maximum load conditions and a train departure of 1500 passengers during a 5-min peak period. Evaluate the differences of (a) using two stairways, one at each end of the platform, and (b) using three stairways, one at either end and one in the center. Note that the average walking distance is half the maximum walking distance from either end of the platform.

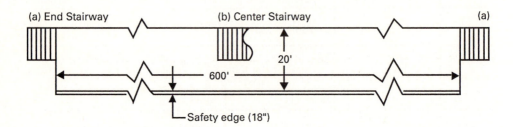

Solutions: The platform will be evaluated using the TS method. The net effective area is determined by deducting the 18-in (457-mm) safety edge along the length of the platform and any stairway footprint. All the departing passengers will both walk and wait on the platform. Walk times are determined by the average walking distance from each stairway to the adjacent platform sections, and an assumed "restrained" walking speed of 3.3 ft/s (1 m/s). The average wait time, assuming that passenger arrivals on the platform are uniform, is half of the 5-min headway time, or 2.5 min. In alternative (a) there is no stairway footprint, but in alternative (b) the stairway footprint must be deducted from the net platform area, compensated by a reduction in average walking distances.

(a) Using two stairways

$$\text{Gross area platform} = (20 \text{ ft})(600 \text{ ft}) = 12{,}000 \text{ ft}^2$$
$$\text{Less safety edge} = (1.5 \text{ ft})(600 \text{ ft}) = \underline{-900 \text{ ft}^2}$$
$$\text{Net effective area} = 11{,}100 \text{ ft}^2$$

$$\begin{aligned}
\text{TS supply} &= (\text{net effective platform area})(\text{headway min}) \\
&= (11{,}100)(5 \text{ min}) \\
&= 55{,}500 \text{ ft}^2\text{–min}
\end{aligned}$$

$$\text{Average walk distance} = (0.5)(300 \text{ ft}) = 150 \text{ ft}$$
$$\text{Average walk time} = \frac{150}{3.33 \text{ ft/s}} = 45 \text{ s or } 0.75 \text{ min}$$
$$\text{Average wait time} = (0.5)(\text{headway}) = (0.5)(5) = 2.5 \text{ min}$$

$$\begin{aligned} \text{TS demand} &= (\text{no. passengers})(\text{avg. walk time} + \text{avg. wait time}) \\ &= 1500(0.75 + 2.5) \\ &= 4875 \text{ pr–min} \end{aligned}$$

$$\text{Average platform area/passenger} = \frac{\text{TS supply}}{\text{TS demand}} = \frac{55,500 \text{ ft}^2\text{–min}}{4875 \text{ pr–min}} = 11.3 \text{ ft}^2/\text{pr}$$

$$\text{At max. occupancy} = \frac{\text{platform area}}{\text{max. passengers}} = \frac{11,100 \text{ ft}^2}{1500 \text{ psgrs.}} = 7.4 \text{ ft}^2/\text{pr}$$

Platform LOS at average occupancy, 11.3 ft²/pr
Walkway LOS D, queuing LOS B
Platform LOS at maximum occupancy, 7.4 ft²/pr
Walkway LOS E, queuing LOS D

Discussion: This is a functional, but very crowded platform. There are examples of more crowded platforms in the New York City transit system. The platform crowding could be improved by widening of the platform or by adding trains to reduce the passenger volume per arrival.

(b) Using three stairways

$$\begin{aligned} \text{Net effective platform area with 2 end stairs} &= 11,100 \text{ ft}^2 \\ \text{Less footprint of center stair (11 ft} \times 16 \text{ ft)} &= \underline{-176 \text{ ft}^2} \\ \text{Net effective area with 3 stairs} &= 10,924 \text{ ft}^2 \end{aligned}$$

$$\text{TS supply} = (10,924 \text{ ft}^2)(5 \text{ min}) = 54,620 \text{ ft}^2\text{–min}$$

TS demand: average wait time remains the same, average walking distance cut in half by center stair (from 150 ft to 75 ft), and average walk time from 0.75 min to 0.38 min.

$$\text{Average platform area/passenger} = \frac{54,620 \text{ ft}^2-\text{min}}{4320 \text{ pr}-\text{min}} = 12.6 \text{ ft}^2/\text{pr}$$

$$\text{TS demand} = 1500(0.38 + 2.5) = 4320 \text{ pr}-\text{min}$$

Platform LOS at average occupancy, 12.6 ft^2/pr
Walkway LOS D, queuing LOS B
LOS at maximum occupancy remains the same

Discussion: The addition of the stairway at the center of the platform reduces the time–space supply, but shortens walking distances. This impact is not sufficient to improve the platform LOS, but the TS analysis does show that the average level of crowding is reduced and passenger convenience is improved. In practice, it is known that passengers tend to cluster around platform access stairs, so the center stairway design will also result in a more even distribution of passengers on the platform. This also results in a more even distribution of passengers on the train, a desirable objective to improve passenger perceptions of service.

ESCALATOR AND MOVING WALKWAY LOS

Escalators and moving walkways are high-capacity, continuous-service mechanical aids that can facilitate vertical and horizontal pedestrian movement. Escalator and moving walkway technology has evolved over a period of 100 years, and there are examples of well-maintained escalator installations that have provided continuous service for more than 50 years. Photographic studies of escalator and moving walkway use indicate that escalator utilization and capacities are closely related to human factors such as shoulder width, personal space preferences, and ability to adjust to system speed. Even under heavy queuing, vacant steps can be observed on most escalators, with similar preferred personal spacing on moving walkways, rather than that assumed by the manufacturer. Most escalators in transit applications in the United States operate at a speed of 90 ft/min (0.45 m/s), but higher speeds are observed in Europe, reportedly more than 164 ft/min. The U.S. Code limits escalator speeds to 120 ft/min (0.60 m/s), and moving walkway speeds to 180 ft/min (0.91 m/s).

Escalators are preferred for vertical movement in transit applications because of their high capacity. It would take three or more large elevators to equal the capacity of a single escalator. Disadvantages of escalators are that they take up significant space, are not accessible to wheelchair users, and, because of their 30° slope, may be difficult to integrate with other movement facilities such as elevators. Escalators and moving walkways tend to experience more accidents than elevators because of the direct exposure of passengers to moving elements of the system, passenger difficulties in adjusting to escalator and walkway movement, and their mechanical discharge characteristic. Escalators and moving walkways will continue to mechanically discharge passengers until stopped. This has resulted in accidents where there is limited landing area to disperse exiting passengers or where the discharge end of the escalator cannot be cleared quickly enough for some reason. Since escalators and walkways can mechanically discharge up to 90 persons/min and these persons minimally require at least 5 ft²/pr (0.5 m²/pr) each to move away from the escalator, it can be seen that even a temporary blockage at the discharge end of an escalator can create a large demand for circulation space. Escalator data and theoretical and practical design capacities are shown in Table 8-4.

Estimates of moving walkway use can be developed from Eq. (8-1) by using the speed of the walkway and assuming the average standing area of passengers, or by the TS method, Eq. (8-3), if it is necessary to determine attainable capacities where there is a mix of standing and walking passengers.

TABLE 8-4
Theoretical and Nominal Escalator Capacities

Width at Hip		Width at Tread		Theoretical Capacity	Nominal Capacity	
in	mm	in	mm	pr/hour	pr/h	pr/min
32	813	24	610	5000	2040	34[a]
				6700	2700	45[b]
48	1219	40	1016	8000	4080	68[a]
				10,700	5400	90[b]

[a]Incline speed of 90 ft/min (0.45 m/s), 68 steps/min.
[b]Incline speed of 120 ft/min (0.60 m/s), 89 steps/min.

Example: Determine the practical capacity of a 300-ft (81.5-m)-long (l), 120-ft/min (0.6-m/s), 4-ft (1.2-m)-wide (w) moving walkway under the assumption that half of the passengers stand and half walk at a speed of 3 ft/s.

Solution: There are two types of passengers on the moving walkway, standees who occupy less space but are on it for a longer time and walkers who need more space and who are on it for a shorter time. To solve the problem it is necessary to assume the space needed by standees and walkers. For purposes of this example, a crowded moving walkway at 7 ft²/pr (0.7 m²/pr) for standees and 20 ft²/pr (1.9 m²/pr) for walkers is assumed. The capacity per minute, $T = 1$ min, will be determined.

n_1 = standees, a_1 = 7 ft²/pr, t_1 = 300 ft/2 ft/s = 150 s or 2.5 min
n_2 = walkers, a_2 = 20 ft²/pr, t_2 = 300 ft/(3 + 2 ft/s) = 60 s or 1 min
N = capacity (p/min), n_1 = 0.5N, n_2 = 0.5N

From Eq. (8-3),

$$(a_1 n_1 t_1) + (a_2 n_2 t_2) = wlT$$
$$(7)(0.5N)(2.5) + (20)(0.5N)(1) = (4)(300)(1)$$
$$8.75N + 10N = 1200$$
$$18.75N = 1200$$
$$N = 64 \text{ pr/min, practical capacity of walkway}$$

ELEVATOR LOS

Elevators have had limited application in transit stations, except for vertical movement of physically impaired persons. Their use has not been more widespread because elevators generally have less movement capacity than escalators and stairs and because users must wait for elevator arrivals. It would take a group of three or more large elevators to equal the capacity of a single escalator. Elevators have the advantage of fast trip times, lower accident rates than escalators, and, in some installations, lower life-cycle cost. Other advantages of elevators are that they provide for bidirectional movement and standby service where there is a mechanical failure of one unit in a group. From a station planning viewpoint, elevators simplify the location of vertical movement access and fare control areas as compared to inclined escalators.

Elevators should receive greater consideration as a vertical movement alternative in transit stations particularly since at least one elevator is required for the needs of the physically impaired. The elevator alternative should be examined for deep stations where escalator trip times are long and for outlying stations where passenger volumes are likely to be lower. Escalator trip times in deep stations can exceed 2 min, whereas the comparable trip by elevator could be less than 30 s, excluding waiting time. It is not unusual to see the non-physically-impaired competing to use the elevator in the deeper stations of the Washington, D.C., Metro transit system to avoid longer escalator trip times. Elevators can be programmed to meet an arriving train to help offset the waiting time disadvantage.

Elevator capacity is determined by the floor or standing area of the cab, average speed allowing for acceleration and deceleration, and dwell times for the loading and unloading of passengers, plus the opening and closing of doors. Elevator travel speeds of up to 1,800 ft/min (9 m/s) have been attained in high-rise building applications, but a speed of about 400 ft/min is the more likely maximum for transit stations. Approximate estimates of elevator capacity for preliminary planning purposes can be developed by assuming cab standing areas at 2 ft^2/pr (0.2 m^2/pr), an allowance of 10 s for each cab acceleration and deceleration set, 10 s for each door opening and closing set, and the travel speed of the elevator. Elevator suppliers should be consulted if preliminary estimates indicate that an elevator alternative to escalators may be feasible. They have elaborate computer simulation programs that would confirm the relative service statistics of the two alternatives.

Example: Determine the number of elevators required to meet a peak-period train discharging 150 passengers at an outlying station. The station has a 50-ft (15.2-m) rise. Compare with the alternative of a 48-in (1220-mm) nominal-width escalator operating at a speed of 90 ft/min (0.45 m/s) and with a practical capacity of 68 pr/min or 1.1 pr/s.

Solution: As a trial assumption, three large elevators with a cab area of 50 ft^2 (0.5 m^2) will be used. The standing passenger capacity of these elevators at 2 ft^2/pr would be 25 persons. Dwell time to load and discharge passengers via double opening doors at a headway of 1 s/pr/door would be about 13 s. The shaft time or elevator travel time for the 50-ft trip at a speed of 400 ft/min would be 8 s, with the addition of approximately 10 s for each acceleration and deceleration set and 10 s for each door opening and closing set.

The three elevators would be programmed to meet the arriving train, pick up 75 passengers, and return for the remaining 75. The trip time for the first group of passengers unloaded at the surface would be:

2 (13 s) load/unload + 8 s travel + 10 s accel/decel + 10 s door close/open = 54 s

The trip time for the first person using the escalator to reach the surface would be

$$100 \text{ ft slope}/1.5 \text{ ft/s} = 67 \text{ s}$$

The seventy-fifth escalator passenger would reach the surface after 2 min. The maximum wait for the second group of 75 elevator passengers left on the platform after the first pickup would be

54 s + 10 s door close /open + 8 s travel + 10 s accel/decel = 82 s

This compares with the average waiting time of about 1 min experienced by 150 passengers boarding an escalator with a capacity of 68 pr/min.

The total time for the second group of 75 elevator passengers to reach the surface level would be

82 s + 2 (13 s) load/unload + 10 s door close/open + 8 s travel + 10 s accel/decel
= 136 s

This compares with the time for the last escalator passenger to reach the surface of

$$67 \text{ s} + 150 \text{ pr}/1.1 \text{ pr/s} = 203 \text{ s}$$

The people movement capacity of the three elevators is

$$150 \text{ pr}/136 \text{ s} = 1.1 \text{ pr/s}$$

exactly the same as the escalator.

Discussion: The theoretical analysis shows that overall passenger service statistics for the three elevator alternative are comparable to the escalator. The movement capacity in pr/s for the three large elevators is 150/136 s = 1.1 pr/s, equal to the escalator. The elevators have a faster total delivery time than the escalator. Escalators are viewed by many as continuous-service, no-wait systems. But the short-term capacity of the escalator would be exceeded even with the relatively low demand of 150 train passengers. This results in a wait to ride the escalator, which should be considered in comparing the service of the two alternatives. In the long term the three elevators could have functional and life-cycle cost advantages, particularly considering that a mechanical failure of the escalator would have serious consequences. The failure of one elevator would still leave two available at reduced levels of service.

PLANNED PEDESTRIAN SYSTEMS

There is much evidence of a growing awareness of pedestrian needs. The benefits of urban pedestrianization include reduced air, noise, and visual pollution and reduced pedestrian accidents and other improvements in the quality of life. Pedestrianization has many forms including auto-free zones and malls within existing city street systems, vehicle-free business or activity centers, elevated pedestrian "skyway" systems, and underground networks. Skyway systems have been built in such cities as London, Minneapolis, and Cincinnati, and underground networks in Montreal, Tokyo, Houston, and New York.

The classic approach to pedestrian improvements is the separation of the pedestrian from the vehicle either by space or time. Traffic signalization represents an example of separation of pedestrians and vehicles in time, but pedestrians are still exposed to turning vehicles. Traffic signalization also has the disadvantages of causing pedestrian delay, queuing at crosswalks, and the creation of denser platoons of pedestrians than would normally occur in uninterrupted free flow. The spatial separation of pedestrians and vehicles, either horizontally by pedestrian malls or vertically through elevated or underground pedestrian convenience networks, represents the ultimate improvement objective, but more modest improvements can be quickly and inexpensively attained.

There is a high pedestrian-accident exposure due to vehicles turning through crosswalks while people are crossing. Many cities already have extensive vehicle turn restrictions in downtown areas, but they are not planned on a systemwide basis. This may not cause as much hardship to motorists as might be thought since the predominant downtown vehicular movement is the through one.

Low-capital improvements include upgrading pedestrian circulation, better street lighting, and standardization of street furniture and signs. Improved circulation is attained by special pedestrian signal cycles and vehicular turn restrictions, sidewalk widenings through the use of building setbacks and arcades, better location of street furniture, and shortening of walking distances by means of midblock connectors. The control of street furniture location is necessary to provide maximum clear width on sidewalks and to eliminate obstructions in the vicinity of crosswalks, particularly those that can obscure the turning driver's view of pedestrians. Street lighting improvements upgrade area image and significantly reduce pedestrian accidents and street crime. Many cities have found that lighting improvement programs receive quick popular support and even supplementary private financing on a voluntary basis. Additionally, the change to more efficient modern luminaires often results in reductions in total energy use.

Building setbacks, arcades, pedestrian plazas, and other such amenities can be obtained by bonus zoning amendments that allow larger building areas to developers who provide them. When pedestrian plazas are provided by private developers, care must be taken that the improvement is carefully integrated into the pedestrian system. Above- or belowgrade building plazas do not add to sidewalk capacity and may actually isolate and inconvenience some pedestrians.

The pedestrian mall is becoming a common improvement, but it must be carefully planned to be successful. The requirements for a viable mall program include complete exclusion of all but emergency vehicles; development of adequate perimeter street capacity to replace that eliminated by the mall; provision of adequate transit and highway access and sufficient parking; upgraded street lighting; and the development of an active and cooperative promotional program based on aesthetic improvements, special events, and coordinated advertising. The locations of walking trip generators must be considered when planning malls. Transit operations within the mall can discourage walking trips and exposure to retail edges, whereas strategically located stops at the ends of the mall can encourage walking and retail exposure.

The ultimate pedestrian improvement program is the grade separated pedestrian convenience network. These networks are being built above or below street level, depending on local requirements. The network aspect, particularly the need for continuity within these systems, must be emphasized. New York City has several miles of underground passages serving individual buildings and subway stations. Because these are not interconnected, their use is limited except in the most inclement weather. This is in sharp contrast to the well-planned and heavily utilized 3.6-mi (6-km) underground system in Montreal, Canada.

Underground systems need only be about 10 ft (3 m) below street level to provide full weather protection and efficient climate control. They can be easily connected to subway transit stations. Disadvantages of underground systems include their high construction costs, possible conflicts with subsurface utilities, and loss of visual identity with the cityscape above. Aboveground pedestrian convenience networks have the advantage of lower construction costs and greater opportunities for integration and identification with the cityscape. The primary disadvantage of aboveground networks is that their greater height above street level, required to provide vehicle clearances, makes them difficult to relate to belowground transit. Both systems provide the developer or owner with added valuable commercial space.

Figure 8-3 *Pedestrian transit mall and skyway—Nicollet Mall, Minneapolis. The Minneapolis skyway system consists of an elevated network of connecting bridges and passageways serving many of the major buildings in the downtown areas. (courtesy of Greater Minneapolis Chamber of Commerce)*

Pedestrian system planning in transportation terminals and stations follows the same basic pedestrian improvement objectives but requires greater consideration of the heavy pedestrian traffic movements typically occurring in these facilities, the magnified value that the traveler is likely to place on time and delay, and the increased need for information and orientation. Also, transportation planners rarely examine the effectiveness of the external walkway network surrounding a transportation terminal or station. The service area of transit, and therefore its potential utilization, could be increased by more effective planning of this external pedestrian system. Pedestrian processing times through transportation terminals should be minimized because of the tendency of the passenger to magnify this time over the equivalent time spent in transit. This human tendency for exaggeration of time spent making intermodal transfers has been noted by transportation system analysts, with some applying a factor of 2.5: 1 for time spent in a station.

Figure 8-4 *Place Bonaventure, Montreal, Canada. Smart shops line three levels of corridors in a giant merchandising mart in the heart of the city. The mart is part of the Montreal underground pedestrian network that connects major transportation lines and many of the hotels and major retail establishments in the downtown area. (courtesy of City of Montreal)*

Deep subway systems have been built on the basis of construction cost savings without consideration of the value of pedestrian time that is spent, over the life of the system, traveling to and from the surface and platform level. In some deep stations this can involve an escalator ride of more than 2 min. Passenger orientation, information, and way-finding convenience are also important transportation terminal design objectives.

The physically impaired must be considered in the design of all pedestrian systems. Surveys in the United States indicate there are at least 20 million Americans with disabilities severe enough to restrict or discourage their use of public transportation or their finding employment commensurate with their qualifications. Many others with what might be termed minor sight, locomotion, or other impairments are inconvenienced daily by design features that do not consider these common disabilities.

The ranks of the physically disadvantaged are also expanding at a rate faster than the growth of the general population because medical advances are continually increasing survival rates from accidents and illness and extending life spans of the aged. The very heavy automobile accident rate in this country is a contributor to the ranks, with the added reminder that anyone, despite present physical and mental capabilities, can become disabled at any time and possibly rendered inoperable in a society ordered only for the most physically fit.

There are other types of impairments that designers sometimes overlook. Passengers in transportation terminals are likely to be physically encumbered by baggage, and subway users by parcels and even heavy winter clothing, a factor that should be considered in designing doorways, turnstiles, stairs, and other similar human interface features. This means that the proportion of physically disadvantaged users in most transportation and building systems constitutes a larger population than is generally realized.

While some may believe designing systems with consideration of the physically impaired is a highly idealized, impractical, and costly philosophy, it is not true. The needs of these persons are only a magnification of the problems that face all system users. By recognizing these needs, designers can project themselves more easily into the problems of all users, creating designs with greater general utility. On the other hand, design-imposed dysfunctions can limit the economic life and viability of building and transportation systems by continual daily inconvenience. Consideration of the needs of the disadvantaged users of a system is not an idealistic design objective, but a pragmatic approach to producing more utilitarian systems for all.

SUMMARY

Walking is a unique transportation mode connector and a key determinant of many aspects of urban quality of life. Transit station planning and design require a careful analysis of the movement of people. Pedestrian facility organization and adequacy within transit stations determine user perceptions of service, convenience, and passenger safety. This chapter provides the basic analytical tools needed to determine new station requirements and adequacy of existing facilities. Two methods of analysis are presented. Level-of-service standards provide qualitative measures for the design and evaluation of simple walkway, stairway, and queuing spaces. The time–space analysis technique provides a means of analyzing more complex pedestrian spaces. Examples include platforms, fare-control areas, and corridor intersections. The capacity and application of escalators and elevators is also discussed. Simple solved problems are presented to illustrate methods of analysis for a variety of pedestrian facilities.

FURTHER READING

BENZ, GREGORY P., "Transit Platform Analysis Using the Time-Space Concept," in *Rapid Rail Transit and Planning Tools*, Transportation Research Record 1152, pp. 1-10. Washington, D.C.: Transportation Research Board, 1987.

FRUIN, JOHN J. *Pedestrian Planning and Design* (rev. ed.). Mobile, Ala.: Elevator World Magazine, Inc., 1987.

——, DILIP K. GUHA, AND ROLF F. MARSHALL. *Pedestrian Falling Accidents in Transit Terminals*, Final Report, prepared by the Port Authority of NY and NJ for UMTA under contract to Research and Special Programs Administration, Transportation Systems Center, UMTA Technical Assistance Program, Report no. DOT-TSC-UMTA-84-36. Washington, D.C.: U.S. Government Printing Office, December 1985.

Proceedings of the Conference on Multimodal Terminal Planning and Design, eds. Al Hollinden and Linda Ahlberg. Irvine, Calif.: University of California, Irvine, Institute of Transportation Studies, March 1981.

STRAKOSCH, GEORGE R., *Vertical Transportation: Elevators and Escalators* (2nd ed.). New York: John Wiley & Sons, Inc., 1983

TRANSPORTATION RESEARCH BOARD, *Highway Capacity Manual*, Special Report 209. Washington, D.C.: Transportation Research Board, 1985, Chap. 13, "Pedestrians," pp. 13-1 to 13-29.

VIRKLER, MARK R., MICHAEL J. DEMETSKY, AND LESTER A. HOEL, *Transit Station Design: Case Studies of a Planning and Design Method*, Final Report, prepared by the University of Virginia, Department of Civil Engineering, for U.S. DOT, University Research Program, Report no. DOT-RSPA-DPB-50/79/14. Washington, D.C.: U.S. Government Printing Office, February 1980.

EXERCISES

8-1 (a) Measure the area of an elevator cab floor and record your observations of pedestrian areas, convenience, and behavior during a number of elevator trips; compare to LOS and discuss.

   (b) Measure the area of a busy street corner and record your observations of pedestrian areas, convenience, and behavior during a number of light cycles; compare to LOS and discuss.

8-2 Conduct walking-speed studies of people walking to a transit stop and people in a shopping mall. Discuss differences in observed speeds and behavior.

8-3 Record your personal walking distances for your different activities during a typical day. Discuss reasons for the long walking distances occurring in large cities.

8-4 Determine the pedestrian LOS for a 10-ft (3-m)-wide corridor (wall-to-wall) and a 6-ft (1.8-m)-wide stair (clear distance between handrails) for a volume of 500 pedestrians during a 5-min peak period. Discuss the differences in LOS and problems at the stair approach at the point where the two intersect.

8-5 Two 16-ft (5-m)-wide corridors intersecting at right angles will be accommodating a forecasted demand of 750 multidirectional pedestrians in a 5-min peak period. Walking speed through the intersection is estimated at 3.3 ft/s (1 m/s) and average occupancy time in the intersection at 6 s, or 0.1 min. Using the TS method, determine the average ft²/pr (m²/pr) and LOS for the intersection.

8-6 For Exercise 8-5, determine the sensitivity of the design to changes in predicted occupancy times to 10 and 12 s. Discuss.

Figure 8-5 *Chicago Transit Authority Terminal Station at O'Hare Airport, Chicago. (courtesy of Harre W. Demoro Collection)*

Figure 8-6 *San Francisco Transbay Transit Terminal. (courtesy of California Department of Transportation)*

PART III

COMPARING

ALTERNATIVES

Chapter 9

COMPARATIVE COSTS

Michael G. Ferreri

Discussions of the importance of continuing and enhancing existing transit service, proposals for development of new systems, and plans for capital investment in existing transit systems are supported by any number of concerns that hold out promise for solution to many urban ills. Public transit has been put forth as part of the solution to:

- Handicapped persons' mobility.
- Economically disadvantaged persons' mobility.
- Cleanup of the environment.
- Urban traffic problems.
- Travel-time savings.
- Shaping urban development.
- Saving energy.

Notwithstanding each of these valid considerations, in the final analysis, urban agencies charged with providing and improving transit service confront an economic resource allocation problem that manifests itself in the estimation of the capital and operating expenses (and resulting deficits) necessary to provide these services. To a substantial degree, transit management has been placed in a position of trying to meet increased costs and requests for service within an environment largely determined by forces beyond its control. One such exogenous factor—the density of development—has impaired the productivity of public transportation, while simultaneously contributing to an escalation in the costs necessary to serve potential travel markets. As indicated in Fig. 9-1, service effectiveness, or the number of passengers generated per vehicle-mi operated, has declined for several decades, while the cost of serving the transit rider has increased greatly. Although some escalation in costs may certainly be attributed to

245

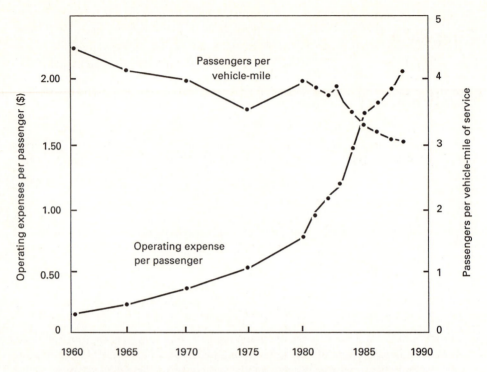

Figure 9-1 *Relationship of expense per passenger and passengers per vehicle-mi, U.S. transit systems, 1960-1988. [Source: American Public Transit Association, Transit Fact Book, 1989 ed. (Washington, D.C.: American Public Transit Association, 1989).]*

inflation and price increases for labor and materials, the growth of automobile ownership and its consequent impact on the location and distribution of urban activities have been a major factor in lower system effectiveness. Similar to many other collective goods and services, urban sprawl has had a deleterious impact on mass transportation.

In response to the economic resource allocation problem, several sound approaches have been developed to analyze comparative costs of alternative solutions for three basic purposes:

1. Urban areas with fully developed multimodal transit systems coincidentally are almost universally faced with financial problems, which have caused the dilemma of maintaining or improving existing operations while trying to control deficits, leading to a search for methods of productivity improvement.
2. Considerations for short-term service expansions require comparative operating cost analysis to ensure the most cost-effective method of expansion.
3. Longer-range planning for capital improvements to existing systems and/or for installation of completely new systems requires detailed estimates of comparative capital and operating expenses so that the most cost-effective solution is assured.

These purposes are driven by the resource allocation question addressed earlier. This question is at issue at all levels of government—federal down to local. The allocation problem has separated itself into the two basic cost areas: capital and operating costs. Historically, capital expenses have involved the replacement of rolling stock and renovation of fixed facilities with substantial assistance from federal grants (at least since 1964). Financial requirements for capital assistance, however, have constituted a relatively minor portion of the total financial problem, while operating deficits are approaching $10 billion per year. Furthermore, the trend of operating losses indicates an aggravation of this disparity in the future. Figure 9-2 illustrates this

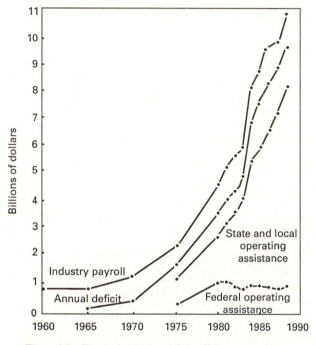

Figure 9-2   *Trend of operating deficit—U.S. transit industry.*

trend and shows further the widening of the gap between federal operating assistance under the Urban Mass Transportation Act and the industry deficit. The gap between federal assistance and operating deficits has been largely filled by increased state and local funds. The figure also demonstrates the labor-intensive nature of public transit wherein the deficit curve is almost in parallel with the industry payroll. This chapter concerns itself with an exploration of these costs and the derivation of methods of estimating their magnitude so that comparative costs can be prepared for use in situations in the three alternative solutions enumerated. The chapter is organized into a discussion of operating costs—their component composition, their variance by mode, and methods of calculation—and then capital costs, which are similarly addressed.

OPERATING COSTS

Figure 9-3 provides an overview of the composition of operating expenses for the U.S. transit industry. These major categories include transportation expense, which is

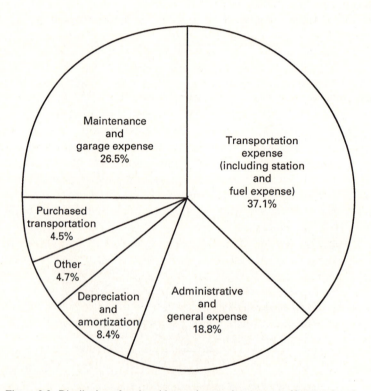

Figure 9-3 *Distribution of nationwide transit operating expenses. [Source: American Public Transit Association*, Transit Fact Book, *1989 ed. (Washington, D.C.: American Public Transit Association, August 1989).]*

basically the cost of providing the service in the form of drivers, supervisory personnel, and fuel and constitutes over one-third of the total costs (37.1%), and maintenance and garage expenses, which involve primarily repairs to rolling stock, including the labor associated with that function—this category constitutes 26.5% on the average. The next largest category involves administrative and general expenses, including personnel costs, insurance, and safety, which constitute 18.8% of expenses. The balance of all other categories is 17.6%. In total, labor-related expenses in the form of wages, salaries and fringe benefits vary by system, but generally constitute 60 to 75% of total cost.

Operating expenses vary significantly by mode of operation and within modes for different operating systems. Table 9-1 compares costs for existing transit modes in 1989: heavy rail (rail rapid transit), commuter rail, light rail/streetcar, and bus. For comparative purposes, it is useful to examine these statistics on unit bases in terms of the cost of providing the service per unit of service provided (number of vehicle-mi operated annually) and per passenger carried.

Heavy rail services (rail rapid transit) display an average cost of $6.53/vehicle-mi with a range from $3.66 in Atlanta to $8.97 in Boston. This variance is partially explained by the fact that the top operator wage rate in Atlanta is $12.71/h, while Boston's is $17.57. Furthermore, Atlanta's system is quite new.

Commuter rail services involve even wider variations, ranging from $5.06/vehicle-mi for Caltrans service to San Diego (which is operated under contract) to $12.39 for SEPTA services in Philadelphia. The average for this mode is $8.06 per vehicle-mi.

The greatest variance in unit cost occurs in light rail systems with a range from $3.71/vehicle-mi on the San Diego Trolley to $17.87 in Boston, with an average value of $9.11. Once again, this difference is partially explained by wage rates, with San Diego's top operator rate at $13.65/h compared to Boston's rate of $17.76. More of the variance is explained by the fact that San Diego is a new system specifically designed for low-cost operation and includes an honor fare collection system that reduces labor costs considerably.

Bus costs average $4.59/vehicle mi, with a range from $3.16 in Portland to $8.82 in New York. In this case, the variance relates to wage rates but is more influenced by speed (for example, fewer mi/h with operators paid by the h). The average speed of Portland's system is 14 mi/h, while New York's is only 8.3 mi/h.

It is important to note in reviewing these expenses that there are differences that, in some cases, result from the methods of allocating expenses where a system operates more than one mode of service.

Examination of operating expenses per passenger carried indicates similar wide swings in unit costs, although the averages among modes are more closely aligned. Heavy rail, light rail, and bus are clustered at $1.98, $1.46, and $1.37, respectively; commuter rail stands out at $5.47, largely because this mode generally serves much longer trips. For example, if the same statistics were examined on a cost per passenger-mi of travel basis, the commuter rail average would be approximately one-half the bus average ($0.24/passenger-mi for commuter rail and $0.46 for bus).

These statistics are presented for overview purposes only; caution is advised in using this kind of simplified unit pricing for cost estimation. Two reasons for caution were previously pointed out; an additional one is the fact that many operating expenses do not vary by vehicle-mi. For instance, wage-related expenses conform more closely to vehicle-hours of operation, with speed being an obviously important variable to examine. Furthermore, costs related to maintenance of fixed facilities (for example, garages) are a function of the size of the fleet required to operate peak service. For

TABLE 9-1
Representative Operating Costs—Existing Transit Modes

City/System	Operating Expenses/Vehicle-Miles ($)				Operating Expenses/Passenger ($)			
	Heavy Rail	Commuter Rail	Light Rail	Bus	Heavy Rail	Commuter Rail	Light Rail	Bus
New York/MTA	7.23	8.58	—	8.82	1.54	5.83	—	1.30
Chicago/RTA	3.88	8.49	—	5.08	1.24	3.73	—	0.89
Philadelphia/SEPTA	7.18	12.39	8.88	4.58	1.20	5.61	1.05	0.92
Washington/WMATA	7.09	—	—	5.51	1.37	—	—	1.61
Boston/MBTA	8.97	6.91	17.87	5.58	1.24	4.54	1.02	1.36
San Francisco/Muni, BART, Caltrain	5.15	9.91	12.19	6.67	2.74	4.38	1.25	1.06
Baltimore/MTA	6.65	N.A.	—	4.11	2.23	N.A.	—	0.96
Atlanta/MARTA	3.66	—	—	3.29	0.75	—	—	1.19
New Jersey/NJT	—	7.24	5.24	3.42	—	5.62	0.88	1.96
Miami/Metro-Dade	7.27	—	—	4.32	3.60	—	—	1.74
Pittsburgh/PAT	—	5.93	10.24	3.87	—	8.19	2.82	1.49
Cleveland/GCRTA	8.17	—	9.04	4.07	3.87	—	2.48	1.32
San Diego/MTDB, Caltrans	—	5.06	3.71	3.37	—	5.89	0.86	1.54
Buffalo/NFTA	—	—	12.82	4.06	—	—	1.59	1.64
New Orleans/RTA	—	—	6.64	4.38	—	—	0.54	0.86
Portland/Tri-Met	—	—	5.53	3.16	—	—	1.40	1.37
Sacramento/SRTD	—	—	8.07	3.75	—	—	2.13	2.11
Average	6.53	8.06	9.11	4.59	1.98	5.47	1.46	1.37
Range as a percentage of average	81%	91%	155%	123%	158%	82%	109%	91%

Source: 1989 Transit Operating and Financial Statistics—American Public Transit Association.

these reasons, methods of calculating operating expense for these modes have been developed utilizing multivariable cost allocation models that are calibrated for the expense conditions of the existing or proposed transit system being analyzed. A second cost allocation technique is utilization of models that have been developed to estimate the incremental cost (or savings) of changes in existing service by isolating fixed and variable costs. Another operating expense estimation technique (more appropriate to situations where no existing system is in place) is to "buildup" expenses by estimating numbers of personnel and materials for each functional department.

These techniques have been developed in response to the common questions of managers and planners of transit systems:

1. What is the relative financial performance of each of the routes in my system (that is, route revenue versus route cost)? This can be answered with fully allocated cost models.
2. What would the cost be if I modified a route (that is, more or less than current cost)?—this can be answered with incremental cost models.
3. What would it cost to institute a brand new service (for example, light rail)? This can be answered with a cost buildup model.

FULLY ALLOCATED OPERATING COST ALLOCATION MODEL DERIVATION

The preferred technique in developing multivariable cost allocation models is illustrated and derived here.[1] The technique is valid for and can be applied to any urban area with proper unit data.

Transit operations can be viewed as an economic input–output model. Money is supplied to the system and transit resources (for example, vehicle-h, vehicle-mi, and peak vehicles) are output by the transit system. Mathematically, this economic relationship can be stated as shown in Eq. (9-1).

$$C_t = f(R_1, R_2, R_3, \ldots, R_n) \qquad (9\text{-}1)$$

where C_t = total cost of transit services (input)
        R = transit resources provided (output)
        n = number of resources provided

Normally, the cost of providing transit services is presented in a standard list of expense accounts. The cost of each expense account can be denoted C_i, which is the cost of expense account i. The total cost of operations, C_t, for all m expense accounts can be mathematically defined as shown in Eq. (9-2):

$$C_t = \sum_{i=1}^{m} C_i \qquad (9\text{-}2)$$

where C_i = cost of expense account i
 C_t = total cost
 m = number of expense accounts

Equation (9-2) represents the input side of transit operations in terms of total cost and the individual cost components. From Eqs. (9-1) and (9-2), it is clear that the input–output relationship for costs and resources can be stated for individual expense accounts as shown in Eq. (9-3):

$$C_i = f(R_1, R_2, R_3, \ldots, R_n) \qquad (9\text{-}3)$$

The primary assumption of the cost allocation model is that each expense account can be attributed to one or more resources. Thus, for each expense account i, a proportion of cost allocated to each resource can be specified. For the most part, this assignment or allocation is a subjective process; however, other research has demonstrated the relationship between certain cost accounts and resource levels. For example, fuel cost for a bus operation would logically be allocated entirely to vehicle-mi. Mathematically, the assumption regarding assignment of cost to one or more resources can be stated as shown in Eq. (9-4):

$$\sum_{j=1}^{n} P_{ij} = 1 \qquad (9\text{-}4)$$

where P_{ij} = proportion of cost for expense account i allocated to resource j

Based on Eq. (9-4), the cost for each expense account can be allocated to each resource as shown in Eq. (9-5):

$$C_{ij} = C_i P_{ij} \qquad (9\text{-}5)$$

where C_{ij} = cost allocated to resource j for expense account i

By summing all the expense account amounts by resource, the total cost can be stratified by resource as shown in Eq. (9-6):

$$C_j = \sum_{i=1}^{m} C_{ij} \qquad (9\text{-}6)$$

where C_j = cost allocated to resource j

Thus, the sum of costs allocated to each resource is a rearrangement of cost by resources provided rather than expense accounts and will equal the total system cost, as shown in Eq. (9-7):

$$C_t = \sum_{j=1}^{n} C_j \qquad (9\text{-}7)$$

The development of the cost allocation model is the computation of unit cost factor as shown in Eq. (9-8):

$$U_j = \frac{C_j}{R_j} \qquad (9\text{-}8)$$

where U_j =   unit cost for resource j

The multivariable cost allocation model can be defined as shown in Eq. (9-9):

$$C_t = U_1 R_1 + U_2 R_2 + U_3 R_3 + \ldots + U_n R_n \qquad (9\text{-}9)$$

Given a set of resource levels for a particular transit route or line, the unit cost can be applied to compute the cost of the particular transit services comprising the transit system. Thus, the cost allocation model is quantified from overall system statistics but is applied on individual components that comprise the system.

OPERATING COST MODEL EXAMPLES

Having defined the theoretical framework of the cost allocation model, let us apply this approach to the transit operators in the Chicago metropolitan area. (Chicago is used as an example because a number of different modes are operated in that area.) A total of five resources were identified as influencing transit operating costs of any mode to be examined:

- Vehicle (car)-miles.
- Vehicle-hours.
- Track-miles.
- Peak vehicles (cars).
- System revenue.

Closer scrutiny of the operations of rail and bus carriers suggested that vehicle-mi, peak vehicles, and system revenue should be included in the development of both rail and bus cost allocation models. Although system revenue is not a resource provided by the operator, it was included as a parameter influencing costs since certain expenditures, such as advertising and liability insurance premiums, are based on revenue generated. Track-miles were not included in the development of the bus cost allocation model, since they operate over public highways and not on an exclusive right-of-way. Vehicle-hours of operation were deleted from the rail cost model since a considerable portion of the payroll structure is related to vehicle-mi of operation. Also, maintenance charges that are related to use are a function of miles of operation rather than vehicle-h. In addition, rail carriers compile operating statistics by vehicle-mi rather than vehicle-h.

Commuter Railroad Cost Models

For each of the eight railroads operating in the Chicago area, the carrier's expenses were allocated to one of four resources or variables: car-mi, peak car needs, track-mi, and system revenue.

Car-miles. A number of costs are related directly to miles of operation. Expenses such as fuel and maintenance of cars and engines are a direct function of the number of miles operated. Train engineer's wages are also assigned to the category of car-miles.

Peak car needs. The cost resulting from providing storage, operation, and maintenance facilities for cars is a function of the number of cars required to operate the service, rather than the number of miles of service provided. Another significant cost item that varies with the number of peak cars is depreciation. Additionally, salaries of general office personnel and train crew wages are assigned to the category of peak car needs.

Track-miles. Several classes of operating expenses in rail service are a function of the number of miles of track. Such costs include, for example, road property depreciation and maintenance of office buildings. The cost of these items is a function of the number of units, rather than volume of service operated.

System revenue. Traffic and certain insurance expenses are assigned to the system revenue category, as they are a function of passenger volume, which is proportional to system revenue.

The classification of each operating expense item into one of the four allocation resources is reflected in Table 9-2. This table presents all the operating expense accounts to which charges were made. To permit fair and unbiased comparisons between carriers, the percentage allocations were the same for all commuter railroads.

TABLE 9-2
Allocation of Expense Accounts—Commuter Railroad

Expense Classification	Basis for Allocation			
	Car-Miles[a]	Peak Car Needs	Track-Miles[a]	System Revenue
Maintenance of way and structures				
Superintendence			100%	
Roadway maintenance	50%		50%	
Ties and rails	100%			
Ballast & other track material	50%		50%	
Track laying & surfacing	50%		50%	
Fences, snowsheds, & signs			100%	
Stations, office, & roadway buildings			100%	
Water & fuel stations			100%	
Shops & engine houses		100%		
Communications systems	100%			
Signals & interlockings		100%		
Power plants & transmission			100%	
Road property——depreciation			100%	
Roadway machines	100%			
Dismantling road machinery			100%	
Small tools & supplies	100%			
Removing snow, ice, & sand			100%	
Public improvements——maintenance			100%	
Insurance & injuries to persons	50%		50%	
Stationery & printing		50%	50%	
Employees' health & welfare benefits	50%		50%	
Maintaining joint facilities——net	50%		50%	
Other expenses	50%		50%	
Maintenance of equipment				
Superintendence		100%		
Shop & power-plant machinery		100%		
Diesel locomotives——repairs	100%			
Passenger train cars——repairs	100%			
Other equipment——repairs		100%		
Equipment depreciation		100%		
Insurance & injuries to persons		100%		
Stationery & printing	50%	50%		
Other expenses	50%	50%		
Traffic				
Superintendence				100%
Advertising, stationery, & printing				100%
Employees' health & welfare benefits				100%
Other expenses				100%

	Basis for Allocation			
	Car-Miles[a]	Peak Car Needs	Track-Miles[a]	System Revenue
Transportation				
Superintendence		100%		
Dispatching trains		100%		
Station employees, supplies, & expenses				100%
Yard employees, supplies, & expenses		100%		
Train engineers	100%			
Train fuel & servicing locomotives	100%			
Train crew		100%		
Train supplies and expenses	50%	50%		
Signal & interlocking operation	100%			
Crossing protection			100%	
Drawbridge operation		100%		
Communication system	100%			
Employees' health & welfare benefits	50%	50%		
Stationery and printing				100%
Operating joint facilities—net	50%		50%	
Insurance & injuries to persons				100%
Damage to property				100%
Damage to livestock on ROW			100%	
Other expenses	100%			
General and miscellaneous				
Salaries & expenses of general officers		100%		
Salaries & expenses of clerks & attendants		100%		
General office supplies & expenses		100%		
Law expenses and insurance				100%
Employees' health & welfare benefits[b]				
Pensions[b]				
Dining and buffet service			100%	
Stationery and printing		100%		
Other expenses		100%		
Taxes				
Payroll taxes[b]				
Property taxes		50%	50%	
Rents payable—equipment rentals		100%		
Fixed charges—interest on equip. obligations		100%		

[a]Metric conversion: 1 mi = 1.6 km.

[b]Allocated on the basis of total employee compensation by major employment categories (e.g., maintenance of way and structures, traffic, transportation, etc.).

Source: Adapted from Walter Cherwony and Brian McCollom, "Development of Multi-Modal Cost Allocation Models,"in *The Proceedings of the Fourth Intersociety Conference on Transportation* (Los Angeles: The American Society of Mechanical Engineers, July 1976), pp. 1-9.

For example, the cost allocation model development for the Chicago and North Western Transportation Company resulted in the apportionment of 39.14% of aggregate cost on the basis of car-mi, 46.11% on the basis of peak car needs, 5.23% allocated on a track-mi basis, and the remaining 9.52% as a function of system revenue. Table 9-3 reflects these apportionments and also indicates the relative weight of each resource variable on a unit cost basis. While actual dollar amounts in these examples are for 1976, the technique and relative results remain valid.

TABLE 9-3
Operating-Cost-Allocation-Model Development—
Chicago and North Western Transportation Company

Basis of Allocation	Total Units	Total Cost Allocated	% of Total Cost	Unit Cost
Car-miles[a]	11,104,691	$ 9,272,264	39.14	$0.83/car-mi
Peak car needs	256	10,923,612	46.11	$42,670.36/peak car
Track-miles[a]	358.9	1,239,684	5.23	$3454.12/track-mi
System revenue	$24,278,000	2,254,440	9.52	$0.09/$1 of system revenue
Total		$23,690,000	100.00	

[a]Metric conversion: 1 mi = 1.6 km.

Source: Walter Cherwony and Brian McCollom, "Development of Multi-Modal Cost Allocation Models," in *The Proceedings of the Fourth Intersociety Conference on Transportation* (Los Angeles: The American Society of Mechanical Engineers, July 1976), pp. 1-9.

For the Chicago and North Western Transportation Company, the four-variable analysis resulted in the following formula of cost allocation:

$$C = 0.83M + 42,670.36V + 3454.12L + 0.09R \qquad (9\text{-}10)$$

where C = annual cost of system operation
M = annual car-miles of service
V = peak car needs
L = track-miles
R = annual system revenue

The results of the cost allocation model development for the eight railroads in the six-county metropolitan Chicago area are presented in Table 9-4. Most of the unit cost factors show wider variability than might be expected among operators in the same geographical region.

It should be noted that a cost allocation model was developed for the Chicago Transit Authority rapid transit operations. Since no other comparable system exists in the Chicago urban area to compare model results, further discussion of this mode is not included here. For completeness, however, the cost model is shown in Eq. (9-11):

$$C = 0.64M + 27,152.17V + 34,119.80L + 0.36R \qquad (9\text{-}11)$$

Bus Service Cost Models

In a similar fashion to that used for the region's rail carriers, expense accounts for the 10 major bus operators were allocated to one of four resources or variables: vehicles, vehicle-mi, peak vehicle needs, and system revenue.

TABLE 9-4
Operating-Cost-Allocation-Model Results—Commuter Railroads

Carrier	Power Source	Unit Cost Factors			
		Car-Miles[a] ($/car-mi)	Peak Car Needs ($/peak car)	Track-Miles[a] ($/track-mi)	System Revenue ($/$)
Burlington Northern (BN)	Diesel	1.25	46,265	6066	0.08
Chicago and North Western (CNW)	Diesel	0.83	42,670	3454	0.09
Chicago, Milwaukee, St. Paul, & Pacific (MR)	Diesel	1.19	67,522	3162	0.10
Chicago, Rock Island, and Pacific (RI)	Diesel	1.29	28,409	4957	0.17
Norfolk and Western (NW)	Diesel	2.31	13,383	235	0.0003
Penn Central (PC)	Diesel	1.23	39,079	839	0.02
Illinois Central Gulf (ICG)	Electric	1.40	35,829	27,222	0.29
Chicago South Shore and South Bend (SS)	Electric	0.98	53,058	3132	0.17

[a]Metric conversion: 1 mi = 1.6 km.

Source: Adapted from Walter Cherwony and Brian McCollom, "Development of Multi-Modal Cost Allocation Models," in *The Proceedings of the Fourth Intersociety Conference on Transportation* (Los Angeles: The American Society of Mechanical Engineers, July 1976), pp. 1-9.

Vehicle-hours. Operating employees wages represent by far the largest single element of cost in most bus transit properties. Employees engaged in operating vehicles are paid on an hourly basis; hence, the allocation of wage expense is most properly made on the basis of hours of service on the system. Similarly, supervision of transportation operations is directly related to the number of hours of service provided, and this item is also properly allocated to the vehicle-h category.

Vehicle-miles. Many costs are related directly to the miles a bus system operates. Expenses such as fuel, tires, and equipment maintenance are a direct function of miles operated. Material expenses for vehicle bodies, brakes, engines, chassis, and transmissions are also a function of exposure in terms of miles of service. Consequently, these costs, together with the cost of motor fuel, taxes, and certain other miscellaneous expenses, are assigned to the category of vehicle-mi.

Peak vehicle needs. Many individual expense items do not vary as functions for either of the foregoing parameters (vehicle-h or vehicle-mi). For example, the cost of providing operating and maintenance facilities for vehicles is determined by the number of vehicles required rather than the number of hours or miles of service provided. Various material expenses are also related to peak vehicle needs, including the maintenance of building, fixtures, shop and garage, service car equipment, and other miscellaneous shop items. A number of broad overhead expenses will vary with the number of vehicles required to operate the system, including depreciation of equipment, general office costs, and the salaries of general office clerks and officials.

System revenue. Operating costs resulting from injuries and damages are logically assigned to the system revenue category. Traffic promotion, station expenses, and federal income and other taxes are also assigned to this category because they relate primarily to system revenue. The classification of each operating expense into one of four allocation variables is presented in Table 9-5. This table aggregates all the operating expense accounts to which charges were made. To facilitate bus operator comparisons, the percentage allocations were the same for all bus systems.

As an example, the development of the cost allocation model for the Chicago Transit Authority bus operations resulted in the apportionment of 14.69% of aggregate costs on the basis of vehicle-mi, 54.62% on the basis of vehicle-h , 25.60% allocated on peak vehicle needs basis, and the remaining 5.09% as a function of system revenue (Table 9-6). For the Chicago Transit Authority, the resultant bus operations cost allocation formula follows:

$$C = 11.13H + 0.28M + 20,059.22V + 0.06R \qquad (9\text{-}12)$$

where C = annual cost of system operation
       H = annual vehicle-hours of service
       M = annual vehicle-miles of service
       V = peak vehicle needs
       R = annual system revenue

TABLE 9-5
Allocation of Expense Accounts—Bus Operations

Expense Classification	Basis for Allocation			
	Vehicle-Hours	Vehicle-Miles[a]	Peak Vehicles	System Revenue
Maintenance expense				
Supervision			100%	
Motor buses—repairs		100%		
Tires and tubes		100%		
Miscellaneous shop expenses			100%	
Other maintenance expenses			100%	
Transportation expense				
Supervision	100%			
Bus drivers	100%			
Fuel		100%		
Lubricants		100%		
Service equipment operation				100%
Other transportation expenses	100%			
General and miscellaneous expenses				
Salaries & expenses of general officers			100%	
Salaries & expenses of general office clerks			100%	
General office rent			100%	
General office supplies & expenses			100%	
Traffic promotion				100%
Other general expenses			100%	
Insurance				
Fire, theft, collision			100%	
Public liability and property damage				100%
Workmen's compensation[b]				
Taxes				
General state and local			100%	
State franchise tax on capital stock				100%
Licenses			100%	
Other local			100%	
U.S. motor fuel and oil				
Payroll[b]				
Depreciation				
Building and fixtures			100%	
Motor buses			100%	
Service equipment			100%	
Garage equipment			100%	
Office furniture and equipment			100%	
Miscellaneous equipment			100%	

[a]Metric conversion: 1 mi = 1.6 km.

[b]Allocated on the basis of total employee compensation by major employment categories (e.g. maintenance, transportation, general office, etc.).

Source: Adapted from Walter Cherwony and Brian McCollom, "Development of Multi-Modal Cost Allocation Models," in *The Proceedings of the Fourth Intersociety Conference on Transportation* (Los Angeles: The American Society of Mechanical Engineers, July 1976), pp. 1-9.

TABLE 9-6

TABLE 9-6
Operating-Cost-Allocation-Model Development—
Chicago Transit Authority—Bus

Basis of Allocation	Total Units	Total Cost Allocated	% of Total Cost	Unit Cost
Vehicle-miles[a]	90,701,804	$ 25,431,448	14.69	$0.28/vehicle-mi
Vehicle-hours	8,500,071	94,572,897	54.62	$11.13/vehicle-h
Peak vehicles	2210	44,330,511	25.60	$20,059.22/peak vehicle
System revenue	$138,832,579	8,806,063	5.09	$0.06/$1 of system revenue
Total		$173,140,919	100.00	

[a]Metric conversion: 1 mi = 1.6 km.

Source: Adapted from Walter Cherwony and Brian McCollom, "Development of Multi-Modal Cost Allocation Models," in *The Proceedings of the Fourth Intersociety Conference on Transportation* (Los Angeles: The American Society of Mechanical Engineers, July 1976), pp. 1-9.

The results of the development of the cost allocation model for the 10 major bus operators in the Chicago metropolitan area are presented in Table 9-7.

INCREMENTAL COST OF SERVICE MODEL

This approach uses the series of operating cost accounts from the previous examples but examines them from the point of view of which will change and which will remain constant if a relatively minor service change is being tested. Under this technique, fixed costs are identified, totaled, and set aside from the analytical process to be added back in at the end.

Variable accounts are addressed in one of two ways. Those that are relatively small or whose value is expected to vary in direct proportion to the service change scale are treated in a standard cost allocation fashion as previously described. Fuel costs are an example of this type of account and a simple unit cost/vehicle-mi would be calculated and applied to the proposed service change variance in vehicle-mi. Those variable accounts that are large or whose value varies disproportionately with a service change are given special analysis. Driver wages and benefits, for instance, are affected not only by the service change scale, but also by the characteristics of the change. For example, service added (or subtracted) during peak periods will have different impacts than service changes during other times of the day.

Table 9-8 is an example result of allocating costs to the categories previously mentioned. The transit system used for this example is an all-bus operation. The 51% of total cost to be "estimated by special analysis" comes from two accounts: operators' salaries and wages and operators' fringe benefits. The 29% allocated on a vehicle-mi basis comprises fuel and lubricants, tires and tubes, vehicle servicing, vehicle inspection and maintenance, accident repairs, and claims. The 4% allocated on a vehicle-h basis includes vehicle movement control and ticketing and fare collection. The 16% fixed costs include primarily administrative services such as personnel, data processing, and marketing. It also includes maintenance of fixed facilities such as garages, offices, and passenger stations/shelters.

TABLE 9-7
Operating-Cost-Allocation-Model Results—Bus Operators

Carrier	Ownership	Unit Cost Factors			
		Vehicle-Hours ($/vehicle-h)	Vehicle-Miles[a] ($/vehicle-mi)	Peak Vehicle Needs ($/peak-vehicle)	System Revenue ($/$)
Urban/suburban[b]					
Chicago Transit Authority (CTA)	Public	11.13	0.28	20,059	0.06
South Suburban Safeways (SSS)	Private	6.21	0.18	11,174	0.11
Suburban Transit System (STS)	Private	4.44	0.21	7645	0.07
United Motor Coach (UMC)	Private	5.08	0.21	5681	0.08
West Towns (WT)	Private	8.31	0.17	6533	0.07
Suburban/local[c]					
Aurora Transit Systems (ATS)	Public	6.03	0.11	13,831	0.11
Elgin Department of Transportation (ELG)	Public	4.54	0.18	5964	0.07
Joliet Mass Transit District (JMTD)	Public	4.49	0.11	3161	0.12
Waukegan North Chicago (WNC)	Private	5.17	0.11	4164	0.06
Village of Wilmette (WIL)	Public	5.23	0.26	5358	0.21

[a]Metric conversion: 1 mi = 1.6 km.
[b]Provides service between downtown Chicago and nearby suburban communities.
[c]Provides service within outlying satellite communities.

Source: Adapted from Walter Cherwony and Brian McCollom, "Development of Multi-Modal Cost Allocation Models," in *The Proceedings of the Fourth Intersociety Conference on Transportation* (Los Angeles: The American Society of Mechanical Engineers, July 1976), pp. 1-9.

TABLE 9-8
Operating Cost by Major Category

	Dollar Amount	Percentage of Total Operating Costs	Percentage of Variable Operating Costs
Variable costs			
Estimated by special analysis	$32,946,460	51%	61%
Estimated by cost allocation			
Miles	$19,179,677	29%	35%
Hours	2,419,229	4%	5%
Subtotal	$21,598,906	33%	40%
Total variable costs	$54,545,366	84%	100%
Fixed costs	$10,636,972	16%	—
Total operating costs	$65,182,338	100%	—

Source: Booz, Allen & Hamilton, *Bus Route Costing Procedures. Interim Report No. 2: Proposed Method*, prepared for UMTA, Report no. UMTA-IT-09-9014-81-1 (Washington, D.C.: Urban Mass Transportation Administration, May 1981), Exhibit 3-2, following p. 8.

The complex part of dealing with incremental costing is developing methods to handle the driver costs "estimated by special analysis." There are 14 identified models (and perhaps as many again that have not been identified) to deal with driver costs. All have advantages and disadvantages, and their analysis and critique could fill a book by itself. For purposes of illustration, one of these models is described here.

LONDON TRANSPORT MODEL

The model developed by London Transport focuses on direct driver cost and assumes indirect driver costs are equal across all time periods.[2] In addition, the model retains the assumption that the impact of peaking on direct driver cost can be generalized from a sample of driver work assignments. The London Transport model assumes, however, that the direct driver cost of a service segment is a function of the number of split shifts and straight shifts required to staff the service. In addition, the London Transport model focuses on driver cost alone. The driver cost procedure is not part of a broad technique for estimating costs.

Input

The London Transport model requires pay-hour data stratified by shift type. These data are obtained from a sample of driver assignments. The model also requires a definition of the daily vehicle-hours and number of vehicles by time period required to operate the service under consideration.

Algorithm. The model's algorithm relates driver cost to the number of straight and split shifts through Eq. (9-13):

$$DL = L_1 s_1 + L_2 s_2 \qquad\qquad (9\text{-}13)$$

where DL =   total driver pay-hours under the London Transport model
  L_1 =   average hours paid per split shift
  L_2 =   average hours paid per straight shift
  s_1 =   number of split shifts
  s_2 =   number of straight shifts

The coefficients L_1 and L_2 are found from a sample of existing driver schedules stratified by shift type and hours paid. The coefficient values are the sample averages obtained by dividing the total hours worked for a particular shift type by the number of shifts of that type.

Though this example utilizes split and straight shifts, alternate categories of work (for example, overtime) can be used as needed to conform with the particular driver assignment practices existing at the application property.

An estimate of the number of split and straight shifts is needed as input to the model to estimate the cost of a proposed service change. The London Transport model contains a procedure for estimating straight and split shifts, unlike most other costing techniques, which do not address the resource requirements estimation task. The shift estimating procedure is illustrated in Table 9-9.

At the beginning of the process, the proportion of straight and split shifts is not known. The total number of shifts required can be easily found, however, by dividing the vehicle-hours required (known from the service change definition) by the average hours per shift obtained from the sample of driver assignments. This step is shown in lines 1 and 2 of Table 9-9. Twenty-seven shifts are required.

Next, the number of peak ends required is obtained from the definition of the service change. A *peak end* is essentially a bus operating in either the morning or evening peak period. Thus, the number of peak ends required equals the number of buses required in the a.m. peak plus the number needed in the p.m. peak. There are 37 peak ends in the example (line 3). Each peak end is staffed with either a straight shift or half of a split shift. Thus, the total number of peak ends equals the number of straight shifts plus twice the number of split shifts.

TABLE 9-9
London Transport Model
Example Driver Cost Calculation

Shift Calculation

(1)	Vehicle-hours	=					=	182
(2)	Total shifts	=	182	÷	6.67 (veh.-h/shift)		=	27
(3)	Peak ends	=	18 morning	+	19 evening		=	37
(4)	Straight shifts	=	2(27)	−	37		=	17
(5)	Split shifts	=	27	−	17		=	10

Cost Calculation

		Straight Shifts	Split Shifts	Total
(6)	Shifts required	17	10	27
(7)	Average pay-hours per shift type	8.0	11.5	
(8)	Driver pay-hours required	136	115	251
(9)	Wage rate per pay-hour	$ 2.00	$ 2.00	$ 2.00
(10)	Driver cost	$272.00	$230.00	$502.00

Source: Adapted from J. W. McClenahan and others, *Two Methods for Estimating the Crew Costs of Bus Service*, TRRL Supplementary Report 364 (Berkshire, England: Transport and Road Research Laboratory, 1978), p. 48.

The remainder of the process involves allocating the 27 required shifts as either splits or straights in conformance with the number of peak ends. The relationships between peak ends, shift types, and total shifts are

$$PE = ST + 2(SP)$$
$$T = ST + SP \tag{9-14}$$

where PE = number of peak ends
ST = number of straight shifts
SP = number of split shifts
T = total shift requirements

Solving this pair of simultaneous equations gives

$$ST = S(T) - PE \tag{9-15}$$

Thus, the number of straight shifts can be found from the known number of peak ends and total shifts. As shown in line 4, the example requires 17 straight shifts. A balance of 10 split shifts (line 5) is required to achieve the total shift requirements of 27.

Once calculated, the shift requirements are multiplied by the coefficient values previously obtained from the sample to produce driver pay-hours required. Driver cost is the product of this pay-hour quantity and the wage rate.

Output

The final product of the model algorithm is driver cost stratified by shift type. The intermediate steps of the model also produce outputs, such as shift and pay-hour requirements, delineated by shift type.

Driver costs estimated by such a model can then be added to the other two categories of cost (fixed and allocated) to obtain the overall incremental cost of a service change.

OPERATING COST BUILDUP EXAMPLE

The preparation of operating expense estimates under this method requires a functional definition of the type of service to be provided and the methods of providing such service. In this example, costs are estimated for a 44.7-mi automated guideway transit (AGT) system with 48 stations. The functional methods of operation are described as follows.

Automatic train operation (ATO). The rapid transit system will be fully automatically controlled from a central tower. It is estimated that ATO will require an average of 10 operators per shift, on a three shift per day basis. One spare shift will be required to cover holidays, vacations, sickness, and so on, producing a total staff requirement of 40 operators. At peak periods, the 10 console operators would be distributed as follows: 4 train controllers, 4 station surveillance, and 2 power controllers. This operator requirement would be reduced in off-peak periods.

Station operation. Station operations will be automated to the extent possible. Ticket vending machines, automatic turnstiles, and bill changers will be available at each station. While the reliability of these is being improved by the manufacturers, failures are apt to occur. When such failures occur, it is necessary to (1) operate affected items manually to afford minimum delay to passengers and (2) repair the failed appliance as rapidly as possible. It is estimated that approximately one man per station, or a staff of 50, will be able to oversee operations and perform ticket-collecting functions in the event of failures.

To provide for repair of vending machine failures, service of escalators, structural repairs, lighting replacements, air conditioning, and plant servicing, a staff of 50 maintenance engineers will be required. Again, these will be allocated among appropriate shifts with cover for holidays and so on.

Other station staff will include the security force. Each station will have closed-circuit television surveillance. If vandalism or a disturbance is detected, however, the security force must respond quickly. Road patrols will visit stations on a random roving basis and be in radio communication with the control center at all times. An additional function of the security staff is to empty the cash from the vending and change machines. It is estimated that a security staff of 50 will be required.

One additional category of station staff required will be cleaners. These will normally work second and third shifts and not be required in peak periods in the day. It is expected that part-time labor will be used extensively for this category. However, for cost-estimating purposes, 50 full-time cleaners are included.

Maintenance and yard operation. In the maintenance shops at two facilities, maintenance engineers in the categories of mechanical, electrical, and electronic will be required. These will be supported by laborers and clerical staff. Yard operations personnel will include 30 hostlers and 40 cleaners, and those categories will both work three-shift operations.

Two categories of maintenance engineers will be concerned with guideway maintenance—the track and power crew and the ways crew. The track and power crew will maintain the running surface, the power system, the communications system, and the trackside units of the control system. The ways crew will maintain and repair the track structure, including support columns.

Other operating costs. Other operating costs will be incurred in the form of replacement parts for vehicles and structures, power purchased, and general accident and other insurance for the system.

The cost of electric power for the entire system, including traction, lighting, heating, console operations, and communication, is estimated at 30 cents/vehicle-mile/year. Annual mileage of 30 million vehicle-miles produces a total power cost of $9 million/year.

These estimates result in a buildup of direct salaries of all operating personnel, including allocations for supervisory personnel and employee benefits. These personnel costs, when added to operating expenses for materials, spares, power, and insurance, produce the overall operating expense estimates indicated in Table 9-10.

Depending upon the problem at hand (that is, estimating operating expenses for changes to an existing system versus installation of a totally new system), either of the preceding two techniques can provide reasonable estimates of operating costs for any mode being analyzed. The advantage of the cost allocation model approach is that it permits not only systemwide cost estimates but also operating expense estimates for individual elements of a system, such as a bus route or a single line of a rail rapid transit/AGT proposal.

TABLE 9-10
Example Summary of AGT Operating Cost Buildup

	Number	Salary ($)	Dollars (000)
Wages and salaries			
Automatic train operation			
Console operators	40	35,000	1400
Station operation			
Custodian/ticket collectors	50	28,000	1400
Appliance maintenance	25	35,000	875
General maintenance	25	35,000	875
Security force	50	30,000	1500
Cleaners	50	20,000	1000
Vehicle maintenance			
Mechanical	80	35,000	2800
Electrical	40	42,000	1680
Electronic	25	50,000	1250
Laborers	30	20,000	600
Clerical	20	25,000	500
Yard operations			
Hostlers	30	25,000	750
Cleaners	40	20,000	800
Roadway maintenance			
Track and power crew	20	40,000	800
Ways crew	20	35,000	700

	$16,930
Employee benefits, pension, etc. (35%)	5,930
Administration/supervision (25%)	4,230
Total	$27,090
Maintenance materials and spares	
Station materials 48 @ $35,000/station	1,680
Roadway materials 45 @ $70,000/mi	3,150
Vehicle materials 380 @ $9000/vehicle	3,420
Power 30 million vehicle-mi @ $0.30	9,000
Insurance	2,000
Estimated annual costs	$46,340
Contingency (10%)	4,630
Total	$50,970

CAPITAL COSTS

Capital costs of transit systems vary significantly and are influenced by design standards, type of equipment, quantity of purchase, local conditions of climate and terrain, and other factors. Bus system capital expenses essentially comprise vehicles and maintenance facilities. Related street furniture, such as shelters and informational signs, are a relatively minor part of the total. Rail transit capital costs contain two of the same elements as bus costs (that is, vehicles and maintenance facilities), but also include guideway, track, stations, power, signals and communications, and other capital expenses.

Unlike the operating expense example, there is no formula approach to capital cost. Each component of a planned new system or for renovation of an existing system should be subjected to a careful engineering analysis that flows from the functional characteristics of the proposed system and estimates of demand for that system. For example, the typical planning process produces modal split data assigning trips to a projected alternative. These trips, in turn, determine the number of vehicles required on the system, the optimum spacing of stations, fixed-facility type, and other elements. While gross unit statistics can be used for very preliminary estimates of the magnitude of expenditure, decisions on implementation of a system require careful engineering analysis.

As this engineering analysis proceeds, typically alternative systems will be examined so that the planned improvement, expansion, or new system construction can be assessed in light of cost effectiveness and other criteria. This analysis is performed by postulating modal options for a given corridor, costing those options, comparing that to the resultant demand and other impacts on the community, and combining all statistics in a cost–benefit or other type of comparative analysis to decide on the appropriate mode.

The variance in capital cost precludes simple unit cost comparisons. For example, recent heavy rail projects in Washington, D.C., Atlanta, Baltimore, and Miami have varied from $60 million $170 million/rte.-mi. Light rail systems built in Buffalo, Pittsburgh, Portland (Oregon), and Sacramento (California) have ranged from $10 million to $110 million/rte.-mi.

Vehicle costs also vary depending on type, specification, and other amenities. Rail cars vary from $1,100,000 to $1,800,000 each. Buses are in the $200,000 range. To truly judge the total cost of different systems, obviously operating expense must be added and both sets of cost placed on an annual expenditure basis by amortizing capital costs. Furthermore, comparative analysis should examine the present worth of future total investment (capital and operating) by, in effect, "capitalizing future operating expenses." In this way, through the use of operating-cost-allocation models and capital-cost engineering estimates, a complete cost analysis can be prepared for utilization in an alternatives analysis to select the appropriate transit mode.

REFERENCES

1   BOOZ, ALLEN & HAMILTON, *Bus Route Costing Procedures, Interim Report No. 2: Proposed Method*, prepared for UMTA, Report no. UMTA-IT-09-9014-81-1 (Washington, D.C.: Urban Mass Transportation Administration, May 1981), Exhibit 3-2, following p. 8.

2   J. W. MCCLENAHAN AND OTHERS, *Two Methods of Estimating the Crew Costs of Bus Service*, TRRL Supplementary Report 364 (Crowthorne, Berkshire, England: Transport and Road Research Laboratory, 1978).

FURTHER READING

Some citations are no longer available from their original source. These citations are often available from the National Technical Information Service, U.S. Department of Commerce, 5285 Port Royal Road, Springfield, VA 22161. We have verified the order numbers for many of these citations, and they are found at the end of the citation. Prices are available through NTIS at the address above.

BHANDARI, ANIL S., AND KUMARES C. SINHA, "Impact of Short-Term Service Changes on Urban Bus Transit Performance," in *Bus and Rural Transit*, Transportation Research Record 718, pp. 12-18. Washington, D.C.: Transportation Research Board, 1979.

CERVERO, ROBERT B., AND OTHERS, *Efficiency and Equity Implications of Alternative Transit Fare Policies*, Final Report. Los Angeles: University of California, Los Angeles, School of Architecture and Urban Planning, June 1980. Now available as PB 80 224 710.

CHERWONY, WALTER, AND SUBHASH R. MUNDLE, "Transit Cost Allocation Model Development," *Transportation Engineering Journal of ASCE*, 106, no. TE1 (January 1980), pp. 31-42.

COUTURE, MICHAEL, ROBERT WAKSMAN, AND RICHARD ALBRIGHT, *A Preliminary Analysis of the Requirements for a Transit Operations Planning System (OPS)*, Staff Study. Cambridge, Mass.: Transportation Systems Center, 1978.

COX, WENDELL, *Application of Transit Cost Allocation Models*. Malibu, Calif.: Pepperdine University, December 1980.

FLEMING, DARYL S., FRANK R. WILSON, AND ALBERT M. STEVENS, "Estimating the Costs of a Subscription Van Service," in *Current Paratransit and Ride-Sharing Activities*, Transportation Research Record 724, pp. 45-52. Washington, D.C.: Transportation Research Board, 1979.

HINDS, DAVID H., "Rucus: A Comprehensive Status Report and Assessment," *Transit Journal*, 5, no. 1 (Winter 1979), pp. 17-34.

LEVINSON, HERBERT S., "Peak—Off Peak Revenue and Cost Allocation Model," in *Planning and Design of Rapid Transit Facilities*, Transportation Research Record 662, pp. 29-33. Washington, D.C.: Transportation Research Board, 1978.

PICKRELL, DON H., AND MICHAEL JACOBS, "A Comparative Analysis of Forecast and Actual Ridership and Costs for Ten Federally-Supported Urban Rail Transit Projects," Draft prepared for the U.S. DOT, Transportation Systems Center, July 1989.

POZDENA, RANDALL J., AND LEONARD MEREWITZ, "Estimating Cost Functions for Rail Rapid Transit Properties," *Transportation Research*, 12, no. 2 (April 1978), pp. 73-78.

R. TRAVERS MORGAN PTY. LTD, *Adelaide Bus Costing Study*, Final Report, prepared for the Director General of Transport, South Australia. Adelaide, South Australia: South Australia Department of Transportation, 1978. Now available as PB 81 124 570.

VITON, PHILIP A., "On the Economics of Rapid-Transit Operations," *Transportation Research, Part A: General*, 14A, no. 4 (August 1980), pp. 247-53.

EXERCISES

9-1 What is the single biggest factor to examine in reducing operating cost?

9-2 You have completed a fully allocated cost model for your system and the results indicate: Cost = ($0.91 × vehicle-miles) + ($22.80 × vehicle-hours) + ($71,400 × peak vehicles). What is the cost of Route 18, which operates 306.20 mi/day, 20.17 h/day, and requires two peak vehicles?

9-3 There is a proposal to add two trips to Route 18, which would increase vehicle-miles to 367.4/day and require an additional bus. Describe the process you would use to calculate the cost.

9-4 You have completed a fully allocated cost model for your bus system. You need to make a financial performance evaluation of every route in the system. Using your cost model and information from other chapters, describe how you would perform this systemwide evaluation.

9-5 Your system opened a light rail line several years ago to augment bus services. There is a proposal to build a new light rail line in another corridor. Describe the method you would use to calculate the cost of this new line, assuming the maintenance facility constructed for the first line has the capacity to handle the new vehicles. Also, comment on why you did not use other methods.

9-6 Using the unit cost data from this chapter and information from other chapters, discuss whether or not there appear to be economies of scale in transit operations.

Chapter 10

COMPARATIVE ANALYSIS

Vukan R. Vuchic

Selection of the best combination of transit modes is the central decision in planning new or expanding existing transit systems. This decision is very important because it not only determines technological, operational, and network characteristics of the planned system, but through these elements it has a major influence on the role the system will assume in the city's physical, economic, social, and environmental conditions and development. Because of their interdependence, all these factors must be considered in the mode selection, making it a very complex task.

It will be shown that some elements of mode comparison and selection can be quantified and thus compared exactly. Many other elements are qualitative, however, so their evaluation must include considerable experience and value judgments. The procedure, therefore, cannot be defined by a quantitative model nor can the results of the comparative analysis be expressed by a single quantitative value. The desire to simplify this process by using a "mechanized" comparative analysis and basing it on a single criterion (usually cost) has sometimes prevailed, but it usually produced erroneous results, contrary to real-world conditions and experience. Particularly misleading have been the studies based on average values and models of hypothetical situations.

Following a brief review of previous works on transit mode comparison, including its theoretical basis and applications, this chapter defines requirements for transit service, including the three major interested parties and characteristics of different transit modes. Utilizing these concepts, a general methodology of comprehensive transit system evaluation is presented. An example of the application of this methodology is also included.

MODE COMPARISON: STATE OF THE ART AND ITS EVALUATION

The studies involving the comparison of transit modes vary considerably in their approach and purpose, as well as in quality. The most common types of these studies are briefly reviewed here.

An extensive conceptual framework for the comparison of different transit modes was developed by Kuhn.[1] He showed the deficiencies of comparisons based on costs only and emphasized the importance of including not only direct quantitative factors, but also indirect and qualitative ones. He illustrated the methodology by a framework for the comparison of a freeway and a rapid transit line. Hill[2] further developed the concepts for transportation plan evaluation, emphasizing the need to consider different affected groups. He proposed a method for systematic handling of nonquantifiable factors that is comprehensive, but extremely complicated for application. Morlok,[3] Manheim,[4] and several other authors emphasized the need to include all major characteristics ("dimensions") of transit modes into their analysis and evaluation. Following these publications, Thomas and Schofer[5] presented a comprehensive report on the evaluation of transportation plans.

Another set of studies focused on the comparison of actual characteristics of different transit modes. Vuchic[6] analyzed the components of different modes, such as types of rights-of-way, technology (guided versus steered), and vehicle size, and on the basis of their characteristics compared light rail transit (LRT) with several other modes for different sets of conditions (network types, passenger volumes, and so on). Deen and James[7] compared the costs of buses and rapid transit for different types of right-of-way (ROW). Other mode characteristics (comfort, speed, environmental impacts, and the like) were intentionally not included. Lehner[8] presented a comprehensive comparison of all major features of light rail transit and rapid transit, utilizing actual data from many operating systems. Other comprehensive comparisons of actual systems involving different modes (commuter buses on a busway, an extensive bus network, and a rail rapid transit line) that serve similar areas but with different types of service were made by Vuchic and Stanger,[9] and Vuchic and Olanipekun.[10]

A third group of studies is those performed for the actual planning of new transit systems in individual cities. The comprehensiveness of these studies varies greatly. The study for San Francisco Bay Area Rapid Transit (BART) was a relatively simple task since the performance specifications mandated by the legislation were such that only modes operating on exclusive ROW could meet them. The choice of rail technology was logical. An early study for Frankfurt, Germany,[11] analyzed alternative modes with some variations in types of service caused by different characteristics of the compared technologies—monorail, LRT, and rapid transit (see Table 5-1). Since a comparison of alternatives became federally required for transit mode selection in the United States during the 1970s, these studies have become increasingly comprehensive and sophisticated. Examples of such studies are those performed for Baltimore, Rochester and Buffalo (New York), Los Angeles and Sacramento (California), Denver, Edmonton (Canada), Miami, Pittsburgh, Portland (Oregon), Honolulu, Dallas,

Houston, and Phoenix (Arizona). These studies have produced a number of excellent conceptual definitions and methodologies for comparisons of modal characteristics.

Finally, several economic studies of mode comparisons have been performed for hypothetical urban corridors, utilizing average costs from different cities or from one specific metropolitan area. Started by Meyer, Kain, and Wohl,[12] this type of study has been followed by several groups of economists, notably including one by the University of California group headed by Keeler and others.[13]

The assumptions and models used in most economic comparisons of modes are so unrealistic that their findings are, in most cases, in sharp variance with the studies of transit in actual cities, mentioned earlier. Their simplistic approach and seemingly clear results, however, give these studies a totally unjustified credibility among some laypersons. It is therefore necessary to discuss briefly the major deficiencies inherent in their methodology.

The economic studies are intended to find optimal domains for individual modes defined by the number of passengers they carry during the peak hour. Actually, choice of mode must be based on a number of factors, such as local conditions, alternative means of travel, service quality throughout the day, and short- and long-term impacts on the served area. Optimal domains of modes in terms of passenger volumes, therefore, are not delineated by a fixed number for all conditions.

The sole criterion used for determining the optimal mode is the minimum cost per passenger-trip. This criterion is valid only in the rare cases when modes with identical level of service (LOS) are compared. In most cases, each mode has a different LOS–cost combination. Thus, if mode I has a lower cost, but also lower LOS than mode II under given conditions, it would be incorrect to conclude that mode I is better because it is cheaper. If the difference in the LOS of mode II is worth its additional cost, mode II is preferred.

A number of important mode characteristics cannot be converted into dollars. But the problem of including these characteristics into mode comparison cannot be solved by elimination of all nonmonetary elements. For example, economic studies often assume that there is sufficient space in central business districts (CBDs) to accommodate freeways and parking facilities for 10,000 or even 30,000 automobiles per hour from a single corridor. Even if this physically infeasible assumption is accepted, the impact of this traffic volume cannot be ignored without making the analysis highly unrealistic.

The computational analysis and the diagrams used by the economic comparisons also have conceptual deficiencies. The basic diagram used presents average cost per trip as a function of passenger volume for different modes, as in Fig. 10-1. Each mode, however, has a different LOS and therefore attracts, under any given set of conditions, a different number of passengers. Rail rapid transit attracts more passengers than does a bus system using busway and streets. Such a bus system, in turn, has a stronger attraction than does a surface bus system. All three systems are so different from the automobile in type of service and potential user groups that their plots on the same diagram have no meaning.

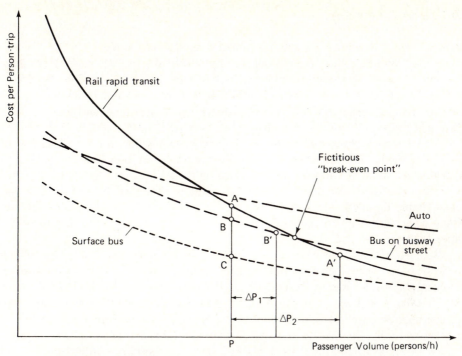

Figure 10-1 *Comparison of modes based on their costs, disregarding differences in level of service and passenger attraction.*

More specifically, the diagram implies that it presents the costs of different modes for any given passenger volume; thus, in Fig. 10-1, cost per trip C for a surface bus appears to compare with cost B for a bus on a busway and street and cost A for rail rapid transit. The fact is that there cannot be a served area in the real world in which these three modes would have the respective unit costs. If a surface bus line would attract P passengers in a given area, then a bus on busway and street would attract a volume $P + \Delta P_1$, and rail rapid transit would attract a volume of $P + \Delta P_2$. Unit cost C therefore should not be compared with costs B or A, but with B' or A'. Moreover, the criterion is not whether, for example, C is lower or higher than B', but whether the cost difference B' − C is worth the attraction of ΔP_1 passengers. Incidentally, this cost difference may sometimes be negative, which makes the higher-quality mode clearly superior even for volumes well below the "break-even point." Actually, the "break-even point" is a fictitious concept: the plotted curves are on different LOS "surfaces" (that is, they cannot be plotted on the same plane, so they do not intersect).

Another problem is that this type of diagram is highly unreliable when it is applied to hypothetical "typical" conditions because of the extreme sensitivity of the curves to the assumptions of the analyst. To change relative positions of curves for different modes by manipulating assumptions of the model is easy. Accordingly, Deen pointed out in his discussion of the study by Miller et al. that the break-even point varied among different studies of this type from the 2000 to 5000 trips/h range to 50,000 trips/h, which is a difference of some 1000%.[14] This characteristic allows use of this methodology to deceptively argue in favor of or against any mode.

These hypothetical economic studies confuse technologies with modes (see Chap. 4). Since the costs of modes are mostly dependent on their type of ROW, the curves in Fig. 10-1 refer more to types of ROW than to bus and rail technologies. For example, a bus on exclusive busway may involve a higher investment and operating cost than light rail transit in a street median.

An example of the application of the same methodology to a comparison of different vehicles illustrates its inherent shortcomings. Suppose that a Cadillac, a Volkswagen, and a motorcycle are compared on the basis of their costs; travel times are included as cost elements, but different riding qualities, safety, and the fact that many people do not want to ride a motorcycle are ignored. Clearly, the motorcycle would come out as greatly superior to the Volkswagen, which would in turn be far superior to the Cadillac.

Because of these deficiencies, the results of the economic studies have little realistic value. Since such important factors as reliability and frequency of service, comfort, and safety enter the economic models only as cost items, while their major influence on passenger attraction is disregarded, these studies greatly distort the relationships among modes in favor of low-investment/low-performance systems.

Those results, implied to be correct, have often been used by various interest groups to argue against improvements of public transportation infrastructure, and particularly rail transit. Their validity, however, has been discredited not only with respect to methodology, but also by real-world events. Comprehensive studies for many cities in this and other countries, previously cited, have clearly shown that real-world conditions are far more complex than the economic hypothetical studies assume: there is a variety of modes—steered and guided—that represent viable alternatives for different cities. A number of cities have found that upgraded buses represent the best solution for many of their corridors (for example, Ottawa, Houston, Pittsburgh); others, or even the same cities, have found that they also have corridors that are best suited to rail transit and that there is a variety of rail modes, rather than one stereotyped "rapid transit." Thus, examples of relatively new successful metro systems include those in San Francisco, Washington, and Atlanta; light rail in Calgary, San Diego, and Portland; and Vancouver's innovative Advanced Light Rail Transit—a fully automated system. This development is continuing in many cities in North America, Europe, and, increasingly, in developing countries.

The diversity of studies comparing transit systems and modes with respect to their assumptions and results is often confusing. An excellent review of the state of the art in this field, with a detailed critical analysis of methodologies used by different authors, was given by Mitric.[15] His study analyzed the correctness of both the conceptual basis and methodologies employed by various authors, as well as the validity of their findings. Following a detailed documentation of their shortcomings, Mitric suggested abandonment of economic modal comparisons and presented the basic guidelines that comparisons of modes should follow.

CONCEPTUAL ANALYSIS OF URBAN TRANSPORTATION MODES

To facilitate an understanding of the individual operating and technical features of urban passenger transportation systems, a growing urban area can be analyzed. The initial condition is a small human settlement with a few dispersed activities and a basic network of paths among them. For this condition, an ideal system of transportation would consist of small vehicles that individual persons or groups would use to travel between different points at the time they desire. The system would be satisfactory in all respects under two conditions: that all persons own vehicles and that everybody can drive them.

If it is supposed that the settlement grows into a small town, then to a city, and finally into a large urbanized area (see Fig. 10-2), it can be shown that, due to increasing volumes of travel, its transportation system would be gradually improved through a sequence of the following steps:

- Introduction of for-hire services by small- and then medium-capacity vehicles (paratransit).
- Introduction of large vehicles as common carriers along the main directions of travel (bus transit).
- Reconstruction of some paths into higher-capacity facilities to accommodate increased traffic volumes (arterial streets, expressways).
- Placement of common carriers on separated ways (first partially, then fully controlled rights-of-way).
- Construction of physical guideways along the controlled ROW, allowing operation of trains with much higher line capacity (LRT, metro, and regional rail).
- Introduction of fully automatic operation of common-carrier vehicles on guideways (AGT, automated metro).

Each of the steps in this evolutionary development of urban transportation would require a certain capital investment, but each would also result in higher capacity, improved service quality, and/or lower operating cost/passenger-km than the preceding systems.

The introduction of higher-performance systems would not necessarily result in elimination of the lower-performance systems; the new systems would serve high volumes of travel with higher efficiency than the preceding systems; thus they would allow those systems to resume the high efficiency of operation they have in their primary domain (that is, at lower volumes of travel).

Owing to the investment required for individual improvements, each successive system tends to have a more limited network than the preceding system. To allow functioning of all models in a coordinated manner, transfer facilities must be provided at various contact points.

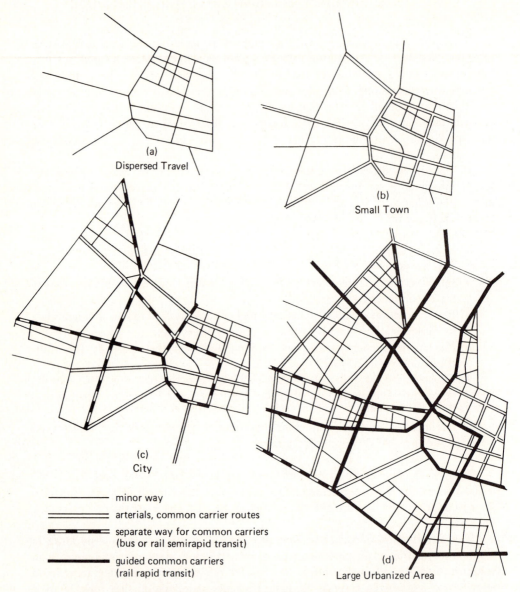

(a)
Dispersed Travel

(b)
Small Town

(c)
City

minor way

arterials, common carrier routes

separate way for common carriers
(bus or rail semirapid transit)

guided common carriers
(rail rapid transit)

(d)
Large Urbanized Area

Figure 10-2 *Change of transportation modes with size of human agglomeration.*

This conceptual analysis corresponds very closely to real-world systems. Urban transportation modes ordered by capacity and performance include private automobiles on local streets, buses, construction of arterials (or freeways), introduction of transit lanes, rail systems with partially controlled ROW (LRT), then with fully controlled ROW (RRT), and finally fully automated intermediate capacity or rapid transit systems. The analysis of individual steps in system improvement can clearly show the trade-offs involved in each upgrading. It can also show that each transportation mode has an optimum domain of operation and no single mode could satisfactorily serve all types of travel: the use of each mode outside its "natural" domain results in high cost, low service quality, and undesirable external effects.

METHODOLOGY FOR MODE COMPARISON AND SELECTION

Each city, area, or corridor to be served by a new transit mode has a unique set of characteristics. For selection of the optimal transit mode, it is necessary to define all the site-specific conditions, requirements, and constraints, which are designated as a *conditions set*. This set may by considered as the demand side of the selection process. On the supply side are the transit modes, from which the optimal one should be selected for the specific application. The selection procedure includes the following major phases: the definition of the conditions set, preliminary design of alternative modes for comparison, and the comparative evaluation and selection of the optimal mode.

DEFINITION OF THE CONDITIONS SET

Based on the overall transportation policy for the city or individual area and on the defined goals for the planned system, specific requirements and standards are developed. To ensure a systematic and comprehensive accounting of all system characteristics, requirements for transit systems are classified into three groups by "interested parties": passengers, operator, and community. A definition of requirements must be done with considerable care, since some of them are rather difficult to define precisely or to distinguish from others. Also, some of them may be either somewhat differently defined, expanded, or omitted in specific cases. However, the framework of this type of analysis has a general validity for virtually all modes of transportation. The more similar the compared modes and their studied applications are, the more precise their comparative analysis can and should be.

The various requirements are listed in Table 10-1; they will be defined briefly. Those requirements that are generally common to different interested parties are defined only once, since they differ only for specific cases. These attributes and their definitions closely agree with factors based on users' perceptions cited in Chap. 22.

Passenger Requirements

Availability. This requirement, without which the population cannot use a transit system, has two aspects: *locational*, closeness to a system's terminals, and *temporal*, expressed as frequency of service. For good availability, users must have both reason-

TABLE 10-1
Transit System Requirements

Passenger	Operator	Community
Availability	Area coverage	Level of service/passenger attraction
Punctuality	Frequency	Economic efficiency
Speed/travel time	Speed	Environmental/energy aspects
User cost	Reliability	Social objectives
Comfort	Cost	Long-range impacts
Convenience	Capacity	
Safety and security	Safety	
	Side effects	
	Passenger attraction	

ably close terminals and an adequate frequency of service. Because of cost constraints, trade-offs between the two must often be made. At one extreme is a dense route network with low frequency of service. At the other extreme is frequent service on few routes; users far from terminals do not have the service unless they use feeders. Most urban transit lines utilize a compromise solution: they provide a certain network density and frequency of service. Naturally, with higher demand both can be increased.

Punctuality. Punctuality is defined as schedule adherence. Variance from scheduled times may result from traffic delays, vehicle breakdowns, or adverse weather conditions. Since traffic delays and interference dominate as causes, by far the most significant factor for securing punctuality is control over the system (that is, separation of transit ROW from other traffic).

Speed/travel time. The total door-to-door travel time can be composed of five parts: access, waiting, travel, transfer and departure times. Relative weights of these time intervals vary, since passengers perceive them differently. Therefore, based on various studies reported in literature, a *weighting factor* of 2.0 to 2.5 can be used for waiting and transfer times to obtain perceived travel times. The relative weight of walking time depends heavily on the attractiveness of the area, weather, and other conditions for walking.

User cost. The price of transportation is another important factor for travelers. Transit fare is the most significant portion of it, but other out-of-pocket costs may also be included, particularly for commuters. In a broader sense, cost of access by automobile and even its fixed costs (if an auto is owned only for that purpose) should also be considered in the cost of travel.

280

Comfort. Comfort is a difficult concept to define precisely because it encompasses many qualitative factors. Paramount are the availability of a seat and the quality of ride (affecting users' ability to read and write). The physical comfort of the seat itself naturally enters in, as does the geometry of the vehicle entrances and exits, width of aisles, presence of air conditioning, jerk and noise level, image of passengers relative to one's self-image, and the degree of privacy offered, to name a few.

Convenience. While comfort is related to the vehicle, convenience refers to the overall system. Lack of the necessity to transfer is a convenience. Good off-peak service, clear system information, well-designed and protected waiting facilities, and sufficient, close parking (if required) are all user conveniences. By nature, evaluation of conveniences is predominantly qualitative.

Safety and security. Passenger safety in terms of accident prevention is very important; however, since safety in transit is usually quite high, this aspect is often less important for passengers than protection from crime. Security is measured by statistical records of crime incidents on the system.

Operator Requirements

Area coverage. Area "covered" or served by transit is defined as the area within 5-min walking distance from transit stops for surface transit and the area within 10-min walking distance from stations for rapid transit. Overall area coverage by a transit network can be expressed as the percentage of the urban area which is the transit service area. In examining area coverage, however, in addition to network extensiveness, provision of and for access modes and central business district (CBD) coverage should also be considered.

Frequency. Frequency is expressed by the number of transit unit (vehicle or train) departures per unit time (hour). It is often incorrectly believed that frequency is not important for commuters. While its significance is greater for off-peak users, it also seriously affects regular riders. For example, there are no residential areas in which only two or three departures during an entire 2-h peak period would be convenient for all potential users. Short, regular headways (that is, high frequency) are an essential element of attracting all categories of passenger trips.

Speed. While passengers are more sensitive to transfer and waiting than travel times, they also prefer high operating speed on the line; the operator is primarily concerned with high cycle speeds on the lines, since they affect the fleet size (investment costs), as well as labor, fuel, maintenance, and other operating costs. Consequently, several speeds are used in different analyses of transit systems:

- Travel speed—one-way average speed of transit units, including stops.
- Cycle speed—average speed, including terminal times.

- Platform speed—overall average speed, including travel to and from garages.
- Pay-time speed—average speed based on drivers' paid time.

Cost. Financial aspects—costs and revenues—often represent the most important single factor of transit system evaluation for the operator. In most cases, three aspects of costs are analyzed: investment cost, operating cost, and revenue. All three vary greatly with local conditions and system characteristics, as well as with time (because of inflation). In evaluation, unit costs rather than total costs of individual modes should be compared.

Capacity. Two different capacities can be defined for a system: way capacity and station capacity. The latter, capacity of lines at stations along the line, governs line capacity since it is smaller in all cases except when vehicles from a line-haul section branch out into several terminals; such cases have few applications at present.

Safety. The operator must pay attention not only to passenger security, but also to the operational safety of the system. Modes with inherently high safety (controlled ROW, guidance, and fail-safe signal systems are the major factors), therefore, have a major advantage over manually controlled vehicles operated on streets.

Side effects. System effects on the nonusers and the urban environment for which the operator is responsible include such physical impacts as enhancing the aesthetics of an area (for example, through construction of attractive stops or stations) or minimizing noise and air pollution. These effects are achieved not only through careful design of vehicles and infrastructure, but also by attracting travel from private automobiles, which generally have much higher negative side effects on the urban environment per person-kilometer than transit vehicles.

Passenger attraction. The number of passengers that a transit line carries is usually the most important indicator of its success and role in urban transportation. The attraction is obviously a function of the type and level of service, but there is also an additional factor, probably best described as *system image*, which can be very important. This image is difficult to define, but it is composed of such aspects as the simplicity of the system, reliability of service, frequency, and regularity, as well as the physical characteristics of facilities, primary fixed-line facilities (wires for trolleybuses, tracks for rail modes, or separate ROW for any technology), which give it clear visibility and presence in the eyes of users.

Community Requirements

Items included in this category, listed in Table 10-1, are generally self-explanatory. Due to the fact that they consist largely of qualitative, indirect, and long-run effects, their characteristics and relative importance vary from case to case. In each specific case they must be carefully defined and analyzed.

In the United States, comparison of transit modes is a legal requirement for any major transit system investment involving federal funds. The comparisons, designated as Environmental Impact Statements, are comprehensive documents that include not only technical and quantitative comparisons of candidate systems (alternatives), but also, in great detail, all short- and long-run community impacts. These include physical, environmental, historic preservation, economic and social aspects.

DEFINITION OF TRANSIT MODES

As explained in Chap. 4, transit modes are defined by three characteristics: (1) right-of-way category, (2) technology, and (3) type of service.

Right-of-Way Categories

It is reemphasized here that, as shown in Chap. 4, the ROW category is the most important element that influences the performance/cost "package" and thus also the level of service/cost characteristics of individual modes. Transit modes sharing the same facilities with other traffic (ROW category C) can *never* be competitive with the private automobile either in speed or in overall LOS, because transit vehicles are subject to the same traffic delays as automobiles, but, in addition, they must stop for passenger stops along their way. This is true for streetcars, trolleybuses, or buses (that is, regardless of technology). Modes with category B ROW, often designated as semirapid transit (for example, light rail), have a considerably higher speed, reliability, capacity, and so on, than those with category C. The highest LOS in all respects is provided by category A, but at the highest investment cost. This factor usually limits the extent of the network of this category, and requires that it be supplemented by other modes as feeders.

Often the alternatives considered are a smaller network of a higher-performance system with feeders or a larger network of a lower-performance system. Many factors influence this choice, but the basic trade-off from the passenger's point of view is between higher LOS (speed, safety, comfort, and so on) on the former and fewer transfers on the latter. Better area coverage is advantageous, but only if the overall LOS remains above a certain acceptable level. If not, passenger attraction may be drastically reduced. The possibility of system upgrading at a later date into a higher-performance system is also an important consideration in planning. The most important characteristics of the three ROW categories of transit modes are presented in condensed form in Table 10-2.

A particularly important factor in selecting the category is passenger attraction, which is a direct function of LOS, that is, of competitiveness of the transit system with private automobile. The three categories present different investment cost/level of service combinations, as Fig. 10-3 conceptually shows. This diagram is closely related to Fig. 4-4: the LOS shown here is a direct function of system performance shown in Fig. 4-4.

TABLE 10-2
Characteristics of the Three Right-of-Way Categories

ROW Categories Characteristics	A	B	C
System performance	Very high	High	Low
Service quality	Very high	High	Low
Passenger attraction	Very high	High	Low
Image/identification	Very good	Good	Poor
Impact on urban form	Very strong	Strong	Weak
Investment cost	Very high	High	Very low
Automation possibility	Full	Partial	None

The relationship between LOS and passenger attraction is presented in Figs. 10-4 and 10-5. Figure 10-4 is the conventional diversion curve showing modal split (or distribution of traffic between two highways) as a function of ratio (or difference) of their travel times (or costs). Figure 10-5 shows the same type of diversion curve as a function of transit LOS, which includes such elements as reliability, comfort, and convenience, in addition to travel time and cost. An increase in the total volume of travel, which occurs when LOS increases, is also shown. Assuming that auto travel has a certain fixed LOS for the given direction of travel, the share of transit grows with its LOS. Since LOS is strongly dependent on the ROW category, domains of each category can be plotted along the abscissa with some mutual overlap, as shown. Thus, the diagram shows conceptually the different volumes of passengers attracted by each category of transit modes, the phenomena always observed in cities with buses and rapid transit, or other types of modes with different ROW categories.

The selection of the ROW category is more closely related to the overall characteristics of the transit system, its anticipated relationship with other modes, and economic, social, and other goals of the city than to specific technology and operating characteristics of modes. It is therefore not only a technical, but also a high-level planning and political decision. Conversely, the selection of a ROW category does influence the technology: for category C, bus is usually the optimal choice; as the separation of transit ROW increases, rail becomes more advantageous; when ROW A is used, rail technology completely dominates for a number of physical, operational, and network reasons.

Technology and Type of Service

The next step in the comparison and selection of modes focuses on determination of the technologies and types of service for candidate modes. Two groups of technology are most commonly used: highway and rail. Other systems can be classified into

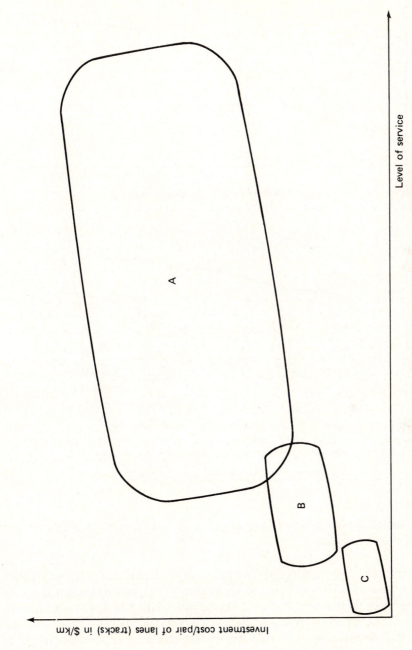

Figure 10-3 *Level of service/investment cost relationship for transit modes with different right-of-way categories.*

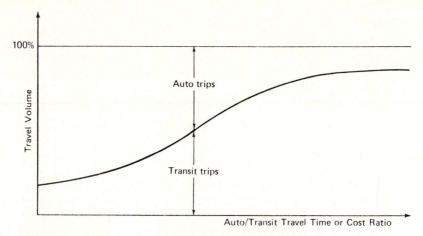

Figure 10-4 *Standard auto/transit modal split or diversion curve.*

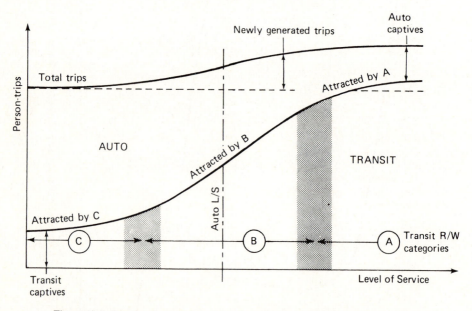

Figure 10-5 *Travel volume and modal split as functions of level of service and ROW categories of transit.*

rubber-tired guided or semiguided technologies, which include trolleybus and rubber-tired transit, and a special category, which includes ferryboats, inclines, and several other technologies, as shown in Table 4-2. On the basis of the established requirements for the specific case, several modes are selected as combinations of technologies and types of service for the adopted ROW category. The technologies and types of service are closely related, although not identical. For example, skip-stop service is used mostly on rapid transit systems, but has been used with express bus service and could be used on any other technology.

286

Comparative analysis of different technologies within the same ROW category is based primarily on a deeper analysis of specific technical and operating system characteristics, and somewhat less on the overall system impact. The analysis is therefore predominantly technical. It is better defined and more quantitative than the one of ROW categories, and yet it is far from simple: it must include a great number of factors, both quantitative and qualitative, and evaluate all of them.

Selection and Functional Design of Candidate Modes

In each specific case of transit mode selection, the engineer–planners must select candidate modes on the basis of an examination of the conditions set for the planned system and a knowledge of the characteristics of different ROW types, transit technologies, and operations. Planners select those modes that may conceivably satisfy the defined requirements. The more expertise and experience planners have, the more precise their choice, and the fewer candidate modes they will select. Accordingly, in no case will an experienced transit planner compare such drastically different modes as buses on street and rapid transit, automated guided transit and minibuses, or dial-a-ride and light rail: the condition sets making the application of the former modes likely will clearly not be suitable for use by the latter ones.

Once these candidate modes are selected, a functional design must be developed for each. The network, specific technology, and operation must be determined so that they are compatible with the given conditions. This preliminary design is necessary since different characteristics of modes make their optimal employments different. For example, rapid transit, light rail, regional rail, and buses on busways would each have its own optimal station locations, connections with other modes, and so on.

THE EVALUATION PROCEDURE

Each candidate mode must now be evaluated with respect to each requirement. The type and depth of evaluation that are reasonable and practical with respect to data availability and objectivity of evaluation of qualitative aspects should be determined. The evaluation of each parameter can be expressed in one of three basic ways: (1) monetary units of measure (dollars), (2) other quantifiable units, or (3) qualitative evaluation.

To derive an overall evaluation of different modes expressed by a single quantitative criterion, two highly subjective and therefore potentially controversial steps have to be made. First, all parameter evaluations have to be quantified; and, second, their relative weights have to be assumed. Although in some rather simple cases this can be done with reasonably satisfactory results, in transit system evaluations this is seldom the case. The reader, analyst, or decision maker will usually get a better picture of compared modes through a complete list of evaluated items than if presented with a single number based on numerous subjective values that often cannot be tracked down.

An Example

An example of this type of comparative analysis is presented in an abbreviated form in a complex comparison of a rapid transit line (Lindenwold) with express bus service (Shirley Express)—modes with different ROW categories, different technologies, and, related to these, different types of service. Although extensive quantitative analyses were made, it was considered that the numbers could sometimes be misleading because the lines operate under similar, but not identical, conditions sets. Therefore, the final comparative evaluations were made in qualitative terms. The results of the comparison are summarized in Table 10-3. This evaluation was

TABLE 10-3
Summary of Comparative Analysis:
Lindenwold Rail Line and Shirley Busway

Requirement	Lindenwold	Shirley	Higher-Rated System
Passenger			
Availability	Good	Poor	Lindenwold
Speed-travel time	Good	Very good	Shirley
Reliability	Very good	Poor	Lindenwold
User cost	Good	Very good	Shirley
Comfort	Good	Poor	Lindenwold
Convenience	Good	Fair	Lindenwold
Safety and security	Very good	Good	Lindenwold
Operator			
Area coverage	Good	Very good	Shirley
Frequency	Very good	Very good	Lindenwold
Speed	Very good	Poor	Lindenwold
Cost: investment	Very poor	Fair	Shirley
Cost: operating	Good	Fair	Lindenwold
Capacity	Good	Poor	Lindenwold
Side effects	Good	Fair	Lindenwold
Passenger attraction	Very good	Good	Lindenwold
Community			
System impact	Very good	Good	Lindenwold

Source: V. R. Vuchic and R. M. Stanger, "Lindenwold Rail Line and Shirley Busway: A Comparison," in *Evaluation of Bus Transit Strategies*, Highway Research Record 459 (Washington, D.C.: Highway Research Board), pp. 13-28.

supplemented by a description of the analysis of each parameter supported by all important data relevant to it. The findings show more clearly the causes of a 70% higher passenger attraction by the Lindenwold rail line than a comparison limited to cost and travel time only could explain. The study separated differences caused by different local conditions from those caused by inherent characteristics of rail and bus technologies, ROW categories, and types of operations.

A similar comparison of two existing systems was performed by Vuchic and Olanipekun[16], on the Lindenwold rail line and New Jersey Transit (NJT) buses. The difference from the preceding study was that these two modes are even more different than Lindenwold and Shirley: NJT buses do not have ROW B—they operate on streets and freeways in mixed traffic. This makes the comparison more difficult. On the other hand, the two systems serve the same general area, so the local conditions are virtually identical. The comparison showed the drastic differences in the types of services buses and rapid transit provide. As a result of these differences, passenger attraction is very different: due to its very high LOS, the single rapid transit line, Lindenwold, attracts a 43% greater ridership than 26 bus lines, which have a much more extensive area coverage, but significantly inferior type and level of service. The rail line has a 44% higher cost recovery ratio (operating revenue/operating expenses) than the bus lines.

SUMMARY AND CONCLUSIONS

In summary, the procedure for the comparative analysis and selection of transportation modes follows these major steps.

- *Step 1:*   Based on urban transportation *policy,* develop *goals* for the transit system.
- *Step 2:*   Define *conditions* for the area to be served.
- *Step 3:*   Utilizing results from preceding steps, define specific *requirements and standards* for the planned system.
- *Step 4:*   Select *ROW type* for candidate modes.
- *Step 5:*   Select *technologies* and *type of operation* for candidate modes.
- *Step 6:*   Develop *functional designs* for candidate modes.
- *Step 7:*   *Evaluate* candidate modes.
- *Step 8:*   *Compare* evaluation results and *select* the optimal mode.

In conclusion, it must be stated that a comparative analysis of transit modes is a very complex problem. There is often a strong tendency to simplify this process, even to the extent that only a single item (usually cost) of peak-hour operation is used as the sole evaluation criterion. Considerable literature exists on "thresholds" of individual technologies, often not recognizing the importance of ROW types and of a great number of performance and LOS characteristics. This tendency for simplification has, in combination with pursuit of a wrong objective in transit system planning (to provide the minimum-cost system), led to many incorrect decisions.

Different transit modes must be compared in a systematic manner and on a comprehensive basis, utilizing many different factors. The methodology presented here facilitates the comparison by classifying transit systems first by their ROW type, affecting strongly their LOS, then by technology, and then by type of operation.

Although the methodology is not exact due to many subjective elements that must be included, it is greatly superior to the simplistic comparisons based on system costs only.

It should be expected that further work and experience with the methodology outlined here will bring additional improvements. However, these improvements should not be expected in the quantification of individual parameters and mechanization of the evaluation procedure, which is usually accompanied by a reduction in an understanding of systems. Rather, the improvements should be made in further formalization of a systematic methodology and comprehensive approach, which will require a much better understanding of transit systems, their operations, and their role in urban transportation than is presently the case.

REFERENCES

1   TILLO E. KUHN, *Public Enterprise Economics and Transport Problems* (Berkeley, Calif.: University of California Press, 1962).

2   MORRIS HILL, "A Method for the Evaluation of Transportation Plans," in *Transportation System Analysis and Evaluation of Alternate Plans*, Highway Research Record 180 (Washington, D.C.: Highway Research Board, 1967), pp. 21-34.

3   EDWARD K. MORLOK, "The Comparison of Transport Technologies," in *Transportation System Evaluation*, Highway Research Record 238 (Washington, D.C.: Highway Research Board, 1968), pp. 1-22.

4   MARVIN L. MANHEIM, "Principles of Transport Systems Analysis," in *Transportation System Analysis and Evaluation of Alternate Plans*, Highway Research Record 180 (Washington, D.C.: Highway Research Board, 1967), pp. 11-20.

5   EDWIN N. THOMAS AND JOSEPH L. SCHOFER, *Strategies for the Evaluation of Alternative Transportation Plans*, NCHRP Report 96 (Washington, D.C.: Highway Research Board, 1970).

6   VUKAN R. VUCHIC, "Place of Light Rail in the Family of Transit Modes," in *Light Rail Transit*, proceedings of a national conference, June 23-25, 1975, Special Report 161 (Washington, D.C.: Transportation Research Board, 1975), pp. 62-76.

7   THOMAS B. DEEN AND DONALD H. JAMES, "Relative Costs of Bus and Rail Transit Systems," in *Transportation Systems Planning*, Highway Research Record 293 (Washington, D.C.: Highway Research Board, 1969), pp. 33-53.

8   FRIEDRICH LEHNER, "Light Rail and Rapid Transit," in *Light Rail Transit*, proceedings of a national conference, June 23-25, 1975, Special Report 161 (Washington, D.C.: Transportation Research Board, 1975), pp. 37-49.

9   V. R. VUCHIC AND R. M. STANGER, "Lindenwold Rail Line and Shirley Busway: A Comparison," in *Evaluation of Bus Transit Strategies*, Highway Research Record 459 (Washington, D.C.: Highway Research Board, 1973), pp. 13-28.

10 Vukan R. Vuchic and Olayinka A. Olanipekun, "Lindenwold Rail Line and New Jersey Transit Buses: A Comparison," in *Urban Public Transportation Research 1990,* Transportation Research Record 1266, Public Transit (Washington, D.C.: Transportation Research Board, 1990), pp. 123-38.

11 Wolfgang S. Homburger, "An Analysis of Different Forms of Rapid Transit," in *Urban Mass Transit Planning* (Berkeley, Calif.: University of California, Institute of Transportation and Traffic Engineering, 1967), pp. 197-203. A summary of a report by K. Leibbrand for Frankfurt, Germany.

12 J. R. Meyer, J. F. Kain, and M. Wohl, *The Urban Transportation Problem* (Cambridge, Mass.: Harvard University Press, 1966).

13 Theodore E. Keeler and others, *The Full Costs of Urban Transport*, a series of monographs (Berkeley, Calif.: University of California, Institute of Urban and Regional Development, 1974-1975).

14 D. R. Miller and others, "Cost Comparison of Busway and Railway Rapid Transit," with discussions, in *Evaluation of Bus Transit Strategies*, Highway Research Record 459 (Washington, D.C: Highway Research Board, 1973), pp. 1-10.

15 Slobodan Mitric, *Comparison of Modes in Urban Transport: A Methodological Analysis*, Technical Report (Columbus, Ohio: Ohio State University, Department of Civil Engineering, July 1976). A summary entitled "Comparing Modes in Urban Transportation" appears in *Transportation Evaluation Techniques*, Transportation Research Record 639 (Washington, D.C.: Transportation Research Board, 1977), pp. 19-24.

16 Vuchic and Olanipekun, "Lindenwold Rail Line."

EXERCISES

10-1   A number of studies have been made with the purpose of finding which modes are "better" than others. Typically, the focus has been on the bus versus rail question, using peak-hour passenger volume as the only variable. Is this problem formulated correctly? What is the answer to it, and under what conditions can there be a correct answer?

10-2   What are the typical problems with comparisons of transit modes based on hypothetical models of cities and analyses of costs only? Which type of modes do these studies tend to evaluate unrealistically highly, which modes are usually unjustifiably downgraded and why?

10-3   Compare major modes of higher-quality bus transit: express bus, semirapid bus, and guided bus (O-Bahn) with regular bus, using their basic characteristics (that is, those conditions independent of local conditions).

10-4   There are opinions that light rail transit (LRT) can have performance similar to that of rapid transit, but it requires much lower investment. Contrary claims are that LRT compromises many operational features because it does not have exclusive ROW, so it is not much better than conventional streetcars. Define the basic characteristics in which the three modes differ and compare them. Evaluate the two opinions and express your conclusions about the merits of

LRT compared to streetcars and to rapid transit.

10-5 Define the following characteristics of transit modes: travel speed, flexibility, long-range impacts, comfort.

10-6 Which transit mode characteristics are included in "side effects"?

Chapter 11

EVALUATING RAPID TRANSIT

Thomas B. Deen and Richard H. Pratt

Throughout most of the world's urbanized areas, public transit needs can be adequately served by local fixed-route bus service operating on streets, mixed with other traffic. Such service is constrained, due to its required stops and delays from other traffic, to average scheduled speeds of 10 to 12 mi/h (16 to 19 km/h). While not competitive with the automobile, these conditions are adequate as long as trip lengths in the corridors served tend to be 5 mi (8 km) or less—about a 30-min trip at average speeds—and maximum hourly passenger volumes in one direction are 5000 to 7000 or less.

Many corridors in larger cities do not fit one or both of these limitations, however, and ways must be found to devise transit service that operates at higher speeds and with higher capacity than local bus service can provide. Provision of express bus service on freeways can sometimes meet the speed requirements, and if no stops for loading are necessary, higher capacity can also be achieved. The acceptable performance range for bus service can often be extended by use of transportation system management (TSM) techniques, which can give buses and other high-occupancy vehicles (HOVs) traffic priority (see Chap. 12). Freeways with bus or HOV lanes or separate HOV facilities provide an opportunity for service at higher speeds and volumes than would be possible in mixed traffic.

On the other hand, reserving lanes for buses, with or without other HOVs, may be physically impractical or publicly unacceptable or may not suffice to meet transportation objectives. Freeways themselves are often congested during peak periods and do not even exist in some corridors. In such situations, strong consideration is often given to the construction of rapid transit.

Rapid transit is defined for purposes of this discussion as express, limited-stop transit service provided entirely or primarily on exclusive or reserved rights-of-way.

Vehicles can be steered by a fixed guideway or by professional drivers, suspended on steel wheels or rubber tires, and propelled by electric motors or petroleum engines. Within rapid transit, there is a choice between rail or bus systems and their variants.

This choice has been made more complex by the increasing opportunity and tendency to opt for "mixed" systems of rail, bus, HOVs, people movers, and so on. It is indeed appropriate to consider the full spectrum of options extending from local transit, through express bus service enhanced by TSM, to semirapid transit and full rapid transit in its various forms. Even so, the decisions and trade-offs for mode selection in any given corridor must still consider the same essential points.

Development costs for rapid transit are always several orders of magnitude greater than for local transit, which benefits from the established street and highway network. Moreover, the high-cost guideways, stations, and maintenance facilities of rapid transit are fixed in place, and thus very careful consideration must be given to their location. They must effectively serve the community for many decades in order to amortize the large investment. All this means that the planning and decision-making process for rapid transit development is much more rigorous, expensive, time consuming, and potentially frustrating than for local transit.

In addition to system location, questions of financing, phasing, performance, social impacts, economic impacts, environmental impacts, and extent of the system must be resolved. Two of the most difficult decisions have to do with:

- Whether rapid transit development should be undertaken at all.
- Which rapid transit mode would be most suitable in the local environment.

WHETHER TO BUILD

In the United States, three primary influences on the decision of whether to embark on rapid-transit development can be identified:

1. Financial and institutional factors—those institutional arrangements that dictate the constraints within which the system is to be financed.
2. Attitudinal factors—those predispositions of the community that exist independent of the plan and planning process associated with rapid-transit development.
3. Physical and analytical factors—those intrinsic attributes that involve the physical layout of the system and the ridership it will serve; its costs, performance, and interaction with other elements of the transportation system; and benefits and cost effectiveness.

These three primary influences structure the following discussion, but not without reference to another division of influences, that of political concerns versus technical concerns. It is unrealistic and therefore detrimental to constructive planning to ignore the influence of political concerns and motives. At the same time, sound, objective, and instructive technical findings are at the heart of good decision making in the high-stakes process of rapid transit planning and development.

FINANCIAL AND INSTITUTIONAL FACTORS

To understand the financial and institutional factors influencing the decision to build or not build a project of the monumental proportions normally included in a rapid transit system, one must have some concept of the motivational context of the agency charged with implementation. This context can be markedly different depending on whether there is an established local/state funding source adequate for the scale of nonfederal funding required. Frequently, there is no adequate funding mechanism in place, and the agency charged with rapid transit construction is also charged with developing the financing.

In one common scenario of this type, which will serve to illustrate the interplay that can arise, the substantive beginning of a rapid transit project comes from a source not even equipped to carry out implementation, such as the comprehensive transportation planning process. The recommendation of rapid transit is made as part of a long-range transportation plan, including suggested designation or formation of an agency to begin work. Often, questions of timing, technology (rail or bus), and locational details are addressed only in schematic form. The legislature acts on the strength of this general recommendation to enact legislation for "an Authority to plan, design, build, and operate a rapid transit system," usually leaving the question of financing unresolved, contingent on a successful application for federal funding, a successful bond referendum, and/or enactment of additional legislation.

The members of the transit authority very quickly perceive that its success will be judged by how quickly they get a system planned, financed, designed, and under way. They also intuitively comprehend that getting anything built at all will require broad-based political and public support, which, in turn, is much more easily achieved with a system that is big, bold, glamorous, fast, extensive, and, above all, which appears to serve as much of the affected area as possible from the day the system first opens. Since even a small start on one short line will in itself be a huge public works project, it is much easier to sell the full system if it appears to serve more people. It may be easier to sell a major urban area a $3 billion project than a $300 million project.

At this point the authority finds itself pulled by opposing forces: the local desire or political requirement for an extensive system and the demand of others, especially the senior governments being called on to finance much of the project, for a truncated, less costly undertaking. The senior government knows it cannot get enough money to fund all the system being planned and suspects that good transportation planning, economic analysis, and common sense would dictate a plan that begins small and develops over time.

The federal government, specifically the U.S. Department of Transportation's Urban Mass Transportation Administration (UMTA), was made the prime example of such senior government in the United States by the Urban Mass Transportation Act of 1964. To conserve scarce federal resources, UMTA has established the policy of funding only one minimum operable segment of new systems at a time and requires a major capital investment planning process that includes the determination of cost effectiveness through a detailed analysis of transportation alternatives.[1]

The dominance of financial influence on planning decisions and the different effect of alternative funding arrangements can be clearly identified from actual cases. Toronto and Baltimore began their rapid transit systems with funding sources that were constrained but required no referendum, and their first sections were the central portions of single lines. In contrast, Washington, San Francisco, and Atlanta all required bond authorization referenda, and all proposed multiple-line, total systems, originally scheduled for completion as a package so that all areas received a commitment for service on a defined schedule. Seattle and Houston, after initial failures at bond referenda, changed course and proceeded incrementally using available funding sources. With expanded availability of federal funding, coupled with the federal policy of starting with no more than one minimum operable segment, Miami, Buffalo, Portland (Oregon), and Santa Clara County (California) all moved forward with single lines. Minneapolis–St. Paul and Dallas, having aspirations far in excess of likely federal involvement, illustrate a possible resurgence of multiple-line system proposals.

ATTITUDINAL FACTORS

Decisions relating to the building of rapid transit, as well as the type of system, are heavily influenced by local attitudes and preconceived notions about the importance of transit improvements quite apart from the analytical presentations of the planning studies.[2] All the larger cities of the United States had comprehensive transportation studies performed as part of the requirements of the 1956 Federal-Aid Highway Act, and most of these recommended a much more modest role for transit than has been subsequently proposed. Improvements in analytical techniques do not explain the differences; the differences relate to the value systems of the citizenry. Major concerns with environment, urban development patterns, and social issues have all surfaced since that time, and in response the evaluative processes and starting assumptions have shifted more to transit's favor.

Often the attitude is not necessarily pro-transit so much as it is antihighway or anti-automobile. San Francisco, Washington, Baltimore, Boston, Sacramento, and Portland are all cities that over time have experienced antifreeway movements that have helped promote the cause of transit. Concern for the environment was perhaps the factor uppermost in the minds of voters in the Denver area in 1975 when they approved the development (never carried out) of a system to cost more than $1 billion before being presented with details of the system's hardware, performance, or required time for development. Sometimes civic boosterism is a motivating factor, especially when two areas that have a tradition of rivalry consider transit development.

Executive interviews in Atlanta, Miami, Portland, and San Diego, conducted in 1989 after rail transit implementation, identified rapid transit as being perceived to bring cities an enhanced quality of life, an improved civic image, an assist to marketing and promotion, and a favorable impact on intraregional development and land-use decisions.[3] The most cited reason for building rapid transit was the perceived need to move large numbers of people; some individuals in Miami admitted that the initial image of their rail system suffered due to low ridership, among other things. Perceptions in Atlanta, Portland, and San Diego were reportedly very positive, notably so in Portland where downtown retail activity and sales increased and public policy favoring development along the rail line with all sorts of supporting incentives was having the desired effect, even during a depressed economy.

For years the federal government has explicitly promoted the concept of carrying out transportation planning at the local level, with local planning officials responsible for the outcome. It is therefore inevitable, and perhaps even desirable, for each community to develop criteria that are responsive to its unique values and aspirations. The problem comes when these predispositions fly in the face of physical or economic reality. It makes no economic sense to build a $300 million rapid transit line to carry 5000 passengers/day no matter what one's aspirations, especially if financial assistance is being asked of some other level of government.

PHYSICAL FACTORS

Regardless of attitudes or institutional arrangements in a community, the size and physical relationships of activities and geography either lend themselves to the type of service that rapid transit provides or they do not. These physical factors are the primary determinants of the ultimate cost of constructing the system and of the number of riders over whom this cost can be distributed. No degree of rapid transit attractiveness can make up for ridership potential that is not there because of urban configuration.

There have been numerous efforts to measure city attributes in ways that will quickly identify those that can justify rapid transit. Table 11-1 lists several such indicators. Most are directly related to measures of potential passenger demand, and many could be accepted as valid for most cases. There are unquestionably minimum city and central business district (CBD) sizes and densities below which no form of rapid transit makes economic sense.

Criteria related to corridor flows, central-city density, or CBD size must be used with caution, however, since the definition of a corridor, what constitutes a CBD, and the boundaries of the central city vary among urban areas. The degree of travel dispersion likewise varies. There are inevitably exceptions to aggregate criteria.

One major factor often omitted in lists of indicators is city configuration. Figure 11-1 shows four representative city configurations, assumed for purposes of discussion to have equal population. Configuration B is a typical city with a CBD in the center and the urban area spread in a 360° pattern around it. On average, only one-eighth of CBD-oriented travel will occur in any one 45° corridor. A rapid transit system serving such an area might require eight spokes. Examples are Washington and Denver.

TABLE 11-1
Selected Rapid Transit Feasibility Criteria

Criterion	Desired or Minimum Threshold for System Development		
	Rail (desired)	Rail (minimum) or Bus	Busway (minimum)
Urban-area population	2,000,000	1,000,000	750,000
Central-city[a] population	700,000	500,000	400,000
Central-city[a] population density (people/mi^2)[b]	14,000	10,000	5000
CBD floor space (ft^2)[c]	50,000,000	25,000,000	20,000,000
CBD employment	100,000	70,000	50,000
Daily CBD destinations/mi^{2b}	300,000	150,000	100,000
Daily CBD destinations/corridor	70,000	40,000	30,000
Peak-hour cordon person movements leaving the CBD (four quadrants)	75,000–100,000	50,000–70,000	35,000

[a]Central city refers to the effective central city, including the central city and contiguously developed areas of comparable density.
[b]Metric conversion: 1 mi = 1.6 km.
[c]Metric conversion: 1 ft = 30.5 cm.

Source: Adapted from Herbert S. Levinson, Crosby L. Adams, and William F. Hoey, *Bus Use of Highways: Planning and Design Guidelines*, NCHRP Report 155 (Washington, D.C.: Transportation Research Board, 1975), p. 26.

Configuration C would require only five spokes to provide the same effective coverage, with each spoke serving a higher percentage of all travel. Examples are Toronto and Chicago. Configuration D can be served with only two spokes, each carrying heavy volumes. Examples are Honolulu and Caracas, Venezuela.

The most difficult configuration of cities is shown in configuration A. An example is the Twin Cities of Minneapolis and St. Paul. A line linking the two CBDs in such a configuration may be singularly effective, but 14 other spokes are required to provide full coverage.

Clearly, the rapid transit systems for each area shown decrease in price from configurations A to D. Moreover, the level of service goes up, since requirements for passenger transfers go down. Finally, within the assumption of equal population, the number of passengers per line goes up. Highway capacity deficiency and auto congestion problems, measures of rapid transit need and viability, also increase as one goes from A to D, since all travel is concentrated into fewer corridors. Aggregate criteria that do not recognize the configuration factor will encounter many exceptions.

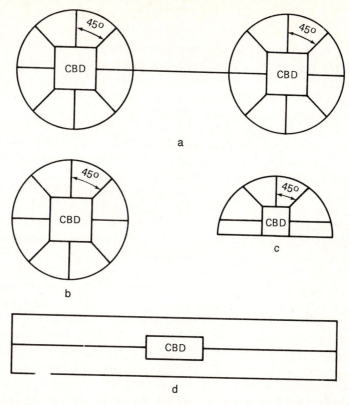

Figure 11-1 *Representative city configurations (equal population). [Source: Adapted from Thomas B. Deen, Walter M. Kulash, and Stephen E. Baker, "Critical Decisions in the Rapid Transit Planning Process," in* Transit Planning, *Transportation Research Record 559 (Washington, D.C.: Transportation Research Board, 1976), pp. 33-43.*

Configuration is a major reason why Honolulu, even though projected to have less than 1 million persons in the standard metropolitan area, can be in project planning for fully grade separated fixed-guideway rapid transit. Thanks to configuration D, their system can serve the city with a single through line and is projected to carry daily volumes of over 80,000 passengers on each of the two approaches to the city center. In contrast, the configuration A cities of Minneapolis and St. Paul, with 2.3 million population, are in the initial steps of a 20-year plan for lower-volume semirapid transit, which attempts to serve many but not all the multitude of corridors.

The worst situation for rapid transit is when individual lower-density suburban centers approach or exceed the size of employment in the CBD, creating a proliferation of travel patterns and corridors exceedingly difficult to serve effectively. The classic example has been Los Angeles, where now sheer size (the second-largest city of the United States, with the seventh largest CBD), accompanying congestion and pollution, and a large transit-dependent population have led to the introduction of heavy and light rail and bus rapid transit in individual corridors. A more typical example of the increasingly common phenomenon of a spread-out city, with dispersed employment rivaling that of the CBD, is Phoenix. The voters of the Phoenix area, with 2.0 million population, in 1989 rejected fixed-guideway transit proposals.

Note that both the aggregate criteria of Table 11-1 and the examination of city configuration implicitly focus on radial travel to the CBD as the primary source of rapid transit riders. With suburban to suburban travel growing faster than other urban travel, interest has increased in serving intrasuburban travel with rapid transit. Table 11-2 uses as examples the extensive San Francisco BART and Washington, D.C., Metrorail systems to illustrate the relative ineffectiveness of rapid transit in serving non-CBD trips. Intrasuburban trips per mile of suburban track are only a fraction of total trips per mile of total system. While it can make sense to align a radial rapid transit route to serve non-CBD trips as an adjunct to carrying the 80% or so of system riders who travel to the CBD, investing the total cost of a rapid transit line in service to intrasuburban travel alone is another matter. Suburban centers will have to achieve the size, density, convenience to pedestrians, and disincentives to auto use of center-city CBDs before intrasuburban rapid transit offers real promise.

The other major factor, in addition to city configuration, that causes exceptions is the availability of cheap right-of-way. If rail rapid transit can be built, for example, on the surface in the median strip of a highway (and thus avoid subway or elevated construction), construction costs (including stations, equipment, and right-of-way) might typically run $40 million/rte.-mi ($25 million/rte.-km). If the line is required to run underground, however, costs for subway construction might be 6 times this amount. Cleveland, Ohio, built their modest but effective rail rapid transit system even though patronage was only 4000 persons/h on one of their lines. Building rail rapid transit for such a low patronage made sense only because of the very low cost of the system when built in 1955, which in 1990 dollars would be $23 million/rte.-mi. The low cost was possible only because of the availability of an inexpensive right-of-way along existing railroad lines that required no tunneling and very little elevated construction.

Figure 11-2 shows the importance of construction costs in determining the total cost of transporting people. It should be noted that the total capital, operating, and maintenance cost of transporting people in automobiles or on the local buses of major cities is in the range of 25 to 50 (16 to 31) cents/passenger-mi (passenger-km) overall, or 25 to 75 (16 to 47) cents/passenger-mi (passenger-km) if the upper end of the range is keyed to the incremental cost of new facilities to accommodate commuter travel by auto. From Fig. 11-2 it can be seen that 20,000 passengers/day might be all that is required to maintain a 50 cent/passenger-mi cost if a rapid transit line can be built for $10 million/mi, whereas if capital costs are $100 million/mi, patronage must be 100,000/day to achieve a 75 cent/passenger-mi cost.

The all-important issue of physical factors boils down to the bottom-line question of what it is going to cost per passenger-mile to transport people via rapid transit. If this cost exceeds the cost of other options by significant amounts, then any justification offered in terms of overall community benefits must be examined more critically before

TABLE 11-2
Crosstown and Intra/Intersuburban Travel via Rapid Transit

San Francisco Bay Area Rapid Transit District: April 26, 1989 BART Ridership[a]

	Weekday Trips		Stations		Length of Track		Trips per Station	Trips per Mile[c]
	Number	Percent	Number	Percent	Miles[c]	Percent		
Total system	216,900	100	34	100	71	100	6400	3100
System excepting CBD	47,800	22	27	79	67	94	1800	700
Intra- and intersuburbs only	19,800	9	18	53	41	58	1100	500

Washington Metropolitan Area Transit Authority: 1990 Metrorail Passenger Survey[b]

	Weekday Trips		Stations		Length of Track		Trips per Station	Trips per Mile[c]
	Number	Percent	Number	Percent	Miles[c]	Percent		
Total system	519,000	100	61	100	70	100	8500	7400
System excepting CBD	77,800	15	43	70	56	80	1800	1400
Intra- and intersuburbs only	35,300	7	28	46	39	56	1300	900

[a]CBD includes Oakland and San Francisco CBDs; suburbs exclude Oakland and San Francisco. BART ridership is pre-Loma Prieta earthquake. Source: Metropolitan Transportation Commission.
[b]CBD includes Rosslyn and Pentagon; suburbs exclude District of Columbia, Rosslyn, and Pentagon. Metrorail ridership is pre-Wheaton extension. Source: Washington Metropolitan Area Transit Authority.
[c]Metric conversion: 1 mi = 1.6 km.

an affirmative decision is made. On the other hand, if the cost is equal to or less than other existing modes, then the "go" decision can be made more easily. Unfortunately, the cost effectiveness of proposed and operating U.S. transit systems, both rail and bus, is often not presented in terms of the ultimate product, a "passenger-mile." Table 11-3 shows costs of operating rapid transit systems, both per passenger and per passenger-mile.

WHICH TECHNOLOGY?

Technology provides the planner with five alternatives that have at least the potential for supplying rapid transit service within an urban area or individual corridor. These five modes are:

- Rail rapid transit (RRT).
- Light rail transit (LRT).
- Bus rapid transit (BRT).
- Commuter railroad (CRR).
- Automated guideway transit (AGT).

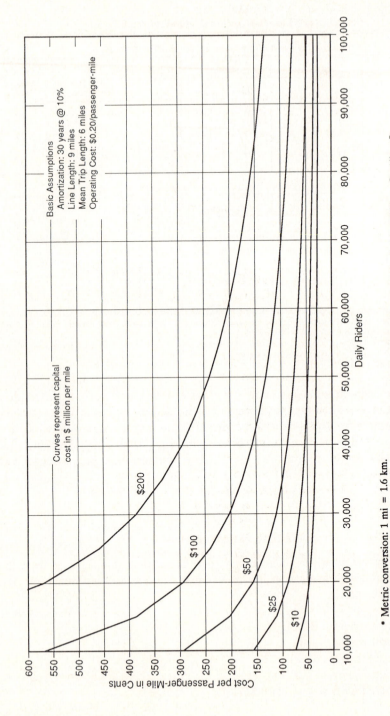

* Metric conversion: 1 mi = 1.6 km.

Figure 11-2 *Cost per passenger-mile versus daily patronage. [Source: Compiled by William G. Allen, Jr., for the Transportation Research Board, adapted from report by Alan M. Voorhees & Associates, Inc., A Long Range View of Transit in Nashville (McLean, Va.: Alan M. Voorhees & Associates, Inc., September 1970, rev. September 1971).]*

TABLE 11-3
Costs for Several North American Rapid Transit Systems

Item	Rail Rapid Transit				Light Rail Transit				Busway[a]		Automated Guideway Transit		
	Atlanta	Baltimore	Miami	Washington	Buffalo	Pittsburgh	Portland	San Diego	L.A. El Monte	Pittsburgh E & S	Detroit DPM	Miami DPM	Vancouver
Year of primary data	1987	1987[b]	1988	1986	1987	1989	1989	1988	1983-86	1987	1988	1988	1987
Annual patronage (millions)	53.7	11.9	10.4	116.0	8.1	9.0	6.4	8.4	5.7	12.2	3.2	3.2	18.0
Daily patronage (thousands)	184.5	42.6	35.4	411.6	29.2	30.6	19.7	27.0	22[c]	47.0	11.3	10.8	58.0
Capital costs (millions of 1988 $)	2720	1289	1341	7968	722	622	266	176	144	216	215	175	640
Annual capital costs (millions of 1988 $)	278.1	131.8	137.1	814.8	73.8	63.6	27.2	18.0	8.1[d]	22.1	22.0	17.9	65.4
Annual operating costs (millions of 1988 $)	40.3	21.7	37.5	199.9	11.6	8.1	5.8	7.2	10.9	6.7	10.9	4.6	19.1
Total annual costs (millions of 1988 $)	318.4	153.5	174.6	1014.7	85.4	71.7	33.0	25.2	19.0	28.8	32.9	22.5	84.5
Cost per passenger-trip (1988 $)	5.93	12.90	16.79	8.75	10.55	7.97	5.16	3.00	3.34	2.36	10.28	7.03	4.70
Average trip length (mi)[e]	5.3	3.6	7.8	6.2	3.6	6.1	6.1	9.5	7.1[f]	4.5	1.5[f]	1.0[f]	7.2[f]
Cost per passenger-mi ($)	1.12	3.58	2.15	1.41	2.93	1.31	0.85	0.32	0.47	0.52	6.85	7.03	0.65

Metric conversion: 1 mi = 1.6 km.

[a]Includes the cost of purchasing and operating buses (busway portion of affected routes only).
[b]Data does not include Owings Mills extension.
[c]Bus passengers only (does not include carpool/vanpool passengers).
[d]Computed by allocating 55% of cost to bus operation (in proportion to bus ridership vs. total HOV facility person volume).
[e]Revenue (linked trip) guideway trip length.
[f]Estimated by the authors as a function of line length.

Sources: Compiled by William G. Allen, Jr., for the Transportation Research Board from various sources, including: Don H. Pickrell, *Urban Rail Transit Projects: Forecast Versus Actual Ridership and Costs* (Washington, D.C.: Urban Mass Transportation Administration, 1989); A. D. Biehler, "Exclusive Busways Versus Light Rail Transit: A Comparison of New Fixed-Guideway Systems," in *Light Rail Transit: New System Successes at Affordable Prices,* Special Report 221 (Washington, D.C.: Transportation Research Board, 1989), pp. 89-97; Texas Transportation Institute, *Transit System Comparison Study—Comparative City Data Base,* Rail Research Project, prepared for the Metropolitan Transit Authority of Harris County (Houston, Tex.: Texas Transportation Institute, August 1989); Crain & Associates, Inc., *The Martin Luther King, Jr., East Busway in Pittsburgh, PA,* prepared for UMTA (Menlo Park, Calif.: Crain & Associates, October 1987); N. D. Lea & Associates, Inc., *Assessment of the San Diego Light Rail System* (Washington, D.C.: N. D. Lea & Associates, November 1983); Samuel L. Zimmerman, "UMTA and Major Investments: Evaluation Process and Results," in *Transit Administration and Planning Research,* Transportation Research Record 1209 (Washington, D.C.: Transportation Research Board, 1989), pp. 32-36; H. S. Levinson and others, *Bus Use of Highways: State of the Art,* NCHRP Report 143 (Washington, D.C.: Highway Research Board, 1973).

Modal definitions are provided in Chap. 4. Note that for this discussion BRT will be taken to encompass any system utilizing buses operating, for at least the major portion of their routes, on exclusive or reserved paved rights-of-way (busway or transitway), permitting high-speed operation, including priority lanes on limited access roads. The reserved pavement may be shared with other high-occupancy vehicles (HOVs) as long as degradation of bus operations does not result.

Commuter railroad operation is a special case in the selection of technology, since the availability of a well-constructed railroad line appropriately situated is a prerequisite. Most CRR operations, such as those of New York, Chicago, Philadelphia, San Francisco, and Boston, perform their vital transportation role with track and terminal facilities built by the private railroad companies long before changing circumstances removed the profit from railroad passenger service. There have been many studies of the potential for new CRR, but the economic trade-offs almost always look unfavorable, except for the occasional upgrading and expansion of existing service.

Justification of completely new CRR service is likely only in those few metropolitan areas where (1) railroad track is already in good condition, (2) the tracks penetrate deep into the CBD and good distribution is available from the central terminal to other destinations, (3) significant residential population can be served by the outlying track locations, and (4) the commuting distances involved are long, typically 10 to 50 mi (16 to 80 km) for most passengers. Toronto's GO Transit is the preeminent example of a new system.

Within the emerging family of technologies classified as automated guideway transit (AGT), two major subgroups have achieved operational status. One group, typified by people-mover systems of modest speed, serves the relatively short trip movements found in major activity centers, including a few downtowns and campuses and a relatively large number of major airports. The other group consists of higher-speed line-haul applications and represents the type of AGT of primary interest as a rapid transit option. These line-haul applications hold promise but still exhibit "teething problems." The only installations presently approaching metropolitan scale are those in Lille, France (VAL), and Vancouver, B.C. (SkyTrain). As a rapid transit technology, this form of AGT is close to RRT, but can employ vehicles that are still small compared to RRT or LRT, structures that are lighter, and service envelopes that require less horizontal and vertical clearance. All AGT must be fully grade separated. (See Chap. 24 for a detailed discussion of AGT systems.)

This leaves most cities with two sets of technology choices, as a practical matter, within the widening spectrum of rapid transit options. One set of choices is bounded by heavy and light rail transit, with line-haul AGT as a promising variation, and the other set is comprised of BRT and the various opportunities for BRT integration with HOV facilities. In area after area, the choice is agonizing, being made only after years of debate, delays, and great frustration. The record suggests that in some cases the choice gets confused and is used by those who prefer no system to delay the process altogether. In many cases the arguments are waged at a superficial and emotional level and often overlook the fact that the choice of technology is only one of a number of choices necessary, some of which can affect costs and service more than the technology issue.

Several studies have been made that try to compare the relative costs of the systems (particularly RRT and BRT), with widely varying results. For example, Miller and others[4] found that RRT was almost always cheaper, whereas the Institute for Defense Analyses[5] found that BRT is always cheaper. Deen and James[6] found that either could be cheaper, depending on the volume to be carried and on the extent of the subway segments required. Subsequent studies continue to cover the spectrum of findings.[7, 8] The reasons for such variance among responsible investigators are many, but there are two that dominate the confusion.

1. A failure to recognize the huge differences in costs associated with alternative vertical alignment configurations.
2. A failure to recognize the complexities intrinsic to the decision to select subway versus elevated versus surface on exclusive right-of-way versus surface in mixed or restricted traffic.

Even including all components unaffected by vertical alignment (such as power and signal systems, yards and shops, and rolling stock), underground construction costs 2 to 3 times that of elevated, and elevated construction costs 2 to 3 times that of surface construction. Finally, surface systems (or segments) themselves can vary by a factor of 2 to 3, depending on whether they must be located on an exclusive right-of-way or can be located on streets mixed with or alongside other traffic. These ratios tend to hold true for all fixed-guideway technologies and become more pronounced (2 to 5) in the case of BRT. Their sheer magnitude guarantees that any analysis that does not explicitly account for them is probably going to get unreliable answers.

Figures 11-3 and 11-4 illustrate several phenomena including the very large differences in cost of rapid transit construction, depending on the extent of surface, elevated, or underground alignment. Figure 11-3 plots the per-mile costs of RRT, LRT, AGT, and BRT as a function of the percentage of the line or system that is underground, the dominant cost determinant. Figure 11-4 plots the same data points over time for those examples with less than 20% of their alignment underground so that they can be seen more clearly (note the change in the cost scale).

One pattern that stands out in Figures 11-3 and 11-4 is the increase in construction cost over time, even after conversion to 1990 constant dollars, with the early 1970s being a watershed between lower and higher cost systems. It can be hypothesized that the higher costs of the newer projects reflect additional expenditures associated with environmental impact mitigation requirements, handicapped accessibility requirements, and increased pressure from the citizenry for nonintrusive construction, along with the provision of more amenities such as escalators, possibly coupled with taking advantage of expanded funding sources to include more niceties and peripheral improvements than would previously have been contemplated.

What appears in Figure 11-4 to be an enormous growth in cost over time in the case of systems with 20% or less underground construction is, however, predominantly the result of the type of alignment involved. Most of the newer, higher cost systems in Fig. 11-4, specifically the AGT systems and Miami RRT, have large components of

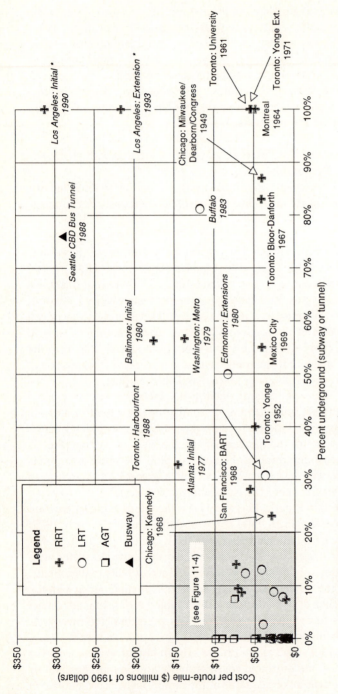

Figure 11-3 *Fixed-guideway system costs versus percentage underground. [Source: Compiled by William G. Allen, Jr., for the Transportation Research Board; adapted from various sources, including: J. Hayden Boyd, Norman J. Asher, and Elliot S. Wetzler, Evaluation of Rail Rapid Transit and Express Bus Service in the Urban Commuter Market (Arlington, Va.: Institute for Defense Analysis, October 1973). Don H. Pickrell, Urban Rail Transit Projects: Forecast Versus Actual Ridership and Costs (Washington, D.C.: Urban Mass Transportation Administration, 1989). Parsons Brinckerhoff Quade & Douglas, Inc., Company files. J. W. Schumann, "What's New in North American Light Rail Transit Projects?" in Light Rail Transit: New System Successes at Affordable Prices, Special Report 221 (Washington, D.C. Transportation Research Board, 1989), pp. 8-42. Arlee T. Reno and Ronald H. Bixby, Characteristics of Urban Transportation Systems, prepared for UMTA (Washington, D.C.: System Design Concepts, Inc., October 1985).]*

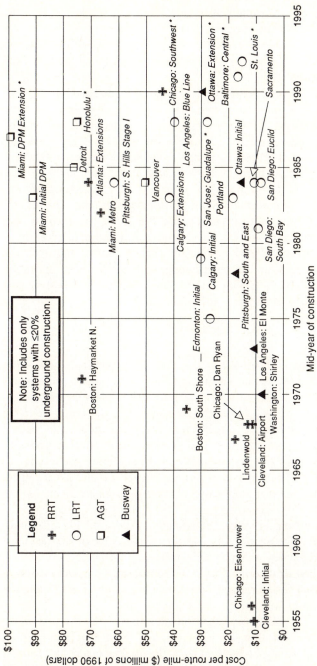

Figure 11-4 *Fixed-guideway system costs versus mid-year of construction. [Source: Compiled by William G. Allen, Jr., for the Transportation Research Board; adapted from various sources, including: J. Hayden Boyd, Norman J. Asher, and Elliot S. Wetzler, Evaluation of Rail Rapid Transit and Express Bus Service in the Urban Commuter Market (Arlington, Va.: Institute for Defense Analysis, October 1973). Don H. Pickrell, Urban Rail Transit Projects: Forecast Versus Actual Ridership and Costs (Washington, D.C.: Urban Mass Transportation Administration, 1989). Parsons Brinckerhoff Quade & Douglas, Inc., Company files. J. W. Schumann, "What's New in North American Light Rail Transit Projects?" in Light Rail Transit: New System Successes at Affordable Prices, Special Report 221 (Washington, D.C.: Transportation Research Board, 1989), pp. 8-42. Arlee T. Reno and Ronald H. Bixby, Characteristics of Urban Transportation Systems, prepared for UMTA (Washington, D.C.: System Design Concepts, Inc., October 1985).]*

* Projected (year is mid-year of cost data).
Note: Costs include right-of-way and equipment. Systems 1975 or newer shown in *italics.*

307

elevated construction. When Figs. 11-3 and 11-4 are looked at together, and either the pre-1975 or the newer projects are examined as a separate set of data points, the importance of underground construction can be seen. The data points of either time period indicate that the cost per mile of underground has for the most part been on the order of 3 to 6 times the cost of surface systems. (The newer projects are identified in italics to make them stand out.)

It is fair to say that decisions made on vertical configuration are fundamental with respect to the ultimate costs of the system, and that they can easily transcend the related, but often separate, question of technology selection. The lack of understanding of these relationships has caused no end of confusion where system costs are compared. For example, many past proposals for new technologies suggested that very large cost savings would be possible because it was assumed that they could be built elevated anywhere they could not be on the surface, whereas the cost comparison was with conventional RRT systems that normally had a portion underground. The reasons for placing RRT underground were not recognized; had they been, there would have been less optimism about locating other technologies in an elevated configuration.

Probably the only technology-related cost factor that begins to approach the importance of vertical configuration in determining cost is the cost allocation opportunity afforded by BRT/HOV facility sharing. Such facility- and cost-sharing opportunities would rarely apply in underground configurations.

RELATIONSHIP OF PLANNING ELEMENTS

Figure 11-5 depicts some basic relationships in the planning process that shape the decision on the vertical configuration and technology issues for rapid transit systems or individual lines. The process begins with a recognition of the planning and design goals: to maximize benefits, which are always closely related to maximizing ridership (for example, air pollution reduction is directly related to the number of people attracted from their cars); to minimize costs; to minimize any adverse social or environmental impacts; and to design a system to attract the public support needed to generate the financing required. In circumstances where financing is already arranged, the goal of public support has the narrower scope of ensuring popular acceptance of actions taken.

The designer–planner must maximize goal achievement using available technology with its constraints of space requirements, costs, and performance. He or she also must allow for the topography and physical shape and dimensions of the city, which, in turn, influence the horizontal and vertical configuration of the system. The combination of the elements produces a system design with attributes such as speed, service frequency, capacity, and costs, which satisfy, in part, the goals.

The designer–planner can and should develop alternative systems that make different trade-offs among configuration, service, costs, and technology and produce different system attributes that satisfy, in different ways, the original goals. This process of trying and testing alternatives produces results that are extremely useful in improving many aspects of system design, but are never entirely conclusive or compelling with respect to some of the most major issues, since no system will fully achieve all the goals. In the end, the choices between the realistic alternatives available must be resolved through political compromises achieved by the many varied interests involved. The main point from Fig. 11-5 is that the attributes of the selected system are influenced by goals and configuration, as well as technology constraints.

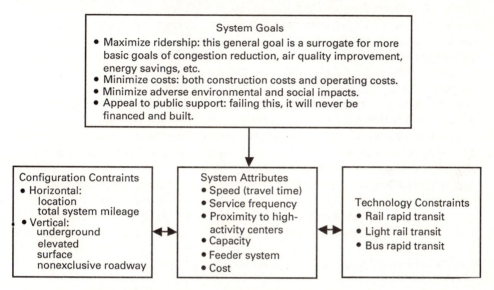

Figure 11-5 *Relationship between elements influencing system planning.*

One of the fundamental trade-offs that must be made in system planning is among:

- The system's total mileage.
- The ease of access the system affords to the high-activity centers of the city.
- The scheduled speed of the system.
- The selection of vertical configuration.

One of the first difficulties faced by the transit planner in developing alternative system plans for evaluation is that no system can provide much of a boost to service unless it can provide service within a convenient walking distance of the traveler's ultimate destination or origin. Secondary feeder services can often be used at one end of the trip (thus inducing one mode transfer), but rarely can the traveler be induced to make two mode transfers. Therefore, there is a high priority on locating stations very close to the centers of the highest-density areas of the city, the very locations where land costs are at a premium, where existing rights-of-way are least likely to exist, where elevated segments are most likely to meet strong resistance, where the demolition associated with any grade separated construction on the surface is difficult, disruptive, and expensive, and where the traffic and pedestrian conflicts of operation at grade are the toughest to resolve. Because of the cost multiples involved in going underground, it is safe to say that the choice of underground would almost never be made were it not for these factors. In many instances, if underground is not practical, then the proposed transit improvements will not be made.

Planners can reach more activities within a given rapid transit mileage allotment through the use of more underground. In so doing they increase potential ridership and the benefits to be derived from the system. Unfortunately, by so doing they also increase the costs. Whether the underground is worth the extra costs depends on how much is required, how many passengers will be obtained, and how noxious the alternatives are. Clearly, these are complicated issues that can only be determined by a detailed study of the specific site in question, and even then they can reasonably be debated.

Generally, all the foregoing tends to apply for any of the technologies; nevertheless, it is true that some technologies lend themselves to some situations better than others. For example, if one is certain that a given line must be underground for its entire 12-mi (19-km) length, must have an average of one station a mile, and must carry 25,000 passengers/h in one direction, then the choice is clearly RRT. The large underground stations required for the high volume of required buses eliminate BRT from contention, and the high-capacity need eliminates LRT and AGT. Other scenarios could be developed that would favor BRT or LRT or AGT in a compelling fashion. Unfortunately, the more typical situation is not so clear; indeed, no existing rapid transit line in North America outside of New York City, Toronto, Montreal, and Mexico City comes anywhere close to the 25,000 passenger hourly volume used in the example above.

Table 11-4 shows in tabular form some of the more frequently encountered relationships involved in translating system goals into design objectives and, in turn, into design methods and technology attributes. For example, to meet the goal of minimizing construction cost, the designer might choose the objective of maximizing the use of shared facilities, seeking to run on HOV lanes and transitways open to carpools and vanpools. In this case, BRT would be the favored technology, being capable of operation in all types of HOV configurations. LRT would be second choice, being appropriate for limited running in arterial HOV lanes only, and the last choice would be RRT and AGT with their requirement for exclusive guideways.

RAIL SYSTEMS VERSUS BUS SYSTEMS

While the choice between RRT, LRT, and AGT is often difficult, the really intense controversies seem to be generated in making the choice between these rail/fixed-guideway systems and bus systems. Understanding these controversies requires a recognition that very large economic interests are differentially affected by the final choice, with highway–automobile interest groups tending to favor bus systems, while interest groups aligned with the providers of rail equipment and related industry tend to support rail systems.

Perhaps the greatest factor working against the use of buses is related to the public's attitude. Existing local bus transit, particularly in the United States, has a

TABLE 11-4
Some Relationships Between Design Goals and Technology Attributes

Goal/Design Objective	Design Method	Technology Suitability Rank			
		RRT	AGT	LRT	BRT
Maximize ridership/					
Locate stations within easy walk of many major centers	Locate system underground to allow unobtrusive/nondisruptive high-capacity entry into high-density areas	1	2	2	3
	Locate system in surface streets/malls of major centers, with first-floor-level stops	2	1	1	1
	Use high line mileage and many stations systemwide	1	1	1	1
Provide high-frequency service	Use short trains or single-vehicle trains with short headways	3	1	2	1
Maximize scheduled speed	Provide grade separation and high-speed alignment for entire system	1	2	3	4
	Provide skip-stop and express service	2	2	2	1
Reorganize transit service systemwide	Remove radial bus service; provide focus to reorient bus routes into community/cross-town operation	1	2	3	4
Maximize development impact/					
Stress accessibility and permanence	Use fixed-guideway with substantial stations central to areas of potential development/redevelopment	1	2	3	4
Minimize construction cost/					
Use of existing ROW to avoid underground/elevated construction	Use freeway medians, railroad/power-line rights-of-way though these may be distant from activity centers	1	1	1	1
	In lower-density areas, let system run on streets/highways mixed with other traffic	3	3	2	1
Maximize use of shared facilities	Run on HOV lanes and other facilities open to carpools/vanpools	2	2	2	1
Reduce total construction required	Reduce system mileage, number of stations	1	1	1	1
	Use shorter, simpler stations, low platforms, etc.	2	2	1	1
	Use smaller horizontal and vertical clearances, lighter structures	2	1	2	2
Reduce system complexity	Eliminate power distribution and control systems	3	3	2	1
Minimize operating cost/					
Reduce operating personnel	Use long trains to reduce personnel/passenger ratio	1	2	2	3
	Use more complex systems affording greater automation	2	1	3	4
	Use short trains in off-peak	3	1	2	1
Reduce maintenance personnel	Use simpler systems with less electronics and hardware	3	4	2	1
Maximize public support/					
Provide service to widest possible area	Use low cost/mile systems, maximum use of at-grade, nonexclusive right-of-way	4	3	2	1
Fit predispositions of public	Use rail/fixed-guideway systems; avoid bus systems	1	1	1	2

tarnished image with most urbanites, and proposals for bus rapid transit tend to be marked with the stigma. New rail/fixed-guideway transit systems, on the other hand, tend to have a very favorable image in the public mind. Thus, the agency proposing a bus system, particularly one requiring a large capital investment and voter approval, must make an uncommonly convincing case. Transit authorities sense this public sentiment and, partly as a result, have rarely gone to a bond referendum to build bus rapid transit with significant busway mileage. The Ottawa and Pittsburgh busways and the Los Angeles, Northern Virginia, and initial Houston bus/HOV facilities were all built with monies available without recourse to bond referenda. The successful 1988 Houston bond referendum, however, did cover additional bus/HOV facilities (transit-ways) in conjunction with a fixed-guideway component and highway improvements.

Institutional arrangements also tend to conspire against buses. The operator of the existing bus system may be a different agency than the one charged with rapid transit development, and the agency that would build busway/HOV facilities may be different yet. When control of the construction or the service that would be operated lies with others, the self-interest of transit development agencies and even their consultants has been known to weaken their interest in proposals to build busways, bus stations, and other such facilities.

Aside from attitudinal and institutional factors, inherent physical features distinguish the performance and cost characteristics of bus and rail/fixed-guideway systems. Achieving comparison of these features in such a way as to receive broad agreement is elusive; arguments about the relative efficiency of the two modes continue unabated. Both bus and rail systems have advocates that present their arguments in superficial terms that tend to obscure the real differences, which are already sufficiently complex. It is useful to examine some of the various claims as a way of highlighting the real differences between systems.

Bus advocates claim that:

1. *Buses are more flexible and can offer no-transfer service in response to diffuse trip patterns.* There is little doubt that buses have advantages over rail in the provision of direct service: buses are operated as single units, can be dispatched along individual routes set up for different travel markets, and can leave bus rapid transit facilities to access off-line sites. Nevertheless, direct bus service has its limits. No-transfer rides between many points can be provided only by sacrificing service frequency. An analysis for the Los Angeles area showed that providing for direct service between all potential bus collection areas would result in an average of two bus trips/day/route, clearly unacceptable.

2. *Buses can provide higher speeds than rail when used on a busway or HOV lane, since they can provide nonstop service.* This tends to be true in those cases where patronage is sufficient to support nonstop service. Buses can travel at nonstop speeds of 40 to 50 mi/h (64 to 80 km/h) on an urban busway. If stops are introduced to serve more origins and destinations, scheduled speeds may be somewhat lower than for rail transit with equivalent stops, owing to acceleration limitations. RRT systems run at scheduled speeds (including stops)

of 25 to 45 mi/h, depending on station spacing. LRT, as presently operated in the United States and Canada, operates at scheduled speeds of 10 to 21 mi/h.

3. *Buses are cheaper than rail, which is altogether too expensive.* The real cost issue between systems is not whether the use of buses on existing streets and highways is cheaper—it probably is—but whether comparable service free of traffic delays and congestion can be provided at lower cost. Buses using specially constructed busways may or may not be cheaper, depending primarily on passenger volume and whether the transit route must operate partially or wholly in subway. Costs of busway construction, including right-of-way (land) and vehicles, and excluding the one example involving a trolleybus subway, have ranged from $8 to $30 million/mi ($5 to $19 million/km), as illustrated in Fig. 11-4. The cost range for those RRT and LRT systems that are almost entirely on the surface starts at the same point but extends about 50% higher.

4. *If buses are given priority treatment, then buses can provide high-level service at much lower cost than rail.* Taking existing freeway lanes away from general traffic has proved impractical or politically infeasible in most instances. When new lanes can be built for HOVs including buses, a high level of service does become quite economical, the cost of the new lanes being spread across both carpools/vanpools and buses. Another cost-saving potential for buses in rapid transit service is that they have the flexibility to use any combination of running on busways, lanes reserved for buses or for all HOVs, freeways in mixed traffic, and/or streets in mixed traffic, so the more expensive options need only be used for those portions of a route where they are critical to bypass congestion and bring service close to high-activity centers.

Rail advocates claim that:

1. *Rail systems are more attractive to prospective users and thus can achieve a higher shift from auto to transit use.* Rail rapid transit, and *new* rail rapid transit in particular, is obviously more attractive than ordinary slow local bus service. However, most travel choice investigations have identified no special attractiveness for rail when bus service is equivalent in time, cost, and convenience. A few have shown a modest, unexplained preference for rail. This preference, if it exists, may be less a function of rail transit "sex appeal" than features often (but not uniquely) associated with rail transit, such as the service reliability afforded by separate rights-of-way, readily recognizable and weather-protected stops, off-vehicle fare collection, simple and easy-to-remember routings, and good service frequency.

2. *Rail systems have more capacity.* This is true for RRT, but in a vast majority of cases, capacity is irrelevant. Many existing and proposed rail systems have peak loads that are well within the capacity range of bus systems. Present maximum load-point volumes on North American RRT lines exclusive of New York City, Toronto, Montreal, and Mexico City are in the range of 3000 to 15,000 passengers/h/track, and LRT maximum load-point volumes are in the range

of 1000 to 10,000 passengers/h/track. RRT systems can be designed to carry 30,000 passengers/h/track and more; bus systems can carry a similar number per lane *as long as the buses do not stop on the roadway*. If passenger pickup along the way is required, then the bus lane is limited to 8000 or so passengers/h, unless multilane, multiberth stations are provided. Such bus stations require more space than rail stations, and the space may not be available.

3. *Rail systems are more energy efficient and do not cause as much air pollution.* Superior energy efficiency may or may not be an attribute of a rail system, depending largely on the average occupancy of the vehicles. Research has shown, for example, that buses in large cities can be at least as energy efficient as RRT.[9] Rail systems are less polluting in those instances where electrical power generation does not involve emissions, as in the case of hydroelectric or solar generation. Even if the power generation is polluting, the emissions problem at the site of the power plant may be less acute than in the city.

4. *Rail systems have lower operating costs than bus systems.* This may be true on systems not saddled with labor rules requiring superfluous personnel, at least as long as passenger volume is large enough to take advantage of the multiple-car per operator capacity of most rail systems. However, the need for skilled electronic maintenance personnel, station attendants, and in some cases special police, takes away from the staff cost savings once projected for automated systems. Rail systems, unlike many busways, are almost always restricted to one agency, limiting opportunity to foster service competition.

Representations about rail system attractiveness and lack of pollutant emissions are examples of arguments that obscure more fundamental underlying issues. Overall door-to-door travel time and convenience are of such importance to the prospective transit user that any special technology attractiveness that may exist is assuredly secondary to route and station location, service frequency and connectivity, and avoidance of congestion. Facility location and service requirements may in turn determine which affordable technology will work best. Likewise, the pollution issue may be overshadowed to the extent that both bus or rail with reasonable patronage cause relatively little pollution per passenger-mile compared to autos (assuming that bus emissions are, as presently mandated, brought more in line with auto emissions). The alternative providing superior service generally produces the most riders and the greatest diversion from autos, in turn resulting in the least pollution.

Flexibility is a broader concern than suggested by the directness of service question alone. The ability to adjust routings in response to changed travel patterns is another issue. There is little doubt that bus routes can be more easily changed than rail routes. Yet, if busways are built, those bus-route segments that use them are as fixed as a railway. Moreover, routing flexibility can be a disadvantage if one purpose of building a transit system is to encourage denser land-development patterns. Not to be overlooked is the ability of a radial rail system (or other technology similarly operated) to foster restructuring of the remaining bus service into a combined rail access (feeder) and local access (community- and activity-center-based) transit service.

Flexibility of alignment configuration is offered by LRT, in that it can combine segments of on-street operation with segments of rapid-transit-type operation. Flexibility of implementation phasing is cited as a major reason for choice of BRT in Ottawa.[10] The non-CBD busways opened first, starting in 1983; in the CBD buses will use downtown streets until a planned bus subway is needed. The already mentioned flexibility of buses to use any combination from running on streets to busways to HOV lanes becomes increasingly advantageous as planners seek forms of rapid transit suitable for adaptation to an auto-dominant land-use environment. A number of transit agencies have formed a partnership with ridesharing by including carpools and vanpools in their toolkit of solutions to suburban congestion and mobility needs, and similarly the opening of some busways and most priority lanes to pool vehicles provides a form of rapid transit service whereby BRT and HOVs together can penetrate markets too dispersed for any of the "pure" forms of rapid transit.

It is around the question of costs that the greatest controversy is centered. Both busways and rail systems require land, grading, drainage, structures, and roadway preparation. The most significant capital cost differences result from the need of rail transit for power distribution and control systems, which for the most part are not required for nonelectric bus systems. These elements account for about 40% of rail costs for at-grade construction, 20% for aerial, and less for subway, at which point such costs tend to be more than counterbalanced by complex BRT station requirements. Rail construction costs will therefore tend to be somewhat higher than for busways, as long as alignment in subway is only a small part of the system, and passenger volumes are low enough that large bus stations are not required.

From the foregoing discussion it should be evident that the passenger load, the length of system located in tunnel, and the space (right-of-way) available will all influence cost. Other factors include the size of the bus or train units to be operated, the ratio of peak to off-peak traffic loads, and the frequency of service provided in excess of load requirements during off-peak periods. Figure 11-6 indicates that where peak-h volumes exceed 12,000 passengers/h and more than 20% of the line must be in subway, rail systems can be cheaper per passenger carried. At volumes of 4000 passengers/h, and at 12,000 passengers/h when no subway is required, buses are likely to show a cost advantage. Bus cost advantages for a total system may be greater if circumstances allow extensive use of HOV facilities and lanes.

HOW TO EVALUATE

Decision makers faced with questions of "whether to build" and "which technology" have the opportunity to make use of evaluation procedures that have been continuously evolving over the last several decades. The evolution has progressed through cost-benefit analysis into the present use and continued development of both effectiveness analysis and alternatives analysis with its cost-effectiveness measures.

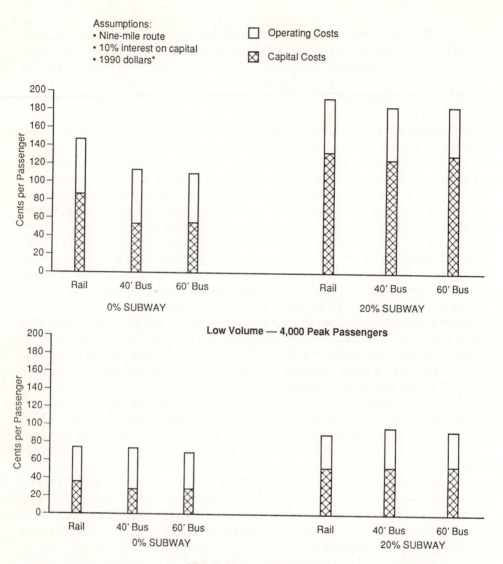

Figure 11-6 *Total rail and busway costs (cents/passenger). [Source: Compiled by William G. Allen, Jr., for the Transportation Research Board; adapted from Thomas B. Deen and Donald H. James, "Relative Costs of Bus and Rail Transit Systems," in* Transportation Systems Planning, *Highway Research Record 293 (Washington, D.C.: Highway Research Board, 1969), p. 52.]*

* In converting to 1990 dollars, no attempt has been made to introduce the effects on capital cost of environmental, handicapped accessibility, or other requirements or trends since the original study. The costs per passenger are thus lower than current experience, but are valid in relative terms for purposes of rail versus bus comparison.

Alternatives analysis and associated systems and project development planning steps are at present required for almost all rapid transit projects receiving federal capital funding in the United States.

COST-BENEFIT ANALYSIS

Economic analysis has long been an important element of determining the feasibility of large capital-intensive projects. Historically, such examinations have attempted to measure the magnitude of total benefits expected to accrue over the entire life-cycle of the project compared to its total costs, a process often called cost-benefit analysis. Both benefits and costs expected in the more distant future are heavily discounted compared to short-term effects. In the application of cost-benefit analysis to a rapid transit project, the costs include the one-time costs of land acquisition and system construction as well as the continuing costs of system operation. Benefits include time savings of the passengers of the preexisting transit service, operating cost and/or time savings of passengers who otherwise would have used private cars or other modes of travel, and any time savings estimated for those choosing to remain in their cars but projected to experience less congestion.

Cost-benefit analysis is an effective way to compute and compare those costs and benefits that can reasonably be translated into monetary terms. Urban goals of the late twentieth century, however, have been increasingly oriented toward values that are difficult if not impossible to measure monetarily. For example, determining the dollar value of increasing the mobility of the poor or of encouraging particular land-use patterns, or of reducing air pollution is a daunting task. Such calculations must necessarily depend on some heroic and less than totally agreed on assumptions.

The benefits that the rapid transit cost-benefit analyses of the 1960s and 1970s attempted to encompass can be divided into three categories:

1. *Transportation (direct) benefits.* Includes travel-time and operating cost savings for various classes of users of the transport system (all modes).
2. *Community (indirect) benefits.* Includes those other benefits deemed by the analysts to be quantifiable but stemming from secondary effects of the transportation improvement.
3. *Miscellaneous benefits.* Includes items not conveniently classed into the other two categories.

A critical evaluation of cost-benefit analysis as applied to rapid transit, prepared in 1975, concluded that, while the direct benefits included in the various studies were relatively uniform in concept and in components included, indirect benefits varied widely, with seemingly little agreement as to what items to include and what methodologies to employ, and the miscellaneous benefits included seemed to represent further departures from rigorous cost-benefit methodologies.[11] In the face of such analytical disarray, transportation planning professionals called for critical study elements to be prescribed and standardized.

Examples of problem areas identified in various cost-benefit analyses included double counting within direct benefits by including both accident and insurance cost reductions probable multiple counting within indirect benefits involving different ways of measuring the same benefit, and selection of inappropriate bases for comparison in computing benefits such as "savings from transport investments no longer needed." "Savings in fare expenditures" were often treated as benefits but are simply revenue reductions, and should have been excluded, since system revenue is neither a benefit nor a cost but a component of system financing. "Savings in bus system operation costs" should have been regarded as a reduction in system cost (to be found in the denominator of the benefit-cost ratio) instead of as a benefit (in the numerator).

As part of the critical evaluation, benefits from several studies were converted to constant (1973) dollars and normalized by dividing the benefits by the number of transit system riders that had been estimated for the design year. Even the direct benefits per rider were found to vary widely in value. Operating cost savings by persons estimated to divert to the improved transit system varied from over $6.90 for Honolulu and Los Angeles to only $0.74 in Atlanta. Time savings for trips that continue to use autos after transit improvement, attributed to estimated reduction in highway congestion, varied from Honolulu's $16.14 down to Baltimore's $0.40. Table 11-5 summarizes the values and direct benefit percentages estimated for different cities.

The absolute value of total benefits per design-year rider varies from Baltimore's $41.34 down to Buffalo's $4.86. It is difficult to explain why there should be a tenfold difference. The proportion of all benefits that were related to direct transportation benefits varies even more, from more than 100% in Buffalo and Honolulu to only 36% in Baltimore. The table also suggests some of the reasons for the wide variations encountered. The *discount rate*, the presumed time value of money used to discount the value of future benefits and costs back to present worth, is a critical assumption used in cost-benefit analysis and can make a big difference in the results when comparing systems with different degrees of capital intensiveness. This value varied from 4% in Buffalo to 6% in Atlanta. The value of travel-time savings varied from $0.60 to $3.60 per hour.

Clearly, the relative value of rapid transit systems could not even be hinted at when the input assumptions were so variant. Economic analysis of benefits and costs fell into disfavor in the United States, partly because of the lack of standards (an open invitation to add benefits from as many sources as imagination could produce), partly because of the necessary dependence on a number of difficult and therefore frequently questioned assumptions, and partly because of attempts by authorities to bend the process into a tool for justifying actions they fervently desired to take for various reasons. Although the cost-benefit analyses of the 1960s and 1970s are now history, the lessons learned are invaluable, and many of the more desirable attributes of cost-benefit analysis are systematized and included in evaluation methodologies described in the following sections.

TABLE 11-5
Selected Differences in Benefit/Cost Assumptions and Corresponding Total Benefits Estimates

Metro Area	Discount Rate (%)	Value of Time ($/hour)	Direct Benefits as % of Total	Total Benefits per Design-Year Rider (1973 dollars)
Buffalo	4	1.72	119	4.86
Atlanta	6	3.00	98	24.85
Baltimore	4	0.60	36	41.84
Honolulu	5	3.19	113	33.63
Los Angeles	6	3.60	62	31.88
Washington	4	2.95	98	13.03
Cleveland	6	2.80	66	13.82

Source: Adapted from Thomas B. Deen, Walter M. Kulash, and Stephen E. Baker, "Critical Decisions in the Rapid Transit Planning Process," in *Transit Planning*, Transportation Research Record 559 (Washington, D.C.: Transportation Research Board, 1976), pp. 33–43.

EFFECTIVENESS ANALYSIS

The inability of cost-benefit analysis to address nonmonetary factors led to the utilization of what is called effectiveness analysis or goal attainment evaluation. Introduction of effectiveness analysis did not necessarily require new analytical techniques, although it tended to encourage them; it was and is primarily a means of organizing and dealing with analytical results. It is a systematic procedure for examining the relative merits of different transportation proposals in a manner that allows taking into account important concerns not encompassed by cost-benefit analysis. When the proposals examined include transportation options without rapid transit and options with alternative rapid transit modes, effectiveness analysis directly addresses both the "whether to build" and "which technology" questions.

Effectiveness analysis allows all types of evaluation measures: (1) those that can be meaningfully described in monetary terms, (2) those that are not meaningful in monetary terms but can be quantified in other units, and (3) those that, while important, can only be described qualitatively. Cost-benefit types of measures are not excluded from effectiveness analysis. They can be included as part of the broader evaluation provided by the methodology.

The steps necessary to carry out an effectiveness analysis are:

1. Explicit definition of *goals* (generalized end states or directions of desired movement), *objectives* (specific end states or targets to be hit), *criteria* (ways to measure objective attainment), *measures* (attributes to be tested to determine the degree of objective attainment), and, if applicable, *standards* (acceptable levels of objective attainment).

2. Assembly of forecasts, estimates, and other analysis results into an evaluation matrix, relating the analysis findings to the evaluation criteria used and to the different alternatives examined.

Table 11-6 illustrates one example each of a number of possible goals, objectives, and criteria, along with associated measures. Figure 11-7 illustrates an evaluation matrix. Criteria that are measured in monetary units, quantitative nonmonetary units, and qualitative terms are separately identified.

TABLE 11-6
Example Goal, Objective, Criterion, and Measures

Goal:	Quality transit service competitive with the auto
Objective:	To provide a high level of transit service from trip origin to trip destination
Criterion:	Door-to-door transit travel time, convenience and reliability for corridor travel
Measures:	Peak-period and off-peak in-vehicle transit travel time between residences and CBD
	Number of transfers required between residences and CBD
	Peak-period and off-peak service frequency for collector and trunk-line transit service
	Amount of corridor dwelling units within walking distance of stations or stops
	Amount of corridor employment within walking distance of stations or stops
	Segregation of transit vehicles from traffic delays

The extensive inclusion of highway performance measures within the evaluation matrix of Fig. 11-7 would be inappropriate for a purely rapid-transit evaluation. The evaluation matrix is from the 1989-1990 *Commuter Assistance Study* of the Maryland Department of Transportation, a new breed of multimodal study that simultaneously evaluates not only alternative rapid transit modes, but also all kinds of highway and HOV improvements along with low-cost transit options.[12] Such multimodal evaluations may become more common in the future in light of efforts within the U.S. Department of Transportation (DOT) to achieve better consistency and coordination between the capital project evaluation processes of the Urban Mass Transportation Administration (UMTA) and the Federal Highway Administration.

When effectiveness analysis began to supplant cost-benefit analysis, the pendulum swung away from economic assessments, exposing a potentially major weakness. While the many evaluation measures of effectiveness analysis may be of great assistance in the local determination of whether to build rapid transit or not and in the choice of rapid transit mode, they may obscure the economic deficiencies of those proposals that should rank as "crazies" and do not necessarily provide a simple indicator for use by senior governments faced with prioritization needs. Thus, while UMTA encourages the use of effectiveness analysis techniques in the systems analysis process and the choice of a locally preferred alternative, it mandates as part of its alternatives analysis process the development of a specific economic measure that can be compared from project to project. One way to strengthen effectiveness analysis is to make sure that one or more such economic measures are included in the evaluation matrix.

Measures of the Problem/Solution	Existing Conditions	Future Null Alternative	Alternative 1	Alternatives 2, 3 ...
Screen-line highway volume/capacity ratio	####	####	####	####
Percentage of highway lane-miles operating at LOSs A–F	####	####	####	####
Person-miles traveled via LOV, HOV, transit	####	####	####	####
Transit boardings	####	####	#####	####
Percentage of commuter miles carried via LOV operating at or above LOS D; via HOV; via transit	####	####	####	####
Travel times for selected locations	####	####	####	####
Reduction in highway VMT	NA	NA	####	####
Capital cost	NA	NA	$$$$	$$$$
Annual operating cost	NA	NA	$$$$	$$$$
Annualized cost per transit trip	NA	NA	$$$$	$$$$
Ability for transit to meet specified cost/revenue ratio	NA	NA	≈≈≈≈	≈≈≈≈
Enhancement of access to existing or planned economic development	NA	NA	≈≈≈≈	≈≈≈≈
Compatibility with local transportation plans	NA	NA	≈≈≈≈	≈≈≈≈
Fatal flaw evaluation	NA	NA	≈≈≈≈	≈≈≈≈
Right-of-way opportunities	NA	NA	≈≈≈≈	≈≈≈≈
Other issues including safety	NA	NA	≈≈≈≈	≈≈≈≈

Legend:
LOV   Low-occupancy vehicle.   HOV   High-occupancy vehicle.
LOS   Level of service.   VMT   Vehicle miles of travel.
Measure described quantitatively in nonmonetary terms (e.g., travel time).
$$$$ Measure described quantitatively in monetary terms (e.g., millions of dollars).
≈≈≈≈   Measure described in qualitative terms (e.g., good/fair/poor).
NA   Not applicable to evaluating base case conditions.

Figure 11-7 *Multimodal Alternatives Evaluation Matrix. [Source: Adapted from COMSIS Corporation, Parsons Brinckerhoff Quade & Douglas, and Richard H. Pratt, Consultant, Inc.,* Maryland Statewide Commuter Assistance Study Corridor Profile Reports, *prepared for Maryland DOT (Baltimore-Washington International Airport, Md.: Maryland Department of Transportation, 1990).]*

Whether or not a formal effectiveness analysis is conducted as part of the evaluation process, formulation of transportation goals and objectives is a step that should not be omitted for any city considering investment in rapid transit. These goals and objectives need to be comprehensive and specific, avoiding vague "motherhood and apple pie" protestations. Goals and objectives are the mechanism whereby regional and local decision makers can guide planners and engineers toward achieving the desired ends and can then check (using the evaluation results) that the desired ends are in fact best served by the solutions offered.

ALTERNATIVES ANALYSIS

In the mid-1970s, with cost-benefit analysis of rapid transit proposals in growing disrepute, it was suggested that the U.S. DOT should require studies of rapid transit feasibility to meet prescribed standards prior to application for federal funds. The U.S. DOT and UMTA themselves strongly felt this need, given their responsibility for equitable and politically defensible distribution of federal funding. UMTA's response has been their "Major Capital Investment Policy," which in turn is embodied in the UMTA "Major Capital Investment Planning" process.[13]

This policy and process is not intended to be a substitute for a region's own comprehensive planning. The cost-effectiveness measures prescribed are the product of a limited goal set oriented toward rating projects for suitability of federal funding in an era of scarce federal resources. Nonetheless, the major capital investment process, including environmental analysis requirements linked with it, has influenced planning well beyond that done in support of applications for U.S. federal funds. The key UMTA major capital investment policy tenets are (abridged):

- Proposed guideway projects shall be consistent with the area's comprehensive long-range transportation plan.
- Where the plan calls for a fixed guideway, it should be proposed for implementation incrementally, one usable segment at a time.
- Projects must be cost effective as determined through an analysis of transportation alternatives, including low-cost improvements to the existing infrastructure and better management and operation of existing transportation facilities.
- There should be full opportunity for the timely involvement of the public, local elected officials, and all levels of government in the alternatives analysis process.
- Project decisions should be based upon realistic cost estimates and financing proposals that take into account operating expenses.
- The local area should consider local supportive actions to enhance cost effectiveness, including land-use planning, zoning, joint development, feeder bus services, adequate parking, and other pricing, regulatory and enforcement measures.

The UMTA major capital investment project development process encompasses

(1) system planning, (2) alternatives analysis, (3) preliminary engineering, (4) final design, and (5) construction. The system planning and alternatives analysis phases are where "whether to build" and "which technology" questions are normally resolved, but decisions may be changed during preliminary engineering as well, as more refined costs and other information become available. The system planning phase is viewed as being integrated with the ongoing urban transportation planning process during which local officials update regional goals and objectives, project future land use and travel, identify current and anticipated transportation problems, examine a wide range of alternative solutions, assess the availability of financial resources for future capital and operating costs, and develop short- and long-range implementation programs reflecting financial resources. UMTA equates system planning with the ongoing 3C urban transportation planning process (see Chap. 3) conducted in each urbanized area by its metropolitan planning organization, but equivalent planning processes can occur at the state level. For example, the Maryland DOT intends to transition its previously mentioned *Commuter Assistance Study* into such an ongoing process covering all transportation modes statewide.

The alternatives analysis phase may be initiated if local officials find that one or more corridors in the region are candidates for fixed-guideway transit investments. They select a priority corridor and identify a small set of potentially cost-effective alternatives for detailed study. Upon receiving approval to initiate an alternatives analysis, the designated local lead agency studies the priority corridor in detail, looking at alternative solutions to the transportation problems identified in system planning. For each alternative, estimates are prepared of measures of transit service quality, patronage, farebox revenues, operating and maintenance costs, and operating deficits; station access and parking impacts, highway congestion effects, and any other transportation system impacts; environmental impacts; capital costs; and financial requirements. The analysis is brought together in a comparative assessment of the benefits and costs of each alternative, essentially an effectiveness analysis.

The range of alternatives analyzed will typically include one or more rail rapid transit options (RRT, LRT, or other fixed guideway) and a BRT alternative, often with provisions for joint use with other HOVs, and must include both a null (no-action) alternative to meet National Environmental Policy Act regulations and a nonguideway bus/transportation systems management (TSM) alternative. This TSM alternative includes such low-cost actions as traffic engineering and transit operational changes, along with significant (but not major) capital improvements as appropriate, all accomplished within realistic limits imposed by such constraints as street capacity and funding for operating deficits. The TSM alternative is intended in part to place cities competing for U.S. federal funds on a level playing field, recognizing that existing conditions will vary from city to city in the amount of TSM that has already been accomplished. It is also designed to demonstrate the extent to which transportation problems can be resolved without recourse to a major investment in new facilities, thereby providing technical findings relevant to the "whether to build" decision. Analysis of the other alternatives provides information for the "which technology" decision.

The alternatives analysis phase includes the development of a draft environmental impact statement, selection of what UMTA calls the locally preferred alternative, and preparation of a realistic funding plan. Lest the earlier discussion of financial, institutional, and attitudinal factors makes it seem that this comprehensive and involved process may be no more than an expensive and contrived justification of decisions already made, it should be pointed out that—at the very least—a properly done alternatives analysis, in addition to guarding against a major mistake, can provide a wealth of highly useful information pertinent to rapid transit alignment choice, station and terminus location decisions, determination of local bus service policy, and design of distributor, feeder, and complementary transit routings.

A crucial element of alternatives analysis, particularly from the federal perspective, and the element most subject to criticism is the computation of cost effectiveness. Along with local financial effort, the cost-effectiveness measure is the primary nonpolitical determinant of priority for federal funding. *Cost effectiveness* means the extent to which a project returns benefits relative to its costs. In an UMTA alternatives analysis, the cost effectiveness of a rapid transit project is measured in terms of its added benefits and added costs when compared to the TSM alternative. The cost-effectiveness measure initially prescribed by UMTA, one of two accepted cost effectiveness measures as of 1990, is called the incremental index. The *incremental index* takes the form

$$\text{Incremental Index} = \frac{\Delta \$CAP + \Delta \$O\&M + \Delta \$TT}{\Delta \, RIDERS} \qquad (11\text{-}1)$$

where Δ = difference relative to the TSM alternative
       $\$CAP$ = total capital costs, annualized over the life of the project
       $\$O\&M$ = annual operating and maintenance costs
       $\$TT$ = annual value of travel time for existing riders
       RIDERS = annual transit ridership, measured in linked trips

The lower the index is, the better the project. Note that the denominator, being the difference in ridership relative to the TSM alternative, causes the measure to place a very high value on the attraction of new transit riders, thereby acting as a surrogate for the intangible benefits associated with reduced automobile use. The other potential benefit included in the equation, reduced travel time for existing riders, is expressed as a negative cost when there are time savings. UMTA specified values of time in 1984 of $4.00/h for work-purpose trips and $2.00/h for other trips. The plan is to update these values as conditions require.

The second cost-effectiveness measure accepted by UMTA uses consumer surplus as the benefit measure, expressed in terms of hours of user benefits. The corresponding cost-effectiveness equation, known as the *user index*, is

$$\text{User Index} = \frac{\Delta \$CAP + \Delta \$O\&M}{\Delta \text{ USER BENEFITS}} \qquad (11\text{-}2)$$

where Δ = difference relative to the TSM or other less expensive alternative
$\$CAP$ = total capital costs, annualized over the life of the project
$\$O\&M$ = annual operating and maintenance costs

and Δ USER BENEFITS are calculated in hours, in a manner based on micro-economic theory, according to Eq. (11-3).

$$\Delta \text{ USER BENEFITS} = [(P_0 - P_1) \times R_0] + [\frac{(P_0 - P_1)}{2} \times (R_1 - R_0)] \quad (11\text{-}3)$$

where P_0 = price of travel paid by TSM or other base-case riders
P_1 = price of travel for the same trips with further investment
R_0 = number of TSM or other base-case riders
R_1 = number of riders with further transit investment

Price of travel in this context includes travel time, fares, and charges at park-and-ride lots, all the time and out-of-pocket costs incurred by the transit user. The price of in-vehicle travel time is as measured, expressed in hours. The price of out-of-vehicle travel time is calculated, borrowing a relationship derived from transit ridership forecasting (mode choice models) by weighting the measured walking, waiting, and transferring time by a factor of 2. The price of fares and other charges is expressed in hours using values of time to convert from dollars. The units of the user index cost-effectiveness measure thus are dollars per hour, in other words, the amount of expenditure it will take to achieve an hour of travel-time savings or equivalent benefit. Required expenditures out of scale with prevailing wage rates should raise a red flag, suggesting the need for extra scrutiny of the transit investment involved.

Table 11-7 summarizes five case studies presented by Samuel Zimmerman to illustrate how the investment rating system developed by UMTA has worked. Of the five proposals, the Seattle Bus Tunnel, Houston Transitways, and Los Angeles Metro Rail are projects that were highly rated as potential federal transit investments, whereas the St. Louis LRT and Miami Downtown People Mover (DPM) extension are projects that did not fare well in the rating process, although they later did receive funding by the U.S. Congress. Common features of the highly rated projects are that they are generally a critical piece of a much larger system, the benefits are substantially higher than the level that could be achieved with more modest investment (as exemplified by the TSM alternative), and they are backed by stable and dependable local financing of transit. Contrasting common features of the poorly rated projects are their inability to produce significant incremental transportation and other benefits over more modest investments and the precarious state of local transit financing.[14]

TABLE 11-7

Five UMTA Major Investment Rating System Case Studies

Project	Total Cost (millions)	UMTA Share (millions)	Incremental Index (per trip)	Local Fiscal Effort		
				Nonfederal Share (%)	Capital Financing Plan	Reliability of Operating Assistance
Seattle Bus Tunnel	$394	$179	$1.44	50	acceptable	acceptable
Houston Transitways	$356	$210	$3.78-4.94	40	acceptable	acceptable
L.A. 8-mi Metro Rail	$1250	$696	$3.30	44	acceptable	acceptable
St. Louis LRT	$384	$289	$9.50	25	no cash match	deficient
Miami People Mover Extensions	$248	$186	$15.20	25	acceptable	deficient

Source: Adapted from Samuel L. Zimmerman, "UMTA and Major Investments: Evaluation Process and Results," in *Transit Administration and Planning Research*, Transportation Research Record 1209 (Washington, D.C.: Transportation Research Board, 1989), pp. 32-36.

The alternatives analysis evaluation processes are not without problems. Systems covered by alternatives analyses and earlier economic analyses are now in operation, and some analysts have concluded that the underlying estimates upon which the original evaluations were based have tended to be decidedly optimistic. A review by Don Pickrell covering ten federally funded projects, summarized in Table 11-8, suggests that actual ridership results have ranged from 28 to 85% lower than the forecasts available when the "whether to build" decision was made. Taken in combination with capital cost experience averaging 50% above estimates and operating costs even further in excess, the annual capital and operating cost per passenger has been calculated as running from almost 3 to almost 10 times the originally estimated value in constant dollars.[15]

Such findings raise the possibility that decision makers might have made different choices if more accurate forecasts were available and underscore the importance of steps to improve the accuracy of forecasts prepared to support future transit investment decisions. The temptation to overestimate ridership and underestimate costs is strong during the planning phase. However, operating cost estimation should now have benefited from actual experience with running automated systems, and ridership estimation procedures have improved, particularly in the representation of transit usage by those beyond walking distance of transit service. Likewise, the capital cost estimation procedures applied in U.S. planning ought now to reflect previously unforeseen obstacles to cheap construction, such as environmental impact mitigation requirements, handicapped accessibility requirements, and requirements resulting from the NIMBY (not in my back yard) syndrome, coupled with the litigious nature of our citizenry, all likely contributors to the increase in constant-dollar costs from the 1950s and 1960s to the 1970s and 1980s clearly seen in Figs. 11-3 and 11-4.

Caution is required in the application of hindsight. For example, attempts to evaluate performance by recalculating the UMTA incremental index with systemwide ridership data obtained before and after the opening of new systems are particularly problematic. The results have been highly variable, and if, for whatever reason, systemwide transit ridership declined as the guideway system was introduced, no cost per new transit trip can be computed at all. Some such situations, as has been inferred, may occur because the new system performed poorly. In other cases, the cause may be exogenous factors such as local economic conditions (for example, economic recession) and systemwide transit service and fare changes (for example, fare increases). Transit systems reported to have lower ridership in some period after guideway implementation have included not only certain U.S. operations with UMTA-funded rail lines, but also at least one LRT and the Ottawa busway[16] from among the heavily used Canadian systems.

Concerns about decisions made on the basis of faulty estimates come closest to the mark in the cases where the discrepancy is greatest, such as Miami. One would have to know a system's performance relative to the broader range of regional goals and objectives to make full judgment. Even though past forecasting has been highly imperfect, it would be unwise to reject economic analysis and related measures outright. Consider case examples from the planning of Washington's Metrorail. During planning, a number of transportation professionals and political leaders were concerned that a new system in the automobile age could never carry as many riders as the established RRT systems in cities such as Chicago, Philadelphia, and Boston. The forecasts, however, given Washington's unique travel patterns, projected that Metrorail would generate more ridership. It now does so. There were other critics who thought the system needed express and local tracks, like New York's. The forecasts projected that Washington Metrorail would carry only a fraction of New York's RRT ridership, and that is also the case. Thus transportation planning analysis allowed major issues to be put in the proper context.

There are technical difficulties with the UMTA cost-effectiveness measures to consider. Experience has shown that the incremental index has these deficiencies:

- The use in the denominator of "new transit trips," a number derived by subtracting one forecast from another, makes the index statistically volatile and highly sensitive to forecasting errors of the type cited by Pickrell.
- Benefits to existing riders are valued in the dollar equivalent of travel time saved and subtracted from costs inconsistent with the treatment of benefits to new riders, which are valued simply in numbers of new transit trips.
- Although many benefits are related to the attraction of new transit trips, the measure does not address such factors as the length of trips served.
- The index cannot be used for all modes in a multimodal study; even the introduction of HOV facility components creates "new trip" definitional problems.

The consumer surplus cost-effectiveness measure was developed to address some of these problems, however, there seem to be two criticisms applicable to this index:

TABLE 11-8
Forecast and Actual Results for Recent Rail Projects

	Rail Rapid Transit Projects					Light Rail Transit Projects			Downtown People Mover Projects	
	Washington	Atlanta	Baltimore	Miami	Buffalo	Pittsburgh	Portland	Sacramento	Miami	Detroit
Weekday Rail Passengers (thousands)										
Forecast	569.6	NF[a]	103.0	239.9	92.0	90.5	42.5	50.0	41.0	67.7
Actual	411.6	184.5	42.6	35.4	29.2	30.6	19.7	14.4[b]	10.8	11.3
Difference	-28%	—	-59%	-85%	-68%	-66%	-54%	-71%	-74%	-83%
Rail Project Capital Cost (millions of 1988 dollars)										
Forecast	4352	1723	804	1008	478	699	172	165	84	144
Actual	7968	2720	1289	1341	722	622	266	188	175	215
Difference	83%	58%	60%	33%	51%	-11%	55%	13%	106%	50%
Annual Rail Operating Expense (millions of 1988 dollars)										
Forecast	66.3	13.2	NF	26.5	10.4	NF	3.8	7.7	2.5	7.4
Actual	199.9	40.3	21.7	37.5	11.6	8.1	5.8	6.9	4.6	10.9
Difference	202%	205%	—	42%	12%	—	45%	-10%	84%	47%
Total Annualized Cost Per Annual Rail Passenger (1988 dollars)										
Forecast	3.04	NF	NF	1.73	2.15	NF	1.68	1.53	0.90	1.14
Actual	8.75	5.93	12.92	16.77	10.57	7.94	5.19	6.53	7.11	10.21
Difference	188%	—	—	872%	392%	—	209%	328%	693%	795%

[a]NF = not forecast

[b]Sacramento daily LRT patronage is reported to be 23,000 in 1990.

Source: Don H. Pickrell, *Urban Rail Transit Projects: Forecast Versus Actual Ridership and Costs* (Washington, D.C.: Urban Mass Transportation Administration, 1989), p. vii.

- The computation of benefit includes fares and other user fees. As in the case of cost-benefit calculations, user-fee savings to the transit riding public have to be counterbalanced by higher subsidy by the public at large and therefore should not be a part of benefit computations.
- The benefit assigned to a new transit rider, being calculated on the basis of travel time and user-fee savings alone, is one-half the benefit assigned to an existing transit rider making the same trip and cannot serve as a surrogate for indirect benefits such as congestion reduction or reduction in pollutant emissions.

It is arguable that the travel-time savings benefit in the user index does serve as an adequate proxy for such indirect or miscellaneous benefits as mobility enhancement and economic development in the user index. The first of the two criticisms can be addressed by simply leaving saving in fares and other user charges out of the benefit equation. The second can be addressed by recognizing that the incremental cost-effectiveness measure should not be used in isolation, but rather in conjunction with other measures in a comprehensive evaluation such as encompassed by effectiveness analysis.

Clearly, economic analysis is not a substitute for good sense; the judgment of those involved in the decision making must be relied upon to weigh the relative importance of cost effectiveness and nonmonetary factors. It would seem, however, that effectiveness analysis, including the use of quantitative economic criteria and full consideration of alternatives, is a good way to approach rapid transit evaluation. If U.S. federal money is sought, then the planning process may require some adjustment to ensure compliance with mandated UMTA alternatives analysis requirements. This is not to say that there is anything intrinsically superior, from the local decision-making point of view, with the UMTA process. Nevertheless, low cost effectiveness should serve as a warning that nonmonetary benefits must be extremely important if such a system is to be justified.

SUMMARY

Decisions of whether to build rapid transit and which technology to adopt take place in a dynamic political and institutional environment that makes evenhanded evaluation difficult. When officials responsible for building a system must get voter support for bond issue financing, the support must come from the entire area if they are to build anything. The amount of investment then is a function of what it costs to cover the area, and, in such an environment, investment analysis becomes foreign.

The cost and effectiveness of providing rapid transit is determined in a major way by urban area configuration and availability of rights-of-way. Arguments about the relative costs of rail rapid transit and bus rapid transit are seen to be transcended by the cost implications of more complex decisions about whether the system—whatever the technology—must be underground, elevated, or on the surface.

Public acceptance tends to lean toward rail systems, even when bus systems might serve better for less cost. Bus rapid transit cost advantages may be enhanced by opportunities for taking advantage of high-occupancy vehicle facilities and lanes. Otherwise, the differences between costs of rail and busway systems are not as great as is often supposed. Many times the decision will have to be made on factors other than cost.

Evaluation procedures are imperfect, but honest attempts to develop sound, objective, and instructive information can contribute greatly to informed choices. A properly done alternatives analysis or comparable economic and effectiveness assessment will first and foremost help guard against a truly bad public investment decision. The required evaluations also provide highly useful direction as to the location and design of the high-cost guideways, stations, and appurtenances of any rapid transit that may be decided upon.

ACKNOWLEDGMENTS

Major assistance in data development for this chapter was provided by Winfield O. Salter of Parsons Brinckerhoff Quade & Douglas and William G. Allen, P.E., with vital help from others too numerous to list. The text has benefited significantly from the helpful comments of several reviewers, with particularly extensive input from Messrs. Salter and Allen; Samuel L. Zimmerman, Urban Mass Transportation Administration; Katherine F. Turnbull, Texas Transportation Institute; and David M. Levinsohn, COMSIS Corporation.

REFERENCES

1   URBAN MASS TRANSPORTATION ADMINISTRATION, "Urban Mass Transportation Administration Major Investment Policy: Notice," *Federal Register*, 49, no. 98 (May 18, 1984), pp. 21284-91.

2   MARK A. EURITT, M. ALLEN HOFFMAN, AND C. MICHAEL WALTON, "Conceptual Model of the Fixed-Guideway Decision Process," in *Urban Public Transportation Research 1990*, Transportation Research Record 1266, Public Transit (Washington, D.C.: Transportation Research Board, 1990), pp. 152-62.

3   TEXAS TRANSPORTATION INSTITUTE, *Rail Research Project*, prepared for the Metropolitan Transit Authority of Harris County. (Houston, Tex.: Texas Transportation Institute, 1989).

4   D. R. MILLER AND OTHERS, "Cost Comparison of Busway and Railway Rapid Transit," in *Evaluation of Bus Transit Strategies*, Highway Research Record 459 (Washington, D.C.: Highway Research Board, 1973), pp. 1-10.

5   J. HAYDEN BOYD, NORMAN J. ASHER, AND ELLIOT S. WETZLER, *Evaluation of Rail Rapid Transit and Express Bus Service in the Urban Commuter Market*, prepared by the Institute for Defense Analyses for U.S. DOT (Washington, D.C.: U.S. Government Printing Office, October 1973). Now available as PB 265 236.

6   THOMAS B. DEEN AND DONALD H. JAMES, "Relative Costs of Bus and Rail Transit Systems," in *Transportation Systems Planning*, Highway Research Record 293 (Washington, D.C.: Highway Research Board, 1969), pp. 33-53.

7   BORIS S. PUSHKAREV, WITH JEFFREY M. ZUPAN AND ROBERT S. CUMELLA, *Urban Rail in America: An Exploration of Criteria for Fixed-Guideway Transit* (Bloomington, Ind.: Indiana University Press, 1982).

8   LOUISE E. SKINNER, *Comparative Costs of Urban Transportation Systems*, Final Report, prepared by the FHWA (Washington, D.C.: U.S. Government Printing Office, June 1978).

9   PHILLIP S. SHAPIRO AND RICHARD H. PRATT, "Energy-Saving Potential of Transit," in *Environmental and Conservation Concerns in Transportation: Energy, Noise and Air Quality*, Transportation Research Record 648 (Washington, D.C.: Transportation Research Board, 1977), pp. 7-14.

10 JOHN A. BONSALL, *Transitways—The Ottawa Experience* (Ottawa, Canada: OC Transpo, 1987).

11 THOMAS B. DEEN, WALTER M. KULASH, AND STEPHEN E. BAKER, "Critical Decisions in the Rapid Transit Planning Process," in *Transit Planning*, Transportation Research Record 559 (Washington, D.C.: Transportation Research Board, 1976), pp. 33-43.

12 COMSIS CORPORATION AND LOUIS E. KEEFER ASSOCIATES, *Maryland Statewide Commuter Assistance Study   Corridor Profile Reports*, prepared for Maryland DOT (Baltimore—Washington International Airport, Md.: COMSIS Corporation, 1990).

13 JAMES M. RYAN AND DONALD J. EMERSON, *Procedures and Technical Methods for Transit Project Planning*, Review Draft (Washington, D.C.: Urban Mass Transportation Administration, 1986).

14 SAMUEL L. ZIMMERMAN, "UMTA and Major Investments: Evaluation Process and Results," in *Transit Administration and Planning Research*, Transportation Research Record 1209 (Washington, D.C.: Transportation Research Board, 1989), pp. 32-36.

15 DON H. PICKRELL, *Urban Rail Transit Projects: Forecast Versus Actual Ridership and Costs* prepared by the Transportation Systems Center for UMTA (Washington, D.C.: U.S. Government Printing Office, October 1989).

16 JOHN F. KAIN, *Increasing the Productivity of the Nation's Urban Transportation Infrastructure: Measures to Increase Transit Use and Carpooling*, Draft Final Report (Washington, D.C.: Urban Mass Transportation Administration, March 1990).

FURTHER READING

"Techniques for Modal Comparison," in *Canadian Transit Handbook* (2nd ed.). Toronto, Canada: Canadian Urban Transit Association and the Roads and Transportation Association of Canada, 1985.

TRANSPORTATION RESEARCH BOARD, *Light Rail Transit: New System Successes at Affordable Prices*, papers presented at the National Conference on Light Rail Transit, May 8-11, 1988, San Jose, Calif., Special Report 221. Washington, D.C.: Transportation Research Board, 1989.

EXERCISES

11-1   Identify three major influences that effect the decision of whether to build rapid transit in U.S. cities. Which of these do you think are most important? Why?

11-2   Name several factors that tend to argue for beginning rapid transit with a single line. What factors argue for an initial commitment for a full regional system?

11-3   What factors are most important in determining the likely patronage, cost, and cost effectiveness of rapid transit in a regional corridor?

11-4   Why has rapid transit not been used for non-CBD-oriented corridors? What factors tend to limit the utility of rapid transit for intrasuburban travel?

11-5   What attributes of commuter railroads preclude their use in all but the largest U.S. cities, and not all of those?

11-6   Which of the newer rapid transit systems have total costs per passenger mile significantly exceeding the cost range for travel by auto and local bus?

11-7   What justification might there be for building such systems? In hindsight, what decisions might you have made on whether or not to build rapid transit and what technology to select? Why?

11-8   Assume you were given the task of evaluating a new rapid transit proposal. Develop an evaluation process including goals, objectives, criteria, and measures.

11-9   What do you consider to be the appropriate division of roles between transportation planners and politicians in rapid transit evaluation and development?

PART IV

PLANNING

Chapter 12

TRANSPORTATION SYSTEM MANAGEMENT

DENNIS C. JUDYCKI AND WAYNE BERMAN

Well-planned, cost-effective transportation system management (TSM) strategies can improve mobility on existing systems for urban transportation users. This is particularly important considering the high cost of constructing new facility capacity and the current and projected increase in travel. By the year 2000, it is estimated that new development, demographics, family composition, and trip-making trends will result in an increase of nearly 50% in travel within urban areas.[1] Because of the burden on the transportation system, maximizing the usefulness and effectiveness of existing facilities and services is essential, even in those situations where new capacity is available.

TSM is the application of construction, operational, and institutional actions to make the most productive and cost-effective use of existing transportation facilities and services. It is through the application of TSM strategies such as operational changes and land-use policies that an urban area is able to maintain mobility and safety in the face of growing demand for travel and limitations on system capacity growth.

The primary purpose of this chapter is to present contemporary operational concepts, applications, and analyses of TSM strategies. The presentation is drawn from references, existing and ongoing research, and current views of national organizations such as the Transportation Research Board, the Institute of Transportation Engineers, and the Association for Commuter Transportation.

BACKGROUND AND PHILOSOPHY

TSM practices in the 1990s are the byproduct of fundamental traffic engineering actions taken to improve the operation of the highway system beginning in the early 1930s. Decisions such as increasing or decreasing the parking supply, incorporating left-turn bays at intersections, or implementing progressively timed traffic signals would later become part of the overall concept of transportation system management.

Urban areas received a great deal of attention between the early 1960s and mid-1970s. In the United States, Congress recognized the importance of metropolitan planning in the 1962 Highway Act, which included the framework for an urban planning process. In the late 1960s, there was a great deal of pressure to establish a federally aided highway public transportation program for larger cities. The 1970 Federal-Aid Highway Act addressed this issue through authorization for a federal-aid urban system and funding allocation for constructing exclusive bus lanes.[2]

Further recognition and support was given to urban operational planning and improvement needs with the creation of the Urban Area Traffic Operations Improvement Program in the 1968 Highway Act. This program became known as TOPICS (Traffic Operations Program to Improve Capacity and Safety). One of the problems identified by this program was that while earlier extension of the freeway system into urban areas had relieved traffic congestion on many arterials, volumes had increased on other arterials and city streets on which local jurisdictions were unable to finance improvements. In establishing the TOPICS program, Congress also recognized that urban system traffic operational improvements were not receiving the full advantage of modern traffic engineering techniques.[3]

The concept of transportation system management received formal recognition in the United States as part of the 1975 Joint FHWA–UMTA Urban Planning Regulations. The intent was that TSM include solid practices and applications for the management of supply and demand strategies. As reflected in the appendix to the regulations, TSM includes "operating, regulatory, and service policies so as to achieve maximum efficiency and productivity for the system as a whole."[4]

In theory, TSM actions are intended to improve the operating efficiency of the existing transportation system (facilities, services, and modes). TSM actions consist of both supply management elements (for example, traffic engineering and signal improvements) and demand management elements (for example, projects to increase the number of high-occupancy vehicles used for commuting). TSM actions must be considered throughout a metropolitan area when addressing system, corridor, individual facility, and site improvements at the planning and project development stages.

The contemporary approach to TSM attempts to bridge the gap between plans, policies, and operational actions used in managing a transportation system. In this regard, two concepts are fundamental to understanding TSM. The first concept is that there will always be a need for *continuously managing and improving* the operation of the transportation system. Because traffic congestion can always be a problem, projects must always be monitored, adjusted, or revised to be effective at providing relief and improvement. The second concept is that TSM plans, policies, and operational actions must *interact and blend* with each other to support the overall long- and short-term mobility goals of a community. The transportation modes, services, policies, and programs must be designed to work together rather then compete. Plans must be developed to provide opportunities for packaging and applying a combination of policies, programs, and operational actions to effectively meet mobility needs. Interaction is critical to the success and effectiveness of this management concept.

TSM ACTIONS

TSM actions are generally implemented to address problems in two types of environments within a metropolitan area: corridors and activity centers. Corridors include the radial and circumferential travel ways within a region. These travel ways generally include freeways, arterials, and public transit lines. Activity centers are the employment, retail, commercial, educational, special event, and/or recreational areas that generate (or attract) trips (for example, a suburban office park, a shopping center, or a central business district).

TSM actions are usually categorized as supply-side or demand-side actions. *Supply-side actions* are intended to increase existing vehicle capacity on the system. *Demand-side actions* are designed to reduce vehicle demand on the system by increasing vehicle occupancy. Both supply-side and demand-side actions, when applied in a coordinated manner, give transportation professionals powerful tools with which to manage the existing system. Following is a discussion of various TSM actions and whether they have supply-side or demand-side application.

TRAFFIC ENGINEERING IMPROVEMENTS

Traffic engineering improvements such as channelization, left- or right-turn lanes, one-way streets, reversible traffic lanes, intersection widening, bus turnout bays, and improved signing and pavement markings are the most widely implemented TSM strategies in corridors, activity centers, and surrounding regions. Based on experience in small, medium and large communities, capacity and safety (usually a reduction in vehicle accidents) improvements have been realized as a result of the action. The cost of these improvements varies considerably, but the benefits usually exceed the costs. Traffic engineering improvements improve capacity; thus they are considered to be supply-side actions.

TRAFFIC CONTROL IMPROVEMENTS

Traffic control systems are designed to reduce travel times, delays, and stops, while also improving average speeds on arterial roadways and freeways. These systems

Figure 12-1 *Contraflow bus lane on CBD street in Los Angeles. (courtesy of Federal Highway Administration)*

include strategies like coordination of traffic signals, continuous optimization of timing plans, use of bus priority signal control systems, and implementation of computer-based traffic control and freeway traffic management. Typical experiences have shown decreases in travel times and vehicle delay on arterials as a result of improved traffic signal systems. Traffic control systems are considered to be supply-side actions due to their impact on capacity.

FREEWAY MANAGEMENT STRATEGIES

A comprehensive freeway management system is used to help relieve the traffic delay that accounts for the majority of urban congestion.[5] On a nationwide basis, benefits from these systems indicate an average increase in vehicle speeds combined with an average reduction in delay. These actions improve the vehicle-carrying capacity of the freeway and, therefore, are considered to be supply-side actions. A comprehensive freeway management system includes the following elements and implements those that are needed.

- Surveillance systems to monitor traffic conditions and collect traffic data.
- Ramp meter signals to smooth traffic flow and improve freeway speeds.
- Control systems to regulate traffic flow to prevent the onset of congestion and restore free flow more quickly when traffic breaks down.

- Incident management programs to reduce the number and duration of incidents.
- Motorist information systems to provide real-time information to drivers on traffic conditions.
- Spot geometric/capacity improvements to reduce or eliminate bottlenecks.
- HOV systems to provide reliable time savings incentives to encourage carpooling, vanpooling, and bus use.

PRIORITY TREATMENT FOR HIGH-OCCUPANCY VEHICLES

High-occupancy vehicles (HOVs) are passenger vehicles that meet or exceed a certain predetermined minimum number of passengers, for example, more than two or three people per automobile. Carpools, vanpools, and buses are HOV vehicles.[6] Priority treatment for HOVs is aimed at encouraging multiuser transportation by offering a cost, travel-time, or walking distance savings over non-HOVs. On freeways and arterials, priority treatment is achieved by designating a new or existing lane(s) for the exclusive use of HOVs, usually during peak commuting periods. This strategy is especially important on congested arterials or freeway corridors with limited potential for building additional lanes. HOV programs also help during periods of major bridge or highway reconstruction. While these actions may increase capacity on a facility, they also increase the use of HOVs. Therefore, priority treatments for HOVs can be considered as both supply-side and demand-side actions.

Ramp meter bypass lanes for HOVs, in coordination with ramp meters, are also being used on corridors as part of a freeway traffic management system. (See Fig. 12-2.) These bypass lanes allow HOVs to go around the traffic signal used for ramp metering and enter the freeway with minimal delay from the signal or the vehicle queue.

In activity centers, the opportunities for preferential treatment include providing parking spaces for carpools that offer a cost and/or walking distance savings and providing more green time for buses at signalized intersections. Both concepts have been effective in congested areas at supporting and enhancing ridesharing and transit programs.

During the planning of HOV preferential treatment programs, the following factors must be taken into account:

1. The ability to enforce the preferential treatment in order to minimize violations.
2. The location/placement of preferential treatment so as to promote HOV use.
3. The impacts on non-HOVs.
4. The expenditures/savings to implement HOV programs.
5. The demand for HOV programs.
6. Other actions that might reinforce or enhance the operation of the preferential treatment (for example, an employer-based ridesharing program).

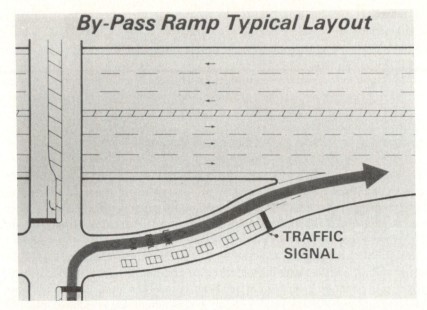

Figure 12-2 *Typical layout of ramp meter bypass lane. (courtesy of Federal Highway Administration)*

When implemented on a congested freeway or arterial, preferential treatments can increase the people-moving capacity of the facility. HOV lanes (on the mainline, at ramps, or at toll plazas) can also significantly improve the efficiency and economy of public transit and ridesharing operations by providing a time (and a cost) savings to commuters using these services. The travel-time savings may vary depending on the length of time on the HOV lane and the level of congestion on the facility. If implemented and operated in an effective manner, preferential treatments can defer or eliminate the need to construct additional roadway lanes.

RIDESHARING PROGRAMS

Ridesharing programs, also referred to as travel demand management (TDM) programs, are institutional and operational actions needed to implement and support the use of HOVs (carpooling, vanpooling, and public transit programs). Ridesharing has been most effective at increasing the use of HOVs when implemented at employment sites where strong management support for the programs exists. Ridesharing programs reduce vehicle trips to the site, thereby relieving congestion at the site entrance or adjacent intersections or both.

To effectively implement ridesharing programs, some or all of the following policies and incentives need to be in place: HOV lanes and ramps, preferential parking for HOVs, employer transportation coordinator(s), flexible work-hour policies, marketing and promotional programs, pricing policies (for example, for parking and transit), revised parking codes and zoning, and matching services. The private sector, as an active participant in the provision of ridesharing services, can benefit through reduced costs for providing employee parking, increased ability to hire and retain employees (especially during periods of company relocation), and a reduction in employee stress levels resulting from an easier commute.

Figure 12-3 *HOV lane. (courtesy of Federal Highway Administration)*

PARKING MANAGEMENT

Parking management programs are considered to be demand-side actions that strongly influence whether a commuter drives alone or uses an HOV. In a corridor environment park-and-ride lots serve to shift the parking supply from the central business district to the outlying area, reducing congestion and vehicle travel demand through a corridor. These lots support the use of public transit or rideshare programs. The lots can be located at shopping centers or churches or on vacant land that is at or near major freeways.

Parking management programs in activity centers include on-street parking restrictions, residential parking permit programs, on-street parking meters (short- or long-term), on-street parking enforcement or adjudication programs, off-street parking pricing programs (to encourage ridesharing or short-term use), off-street parking discounts in shopping areas, carpool/vanpool preferential parking (both on- and off-street), and modifications of parking provisions of local zoning codes to encourage carpool and transit use. The amount of parking provided, the location of parking, and the use of the parking spaces all have a direct impact on mode choice. In this regard, parking management actions influence the extent of ridesharing and transit use at an activity center.

TRANSIT SERVICE IMPROVEMENTS

Transit service improvements in corridors include express bus service, more frequent runs, limited stop bus routes, and transit centers. The *transit centers* provide a point where several routes converge with coordinated "timed" schedules to improve connections with a minimum of waiting time. The centers may also be used to coordinate transfers between different modes of transportation, such as bus, taxi, and rail service.

In congested activity centers, where bus volumes are high, special roadway lanes or streets dedicated for transit vehicles can improve bus travel time and schedule adherence, especially during peak periods. In suburban areas, particularly where active development is taking place, transit service improvements can include special bus lanes, transit centers, bus turnout bays, shelters, reduced transit fare/pass programs, and loop or shuttle service between retail and employment sites. Other types of transit service improvements, especially between activity centers and residential areas, can include minibuses, taxis, or other demand-responsive systems.

Transit service improvements are demand-side actions in that they attempt to relieve congestion by reducing vehicle trips. They can be enhanced further when actions like preferential lanes, signal priority, freeway ramps for buses, and park-and-ride lots are also applied to enhance transit service. With any type of transit improvement, a market research effort is necessary to identify the service needs of specific markets (for example, office parks or educational centers). The development and promotion of new services can be based on the results of the market research effort.

ORGANIZATIONAL AND INSTITUTIONAL CONCEPTS

Transportation planners and engineers, particularly those working in urbanized areas, recognize that public and private agencies must work together to safely and efficiently operate the transportation system. One agency's role can no longer be considered exclusive of another agency's. Consequently, TSM planning involves pooling the individual resources of various agencies to deal with congestion and mobility issues. Communication, cooperation, and coordination between and within the public and private sectors are essential to effective TSM planning.

ROLE OF GOVERNMENT AGENCIES

Government agencies at state, local, and regional levels are responsible for facilitating and funding the planning, development, implementation, and operation of TSM actions. Implementation of TSM strategies is often constrained by institutional problems associated with the coordination of many groups in the public sector. The authority for decision making is dispersed among several agencies and often between several levels within each agency. Often the state transportation agency and/or local transportation agencies (city, county, and/or transit operator) share responsibility for the decision making and implementation for TSM.

In some metropolitan areas, the challenge created by transportation problems has resulted in transportation agencies reexamining their mission and function. For example, many transit agencies have responded to new, nontraditional suburban markets with new types of services. Transit agencies are viewing themselves as "managers of mobility" rather than just operators of traditional bus or rail services. In other metropolitan areas, subregional planning groups have been formed to deal with the transportation problems in their community.[7] In still other metropolitan areas, local governments have enacted trip-reduction ordinances that require developers (and employers) to share in the cost and provision of transportation service (for example, traffic signalization, ridesharing, and transit) to their commercial or residential sites.

The metropolitan planning organization (MPO) is one group that can play a key role in the development of TSM within an urban area. Because the MPO is responsible for developing the regional long-range and TSM elements of the transportation plan, it can be the focal point for coordination among agencies on critical issues pertaining to the application of TSM. Often, the MPO is also responsible for collecting the important regional or corridor travel data that are essential when planning, monitoring, and evaluating TSM projects. The MPO can also play a key role in involving the major private sector groups (for example, the chamber of commerce or private developers) in the planning process or when a regional trip-reduction ordinance is being developed.

TRAFFIC MANAGEMENT TEAMS

One of the most effective means of implementing transportation management strategies is through a traffic management team (TMT). A TMT brings together individuals representing various transportation and support agencies within a specific area. The purpose of the TMT is to improve the overall operation and safety in urban corridors by coordinating the activities of the principal operating agencies in the area (for example, the state highway agency, the local traffic engineering agency, and the transit agency). Subsequently, the TMT is able to provide participating agencies with the following opportunities:

- Direct communications that enhance information exchange among team members and with the public.

- Cooperation and coordination in the daily traffic operation activities of each agency.
- Coordination among agencies on the best means of allocating funds for traffic operations.
- Evaluations of proposed improvements from different points of view (for example, police, fire, emergency rescue, traffic, and transit).
- Meetings with planners and engineers to review and discuss long-range plans.
- Coordination of schedules for construction projects on freeways, arterials, and bridges.
- Review of construction traffic control plans to assure that all agencies understand how they will be affected.
- Cooperation in determining how to handle traffic during periods of both recurring (daily) and nonrecurring congestion (for example, incidents).
- Cooperation in planning and carrying out traffic management during incidents, special events, and unusual weather conditions (ice storms, snow, hurricanes).
- Joint studies on decreasing the number of incidents in high-accident locations.

TMTs are generally formed to address a tangible problem, need, or circumstance for a given urban area. For example, they can address a specific transportation issue for a freeway corridor such as incident management or traffic management during a freeway reconstruction project. TMTs can also address a wider range of transportation management issues, such as rerouting downtown traffic during street construction, implementing a bus lane on a city street, handling traffic for special events, and correcting traffic and safety problems in a community. A successful team was established for traffic management during the 1984 Los Angeles Olympic Games. TMTs can be used in whatever manner is most appropriate to achieve specific transportation management objectives.

Elements that are common to all successful TMTs include the following: (1) commitment, (2) an understanding of the scope and role of the team, (3) clearly defined objectives, (4) strong representation of participating agencies, (5) a leader, (6) regular meetings, and (7) agreement on the expected duration of the team's existence.[8] Successful teams have the common denominator of being able to develop a working partnership among participating agencies and to avoid turf battles that can inhibit progress.

Members of a TMT should be more than just representatives for their respective agencies—they should be action oriented and have the strong support of their superiors. Team members are generally second- or third-level officials (for example, district or city traffic engineers and chief of police of the traffic operations/enforcement unit). The idea is to have members who not only are aware of the daily operations of their respective agencies, but are also able to speak for their agencies and commit them to a course of action agreed upon by the TMT. Regardless of whether the formation of a TMT evolves from existing communications among agencies or is the result of a planned and organized effort, the team's formation should never be forced. The expected duration of a TMT is essentially based on its scope. The agencies that are typically represented on a TMT are listed in Table 12-1.

TABLE 12-1
Agencies Typically Represented on Traffic Management Teams

- State highway agency (district traffic engineer plus other members as needed)
- City traffic or transportation office(s)
- County traffic or transportation office(s)
- State police or highway patrol
- Police, fire, and rescue department(s)
- County sheriff's office(s)
- Regional or metropolitan transit authority
- Federal Highway Administration
- Public relations specialists
- Other groups where and when needed (e.g., utility companies, public works agencies, private trucking firms, private employers and developers, taxi services)

Source: Adapted from Sheldon G. Strickland and Jonathan D. McDade, "Transportation Management and the 3 C's for Dealing with Urban Congestion," in *Compendium of Technical Papers for the 57th Annual Meeting of the Institute of Transportation Engineers, August 16-20, 1987* (Washington, D.C.: Institute of Transportation Engineers, 1987), pp. 228-32.

In summary, when using TMTs as a means of implementing TSM strategies, it is important to keep a positive atmosphere. By starting out slowly and setting realistic goals, TMTs can be very effective. It is not practical to assume that you can use a "template" in forming a TMT because they are not all alike. They should be formed to meet the local needs. A well-organized TMT can help maintain a high level of cooperation, communication, and coordination among transportation agencies in an urban area.

INVOLVEMENT OF THE PRIVATE SECTOR

Traditionally, TSM strategies have focused on public initiatives such as traffic signal improvements, roadway widening, preferential treatment for high-occupancy vehicles, and public transit improvements. Nonetheless, traffic congestion caused by private sector development in urban and suburban areas indicates that the provision of transportation services is not a problem to be addressed solely by public agencies. Employers and land developers are particularly instrumental groups because they help to generate traffic and are in a position to influence employee mode choice either directly through various incentives or indirectly through the design of a building or parking facility. Employers also serve as a key channel through which employees receive transportation information and services.

Public agencies can create opportunities for private–public partnerships by requiring that TSM projects complement the private sector development. One of the critical links between public objectives and private sector actions is the local zoning ordinance.[9] Most local zoning ordinances contain a set of off-street parking requirements that are intended to control the amount of parking supply created during private land development. Reducing these required parking space amounts when the developer implements TSM actions can reduce vehicle trips and the traffic impacts of the new development. These parking requirements are a potentially valuable tool in enabling the public sector to influence private sector decisions in the area of TSM, with benefits potentially accruing to both the public and private sectors.

The application of a parking code to involve the private sector in the provision of transportation services has proved to be legally and institutionally acceptable in many communities. A number of cities and counties are using the parking codes and other newly developed *trip-reduction* ordinances to establish incentives for developers, landowners, and employers to institute ridesharing and transit programs in exchange for reductions in the amount of parking spaces required—a major incentive for the developer being a reduction in the cost of development. Table 12-2 illustrates typical cost savings based upon increased vehicle occupancy levels.

Locations that have instituted such parking code/zoning changes all share a land-use environment where traffic congestion, pollution, and developmental growth all threaten the balance of public services. Other areas undergoing business declines have shown little interest in revising their parking codes or local ordinances to require developers to implement TSM actions as a condition to building.[10]

TRANSPORTATION MANAGEMENT ASSOCIATIONS (TMAs)

In an attempt to channel the private sector's energy to be involved in the provision of transportation services, public–private partnerships have developed through transportation management associations (TMAs). TMAs are made up of several businesses who work together to form a partnership with local governments in order to help solve local transportation problems associated with rapid urban/suburban growth.

TMAs give the business community a voice in local transportation decision making, provide ridesharing and transit services to their employees, and serve as a forum for public–private consultations on issues of transportation planning, financing, and implementation. TMAs have been active participants with government, including the MPO, in discussions on issues as varied as establishing highway funding priorities, restructuring public transit routes, improving public transit service, minimizing the disruption caused by road reconstruction, and instituting traffic management strategies to mitigate congestion.[11] TMAs have been found to be supportive of the goals set forth by the MPO.

The initiative to form a TMA may be sparked by a variety of motives and circumstances. In some cases, TMAs have been formed, voluntarily, by local employers and property owners who are concerned that traffic congestion or the costs of providing more parking may adversely affect the productivity of their operations and stifle future economic prospects. In other cases, the formation of a TMA has arisen

TABLE 12-2
Sample Cost Savings for Increases in Auto Occupancy

Auto Occupancy[a] Increased to:	Parking[b] Reduction		Construction Cost[c] $ savings		Land Cost[d] $ savings		Commute Cost[e] $ Savings (annual)	Constr. & Maint. Cost $ Savings (annual)	
	%	spaces	surface	structured	surface	structured		surface	structured
1.2	4	24	24,000	120,000	79,000	26,000	12,500	2,600	9,600
1.3	12	72	72,000	360,000	238,000	79,000	34,700	7,900	28,800
1.4	18	108	108,000	540,000	356,000	119,000	54,000	11,900	43,200
1.6	28	168	168,000	840,000	554,000	185,000	85,000	18,500	67,200
1.8	36	216	216,000	1,080,000	713,000	238,000	109,000	23,800	86,400
2.0	42	252	252,000	1,260,000	832,000	277,000	128,000	27,700	100,800
2.5	54	324	324,000	1,620,000	1,090,000	356,000	162,000	35,700	129,600

[a]Base auto occupancy = 1.15 (typical of a non-CBD site with no ridesharing program).

[b]Assume 200,000-ft^2 (18,000-m^2) office building with 800 employees with minimum parking requirement of 600 spaces.

[c]Assume cost of parking construction per space = $1000 surface, $5000 structured, $10,000 underground.

[d]Assume land cost = $10/ft^2 ($10/0.09 m^2).

[e]Assume vehicle operating costs = $0.15/vehicle-mi ($0.09/vehicle-km) (approximate travel-related cost of vehicle operation, based on AASHTO's *Manual on User Benefit Analysis*). Assumed average trip length = 8 mi (13 km) one way.

Source: Adapted from Steven A. Smith and Stuart J. TenHoor, *Model Parking Code Provisions to Encourage Ridesharing and Transit Use (Including a Review of Experience)*, Final Report, prepared by JHK & Associates for the FHWA (Washington, D.C.: Federal Highway Administration, September 1983), p. 7.

out of local ordinances that set traffic reduction or parking space requirements on new development, thus requiring the private sector to provide TSM actions as a condition for going forward with their projects. In either case, TMAs enable their members to consolidate their efforts, pool their resources, and reduce the cost of compliance with local requirements through shared services and joint programs.[12] Table 12-3 contains a listing of the typical activities of a TMA.

PLANNING AND ANALYSIS FACTORS FOR TSM

Systematic planning is an essential ingredient in the development of effective TSM actions. It has four important purposes that, when achieved, can lead to successful actions:

1. *Focuses the program effort.* Planning attempts to answer important questions on what, where, why, when, and how various TSM projects will be undertaken. These questions include who will conduct the programs and for whom the programs will be undertaken. Finally, any TSM plan should attempt to assess the impact that various strategies will have on such issues as travel behavior and mode choice, traffic congestion and vehicle volumes, auto occupancy, delay, parking supply and cost. If these questions are answered in a systematic and explicit manner, the focus of TSM strategies will become clear.
2. *Defines a course of action.* The primary purpose of planning is to define a results-oriented course of action that is based on conditions existing in the marketplace or the system. The planning process recommends a course of action and assures that the selected projects have a reasonable opportunity for success.
3. *Evaluates achievements.* The plan also serves as a guide for monitoring whether TSM activities are being conducted as planned and evaluating whether the desired results are being attained. These results are critical to revising or adjusting TSM actions to meet intended goals and objectives.
4. *Strengthens internal accountability.* A well-conceived plan outlines staff responsibilities in the areas of marketing, implementation, and evaluation. It also gives staff members insight into the relationship of their specific assignments to the overall project and institutional goals.

DATA COLLECTION EFFORTS

In order to develop effective TSM plans, relevant information is needed. This information (or data) could relate to issues such as costs, performance characteristics of the transportation system, and changes in performance resulting from the

TABLE 12-3
Typical Activities of a TMA

Offer a forum for public–private consultation on:
- Highway funding priorities.
- Minimizing disruptions from road repairs.
- Transit service improvements.
- Traffic engineering improvements (placement of new signals, changes in traffic flow, etc.).

Represent and advocate the needs and interests of TMA members before public agencies, legislative bodies, and the transportation planning process by:
- Monitoring traffic conditions and recommending appropriate "quick fix" road improvements.
- Conducting employee travel surveys, assessing commuter travel needs (market research), and recommending appropriate changes in transit routing and level of service.
- Monitoring development and employment trends and assessing their impact on future road and transit needs.
- Advising on alignment and new locations for transportation facilities.

Build a local constituency for better transportation and raise funds for local transportation improvements.

Promote, coordinate, and provide travel demand management actions to reduce peak-hour demand on transportation facilities and help TMA members comply with local traffic reduction requirements (trip-reduction ordinances, parking codes, conditions of development, permits, proffers, etc.):
- Ridesharing (carpooling, vanpooling, public transit).
- Variable work hours to spread peak-hour traffic.
- Parking management.
- Market research, promotion, and evaluation.
- Emergency (or guaranteed) ride program.

Facilitate commuting and provide internal circulation within the area through:
- Daytime circulators.
- Subscription van/buses.
- Short-term car rentals.
- Shuttles to rail stations and fringe parking lots.
- Emergency rides for employees who rideshare.
- Reverse commute services for employees.

Provide specialized membership services to TMA members:
- Conduct employee "travel audits" and provide relocation assistance to new employees.
- Train in-house transportation coordinators.
- Manage shared tenant services, such as day-care centers, security, sanitation, landscaping.

implementation of different TSM projects. To this end, information is needed to achieve the following:

- To provide data for applying analytical procedures and/or calibrating computer models to estimate the impacts of various strategies.
- To compare the actual results to predicted impacts.
- To compare the results at one site to the results at another.
- To provide data to other areas considering similar projects.
- To monitor the operation and effectiveness of projects for possible revisions or adjustments.

Collecting information/data needs to be considered as standard procedure when planning and implementing any TSM action; however, this effort can utilize significant amounts of resources and is often considered to be time consuming and not cost effective. To make the effort more cost effective, consideration must be given to selecting the measures of effectiveness and identifying data sources as a prelude to actually collecting the information.

Selecting Measures of Effectiveness

Measures of effectiveness (MOEs) are used to determine the extent to which a TSM strategy has attained a particular goal or objective. Within the context of TSM, these measures are used as a gauge to evaluate the effectiveness or success of a particular action at meeting its goal. Any action taken by the transportation professionals is intended to satisfy a community goal or objective. The goal may be stated explicitly: "reduce congestion in the core area of the city by minimizing stops and delays." It may also be implied by an elected official's or business leader's pledge to "increase accessibility to a decaying portion of the downtown." Both the explicit and implicit goals are easy enough to state, but may be impossible to measure. Therefore, MOEs are used as yardsticks by which to measure how well goals are being met.[13]

There are four approaches to developing the measures of effectiveness. One approach has often been viewed as a top-down process. That is, the broad goals are identified, more explicit objectives are stated, and then the measures of effectiveness are used to determine the extent to which the goals and objectives are satisfied.

A second approach is to examine possible actions to be implemented and to attempt to assess what effect the implementation might have under specific conditions. This approach requires the formulation and testing of hypotheses using the planning analysis methods to estimate impacts (as discussed in a later section of this chapter). The measures can then be identified to determine the correctness of the test and estimate the magnitude of the impact.

A third approach is to determine what data are available or easily collected and what measures can be derived from these data. This approach may have the greatest chance of success, given real-world constraints of limited funds and professional staffs.

A fourth and more attractive approach is to use all the approaches in concert. Augmented by tests of sensitivity, relevance, and computational ability, this combined approach allows the planner to proceed with greater assurance of success in measuring goal attainment. Table 12-4 presents a list of 14 of the most frequently used measures of effectiveness. Not all these measures would necessarily be used to evaluate a particular TSM project. They should be used selectively.

TABLE 12-4
Frequently Used Measures of Effectiveness

- Point-to-point travel time
- Traffic volumes (for an intersection, driveway, or route)
- Vehicle (or person) delay
- Number of vehicles by occupancy
- Vehicle-miles of travel (VMT)
- Vehicle-hours of travel (VHT)
- Person-miles of travel (PMT)
- Person-hours of travel (PHT)
- Transit passengers
- Transit passenger miles of travel
- Energy consumption
- Air pollution emissions
- Capital costs
- Vehicle requirements

Source: Adapted from Charles M. Abrams and John F. DiRenzo, *Measures of Effectiveness for Multimodal Urban Traffic Management, Volume 2: Development and Evaluation of TSM Strategies*, Final Report, prepared by JHK & Associates and Peat, Marwick, Mitchell & Company for the FHWA, Report no. FHWA-RD-79-113 (Washington, D.C.: U.S. Government Printing Office, December 1979), p. 62. Now available as PB 80 198 682.

Selecting an appropriate MOE depends on two important criteria: (1) the level of importance of the measure and (2) the level of effort required to collect the data for that measure.[14] The *level of importance* of a measure of effectiveness indicates its need in the analysis or evaluation. Some measures are absolutely necessary since they uniquely indicate how well a particular objective has been attained. Most may be less important due to the availability of other measures of effectiveness that are easier to use or more descriptive. The *level of effort* of a measure of effectiveness relates to the ease of field measurement (that is, collection of the data) and/or the ease of modeling. Regardless of the importance of a measure, it cannot be used in an evaluation if the costs (both money and resources) of obtaining the MOE are prohibitively expensive. More specific criteria for developing the measures are contained in Table 12-5.

TABLE 12-5
Criteria for Developing Measures of Effectiveness

Relevancy to objectives
> Each MOE should have a clear and specific relationship to TSM objectives in order to ensure the ability to explain changes in the condition of the transportation system.

Simple and understandable
> Within the constraints of required precision and accuracy, each MOE should be simple in application and interpretation.

Quantitative
> MOEs should be specified in numerical terms whenever possible.

Measurable
> Each MOE should be suitable for application in preimplementation simulation and evaluation (i.e., have well-defined mathematical properties and be easily modeled) and in postimplementation monitoring (i.e., require simple direct field measurement attainable within reasonable time, cost, and personnel budgets).

Broadly applicable
> MOEs that are applicable to many different types of strategies should be used wherever possible.

Responsive
> Each MOE should be specified to reflect impacts on the various actor groups, taking into account, as appropriate, geographic area and time period of application and influence.

Sensitive
> Each MOE should have the capacity to discriminate between relatively small changes in the nature or implementation of a control strategy.

Not redundant
> Each MOE should avoid measuring an impact that is sufficiently measured by other MOEs.

Appropriately detailed
> MOEs should be formulated at the proper level of detail for the analysis (e.g., if conceptual-level sketch planning is involved, the appropriate MOE is probably less detailed than one useful for more detailed implementation planning and design).

Source: Adapted from Charles M. Abrams and John F. DiRenzo, *Measures of Effectiveness for Multimodal Urban Traffic Management, Volume 2: Development and Evaluation of TSM Strategies,* Final Report, prepared by JHK & Associates and Peat, Marwick, Mitchell & Company for the FHWA, Report no. FHWA-RD-79-113 (Washington, D.C.: U.S. Government Printing Office, December 1979), p. 68. Now available as PB 80 198 682.

Identifying Data Sources

Data used for the analysis of TSM actions (particularly for estimating measures of effectiveness to be used in before-and-after studies) can come from existing records or from new field data collection or both. Potential data sources based on objectives and relevant measures of effectiveness are shown in Table 12-6. The table indicates the source of data (field data collection, surveys and questionnaires, or agency records) for different measures.

TABLE 12-6
Potential Data Sources

| Objective | MOE | Primary Data Source | | |
		Field Counts/ Data Collection	Type of Survey	Agency Records
Maximize capacity	Critical lane volume	Manual traffic counts		
	Parking supply	Parking inventory		Municipal
	Volume/capacity ratio	Manual traffic counts		
Maximize productivity	Operating cost/passenger trip			Transit co.
	Operating cost/revenue vehicle-mile			Transit co.
	Operating revenue/operating cost			Transit co.
	Passengers/revenue vehicle-hour	Transit boarding-alighting counts	On-board	Transit co.
Minimize operating costs	Operating and maintenance cost			DOT/DPW Police Planning Transit co.
	Operating deficits			Transit co. Municipal
	Operating revenue			Transit co. Municipal
Minimize auto usage	Intersection turning movements	Manual traffic counts		
	Number of carpools		Employee Household	
	Number of vehicles by occupancy	Occupancy counts		
	Person-miles of travel (PMT)	Auto-occupancy counts Transit boarding-alighting counts		
	Person trips	Transit boarding-alighting counts Occupancy counts	Household Roadside	Transit co.
	Traffic volume	Mechanical counters Manual traffic counts		
	Vehicle-miles of travel (VMT)	VMT counts		
Maximize transit usage	Passenger-miles of travel	Transit boarding-alighting counts	Household On-board	
	Transit passengers		Household On-board	Transit co.
Reduce travel time	Person-hours of travel	Transit boarding-alighting counts Occupancy & VMT counts with floating car technique or license plate survey or moving vehicle methods		
	Point-to-point travel time	Floating car technique, time-lapse photography, moving vehicle method, license plate survey		

353

| Objective | MOE | Primary Data Source | | |
		Field Counts/ Data Collection	Type of Survey	Agency Records
	Vehicle delay	Manual intersection delay technique, Floating car technique, license plate survey, moving vehicle method		
	Vehicle-hours of travel	VMT counts with floating car technique, license plate survey, moving vehicle method		
	Vehicle stops	Manual intersection delay technique, test car method Time-lapse photography		
Minimize travel costs	Parking cost		Parker Employee	Municipal
	Point-to-point out-of-pocket travel costs		Household Parker Employee	
	Point-to-point transit fares			Transit co.
Maximize safety	Accidents			Accident
	Accident rate			Accident Traffic count
	Traffic violations	Field observation Time-lapse photography		
Maximize comfort and convenience	Parking accumulation	Parking usage study		
	Perceived comfort and convenience		On-board attitudinal	
	Transit load factor	Field observation Transit boarding-alighting counts		
	Trip distance		Employee Household	
	Walk distance from parking location to destination		Parker Employee	
Maximize reliability	Perceived reliability of service		On-board attitudinal	
	Schedule adherence	Field observation		
	Variance of average point-to-point travel time	Floating car technique, time-lapse photography, moving vehicle method, license plate survey		

Source: Adapted from Charles M. Abrams and John F. DiRenzo, *Measures of Effectiveness for Multimodal Urban Traffic Management, Volume 2: Development and Evaluation of TSM Strategies*, Final Report, prepared by JHK & Associates and Peat, Marwick, Mitchell & Company for the FHWA, Report no. FHWA-RD-79-113 (Washington, D.C.: U.S. Government Printing Office, December 1979), pp. 131-32. Now available as PB 80 198 682.

The data collection effort must be completed within certain budget and time constraints in order to be cost effective. Generally, the sample size and reflected cost estimates of a data collection program result in a desirable study. In some cases, however, projected data needs may exceed the available resources. Possible means of reducing the costs of data collection are contained in Table 12-7.

In most cases, a combination of the methods shown in Table 12-7 is used. As a general guide, it is preferable to sacrifice the coverage of a program (for example, the number of sites) rather than the quality of data at a particular location. Subsequently, when putting together a data collection program, it is important to perform a trade-off analysis. It is also important to perform cost analyses since program costs are affected when data collection procedures are revised. A cost analysis should be repeated until costs are brought within budgetary constraints.[15]

TABLE 12-7
Methods to Reduce the Costs of Data Collection

- Eliminate less important data
- Reduce the number of data collection locations
- Reduce the time period of data collection
- Scale down experimental control activities
- Reduce the desired precision of the estimates
- Modify the data collection procedures

Source: Adapted from Charles M. Abrams and John F. DiRenzo, *Measures of Effectiveness for Multimodal Urban Traffic Management, Volume 2: Development and Evaluation of TSM Strategies*, Final Report, prepared by JHK & Associates and Peat, Marwick, Mitchell & Company for the FHWA, Report no. FHWA-RD-79-113 (Washington, D.C.: U.S. Government Printing Office, December 1979). Now available as PB 80 198 682.

ANALYSIS TECHNIQUES FOR TSM PLANNING

To interpret or analyze the information/data that have been collected, certain planning procedures or techniques are used by engineers and planners. Many techniques are available for analyzing information used in the planning of TSM projects.[16] These techniques cover a range of complexity and generally fall into the following categories:

Specification. Specification is generally used to set a value or goal on the transportation and activity measures used in an analysis. Although not an estimation technique directly, specification can set a standard from which to measure the performance or impact of a TSM action. Examples are 12 vans placed in service for employees in the next 12 months, 15-min headway on a proposed bus route, and level-of-service C on an improved arterial street.

Direct measurement. Direct measurement of the existing environment can provide valuable information for estimating potential services or proposed designs. Even in an analysis of proposed conditions, values of some measure can be obtained directly through field surveys and maps. Such measures as lane-miles, length of a bus route, adequate turning radii for fire trucks or buses, potential ridership, or employee attitude for a new service can all be assessed using some form of direct measurement.

Market research. A form of direct measurement, market research can lead to improved information on attitudes, trends, needs, status and acceptance for a proposed action. Most market research is done through surveys at the workplace, at some point along a trip, through the mail, over the telephone, or through one-on-one interviews. Information from market research can serve as the impetus for TSM programs better suited for transportation users. Examples of market research include transit ridership surveys, employee surveys for a proposed company ridesharing program, and mail-out surveys to identify or monitor travel changes due to a highway reconstruction project.[17]

Direct calculation. Some measures of interest are sums, products, or ratios of other measures. Both travel-related measures (such as cost per person-minutes saved) and financial measures (such as revenue and subsidy requirements) are usually calculated using other estimated values. Summary measures for a study area (such as vehicle-miles of travel) are often the sums of values estimated for components such as intersections and street segments.

Before-and-after studies. Before-and-after studies are the traditional method used when evaluating TSM actions. Numerous reports and texts have been prepared on undertaking a before-and-after study.

Analogy. Performance levels and impacts observed at other sites are often the only simple means of estimating the outcome of a program. Analogy can be used when there is a lack of data or data are difficult to obtain at the proposed location. Analogy is less costly than other programs and leads to a quicker summation of the impact of a TSM action. Data from a single case study or a compilation of several studies may be used with or without modifications to reflect differences between the characteristics of the sites. Examples of the use of analogies include estimating the patronage on a proposed community transit service by using data developed for a similar service, or estimating auto occupancy, mode share, and traffic volumes at an employment site, for a proposed ridesharing program, by using information from a similar program.

Look-up. Performance and impact levels of TSM programs can sometimes be synthesized into a graph or table format. The results of research studies employing analytic or simulation models may also be presented in nomographs, graphs, tables, or similar formats from which estimates can be directly extracted. Graphs relating to intersection capacity, critical gap, and conflicting flows are examples.

Simple equations and formulas. Estimates are often obtained by applying simple equations, unit rates, or formulas. Examples include trend lines or growth rates used to estimate traffic volume, accident and emission rates (per vehicle-mile) used to estimate safety and air quality factors, formulas used to allocate transit operating costs among routes based on measures such as vehicle-miles and vehicle-hours, and elasticities used to estimate changes in volume measures.

Analytical or simulation procedures. Analytical procedures (manually operated or computerized) may be required to obtain accurate estimates of impacts. Some of the analytical procedures may be simple work sheets; others are best applied with the assistance of a calculator or computer programs. Analytical procedures currently available for estimating the travel impact of different TSM proposals can be grouped into five categories:[18]

1. Network-based highway and transit planning models—used in travel demand forecasting functions (such as traffic assignment and mode split analyses) that are required to estimate changes in travel patterns within a corridor or network as a result of TSM projects.
2. Quick-response estimation techniques—simplified network-based procedures applicable when data, funds, and resources are limited and results are needed within a short time frame.
3. Highway capacity analysis procedures—used to estimate the capacity of the affected roadway as well as affected modes; also used to estimate operational measures of effectiveness, including level of service and average speed on the affected highways or arterials.
4. Traffic simulation models—used to estimate traffic conditions and to estimate operational or economic measures of effectiveness, particularly when the time-varying nature of traffic flow is important or roadway geometrics are complex.
5. Traffic optimization models—used in the impact estimation process to assess, refine, or improve plans for a particular highway or route; also provide estimates of operational and economic measures of effectiveness.

Table 12-8 lists the significant factors that need to be considered when deciding which planning technique to select for the situation.

TABLE 12-8
Considerations in Selecting Planning Techniques

- Nature, magnitude, and complexity of the project
- Type of facility (e.g., freeway or arterial)
- Amount of time and level of effort needed
- Size of the affected corridor
- Volume of traffic that will be impacted
- Size/complexity of the affected corridor or area
- Experience of the professional staff
- Availability of accurate data
- Availability of resources (cost, time, labor)

Source: R. A. Krammes and others, *Application of Analysis Tools to Evaluate the Travel Impacts of Highway Reconstruction with Emphasis on Microcomputer Applications*, Final Report, prepared by Texas Transportation Institute, Texas A&M University System, for the FHWA, Report no. FHWA-ED-89-023 (Washington, D.C.: Federal Highway Administration, June 1989 [cover March 1989]), p. 28. Now available as PB 89 187 181.

TSM AS A COMPONENT IN AIR QUALITY ATTAINMENT

The automobile as presently utilized and powered is a major contributor to air quality degradation. To improve air quality in urban areas, many metropolitan planning organizations/air quality districts have developed transportation control measures (TCMs). TSM activities are universally a major component of such plans.The full TCMs often contain actions beyond transportation system management, such as enhanced vehicle inspection and maintenance requirements, improved vehicle technology and fuels, market-based economic elements, and land-use strategies, as well as alternative transportation services to replace auto trips. TSM actions, however, are usually the dominant strategy.

TECHNOLOGY APPLICATIONS FOR TSM

There are many reasons for using advanced technologies in TSM applications. New and advanced technology can improve the efficiency and traffic-handling capacity of existing roadways. Technology can address and reduce inherent safety limitations attributable to both human factors and the roadway system. New technology has the potential to improve mobility and commercial productivity by alleviating traffic congestion and roadway incidents. Finally, new and advanced technology can improve the comfort and convenience of the driver and passengers on the system.[19]

Figure 12-4 *Freeway management center. (courtesy of Federal Highway Administration)*

The accepted terminology describing the application of new advanced technology to transportation systems management is *intelligent vehicle/highway systems* (IVHS). IVHS technologies can be expected to improve the management of the existing infrastructure, given its operating limitations, primarily by providing significant amounts of real-time information to the motorist and to public and private operating agencies so that travel can be made safely and efficiently.

The information provided by IVHS technologies has three important implications for improved management of the existing system. First, the information can make the operations of the system more efficient by effectively using the available facilities, services, modes, and routes. Second, the efficient operation of the system, because of IVHS technologies, may preclude the urgency or need for major system expansion. Third, efficient operations can also lead to an extension of the life of a particular facility, thereby postponing the need for replacement.

Improved management of the existing infrastructure is tied to the efficiencies gained through the use of information provided by IVHS technologies. The real-time information made possible by implementing IVHS technologies can include the following:

1. Location of reconstruction and maintenance activities.
2. Location of underused or overused facilities and services.
3. Identification and location of good operations.
4. Identification of restricted or out-of-service facilities.
5. Identification of alternate routes (detours), modes, services, and conditions.
6. Identification of ridesharing and transit opportunities.
7. Monitoring and routing of heavy and hazardous shipments.

There are four IVHS components that stem from advances in electronics, communications, and information processing. IVHS technologies will be discussed briefly, along with their near- or long-term impact on the improved management of the existing infrastructure.

ADVANCED TRAFFIC MANAGEMENT SYSTEMS (ATMS)

ATMS provide the real-time means for transportation operators to effectively monitor traffic conditions, quickly adjust traffic operations, and effectively respond to accidents. They include traffic detectors, computerized signals, adjustable speed limit signs, and changeable roadside information signs and lights. ATMS can reduce traffic congestion and delays and permit shorter response times for traffic incidents. There are many examples of this type of technology:

- Computerized traffic control systems, in place at about 20% of the signalized intersection locations.
- Adaptive and interactive signal control, now in the developmental stages.
- Incident detection and response systems, being developed in a number of urban areas.

- Automatic vehicle identification systems being used to provide smooth access to restricted highways or for quicker toll collection or automatic payment.
- Identification systems to monitor hazardous cargoes or track stolen cars.

ADVANCED TRAVELER INFORMATION SYSTEMS (ATIS)

ATIS provide drivers with in-vehicle information on congestion, navigation and location, traffic conditions, and alternative routes. ATIS could also be designed to provide travelers with trip information at the home or in the office on bus schedules, congestion, and so on. These systems are the link to travelers, providing them with the necessary information on opportunities for trip making. Additional information could be provided to include local accidents, construction areas, weather and road conditions, alternate routes, and ridesharing and transit services. In consort with other IVHS technologies, information could be provided on potentially dangerous driver, vehicle, road, or environmental conditions. Specific types of ATIS technologies include:

- On-board replication of maps and signs.
- Pretrip electronic route planning.
- Traffic information broadcasting systems.
- Safety warning systems.
- On-board navigation systems.
- Electronic route guidance systems.

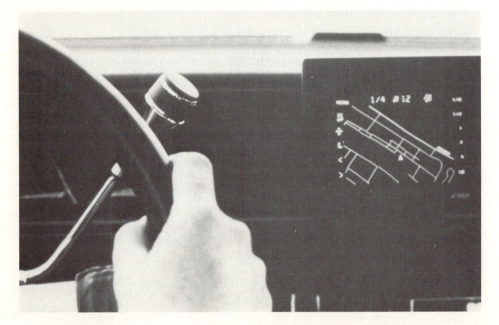

Figure 12-5 *In-vehicle electronic map. (courtesy of Federal Highway Administration)*

COMMERCIAL VEHICLE OPERATIONS (CVO)

CVO include technologies and fleet-control operations intended to enhance the efficiency of operating trucks and fleets of vehicles. Such systems also improve the efficiency of regulatory compliance, vehicle inspection, and fleet monitoring operations. Several of these types of systems are being used and many more are being planned. It appears that the effect of this technology on infrastructure management is near term.

ADVANCED VEHICLE CONTROL SYSTEMS (AVCS)

AVCS are those technologies designed to help the driver perform certain vehicle control functions. Using data collected by on-board sensors, AVCS provide information to vehicle operators that allows them to make decisions quickly and accurately or that allows action to be taken independent of the operator. A number of AVCS technologies are available or under development. Some of these include:

- Antilock braking systems.
- Speed control warning systems.
- Adaptive speed control.
- Driver assist systems.
- Radar braking.
- Automatic headway control.
- Automatic lateral control.
- Proximity warning.
- Smart cruise control.
- Automatic speed control.
- Automatic highway systems.

CASE STUDIES

The following case studies provide illustration and insight into the application of the key concepts presented in this chapter.

INTEGRATED TRAFFIC CONTROL—THE SMART CORRIDOR—LOS ANGELES, CALIFORNIA

The "Smart Corridor" (see Fig. 12-6) consists of 12.3 mi (19.7 km) of the Santa Monica Freeway and five parallel arterials. Traffic data and management strategies will be coordinated among the California Department of Transportation, the California Highway Patrol, the city of Los Angeles Police Department, and the Los Angeles County Transportation Commission. This coordination will be accomplished by linking together the five existing traffic control centers operated by these agencies and developing a common data base of information that they all can share. Through this mechanism, traffic management strategies such as ramp metering policies, parking enforcement, signal timing, and detours around major congestion or incidents will be coordinated.

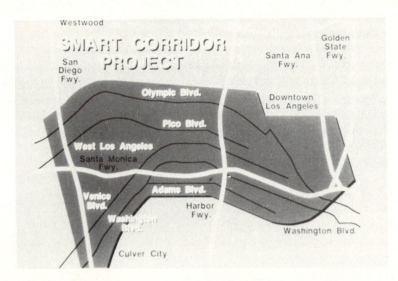

Figure 12-6 *Smart Corridor map. (courtesy of Federal Highway Administration)*

The project also involves consideration and potential application of advanced traffic management strategies. Strategies considered include coordination of ramp meter signals with traffic signals, use of changeable message signs on arterials and at parking garage exits to advise motorists of the best routes, application of expert systems theory to the problems of incident detection and response, freeway-to-freeway connector metering, and a critical examination of various innovative mechanisms for communicating motorist information, such as areawide highway advisory radio, computer bulletin boards, telephone dial-in systems, commercial television, and videotext.

Finally, the project will incorporate consideration of improving the policy elements of traffic management. This will include an examination of freeway service patrol ideas, establishing incident management teams for both freeways and arterials, applying enforcement, and selecting accident investigation sites. A 7-month conceptual design study for the Smart Corridor was completed in 1989. Following completion of this effort, it will take 3.5 years and $30 million to complete the design and install the system. The project is not expected to be operational until late 1992.

Freeway Management—The Flow Program—Seattle, Washington[20]

In the Seattle area, the Washington State Department of Transportation (WSDOT), working closely with the city, and the transit operator (Metro) implemented a comprehensive package of freeway management actions along Interstate 5 North (north from Seattle). Freeway management strategies incorporated into the "Flow Program" have enabled the WSDOT to maintain a viable freeway operation without the expensive construction of new facilities. The program includes the use of HOV lanes, a ramp metering system with HOV bypass lanes, express bus service with designated freeway transit stops (known as "freeway flyer stops"), a corridor ridesharing program with park-and-ride lots, and a civilian-assisted fast-lane enforcement plan. The Flow Program, in conjunction with programs like reduced carpool parking fees, variable work hours, transit service improvements, and vanpool incentive actions, provides a realistic package of actions to maintain future mobility through the I-5 corridor.

The WSDOT had three primary objectives for implementing the Flow Program: (1) improve I-5 freeway operating efficiency in order to save time and money, (2) reduce merging and congestion related accidents, and (3) maximize the people-moving capability of the freeway through on-ramp metering and HOV lanes.

In the Seattle area, coordination and cooperation between state and local agencies have made the Flow Program a success. The early involvement and subsequent support of the media and the public also played a key role in the success of the effort.

Public—Private Agreements and TMOs—Montgomery County, Maryland[21, 22]

Montgomery County is located immediately northwest of Washington, D.C., with a population of 700,000 and an employment base of over 250,000. Since 1973 the county has had an Adequate Public Facilities Ordinance (APFO) that requires local officials to examine the adequacy of transportation facilities and services before approving new land developments. Over time, the requirements have become progressively stronger and more effective, with increasing emphasis on public–private sector solutions. The ordinance has been the stimulus for a number of far-reaching traffic congestion alleviation requirements in the county.

The county's APFO requires that public facilities be adequate to handle new demands before development can take place. The ordinance technically covers all public facilities, but it is transportation that has grown to be the most significant issue with respect to new development. If a proposed development will produce unacceptable levels-of-service conditions on the nearby roads, then public or private sector solutions must be found to either reduce trips or increase the capacity of roads.

The APFO spells out two approaches to determining the adequacy of public facilities to meet the demands of new development: (1) a local area review test and (2) a policy area review test. The local area review is basically an intersection analysis on the roads in an area surrounding the development site. For large sites (for example,

1000 dwelling units or 1 million ft^2 of commercial space), this area could cover 1 mi or more. This review requires that traffic on the roads in the surrounding area operate at no worse than level-of-service E. If the required conditions for traffic flow are not met, the developer must work with the county to implement acceptable TSM actions.

The policy area review follows the local area review and is intended to identify the downstream and upstream impacts of the additional development within one of the 19 general subareas of the county. Each subarea has predetermined levels of acceptable traffic congestion. The subareas with good levels of transit service have higher levels of acceptable traffic congestion than subareas with low levels of transit service. Based on these levels, a determination is made as to whether sufficient transportation capacity exists within the policy subarea to allow additional development to take place.

To provide transportation improvements to existing developments, Montgomery County has also embarked on an effort to establish *transportation management organizations* (TMOs) in certain subareas of the county with high-density existing development. The organizations are voluntary, nonprofit, membership associations that include both the private and public sectors. The organizations have the following primary purposes:

1. To serve as a forum for private and public sector responses to transportation problems.
2. To identify and implement actions to reduce traffic congestion, air pollution, and energy consumption.
3. To facilitate orderly growth.
4. To ensure adequate access and internal mobility.
5. To coordinate "demand management" programs that include promoting transit and ridesharing services, spreading employee arrival and departure hours, and implementing parking management and other programs to encourage the use of high-occupancy vehicles for commuting.
6. To organize, manage, and promote bus or van programs.
7. To develop and coordinate common parking policies and other incentives and disincentives aimed at reducing the use of single-occupant cars.
8. To help members meet trip-reduction obligations.
9. To conduct a cooperative planning program to meet future needs.

SUMMARY

Transportation system management actions are tools for the transportation professional to meet the management and operational challenges of relieving congestion, maintaining mobility, and improving the efficiency of transportation facilities, services, and modes. TSM actions must interact and blend with other construction and land-use actions to meet the long- and short-term goals of the community. The key ingredients to achieving success with TSM actions are the following:

- Have institutions and organizations that recognize the need for a variety of TSM actions.
- Undertake thoughtful planning to make TSM actions an integral part of the transportation plans and programs.
- Coordinate among the public and private providers of transportation.
- Have a willingness to apply TSM actions in an innovative manner.
- Have an ability to market and inform the public on the TSM action(s).

This chapter presented the contemporary approach to the planning and application of TSM actions. It has also presented the philosophy that TSM has evolved from a planning concept to include the actual operation and management of transportation. The chapter emphasized the need for coordination among institutions and between the public and private sectors to make TSM actions effective. The traffic management teams, metropolitan planning associations, and transportation management associations discussed in the chapter are creative approaches that can be used to achieve coordination.

Simplified and complex approaches to analyzing the effectiveness of TSM actions were also presented in this chapter as essential ingredients to a thoughtful TSM planning process. Traditional and innovative TSM actions were included to demonstrate the variety of actions to better manage traffic and improve mobility. Advanced technologies (known as intelligent vehicle/highway systems or IVHS) were also addressed to illustrate their potential application to improving mobility. Finally, case studies were presented to illustrate the concepts presented.

It is important to bridge the gap between TSM as a systems concept developed by states and metropolitan planning organizations and the application of operational actions implemented by states and local operation agencies. Effective TSM is critical to metropolitan areas and should recognize and build upon the strength of urban planning and traffic operational disciplines.

REFERENCES

Some citations are no longer available from their original source. These citations are often available from the National Technical Information Service, U.S. Department of Commerce, 5285 Port Royal Road, Springfield, VA 22161. We have verified the order numbers for many of these citations, and they are found at the end of the citation. Prices are available through NTIS at the address above.

1   JEFFREY A. LINDLEY, "Urban Freeway Congestion: Quantification of the Problem and Effectiveness of Potential Solutions," *ITE Journal*, 57, no. 1 (January 1987), pp. 27-32.

2   TRANSPORTATION RESEARCH BOARD, *America's Highways: Accelerating the Search for Innovation, Strategic Transportation Research Study: Highways*, Special Report 202 (Washington, D.C., Transportation Research Board, 1984), p. 302.

3   Ibid., p. 300.

4   FEDERAL HIGHWAY ADMINISTRATION AND URBAN MASS TRANSPORTATION ADMINISTRATION, "Transportation Improvement Program," 23 CFR, Part 450, Subparts A and C, *Federal Register*, 40, no. 181 (September 17, 1975), pp. 42976-84.

5   LINDLEY, "Urban Freeway Congestion."

6   TRANSPORTATION RESEARCH BOARD, *Urban Public Transportation Glossary*, ed. Benita H. Gray (Washington, D.C.: Transportation Research Board, 1989), p. 72.

7   MICHAEL D. MEYER AND OTHERS, *A Toolbox for Alleviating Traffic Congestion*, Draft Report (Washington, D.C.: Institute of Transportation Engineers, 1989).

8   SHELDON G. STRICKLAND AND JONATHAN D. MCDADE, "Transportation Management and the 3 C's for Dealing with Urban Congestion," in *Compendium of Technical Papers for the 57th Annual Meeting of the Institute of Transportation Engineers, August 16-20, 1987* (Washington D.C.: Institute of Transportation Engineers, 1987), pp. 228-32.

9   Ibid.

10   STEVEN A. SMITH AND STUART J. TENHOOR, *Model Parking Code Provisions to Encourage Ridesharing and Transit Use (Including a Review of Experience)*, Final Report, prepared by JHK & Associates for the FHWA (Washington, D.C.: Federal Highway Administration, September 1983).

11   KENNETH C. ORSKI, "Transportation Management Associations: Battling Suburban Traffic Congestion," *Urban Land*, 45, no. 12 (December 1986), pp. 2-5.

12   MEYER, *A Toolbox*.

13   CHARLES M. ABRAMS AND JOHN F. DIRENZO, *Measures of Effectiveness for Multimodal Urban Traffic Management, Volume 2: Development and Evaluation of TSM Strategies*, Final Report, prepared by JHK & Associates and Peat, Marwick, Mitchell & Company for FHWA, (Washington, D.C.: U.S. Government Printing Office, December 1979). Now available as PB 80 198 682.

14   Ibid.

15   Ibid.

16   J. H. BATCHELDER AND OTHERS, *Simplified Procedures for Evaluating Low-Cost TSM Projects: User's Manual*, NCHRP Report 263 (Washington, D.C.: Transportation Research Board, October 1983).

17   FEDERAL HIGHWAY ADMINISTRATION, *Strategic Marketing for Ridesharing Professionals*, prepared by the Alliance to Save Energy, 1982, reproduced by the FHWA (Washington, D.C.: Federal Highway Administration, 1984).

18   R. A. KRAMMES AND OTHERS, *Application of Analysis Tools to Evaluate the Travel Impacts of Highway Reconstruction with Emphasis on Microcomputer Applications*, Final Report, prepared by Texas Transportation Institute, Texas A&M University System, for the FHWA, Report no. FHWA-ED-89-023 (Washington, D.C.: Federal Highway Administration, June 1989 [cover March 1989]). Now available as PB 89 187 181.

19   FEDERAL HIGHWAY ADMINISTRATION, *The Future National Highway Program: 1991 and Beyond; Working Paper No. 7: Advancements in Vehicle and Traffic Control Technology* (Washington, D.C.: Federal Highway Administration, 1987).

20 FEDERAL HIGHWAY ADMINISTRATION, OFFICE OF PLANNING, *Transportation Management for Corridors and Activity Centers: Opportunities and Experiences*, Final Report, Technology Sharing Program, Report no. DOT-I-86-21 (Washington, D.C.: U.S. Department of Transportation, May 1986).

21 ALEXANDER J. HEKIMIAN, "Public/Private Agreements and Transportation Management Organizations in Montgomery County, Maryland," in *Proceedings of the ITE's 1987 National Conference on Strategies to Alleviate Traffic Congestion* (Washington, D.C.: Institute of Transportation Engineers, 1988).

22 JOHN J. CLARK, "The Adequate Public Facilities Ordinance in Montgomery County, Maryland," paper presented at The Private Sector and Public Transit Symposium, sponsored by the Urban Mass Transportation Administration, Denver, Colorado, April 1989.

EXERCISES

12-1   Identify five existing transportation system management actions in your community. Why would you consider each of these actions to be TSM? What do you think is the goal of these actions? How would you assess the effectiveness of these TSM actions at achieving the goal you have identified? Who is responsible for planning, implementing, and operating each of the TSM actions that you have listed?

12-2   Discuss how the Federal-Aid Highway program, between 1960 and 1975, recognized the importance of a program to improve traffic operations in urban areas. How did this lead to the formal establishment of TSM in 1975? How has the federal role in urban transportation evolved from 1975 to today?

12-3   Compare and contrast the TSM planning requirements for a corridor to that of an activity center. Account for the types of actions, institutional and organizational factors, data needs, and analysis considerations.

12-4   Using examples, discuss the differences in the application of supply-side TSM actions and demand-side TSM actions.

12-5   Select one or more TSM actions and develop a plan for implementing the project in a congested corridor. What type of supply-side and demand-side actions would be considered? Include in the plan recommendations for organizational and institutional arrangements that would need to be established, data collection factors, measures of effectiveness, and analysis techniques that could be used. Justify your recommendations.

12-6   Develop a plan as in Exercise 12-5 to relieve congestion at a major suburban employment center.

12-7   What factors need to be considered when evaluating the effectiveness of a TSM action? What role do MOEs play? How can the cost of data collection be minimized?

12-8   What are the important impacts provided by IVHS technologies on transportation system management? What are the issues that need to be addressed when applying IVHS? What organizational arrangements would be needed?

12-9   What are the potential roles and responsibilities of the private sector in TSM? What types of TSM projects would be enhanced by the private sector? How can the public sector involve the private sector in TSM?

12-10   Discuss the critical barriers that you feel need to be overcome in order to implement effective TSM actions.

Chapter 13

SYSTEM AND SERVICE PLANNING

HERBERT S. LEVINSON

The planning of urban transit systems and services should reflect the history, geography, and economy of the particular area. Past practice and precedents, the city's physical setting and features, the patterns of population and employment, the attitudes and perceptions of residents, and the prospects for growth and change influence the form of the city, the importance and use of public transportation, and the role of the various transportation modes.

Factors such as population and employment density, per capita income and car ownership, and transportation cost by public and private conveyance are among the key quantifiable factors for transit planning and service decisions.

This chapter presents the parameters and principles that underlie system and service planning. It describes the relationship between transportation (public transportation in particular) and urban development, sets forth general approaches to transportation system planning, gives guidelines for rail transit system and operations planning, and contains service planning methods for bus transit.

TRANSPORTATION AND DEVELOPMENT

Transportation technology has been closely linked with the density of human settlement and with the uses of urban land. It has continually influenced the location, form, and economy of urban areas throughout the world. Mechanized transportation (both public and private) has enabled cities to intensify at their centers and expand at their parameters; it has made the modern urban region a reality. The specific impacts have varied, depending upon the degree of economic development, extent of urbanization, social and cultural patterns, antecedents, and public policy.

Cities were first built to a pedestrian scale. Travel distances were short, development was compact, and densities were high. As urban transportation became mechanized, the scale of the city expanded. Each transportation mode—streetcar, rail transit line, and motor vehicle—expanded the area of urban development, and each contributed to the employment concentration at the city center and population dispersion on the periphery. Between 1875 and 1900, the steel-frame skyscraper, vertical elevator, and electric railway changed the scale of the city and its center. The "electric railway city" replaced the "pedestrian city" as the radius of development increased from 3 to over 10 mi. This trend reached its peak prior to the Great Depression of the 1930s.

As the automobile, the bus, and other motorized vehicles became more reliable and popular, areas that had not been reached before by rail became accessible. This filling in of outward expansion between transit corridors continued and accentuated the decentralization process already started by street railway, rapid transit, and commuter rail lines. Although these changes began about 1925, the trend toward decentralization was constrained by depression and war for almost a quarter-century. Between 1950 and 1970 the "automobile city" became a reality, and the "urban region" blurred the differences between city and country.

The pertinent characteristics of the pedestrian, electric railway, and automobile city and their density implications are shown in Table 13-1.

TABLE 13-1
Transportation Mode and Urban Form

Item	Type of City		
	Pedestrian	Electric Railway (Rapid Transit)	Automobile
Population	3,000,000	3,000,000	3,000,000
Area (mi^2)	30	200	1000+
Density (pers./mi^2)	100,000	15,000	5000
Jobs in city center	200,000	300,000	150,000
Development pattern	Compact	Major corridors	Dispersed
Example	Paris, 1900	Chicago, 1920	Houston, 1980

Today's major transit improvements in American cities are superimposed on an auto-oriented environment. In location, lines are fitted to major thoroughfares, freeways, topography, and open areas—not directly to density patterns. Therefore, they do not provide the dramatic improvements in overall access that was common before 1930. These systems by themselves do not have strong impacts on residential developments unless they are complemented by many other factors. Also needed are the availability of attractive sites for development, strong zoning incentives, and a vigorous demand for residential and commercial space in the system's service area. Even then, for the North American city, the primary function of new transit lines is to serve and reinforce the core area rather than to create the opportunity for high-density residential development along corridors.

INTERACTIONS

The effects of public transportation investment on urban development vary widely from city to city and within each city. The impacts depend on the changes in accessibility resulting from improved transport, the conditions of the land (whether vacant or built up and whether right or wrong location), the demand for housing and commercial development, and the presence or absence of government policies. (See Fig. 13-1.)

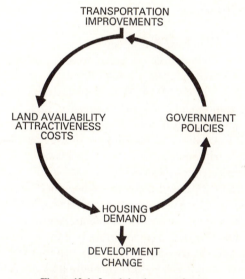

Figure 13-1 *Land development factors.*

Thus, transportation improvements have important *differential* impacts on urban land.[1] The extent of these impacts depends upon the relative changes in accessibility introduced into the overall transportation system in relation to other development factors—anticipated future growth, availability of developable land, utilities, topographic constraints, and inducements. Impacts are most pronounced in developing areas, since it is relatively difficult to change the use and intensity of existing built-up land. Impacts are greatest in rapidly growing high-income areas and least in established medium- or low-income areas.

These phenomena suggest the following theory of urban development. Where transportation improvements increase accessibility in high-income, low-density areas, they may bring about multifamily dwellings, offices, or mixed-use developments. Initial occupants of the land are replaced by a second group. The second group eventually may be displaced by a third lower-income group of families at a higher density. In contrast, many areas built initially for lower-income groups do not change appreciably as new transportation facilities are introduced. There is usually little short-term change in already built-up areas.

This cyclical theory of urban change assumes that the urban area has a high level of dynamism. It also assumes that urban growth patterns will not be unduly impacted by social and demographic changes. These interactions have important implications for the planning of rail transit systems. A key planning decision is the extent to which new lines should (1) serve existing demands from already built-up areas or (2) serve future demands that might result from or be enhanced by building along the line. Ideally, system design should capture both markets and preserve rights-of-way for future expansion.

DENSITY AND TRANSIT RIDERSHIP

Transit works best where travel is concentrated in space and time. It is well suited to serving areas with high population and employment densities. It is effective where street travel is slow and parking costs are high. (Parking costs usually correlate with employment density.) Low levels of car ownership also reinforce transit ridership.

The effects of population and employment densities (and car ownership) on urban travel patterns and public transportation ridership are well documented. Many origin–destination and travel demand surveys have shown how these densities influence the number and type of trip and the modes of travel used.[2]

As population density rises, there is an increase in the total number of person trips, including pedestrian trips, and a corresponding decrease in the number of trips in vehicles. This is because many shopping, social, and school trips, and some work trips, are made on foot in high-density environments. Also, a greater proportion of the nonwalking trips are made by public transportation in these areas. Moreover, in high-density areas, income and car ownership—the two important explanatory factors that influence trip rates and mode choice—are normally less. As densities decline, travel becomes more dispersed and transit becomes less effective in serving travelers.

In almost every city, overall person-trip rates (in vehicles) decrease and transit-trip rates increase as cities or neighborhoods become more dense. This is apparent from the relationships between person trips and residential densities shown in Fig. 13-2 for six U. S. urban areas.

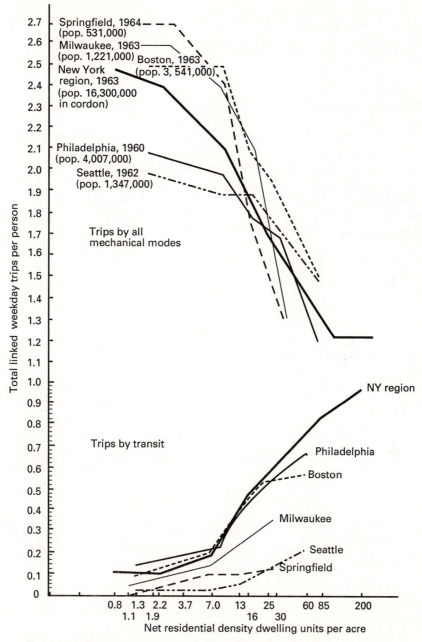

Figure 13-2 *Total trips per person by mode related to residential density in six urban areas. [Source: Boris S. Pushkarev and Jeffrey M. Zupan,* Public Transportation and Land Use Policy, *a Regional Planning Association Book (Bloomington, Ind.: Indiana University Press, 1977), p. 31.]*

At every density level, larger cities tend to have higher transit ridership than smaller communities. This is explained in part by the concentrations of employment in major activity centers, the clustering of activities (such as universities) along transit lines, and the existence of rapid transit lines.

There is strong correlation between downtown employment density measured in employees per acre and public transportation use. For example, more than 90% of all travelers to Manhattan (New York), where employment density approximates 800 persons per acre, arrive by transit, compared to Denver, where 20% arrive by transit and employment approximates 150 persons per acre.[3]

The trends toward dispersed urban development, rising car ownership, and growing per capita incomes have created an adverse environment for public transportation in the United States. (See Fig. 13-3.) Maintaining and increasing transit ridership, therefore, will call for positive policy actions regarding transit service improvements, concentrations of population, and employment and parking policy.

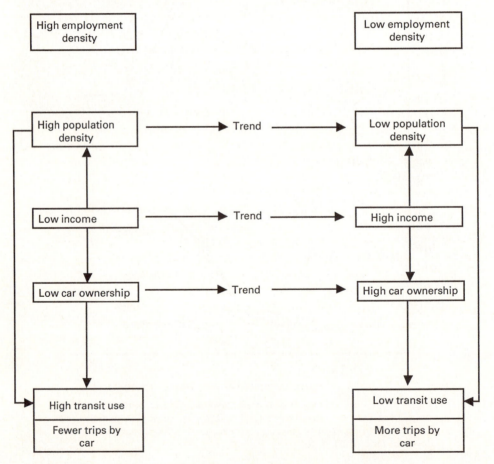

Figure 13-3 *Modal use factors.*

GUIDELINES FOR TRANSIT MODES

Each transit mode has an important role depending upon urban area size, population density, structure, and CBD activity. The guidelines in Table 13-2 are useful in system and service planning. They show minimum residential densities suggested for each transit mode. The corresponding minimum CBD floor-space guidelines are:

Mode	Millions of Square Feet
Commuter rail and rail transit	75
Light rail transit	35
Express bus	20–50
Local bus	
10-min service	18
30-min service	5–7

Chapter 11 discusses another set of conditions that are conducive to rail and bus rapid transit development in the U. S. based upon past experience: an urban area population of at least 2 million persons, 50 million ft^2 of CBD floor space, and a CBD employment of at least 100,000. Lesser conditions are indicated for light rail transit (LRT) and busway development. (See Table 11-1, p. 299.)

Many other factors influence the feasibility, type, and extent of rapid transit development, including the size and shape of the city—for example, the angle or length of arc subtended by the city center; topographic barriers, notably the presence of water bodies or mountains; the type of downtown street system and its suitability for on-street transit distribution; and the availability of suitable rights-of-way. Equally important are the operating speeds of the existing bus system, both in the city center and throughout the region. The rates of regional and CBD growth also must be considered, as well as the extent and adequacy of the existing freeway system.

The number of riders needed to justify a major transit investment depends upon the cost to build the system and the expected time savings to passengers. Table 13-3 gives daily ridership threshold volumes suggested for various types of construction and fixed-guideway transit. Values are shown in terms of passenger miles per mile of line. The required passenger volumes can be estimated as follows:

$$V = \frac{pM}{r} \qquad (13\text{-}1)$$

where V = passenger-volumes on line
M = length of line in mi
r = average length of ride
p = passenger-mi/mi of line

The key point is that the threshold volumes increase with the cost and complexity of construction.

TABLE 13-2
Transit Modes Related to Residential Density

Mode	Service	Minimum Necessary Residential Density (dwelling units/acre)	Remarks
Dial-a-bus	Many origins to many destinations	6	Only if labor costs are not more than twice those of taxis
	Fixed destinations or subscription service	3.5 to 5	Lower figure if labor costs are twice those of taxis; higher if thrice those of taxis
Local bus	Minimum, ½-mi route spacing, 20 buses/day	4	Average, varies as a function of downtown size and distance from residential area to downtown
	Intermediate, ½-mi route spacing, 40 buses/day	7	
	Frequent, ½-mi route spacing, 120 buses/ day	15	
Express bus reached on foot	5 buses during 2-h peak period	15 (average density over 2 mi^2 tributary area)	From 10 to 15 mi away to largest downtowns only
reached by auto	5 to 10 buses during 2-h peak period	3 (average density over 20 mi^2 tributary area)	From 10 to 20 mi away to downtowns larger than 20 million ft^2 of nonresidential floor space
Light rail	5-min headways or better during peak hour	9 (average density for a corridor of 25 to 100 mi^2)	To downtown of 20 to 50 million ft^2 of non-residential floor space
Rapid transit	5-min headways or better during peak hour	12 (average density for a corridor of 100 to 150 mi^2)	To downtown of larger than 50 million ft^2 of nonresidential floor space
Commuter rail	20 trains a day	1 to 2	Only to largest downtowns, if rail line exists

Source: Boris S. Pushkarev and Jeffrey M. Zupan, *Public Transportation and Land Use Policy*, a Regional Plan Association Book (Bloomington, Ind.: Indiana University Press, 1977).

TABLE 13-3
Threshold Volumes for Rapid Transit Development
(keyed to type of structure)
(minimum service frequency, 8 min)

Mode	Type of Construction	Daily Pass.-Mi/Mi of Route
Rail rapid	Above ground	14,000
	One-third tunnel	17,000–24,000[a]
	All tunnel	24,000–42,000[a]
LRT	Low capital	4000
	Considerable grade separation	7000
	One-fifth in tunnel	13,500
	All tunnel	40,000
Downtown people mover	Above ground	12,000
	All tunnel	30,000

[a]Range reflects varying criteria for cost/weekday passenger-mi of travel

Source: Adapted from Boris Pushkarev, with Jeffrey M. Zupan and Robert S. Cumella, *Urban Rail in America: An Exploration of Criteria for Fixed-Guideway Transit* (Bloomington, Ind.: Indiana University Press, 1982), p. 116.

THE TRANSIT PLANNING PROCESS

Transit planning takes many forms. It includes *strategic planning*, which takes a broad global look at how an agency might function in its surrounding environment; *long-range system planning*, which generally relates to major facility development (and in the United States, UMTA's alternatives analyses process if federal funding is expected); *short-range planning*, which traditionally produces a transit development plan; and *service or operations planning*, which looks at service changes on a continuing basis.

The appropriate type of planning depends upon specific circumstances. *Strategic planning* is appropriate when a transit agency wants to reassess its role, mission, and organization. *Long-range system planning* is needed wherever a community wants to expand its existing rail transit or busway systems or develop new capital-intensive facilities. High rates of population and employment growth normally underlie these efforts. Procedures are similar to those used in traditional comprehensive, cooperative, continuing transportation studies (the federal 3C process). *Short-range planning* (usually for a 5-year period) is desirable where administrative, funding, and service charges are contemplated. *Service or operations planning* is an ongoing activity—often on a route or corridor basis—to improve service efficiency and effectiveness as well as to respond to immediate community concerns.

Transit planning studies should assess existing problems and how they are likely to change, identify improvement options, and suggest directions. They should provide essential information for a community's decision makers relative to ridership, costs, performance, and environmental and economic impacts. They should produce transit plans that are compatible with an area's needs, goals, and resources. These studies are necessary wherever major fixed-guideway systems (rail or bus) are implemented. See Chap. 11 for a detailed discussion of this process.

TRANSIT PLANNING AND PUBLIC POLICY

Transit is an important asset to metropolitan areas, especially their city centers. It is logical, therefore, that transit planning be complemented by appropriate public policies to reinforce transit ridership. It does not make good public investment sense to spend a billion dollars on a new fixed-guideway system (rail or bus) and then to undercut its ridership by expanding radial freeway capacity or doubling the downtown parking supply. Furthermore, it does not make sense to let the city's bus system languish while the guideway is being built.

URBAN DEVELOPMENT AND TRANSIT

Urban development and transit decisions should be coordinated to the maximum extent possible. Expanding development in the city center and clustering commercial and residential activities around transit stations will provide both environmental and transportation benefits over the long run. Opportunities for transit-friendly environments also should be realized in newly developing parts of the urban region.

Zoning policies and tax incentives should encourage integrated development corridors in which the transportation facility and its adjacent development are viewed as a total environmental system. This concept has been successfully applied in places like Singapore and Stockholm where new-town developments are keyed to rail transit lines. Conversely, where high-density developments exist, appropriate investments in transit should be encouraged.

Improving the transit orientation of suburban areas is a desired long-range objective. Transitways, and attractive bus terminals where transitways are not practical, are desirable at major activity complexes. (Obviously, many new suburban streets are needed to cope with traffic congestion.)

Residential subdivisions should be transit friendly. Street continuity should be sufficient to allow bus service through larger residential clusters, and adequate pedestrian access to bus stops should be provided (see Fig. 6-10). Clustering of activities in new developments is conducive to good bus service. Ideally, each new subdivision or major commercial development should be checked for its transit service as well as its traffic adequacy. Zoning should be conditional on the provision of suitable transit services. (See also Chap. 6.)

FREEWAYS AND TRANSIT

Radial freeway design and location should be coordinated with public transportation services. In larger cities, this may involve joint multimodal transportation corridors or development in separate corridors. In some settings (such as the penetration of high-density areas), effective rail or bus transitways may reduce the need for freeway development.

Bus priority schemes (for example, ramp metering, reserved bus lanes, special bus ramps) can improve line-haul transit. These are best accomplished by integrally incorporating them into the basic freeway design. Median strips along radial freeways could be reserved for future bus or fixed-guideway rail transit, particularly in urban areas that exceed 1 million persons. Figure 13-4 illustrates the evolutionary development of such a multimodal transportation corridor. (See also Chap. 12.)

PARKING AND TRANSIT

Urban parking policy should complement transit planning decisions. This can be done in two basic ways: (1) provision of extensive park-and-ride facilities along express bus and rail transit lines and (2) managing downtown parking supply and price.

Zoning ordinances in large cities should either prohibit additional off-street parking in the city center or limit the amount of off-street parking for offices. (Boston, Chicago, New York, Portland, San Francisco, and Seattle are among the U. S. cities where such policies have been established.)

In cities with a high dependence on transit, maximum and minimum parking requirements should be established for various parts of the city based upon land-use intensity and proximity to transit. The standards should be realistic, however, and should not inhibit continued development.

Urban transportation policies designed to support transit must be rooted in economic realities. They must be practical and politically viable.

BUS TRANSIT PLANNING

Bus transit planning is mainly service planning. It is short-range and operational, rather than long-range and capital intensive. It involves changes in where, when, and how services run in response to changing land use, travel patterns, and resources.

Most changes in service patterns reflect small-scale, fine-grained adjustments that reflect ridership changes caused by population growth or decline; service to new employment centers, schools, hospitals, shopping centers, and residential areas; service via new streets and expressways; and restructured or reduced service to bring costs and revenues into better balance. In almost every case, the amount of financial support beyond farebox revenues influences the amount and type of service.

STAGE CONSTRUCTION OF
FREEWAY-TRANSIT CORRIDOR

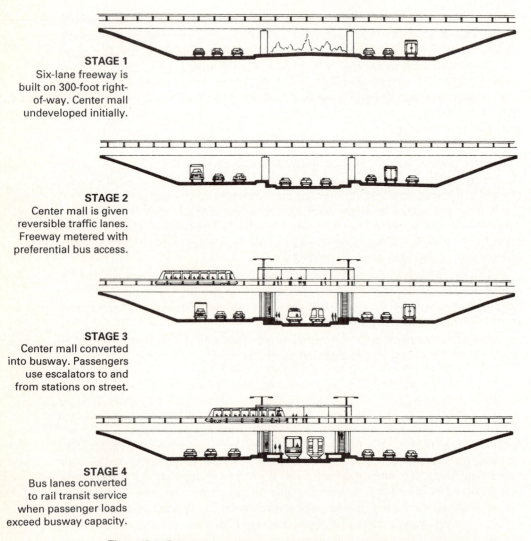

STAGE 1
Six-lane freeway is
built on 300-foot right-
of-way. Center mall
undeveloped initially.

STAGE 2
Center mall is given
reversible traffic lanes.
Freeway metered with
preferential bus access.

STAGE 3
Center mall converted
into busway. Passengers
use escalators to and
from stations on street.

STAGE 4
Bus lanes converted
to rail transit service
when passenger loads
exceed busway capacity.

Figure 13-4 *Evolutionary development of transportation corridor. [Source: Wilbur Smith and Associates,* The Potential for Bus Rapid Transit *(Detroit, Mich.: Automobile Manufacturers Association, 1970), p. 98.]*

Major changes in routes and services come about when (1) urban and regional services are integrated into one system, (2) the service area is expanded to cover surrounding communities, or (3) rail transit, busway, or HOV-lane development allows reorienting of routes.

RELEVANT FACTORS

Bus transit service planning should reflect the specific needs and operating requirements of each urban area. Relevant planning factors include past operating practices and procedures; the current operating authority and system extent; farebox cost-recovery requirements; land use, population density, and employment features; street patterns; and the availability of off-street rail transit. These factors, singly and in combination, influence the pattern of bus services and the opportunities for change and expansion.

Street Patterns

Service planning should recognize the type of city and its basic physical and economic structure; the strength and character of the city center; and the locations of residences, shops, schools, and employment areas. These factors, coupled with the ease or difficulty of driving and parking, influence riding habits and the locations and amount of service. High development densities, concentrated travel corridors, topographic barriers, a growing economy, and strong central areas make for a good transit city. Conversely, low densities, dispersed development, and weak central areas limit ridership.

Street patterns influence service in several ways. First, the presence or absence of suitable streets limits where buses can travel. The lack of suitable streets in many suburban areas makes it difficult to provide effective bus service. Cities with radially developed street patterns have radial bus service with no or limited crosstown routes. Even the large Boston metropolitan area has relatively few crosstown (circumferential) routes because of the restricted street patterns. Conversely, systems with grid street patterns, such as Chicago, Toronto, Los Angeles, and Milwaukee, develop many crosstown bus routes, and passenger transfer becomes an important part of the bus system. Second, the old, established transit routes are often the locations of apartments and retail areas, which are developed in a ribbon along these streets. Moreover, traffic engineering improvements are usually concentrated along arterial streets, making these streets better suited for bus operations.

Rail Transit

The availability of rail transit lines operating on exclusive (or semiexclusive) rights-of-way also influences bus service patterns. The presence of rail transit tends to limit the number of radial bus lines and, in some cases, the amount of express bus service. The rail lines should provide the line-haul part of the trip to the city centers, and the bus routes should feed the rail lines as much as possible. This arrangement can provide faster rides for CBD-based travelers, reduce service duplication, maintain schedule reliability, and minimize operating costs. Cities without rail transit must provide radial line-haul local and express buses. This usually leads to a radial bus pattern, even with a grid street system.

Ridership

Ridership demands also influence route structure and service frequency. Family income, car ownership, and residential and employment density have important bearing on line and system patronage—socioeconomic and land-use variables that are normally outside of the control of the transit operator. Fare structure, system speed and reliability, and the actual service provided, which also affect ridership, can be influenced by operating policy and service planning. In most cities, about two-thirds to three-quarters of all bus trips are made by people without driver's licenses. The proportion of "choice" and "captive" (transit-dependent) riders, however, varies widely by city, route, service type, and time of day.

It is necessary, therefore, to know the types of riders along any route or group of routes. This means identifying the mix of riders by trip purpose (work, shop, school, medical, and so on), time of day (peak, off-peak), and age group (young, school children, adult, elderly). Special travel pattern surveys (such as home interviews) usually are needed for new systems or major route changes. Schedule, ridership, and transfer data can be augmented by on-vehicle rider surveys for existing bus lines.

SERVICE GOALS AND GUIDELINES

Goals and policy guidelines enable transit agencies to plan services and allocate available resources in a consistent, rational, and systematic manner. Guidelines also provide a context for developing detailed service standards and planning criteria and for establishing performance measures. When service policies conflict with economic limitations, funding resources should be administered in the most cost-effective manner.

Goals

Typical underlying community goals are:

- To establish and maintain a network of high-quality urban transit services for residents and visitors.
- To provide access to places of residence, work, school, personal business, shopping, and recreation with the amount and type of service appropriate to each. This goal implies a minimum level of service on routes where minimum acceptable levels of ridership and revenues cannot be realized.
- To decrease auto use by attracting new customers (that is, choice riders),

thereby helping to reduce traffic congestion, air pollution, and energy consumption.

- To provide and ensure reasonable service for elderly, handicapped, young, and low-income people.
- To operate buses in a safe, clean, and comfortable manner.

Corollary goals may include (1) meeting a specified farebox cost-recovery ratio, (2) achieving a specified increase in annual ridership with no increase in employees, (3) maximizing benefits to the regional economy, and (4) contributing to an improved environment.

Service Objectives

The bus system should provide the best possible service to the greatest number of people within the governing economic constraints. Planning must balance the amount and type of services provided with the net cost of service.

Conventional fixed-route bus service should meet the travel needs of most residents in the service area. System design should emphasize bus service to vital activities such as employment, shopping, medical, and education.

A well designed service should have:

1. An up-to-date route system consistent with current demands and understandable to riders.
2. Convenient schedules.
3. Reliable services.
4. Coordinated transfer opportunities.
5. Effective integration with rapid transit systems and other public transportation services and/or systems when they exist.
6. Amenities at bus stops.
7. Reasonable fares.
8. Park-and-ride facilities where appropriate.

Guidelines

The goals and objectives are generally translated into service guidelines and standards. These guidelines give each transit agency a systematic basis for making changes in routes, hours of service, or service frequency. Representative guidelines are summarized in *Bus Route and Schedule Planning Guidelines*.[4]

ROUTES AND SERVICE

Providing the best possible bus service to the greatest number of people calls for carefully relating service to existing and potential markets. Bus services should be concentrated in heavy travel corridors, with the greatest service frequency and route coverage usually provided on approaches to the city center. Route structure should be clear and understandable, and service duplication should be avoided. Changes in bus service must be coordinated with planning and traffic agencies to expedite bus flow and to assure that streets in nearby developing suburban areas are able to accommodate buses. These changes in service should minimize the disruption of existing riding patterns.

Service Area and Route Coverage

Bus service coverage and frequency should reflect the density of the population and the density of the street system. United States and Canadian experience suggests that bus service should be provided where population density exceeds $2000/mi^2$ and ridership exceeds 20 to 25 passengers/bus-h on weekdays, 15 on Saturdays, and 10 on Sundays. Route continuity and transfer requirements may lower these factors.

The actual service area is usually defined by legislation. Within this area, the delineation of areas served or "covered" provides a measure of transit accessibility and a method by which to judge duplicate service. Area coverage expresses the extent of population within a reasonable walking distance. The area within a 5-min walking distance from bus stops is traditionally considered the primary service area, and areas between 5 and 10 min are considered secondary service areas. For park-and-ride facilities, where passengers come by car, longer distances are acceptable. The following general guidelines are suggested:

- 90% of the residences should be within 0.25 mi of a bus stop where population density exceeds 4000 persons/mi^2 or three dwellings per acre.
- 50 to 75% of the population should be within 0.5 mi of a bus stop where population density ranges from 2000 to 4000 persons/mi^2.

These criteria translate into parallel bus routes every 0.5 mi in urban areas and every mile in suburban areas.

The desired spacings of bus routes are not always possible because of the configuration of the street system, the interposition of physical barriers, and the occasional need to reach closer points of heavy passenger travel demand. Thus, the spacing standards for any given transit system are subject to modification where physical barriers (such as unbridged rivers, severe differences in elevation, or lack of cross streets) prevent access to the route and impel a closer spacing. Where the blockage of access is due to lack of cross streets, efforts should be made to have the necessary streets or pedestrian ways opened, because the transit system should not have to bear the cost of adapting to an inadequate street design.

The effect of grades should be considered in evaluating route coverage. A 5-min walk on a level grade, based on 3 mi/h, results in a 0.25 mi walking distance. This distance drops to 1200 ft for an 8% grade and 900 ft for a 14% grade.

Route Structure

Transit routes in smaller communities normally include a few radial lines that meet in the city center. As the size of the service area and system increases, there is a corresponding increase in the number and complexity of the route structure. Large bus systems, in particular, include a combination of radial, circumferential, and grid route structures. Sometimes, as in Pittsburgh, complex or irregular systems emerge due to topographic barriers or irregular street networks. In all cases, the route structure should rationally relate activity centers to residential areas over the available street network. See Chap. 6 for a discussion of the different types of bus route networks.

In general, a few lines with frequent service are preferable to many lines with infrequent service. Operation of similar lines parallel to each other at short distances is a duplication of service and lowers the quality of service. In areas of very low demand, however, it is preferable to reduce the frequency rather than increase separation of lines farther than 1 mi (to avoid poor area coverage). Moreover, if service is infrequent, riders must rely on schedules.

Bus routes in the city center that are concentrated on key streets will give riders a sense of transit identity and a clear idea of the service. Such routes will result in enough use to make a priority treatment feasible. Accordingly, depending on the size of the business district, as many routes as possible should operate on the same street or the same few streets. Unless prevented by a one-way street pattern or by looping requirements, buses should operate in both directions on the same street to simplify routes, improve passenger understanding, and minimize excess bus travel. These factors underscore the desirability of downtown bus malls.

Dispersed routing patterns may be necessary in larger city centers because of dispersed employment areas or capacity limitations on the curb bus lanes. Los Angeles, Washington, D.C., and Manhattan are obvious examples; however, similar conditions exist on a smaller scale in other city centers.

Bus routes entering the city center should be spaced to traverse the center of the area within three city blocks (900 to 1200 ft). The goal is to bring major downtown employment and shopping concentrations to within 600 to 800 ft of a bus stop. Routes generally should cross the entire central area to provide convenient passenger delivery to all points and to minimize bus turns on congested downtown streets. Through routing is often desirable, but buses that must terminate and lay over downtown should pass through the CBD so that their curb layovers are located in less congested areas.

Passengers leaving major CBD activities should be able to board and alight from buses without having to cross major traffic flows.

Express Bus Service

Although most cities of more than 25,000 people can sustain some sort of local bus service, express service generally requires a population of more than 250,000. Express service has greatest potential in metropolitan areas larger than 1 millon, where it may account for 25 to 30% of the total route mileage. Where local routes go beyond 3 mi of the CBD and passenger volumes are great enough (especially for longer trips), express or limited-stop service may complement local service. In addition, the following should be considered:

- The CBD is generally the primary area that can be served successfully by express buses. CBD employment should exceed 30,000. Occasionally a major airport or outlying commercial center can be served, as can special events at stadiums or sports arenas.
- The journeys to and from work usually represent the greatest proportion of express trips, and the system should be designed to meet these demands.
- In cities with rail transit, express buses should not serve the same corridors as the rail lines.
- It is usually easier to draw patronage for a new express bus service from local buses than to get people to shift from automobiles. Where service is competitive with automobile travel, however, some diversion of motorists can be expected.
- Residential population densities must be high enough to generate a full or nearly full bus load with as few local service stops as possible. Unless a strong CBD orientation has been fostered by using express bus (or rail) service in promoting an area's development, a gross density of about 7000 to 10,000 people/mi is usually necessary to support direct express bus service. This density is common in older, small-lot, single-family developments and is found in recent garden apartment and town-house developments. At least 30 potential peak-hour CBD passengers per mile of route appear necessary for direct express bus service to a residential area.
- Park-and-ride lots, needed in suburban areas where densities are too low to generate walk-on traffic, enable express buses to attract riders who might otherwise drive. These lots should be located where off-peak service is provided so that patrons can reach their cars, for example, in case of emergency.
- Buses should operate at or near free-flow traffic conditions for all or most of their trip. The best routes are along busways, freeways, or other roadways where buses can travel quickly without congestion once satisfactory passenger loads are achieved. Express bus service along arterial streets may be desirable where employment and population are clustered at major intersections and there is no freeway in the corridor.
- Express bus service on freeways should be offered in peak periods only, except in very large cities or under unusual circumstances. Express bus service on arterials can be provided during both base and peak periods, although base (midday) service will depend on traffic density.
- Service may operate nonstop in the express zone (typical freeway "closed- door" operations) or limited stop (typical "open door" arterial operations). Where limited-stop service is provided, buses should stop at major transfer points and cross streets but not more often than about every 0.5 mi.
- An attempt should be made to give every passenger a seat, even during the

peak 20-min periods. This is especially important where long (more than 5-mi) nonstop runs operate at relatively high speeds.

- Express and local bus service may be mixed effectively in high-volume corridors (Archer Avenue, Chicago, is one such example; Geary Street, San Francisco, is another). Where the two services operate on the same street or in the same corridor, the express service should provide a means of obtaining better overall passenger distribution and load control in the corridor.
- Express service at spacings closer than 0.5- to 1.0-mi intervals should be discouraged to minimize service duplication.
- Express buses should save at least 5 min over local bus travel. This calls for a minimum 3-mi express bus run from the CBD. The time saved by express buses compared to local buses operating on the same streets is usually 1 to 2 min/mi. Where buses enter the downtown area, every effort should be made to give them preferential treatment to reduce delays and improve service dependability.

The extent to which express runs can draw substantial patronage depends on (1) the size and compactness of the group of transit patrons or potential transit patrons with CBD destinations to be served; (2) the availability of a busway, freeway, other type of limited access highway, or multilane arterial street; (3) a reasonably free flow of traffic on that highway during weekday rush hours; (4) extensive congestion in the area to be bypassed, which makes it rewarding to avoid the surface streets; and (5) the practicality of bypassing a 3-mi annular ring around the CBD without creating demand for uneconomical duplication of bus services and without eroding existing local bus patronage.

Service Coordination

Service coordination implies (1) the ability to transfer freely and conveniently between modes, (2) distinct service areas for each mode, thereby minimizing duplication, (3) adjustments and interrelationships of schedules (especially during midday and evening hours), and (4) joint fare structures. Coordination may take place between urban and suburban carriers, rail and bus transit, and bus and car. It may involve coordination of routes and schedules within a single bus system or between bus and paratransit services. It implies adequate park-and-ride lots at express transit stations and the use of express bus or rail for long line-haul trips.

Convenient and easy transfer between routes and services is the key to effective coordination. The experience of cities with effective transfer facilities (including Atlanta, Boston, Chicago, Cleveland, and Philadelphia in the United States and Edmonton, Vancouver, and Toronto, Canada) indicate that:

- A network of routes can operate much more economically and offer higher frequency of service if transfers are given than if attempts are made to avoid them at all costs.
- Transfer stations can be very efficiently integrated with such facilities as long-

distance terminals, shopping centers, and administrative complexes.
- When transfers are well designed and operated, passenger objections to transferring are diminished. Timed transfers are increasingly popular.
- Transfers simplify service patterns, especially in a grid system.

SERVICE LEVELS

Bus service levels reflect past practices, ridership requirements, and economic constraints. Peak-hour service frequencies generally reflect ridership levels and capacity needs, whereas base-period and evening services often reflect policy headways.

Service Periods

Twenty-four hour service, 7 days per week is normally limited to major systems such as New York, Chicago, Philadelphia, Pittsburgh, San Francisco, and Washington, although many large cities do not provide overnight service. Medium-size cities provide service 7 days a week, usually about 18 hours per day.

In most cities, regular weekday service should be provided from about 6 a.m. to 11 p.m. on weekdays on principal routes. Suburban feeder service should operate from 6 a.m. to 7 p.m., and in some cases only during peak periods. Saturday and Sunday service should be provided on principal routes, although Sunday service may be optional in smaller communities. (See Chap. 6 for a discussion of scheduling.)

Loading Standards

Loading standards should reflect the type of service and time of day. Seats should be available for passengers at all times on freeway express bus service and on local routes during midday and evening periods. Desirable loading standards for local bus service are: peak 30 min, 125 to 160% of seats; peak 60 min, 100 to 140%; transition periods, 100 to 120%.

New Routes and Service Changes

Service changes are initiated in response to requests from the community, metropolitan planning organization (MPO), or transit agency board; as a result of on-going system evaluation by the transit property; or to reflect major changes in the system's financial requirements. Changes should be evaluated by the transit management, including appropriate boards of the transit agency. The flexibility of bus operations makes it easy for transit systems to experiment with service changes without major capital cost expenditures.

Service experiments should be tried for a sufficiently long time to allow ridership patterns to develop and to give riders a sense of route permanence. Trial periods should be at least 6 months long.

Because of funding constraints, bus service extensions and changes in the United

States normally follow development. This contrasts with some Canadian and European experience, where bus service often precedes development. When bus transit comes first, it has the opportunity to help shape the development and establish the riding habit. In some recent major developments, the community has required that the developer bear the cost of providing timely bus service.

Service Planning Process

Bus service planning is a short-range process that is usually done on a route-by-route basis. Therefore, many of the procedures developed for analysis of major transit investments usually do not apply.

Planning service changes involves estimates of costs, revenues, and community benefits associated with new, expanded, or restructured bus routes. The key steps include (1) reviewing characteristics of the service area—including the physical feasibility of the proposed bus routes, (2) estimating ridership, (3) estimating revenues, (4) simulating bus travel times, (5) estimating service requirements and costs, and (6) assessing economic performance. These steps are outlined in Fig. 13-5.

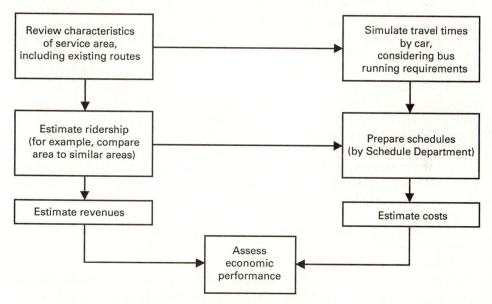

Figure 13-5 *Generalized procedure for planning new bus routes. [Source: Transportation Research Board,* Bus Route and Schedule Planning Guidelines, *NCHRP Synthesis of Highway Practice 69 (Washington, D.C.: Transportation Research Board, May 1980).]*

The analysis of the territory to be served should consider (1) the density and distribution of income and age structure of the population; (2) the nature of the terrain and the available street pattern, with particular regard to the suitability of the bus service; and (3) locations of employment, retail and recreational areas, hospitals and medical centers, churches, and schools. Aerial surveys provide a useful tool for quick analysis.

After examining the existing route structure, service concepts for the proposed change should be prepared. These concepts should be checked in the field for their practicality. Consideration should be given to (1) how the route serves the areas of passenger generation, (2) potential interchange points with other bus and rail lines, (3) adequacy of the street system, (4) ability to turn buses back at the end of the line, (5) opportunities to provide terminal facilities for drivers, and (6) adequacy of bus stops. Bus running times should be simulated in the field.

Ridership Estimates

Potential new patrons are perhaps the most important criterion for deciding to make a route or service change. A variety of ridership estimation techniques has been developed to assess the effects of various road and transit system changes. Most of these techniques explicitly or implicitly use such factors as car ownership (or income and residential population density), employment density, and relative travel times and costs by bus and car. But they vary widely in ease of application, treatment of parameters, precision afforded, and responsiveness to fine-grained service changes. From the perspective of most transit operations, the best available estimating techniques are as much art as science, but they can be effectively applied by an experienced transit planner.

Long-range transportation planning studies derive relations based on modal choice models that relate *disutilities* (car–bus travel times and costs) to choice and dependent users. The current state-of-the-art involves logit modal choice curves, which can be applied on a network basis to person-travel between zones. These techniques apply to large-scale, long-range changes in system capabilities, but they are not suited to short-range, small-scale service changes.

Elasticity relations have been used to estimate the effects of fare and service frequency changes on ridership of existing routes. *Fare elasticity* (change in ridership per unit change in fares) has ranged from -0.1 to more than -0.5, depending on market segment and trip purpose. Fare elasticities of about -0.15 to -0.20 have been found in recent years for several medium-size bus systems. Headway elasticities have been found to range from -0.3 to -0.8, which implies that a 100% increase in headways would result in a 30 to 80% drop in patronage.

Transit agencies have traditionally estimated ridership by analogy methods that compare a route under consideration with ridership on a similar route in terms of service, land-use, and demographic characteristics.

Ridership estimation includes the following steps for each route under consideration:

1. Estimate the dwelling units and population within the coverage area, preferably by block. This may include use of census data, mail drops by zip code area, or analysis of aerial photographs.
2. Estimate the nature of the area. This includes median family income, type and

age of dwelling units, and car ownership.

3. Conduct telephone surveys as needed to identify market and travel attitudes and patterns.
4. Apply the *riding habit* (daily or annual rides per capita) to the population base to obtain ridership potentials for residential areas served.
5. Identify schools, shopping centers, offices, and industries within the service area. Obtain estimates of enrollment, employment, places of residence, and probable travel modes. Estimate the ridership potential of these activities and add it to the residential ridership identified in step 4.

IMPROVING BUS MOVEMENT

System and service planning should encourage high bus speeds, since an increase in speeds benefits both the transit passenger and operator. Higher speeds give the passenger a more attractive ride and, in some cases, may attract new riders. They benefit the transit agency by increasing driver and vehicle productivity, reducing fleet size, and cutting costs.

High bus speeds may be attained by (1) reducing the number of stops, (2) reducing the dwell times at stops, (3) improving traffic conditions along the route, and (4) giving buses priority over other traffic.

Reducing Time at Stops

Bus dwell times can be reduced by providing multiple-berth stops, fare prepayment at major boarding points, use of exact fares (preferably single-coin fares), auxiliary fare collection personnel that board passengers through the rear door, and use of honor fare systems. Wider, double-channel entrance and exit doors can expedite passenger loading. To expedite CBD bus boarding, several systems (for example, Pittsburgh and Seattle) use a pay-as-you-enter system for inbound trips and a pay-as-you-leave system for outbound trips.

Reducing Traffic Delays

Effective traffic engineering along bus routes will benefit overall bus movement. At many locations, turn controls, parking restrictions, especially during peak hours, widened radii, and intersection channelization will allow buses to operate more effectively. Enforcement of parking restrictions with prompt towing of illegally parked vehicles is especially desirable.

Giving Buses Priority

Bus priority measures have proved successful in rationalizing street use and reducing bus travel times. Most priority measures involve normal-flow curb bus lanes on city streets. A growing number of cities, however, have provided reserved bus lanes on freeways, often for use by carpools as well. Houston, for example, has instituted an extensive series of such transitways, complete with large park-and-ride lots from which express buses run nonstop to the city center.

Busways in Ottawa, Canada, Los Angeles, and Pittsburgh provide stations and, in many respects, operate similarly to light rail lines. Buses operate in mixed traffic in residential areas and then run local or express on the busway to the city center, which they traverse via reserved bus lanes. Seattle has a CBD bus tunnel, which connects directly to bus lanes along I-5. Because the guideway sections form only over part of the overall bus route, the investment cost is less than would be needed for rail transit.

Busways, transitways, and priority lanes properly applied can produce major time savings. Their successful implementation requires a reasonable concentration of bus services, a high degree of bus and car congestion, community willingness to enforce the lanes, and overall support of public transportation services. Planning calls for a realistic assessment of demands, costs, benefits, and impacts.

RAIL TRANSIT PLANNING

Many types of rail transit operate in cities throughout the world. Their arrangements, designs, and operations reflect when they were built and the environment in which they operate. The more common systems include commuter rail, rail rapid transit, and light rail transit (discussed in Chap. 5) and automated guideway transit (discussed in Chap. 24).

The differences among these systems mainly reflect degree of access control, amount of automation, method of operation (including fare collection, train consist length, station frequency), and vehicle design. The fully automated systems *must* be completely grade separated, while the other technologies may permit grade crossings, or in some cases, running in mixed traffic.

REASONS FOR RAIL TRANSIT

The main reasons for building a new urban rail transit line or other fixed-guideway system are to improve the movement of people in a densely developed area in an environmentally attractive manner, to increase the CBD orientation of residential areas, to provide transportation capacity for future growth, and to strengthen the city center. (Many of these reasons also apply to bus rapid transit systems that provide similar alignment and performance.)

Rail transit services operating mainly or completely on exclusive rights-of-way can provide fast, dependable service, especially during peak periods. They can help structure urban development to permit more intensive development in the city center, and they provide radial transportation capacities that cannot be achieved by highways and surface transit. These benefits often offset the long lead times and high development costs.

Rail transit is especially important where public transportation delivers a large number of peak-hour trips to the city center. It enables the CBD to be built upward rather than outward without unnecessary street and parking requirements. Rapid transit and commuter railroads are the main means of traveling to or from the downtown areas in most large cities. They account for more than half of all peak-hour entrants into downtown New York, Chicago, Philadelphia, and Boston.

Rail transit complements (or supplements) freeways in major travel corridors. It can penetrate areas where freeway construction is difficult, impractical, or impossible. It can provide high peak-hour capacities in the radial corridors that lead to the city center without extensive land-taking for streets and parking. Thus, in some cases, it can reduce radial freeway capacity requirements and the extent of freeway construction.

Rail transit reduces travel times to the city center. Operating speeds range from 20 to 35 mi/h on most rapid transit systems, as compared with 10 to 20 mi/h by surface mixed-traffic transit. This time saving serves to increase the downtown orientation of outlying parts of metropolitan areas located near transit stops.

Rail transit is sometimes perceived as symbolic of a modern metropolis. More significantly, the permanence of the right-of-way provides a basis for investment along the line. The extent of this investment depends upon market forces and incentives provided by the community.

PLANNING NEW SYSTEMS

The geography of each urban area should help determine the type, location, extent, and design of rail transit. The goals should be to (1) maximize ridership, (2) facilitate efficient operations, (3) maximize development impacts, and (4) minimize construction costs.

The various lines should serve the corridors that produce the maximum patronage. Frequently, but not always, these are the corridors of existing transit ridership. Availability and costs of right-of-way, however, may require modifications in optimum alignment to cut costs and build an affordable system. Use of freeway medians and rail rights-of-way and minimizing underground construction may be desirable to cut costs.

System Extent

There is no simple formula for determining how far a proposed rail line should extend. Political, market, and physical factors and operating conditions influence the location and length of line. The following guidelines emerge from the differing perspectives on the desired length of line.

1. It should be as short as possible to provide the desired service and attract the needed ridership. Once the line is opened and its ridership is established, it can be extended.
2. It should be long enough to provide a "few good stations" at its outer end that will develop the desired ridership.

3. It should extend out far enough so that sufficient park-and ride facilities can be provided at outer stations.
4. It should serve existing markets, and it should capture new markets as well.

It is important to determine the extent that a new line should serve existing demands versus capturing new markets. Ideally, both the coverage of the system and the spacing of stations should capture *both* markets. At minimum, new lines should extend beyond the limit of existing urban development, and right-of-way should be preserved for subsequent extensions as land is developed. Experience with rail transit developments in U.S. and Canadian cities indicates that many of today's most successful lines and markets did *not* exist when the lines were built.

Typically, rail lines in North American cities should extend about 12 to 20 mi distance from the city center. Because speed is essential, corresponding travel times should not exceed 30 to 40 min. Rail transit speeds should compare favorably with freeway automobile speeds; otherwise, both passenger attraction and the long-term value of the service will be limited.

For maximum development impact, lines should extend beyond the built-up area. This is apparent from the evolving population density profiles shown in Fig. 13-6. Residential densities in New York, Chicago, Philadelphia, and Boston clearly reflect the result of rail transit development during the first half of the twentieth century. In all these cities, the patterns were similar. Rail transit lines had their greatest impact around station areas located *farthest* from the city center, which were previously undeveloped and unserved by public transport. Settlement generally was as close to stations as land availability allowed; impacts were much less in already built-up areas.

Neighborhoods change along rail lines over time. When transit serves built-up areas, there is a slight growth that is often followed by a decline. The peak ridership at a particular station usually occurs about 5 to 10 years after the line is opened. In contrast, when an unbuilt area is served, ridership may grow dramatically for a 10- to 15-year period before the neighborhood and ridership stabilize. (See Fig. 13-7.)

System Configuration and Design

Desirable (and undesirable) aspects of rapid transit system configuration and design are shown in Fig. 13-8. They reflect the following guidelines:

1. *Radial character*. Rail transit lines should radiate outward from the city center. Crosstown or circumferential lines should be avoided. United States and Canadian experience indicates that about 75% of all rapid transit riders begin or end their trips in the CBD (or travel through the city center).
2. *Market penetration*. Rail transit lines should penetrate, rather than skirt, major market areas such as high-density residential neighborhoods, schools, medical centers, and outlying business areas. This makes it possible to augment the home-to-CBD work-trip ridership base.

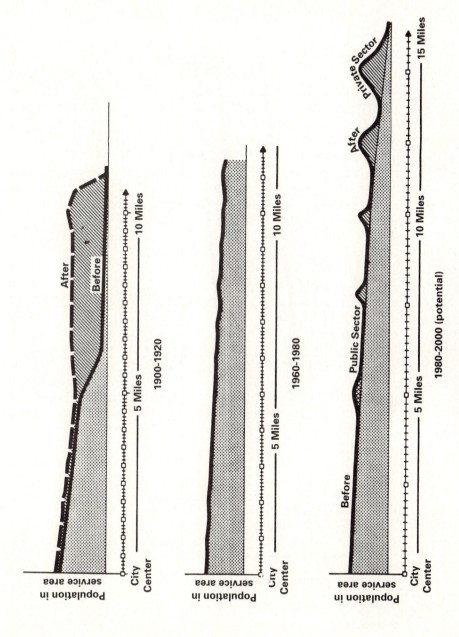

Figure 13-6 *Residential density profiles along rail transit line.*

395

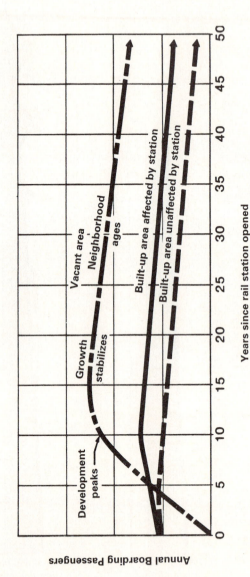

Annual Boarding Passengers

Years since rail station opened

Development
peaks

Growth
stabilizes

Vacant area
Neighborhood
ages

Built-up area affected by station

Built-up area unaffected by station

Figure 13-7 *Generalized effects of urban change on rail transit ridership over time.*

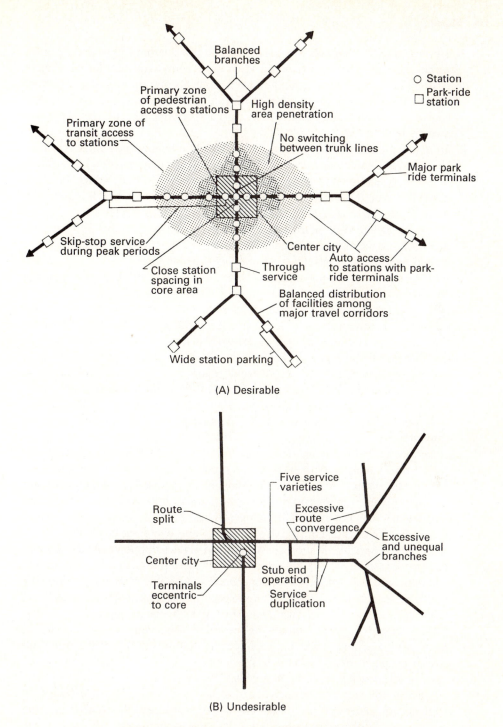

(A) Desirable

○ Station
□ Park-ride station

Balanced branches

Primary zone of pedestrian access to stations

High density area penetration

No switching between trunk lines

Primary zone of transit access to stations

Major park ride terminals

Skip-stop service during peak periods

Center city

Auto access to stations with park-ride terminals

Close station spacing in core area

Through service

Balanced distribution of facilities among major travel corridors

Wide station parking

(B) Undesirable

Five service varieties

Route split

Excessive route convergence

Excessive and unequal branches

Center city

Stub end operation

Terminals eccentric to core

Service duplication

Figure 13-8 *Rapid transit route configuration concepts.*

3. *Through service*. Through routing patterns are preferable to terminating lines within the city center: (a) they provide a more convenient ride for passengers passing through the center, (b) they avoid problems of train storage and turning trains back, (c) they achieve a better line utilization by directions, and (d) they enable one underground tunnel to serve two corridors, thereby capitalizing on a costly investment.

4. *Minimum branches and switching*. Routes should minimize the number of branches. A single route per track simplifies scheduling, equalizes train loads, maximizes service reliability and capacity, and is easiest to understand. In some cases, however, it is necessary to operate several lines on a route. It is generally desirable to provide a maximum of two branches per route. The branches should be balanced in their route lengths and service requirements. Thus, a 4-min peak service on each branch would result in 2-min trunk-line service. There should be minimum switching between major trunk lines.

5. *High speeds*. Portal-to-portal speeds between the city center and outlying areas should be comparable to those by automobile. High operating speeds require good geometric design standards (grades, curvature, grade separation), high-performance cars, and comparatively long distances between stops. Distances between stops can be increased by (a) wide spacing between stations, such as on Chicago's Dan Ryan and Skokie Swift routes; (b) express and local services, such as on New York City's major trunk routes; and (c) alternate or skip-stop services, such as on Philadelphia's Market–Frankford line and Chicago's North–South route. Several speed-related concerns relate specifically to light rail transit. These concerns include identifying when and where to grade separate; the type of protection needed for at-grade intersections, signal preemption opportunities; treatment, design, and operation in on-street reservations; analyses of impacts to street traffic; and methods of signal control. Ideally, the amount of street running should be less than 25% of the total route mileage. (Street running in the city center should not produce a time loss of more than 4 to 5 min over off-street operations.) Single-track operations should be avoided since they limit service frequency and operating flexibility.

6. *Wide station spacing*. Station spacing should reflect development density and likely modes of arrival to stations. Relatively close station spacing is desirable where people walk to stations; wider spacing is desirable when people arrive by bus or drive to stations. Representative spacing by modes of arrival are walking, 0.5 mi; bus, 0.5 to 1 mi; and automobile, 2 to 3 mi. In general, the widest station spacing possible should be provided. The wide station spacing is necessary to achieve high line-haul speeds. Station spacing of 0.5 to 0.7 mi results in speeds of 20 to 25 mi/h; spacing of 1 mi, 30- to 35-mi/h speeds; and spacing of 2 mi, 40- to 45-mi/h speeds.

7. *Ample station access*. Attractive pedestrian access should be provided to stations, especially within medium- and high-density areas. Convenient bus–rail interchange is necessary where bus lines serve stations. Facilities may range from a simple bus stop adjacent to a station entrance, to an elaborate bus

terminal (for example, Jefferson Park, Chicago). The Toronto Transit Commission designs its major rail–bus interchange facilities to permit barrier-free transfer between bus and rail lines.

Park-and-ride facilities are essential along rail lines in suburban areas. Experience with existing park-and-ride lots and garages indicates that occupancies often exceed capacity; in these cases, transit ridership is inhibited by the lack of parking.

Facilities range in size from small lots along Cleveland's Shaker Heights rapid transit lines to the 2500-car parking garages located along the Massachusetts Bay Transportation Authority Red Line in Braintree and Quincy. When more than 2000 spaces are required, garages should be provided to keep walking distances less than 1000 feet.

8. *Maximum operational efficiency.* System layout and design should permit maximum operational efficiency. Yards and shops should be placed at strategic locations (the end of line). Frequent crossovers and turn-back opportunities should be provided. Automation should be used to the maximum extent possible in train operation, service monitoring, fare collection, and train control.

The downtown end of the rail transit trip offers an excellent opportunity for time savings over automobile travel. It is essential, therefore, to maximize service convenience by placing routes through areas of heavy demand, providing frequent stations, and interconnecting stations and mezzanines with major pedestrian movement corridors. To the maximum extent possible, facilities should serve as their own distributors, thereby minimizing transfers to other transit vehicles or changes in travel mode.

OPERATIONS PLANNING

Rail transit operations are affected by the system layout and ridership patterns and by work rules. Operations are also influenced by past practices and the institutional setting: is the rail system run as an independent entity or is it coordinated with the bus system?

Service Periods

Systems may operate around the clock, from early morning to late evening, or just during peak hours. The choice depends upon precedent, local policy, and system design. When systems are shut down overnight, provisions must be made for securing stations.

Fare Collection

Most of the older rapid transit and LRT systems utilize a flat fare, payable at stations or on vehicles upon entering. Fares are paid to station attendants, turnstiles, or directly to fareboxes on vehicles. Zone fares are limited to a few long trips on special services. Commuter rail lines, in contrast, utilize a zone fare system, with peak-period schedules often keyed to the zones to facilitate ticket collection; traditionally, tickets are purchased from station attendants and collected on trains.

The newer rapid transit systems utilize automatic farecards, which are keyed to zone fares. New LRT lines (Los Angeles, Portland, Sacramento, Santa Clara, San Diego) also utilize zone fares. Tickets are obtained from fare vending machines, and there is no on-vehicle fare collection; an honor system is used, with random on-board inspection for compliance.

Service Patterns

A single service per route is the preferred service pattern. A single service simplifies schedules, assures uniform intervals between trains, equalizes train loads, and is the easiest for riders to understand. Many lines have branches, however, and require more than one service per track. For rail rapid transit systems, there generally should not be more than two services per trunk-line route. This restriction can be relaxed for LRT and commuter rail services.

LRT lines generally have all trains make all stops. Many commuter rail lines operate zone express service, especially during peak periods, because headways are relatively long. Sometimes different services are scheduled on the same track.

Most North American rapid transit lines have all trains stop at each station along a route. New York City, Chicago, and Philadelphia, however, utilize zone express service on three- and four-track lines and skip-stop service on two-track lines. The skip-stop operation lets alternate trains serve lightly used stations; all trains serve major stops. This operation speeds service for most riders and equalizes train loads. (See Table 13-4.)

TABLE 13-4
Comparison of Skip-Stop and Zone Express Service

Mode	Advantages/Disadvantages
Skip-stop	Balances passenger loads on trains.
	May pose problems of speed difference with short headways.
Zone express	Needs multiple tracks in same direction (except where headways are long).
	Facilitates ticket collection on trains.
	Increases transfer between services.

Train Length

The length of train consists can remain the same throughout the entire period of operation, with intervals between trains varied to reflect variations in ridership. This policy (used by the New York City Transit Authority, the Toronto Transit Commission, and BART) works well where ridership is high; it also avoids the need to couple and uncouple trains.

Where rail ridership is light, however, it is desirable to maintain frequent service. This may call for tailoring the train consist length to the ridership demand. (Examples of systems changing train length throughout the day include Boston, Chicago, Cleveland, and Philadelphia.)

FLEET AND CAPACITY REQUIREMENTS

Most transit agencies are concerned with (1) the number of rail cars or buses needed to serve passengers on a given transit line at the maximum load point or section and (2) the ability to accommodate these cars at major passenger boarding points or interlocking points. Capacity standards and computational approaches vary among properties.

FLEET REQUIREMENTS

The number of rail cars or buses that are required depends upon (1) the peak passenger demand, (2) the car or bus size and seating arrangement, (3) the passenger loading standard per vehicle, (4) the number of cars per train, and (5) the round-trip travel time. Computational steps are as follows:

1. *Apply passenger loading standards*. Each transit agency has its own standard for vehicle loading. This standard reflects the size of vehicle, number of seats, area available for standees, and allowable space per standee. Commuter rail lines generally base car requirements on seated loads. Subway and LRT services normally allow standees and base service requirements on *schedule design loads*—approximately 2 passengers/ft of car length. *Crush capacity*—about 3 passengers/ft of car length—should *not* be used for scheduling or planning purposes. Because it is not possible to load all cars of a train equally, under schedule design loads, some cars will operate at crush capacities. Examples of rail loading standards are as follows:

   • The Metropolitan Atlanta Rapid Transit Authority, Georgia, uses 4.25 ft^2/passenger as a basis for estimating the number of cars needed.
   • Pushkarev, in *Urban Rail in America*,[5] suggests 5.4 ft^2/passenger.
   • The *1985 Highway Capacity Manual*[6] suggests 5.0 ft^2/passenger for level of service D, and 3.3 to 3.0 ft^2/passenger for the maximum scheduled load.
   • Fruin (Chap. 8) states that 2.3 ft^2/passenger is the absolute value used for scheduling services by the New York Transit Authority.

2. *Compute minimum headways.* The peak-hour, peak-direction passenger demand at the maximum load point or section, related to the specified loading standard, determines the number of rail cars needed. The *number of* cars per train is dependent on length of platforms and is established by the transit agency, based upon operating policy for the number of trains per hour. (Commuter rail trains may range up to fourteen 85-ft cars; rail transit trains range from six to ten cars, with 400 to 600 ft as a typical train length; LRT trains may range up to four cars).

Given the peak rate of passenger flow and the passenger capacity of individual transit vehicles, the required headway can be determined as follows:

$$h = \frac{60nc}{p \ \max} \qquad (13\text{-}2)$$

where c =   passenger capacity of individual cars (persons/car)
n =   the number of vehicles or cars per transit unit (n is 1 for a single unit)
$p \max$ =   peak flow rate (persons/h)
h =   headway between individual trains (min)

It is important to assure that this headway can be maintained at critical points along the line. United States and Canadian experience indicates that up to 30 rapid transit trains per track per hour can be accommodated assuming block signal control. (When trains become overloaded and dwell times increase, this figure may drop to about 26 to 28). A maximum of 20 commuter rail trains per track per hour can be accommodated. Current experience suggests that 60 to 90 LRT cars per track per hour can be accommodated. The precise number of LRT trains depends upon train length, method of CBD distribution (on- versus off-street), and traffic and/or block signal controls. CBD bus lanes can carry 80 to 100 buses/h.

3. *Estimate fleet size.* Once the headways have been computed, estimating fleet size is straightforward. It can be done by tracing individual vehicles on a time–space or "string" diagram or computed by formula. It also can be estimated from the relationship shown in Eq. (13-3). The values derived by this formula should be increased by the number of trains waiting in the terminal and by about 10% for spare cars.

$$N = \frac{n(2L)(60)}{Vh} \qquad (13\text{-}3)$$

where N = number of rail cars or buses needed
n = cars/train (n = 1 for buses)
V = average speed (mi/h)
L = length of line (mi)
h = headway (min)

CAPACITY ESTIMATES

The passenger capacity of a rail or bus line is the product of the *vehicle flow rate* (the number of vehicles per hour past the busiest stop or other point of constriction) and the *load factor* (the number of passengers per vehicle that could be carried). Capacity is influenced by (1) passenger capacity of individual vehicles at the designated loading standard, (2) minimum possible headway or time spacing between successive trains, and (3) the number of tracks and station platforms.

The minimum possible headway is influenced by the signal control system, the passenger service times at the busiest CBD and terminal stations or stops, and the constraints posed by junctions and interlocking points. For light rail systems with street running and buses, street traffic and traffic signal controls should be considered.

Equation (13-4) is a general formula for estimating the capacity of a transit line.

$$c_p = \frac{(g/c)(3600)nSR}{(g/c)D + t_c} \qquad (13\text{-}4)$$

where c_p = people/h/track (or lane)
t_c = clearance between successive trains (or buses)
D = dwell time at major stops
S = passengers/car
n = cars/train (for buses use n_b = number of effective berths/stop)
R = reductive factor to account for variations in dwell times and arrival variations (0.833 for on-street; 0.90 to 0.95 for off-street operation)
g/c = green/signal cycle (1.00 for off-street operations)
h = headway between successive trains (or buses) = $(g/c)D + t_c$

This formula shows how important it is to maximize the number of passengers accommodated per unit and to minimize the dwell times at stops. Each of these factors has important bearing on vehicle design and operation. (See references 6 and 7 for further details on estimating transit capacities.)

SUMMARY

This chapter contains guidelines for transportation system and service planning. It indicates how transit can service and shape urban development and how factors such as population and employment density, car ownership, and parking costs influence the demand and role of public transportation in today's metropolis.

Public transportation works best where travel is concentrated in space and time. Thus, CBD employment levels and residential population densities define the roles of the various types of transit. Equally important is the need for public policy decisions that reinforce transit ridership, especially where major new systems are planned.

Bus service planning should reflect the specific needs, operating requirements, and financial constraints of each urban area. The underlying goal is to provide the best possible service to the greatest number of people at least total cost and least adverse impact.

The chapter shows when, where, and how rail transit systems should be developed. It stresses the importance of high-speed radial routes and services that can compete favorably with the automobile in terms of speed and reliability. Finally, it sets forth procedures for estimating fleet requirements and transit capacities.

REFERENCES

1   HERBERT S. LEVINSON, "Coordinating Transport and Urban Development," *ITCC Review*, no. 4 (10) (October 1976) [Tel Aviv Association of Engineers and Architects in Israel].

2   BORIS S. PUSHKAREV AND JEFFREY M. ZUPAN, *Public Transportation and Land Use Policy*, a Regional Plan Association Book (Bloomington, Ind.: Indiana University Press, 1977).

3   HERBERT S. LEVINSON, "Modal Choice and Public Policy," in *Engineering Issues, ASCE Journal of Professional Activities*, 99, no. PP1 (January 1973), pp. 65-75.

4   TRANSPORTATION RESEARCH BOARD, *Bus Route and Schedule Planning Guidelines*, NCHRP Synthesis of Highway Practice 69 (Washington, D.C.: Transportation Research Board, May 1980).

5   BORIS PUSHKAREV, WITH JEFFREY M. ZUPAN AND ROBERT S. CUMELLA, *Urban Rail in America: An Exploration of Criteria for Fixed-Guideway Transit* (Bloomington, Ind.: Indiana University Press, 1982).

6   TRANSPORTATION RESEARCH BOARD, *Highway Capacity Manual*, Special Report 209 (Washington, D.C.: Transportation Research Board, 1985).

7   VUKAN R. VUCHIC, *Urban Public Transportation Systems and Technology* (Englewood Cliffs, N.J.: Prentice-Hall, Inc., 1981).

FURTHER READING

Canadian Transit Handbook (2nd ed.). Toronto, Canada: Canadian Urban Transit Association and the Roads and Transportation Association of Canada, 1985.

CHARLES RIVER ASSOCIATES, INC., AND HERBERT S. LEVINSON, *Characteristics of Urban Transportation Demand—An Update* (rev. ed.), prepared for UMTA, Technology Sharing Program, Report no. DOT-T-88-18. Washington, D.C.: U.S. Department of Transportation, July 1988.

FIELDING, GORDON J., *Managing Public Transportation Strategically: A Comprehensive Approach to Strengthening Service and Monitoring Performance*. San Francisco, Calif.: Jossey-Bass Publishers, 1987.

——, "Transit in American Cities," in *The Geography of Urban Transportation*, ed. Susan Hanson. New York: The Guilford Press, 1986.

JACOBS, MICHAEL, ROBERT E. SKINNER, AND ANDREW C. LEMER, *Transit Project Planning Guidance: Estimation of Transit Supply Parameters*, prepared by the Transportation Systems Center for UMTA. Washington, D.C.: Urban Mass Transportation Administration, October 1984.

LEVINSON, HERBERT S., CROSBY L. ADAMS, AND WILLIAM F. HOEY, *Bus Use of Highways: Planning and Design Guidelines*, NCHRP 153. Washington, D.C.: Transportation Research Board, 1975.

MAYWORM, PATRICK, ARMANDO M. LAGO, AND J. MATTHEW McENROE, *Patronage Impacts of Changes in Transit Fares and Services*, prepared for U.S. DOT, Office of Methods and Demonstrations, Report no. 1205-UT. Washington, D.C.: U.S. Department of Transportation, 1980.

TRANSPORTATION SYSTEMS CENTER, *Urban Rail Transit Projects: Forecast versus Actual Ridership and Cost*, prepared for UMTA. Washington, D.C.: Urban Mass Transportation Administration, October 1989.

VUCHIC, VUKAN R., AND OTHERS, *Transit Operating Manual*. Harrisburg, Pa.: Pennsylvania Department of Transportation, 1976.

WHITE, PETER R., *Public Transport, Its Planning, Management and Operation*. London: Hutchison, 1986.

EXERCISES

13-1   Discuss the desirability of developing a rail transit system in Phoenix, Arizona, based upon the guidelines set forth in this chapter and Chap. 11. CBD employment is estimated at 35,000, and 1980 population, area, and density characteristics were as follows:

	City	Urbanized Area
Population	789,704	1,409,279
Land area (mi^2)	324	641
Density (persons/mi^2)	2437	2199

13-2   Transportation planning studies for a proposed LRT line that will have considerable grade separation, but with no tunnels, showed a volume of 15,000 riders per day. The line would be 15 mi long, and the average trip length would be 7.5 mi. Comment on the desirability of this line based upon the criteria set forth in Table 13-3.

13-3   The fare elasticity for local bus service has declined from about -0.30 in 1950 to about -0.20 in 1990. Cite the reasons for this decline.

13-4   An urban bus line carries 10,000 riders per day. The fare charge is $1.00. If the fare is increased to $1.25, what would be the change in daily ridership and revenues?

13-5   Estimate the number of LRT cars needed to carry a peak load of 7500 passengers/h in 2-car trains. Assume that each car can carry a maximum of 150 people and that 15% spare cars should be provided.

13-6   A bus lane on a CBD street provides the equivalent of two effective berths at each major stop. Assuming 60 passengers/bus, a g/c ratio of 0.6, a dwell time of 60 s, and 15 s clearance between buses, how many people/h can the bus lane accommodate?

13-7   Conduct a speed-and-delay study of a bus line. Estimate the amount of time spent moving, in traffic delays, and at bus stops. What actions should be taken to improve speeds?

13-8   Develop a service pattern and schedule for the line profile shown in the following table. Assume 43-passenger buses and an acceptable load factor of 1.4.

P.M. Peak-Hour Line Profile for a Hypothetical Bus Route
(passengers/hour)

Section	Distance (mi)	On	Off	On bus
A (CBD)	0.0	600	0	
A - B	1.0	0	100	500
B - C	2.0	50	150	400
C - D	3.0	30	200	230
D - E	4.0	20	50	200
E - F	5.0	25	50	175
F - G	6.0	25	100	100
G - H	7.0	0	100	0

Chapter 14

RURAL PUBLIC TRANSPORTATION

Peter Schauer

This chapter traces the history of rural public transportation, presents issues that are critical to the planning and design of rural services, and concludes with models for evaluation of rural public transit. Rural public transit services are those transit services that are provided in rural or small urban areas with under 50,000 population and are open to the public, as opposed to closed-door special client services. Rural public transportation for the purposes of this chapter does not include air, rail, intercity bus, or private auto transportation.

Rural public transportation is characterized less by the scale or magnitude of individual projects than by unique operating strategies in specific geographic planning areas. Rural public transportation in one area of a state may mean a small fixed-route service operating on 20-min headways. Yet, in another area of the same state, rural public transportation may involve the local senior citizens center station wagon, with volunteer drivers, that takes people on trips with headways of days for life-support shopping and medical services. The range of services are illustrated by the following descriptions.

- The Community Action Agency, Mercer County, West Virginia, provided individuals with automobiles and they, in turn, were responsible for transporting others.[1]
- New Castle, Indiana, (population 20,056), operates seven vehicles in fixed-route service.[2]
- In 1974 West Virginia initiated a statewide Transportation Remuneration Incentive Program (TRIP) based on a user-side subsidy similar to food stamps.[3]

While at least one rural public transportation service started about 1860 (the

Kernville Stage and Freightlines, a private operation in California),[4] the majority of the current rural public transit systems have been established since about 1960. Many services were funded through the Older Americans Act of 1965 and the Office of Economic Opportunity's Community Action Program. In a 1976 study of 75 projects, it was found that 35 had received subsidies from the Office of Economic Opportunity and 23 had received federal funds for the elderly.[5] In a 1989 study, it was found that of 1161 rural transit providers in the United States, 57% received some social service funding and of that group 41% received funds from programs for the elderly.[6] Most of the early rural transportation systems were not-for-profit providers or public agencies, and this arrangement continued through 1990, with approximately 57% of all rural systems operated by a public agency, 41% operated by a not-for-profit agency, and 2% operated by for-profit companies.[7]

The not-for-profit agencies' interest in transportation traditionally focused on identifying the need for services. These same agencies, however, frequently lacked planning and operation capabilities. In the West Virginia TRIP, this weakness was identified as a major problem.[8] Deficient planning and operational expertise caused some defective initial service design and operational errors in early (1960s) projects. Almost all the early projects intended to become self-supporting in some fashion— through fares from riders, through contracts with public or private groups, or through a continuing commitment of operating subsidies from a state or local government.[9] One program, for example, established a sequence of five operational goals for each new route as follows:

1. Operating revenue equal to driver wages.
2. Operating revenue equal to driver wages plus variable costs.
3. Operating revenue equal to driver wages plus variable costs plus operation costs minus depreciation.
4. Nonoperating revenue plus operating revenue equal to total costs minus depreciation.
5. Nonoperating revenue plus operating revenue equal to total costs.[10]

While these goals are admirable and undoubtedly helped guide the program in a sensible fashion, the realities of providing service in an environment characterized as "high need and low demand"[11] meant that the ultimate goal, to become self-supporting, was unrealistic. In 1974, assessment of a selected group of systems revealed that few had succeeded in becoming self-supporting.[12] Lack of monetary success coupled with the social service advocacy base of the systems started a movement in the early 1970s to secure federal subsidies to offset system deficits. These efforts resulted in Section 147 of the 1973 Federal-Aid Highway Act, enacted to implement rural transportation demonstration projects. In 1978 the United States Congress enacted Section 18 of the Urban Mass Transportation Act. The Section 18 program established a formula grant program for areas other than urbanized areas larger than 50,000 population. Section 18 required a minimum 50% local match for operation subsidies and a minimum 20% match for capital and project administration. (See also Chap. 3.)

The importance of the link between rural public transportation and social services was affirmed in 1985 when an amendment to the Urban Mass Transportation Act allowed contract revenue (monies secured through contracts for services with social services agencies, cities, towns, and others) to be used as local match on Section 18. This meant that federal funds could be utilized in certain contract situations to match Section 18 federal funds. The amendment lessened the burden on local government for match, and it also encouraged additional coordination of services in rural areas. The dependence on federal funds is shown in Table 14-1: 26.5% of nonurban costs are supplied by federal funds as compared with 7.7% of urban costs. Although 49% of the U.S. population resides in rural and small urban areas dependent on federal funding, these areas receive less than 10% of the total available Urban Mass Transportation Act funding. Furthermore, Section 18 assistance has declined since 1980, while rural public transit systems using the programs have greatly expanded.[13] Lack of funding and the continuing need for services mean new services must often be planned with less federal funding, and existing services must be made more efficient.

TABLE 14-1
Operating Costs for Public Transportation

Revenue Generator	% Urban Costs	% Nonurban Costs
User	44.3	27.8
Local	30.3	34.7
State	17.6	11.0
Federal	7.7	26.5

Source: Adapted from American Association of State Highway and Transportation Officials, *1985 Survey of State Involvement in Public Transportation*, a report to the Standing Committee on Public Transportation (Washington, D.C.: American Association of State Highway and Transportation Officials, October 1985), p. 21. *Survey of State Involvement in Public Transportation*, Copyright 1985. The American Association of State Highway and Transportation Officials, Washington, D.C. Used by permission.

DEFINING AND ESTIMATING RURAL TRAVEL NEEDS[14]

THE CONCEPT OF NEED

It is extremely difficult to provide a quantitative response to the problem of defining the magnitude of rural public transportation needs. Nonetheless, it is not difficult to establish conceptually the critical need for adequate transportation services to rural residents. The energy crisis and inflation of the early 1970s focused attention on the singular dependence of the rural population on the automobile. Few economical alternatives to automobile travel existed. Particularly acute problems faced the transportation-disadvantaged sector of the population, including the elderly, handicapped, youth, and those limited by single-auto ownership. Difficulties were also particularly evident for those elderly and poor who desired to travel to points of human services delivery in nearby town centers.

On a national scale, data from the Nationwide Personal Transportation Study (conducted by the Bureau of the Census for the Federal Highway Administration, 1969–1970) helped to illustrate the magnitude of rural travel problems and needs.[15] The data confirmed that those living in unincorporated areas traveled more frequently and generally made longer trips than average. Public transportation was used for work trips by only 2.6% of the people in unincorporated areas and 3.1% of those in towns with less than 5000 population. In addition, only 12.4% of all households in unincorporated areas did not own cars (mostly the poor and elderly).

While these data were only nationwide averages, they suggest some definite trends in rural travel. First, there is an overwhelming reliance on automobile travel. Second, those rural households in reasonably stable and comfortable financial positions are willing to drive more often and longer. These households may not perceive any pressing travel needs or problems. Third, the small fraction of those rural families who are transportation disadvantaged have urgent travel needs. Thus, in many cases the transportation problem can be summarized as a question of whether or not a privileged majority is willing to subsidize the transportation costs for a dependent minority.

Since rural transportation problems and needs are so closely correlated with auto availability, several analysts have measured needs in terms of automobile accessibility. In a report to the U.S. Senate, Ira Kaye suggested that "transportation-deprived" households were those that did not own an automobile and "transportation-handicapped" households were those that owned no more than one automobile.[16] The latter definition recognized the fact that the breadwinner was expected to utilize the only car available for work trips. A survey indicated that in at least 28 states, over two-thirds of the rural population could be classified as transportation handicapped and that in 12 states at least 20% of the households were transportation deprived.

Burkhardt and Eby procured a refined algorithm for assessing rural transportation needs.[17] They recognized that need must include both the factors of transportation availability (for example, car, taxi, shared rides, walking, bus service) and the concomitant factors of transportation affordability (for example, level of income per household). A numerical rating scheme was devised to produce composite levels of need based on the degree of modal accessibility plus the level of income. The authors, however, recognized the arbitrary nature of the needs estimation process and suggested a probing of consumer behavior through demand analyses.

Unfortunately, since the concept of need for rural transportation services has not been rigidly defined, this need has been difficult to measure. Various analysts have taken different approaches to evaluate needs, and there is not a clear uniformity of opinion. Basically, three broad approaches are available. Perhaps the most common approach is for experts, such as transportation engineers, planners, sociologists, and/or transit managers, to assess relative needs based on various social indicators combined with their best judgments. Second, need may be gauged from a survey of potential users, developed through a home-interview questionnaire. Finally, need may be estimated by comparing the travel behavior of a target group against a standard taken from local or national travel surveys.

CONTRASTING DEMAND WITH NEED

The distinction between rural transportation needs and rural travel demands is most crucial to the eventual development and implementation of transit services and should be recognized. Unlike need, demand is based on the economic willingness-to-pay concept and is measured (for example, the price of travel). Demands are registered in a market and are, therefore, related to the user's income level. Those with low incomes, or no automobiles available, are less likely to demand travel.

Travel demand contrasts sharply with the social concept of need. Travel needs are a fixed amount of travel that is deemed necessary to provide an adequate standard of living, a quantity not affected by the price of travel. One may have a need to travel independent of the ability or willingness to pay. In this context, need is an equity criterion, indicating a deviation from an established norm that should be corrected.

TECHNIQUES TO ESTIMATE NEED

Techniques used to estimate the magnitude of rural transportation needs are somewhat arbitrary, and their limitations should be recognized by planning agencies developing a need estimate. For example, the technique of solely *using the judgments of experts* is inadequate because it is completely devoid of community participation in a project that is pertinent to the community's welfare.

A second technique, *using an opinion poll of area residents*, poses severe measurement problems. Home interviews by both Jon Burkhardt and R. N. Robertson failed to identify significant need when respondents were asked what trips they would like to make that they currently were not making.[18] In both studies, the "desired" trips were found to be less than 6.0% of the existing ones, although the investigators commented that many of the respondents had difficulty grasping the idea of "desired trips" and thus probably substantially underestimated them. In any case, it is exceedingly difficult to find any major unserved demand in this manner.

A third technique, *comparisons against a standard*, is the most realistic, although it also suffers drawbacks. Comparisons cannot be made with travel in urban areas, for example, since rural households are usually more self-sufficient. In addition, rural travel distances are generally longer. Consequently, rural trip-making needs are different from trip-making needs in an urban area.

Another difficulty in making comparisons is that in most states the rural population tends to be older and poorer.[19] These are precisely the types of people that make fewer trips, even in urban areas. Any comparison, therefore, should be with population groups of similar characteristics. Even then we may find that older people in rural areas "need" to make fewer trips because of the locational self-sufficiency and because of the traditional helpfulness of nearby relatives and neighbors in providing transportation.

A fourth technique, *gap analysis*, has been utilized in several studies.[20] This technique is based on the hypothesis that a difference in trip-making rates (for example, the gap) is a direct indicator of transportation need. To apply this procedure, a minimum trip-making rate is set as the standard amount of transportation to be supplied. Usually, an areawide average volume of trips generated per household per day is used for the standard. The choice of an average value is crucial to the magnitude of the needs estimate, and the transportation analyst should clearly state all assumptions. For example, a study of Raleigh County, West Virginia, noted that either a national average, a statewide average, a county average, or averages of rural and poor populations might be used.[21]

Trip-making rates may be cross-classified to attain a more realistic estimate of transportation needs. This approach depends only on the detail of the data collected. One strategy is to cross-classify the travel data by target groups (also known as market segments) and by trip purpose. A target group is an identifiable unit of rural trip makers such as the elderly or the handicapped. Trip purposes could include grocery shopping, other shopping, health care, personal business and recreation. Travel rates for the target groups are determined, and needs estimates, specific to the study area, are then developed.

A continuing problem has been the lack of a comprehensive data base. While urban transportation studies have been substantial and voluminous in terms of data collection efforts, rural areas have been almost completely ignored. One reason for this, of course, is the large expanse of rural territory in this country and the resultant prohibitive cost of conducting home-interview origin-destination surveys similar to those done in urban areas. Another reason is the comparative lack of congestion and related problems such as air pollution and accidents, which may inspire local officials to study rural needs. Even census data are less helpful in rural areas, since the smallest geographic unit usually is the enumeration district and much valuable information (for example, income and trip to work) is not collected.

PLANNING RURAL PUBLIC TRANSPORTATION SYSTEMS

In 1977, Tardiff, Lam, and Dana noted in a review of small-city and rural transportation planning that "The state of the art in non-metropolitan transportation planning is one in which there has been considerable disjointed effort in providing services, but little systematic development of policies, planning theories and methods."[22] Little refinement of rural planning methods or theories has been conducted since that statement was made. Nonetheless, many rural systems have been planned. Figure 14-1 presents a typical planning sequence for a new transit service. The definition of unmet need and goal setting, combined with community input, are critical steps in planning

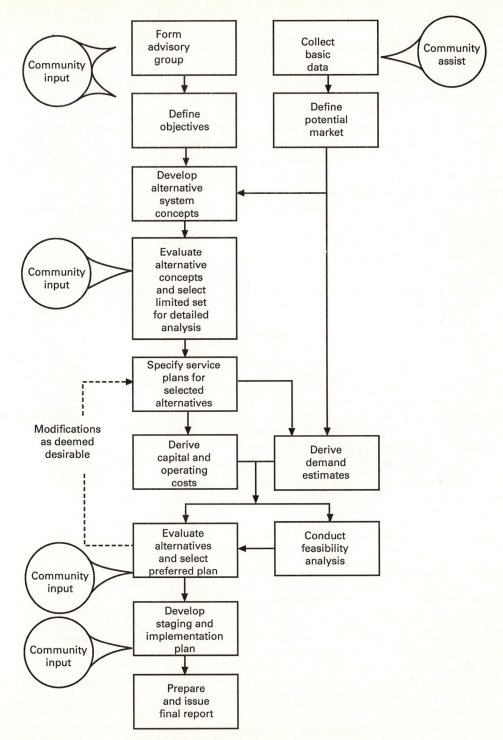

Figure 14-1 *Flow diagram for public transit study.*

for transit services, not unlike the situation in urban areas, except that in rural areas the planner usually has less data and a smaller staff to complete the study. Furthermore, given the great diversity of rural communities and the necessary involvement of local officials, prescribing a process for planning is hazardous if not impossible. Consistent with that difficulty, the Urban Mass Transit Administration has never published rural and small-urban planning requirements. Some states require a 5-year plan, but, in general, no plan is required in most states to secure UMTA Section 18 funding. The state of North Carolina has, since 1979, recommended the 20-step planning process outlined in Table 14-2. This planning process is strategic due to the emphasis on a cyclical process. Step 19 requires procedures for updating and evaluation of the plan. Furthermore, the initial steps evaluate the area environment and operating capacity to develop goals and objectives based on community involvement, all characteristics of strategic planning.[23]

TABLE 14-2
Planning Steps

1.	Form steering committee.
2.	Hold preliminary meeting.*
3.	Gather background information on county.
4.	Inventory public bus operator.
5.	Inventory taxi and private bus operators.
6.	Inventory human service agencies.
7.	Summarize existing arrangements among providers.
8.	Present inventory data to steering committee.*
9.	Identify and enumerate user groups.
10.	Identify public transportation trip needs of user groups.
11.	Identify trip needs of human service agencies.
12.	Identify unmet need.
13.	Identify major attracters and generators.
14.	Present trip needs, unmet demands to steering committee.*
15.	Revise goals, discuss objectives.*
16.	List and analyze alternatives.*
17.	Choose and service design.*
18.	Detail the chosen service design.
19.	Adopt procedures for updating and evaluation.*
20.	Get county commissioner adoption

* Planning steps which require meetings of the steering committee.
Source: Adapted from Public Transportation Division, North Carolina Department of Transportation, *Transportation Development Planning for Nonurbanized Areas: A Guidebook for Local Governments and Service Providers* (Raleigh, N.C.: North Carolina Department of Transportation, January 1979), p. 4.

Miller and Goodnight emphasized the process of community involvement in the analysis of alternatives because:

1. Analytic techniques, no matter how sophisticated and detailed, do not provide completely

accurate estimates of transit patronage. This is especially true for small communities that do not have transit services.

2. For many of the smaller communities a set of feasible alternatives is limited and the cost of testing the most promising alternatives by actually implementing the services is not great.

3. For small systems, the cost of error is not great. Change in routes and additions of buses can be achieved at little cost addition.

4. Factors entering into the decisions pertinent to implementation include social, political, economic, and technical considerations. The transportation related estimates should be balanced in accordance with the roles each of these considerations play.[24]

DEFINING ALTERNATIVES[25]

A variety of vehicle types and operating strategies has been suggested as applicable to rural public transportation, and rural transportation planners are encouraged to consider many vehicle choice options and operating strategies in developing prospective systems. In addition, they are expected to survey all existing providers and supply options and to consider other usually neglected alternatives for improving rural mobility. These include carpools, community volunteer groups, and mobile delivery of human services. In general, it is expected that alternatives would be selected on a cost-effective basis, but this may not always be the case. For example, some agencies may choose to provide fewer vehicles with more expensive equipment (for example, lifts for handicapped), although the actual demand for these facilities may be extremely limited. A representative list of technological alternatives for transit service follows.

1. *Conventional fixed route, fixed schedule system*. A conventional bus system would have vehicles operating on fixed routes and fixed schedules. One variation that seems to be more feasible for low-density rural areas is periodic scheduling, where, instead of daily service, buses serve different areas on different days of the week. Every citizen is offered a dependable means of transportation to the local town or closest urbanized area at least once a week. In this manner, capital and maintenance costs are kept low.

2. *Dial-a-ride (dial-a-bus)*. One of the largest components of the total operating costs of either conventional or demand-responsive service is the drivers' wages. Rural transit systems, like their urban counterparts, are highly labor intensive and, no matter how small and economical the bus, the demand in many rural areas is often too small or too scattered to warrant fixed schedules and routes. Some economies may be achieved by providing demand-responsive services that minimize vehicle-miles and vehicle-hours of service, yet still provide a minimum acceptable level of service to the users. Dial-a-ride is one such system, using minibuses or vans and offering door-to-door service on a telephone demand-scheduled basis. In many situations an advance sign-up system for riders, such as those found in many rural systems, is more practical. This option is termed *planned demand* and usually requires 24-h or longer advance notice to a

dispatcher. An extensive planned demand service has been operating in rural Missouri counties since 1971.[26] This type of service is particularly attractive to elderly and handicapped segments of the population who would have difficulty obtaining access to fixed-route service.

Little used but possible modifications for demand-responsive systems include *mail-a-bus* and *porchlight bus*. In the early 1970s in one community in Missouri, the bus would travel a specific route and stop at any residence where the porch light was illuminated. If the rural area is characterized by low telephone ownership, it may be more effective to use the postal system as a means of transmitting information concerning desired rides. Requests put in the mailbox during the day could be collected that night by a dispatcher at the post office, who would then schedule buses for pickups and deliveries the following day. In some situations it may even be possible to have the mail truck itself serve as a passenger conveyance as is done extensively in Switzerland.

3. *Jitneys*. The jitney is analogous to dial-a-ride in that it is partially demand responsive, but instead of being a bus or van it is usually a private passenger car or station wagon that travels along a semifixed route. These vehicles travel basically one route, but vary somewhat to offer door-to-door service. The jitney driver may offer reserved seating, but more often cruises along until waved down by an individual desiring a ride. In urban areas, no strict schedules are adhered to, but in rural areas a somewhat fixed schedule would be necessary because of the probable few number of jitneys traveling on the back roads. Jitneys have not been extensively used in rural transport systems, but could be applicable to areas with well-defined travel corridors, such as the mountain valleys of Appalachia.

4. *School buses*. Most rural areas are served by a central school system that usually requires an extensive fleet of school buses. These buses generally are idle most of the day and could be used for other needed transportation functions. However, in many states there are legal restrictions on their use. In addition, certain design characteristics (such as a high first step, stiff ride, and narrow seat width) in most school buses make them unsuitable for adults and particularly unsuitable for the elderly. Another difficulty is that of scheduling, because school buses are available for nonschool purposes only in the late morning and early afternoon, thereby eliminating their use for work trips. Part-time drivers for the short nonschool use period would have to be found. Also, use during the off-peak periods might hinder maintenance operations in the bus garages. Despite these problems, some state legislatures have passed laws allowing certain entities to use school buses for purposes other than the transportation of children. Florida has been notable in this regard and has a joint-use program with coordinated transit providers and school districts.[27]

5. *Taxis*. This alternative, unlike the jitney, is completely demand responsive. One problem with the taxi is that the usual practice of servicing only one request at a time forces up the cost of using this mode and makes it prohibitive to many rural families. Yet, if subsidized or coordinated with other modes, the taxi could

become more valuable in solving the rural transportation problem. Situations where the taxi might be used include:

a. Where dispatching ensures filling the taxi to capacity, with the cost being split between all the parties (known as shared-ride services).
b. Where, by pooling resources and hiring the taxi by the day, service organizations find they save money in the long run by not having to purchase and maintain their own vehicle. Also, they do not waste valuable employee time by sending them out in departmental cars to pick up patients or other service recipients.

The basic objections to utilizing existing taxi companies for the provision of rural transportation are the regulations eliminating the possibility of shared rides and also the difficulty that aged or handicapped persons have using small vehicles. However, financially sound taxi companies generally have smoothed out the types of operational and administrative start-up problems that may plague some newly formed rural systems (for example, maintenance, dispatching, and management). Such companies would be logical choices to operate rural public transportation systems.

6. *Rural feeder services*. Any operating scheme could be combined to feed intercity buses. Systems would collect passengers on the back roads and drop them off at waiting stations on the main routes where larger buses operate, or the systems would be the final link in the reverse trip. Intercity bus passengers left off in town could rely upon the taxi to complete the journey. The Rural Connector Service initiated by Greyhound Bus in 1987 and even earlier by Vermont Transit and StageCoach of Randolph, Vermont, are examples of this type of service scheme.[28]

7. *Innovative services*. An enormous array of innovative services, such as organized hitchhiking, cars supplied to individuals who agree to carry others, and even supplying car loans, have been attempted.[29] Some innovations are no longer in existence, but innovative utilization of volunteers as staff and drivers continue in many rural areas. The rural transit planner should be alert to utilizing the unique qualities and resources of an area when designing an alternative.

Although small vehicles are cheaper to run than large ones, the total cost of transportation/seat-mi decreases markedly with increasing vehicle capacity. For most rural systems, however, vehicle load factors are low, so high-capacity vehicles are not needed. Vehicle selection should not be made solely on the basis of capital and operational costs; the degree of capital subsidization, the user level of service provided, and the type of demand to be satisfied should also be considered.

Minibuses, with capacities ranging from 8 to 20 passengers, are the most popular vehicles for meeting the transportation needs of the rural areas where demand does not warrant the use of larger vehicles. Also, they can be more easily maneuvered on the substandard roads often found in rural areas. Due to their low capital and operating costs, minibuses may be able to run routes that were considered economically infeasible with larger conventional buses.

Most rural transit systems have chosen to purchase either van-type vehicles or small transit buses. In general, they also tend to buy new vehicles rather than used ones. The reasons for new vehicles are twofold. First, the purchase of older vehicles involves a trade-off of depreciation for maintenance costs. Maintenance costs for older vehicles may prove to be unacceptably high, especially when the purchase price of new vehicles is fully or partially subsidized from outside sources. Second, operators are especially cognizant of the impact of a clean and reliable vehicle on ridership. They prefer the positive community impact of shiny new vehicles.

A number of operating strategies are feasible for rural localities. The alternatives may be analyzed by considering different types of routing and headways. Many operating systems provide both fixed-route/fixed-schedule and demand-responsive services or innovative service that features aspects of all the alternatives. The fixed routes generally serve work trips, are used as connectors between town centers, or are closely tied to a human services delivery system (such as a senior-citizen lunch program). Occasionally, the topography of a rural county is ideally suited for fixed routes, such as the Appalachian corridors or the coast of California.

Partially demand-responsive systems include those using route-deviation or point-deviation systems. These services have been operated in small-town environments and provide more flexibility than the fixed-route/fixed-schedule system. Fully demand-responsive services, operating on real time with dynamic routing, have generally not been applied in rural scenarios, especially if the system is to cover an entire county, since demand densities are too low.

The door-to-door service characteristics of demand-responsive systems are highly desirable. Therefore, some rural counties have provided door-to-door transportation services on a scheduled (for example, planned-demand) basis. Often the same vehicles that carry peak-hour work trips will operate in the planned-demand mode between the peak hours. To increase the economic efficiency of these systems, the county is often divided into sectors, with service in a sector only being offered on specific days of the week.

The most vexing problem facing rural transit planners is how to allocate scarce resources for the most public good. Sooner or later all service providers or planners are forced to make relative value judgments on whether, for example, in a managed demand system, they allocate vehicles to transport one person to regular kidney dialysis or to provide service to seven people who want to go grocery shopping. Although most systems do not formally establish priorities, an informal priority often is adopted whereby the number of people transported is roughly weighed against the trip purpose so that one person requesting service for recreational purposes would receive service after another individual receives service for a medical purpose. While, in general, the rule of first come, first served is observed, trips are judiciously prioritized, and dispatchers often negotiate with potential passengers on the most advantageous time to make their trip.

There are numerous routing and scheduling options for rural transit systems.

However, few guidelines exist to aid in the development of routes or schedules for a new rural service. Operating experience is perhaps the best source for current guidelines. Experience with rural transit systems in North and South Carolina led to the following conclusions about scheduling.[29]

SCHEDULING PRACTICES

1. Rural worker schedules should rarely exceed 1.5 h total run time from origin to destination. Workers tend to resist trip time that is more than double car-trip time.
2. Rural social delivery schedules can be somewhat longer in overall duration (about 2 h is maximum). As a rule, trip needs in this category have less urgency, and passenger demands on the schedule are less critical.
3. Rural social delivery schedules should allow 2 h between arrival time and return time for general business and shopping needs.
4. Rural demand-route schedules should have generous time allowances built in for passengers embarking with groceries and for elderly passengers, who are slower to board and discharge. Stop allowances should be roughly estimated at 2 to 3 min apiece. This is more difficult to achieve on fixed-route schedules.
5. Fixed-route schedules should be geared for an average open road speed of 40 to 45 mi/h (64 to 72 km/h), with a time insertion of about 2 to 5 min at each mainline stopping point. Very little allowance is required (at first) for flag-stop possibilities. These will usually be rare during the first year of operation.
6. All schedules should consider allowing at least a 5- to 10-min delay at each end of a long—about 25 mi (40 km)—run. This scheduled slack time permits drivers to catch up on any unplanned delays on the prior leg.
7. Worker buses should always have at least a 10-min prior arrival time at the factory gate to allow time for workers to check in. Less than that will produce a drastic and immediate drop in worker ridership, since they are by far the most critical riders in the system.

ROUTING RULES

Routing rules have been gained as a product of operating experiences. Most are stated as rules of thumb that should not be blindly adhered to in all cases. The following guidelines are often used.

1. Rural passengers are reluctant to walk as much as 0.4 km (0.25 mi) to a fixed-route bus stop.
2. For many-to-one demand-responsive services, loop routes radiating about a central destination are desirable. Passengers are returned home as the vehicle leaves the central destination and picked up on the return to town. This procedure shortens the average passenger's in-vehicle travel time.
3. Routes should not be modified to accommodate only one or two people, although route planners should be alert to all suggestions.

4. Variable and irregular scheduling typical of route-deviation bus systems places severe restrictions on reliability. Riders have more confidence in a fixed-route system or an advance reservation door-to-door service.

In summary, the design of a successful rural transportation system (including vehicle selection, routing, and scheduling) is contingent upon the planners' thorough knowledge of the community, its geography, its road network, and the needs of the potential rider. Guidelines are available, but one cannot assess the exact impact of changing any of the design variables without actually operating a system. The *Florida Management Manual for Small Transit Systems* notes that the transit manager of very small transit systems (no more than five buses) will probably want to simplify the planning and scheduling process by basing service on policy decisions involving what the transit system believes it can afford and general marketing considerations.[30] The discovery of what the system believes it can afford and general marketing considerations will be found through the planning process.

Planning for transit in rural areas is a lengthy process. Data from Theodore Wallin and Alice Kidder indicate that it takes approximately 3 years to complete the planning process for an average service from initial problem identification, meetings, writing funding proposals, getting approval for funding, and finally operating the service. Table 14-3 presents the elapsed time to pass selected milestones in the planning process. Planners should be aware that each community has its own peculiarities or strengths, which may lengthen or shorten the planning process.

ESTIMATING DEMAND[31]

The concepts of need and demand are inescapably intertwined in the planning process for rural public transportation. Typically, planners are aware that transportation in rural areas is characterized as high need and low demand. That is, the social consequences of not providing service to low-income households, elderly, or others with a high need is great, yet the ability of these people with high need to pay for service makes for low demand. The difficulty of establishing demand is acute, and no entirely satisfactory process for establishing need and demand in rural areas has been developed.

Although the estimation of potential ridership is a difficult task, it is an essential component to the planning and design of a rural transportation system. The inefficiencies associated with an underutilized vehicle fleet may eventually result in the premature demise of rural transit services. A demand projection should, therefore, serve as the primary basis for the system's design.

TABLE 14-3
Elapsed Time Requirements to Pass Selected Milestones

Task	Mean Months Required to Pass Milestone	Lowest Number of Months Reported	Highest Number of Months Reported
Calling initial organized meeting	5.3	1	15
Getting agreement to start a transportation service	5.2	1	15
Meeting with other organizations to consolidate or coordinate service	24.6	2	99 or more
Writing proposal for funding (only during the initial period before vehicles started on the road)	5.8	1	12
Getting needed funds to get started	5.9	1	15
Meeting with key officials to get approvals (leases, donations of space, permits, etc.)	5.4	0	50
Planning the service and program	17.1	2	99 or more
Hiring staff	16.4	1	99 or more
Recruiting volunteers	33.7	2	99 or more
Training volunteers	5.0	0	9
Training other paid drivers	1.7	0	2
Publicizing service	4.9	2	12
Arranging insurance	3.8	0	14
Setting up routes and schedules	19.0	1	99 or more
Making experimental changes in routes and schedules	34.7	2	99 or more
Completing other tasks involved in start-up	3.7	1	8

Source: Adapted from Theodore A. Wallin and Alice Kidder, *Financing and Sustaining Mobility in Rural Areas: A Manual*, Final Report, prepared by The Franklin Program on Transportation and Distribution Management, Syracuse University, for UMTA, Technology Sharing Program, Report no. DOT-I-87-2 (Washington, D.C.: U.S. Department of Transportation, August 1986), pp. 4-9, 4-10.

As previously discussed, a number of techniques have been used to determine demand. Recent experience, however, has shown that the following methods are not reliable.

- A local "would-you-ride" survey.
- Gap analysis.
- Professional opinions.

A common approach to demand estimation has involved door-to-door attitude surveys prior to the development of the transportation service. Such surveys generally include questions about the number and types of transit trips that would be made under various environmental conditions (for example, quality of service, automobile availability, and frequency). There are two serious flaws with this method of demand projection. The first difficulty is that multipurpose journeys are often not measured properly by the questionnaire. Generally, respondents are asked to indicate how many trips they would make on the service, if it existed, for each trip purpose. In doing so, they often neglect to consider multipurpose trips and provide an overestimate of the actual number of person trips. Second, and of critical importance, the demand forecasts on the basis of attitude surveys of this type generally are not verified by actual travel behavior. In a survey of prospective travel frequencies in a small town in New York (Oneonta), public response indicated that a demand-activated bus service would generate 33,700 trips/week when an actual service in a comparable nearby small town (Batavia, New York) only generated 1500 trips/week.[32] The discrepancy between the estimate and actual demand illustrates the fact that public opinion surveys cannot be directly translated into actual vehicle trips.

Both gap analysis and the use of professional opinion (such as the Delphi technique) also have shortcomings. Gap analysis is better suited as a needs estimation tool. The use of experts' opinions, as incorporated into a "goals attainment" procedure, has not been sufficiently tested to be recommended for use.

It is evident that demand forecasts for a particular area should be tempered by a knowledge of the existing levels of demand for like transportation services in other similar localities. Table 14-4 presents a summary of some existing rural transportation systems and their service characteristics. Some of these programs include special service to the elderly, while others have a broader ridership base. Trip-generation rates in Table 14-4 are presented in terms of annual transit trips (one-way) per capita. Note that most systems are servicing less than 1.0 transit trip per resident per year. This rate of travel might be used as a liberal rule of thumb for maximum anticipated ridership, in the absence of better data. Many systems will not even produce this level of ridership. In a study for the state of Pennsylvania, a range of travel rates between 0.3 and 2.4 annual trips per capita was used to develop a forecast of statewide potential rural transit demand.[33] This is quite a wide range (the highest estimate being 8 times the lowest) and may prove to be of little aid to a planner trying to decide on a realistic demand level to use for a particular county or planning district.

TABLE 14-4
Observed Rates of Transit Use

Trip-Generation Rate (Annual trips per capita)	Location
4.00—10.00	Batavia, N.Y. (dial-a-ride)
3.00—4.00	High estimate, small urban areas (Pa.)
2.00—3.00	High estimate, rural (Pa.)
1.00—2.00	Mid-Delta (Ark.)
0.50—1.00	Raleigh County (W. Va.) Low estimate, small urban areas (Pa.)
0.25—0.50	Venango Action Corp. (Pa.) Low estimate, rural (Pa.)
0.00—0.25	Kingsport, Tenn. Potter County (Pa.) McKean County (Pa.)

Three approaches to estimating demand that are considered acceptable are:

- Trip-generation-rate models.
- Regression models.
- Participation-rate models.

Only trip-generation models have been utilized to any extent and are the obvious choice for preliminary planning, although a regression functional-demand equation developed by Burkhardt and Lago through statistical analysis of fixed-route and demand-responsive systems may prove quite useful.[34] The third technique analyzes the demand for rural transit to social services in terms of the participation rate of those utilizing social services and the likelihood of transit use for travel to the services. This technique may be well suited for those rural transit systems designed to act primarily as a human services delivery system for the elderly.

The trip-generation-rate model is an aggregate approach. That is, trip rates are assumed to hold for an entire population. However, by detailing exact target groups that are expected to utilize the system, a more refined travel estimate is produced.

To compute demand by means of the trip-generation-rate model, the following formula is used:

$$D = \sum_{i=1}^{n} d_i(POP_i) \qquad (14-1)$$

where D = total annual demand for transit trips
    d_i = annual trips per person in the ith target group
    (POP_i) = population of the ith target group
    n = number of target groups

In Pennsylvania studies, planners selected two target groups, the elderly and the nonelderly poor, which were expected to comprise 80% of the public transportation system ridership. The demand equation is

$$D = \frac{12(POP_{elderly}) + 19(POP_{poor})}{0.80}$$

where the trip-making rates for the two groups were projected to be 12 and 19 trips per year, respectively. Subsequent demand studies using Wisconsin data have shown that use of a "no-auto-available" target group produced more accurate demand projections, and a study in California emphasized the importance of income in demand projections.[35] Completely satisfactory demand models have not been developed, and this area has progressed little since the mid-1970s.

Planners developing rural public services typically separate potential ridership to identify high-demand market segments without service, such as an employment center or senior center. Table 14-5 presents a list of potential market segments. The ridership for the high-demand segment is then quantified as trips per day, and other services are incrementally added to the core service. As the planner quantifies other lower-demand market segments, the total estimated demand is then compared to demand estimation models and actual ridership from other similar systems to determine if the estimates by market segment are reasonable. For further discussion of market segmentation, see Chap. 16.

TABLE 14-5
Transit-Dependent Market Segments

1. Frail elderly (those persons no longer able to drive themselves).
2. Children in families with no available transportation.
3. Students who do not have cars of their own, and who need to get to colleges, technical institutes, job training programs, etc.
4. The physically disabled (persons with vision impairment, multiple sclerosis, polio, paralysis, etc.) who have not been able to drive themselves.
5. The mentally disabled (mental retardation, mental illness, brain injury, etc.).
6. The low-income family that does not have one car for each wage earner and for whom at least one adult is transit dependent (for example, welfare mothers without cars).
7. Those who are fearful of driving or who are unwilling to drive to unfamiliar areas such as to hospitals in large cities.
8. Those who have no license to drive.
9. Those who have no transportation to programs designed for special groups, for example, the seniors (e.g., recreations sites and adult day care), the low income (e.g., welfare offices), or the general public (e.g., public hearings).
10. Spouses of wage earners who take the family's only vehicle to work, leaving the spouse with no transportation for part of the day.

Source: Adapted from Theodore A. Wallin and Alice Kidder, *Financing and Sustaining Mobility Programs in Rural Areas: A Manual*, Final Report, prepared by The Franklin Program on Transportation and Distribution Management, Syracuse University, for UMTA, Technology Sharing Program, Report no. DOT-I-87-2 ((Washington, D.C.: U.S. Department of Transportation, August 1986), p. 2-1.

COORDINATION

The concept of market segmentation is particularly important when the issue of coordination of rural passenger transportation is considered. Rural transportation service for some market segments exists in practically every county in the United States. The service may only be for Head-Start children or senior citizens' centers, but the planner for rural transit is encouraged to consider the concept of coordination before initiating a completely new service, because some level of service undoubtedly already exists. The concept of coordination will be initially introduced into the planning effort in an inventory of existing providers. The existing providers may include various social-service providers, public providers, and private for-profit providers. All these groups should be considered in the coordination process. The concept of coordination is not directed specifically at consolidation of services but rather at a family of activities, ranging from communications between operators to the maximum coordination, which is consolidation of services. The benefits of coordination are:

1. Eliminating duplication of transportation services.
2. Making better use of underutilized equipment, expertise, facilities, or other resources.
3. Matching transportation providers with transportation purchasers.
4. Taking advantage of volume purchasing power.[36]

The coordination benefits realized may be more service for the available funding, more available service, and better availability of transportation to those in need. Large monetary savings through any coordination efforts are unusual. The monetary savings of programs have been unclear, and the actual benefits of coordinated services typically are service quality improvements and more available service.

Coordination to achieve these benefits is complex due to the great number of federal programs that supply or have the potential to supply passenger transportation services. Approximately 114 programs exist that pertain to passenger transportation, and the estimate of expenditures by the U.S. Department of Health and Human Services approaches $1 billion per year.[37]

The major impediments to the coordination of public and specialized transportation in rural areas arise from the multiplicity of human-service and related transportation programs provided by the federal, state, and local governments. The issues that will necessitate resolution in most coordination efforts include:

1. Inconsistencies in service boundaries or target population groups.
2. Cost allocation methods and cost accounting requirements.
3. Matching rate type, and percentage variances.
4. Data collection requirements.
5. Vehicle operating costs (insurance, maintenance, gas, license, etc.) and pro rata utilization charges for nonprovider agencies.
6. Public service commission (or public utilities commission) regulation and requirements.
7. Funding levels authorized for programs.

8. Commingling of funds (administrative mechanisms and budgetary procedures).
9. Auditing standards and requirements.
10. Effective utilization of volunteers (in-kind services and facilities) in program planning, development, and implementation)
11. The relationships between human services, transportation systems, proprietary transportation providers, and public mass transportation systems in both urban and rural areas.[38]

Saltzman investigated the coordination of transportation by human service agencies and discovered five factors that influence a given social service agency to participate in a coordinated transportation service, as shown in Table 14-6.[39] Figure 14-2

TABLE 14-6
Factors Influencing Agency Willingness to Coordinate

Relative Rating	Gamma	r	Rank	Variable Description
Influential	-.40	-.42	1	Perceptions of whether the cost savings were worth the loss of control when coordinating.
	-.32	-.28	2	Amount of time an agency had available to negotiate coordination.
Moderately influential	+.25	+.28	3	Whether an agency thought they would not lose much control if they coordinated.
	-.25	-.19	4	Perceptions of how much cost savings would occur from coordination.
	+.22	+.23	5	Whether transportation was an authorized function of the agency.
Negligible or no influence	+.20	+.20	6	Amount of administrative effort an agency thought it would take to coordinate.
	+.001	+.02	7	Whether an agency thought regulations were a barrier to coordination.
	-.04	-.06	8	Whether an agency was sure it would have operating funds the next year.
	-.05	-.02	9	Whether an agency expected an increase in next year's budget.
	-.02	-.02	10	Whether an agency received its approved budget before or after it was required to start operating a system.

Source: Adapted from Arthur Saltzman, *Coordination of Transportation by Human Service Agencies: An Interorganizational Perspective*, Ph.D. dissertation for the University of California, Irvine, reprinted in Technology Sharing Program (Washington, D.C.: U.S. Department of Transportation, January 1980), p. 183.

is the path diagram for Saltzman's "willingness to coordinate hypothesis." The diagram shows that, if an agency believes that their savings are worth the loss of control and

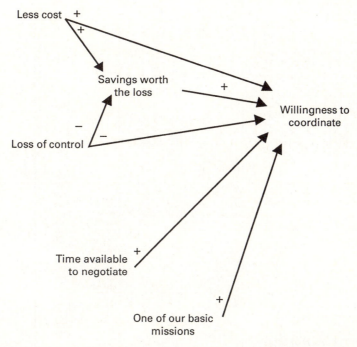

Figure 14-2 *Path diagram for willingness-to-coordinate hypothesis. [Source: Arthur Saltzman,* Coordination of Transportation by Human Service Agencies: An Inter-organizational Perspective, *Ph.D. dissertation for the University of California, Irvine, reprinted in Technology Sharing Program (Washington D.C.: U.S. Department of Transportation, January 1980), p. 185.]*

the lower costs are coupled with time available to negotiate and if the agency has the coordination of services as one of its basic missions, it is likely that the agency will participate in a coordinated service. This macro approach to coordination is then coupled with a micro evaluation of coordination as shown in Fig. 14-3, where a planner must identify underutilized vehicle time or driver time and couple these factors with the unmet transportation needs of various market segments.

Contracting or purchase of services from private for-profit operators has been receiving considerable attention and is a special area of coordination. With private operators, coordination may involve other activities rather than direct service functions. These might include routine maintenance, vehicle cleaning, dispatching services, and other activities. As can be seen from Table 14-7, coordination with private operators goes beyond the mere purchase of transportation services. Practically any activity that is conducted by the transit service is an opportunity to coordinate with the private sector.

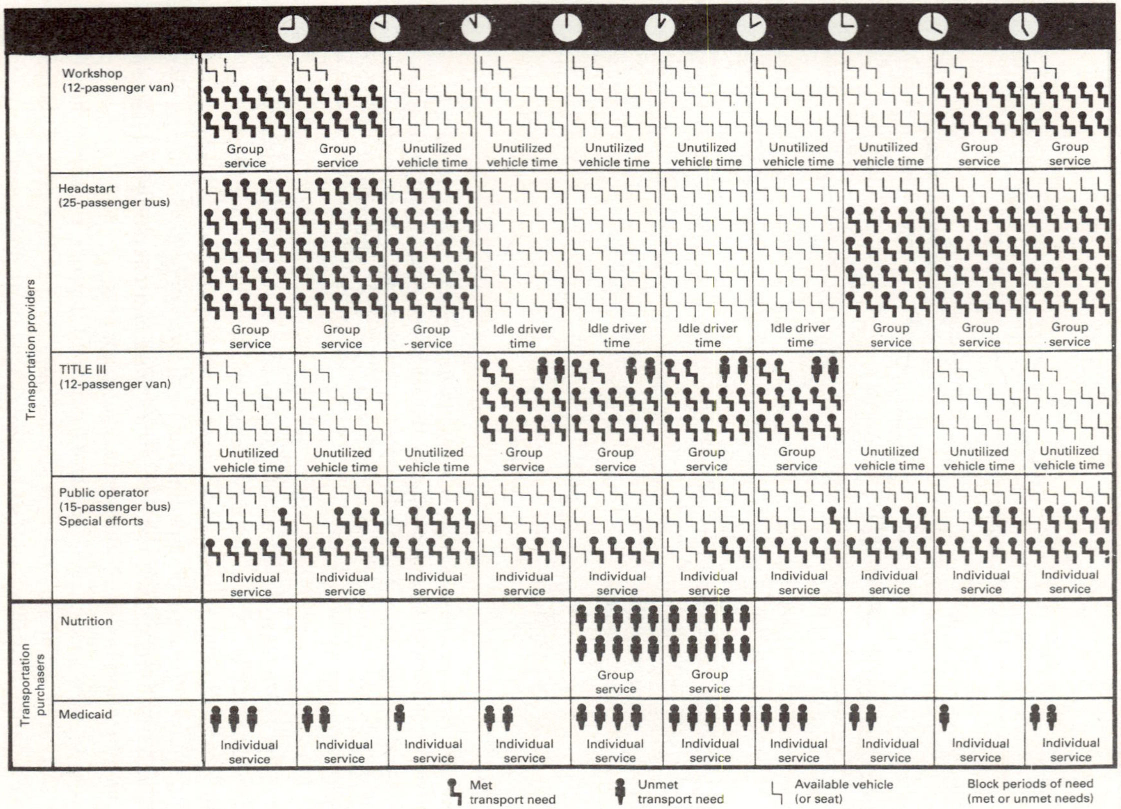
Transportation providers
Workshop (12-passenger van)
Headstart (25-passenger bus)
TITLE III (12-passenger van)
Public operator (15-passenger bus) Special efforts
Transportation purchasers
Nutrition
Medicaid
Group service
Unutilized vehicle time
Idle driver time
Individual service
Met transport need
Unmet transport need
Available vehicle (or seat)
Block periods of need (met or unmet needs)

Figure 14-3 *Transportation resources and needs. [Source: Applies Resource Integration, Ltd.,* Planning Guidelines for Coordinated Agency Transportation Services *(reissued version), prepared for U.S. DOT and U.S. Department of Health and Human Services, Report no. DOT-I-87-33 (Washington, D.C.: U.S. Government Printing Office, April 1980), p. 7.]*

TABLE 14-7
Private Sector Coordination: Contracting Opportunities

Category/Name	Activity	Private Sector Provider
Administration		
Grant Administration	Grant preparation Grant management - record keeping - financial transportation - regulatory compliance	Consultant Service contractor Management company
Reporting	Procedures/forms development Data collection Data analysis	CPA Data processing company
Computer Processing	Software and hardware needs System installation System maintenance System evaluation and updating Turn-key service	Consultant Service contractor Management company
Procurement	Specifications development Production inspection Inspection and acceptance	Consultant Service contractor Management company
Audit/Accounting	Independent year-end audit Overhead audits Monthly accounting	CPA CPA CPA
Planning	Transportation Development Plan Management audits Special studies Route and schedule evaluation	Consultant Consultant/Management co. Consultant/Management co. Consultant/Management co./Service contractor
Marketing	Marketing analysis Campaigns and promotions Vehicle advertising space	Research firms Marketing/PR firms Marketing/PR firms
Maintenance	Vehicle cleaning Vehicle body/paint work Major vehicle repairs/overhauls Routine vehicle maintenance Office equipment	Local garages Specialty service corp. Body/paint shops Engine/transmission shops Local garages Auto/truck dealerships Business machine repair
Operations	Employee recruitment Employee (contract) management Employee training Vehicle operations Safety training	Personnel agency Personnel agcy./Mngement. co. Personnel consult./Mngementt. co. Taxi/limousine Tour companies Paratransit companies Emergency service providers School bus companies Consultant/Management co.

Source: Adapted from Carter–Goble Associates, Inc., *Private Sector Contracting for Rural and Small Urban Public Transportation Providers: Workshop Manual*, Technology Sharing Program (Washington, D.C.: U.S. Department of Transportation, 1990), p. iii-8.

Forty-one states have some type of coordination mechanism, and these efforts can be categorized into one of three methods for coordination of the administration of transit programs: (1) task forces, (2) committees, or (3) mandatory programs.[40] The transit planner should consult with the state agency responsible for public transit to determine the level of coordination necessary as plans are developed.

IMPLEMENTATION

The key element in the implementation process is the coordination of the planning effort with the day-to-day requirements of an implementation program. The initial implementation considerations are many in number, but the following list represents those that are essential to the development of a successful system (they are discussed in this section and the next):

1. Institutional arrangements.
2. Policy making and staffing.
3. Insurance.
4. Finance and funding.
5. Cost and evaluation.

The principal institutional arrangements that are considered in the planning process are:

1. The nonprofit organization, organized according to the laws of individual states.
2. Private for-profit corporations.
3. Regional transit authorities.
4. Transportation districts.
5. Service provision under a governmental agency, typically a city or county government.

No single model has been uniformly successful. Cooperatives at one time were considered promising, but given public funding requirements and tax advantages of other forms of operations, the cooperative mode of organization has been largely avoided as of the mid-1970s. The most notable of the early cooperatives was the OATS (Older Adults Transportation Service) program in Missouri. This program established itself initially as an agricultural cooperative but found that it could not receive tax advantages or certain essential government grants, which it needed to succeed and, therefore, reorganized as a not-for-profit corporation. This illustrates a critical problem for planners in the initial stages: to choose the correct form of institutional arrangement that allows the program to adapt to the operating environment.

The policy board that is established to operate the service will have numerous areas in which to establish policy. A list of areas for developing initial goals and policies is contained in Table 14-8. The most critical decision that a board will effect is the development of an organization chart and the corresponding selection of a chief executive officer. Figure 14-4 presents a generic functional organization chart. The relationship between the functional organization chart and the personnel organization chart for a small service is presented in Fig. 14-5. As an organization grows, the service may have staff members who conduct planning, marketing, and other activities shown consolidated under the manager's office. The board should be alert and monitor the service through a comprehensive taxonomy of goals, objectives, and targets for each of the functional areas of the service.

TABLE 14-8
Governing Body Policy Decision Areas

- Farebox recovery.
- Special fares.
- Geographic area of service (demand-responsive).
- Designation of priority patron (demand-responsive).
- Designation of priority trip purpose (demand-responsive).
- Client eligibility requirements (if applicable).
- Client billing rates, form, and amount (if applicable).
- Fleet deployment and garaging.
- Vehicle maintenance scheduling.
- Capital replacement.
- Hours of service.
- Length and location of routes (fixed-route).
- Days of service.
- Level of service (for example, fixed-route headways).
- Vehicle capacity and vehicle type.
- Ultimate fleet-size.
- Vehicle backup.
- Accessibility features.

Source: Adapted from National Association of County Engineers, *Rural Public Transportation*, NACE Action Guide Series, Vol. II (Washington, D.C.: Federal Highway Administration, 1986), p. 3-2.

The most critical area of initial development in the implementation process is securing insurance, which has proved to be a difficult necessity both in terms of costs and availability. An agency's attractiveness for insurance coverage can be enhanced not only by a good loss ratio but also through the development of a strong risk-management program. The principal areas to develop loss control measures are organizational, vehicle, employee, and passenger safety programs; service factor considerations; physical property protection; and professional liability.[41]

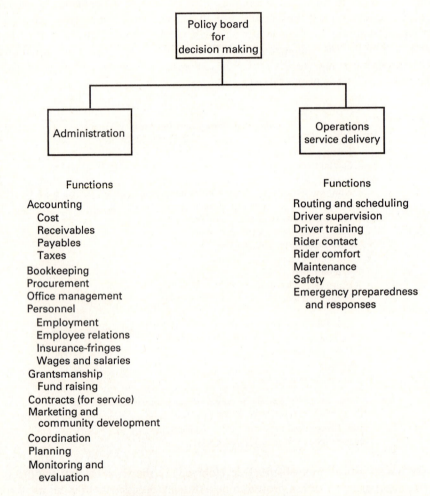

Figure 14-4 *Functional organization chart.*

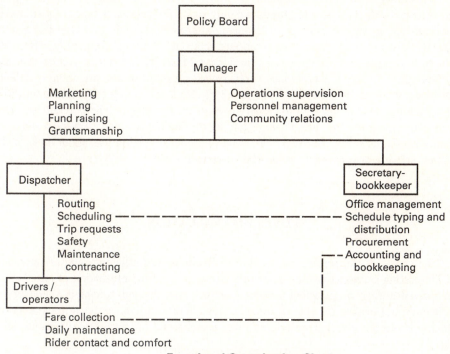

Functional Organization Chart

From the above the personnel chart is developed

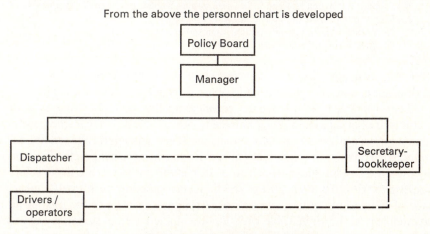

Personnel Organizational Chart

Note: Solid lines indicate direct line authority and supervision. Dashed lines indicate coordination between positions.

Figure 14-5 *Development of organization chart from functional organization chart.*

Financing the selected operating alternative will be partially determined by the alternative itself. That is, some funds are only available for certain types of systems. In the selection process a number of financing alternatives should be examined as they directly relate to the policies that the board sets out. The most frequently mentioned source of funds in a 1989 survey was the Urban Mass Transportation Act (mentioned by 96% of the survey). The typical rural service reported that approximately 29% of its budget came from federal sources, and 34% from state and local government (80% of survey received some state or local government funding).[42] The percentages have been decreasing for the federal share and increasing for the state and local share. In Pennsylvania, as recent as fiscal year 1986, the federal portion was about 48% of the budget subsidy of rural and small-urban systems.[43]

COST AND EVALUATION

The costs of the service are used in determining the efficiency and effectiveness of an existing service, but they also are a component of the evaluation of alternatives conducted during the planning process. Cost recovery through pricing is a measure of efficiency, but pricing for cost recovery is more than simple maximization of recovery. Pricing is often a policy decision and fares are charged for a variety of reasons, such as:

1. To avoid the stigma attached to free-fare systems as poor people or "welfare buses."
2. To generate revenue in order to minimize subsidies.
3. To allocate a scarce resource (seating capacity) among potential users.
4. To attach a cost to the benefits perceivable to the users of the system.[44]

Even the evaluation measure of cost recovery is not simply an issue of subsidy minimization, and the relationship between pricing and policy is complex.

Lee, Tamakloe, and Mulinazzi recommend that cost effectiveness is the most useful type of evaluation when compared to other evaluation techniques, such as cost-benefit ratios, goal achievement or impact incidence, and matrix and ranking and rating methods.[45] However, it is helpful to utilize the goal achievement method as a precursor to cost effectiveness. The goal achievement method has at its core the development of a relevant series of interest groups and then corresponding performance measures for each of the various system alternatives. An interest matrix of the goal achievement methodology is shown in Table 14-9. By developing an interest matrix and arriving at various measures, corresponding to the various groups, a cost effectiveness evaluation can be applied. If measures of convenience, such as frequency of service, are important to one of the interest groups, a measure of frequency (number of vehicles serving a given destination per hour) can be evaluated and referenced back to the interest group.

TABLE 14-9
Impact-Interest Matrix

Impact or Condition Set	Interest Group		
	Passenger	Operator	Community
Availability	X		
Area coverage		X	
Speed	X	X	
Cost	X	X	
Punctuality/reliability	X	X	
Comfort	X		
Convenience	X		
Security/safety	X	X	
Frequency	X	X	
Capacity		X	
Side effects		X	
Passenger attraction		X	X
Long-range impact			X
Environment/energy impact			X
Economic efficiency			X
Social objectives			X

Source: Joe Lee, E. K. A. Tamakloe, and Tom Mulinazzi, *A Public Transportation Needs Study for the Low Density Areas in a Five-State Region in the Midwest (Iowa, Kansas, Missouri, Nebraska, and Oklahoma)*, Final Report (Washington, D.C.: U.S. Department of Transportation, April 1981), p. 91.

For example, in a simulation study of demand-responsive transportation in rural Virginia, alternatives were defined by service-area size (called the sector) and the number of vehicles assigned to a sector.[46] Sector size was defined as either the entire county or one of five wedged-shaped factions of the county. Level-of-service (LOS) factors and system resource utilization and cost factors were then determined for each combination of service area and number of vehicles. From these data, an analyst was able to evaluate three possible demand-responsive service options.

- *Option A*: Purchase enough vehicles (5) to meet the target demand and run them over the entire county (761 rte.-mi).
- *Option B*: Purchase enough vehicles (4) to meet the target demand and run the entire fleet within a sector (571 rte.-mi). Alternate sectors according to the day of the week.
- *Option C*: Confine service to sectors but operate vehicles simultaneously in all sectors (673 rte.-mi). Purchase enough vehicles (5) to meet demand or provide at least daily service in each sector.

Differences in the options lead to some interesting cost base comparisons for the particular area. By restricting service to one sector per day, the fleet size could be reduced by one vehicle and the route mileage by 25% on a countywide service. Also, daily operating costs (including fuel, insurance, license, maintenance, repair, labor, and vehicle depreciation, but not administrative cost) could be reduced by approximately 20%. If through an interest matrix it was revealed that the passengers found a once-a-week service frequency unacceptable, then by purchasing a fifth vehicle, service could be improved. A vehicle could be assigned to each of five sectors, with all vehicles operating simultaneously. This might be an acceptable alternative, although daily operating costs would increase to a level comparable to the cost of option A. If, according to the interest matrix, it was revealed that cost per mile was acceptable with option A to an appropriate interest group, then option C with simultaneous service to all sectors would be slightly preferable to the unrestricted countywide service from an operation standpoint.

Data to evaluate alternatives before operations begin are difficult but not impossible to develop. By developing a sample budget and then comparing the system cost to similar systems, costs can be compared. Evaluation after operations have been initiated is more straightforward, and data are available from most state departments of transportation on operating costs. Table 14-10 presents a cost element structure to

TABLE 14-10
Cost Element Structure for Rural Transportation Systems

Overall Cost Category	Cost Elements
Operating costs	
Per vehicle-mile	Fuel
	Oil
	Tires and tubes
	Vehicle repairs and maintenance—parts
	Vehicle repairs and maintenance—nonvolunteer labor
	Vehicle repairs and maintenance—volunteer labor
Per vehicle-hour	Driver wages—nonvolunteer labor
	Driver wages—volunteer labor
	Dispatcher wages—nonvolunteer labor
	Dispatcher wages—volunteer labor
Per vehicle	Insurance
	Maintenance of dispatching equipment (base and mobile)
	Driver examinations and training, license, and tags
	Vehicle storage (including covered storage)
All other operating costs	General and administrative overhead
Capital costs	Vehicle capital
(including depreciation	Dispatching equipment capital (including
and interest charges)	dispatching base, repeaters, and mobile equipment)

Source: Adapted from Joe Lee, E. K. A. Tamakloe, and Tom Mulinazzi, *A Public Transportation Needs Study for the Low Density Areas in a Five-State Region in the Midwest (Iowa, Kansas, Missouri, Nebraska, and Oklahoma)*, Final Report (Washington, D.C.: U.S. Department of Transportation, April 1981), p. 49.

aid in evaluating costs before operations begin. Table 14-11 represents typical operating costs for various-size systems to aid in evaluating operating systems.

Regardless of whether the evaluation is before or after services have begun, the relationship between goals and costs cannot be ignored. Furthermore, even if a system is meeting goals at a satisfactory cost, monitoring still must take place. The evaluation process and relationship of goals is shown in Fig. 14-6 and reinforces the concept that costs and evaluation are always examined in some interest matrix context.

TABLE 14-11
Operating Costs per Trip and per Vehicle-Mile, by Size of System

	All Trips by All Providers	Fixed-Route Service Only	Demand-Responsive Only
All providers			
Operating cost per trip			
arithmetic mean	$2.98	$2.53	$3.55
median	$3.81	$5.30	$3.64
range*	$1.40–$13.74	$1.43–$12.62	$1.34–$15.84
Operating cost per vehicle-mile			
arithmetic mean	$1.29	$1.94	$1.09
median	$1.19	$1.77	$1.39
range*	$0.59–$13.74	$0.91–$3.67	$0.55–$2.21
Small providers (1-5 vehicles)			
Operating cost per trip			
arithmetic mean	$3.25	$3.03	$3.28
median	$3.62	$5.54	$3.17
range*	$1.69–$16.69	$1.84–$12.62	$1.69–$17.25
Operating cost per vehicle-mile			
arithmetic mean	$1.41	$1.63	$1.31
median	$1.42	$1.65	$1.42
range*	$0.61–$2.40	$0.96–$2.62	$0.74–$2.21
Large providers (6+ vehicles)			
Operating cost per trip			
arithmetic mean	$2.92	$2.40	$3.61
median	$3.87	$3.01	$4.42
range*	$1.30–$12.51	$1.43–$6.81	$1.01–$12.51
Operating cost per vehicle-mile			
arithmetic mean	$1.28	$2.08	$1.01
median	$1.21	$1.78	$1.13
range*	$0.61–$2.52	$1.16–$3.67	$0.51–$2.09

*Range excludes 10% of cases at each end of array.

Source: Adapted from Community Transportation Association of America, "Profile of Section 18 Programs" (draft 1990).

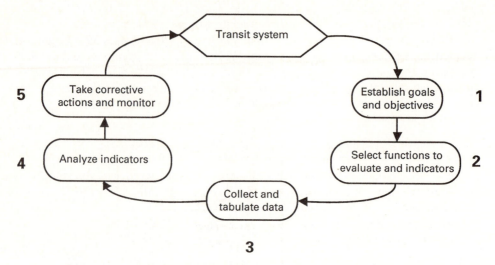

Figure 14-6 *Performance evaluation steps. [Source: Carter-Goble Associates,* Rural Public Transportation Performance Evaluation Guide, *Final Report, prepared for Pennsylvania DOT, reprinted by Technology Sharing Program, Report no. DOT-I-83-31 (Washington, D.C.: U.S. Department of Transportation, November 1982), p. 4.]*

SUMMARY

Identifying the need and demand for rural transit services is an abstract and difficult process. However, the planning process whereby market-segment analysis and involvement of the community are coupled to select a feasible alternative can be systematic and reliable. This planning process that evaluates market segments for their needs and demand is based on the heritage of rural transit, serving those in greatest need.

When evaluating alternatives, there are many different types of strategies that all relate conceptually to cost evaluation. One alternative that should always be evaluated is coordination. While coordination evaluation is a critical planning step, it must be remembered that the American public demonstrates a willingness to support an isolated and fragmented rural transportation service (the school bus system). Consequently, the rural transit planner should not be hesitant to design a service that is somewhat narrow but has wide support on an interest matrix. When evaluating the selected alternatives, at least six principal institutional arrangements may be used; however, the determining factor for the selection of an institutional arrangement should be based on the potential for a strong financial plan that will allow a rural public transportation system to thrive and serve those in need.

REFERENCES

Some citations are no longer available from their original source. These citations are often available from the National Technical Information Service, U.S. Department of Commerce, 5285 Port Royal Road, Springfield, VA 22161. We have verified the order numbers for many of these citations, and they are found at the end of the citation. Prices are available through NTIS at the address above.

1   TRANSPORTATION SYSTEMS CENTER, *Rural Passenger Transportation: State of the Art, Overview*, Technology Sharing Series (Washington, D.C.: U.S. Department of Transportation, October 1976), p. 12.

2   INDIANA DEPARTMENT OF TRANSPORTATION, DIVISION OF PUBLIC TRANSPORTATION, *1988 Annual Report*, Indiana Public Transportation, (Indianapolis, Ind.: Indiana Department of Transportation, July 1989), p. 68.

3   TRANSPORTATION SYSTEMS CENTER, *State-Initiated Transportation Programs: Selected Case Studies*, Technology Sharing Series (Washington, D.C.: U.S. Department of Transportation, August 1980), pp. 26-38.

4   *Proceedings of the Conference on Rural and City Transit Policy*, March 30–April 1, 1977, University of California, Davis, eds. Timothy J. Tardiff, Arthur Saltzman, and Karen Lundegard (n.p.: University of California, Institute of Transportation Studies, June 1978), p. 58.

5   TRANSPORTATION SYSTEMS CENTER, *Rural Passenger Transportation*, p. 17.

6   COMMUNITY TRANSPORTATION ASSOCIATION OF AMERICA, "Profile of Section 18 Programs (draft 1990), Table 1.

7   Ibid., Table A-1.

8   TRANSPORTATION SYSTEMS CENTER, *State Initiated Transportation Programs*.

9   U.S. CONGRESS, SENATE COMMITTEE ON AGRICULTURE AND FORESTRY, SUBCOMMITTEE ON RURAL DEVELOPMENT, *The Transportation of People in Rural Areas* (Washington, D.C.: U.S. Government Printing Office, February 27, 1974), p. 11.

10 Ibid., p. 57.

11 Ibid., p. 7. The term "demand" in this report is used in its economic sense, viz. how much transit service will be consumed at a given price. "Need" on the other hand refers to the social consequences of not having transit service. If the lack of transit prevents persons from reaching essential shopping, medical attention, etc., then there is a "need" for such service. There is "demand" for transit service, however, only when someone is willing to pay for it.

12 Ibid., p. 11.

13 NATIONAL ASSOCIATION FOR TRANSPORTATION ALTERNATIVES (changed name to Community Transportation Association of America), *Equity in Transportation* (Washington, D.C.: National Association for Transportation Alternatives, March 1988), p. 2.

14 Portions of this section previously appeared in the first edition of *Public Transportation: Planning, Operations and Management*, eds. GEORGE E. GRAY AND LESTER A. HOEL (Englewood Cliffs, N.J.: Prentice-Hall, 1978), Chap. 23, "Rural Public Transportation" by Robert J. Popper, Department of Civil Engineering, Virginia Polytechnic and State University and John W. Dickey, Environmental and Urban Studies, Virginia Polytechnic Institute and State University.

15   JOHN W. DICKEY, *Rural Public Transportation Needs and Recommendations* (Blacksburg, Va.: Virginia Polytechnic Institute and State University, Center for Urban and Regional Studies, November 1973), pp. 8-22.

16   NATIONAL AREA DEVELOPMENT INSTITUTE, *Prelude to Legislation to Solve the Growing Crisis in Rural Transportation, Part II: Meeting Rural Transportation Needs*, prepared for the U.S. Senate, Committee on Agriculture and Forestry (Washington, D.C.: U.S. Government Printing Office, February 10, 1975), p. 281.

17   JON E. BURKHARDT AND CHARLES L. EBY, "Need as a Criterion for Transportation Planning," in *Transportation Systems Planning and Analysis*, Highway Research Record 435 (Washington, D.C.: Highway Research Board, 1973), p. 37.

18   JOHN W. DICKEY AND CHARLES B. NOTESS, "Rural Public Transportation: Problems and Needs," in *Toward a Unification of National and State Policy (and Action) on the Transportation Disadvantaged, Part II: Rural Perspectives*, Proceedings of the Fourth Annual Conference on the Transportation Disadvantaged, December 3, 4, 5, 1974, St. Petersburg Beach, Florida, eds. William G. Bell and William T. Olsen (Tallahassee, Fla.: Florida State University, n.d.), pp. 1-32.

19   U.S. DEPARTMENT OF COMMERCE, BUREAU OF THE CENSUS, *County and City Data Book 1972: A Statistical Abstract Supplement*, ed. William Lerner (Washington, D.C.: U.S. Government Printing Office, 1973).

20   ROBERT L. MARTIN AND OTHERS, *Summary Report: Planning and Development Program for Mass Transportation Services and Facilities for the Elderly and Handicapped in the State of Georgia* (Raleigh N.C.: Kimley-Horn and Associates, Inc., April 1975).

21   JON E. BURKHARDT AND OTHERS, *The Transportation Needs of the Rural Poor*, prepared for the Office of Research and Development, U.S. DOT (Bethesda, Md.: Resource Management Corporation, July 1969), p. 14. Now available as PB 185 253.

22   TIMOTHY J. TARDIFF, TENNY M. LAM, AND JAMES P. DANA, *Small City and Rural Transportation Planning: A Review*, Report no. IT-D-SR-77-2 (Davis, Calif.: University of California, Davis, Department of Civil Engineering, January 1977), p. 33.

23   BRENDON HEMILY, *Strategic Planning in Small and Medium-Size Transit Agencies: A Discussion of Practice and Issues*, Final Report, prepared by the Institute for Urban Transportation, Center for Transit Research and Management Development, Indiana University, for UMTA (Washington, D.C.: Urban Mass Transportation Administration, August 1986), p. 3. Now available as PB 87 145 793.

24   N. CRAIG MILLER AND JOHN C. GOODNIGHT, "Policies and Procedures for Planning Transit Systems in Small Urban Areas," in *Transit Planning and Development*, Highway Research Record 449 (Washington, D.C.: Highway Research Board, 1973), pp. 14-20.

25   See reference 14.

26   CENTER FOR SYSTEMS AND PROGRAM DEVELOPMENT, INCORPORATED, *Best Practices in Specialized and Human Services Transportation Coordination*, prepared for HUD and U.S. DOT, Technology Sharing Program, Report no. DOT-T-89-20 (Washington, D.C.: U.S. Department of Transportation, July 1989), pp. 90-103.

27   Ibid., pp. 108-112.

28   FREDERIC D. FRAVEL AND OTHERS, *Innovative Funding for Intercity Modes: A Casebook of State, Local, and Private Approaches*, Final Report, prepared by Ecosometrics, Incorporated, for U.S. DOT,

Technology Sharing Program, Report no. DOT-I-87-21 (Washington, D.C.: U.S. Department of Transportation, July 1987), p. 39.

29 EXPANDED METRO MOBILITY TASK FORCE, *Rural Transportation in the Southeast*, prepared for U.S. DOT (Atlanta, Ga.: Southeastern Federal Regional Council, November 1984). Now available as PB 238 880.

30 FLORIDA DEPARTMENT OF TRANSPORTATION AND TOUCHE ROSS AND COMPANY, *Management Manual for Small Transit Systems* (Tallahassee, Fla.: Florida Department of Transportation, August 1981), p. 110.

31 See reference 14.

32 DAVID T. HARTGEN AND CAROL A. KECK, *Forecasting Dial-A-Bus Ridership in Small Urban Areas*, in *Public Transportation Planning*, Transportation Research Record 563 (Washington, D.C.: Transportation Research Board, 1976), p. 57.

33 JON E. BURKHARDT AND WILLIAM W. MILLAR, "Estimating Cost of Providing Rural Transportation Service," in *Transportation for Elderly, Disadvantaged, and Handicapped People in Rural Areas*, Transportation Research Record 578 (Washington, D.C.: Transportation Research Board, 1976), pp. 8-15.

34 JON E. BURKHARDT AND ARMANDO M. LAGO, "The Demand for Rural Public Transportation Routes," in *Proceedings—Seventeenth Annual Meeting, Beyond the Bicentennial: The Transportation Challenge*, Transportation Research Forum, 17, no. 1 (Boston) (Oxford, Ind.: The Richard B. Cross Company, 1976), pp. 498-503.

35 NORRIS H. MILLIKIN, HERB DROSDAT, AND DONALD DEAN, *Transit Needs in Small California Communities*, Interim Report, prepared by the California Department of Transportation, Divisions of Mass Transportation and Transportation Planning, Report no. DMT 013 (Sacramento, Calif.: Caltrans), p. 46.

36 APPLIES RESOURCE INTEGRATION, LTD., *Planning Guidelines for Coordinated Agency Transportation Services* (reissued version), prepared for U.S. DOT and U.S. Department of Health and Human Services, Report no. DOT-I-87-33 (Washington, D.C.: U.S. Government Printing Office, April 1980), p. 7.

37 MICHAEL J. GREENE, *Coordinating Rural Transit: Stretching State Resources for Better Service* (Lexington, Ky.: The Council of State Governments, 1987), p. vii.

38 SUANNE BROOKS, *Transportation Authorities in Federal Human Services Program* (Atlanta, Ga.: U.S. Department of Health, Education, and Welfare, Office of the Regional Director, March 1, 1976), pp. 7-8. Now available as SHR-0000739.

39 ARTHUR SALTZMAN, *Coordination of Transportation by Human Service Agencies: An Interorganizational Perspective*, Ph.D. dissertation for the University of California, Irvine, reprinted in Technology Sharing Program (Washington, D.C.: U.S. Department of Transportation, January 1980), p. 183.

40 GREENE, *Coordinating Rural Transit*, p. vi.

41 MACDORMAN AND ASSOCIATES AND OTHERS, *Risk Management Manual for the Public Transit Industry*, Vol. 1, prepared for UMTA Technical Assistance Program, Technology Sharing Program, Report no. DOT-T-88-23 (Washington, D.C.: U.S. Department of Transportation, August 1988), p. III.2.

42 COMMUNITY TRANSPORTATION ASSOCIATION OF AMERICA, "Profile of Section 18 Programs" (draft 1990), Table 1.

43   PENNSYLVANIA DEPARTMENT OF TRANSPORTATION, BUREAU OF PUBLIC TRANSIT AND GOODS MOVEMENT SYSTEMS, *Pennsylvania Rural and Small Urban Statistical Report, Fiscal Years 1984-85 and 1985-86* (Harrisburg, Pa.: Pennsylvania Department of Transportation, April 1987), p. 19.

44   Tardiff, *Small City and Rural Transportation Planning*, p. 26.

45   JOE LEE, E. K. A. TAMAKLOE, AND TOM MULINAZZI, *A Public Transportation Needs Study for the Low Density Areas in a Five-State Region in the Midwest (Iowa, Kansas, Missouri, Nebraska, and Oklahoma)*, Final Report (Washington, D.C.: U.S. Department of Transportation, April 1981), p. 91.

46   R. J. POPPER AND M. D. BENT, "Simulation Modeling of Demand Responsive Rural Public Transportation Services," in *Modeling and Simulation 7, Part I* (Pittsburg, Pa.: Instrument Society of America, 1976), pp. 439-44.

FURTHER READING

BEADLE, CHARLES R., AND SHELDON M. EDNER, *The Eighth National Conference on Rural Public Transportation*, prepared for UMTA, Technology Sharing Program, Report no. DOT-T-88-16. Washington, D.C.: U.S. Department of Transportation, August 1988.

E G & G DYNATREND, INC., *Rural and Small Urban Transit Managers Workshop. Student Workbook*, Final Report, prepared by Center for Urban Studies for UMTA, Technology Sharing Program, Report no. DOT-T-90-09. Washington, D.C.: Department of Transportation, July 1989.

HOWARD, DAVID M., *A Handbook on Rural Elderly Transportation Services: A Practical Introduction to Operating and Evaluating a Rural Elderly Transportation System*, prepared by the National Resource Center for Rural Elderly. Kansas City, Mo.: University of Missouri, 1989.

MICHIGAN DEPARTMENT OF TRANSPORTATION, BUS TRANSIT DIVISION, *Small Transit System Management Handbook*, Michigan Public Transportation Program. Lansing, Mich.: Michigan Department of Transportation, December 1985. Now available as PB 87 161 402.

SMERK, G. M., AND OTHERS, *Mass Transit Management: A Handbook for Small Cities*, Parts 1-4 (3rd ed. rev.), prepared by the Institute for Urban Transportation, Center for Transit Research and Development, for UMTA, University Research and Training Program, Technology Sharing Program, Report no. DOT-T-88-12. Washington D.C.: U.S. Government Printing Office, February 1988.

WILLIAM G. BELL AND ASSOCIATES, *Specialized Transportation for Rural Elderly Floridians: A Coordinated Approach*, report of a study by the Multidisciplinary Center on Gerontology, Florida State University, for the International Exchange Center on Gerontology, University of South Florida. Tampa, Fla.: University of South Florida, July 1983. Now available as PB 88 133 962.

EXERCISES

14-1   It has been said that passenger transportation is perhaps the most critical element in the delivery of social services. How can public transportation planners use this to their advantage?

14-2   Develop a matrix rating five agencies and their willingness to coordinate. Scale the matrix so that one agency clearly wishes to coordinate and one clearly does not want to coordinate. Use a semantic differential with 5 a high score and 1 a low score on each of the principal coordination factors.

14-3   Community involvement in the planning process is critical to the success of any planning effort. Who should be on the planning committee and what special issues should the creator of the committee be alert to as the committee is developed?

14-4   Examine the elapsed time for selected planning milestones in Table 14-3 and the planning model in Fig. 14-1 and note that it takes approximately 17 months to complete the planning process. If, as shown in Table 14-3, calling the initial organizing meeting takes 5.3 months, what could the planner for a new service do if she or he must complete the process in 12 months to meet the terms of a planning grant?

14-5   In the process of identifying needs and assessing demand, what factors are least difficult to assess and which are most difficult?

14-6   Develop an organization chart for a service that is large enough to support a planning position and list those functions from Fig. 14-5 that could be the responsibility of the planner.

14-7   Figure 14-7 presents an evaluation process. Which steps will have the most involvement from the policy board or governing body?

14-8   List three performance indicators for monitoring ridership and then list the corresponding data required to evaluate the indicators. Finally, list the possible corrective actions for improving the performance indicators.

14-9   Using the following matrix, which areas of the matrix would be best served by fixed-route, fixed-schedule conventional transit? demand-responsive transit? a volunteer automobile-based transit program? a taxi user side subsidy?

Priority Ranking for Passengers

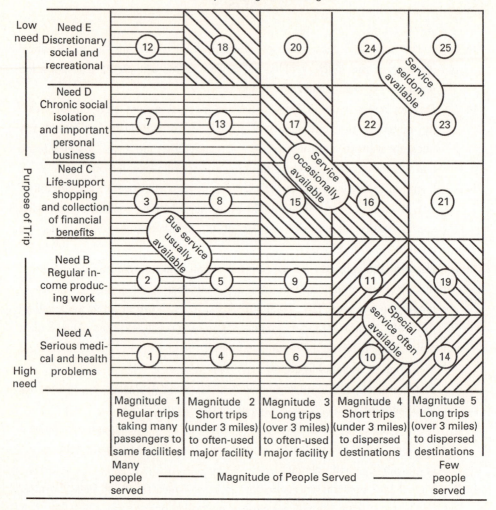

Notes:

1. The numbers in the circles indicate the priority that will be assigned to that trip.

2. The lower the priority number, the greater the chance that the system will be able to provide service.

3. Passengers with high numbers may be able to get service later when the demand is less or may not be able to get service at all.

4. This figure is intended for management use. It is not designed to be understood by laypersons or passengers.

Source: Dave Systems, Inc., Anaheim, Calif., no date.

Chapter 15

FINANCING PUBLIC TRANSPORTATION

RONALD F. KIRBY

Since World War II, the financing of public transportation systems in the United States has become increasingly the responsibility of the federal, state, and local governments and special governmental agencies. In 1945, only 2% of the nation's transit systems and 16% of all transit vehicles were owned by governmental agencies, whereas in 1985 some 30% of the systems and 80% of the vehicles were publicly owned. And while passenger and other revenues covered virtually all the operating expenses of transit systems in the 1940s, almost 60% of total transit revenues in the late 1980s came from public operating assistance funds provided at the federal, state, and local levels.[1]

In the early part of this century, governmental involvement in public transit was limited to regulatory activities. Local governments awarded exclusive operating franchises to streetcar and bus companies in return for their commitment to maintain prescribed fare and service levels. As increasing automobile ownership and low-density suburban development eroded the market for transit after World War I, the financial condition of these private transit monopolies gradually deteriorated, in large part because local authorities would neither approve fare increases and service cutbacks requested by transit managers nor directly subsidize unprofitable services that they insisted should continue to be provided. These policies led many private transit firms to defer capital maintenance and replacement, and eventually to relinquish their financial participation in the urban transit systems by agreeing to public buy outs. This cycle was repeated after World War II.

The financial involvement of governments in mass transit grew initially out of concerns that the deteriorating capital equipment of the private transit companies might lead to the abandonment of much of the existing service structure. The federal Urban Mass Transportation Act of 1964 created a discretionary capital assistance program that provided up to two-thirds (later increased to 80%) of the funds for upgrading transit capital equipment. With the aid of these federal funds, city after city purchased the assets of its private transit company and established a public transit authority. These authorities were directed to offer services and fare structures prescribed by local decision makers, resulting in annual operating deficits that had to be covered by public funds. In the larger cities, public ownership and subsidies often predated federal involvement, with state and local governments providing the funding.

In 1974 the federal government began to provide operating as well as capital assistance for transit, and state and local governments gradually increased their financial contributions to match federal funds and to provide additional capital and operating funds. Total public operating assistance increased steadily from $1.4 billion in 1975 to $9 billion in 1988. Of total industry revenues of $15.4 billion in 1988, 36% came from passengers, 6% came from other operating revenues, 52% came from state and local operating assistance, and 6% came from federal operating assistance.[2]

The nation's public transit systems face a number of major financing challenges over the coming decade. The federal role in financing transit has declined during the 1980s, and the prospects for reversing that decline with the reauthorization of the federal Surface Transportation Act in 1991 are rather uncertain. Although state and local governments have increased their shares of transit assistance as the shares supported by the federal government and farebox revenues have declined, it is not at all clear that this trend can be sustained nationwide. And perhaps most importantly, the growth in suburb-to-suburb travel, especially since the early 1980s, has contributed to a decline in the share of trips served by radial fixed-route transit systems and focused attention on other more flexible forms of public transportation, such as minibuses, organized car- and vanpools, shared taxi, and dial-a-ride systems. This chapter briefly reviews current financing programs, identifies some key issues that need to be addressed, and discusses the prospects for developing more effective financing strategies for public transportation systems in the future.

REVIEW OF CURRENT FINANCING PROGRAMS

The financing of public transportation is currently undergoing significant change as the federal government is redirecting and reducing its role. Its declining participation is expected to be replaced by state, local, and private sector support.

CHANGING FUNDING SOURCES

The most striking trend in the financial structure in the nation's public transit systems since the 1960s has been the declining share of total operating revenues contributed by passenger fares. From almost complete reliance on passenger fares in 1960, the transit industry has seen the percentage of transit revenues attributed to passenger fares decline steadily to around 54% in 1975, 39% in 1980, and 36% in 1988. This shift has been accompanied by a steady increase in the number and scope of governmental mandates on the recipients of public funds and a growing orientation of transit managers toward the requirements of government funding agencies along with traditional obligations to the interests of transit passengers.

Transit funding recipients and managers now have to conform to a range of planning, programming, and reporting procedures, to specifications on vehicles and other capital acquisitions, to reduced off-peak fare provisions for the elderly, to the provision of specialized services for disabled persons unable to use conventional services, and, under the federal assistance program, to labor protection requirements precluding any worsening of the conditions of transit workers. The Americans with Disabilities Act of 1990, though not directly related to transit funding programs, will require transit agencies to make their services fully accessible to disabled persons, as well as to provide paratransit services for those unable to use accessible transit. All these mandates have had significant implications for the costs of transit services, although these costs have rarely been fully quantified or related to the levels of government assistance being provided.

A second significant trend has been the decline since the early 1980s in the level and percentage of operating assistance provided by the federal government. Federal operating assistance peaked in 1981 at $1.095 billion and 17.3% of operating revenues and had declined by 1988 to $950 million and 6.2% of operating revenues. This decline was part of a general cutback in funding for domestic programs by the federal government and will be difficult to reverse in the face of the federal budget pressures that are currently projected for the early 1990s.

INCREASED STATE AND LOCAL SUPPORT

As federal operating assistance has declined, however, state and local assistance has increased. The notable trend in this regard has been the growing role of state governments, many of which had been concerned solely with highway programs until well into the 1970s.[3] According to the most recent report by the American Association of State Highway and Transportation Officials (AASHTO),[4,5] 39 of the 50 states had subsidy programs in 1989, and the total financial commitment of the states of $4.2 billion substantially exceeded the $3.2 billion provided by the federal government. Whereas many of the states entered into transit assistance initially to fill the growing gap between transit revenues and costs, most have now developed proactive assistance programs with their own mandates and requirements. The states have also become increasingly active in the provision of technical assistance to their transit systems and in the monitoring of their financial and operating performance. The states have drawn for their financial assistance programs on a wide variety of revenue sources, including general revenues, sales taxes, fuel taxes, lottery proceeds, and turnpike revenues.

Local government operating and capital assistance is provided almost everywhere (except in a few states that generally operate transit themselves). A wide variety of local revenue sources is used, including general revenues from property taxes, sales taxes, bridge and tunnel tolls, and dedicated highway taxes. Many local transit agencies have sought dedicated taxes for transit services. The Urban Mass Transportation Administration's Section 15 report for 1986 showed dedicated local assistance as 23% of all public operating assistance, compared with 28% for local general assistance, 11% for dedicated state assistance, 24% for state general assistance, and 14% for federal assistance.[6]

The appropriate levels of passenger fares relative to public financial assistance for transit systems have been the subject of much discussion and debate over the three decades or so of extensive public assistance for transit. Cervero[7] conducted polls to determine the percentage of total social benefits that state and local officials thought accrued at the local, state, and federal levels and calculated that, on the basis of perceived distribution of benefits, users should bear 50% of transit costs, local governments 25%, states 12%, and the federal government 13%. In a 1981 study, the U.S. General Accounting Office (GAO) called for local areas to recover more of their operating costs from the farebox and to develop more equitable fare structures, using, for example, distance-based rather than flat fares. The GAO concluded that many simple fare structures were inequitable, because short-distance, inner-city, off-peak trip makers were paying more per mile than suburban work-trip makers.[8]

IMPACTS OF GOVERNMENT SUPPORT CHANGES

Assessments of the impacts of government support for transit operating expenses, particularly federal operating aid, have been controversial. Pickrell[9] concluded that, although there was little evidence that federal operating assistance aggravated historical declines in transit operating and financial performance, the persistence of these declines compromised the effectiveness of federal aid in promoting the goals of service expansion, ridership increases, and fare reductions. He estimated that, of the federal operating aid provided over the period from 1975 to 1984, 42% went to offset higher costs of existing services, 26% for new services, 24% for replacing fare revenues, and 8% for other purposes. He attributed these impacts to rising labor expenses, declining labor productivity, expansion into difficult-to-serve markets, and fare reductions for commuters who would have continued to use the service at higher fares.

By comparison, a 1985 analysis by the American Public Transit Association (APTA)[10] estimated that transit performance and productivity actually stabilized and improved over the period from 1975 to 1980, following the inception of federal operating aid. This analysis showed favorable trends in terms of real expenses/passenger, passengers/employee, passengers/vehicle-mi, vehicle-mi/employee, and stabilization in real expenses per vehicle-mi. APTA designed its study to test the hypothesis advanced by transit critics that federal aid actually caused a decline in transit performance and productivity. Based on comparison of the periods 1970 to 1975 and 1975 to 1980, APTA concluded that the reverse may be true. The period in which transit performance and productivity increased, according to APTA's analysis, was coincident with the initiation and increase of federal operating assistance to transit.

In its 1988 report to Congress, the Urban Mass Transportation Administration

(UMTA)[11] concluded that the federal assistance program, in partnership with state and local assistance, "has made considerable progress in restoring the nation's transit infrastructure." UMTA pointed out that "the nation's bus fleet has been modernized, the needed support facilities have been provided to service bus fleets, a number of new rail systems have been built" and "the older rail systems, built before the advent of the UMTA program, are being modernized."

UMTA also concluded in its 1988 report , however, that transit operating costs per passenger had increased substantially in real terms over the 20-year period of the UMTA program due to declining labor productivity, relatively high employee compensation, extension of service farther into low-density suburban areas, and ownership of rolling stock well in excess of peak requirements. The report also concluded that "the industry has not maximized the benefits of [the] capital investment" provided under the UMTA program. Among several reasons cited for "reduced efficiency in the use of the capital funding provided" were attempting to serve some peak demand that could be served more economically by ridesharing or private-sector operators; focusing too much on capital expansion and not enough on maintenance and modernization of existing equipment; and "reluctance to consider alternative forms of service provision, such as busways, timed transfers, paratransit, and competitive procurement of services."

SUPPORT IN NONURBANIZED AREAS

Various forms of public assistance also have been evolving over recent years in nonurbanized areas with populations less than 50,000. In 1978 a new Section 18 was added to the federal Urban Mass Transportation Act to provide funding for nonurbanized areas. In addition, Section 16(b)2 of the act, added in 1970, has provided capital assistance for services for elderly and disabled persons. The combination of services for nonurbanized areas and for elderly and disabled residents of both urbanized and nonurbanized areas is sometimes categorized under the heading of "community transportation." In a 1986 study, Rural America[12] reported that around $2 billion was being devoted annually to these services. Only 7% of these funds came from UMTA, however; 53% came from other federal agencies such as the Department of Health and Human Services, 16% came from state governments, and the remaining 24% came from local sources, including the farebox. Rural America estimated that community transportation services account for approximately 500 million one-way trips each year, at an average cost of $3.80.

Whereas in urbanized area transit systems farebox and other revenue account for over 40% of total general revenue (excluding capital assistance), in nonurbanized area public transportation systems farebox and other system revenue account for less than 30% of the total.[13] Such systems are much more dependent on operating assistance from the federal, state, and local governments, which provide approximately equal shares of the total public assistance required. The level of support for nonurbanized area transit has continued to be quite strong in the U.S. Congress, with Section 18 program funding having been sustained at around $75 million per year. In addition, a new $5 million per year technical assistance program was initiated in 1987. The low levels of cost recovery from the farebox make these nonurbanized systems quite dependent on public financial assistance, however, and rather vulnerable to any cutbacks that may occur due to budget pressures at any of the three government levels.

THE DIVERSE TRANSIT INDUSTRY

In its compendium of national urban mass transportation statistics for 1986, UMTA reported that the transit industry operates over 60,000 vehicles: 42,000 buses, 7700 rapid rail cars, 560 streetcars, 500 trolleybuses, 3900 commuter rail cars, and 6200 demand-responsive and other vehicles. Much of the service provided by the smaller vehicles is omitted from the statistics collected by UMTA: the statistics collected deal primarily with conventional bus and rail systems. Motor bus services dominate the conventional systems, accounting for almost 80% of the vehicles, over 70% of the vehicle-miles, 68% of the passengers, and 54% of the passenger-miles. The 19 largest motor bus systems make up only 5% of the 379 bus systems, but account for over 50% of the bus-miles of service, 67% of the passengers, and 64% of the passenger-miles.

Of the 438 transit systems reporting to UMTA, only 10 (or 2%) had over 1000 vehicles. Over 60% of the systems operated fewer than 50 vehicles, and over 90% operated fewer than 250 vehicles. These figures indicate that the transit industry comprises a small number of rather large systems together with a large number of very much smaller systems. For this reason, aggregate statistics on the transit industry tend to be dominated by the characteristics of the larger systems and often mask completely the characteristics of the smaller systems. Almost 60% of all the conventional passenger-miles served in the nation are accounted for by the three largest systems: New York, Chicago, and San Francisco–Oakland, with New York alone accounting for over 40%.

This diversity in the size of transit systems complicates government funding. Based on ridership alone, resources invested in the largest systems may have greater impact. The services in the smaller areas, however, are of major importance to those areas. Although they may be considerably more expensive to provide on a per-ride basis, such systems fill a social need and have considerable local and congressional support.

REASONS FOR GOVERNMENTAL SUPPORT

In assessing the appropriateness of alternative financing schemes for transit, it is important to keep in mind the basic reasons or purposes for which transit is used. In its 1988 report to Congress, UMTA noted that urban-area residents use transit for one of the following two reasons: because transit offers a more convenient or economical service for peak-hour commuting than the alternatives, or because they are without immediate access to an automobile and need transit to provide their basic mobility. The first group of users resides primarily in larger urbanized areas where the congestion and out-of-pocket costs of using an automobile make transit an attractive option for the work trip. The second group of users reside in urban areas of all sizes, but make up a larger share of transit trips in the medium and smaller areas.

Current transit financing schemes have grown up over several decades, often starting out as stopgap measures to address short-term problems, such as unexpected growth in annual operating deficits or a worrisome deterioration in the condition of transit capital equipment. The 1990s seem likely to be a period of increasing budget stringency at all levels of government, which will require greater scrutiny of all public assistance programs. The level and type of public transit financing may depend to a greater degree than in the past on how well transit is serving the basic purposes for which public funding is being provided. Several independent assessments of current financing arrangements have found them to be falling short of meeting their objectives for a variety of reasons having to do with the structure and administration of the assistance programs.[14] A careful reassessment of the purposes and performance of public assistance programs for transit will be needed if a strong case is to be made for sustaining these programs in the challenging budget climate of the 1990s.

CURRENT ISSUES

Public transportation systems play important roles in the transportation systems of virtually all U.S. cities, though, as previously discussed, these roles vary considerably with city size and urban form. In very large cities with historically strong central areas, like New York, Chicago, and San Francisco, rail and bus transit systems provide much of the capacity for downtown-oriented travel, accounting for over half of all daily work trips to and from the central core. In medium and smaller urban areas, transit serves much lower proportions of trips, but still provides an important source of mobility for urban residents, particularly those without convenient access to an automobile. Many of the smallest urban areas with little or no fixed-route transit rely instead on various forms of paratransit, including carpools, shared taxis, and minibuses. Such paratransit services also play an important role in larger urban areas, to supplement fixed-route transit in high-density areas and to provide substitute services for low-density travel and for special user groups unable to use conventional transit.

PERFORMANCE EFFECTS ON FINANCIAL SUPPORT

Despite well-known and substantial benefits derived from public transit, public assistance programs for transit have been challenged continually throughout their over 30 years of existence as not adequately meeting expectations. The disappointing performance of transit financing programs can be attributed in part to unrealistic goals that grew up around the various programs, including reviving decaying downtown areas, reducing air pollution, conserving energy, serving the travel needs of the disabled, and reducing traffic congestion. While public transit programs can contribute to the achievement of these goals, other supporting measures must also be enacted, such as the elimination of parking subsidies, regulation of the use of congested roads, implementation of high-occupancy vehicle lanes, higher fuel taxes, and land-use policies that promote higher-density development in transit corridors and around transit stations. In countries like Canada that have enacted such measures, mass transit systems have performed much better.

The disappointing performance of transit financing programs must also be attributed, however, to inappropriate governmental policies and programs.[15] The large capital component of the federal transit program has distorted local decision making toward capital-intensive transit systems that qualify for federal assistance. This distortion has led to the neglect of potentially more cost-effective strategies, such as the provision of high-occupancy lanes for both transit and other high-occupancy vehicles and the greater use of private firms that can supply their own capital equipment, such as taxicab companies and private bus and van operators. Although many of the larger rail transit and bus operations were badly in need of capital assistance and made good use of the UMTA program, political pressures at all levels of government led to some notably poor transit investments, from overly expensive new heavy rail lines in some larger cities to overcapitalized bus fleets and maintenance facilities in many medium and small urban areas. Even the public acquisition of private bus companies facilitated by the UMTA program can be questioned: simply contracting with these or other competing companies for specified services might well have been more cost effective.

PROVIDER-SIDE VERSUS USER-SIDE SUBSIDIES

Another characteristic of current financial assistance programs that limits their potential effectiveness is that they are almost always administered in the form of provider-side subsidies. With provider-side subsidies, funding is disbursed directly to transportation providers for offering services and fare policies that are specified by the funding agency. An alternative approach, user-side subsidies, permits qualified users to purchase transportation vouchers at prices substantially below the value of the vouchers to the transportation providers.[16] The users can exchange the vouchers for the transportation services of their choice, and the providers of the chosen services can redeem the vouchers with the funding agency at values agreed upon in advance. This latter approach encourages competition between providers and tailoring of service offerings to meet the preferences of the users. User-side subsidies have been used extensively to support specialized door-to-door services for elderly and disabled persons in cities like Milwaukee and San Diego and for services to the general public in a few smaller cities like Santa Fe, New Mexico, and Danville, Illinois. User-side subsidies have also been used to provide additional fare discounts to selected users on conventional transit systems, though for reasons of administrative convenience rather than to stimulate competition and service diversification.

Experience to date with user-side subsidies suggests that users can obtain high-quality services from competing providers and that diversity in service offerings and fares is encouraged. Some administrative challenges may be encountered, however, in reimbursing providers and guarding against fraud. Experience with provider-side subsidies, the most common approach for public transportation, suggests that, although administration of the subsidy funds is relatively straightforward, competition between providers is very limited or nonexistent, and serious concerns arise with regard to service costs and efficiency. Both approaches seem likely to continue to be employed to varying degrees in the disbursement of public assistance funds for public transportation.

PRIVATE SECTOR SUPPORT

In the late 1980s, the federal government has focused much of its policy development effort in public transportation on promoting greater private sector participation in the financing and operation of transit services. In large part, this initiative was modeled on the rather ambitious privatization programs undertaken in the United Kingdom during the early 1980s, which restructured the ownership and operation of public transportation and other industries throughout the country. In the United States, the scope of privatization efforts by the federal government was limited by the strong state and local government role in public transportation decision making, and by the fact that the UMTA program has within it several structural features that tend to work against privatization. Local governments that sold off transit assets acquired using federal funds would have had to return the federal share of the proceeds to the U.S. Treasury, for example, and Section 13(c) of the Urban Mass Transportation Act, along with various state and local laws and collective bargaining agreements, essentially precludes any form of privatization that would worsen the condition of existing mass transit employees.

As the various implications of privatization strategies unfolded, the UMTA initiative shifted away from the notion of private ownership as pursued in the United Kingdom and toward the concept of greater competition in service delivery. Under this concept, local transit officials were required by UMTA regulation to consider private sector providers whenever new or substantially restructured services were under consideration. Procedures were developed for using UMTA capital assistance funds to pay for the depreciation and financing costs of privately owned equipment being used in the provision of publicly assisted services. Procedures were also developed for making fair cost comparisons between public and private carriers bidding on the same set of services. Some cities, such as Los Angeles and Miami, undertook major efforts to involve private operators, and significant initial cost savings were reported in several locations. Over time, privately owned and operated transit services may gradually increase their share of the public transit market, and the pressure of actual or threatened competition will likely stimulate efficiency improvements in publicly owned and operated services.

Another important dimension to the privatization initiatives of the federal government is the renewed emphasis on the participation of the private sector in the financing of public transportation. It has long been recognized that private land owners and developers benefit from major transit investments located close to their properties.

There have been a number of interesting case examples of the private sector contributing funding over and above farebox revenues to help support transit services from which they will benefit substantially. Examples include substantial private donations toward the rehabilitation of San Francisco's cable car system, $12 million in annual revenue from development leases around the rail stations of the Washington Metropolitan Area Transit Authority, and special benefit assessment districts in Denver, Miami, and Los Angeles. In Tampa and Pittsburgh, private developers have undertaken the provision of transit infrastructure to link their developments to other city activities. In New York, extensive private sector participation has been obtained in the rehabilitation of the Times Square subway station.

In providing up to 80% of the costs of major transit capital projects, the UMTA program has provided little incentive for local agencies to seek private cost-sharing arrangements for these projects. Recent UMTA guidance suggesting that preference will be given to projects seeking a lower federal share will tend to encourage and reward efforts to involve private financial participation in major projects. Although there is little evidence to suggest that private sector financing arrangements can in themselves underpin major new transit investments, as occurred for example with turn-of-the-century streetcar systems, there is clearly potential for public/private cost-sharing arrangements that match the cost burdens of these investments more closely to the benefits that they generate. Long-range transit investments are more likely to be feasible in the future if they are closely related to land-use policies and partly funded by *value capture* policies that tap part of the land-value appreciation for the transit infrastructure costs.

A further aspect of private sector financing that has been of significant benefit to a number of larger transit agencies is the use of tax-exempt and industrial development bonds and the use of safe-harbor leasing provisions. While these provisions were somewhat restricted in the 1986 Tax Act, under certain conditions they are still available to transit agencies. With regard to safe-harbor leasing, for example, UMTA has been encouraging transit agencies to consider "cross-border leasing," under which transit equipment would be leased from owners outside the United States who would receive tax benefits in their own countries. Agencies in San Diego, California, and New Jersey have concluded such arrangements. The future of these kinds of benefits will be largely determined by federal tax policies, which are likely to be under continual review as the Congress and the administration struggle to get the federal budget deficit under control.

LOCALLY SPONSORED SERVICES

One form of diversification and competition in the financing and operation of public transportation that preceded the federal initiative of the mid-1980s is the growth of locally sponsored services in lieu of services provided by the regional operator. The Washington, D.C., metropolitan area was a leader in this development, when Montgomery County, Maryland, and then Fairfax County and the City of Alexandria, Virginia, established their own local services with smaller vehicles and less restrictive labor arrangements than the regional carrier. While cost savings were an important consideration in these developments, the ability to make local decisions independently of the constraints of the regional system was also important. These systems have begun to contract out some of their services to private operators, although they are primarily publicly owned and operated. None of these systems uses federal funds, since all those funds are needed to support the regional carrier, and there is no point in the local systems assuming all the administrative burdens and requirements associated with the federal funding program. If federal funds continue to decline as a share of the total public funding for public transportation, more metropolitan areas are likely to follow the example of the Washington area in developing their own locally financed and operated services to supplement regional services.

LAND USE AND VALUE CAPTURE

Land use determinations tied to developing or improving transit service offer opportunities to enhance transit financing in many areas. This can take many forms—from rental income from a newsstand at a bus timed transfer station to partial income from a multimillion dollar shopping center with an integrated rail station, as found in Atlanta, Toronto, and Montreal. Increasingly, transit systems are recognizing these opportunities for *value capture* in developing capital programs. The possibilities are as broad as the enterprising organization can implement through legislation, land-use regulations, planning policies, private cooperation, and local support.

Perhaps the most important issue for the future of transit financing lies in the evolving land-use patterns and travel demand in the nation's urban areas. A continuation of the patterns of the past three decades will see the market for conventional fixed-route transit services erode further, with the share of urban travel served by transit shifting more and more to private automobile and more flexible transit modes, such as suburban minibus systems and car- and vanpool services. Under these conditions, the constituency for transit funding will also weaken, and the task of maintaining historical shares of public funding for transit will become increasingly difficult. At the same time, cost pressures will continue to escalate, with new government mandates to provide fully accessible transit to disabled persons, to provide paratransit services to those unable to use accessible transit services, and to reduce emissions from transit vehicles as part of the national effort to improve air quality. If transit is to make a strong case for greater public financial support, the benefits of transit services will have to be convincingly articulated, and the criticisms leveled at transit operating efficiency will have to be effectively countered. In addition,

> If transportation facilities are viewed as an essential utility, similar to sewer, water, or other public services, then they should be constructed as an integral element of any new land development venture. Accordingly, government officials are examining how to extract funds from developers that will help to pay for transportation facilities. Local communities, who are increasingly being asked to bear financial responsibility for providing infrastructure, are finding new ways to finance these improvements by imposing fees on developers. Private and public cooperation is emerging that involves techniques such as special assessment districts,

transportation utilities, exactions, and public–private equity arrangements. These techniques are not panaceas, and each has positive and negative features.

Other nonuser fees have been utilized for transportation projects. These are general revenue items such as taxes on income, sales, and property. Revenue is also raised through lotteries and special fees. Many of these fees have been allocated for local highway improvements where there is a linkage between transportation and land access.[16]

FUTURE PROSPECTS

In 1991 the federal surface transportation legislation will have to be reauthorized. The Interstate Highway System that has been the centerpiece of the federal transportation program since mid-1950 is nearing completion, and the continued participation of the federal government in the surface transportation system will have to be justified on somewhat different grounds. This reauthorization provides an opportunity for all the interested parties to reexamine the basic structure of the federal program that has evolved over the past 30 years and to develop a new structure suited to the needs and priorities of the 1990s and beyond. Although federal funds account for only around 25% of all funding for highways and public transportation, the federal program has had a far-reaching effect on all transportation expenditures and on the local land-use patterns that have evolved around federally funded transportation facilities. Decisions made on the federal program during 1991 will set the overall framework for state and local expenditures on both highways and public transportation and will greatly influence the future role of public transportation in the nation's urban areas.

In recognition of the importance of the federal reauthorization, a number of national associations and interest groups have been developing formal position statements for use in testimony and dialogue as the reauthorization process moves forward. The American Public Transit Association (APTA) has developed a report entitled *Transit 2000* that outlines the transit industry's views and positions on the federal reauthorization.[18] This document argues that "current highway and transit programs do not have the necessary responsiveness nor the flexibility to address current and emerging needs and problems," and that "greater flexibility should be allowed in the use of federal funds and a stronger multimodal approach to planning, funding, and decision making must be established." Other key recommendations of the APTA report include: "Federal transportation policies and programs should require closer integration of transportation investments and land use decisions in order to provide an environment that is conducive to and encourages increased provision and use of high-occupancy shared-ride services," and "The concept of transit should be broadened to encompass and promote increased availability and use of transit and other high-occupancy, shared-ride services in order to better serve diverse travel needs."

Many of the key themes identified in the APTA *Transit 2000* report also appeared in the National Transportation Policy issued by Secretary Skinner of the U.S. Department of Transportation early in 1990.[19] The concepts of flexibility in federal funding and closer integration of transportation investments with land-use decisions were particularly prominent in the secretary's policy. Whereas APTA's report called for "substantial additional federal funding . . . for public transportation," the secretary's policy called for a greater share of the financial burden to be borne by the state and local governments and the private sector. The level of federal funding to be provided for all forms of transportation will be the subject of considerable debate as the reauthorization progresses, with most of the transportation interest groups calling for increases in federal funding, and the congress and the administration currently more concerned about narrowing the federal budget deficit.

While it is too early to judge just what the federal reauthorization will hold for public transportation, it seems likely that the increased costs associated with federal mandates, combined with the traditional pressures for efficiency at the state and local levels and the continued trend toward suburban development of both housing and employment, will present major financing challenges for public transportation systems. It will be necessary for policy makers and managers to examine and utilize to the maximum extent possible all the many promising financing techniques, both traditional and nontraditional, that have been identified and used successfully over recent years. Among the more important strategies are the following:

- Seek opportunities to link transit investment and rehabilitation programs to land-use policies and decisions in ways that will provide for joint public/private financing arrangements.
- Provide more flexibility in the structure and administration of public subsidy programs to encourage and reinforce cost-effective policies at the local level.
- Implement fare policies that maximize the contributions from the farebox (such as distance-based fares and peak-hour surcharges) without jeopardizing the primary transportation objectives to be served.
- Utilize cost-saving measures such as contracting out to private sector operators services they can provide more efficiently.
- Encourage the provision of complementary and even competing services (such as car- and vanpools for peak-hour commuters) that can reduce the more costly demands on conventional transit.
- Promote the development of transit-supportive policies such as high-occupancy vehicle lanes, dense development along transit lines, and the elimination of the preferential tax treatment of employer-subsidized parking.
- Employ user-side subsidies to promote special service discounts for selected groups, particularly where additional subsidy payments can be obtained from nontraditional funding sources.
- Strengthen the case for the use of traditional funding sources at the federal, state, and local levels by demonstrating convincingly how public transportation can contribute to the achievement of the various policy goals of these levels of government, including improved mobility for both captive and choice riders,

reduced demand on congested road facilities, and an improved quality of life in urban areas.

SUMMARY

Since the 1960s, a wide variety of financing sources and mechanisms has been identified and utilized to support public transportation. The steady decline in the portion of transit revenues derived from passengers has increased the pressure on transit policy makers and managers to secure revenues from other sources, including the federal, state, and local governments, and from joint arrangements with the private sector. The declining share of funding provided by the federal government over the past decade has been offset to date by increased shares contributed by the state and local governments, with the states now contributing significantly more to public transportation funding than the federal government. Increasing costs due to government mandates and fiscal stringency at all levels of government suggest that the 1990s will bring major financing challenges for the transit industry.

In the past, public financial support for transit has frequently been initiated in response to some escalating crisis or problem, such as an alarming deterioration in the condition of the transit capital stock or an unexpected increase in the operating deficits of individual systems due to cost increases or ridership declines. Over time, transit assistance programs have gradually shifted away from this crisis mode and toward more proactive approaches that measure and critique the performance of both transit operations and the financial assistance programs themselves. Major efforts have been made to improve transit operating performance and to restructure financial assistance programs to promote the most efficient decisions and policies at the transit-agency level. Much can still be done, however, to improve transit operating performance and to make financial assistance programs more effective.

Many of the prescriptions for more effective transit financing and operations developed over recent years offer real promise: better linkage of transit with land use, greater flexibility in the structure and administration of public financing programs, more rational fare policies, contracting out certain services, encouraging other cost-effective high-occupancy modes, promoting transit-supportive policy measures, employing user-side as well as provider-side subsidies, and strengthening the case for traditional funding sources. As we enter the 1990s, we will need more widespread implementation of these approaches if we are to improve the financial condition and operating performance of the nation's public transportation systems.

REFERENCES

1   AMERICAN PUBLIC TRANSIT ASSOCIATION, *Transit Fact Book*, 1989 ed. (Washington, D.C.: American Public Transit Association, August 1989).

2   APTA, *Transit Fact Book*.

3   AMERICAN ASSOCIATION OF STATE HIGHWAY AND TRANSPORTATION OFFICIALS, *A Study on Future Directions of Public Transportation in the United States*, AASHTO Report (Washington, D.C.: American Association of State Highway and Transportation Officials, 1985).

4   AMERICAN ASSOCIATION OF STATE HIGHWAY AND TRANSPORTATION OFFICIALS, *1989 Survey of State Involvement in Public Transportation* (Washington, D.C.: American Association of State Highway and Transportation Officials, 1989).

5   AMERICAN ASSOCIATION OF STATE HIGHWAY AND TRANSPORTATION OFFICIALS, *Survey of State Capital Funding for Public Transportation* (Washington, D.C.: American Association of State Highway and Transportation Officials, January 1990).

6   URBAN MASS TRANSPORTATION ADMINISTRATION, OFFICE OF GRANTS MANAGEMENT, *Compendium of National Urban Mass Transportation Statistics for 1986 Report Year* (Washington, D.C.: U.S. Department of Transportation, April 1990).

7   ROBERT CERVERO, *Intergovernmental Responsibilities for Financing Public Transit Services*, Final Report, prepared by the Institute of Urban and Regional Development, University of California, Berkeley for UMTA University Research and Training Program, Report no. DOT-I-83-30 (Washington, D.C.: U.S. Government Printing Office, August 1983).

8   U.S. GENERAL ACCOUNTING OFFICE, *Soaring Transit Subsidies Must Be Controlled*, report to the U.S. Congress (Washington, D.C.: U.S. General Accounting Office, February 26, 1981).

9   DON H. PICKRELL, The Causes of Rising Transit Operating Deficits, Final Report, prepared by John F. Kennedy School of Government, Harvard University, for UMTA, Technology Sharing Program, Report no. DOT-I-83-47 (Washington, D.C.: U.S. Department of Transportation, 1983).

10 AMERICAN PUBLIC TRANSIT ASSOCIATION, *Transit Performance and Productivity 1975-1980: Improvements through the Intergovernmental Partnership* (Washington, D.C.: American Public Transit Association, May 1985).

11 URBAN MASS TRANSPORTATION ADMINISTRATION, *The Status of the Nation's Local Mass Transportation: Performance and Conditions*, report of the Secretary of Transportation to the United States Congress, Pursuant to 49USC 308, prepared by UMTA (Washington, D.C.: U.S. Government Printing Office, June 1988).

12 RURAL AMERICA, *Community Transportation: A Growth Industry* (Washington, D.C.: Rural America, n.d.).

13 RONALD F. KIRBY AND ARLEE T. RENO, *Study of Policy Issues in the Public Works Category of Mass Transit*, [cover title] *The Nation's Public Works: Report on Mass Transit*, prepared for the National Council on Public Works Improvement by The Urban Institute, Categories of Public Works Series (Washington, D.C.: National Council on Public Works Improvement, May 1987).

14 Ibid.

15 Ibid.

16   R. F. KIRBY AND R. G. McGILLIVRAY, "Alternative Subsidy Techniques for Urban Public Transportation," in *Urban Transportation Finance*, Transportation Research Record 589 (Washington, D.C.: Transportation Research Board, 1976).

17   LESTER A. HOEL, "Financing Transportation," *Transportation Research, Part A: General*, 24A, no. 4 (July 1990), p. 249.

18   AMERICAN PUBLIC TRANSIT ASSOCIATION, *Transit 2000: Executive Summary of the American Public Transit Association's Transit 2000 Task Force*, Final Report (Washington, D.C.: American Public Transit Association, 1989).

19   U.S. DEPARTMENT OF TRANSPORTATION, *Moving America: New Directions, New Opportunities: A Statement of National Transportation Policy, Strategies for Action* (Washington, D.C.: U.S. Department of Transportation, February 1990).

EXERCISES

15-1   What prompted the reduction in federal operating subsidy programs?

15-2   What are the pros and cons of user-side versus provider-side subsidies?

15-3   What are the financing pressures in your area?

15-4   What is the current status of the national program for federal funding for transit programs?

15-5   Do you feel transit users should pay more for services? Why? For all types of services?

15-6   What are the problems of implementing a fare/distance-traveled system for a conventional fixed-route bus system?

15-7   Discuss congestion pricing strategies that might be effective in reducing congestion in a major urban area.

15-8   Of the strategies listed under "Future Prospects," which might best be applied to your local urban transit system? Why?

PART V

MANAGEMENT

AND OPERATIONS

Chapter 16

MANAGEMENT OF PUBLIC TRANSPORTATION

GEORGE M. SMERK

Interest in the improvement of urban mass transportation was initiated as a result of efforts by the national government through its policy in support of the transit industry. Public policy toward urban mass transportation on the federal level began in 1961 with a small-scale program of demonstrations and loans. After a slow start, the programs established by the federal government picked up momentum; by 1970, federal aid was available through the Urban Mass Transportation Administration (UMTA) for a variety of program purposes, including capital improvements; research, development, and demonstration; planning; and management training. In 1973, certain moneys of the Highway Trust Fund were made available for mass transportation purposes. In 1974, Congress adopted legislation that gave federal transit funds to *urbanized areas* (cities above 50,000 population) on a formula basis. In 1978, the program was expanded to include a formula program for nonurbanized areas. The formula programs covered operating as well as capital costs. In 1982, extraordinary types of capital improvements were given a special source from a penny added to the federal fuel tax. (For details of the history of public transportation see Part I.)

Starting in the 1960s, much of the research sponsored by UMTA was devoted to the development of hardware, in the apparent hope that there would be a breakthrough in technology that would somehow help solve the problems of mass transportation. There was little emphasis on research and development for the purpose of helping to upgrade management or to develop new concepts and new approaches to the management of urban mass transit. Happily, beginning in the early 1970s, UMTA began to turn more of its attention and funds toward the improvement of transit management. Transit properties, especially throughout the United States, and the private contract management companies in particular, sought better ideas and management techniques. This reflected a growing concern with the quality of management in transit and recognition of its importance in making transit more useful and attractive to the urban traveler.

Recognition of the importance of transit management and new and more imaginative means of management is testimony to an often overlooked fact of life in public transportation. Obviously, technology and its improvement are important in any enterprise, but the tools of technology are merely resources and can be only as effective as management skill permits. It is only good sense to examine carefully the concepts and approaches to transit management that will permit the assets of a transit firm—both human and material—to be utilized most effectively.

THE ROOTS OF THE TRANSIT MANAGEMENT PROBLEM

From the early part of the nineteenth century, transit was traditionally managed as a privately owned, monopolistic public utility following the typical ways and means of any regulated, capitalistic undertaking; long ago, changes in population distribution in urban areas and the growth in the use of private automobiles changed the nature of cities and urban mobility, while ending transit's monopoly position. Now that most of the transit industry is publicly owned, the management problem is even more clouded in terms of a rationale to guide managers. The management of publicly owned enterprises poses a major difficulty in the United States, because the country does not really have a long history or well-developed ethic of public enterprise management. Whatever tradition exists is based mainly on the management of truly monopolistic undertakings, such as city-owned water utilities. The lessons learned in the management of the only water company in town provide few clues for management of a mass transportation agency that must operate in direct competition with the private automobile. It takes no genius to see that modern business management techniques could have a revolutionary impact on traditional transit management. As an example, the transit industry and its management have almost always been operations oriented. This means that the conventionally well managed transit property is adept at servicing and maintaining equipment; scheduling, dispatching, and otherwise seeing to it that equipment is on the street and rolling; and utilizing vehicles and personnel in what is hoped to be the least costly manner. What traditional management lacks is a feel for the consumer and, perhaps even more important, the *potential* consumer of public transportation services. On the other hand, modern business management techniques and strategies are generally aimed primarily at serving the consumer. Similar techniques and strategies are applicable to the transit industry, especially in its role as a competitor with the automobile or—in view of potential environmental and energy problems—as an alternative to the private car. The purpose of this chapter is to examine some of the reasons behind the typical management rubric in public transportation and to sketch out the kind of approach that would be most practical in establishing a framework of managerial practice appropriate to today's transit situation.

Not to belabor a point already made but to signify its importance in managerial thought processes, transit management has traditionally been consumed with interest in the operations of transit, rather than concerned with the consumers who use it. Transit is not unique in this orientation; it is common in all the transportation industries. One very good reason for this attitude is that transportation firms, transit included, usually possess very complex operation problems that tend to overshadow other proper concerns of management. In the developmental stages of most modes of transport, the problems of scheduling personnel and equipment, fighting the elements, and overcoming the limitations of equipment and facilities were matters of paramount urgency. Until the advent of the privately owned bicycle, automobile, and truck, most urban dwellers were dependent upon for-hire carriers to move them or their goods.

Finding and retaining good management people is a problem for any enterprise, but transit has had even more difficulty because it has been in the unenviable position of being a declining industry for more than half a century. Low managerial pay and a low self-image often go together, and in the 1950s and 1960s the industry soldiered on, incapable for the most part of attracting and retaining the best people. Perhaps even worse, conservatism of approach is inherent in such declining situations; innovation is avoided and the practices of the past become embalmed in the actions of the present. The painful contraction of service and inevitable decline in the prestige of working in such an industry presents little that is attractive to new blood.

Unfortunately, even before the automotive revolution was under way, the transit industry had been seriously weakened by financial peccadillos, stock jobbing, unscrupulous promoters, and a host of other practices that left the viability of large segments of the transit industry in a financially embarrassed and weakened state. The skyrocketing cost increases of the World War I period and interest due on overinflated capitalization, together with limitations on the amount of fare that might be charged and other statutory obligations connected with operating franchises, led to the bankruptcy of a major portion of the transit industry by 1918.

Forced to meet the challenge of the automobile while much of it was in or near bankruptcy, the transit industry developed a strong and understandable concern with cost cutting. At the same time, vigor was diminished and in some quarters innovation suppressed because of the state of the industry. Some management talent and capital were available from the electrical utility industry, of which many transit firms were a part in the 1920s; however, declining ridership, which was due to the increasing availability of dependable automobiles at reasonable prices, cut revenues and made transit less and less attractive to the parent utility companies, especially after the start of the Great Depression. On top of that, the Holding Company Act of 1935 caused the divorce of many transit firms from their electric utility parents; this effectively diverted segments of the transit industry from major currents of managerial talent and removed many transit firms from any hope of receiving major transfusions of capital from their erstwhile parent firms.

In the wake of the pullout of electric utilities from the transit business, transit holding companies—some controlling a score or more properties—arrived on the scene to fill the vacuum. Many of these holding companies were organized in conjunction with major motor bus equipment manufacturers and suppliers bent on the substitution of buses for streetcars in the transit industry. The focus of attention in this period was generally not one of great concern with the mass transportation consumer or with the development of consumer-oriented management. Rather, it was the superintendence of disinvestment in electric railways and mastering the art of operating buses as nearly like streetcars as possible. Even so, these firms did introduce some wise management practices and probably offered better management to small- and medium-size properties than might otherwise have been the case.

Perhaps even more of a problem in recruiting and retaining the type of management needed in transit was the fact that, since the 1920s, the industry had not been part of the conventional mainstream of American business, which tended to be dominated by growing national firms that required the services of large numbers of professionally trained, middle-management personnel. The challenges and rewards of working with a major national firm are substantial for persons of managerial talent. Transit firms, with the exceptions of a few giants in the largest cities, are relatively small enterprises, and the possibilities of promotion and economic reward appear to be slim to young people looking for a career with real opportunity. In addition, the financial weakness of the transit industry, especially since the end of World War II, has usually made it sadly uncompetitive in salaries. This is not to say that there are not many persons of real skill in the transit industry; there are. But these people generally stumbled into their positions; they did not arrive there as a result of careful recruitment or an early decision to seek out transit as an interesting and rewarding career area. In all truth, because of the lack of outside interest in transit, promoting from within has often been the only option open to the industry. Obviously, this cuts down the field of choice. Moreover, for a person of talent within the transit field, other industry is likely to beckon with higher pay and better working conditions. Transit management offers a stimulating career, but the work is carried out under public scrutiny, and there are strong political pressures. Burnout is not uncommon.

TRANSIT AND THE EXAMPLE OF THE MODERN BUSINESS FIRM

Since the 1960s, the interest of state, local, and federal governments toward public transportation improvements has enhanced the transit industry's importance. The industry is being asked to cope with the national need for improved mobility and overall quality of life and for reduced automobile use in order to protect the environment and cut the demands of transportation on potentially scarce energy resources. In short, there is a vital need to strengthen transit management and to bring transit into line with modern concepts of management in order for it to fulfill its traditional mission and to play properly new and important roles into which it has been cast.

There are lessons for the management of public transportation in the approach used by the modern business firm. A modern, well-managed firm will develop a strategic or long-range view and from that determine its goals—those ideal and broad ends it wishes to achieve. Such firms usually focus on carefully defined objectives (share of the market, return on sales, and the like) and the thoughtful manipulation of human and material resources to reach the objective. Marketing thus becomes a matter of major importance and a central part of the structure of the institution. The market is carefully researched and the pulse of the consumer is taken, not only to determine total demand but also to discover the particular mix of price and service that will appeal to given segments of the market. In the modern business firm, different varieties of product or service are tailor-made for different market segments, along with price and promotional activities aimed at different pocketbooks, life-styles, and viewpoints.

The canny modern firm, after getting a handle on the market potential, turns loose its production experts, product design engineers, and product development staff to see if it can profitably produce what it has determined the public wants. The physical supply and distribution staff smooth the flow and cut the costs of collecting the elements of production and, after the production process, of distributing goods to the market. The financial staff analyzes the potential profit of various products or services and seeks the funds to do the job from internal and external sources. Accountants, electronic data processing experts, and information system developers devise information systems and cost controls, both to provide for a flow of necessary information for management and to prevent waste and inefficiency. Promotion, sales, and advertising personnel work up competitive strategies and plan programs to bring the product to the attention of the public. If, after a careful and complete analysis is made, the firm can, indeed, produce a product or service and sell it in line with its objectives, the final decision will be made to go ahead. Much the same approach can be used in the management of public transportation enterprise.

There is an obvious need for a modern approach to transit management and a new breed of manager with a professional education in business, adept at applying a systematic approach to transit operations and marketing similar to that utilized by most modern business firms. The proper type of management for today's public transportation firm needs a far-sighted strategy and rational goals, and should concentrate on clear-cut, consumer-oriented objectives, organizing the firm to meet these objectives, and utilizing the marketing management concept as a means of turning transit into an industry responsive to consumers.

GOAL SETTING

The value of striving toward defined goals is related to what Samuel Johnson found in the promise of being hanged in the morning—it does wonders in focusing the attention of the mind. What this means in practice is that transit managers and public officials must be specific about what transit is intended to accomplish. The organizational structure and the efforts of the transit property can then be tailored to help meet the goals. Underlying all is strategy, a long-run view. As an example, a transit property may plan to begin to build a rail system and expand it both radially and circumferentially over the years. The strategy aims at keeping transit competitive with the automobile and mindful of the changing demands of the community. Strategic planning must constantly monitor the situation and plans must be reviewed and updated regularly.

Transit objectives have to be precise and workable, not vague, general hopes. Simply "making transit service better" will not suffice. Goals must be concrete and sufficiently practical to enable them to be used in the process of setting realistic objectives, such as providing transit service to meet the needs of the bulk of the members of the community or bringing the operating deficit within reasonable bounds. Such goals can be reasonably translated into objectives.

The rule for formulating practical objectives demands that the goals be clear and definite, attainable, measurable, and reached by a given target date. A good example of such an objective would be "to provide transit service at least every 20 minutes during the major portion of the day, within two blocks of every residence in the city by January 1, 1995." Such an objective must, naturally, fit into the overall plans and goals for urban development within the city. Whole sets of detailed minor objectives and priorities may be established to help in achieving the principal objective.

A multiplicity of objectives of major and minor consequence are no impediment to the fulfillment of major objectives, as long as all the objectives are in concord with the primary thrust of action. A program of vehicle replacement to cut the average age of the transit fleet and reduce maintenance problems and costs would be in accord with the objectives of service on a dependable 20-min headway. On the other hand, the objectives of minimizing maintenance effort and maximizing reliability of service would clearly be in conflict with one another.

Private operators must, of course, focus on profit if they are to remain in business. In a narrow but certainly not improper sense, the private firm can conclude that it is on the right track if, over time, it is profitable. The publicly owned firm must have service as a primary goal; its clue to success in the short run will most likely be an increase in the number of riders. In the long run, the success of the public firm will be in its approach to the realization of the goals and objectives established for it, which most probably will have little or nothing to do with profit.

THE BOARD OF DIRECTORS AND MANAGEMENT

The business of divining strategy, setting goals and objectives, and translating them into action involves interplay between transit management and those who govern the transit entity. This may be a board of directors of a transit authority or, where transit is operated as a city department, the governing body may be the city council. If transit is operated as a city utility, direction may come from a board of public works or a city utility board. Generally, in larger communities the governing body is most apt to be the board of a transit authority or a transit district, the latter usually having taxing authority. Where the governing board has duties embracing more than transit—a city council, for example—there is often conflict between allocating resources for transit and roads and streets or other public purposes. In other situations, as in the case of a board of works, transit may be only a small portion of the total responsibilities; there may be little time to devote to transit. In larger urban places the transit authority may be metropolitan in nature to cover the whole of the urbanized area. Whatever the particular arrangement, the directors of a publicly owned transit agency can be a source of aid or trouble for those engaged in the day-to-day management of the transit property. In situations where a board is trouble, it is usually because the directors or the management do not understand their proper role.

The proper function of directors is to work with the best input from management to understand the long-term environment and to develop a strategy to fit the environment, the needs of the community, and the health of the transit property. From the long-run strategic direction, the board works to set the broad goals of the organization, to provide policy guidelines, and, in conjunction with management, to help establish priorities and objectives. In a public enterprise the directors are representatives of the public; in some cases the directors may be elected, and in other instances they may be chosen by elected officials. The chairman of the modern transit board of directors usually has the chores of keeping political fences well mended and, in company with the other directors and elected officials, of seeing to it that the general thrust of mass transportation is in line with the overall goals and objectives of the municipality served.

Directors should, of course, be concerned with the overall direction in which the transit agency is moving; indeed, they should help set that direction. They should also be involved in helping to obtain and to allocate, in a general way, resources for public transportation. However, directors should not be involved in detailed resource allocation any more than they should be involved in day-to-day management.

Where directors do not understand their proper role, they are likely to hinder the day-to-day affairs of operating transit. Interference in management prerogatives by directors can demolish managerial morale, especially when directors insist on having their way in matters that are unsafe, unwise, or uneconomical or may cause managerial performance to appear unprofessional. Directors have been known to attempt to write schedules, force transit routes into hopeless territories, serve favored shopping centers, order special services, and even commandeer vehicles for private use. Insisting on schedules, routes, and services that are not warranted is probably the worst offense.

One problem that appeared in the switchover of transit from private to public enterprise is the evolution of the board of directors. In the initial stages of public ownership, strong and active members of the community—the so-called "movers and shakers"—apparently can be attracted to serve. Once the enterprise is on its feet, the movers and shakers tend to move on to other undertakings of a more challenging nature; over time, more political individuals or weaker persons with less stature in the community may become directors. It is often at this stage that management is most bothered; being unsure of their role, later generations of directors often meddle in the business of day-to-day management. On occasion, directors will act to raise their political visibility in order to help propel a public career. Part of the problem is simply that the directors must learn what their job really is. It takes time for directors to develop knowledge of transit. For this reason, perhaps the tenure of office should be rather lengthy with staggered terms, with the more senior directors the only ones eligible for the position of chairperson. Above all, of course, those who name directors must choose wisely, animated by the spirit of what is best for the community rather than as a political reward or a place for a designee to gain or increase visibility.

CONSUMER BEHAVIOR

Regardless of whether a transit service is publicly or privately owned, the key to effective goal setting in transit today has to be consumer orientation. This is so because it is not likely that any city would choose to force its citizens to use transit.

However, in these days of concern with strangling traffic congestion, pollution of the environment, and possible shortage of energy, it is appropriate for local government, perhaps at the behest of state and national government, to apply incentives to encourage the use of public transportation, along with disincentives to help discourage use of the private automobile. Public and private partnerships to reduce vehicle miles of travel in urban areas by providing, for instance, low transit fares and a surtax on parking may become common features of U.S. urban life. In any event, the public cannot be expected to utilize transit merely as an expression of civic concern; there must be rewards or real value for the consumer if transit is to attract patronage.

Successful transit operation is mainly a function of marketing, in the broadest sense of the term, as it relates to consumers and potential consumers of transit service. Specific goals will differ from place to place, as will the organizational structure needed to meet the goals; in all cases, however, it is necessary that the goals, objectives, organization, and action be grounded in an understanding of consumer behavior and translation of that understanding into appropriate marketing effort.

It may not appear, at first blush, that consumers act rationally. However, there is both motivation and logic behind consumers' actions, no matter how erratic it may appear to the outside observer. The point is illustrated in the simple model of consumer behavior illustrated in Fig. 16-1. The elements of the model are as follows:

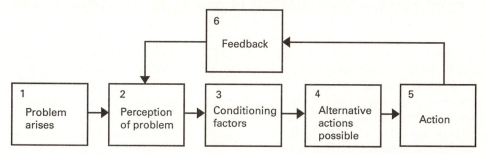

Figure 16-1 *Simple model of consumer behavior. [Source: George M. Smerk, "Mass Transit Management,"* Business Horizons, *14, no. 6 (December 1971), 11.]*

1. *A problem arises.* Behavior is problem solving in nature; consumers will act to solve their problems through purchase and/or use of a product or service.
2. *Perception.* The realization that there is a problem and the nature of that problem is communicated to the brain by the senses. Which of many problems facing the consumer that will have priority is selected at this point.
3. *Conditioning.* Conditioning covers the factors that act as a filter or a preprogramming of consumers' attitudes and approaches to the problem they perceive. Some of these are biological; an example would be a consumer's physical capabilities, such as the need to climb high steps. The most important of the conditioning factors are imposed by society. For example, natives or longtime residents of the United States would be affected and conditioned by Western civilization in general. More specifically, they would be affected by the society of the nation as a whole and the region in which they live, together with the general class in those regions of which they are a part. Also important are the immediate groups of which they are members and the groups with which they identify and which they attempt to copy. All human beings grow hungry, but in the United States hungry persons would be unlikely to eat candied ants or grasshopper in cream sauce as a supper repast at 3 o'clock, nor would they eat their breakfast cornflakes and milk with their fingers. Nature may tell us that we are hungry, but our society determines what we will eat and when and how it will be consumed.
4. *Alternatives.* Consumers must evaluate and select among the various alternatives that are open, acceptable, and known to them. It should be understood that, to the consumer, an option that is unknown does not exist in any meaningful way. In deciding among alternatives, consumers perform rough mental calculations of the time, effort, and money that must be expended on each of the alternatives.
5. *Action.* Consumers act in accordance with the acceptable alternative that meets whatever constraints they face in terms of time, effort, and money. In short, consumers usually will choose the least "costly" acceptable available alternative.

6.   *Feedback*. Feedback is the means by which consumers determine whether or not their problems have been solved by the choices they have made and the actions they have taken. If not satisfied that the problem has been solved, consumers will select alternatives.

For transit management that is trying to attract more patronage, perhaps the most fertile fields for imaginative and useful marketing work are the conditioning factors in conjunction with the alternatives open to the consumer. For example, management might take action in a program that would attempt to affect conditioning so that mass transportation was accepted by an increasing number of sectors of society. To carry this out, objectives and policies should be shaped with improvements of transit's image and acceptability by the public kept in mind. The image of transit as a service for the losers of society has to be changed, or those who identify with winners will not be attracted. By means of good, reliable transit performance, along with careful advertising and community relations work, a more positive attitude toward mass transportation may be developed among consumers and potential consumers.

Promotion of transit as a reasonable alternative to the private automobile is one approach that might be taken in the marketing area. Apart from social stigmas that may be attached to transit, it is fair to say that transit is usually not considered to be an adequate substitute for the automobile. In light of the behavioral model discussed earlier, transit may be more expensive in time, effort, and money than the private automobile. Transit may also be *perceived* as more time and energy consuming and more costly in pecuniary terms even if, in reality, it is not. Consumers will, of course, behave in terms of what they believe to be true.

Under these circumstances, the proper marketing ploy for management is to take steps to reduce the actual and perceived time, effort, and money costs of transit. To effect a real reduction of time and effort, careful rethinking and restructuring of transit routes and schedules are needed. It might also mean fare reduction or restructuring of fares to make the price–service package attractive to consumers. Figure 16-2 provides a graphic presentation of a "walk-ride-walk" home to work trip and possible sites of the cost involved. Assuming that the fare for a transit ride is lower in money cost than the total cost of using an automobile, it is still important to cut other costs. Lengthy walks to transit stops, long running time of vehicles, unattractive equipment or facilities, inconvenient transfers, and grumpy employees all add to the cost of energy and time needed by transit consumers. By reviewing all the segments of a trip, management can make cost reductions where needed; for instance, better coordination of schedules may cut transfer time drastically. Better integration of routes may reduce the need for transit patrons to transfer between routes.

Fare reductions may appear to be the easiest way of making transit more attractive, since it is a direct and obvious action. Even so, the traveling public may not be convinced that transit is much of a bargain if travel time is lengthy. Cutting down on travel time and the other impediments to consumer attraction is not easy. For example, most transit managers—except on grade-separated rapid transit systems—have little or no control over the right-of-way their vehicles must utilize. The typical street shared by automobiles, trucks, transit vehicles, and pedestrians offers many opportunities for delay to the transit service. In such a situation, reserved transit lanes are necessary to speed the movement of transit vehicles.

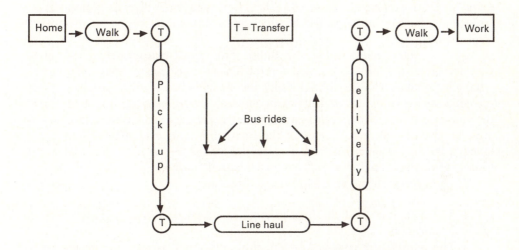

Time Cost	Walk from home	Transfer to pick up	Pick up	Transfer to line haul	Line haul	Transfer to delivery	Delivery	Transfer to walk	Walk to work
Energy cost	Walk from home	Transfer to pick up	Pick up	Transfer to line haul	Line haul	Transfer to delivery	Delivery	Transfer to walk	Walk to work
Money cost	Walk from home	Transfer to pick up	Pick up	Transfer to line haul	Line haul	Transfer to delivery	Delivery	Transfer to walk	Walk to work

Figure 16-2 *Journey analysis: time, energy, and money cost.*

If the general national impression of transit is largely negative, image improvement will need far more than mere cosmetic treatment. Overcoming a bad image is probably a tougher job than creating a new public impression from scratch. The real proof of the pudding lies in the quality of the service–price package that is offered to the public. This can be helped along by careful use of media and personal contact.

ENVIRONMENTS OF THE TRANSIT MANAGER

Transit managers operate within several environments; some of these are not within their control. As an example, the manager of a given transit property must, by and large, live with national and state situations much as they are found. Any real impact on the national environment will probably be slight, although all managers have a right and a duty to inform federal elected and appointed officials of their ideas, needs, and interests. Over time, and in concert with other transit managers, they are more likely to have some impact on state policy, but it will probably not be easy or immediate. The general local situation is also somewhat out of their control, but not totally so. Transit management may be able to work with public officials to ensure that, say, parking bans at bus stops will be enforced or that a local option tax to support transit is adopted.

On the other hand, within the transit firm itself, management exercises a considerable degree of initiative and control. Transit management holds the reins of a fairly large number of variables; through the manipulation of those variables, it can provide a variety of service packages with differing degrees of appeal to the public. If the consumer-oriented marketing–management approach is to be used, recognition must be given to all the elements of the transit firm that may effectively be commanded by management. Moreover, great care must be taken to see that those elements are considered in a systematic interrelated fashion.

Some of the principal aspects of transit firms are:

- The organization of the firm to meet stated goals, as well as input on goal formulation.
- The information collected by the firm and how it is used for management purposes, including accounting and ridership data and other information needed for effective managerial control, reporting to regulatory or control bodies, financial records, and decision making.
- The personnel selected by the firm, how it is recruited and trained, and the methods used in the supervision of personnel and negotiation with organized labor.
- The selection of equipment.
- The maintenance program for equipment and facilities.
- Routing.
- Schedules.
- Communication and control for efficient, effective, and dependable operation, especially between operators and supervisors.
- The overall marketing program.
- The advertising program.
- Studies of potential improved, expanded, or specialized services.
- The public information program, including maps, schedules, and information signs and graphics.
- Community relations programs.

In keeping with the operations-oriented philosophy, the organization chart of the typical transit firm naturally treats operations as the central function with maintenance, clerical work, and administration functions as adjuncts. Marketing is and has been largely neglected in most transit firms. It is not unusual in transit to mistake an advertising program for a real marketing program. If a transit organization is to be geared to carry out the objectives of a truly consumer oriented service, marketing must be the core element about which the organization structure is built. A modern organization structure for transit is illustrated in Fig. 16-3.

In examining Fig. 16-3, it should be recognized that this is a functional organization chart, showing tasks to be performed—not a detailed chart that provides slots for individuals. "Marketing and operations" covers the various jobs related to planning, selling, and running the service. "Information and financial services" includes the office and accounting functions, as well as the gathering of statistics for managerial decision-making, reporting, and planning purposes. "General services" involves the hardware and personnel functions, safety, servicing and maintenance of equipment and facilities, and the purchasing and control of supplies. The precise details of an organization and the number of positions would naturally depend upon the size of the transit property and the degree of specialization possible with a larger firm.

THE MARKETING PROGRAM

Marketing is far more than a stepped-up sales effort. The marketing program of a transit firm must be positively directed to the task of discovering opportunities to serve the public. A private firm will, of course, analyze the results of its services and continue those operations that, in the long run, appear to be most profitable. The publicly owned firm should continue to offer certain needed and desired services, regardless of their profitability, within the context of its stated objectives. At the same time, the publicly owned firm should take steps to increase patronage and revenues so that income is maximized to the greatest extent possible without causing the service to suffer. Obviously, the greater the income, the better the overall level of service that might be provided.

A transit property must adopt a marketing strategy that is appropriate to its situation in a competitive transportation market. Since resources are inevitably limited, to avoid waste, the marketing effort must be focused as finely as possible. The best scheme is to direct the marketing effort toward particular segments of the overall market, rather than to try to reach everyone at the same time. In addition to meeting the needs of obvious patronage groups, marketing should direct a careful promotional effort toward those nonusers who can reasonably be judged as potential transit riders.

One truism: the market for public transportation does not consist of a homogeneous mass of consumers. A single-service approach will not suffice in a real, heterogeneous market because the market is divided into segments of consumers with different needs and desires that require different packages of service. This is addressed more completely in Chap. 17. The market segment, in strategic terms, is the smallest unit for which it is worth tailoring a separate marketing program. The concept of the marketing

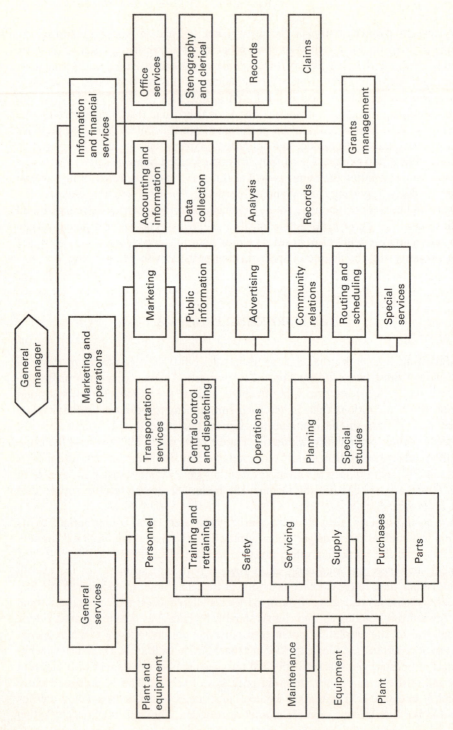

Figure 16-3 *Functional organization for mass transportation. [Source: Adapted from George M. Smerk, "Mass Transit Management," Business Horizons, 14, no. 6 (December 1971), 13.]*

mix is useful in dealing with the segments of the transit market. It includes the product, price, and promotion, and transit managers must try to reach the various segments they hope to influence with various combinations of these elements. The job of the transit marketer is to pick out the worthwhile segments from the mass of travel demand and discover means to serve those for which transit can play an effective and useful role.

A true marketing effort must be based on careful market research. Management must come to know and understand the communities they serve, and that understanding must be based on factual information. Some of the market research will use material gathered by others, such as census data and planning studies. Record keeping and survey research conducted by the transit property will provide material to be sifted, analyzed, and used as the basis of judgment for marketing and other decisions.

Probably the most natural and easy approach to marketing transit is to appeal initially, through a general service offering, to the most accessible segments of the market. In the first stages of the marketing program, these would probably consist of those patrons without an alternative means of travel regularly available to them. The early work would involve approaches pointed at the improvement of the quality of transit service and upgrading the status and general image of mass transportation.

Through concentration on reliability, convenience, comfort, value for money, speed, and other quality factors, the initially served segments should be held and used as a base upon which to build the transit market. Quality improvements and higher standards of service should be promoted through relevant media. Over time, word-of-mouth comments by satisfied customers will help to reinforce and strengthen the transit image. After the potentials of the initial segments are tapped, the next best segment should be sought, held, and so on. Figure 16-4 illustrates the procedure.

The service should be directed toward reducing the time, energy, and money cost of travel and at improving public acceptance. This may be achieved by emphasizing reliable, on-time performance, new and comfortable equipment, service directed to meet consumer needs, and reasonable prices. Once patrons have become accustomed to the service offering, market research should be utilized to derive a cross section of who is using the service. Next, further research into the market should be utilized to determine who is not using transit and the reason for the nonuse. Certain additional segments may be revealed that have promise if some slight adjustment is made to the marketing mix. For example, offering fast express bus service from the outskirts of the city or suburbs to the downtown area may prove to be attractive to those currently using automobiles. Reverse commuting by central city residents to suburban work sites may offer other service opportunities.

Some segments will be ruled out as inaccessible to transit. The salesperson who must carry bulky sample cases on his or her visits to customers is an example; shoppers lugging home two-weeks' worth of groceries is another. Given limited resources, only those segments large enough and accessible enough to warrant cultivation should be pursued.

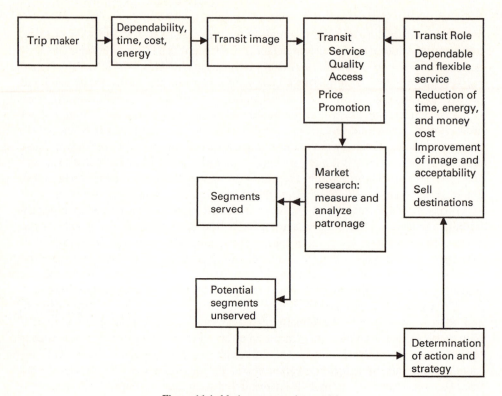

Figure 16-4 *Market segmentation model.*

THE MARKETING MIX

The concept of the marketing mix, as adopted from consumer product industries, is a key element in the process of tapping and holding a given segment of a transit market. The mix consists of all product, price, and promotion activities under the control of management that may be varied to meet the needs of the different transit market segments.

THE PRODUCT

In transit, the first element of the marketing mix—the product—includes the types of service, the quality of service, and the customer's access to it. Transit service types may be divided into the categories of regular route and special services. In regular-route service, the configuration of the routes and time schedules are the principal variables. Special services are those not following regular routes; they may be offered to a sporting event or to particular points for special affairs. Subscription services offering customers curb-to-curb transit service on a monthly basis would also fall into this category. Dial-a-ride—a form of demand-responsive service—is a flexible, curb-to-curb type of service that increases the number of options available to management in serving various market segments where regular service would not meet the needs.

The quality of the service is also important in the product element of the mix. Such factors as air-conditioned equipment, comfortable seating, cheerful decor, reliability, shelters for waiting passengers, courtesy of personnel, transfer requirements, travel time, and distance from origin or destination point to the transit route are all important. Subscription bus service or demand-responsive bus service, both previously mentioned, are other ways of improving access. The latter service is initiated by a telephone call from the consumer, and the bus is dispatched to the consumer by means of two-way radio; the buses travel an irregular route connecting the origin and destination points of several consumers as directly as possible.

PRICING

Pricing is the second major ingredient in the mix. It cannot be considered in total isolation from the rest of the package of product and promotion. It is a matter of providing value for money. Poor service, regardless of price, is still poor service and may not even yield value for money at a substandard fare. High-quality service is far more likely to be perceived as giving good value even at a relatively high price.

How the fare is collected is an integral part of the price. Monthly passes typically provide a discount and offer the convenience of not having to bother finding change. Electronic farecards, tickets, tokens, and transfers are all means of collecting a fare or allowing for a continuing journey. The process must be made as easy as possible and different fare arrangements must be considered and implemented for each segment.

PROMOTION

Promotion is the third part of the mix. It includes advertising in various media, ranging from radio and television through newspapers and circulars. Promotion also includes public information such as maps, schedules, and graphics to inform the public of the service and how to use it. Community relations are also part of the promotional package; this is the process of both meeting directly with the public and keeping the public informed of transit activities. Community relations should be a two-way street of communication and feedback; it is another way that management can find out how the public feels about the service and what the public wishes to have in the way of service changes and improvements. The various means of promotion should be brought into play to inform the public of what is offered and to help build an image of vigor and interest in meeting public needs.

The concept of market segmentation and the marketing mix can be joined together in an operational program.[1] Five customer segments are selected for consideration, and a profile of each of them is developed, as shown in Table 16-1. It is not intended to be definitive, but it does provide a way of thinking about transit marketing and market segmentation. The groups selected include manager/professional, clerical or office workers, inner city, elderly, and suburban housewife. Each segment appears to be large enough to make the efforts of a transit company to attract patronage worthwhile economically. The chosen requirements also provide a cross section of users who have different destinations and different needs and who receive a different mix of benefits from the service.

The manager/professional segment includes persons in the higher-income brackets, who probably tend to place a higher value on their time; travel time and quick and easy access to the service are more important to this segment than are some of the other factors, as shown in the benefits section of Table 16-1. This segment of the market should be appealed to mainly with service improvements rather than with cost savings.

The clerical segment is similar in many ways to the manager/professional segment; the major difference is the lower income level and the increased importance of cost savings as a factor of appeal. Both the manager/professional and clerical segments need transportation between suburban areas and the central city.

Inner-city residents require a different transit service because they not only have travel patterns related to movement within the central city but also between central-city residences and outlying job locations in the suburbs. The need for dependable, low-cost mass transportation service is highly important to the inner-city segment, since many in this group are in the low-income bracket and do not own automobiles. Travel-time savings and ease of access are probably of lesser importance to this segment because of its relative dependence upon transit.

The elderly make up another segment. This is already a large portion of the population and one that is growing rapidly in the United States as life spans slowly increase. Since most persons considered as elderly are retired, their transit needs are not for the journey to work, which is of major importance to the manager/professional, clerical, and inner-city segments. Rather, the elderly are looking for service that will provide mobility for shopping, personal business, and medical visits. Cost savings and accessibility are apt to rank very highly in the list of transit factors, with time savings and travel time of less importance.

The final customer segment is that of the suburban housewife. This segment resembles the manager/professional group in income and car ownership, although travel probably takes place most often during the off-peak times of the day. This is a tough segment to attract to transit because of relatively high income and automobile ownership.

Table 16-1 analyzes the five segments in terms of the benefits that each might receive from transit, the trip purpose, geography (in the sense of origin and destination points), the frequency of use, and the time of the transit trip, plus certain demographic factors.

TABLE 16-1

Profiles of Existing and Potential Customers

Segmentation Base	Customer Segment				
	Manager/ Professional	Clerical	Inner City	Elderly	Suburban Housewife
Benefits[a]					
Travel-time savings	H	H	M	L	M
Dependability	M	M	H	M	M
Cost savings	L	M	H	H	L
Accessibility	H	H	L	H	H
Travel-time options	H	H	M	M	M
Purpose of trip[b]	Work/recreation	Work/shopping	Work/shopping	Shopping/medical	Shopping/recreation
Geography[c]					
Origin	Suburb/CC	Suburb/CC	CC	CC	Suburb
Destination	CBD	CBD	Suburb	CC/CBD	Suburb
Weekly use--potential freq.	Heavy (5+ trips)	Heavy (5+ trips)	Medium (2-4 trips)	Light (1 trip)	Nonuser (0 trips)
Usage time[d]	Peak	Peak	Peak	Off-peak	Off-peak
Demographics[e]					
Income (in thousands)	$15-20	$7-9	$3-5	$3-6	$12-16
Age	35-54	25-34	35-64	65+	35-54
Years of education	13-16	12-15	8-12	5-12	13-16
Availability of car	Yes	Yes	No	No	Yes

[a]Travel-time savings—the reduction in the amount of time required for the user to travel from origin to destination.
Dependability—the increase in the likelihood that the user's expected departure and arrival times coincide with the actual service provided.
Cost savings—the monetary savings to the user from using transit service.
Accessibility—the minimization of user effort required in getting to and from the transit stations.
Travel-time options—the number of alternative travel times available to the user for a given transit trip.
Level of importance: H = high; M = medium; L = low.

[b]Refers to primary trip of each customer segment.

[c]CC = urban area other than central business district; CBD = central business district.

[d]Peak = 7:30 to 9:30 a.m. and 4:30 to 6:30 p.m.; off-peak = 9:30 a.m. to 4:30 p.m. and 6:30 p.m. to 5:30 a.m.

[e]Based on 1970 U.S. Census of Population.

Source: Adapted from Norman Kangun and William A. Staples, "Selling Urban Transit," *Business Horizons*, 18, no. 1 (February 1975), 61.

In Table 16-2 the marketing strategy is laid out in a summary format. Here the marketing mix elements are shown with the variations necessary to serve each of the segments. Contrast the service mix elements for each of the segments, for example, on the item of the characteristics of the vehicles. The manager/professional segment, which will most likely be attracted by service quality, should be wooed by a standard bus that is fitted with a fairly plush interior, including carpet, to lend a bit of eye appeal. Less fancy standard buses (probably air conditioned in this day and age) are supplied for the clerical and inner-city segments of the market. To meet the needs of the elderly and suburban housewife segments, small buses or vans are indicated for a demand-responsive or dial-a-ride service.

Again, the coverage of the services offered to the manager/professional, clerical, and inner-city segments is for the total metropolitan area; the elderly segment is offered a service that covers selected central-city locations, while the suburban housewife is offered a service to selected suburban locations.

In the area of pricing, note that the manager/professional and clerical segments are expected to pay full fare, while discount or promotional fares are offered the other segments, reflecting both the lower income of many inner-city and elderly persons and the difficulty of attracting the suburban housewife away from the automobile.

In the matter of promotion, the benefits of the service are stressed for the manager/professional segment; low price—as well as other factors—is stressed for clerical, inner-city, and elderly segments; and flexibility is stressed for the elderly and suburban housewife segments. The media utilized are also varied for each segment, as is the type of transit information offered.

The plan of attack outlined in the tables is not expected to be the be-all and end-all. However, it does provide a conceptual picture of the starting point in developing a marketing strategy and in putting together different parts of the marketing mix in an operational fashion. In other words, transit management can use this approach to focus on the segments named, or other segments of its choosing (for example, students), and lay out an operating plan. Based on this, a transit firm could make an initial offering of service. Then the process described graphically in Fig. 16-4 should be implemented; that is, research should be aimed at determining if the desired segments were being reached. Various parts of the operational strategy laid out in Table 16-2 could then be tinkered with in order to improve performance.

THE COMPLETE MANAGER

While much time and effort must be devoted to the marketing of mass transportation if modern business management methods are to be adapted to the transit industry, other aspects of management also require major attention.

TABLE 16-2

Conceptual Format for Marketing Strategies

Marketing Mix Element	Manager/ Professional	Clerical	Customer Segment Inner City	Elderly	Suburban Housewife
Service					
Vehicle characteristics	Standard capacity (40-60); carpeted; air-conditioned	Standard capacity	Standard capacity	Bus/van capacity (10-25); carpeted; air conditioned	Bus/van capacity
Routes	Fixed	Fixed	Fixed	Variable	Variable
Hours	6 a.m.-7 p.m.	6 a.m.-7 p.m.	6 a.m.-7 p.m.	9 a.m.-9 p.m.	9 a.m.-9 p.m.
Direct/transfer	Direct	Primarily direct, except at major interchange points	Transfer	Direct	Primarily direct, except with inter-zone transfer
Arr./depar. times	Fixed	Fixed	Fixed	Flexible	Flexible
Interval time/rte.	Peak: 3/hour	Peak: 3/hour	Peak: 2/hour	2/hour	2/hour
Coverage	Total metropolitan area	Total metropolitan area	Total metropolitan area	Selected central city locations	Selected suburban locations
Shelter/station density Origin Destination	High Moderate	High Moderate	Moderate Moderate	Low Low	Low Low
Station parking	Some	Limited	Unnecessary	Unnecessary	Unnecessary
Pricing					
Fares	Full	Full	Discount	Discount	Discount
Vol. discounts	Yes	Yes	No	No	No
Promotion					
Theme	Service benefits, work activities	Service, low price, socializing	Low price, dependability	Time flexibility, low price, socializing	Time/trip flexibility, reduced auto use
Media	Spot TV, local radio, business papers	Spot TV, local radio	Local radio, direct mail	Direct mail, spot TV	Spot TV, local radio, suburban newspapers
Transit information	Central metro. area information center	Multiple ticket locations	Mobile information centers	Special operator	Special operator

Source: Adapted from Norman Kangun and William A. Staples, "Selling Urban Transit," *Business Horizons*, 18, no. 1 (February 1975), 63.

Personnel and labor relations are a prime problem area in transit. Over a large part of the mid-twentieth century, much of the mass transportation industry of the United States was not always able to attract the best human resources. The transit industry's long decline, especially after World War II, made it difficult to attract or retain as many first-rate people for management and nonmanagement positions as would otherwise be the case. Highly qualified, well-educated, well-trained, and highly skilled people do not gravitate to what is perceived as a dying industry. Until the late 1960s, careful recruiting was virtually unknown. In part this was simply because the industry was shrinking and there was not the need to cast wide the recruiting nets.

No management job is easy, and it was particularly difficult in mass transit as the industry shifted from the private sector to the public sector. Managers must work in the goldfish bowl environment of a public enterprise. Political pressures increase, public transit governing board members are often unknowledgeable and difficult to work with, labor unions create the typical adversary relationship in many cases, and the pay in the public sector is typically lower than in the private sector for the same degree of managerial responsibility. Those factors, coupled with the constant search for money that especially typified transit in the 1980s, make the likelihood for managerial burn-out high. Turnover of management is the result. For this reason there is fairly rapid advancement among managers, especially in the smaller transit properties. Transit management offers a high degree of challenge and responsibility and fairly fast advancement, often without much opportunity for sufficient seasoning. There may be insufficient time to hone necessary skills and develop the political savvy demanded of top managers. Even so, many top-quality people have entered the ranks of transit management attracted by the many challenges and the rewarding feeling that comes with the knowledge of a difficult task well done.

Historically, most management employees generally started at the bottom and rose through the ranks in the transit industry. The exception was in the heyday of the electric streetcars around the turn of the century and up to about 1940, when college-educated electrical engineers, along with some civil and mechanical engineers, joined the management team of many transit systems in high-level positions. As the electric railways were abandoned, the need for new engineers slacked off and disappeared except in the largest city rail systems. For the 1950s and 1960s, management most commonly came from internal promotion of operating employees. With the renaissance of transit in the late 1960s and 1970s, there was increased demand for management personnel. The new crop of managers came from people with a background in business, planning, and public administration, and some were engineers in the new rail systems. For the most part, this new crop of managers had little or no transit experience, save perhaps as passengers.

Operating positions in transit are often unattractive because of the working conditions that may involve early and late hours of work, long working days with split shifts because of the peaked nature of demand, and the need for significant seniority before attractive working days and hours are assigned. In large cities many transit operations cover crime-ridden and drug-infested neighborhoods; fear is often the companion of transit operating employees. There is stress from operating under difficult conditions in dangerous places and pressure to operate on a schedule. Bus drivers face the stress shared by all who operate in heavy traffic, with the added strain caused by handling a large vehicle. Many of the older operating facilities lack creature comforts. In some of the older rail systems, the shop facilities are sometimes primitive and, perhaps, even dangerous. In short, transit is a tough job in many places, and there are equivalent jobs that pay well, have decent working hours, and offer less stressful working conditions. Although the pay of transit workers today is often relatively high, even that may not make a difficult job appealing to many potential employees.

Added to the problems of the working conditions in transit is the diminishing work force available in the United States because of the low national birth rate in the wake of the post-World War II baby boom. There are fewer people entering the work force and an increased demand for their services. This makes the job of recruiting transit human resources difficult at best. It means that the work force in transit has to be more productive through labor-saving capital investments and training to use more sophisticated and productive equipment and techniques.

The use of computers for record keeping, payrolls, and management of various activities has been a major means of making employees more productive. Investment in rail facilities has greatly increased the capacity of certain corridors of travel. High-occupancy-vehicle lanes or busways increase the throughput of buses and by speeding up the service may allow more intensive use of human and material resources. Balancing this has been the need for more technically sophisticated personnel to tend the new, complex machines and devices. New buses and rail cars are more complicated than their predecessors, and the labor saved in operations may be partially offset by the need for new types of technicians.

Contracting out certain tasks and the use of consultants has been one response to the shortage of human resources. The push by the federal government to encourage the use of the private sector in transit was to some extent only a continuation of what the transit industry was already doing. Rather than hire full-time personnel, for years transit agencies around the nation were competitively bidding out a range of tasks from money counting and engine and motor rebuilding to marketing studies and vehicle and facilities cleaning.

In a fair number of cities, professional contract management companies have been hired to manage the transit property. Typically, such firms assign one or more of their employees as the resident management team; the local team then can draw upon a central office staff for special expertise in areas such as labor negotiations, maintenance facility design, or market research. Contract management often brings a higher caliber of management and a larger package of skills and experience than would be possible with strictly local management. Indeed, contract management firms, faced by the competitive imperative of contract renewal, often are better practitioners of modern business practice than strictly local management would be in the medium and small cities that are the major market for contract management.

Once the desired people have been hired, careful training must be provided. This has to go beyond just how to operate or maintain vehicles. Rank-and-file personnel need an understanding of the overall direction in which the transit agency is moving, and the importance of the individual employee to the success of the enterprise must be stressed. The careful evaluation of the required tasks and the development of job descriptions will reveal the demands on the employees working in each function. Training and retaining of employees in relevant skills will follow. With changes in technology, such as the introduction of electronics to formerly all-mechanical devices, employees must be upgraded to tackle the new means of performing a task.

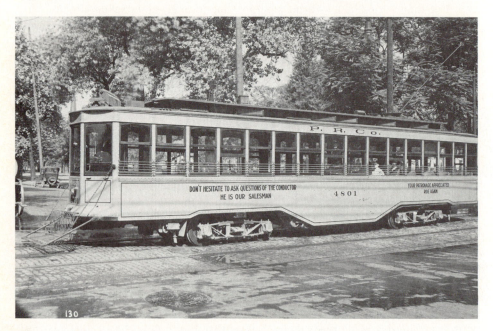

Figure 16-5 *Early sales and courtesy marketing—Pittsburgh Railways Co. (courtesy of American Public Transit Association)*

The operators of vehicles are especially important since they are virtually the only transit personnel who come in contact with the public; in a very real way, they are the salespersons of the mass transportation industry. They *are* the transit system to much of the public. Operators and others who deal directly with the public must be carefully trained in the sales function as well as operations. A good personnel program includes issuing job standards, monitoring job performance, and retraining personnel as necessary. Some transit properties employ quality control officers to make sure that the jobs are being performed to the established standards.

Radio has revolutionized supervision by allowing superior coverage of a transit system with the same or a smaller number of supervisory personnel. Supervisors and dispatchers may be in direct radio contact with any vehicle or train in systems so equipped. Supervisors in radio-equipped vehicles may cover more territory and respond more quickly to calls for help. Television monitoring of stations and other facilities has helped transit security forces to do a better job with smaller staffs and has enhanced public safety. The latest electronic vehicle monitoring and locating systems allow a vehicle's location to be pinpointed; some systems also allow vehicle diagnostics to be performed and routinely monitored while the vehicle is in service. It is also possible to automatically count the number of passengers aboard a bus or other transit vehicle. On-off counts, which typically require a large staff input, may now be carried out on a large-scale basis with a minimum of personnel involved.

Good personnel relations, which include programs of benefits and sincere and honest dealing with employees and their problems, are probably the best way to prevent labor difficulties in public transportation. Moreover, transit agencies receiving federal aid are covered by the provisions of Section 13(c) of the Urban Mass Transportation Act of 1964, as amended. Under Section 13(c), labor must be made no worse off as a result of a federal grant than it was before the grant was made. Because the local union, in effect, is one of the parties who must sign off on the application for these federal funds, good management–labor relations are a necessity; grants may otherwise be jeopardized by refusal of the local union to give its acquiescence.

The transit industry was not spared from the epidemic of substance abuse that struck the United States beginning in the 1960s. All strata of American society were affected by drugs, a plague that appeared more serious and dangerous than the more traditional problem of alcohol abuse. Clearly, operating public passenger vehicles with a work force impeded by drugs was unacceptable. Management response beginning in the 1970s was to begin drug testing for cause. Typically, operating employees were tested for drugs as part of a routine physical examination, but also as a result of involvement in an accident or signs of aberrant behavior. Random drug testing, without any cause, became a controversial issue in the 1980s and one that appears to raise serious constitutional issues. Management also established employee assistance programs (EAPs), often in conjunction with the unions representing employees. EAPs sought to help employees recover from drug and alcohol problems, as well as stress and financial and domestic problems that might affect job performance and safety.

Compounding managerial problems with human resources were changes in the work ethic and the consistency of the work force. Older generations of transit workers had accustomed themselves to the often difficult operating environment and the quasi-military discipline imposed upon them by the transit industry. This was a discipline and managerial style not unlike that military-type model that the railroads had developed in the mid-nineteenth century to manage a dispersed work force that was impossible to supervise closely, as would be the workers in a store, shop, factory, or office. Seemingly arbitrary, and sometimes harsh and capricious, disciplinary methods had to be modified to control and monitor employees in a more modern, cooperative style.

The transit industry's work force, once dominated by male Caucasians, came to involve a large percentage of women and minorities, especially African Americans and Hispanic Americans. Coupled with the overall change in the work ethic, management faced a challenge. Supervisors had to recognize significant differences in culture, background, and attitude among employees. Increased supervisory training was at least a partial solution to this challenge, as management sought to sensitize itself and its supervisory force to the new conditions.

MAINTENANCE

Another critical element that management must deal with realistically is maintenance. Preventive maintenance is indispensable for reliable service; unfortunately, this type of maintenance often falls by the wayside in lean times. Preventive maintenance is very simply the process of finding a problem before it becomes a breakdown or the cause of an accident. It is for this reason, for example, that power-steering-fluid hoses are inspected or replaced on a regular basis rather than waiting until a hose breaks and the power steering on a bus becomes inoperable. Moreover, in these days of high equipment costs, a good preventive maintenance program can reduce the number of pieces of equipment that must be available as a backup to cover breakdowns and other problems that arise in operations. As a result, major savings can be made in capital investment, and greater reliability of service can be offered.

For transit properties with massive fixed facilities, this meant facing up to what often amounted to decades of deferred maintenance on those facilities that totaled nationally many billions of dollars. Enormous sums for capital replenishment have been needed and the job is far from finished. The work is often highly disruptive to operations and operating conditions are difficult.

All the various elements related to the management of transit—personnel, maintenance, routing and scheduling, equipment selection, communications, marketing, and organization—must be related in a systematic fashion by management. None of these elements stands alone; they must be woven together into a total managerial fabric. Understanding the relationship and knowing how best to take advantage of the various resources within a firm is the manager's prime job and must be fully understood in order to provide quality transit service.

MANAGEMENT PERFORMANCE AUDITS

Good management practice demands a regular evaluation of performance. Sometimes called a management performance audit, the evaluation should be carried out either internally or by an external body. The advantage of an external group is that it brings new ideas and a fresh approach to a performance audit, as well as a perception of greater objectivity. Such audits reviewing the whole management of a transit property should be done every 3 or 4 years. Such audits are required regularly in California in order to receive state funding; a few other states also require some auditing. Internal audits should be carried out in depth each year on a few of the managerial functions, such as maintenance, financial management, or marketing.

Most audits start with the goals and objectives of the organization and the individual functions and compare the performance with the desired results. A well-done audit will also carefully examine the various procedures and practices used in carrying out tasks. The performance audits will produce a report of findings and recommendations for management. Constant internal auditing and intermittent external audits should give management help in fine-tuning the system and improving the quality of operations, as well as getting the most out of each dollar.

Performance evaluation also embraces capital projects. Beginning in the 1980s, UMTA required that consultants be employed to monitor major transit capital undertakings. The aim was to avoid unnecessary design changes and the cost overruns that had been a problem from the very start of the federal aid program.

Transit management is a difficult job, but not an impossible one. For example, the success of Tidewater Transit in the Norfolk, Virginia, area is the result of careful route analysis; the use of performance targets; and careful pruning, support, and innovation in the delivery of public transportation. The Champaign-Urbana Mass Transit District in Illinois has used a high degree of innovation, strong market analysis and marketing promotion, careful fiscal management, excellent employee relations, and a passion for on-time performance, to carry 6 million passengers a year in an urbanized area of only a little over 100,000 souls. Port Authority Transit in Pittsburgh has used major capital investments in light rapid transit and exclusive busways, a watchful eye on finances, performance auditing, and innovative fare policies to provide a high quality of service in an area with a very difficult topography.

SUMMARY

Management is a critical but often overlooked element in a successful urban mass transportation service. The use of modern business management concepts and techniques makes sense in the process of improving transit service. The important thing is to focus on consumers and how best to serve them. Only in this way can public transportation meet the reality of today's competitive market for transit service and the need to help improve life in U.S. urban areas.

The transit manager of today is faced with both opportunities and problems that are unlike those of his or her predecessor in the times long gone by, when transit had a virtual monopoly of transportation in American cities. The great opportunity facing transit management is the adoption of modern business practices, which will result in the smooth and effective operation of the transit service, with concomitant benefits to the community. Transit problems are most likely to arise from the industry's poor public image and poor quality of service relative to its competition.

As the director of a public enterprise, the transit manager exists in a new relationship with public officials. This often means that transit is called upon to perform social functions undreamed of in times past. The provision of special lower fares and special services for elderly and handicapped citizens is now required of all transit properties that accept federal funds. Those involved in transit management must constantly arm themselves with facts and figures to make sure that public officials realize the implications of decisions made in regard to public services.

Management opportunities in the public transit field have probably never been more interesting or more exciting than at the present time. What lies ahead is equally as fascinating as the great challenges that faced the transit managers a century ago who mastered the problems of operating horse-railway systems and then were involved in the adventure of the changeover to electric traction. Whether or not the transit industry can meet its new challenges will largely lie in the hands of the coming generation of transit managers.

REFERENCES

Some of the ideas in this chapter originally appeared in GEORGE M. SMERK, "Mass Transit Management," *Business Horizons*, 14, no. 6 (December 1971), 5, 8-16.

1   This very interesting approach was presented in an important article: NORMAN KANGUN AND WILLIAM A. STAPLES, "Selling Urban Transit," *Business Horizons*, 18, no. 1 (February 1975), 57-66.

FURTHER READING

Some citations are no longer available from their original source. These citations are often available from the National Technical Information Service, U.S. Department of Commerce, 5285 Port Royal Road, Springfield, VA 22161. We have verified the order numbers for many of these citations, and they are found at the end of the citation. Prices are available through NTIS at the address above.

ANDRLE, STEPHEN J., AND BRIAN MCCOLLOM, "Space Allocation in Bus Maintenance Facilities," in *Winter and Transit Bus Maintenance and Highway Maintenance Management*, Transportation Research Record 1019, pp. 62-68. Washington, D.C.: Transportation Research Board, 1985.

CHENG, PHILIP C., *Accounting and Finance in Mass Transit*. Totowa, N.J.: Allanheld, Osmon & Co., Pubs., Inc., 1982.

FIELDING, GORDON J., *Managing Public Transit Strategically: A Comprehensive Approach to Strengthening Service and Monitoring Performance*. San Francisco: Jossey-Bass Publishers, 1987.

HOVELL, PETER J., WILLIAM H. JONES, AND ALAN J. MORAN, *The Management of Urban Public Transport: A Marketing Perspective*. Lexington, Mass.: Lexington Books, D.C. Heath & Co., 1975.

INDIANA UNIVERSITY TRANSPORTATION RESEARCH CENTER, INSTITUTE FOR URBAN TRANSPORTATION, *Handbook for Management Performance Audits* (2nd ed. rev.), prepared for UMTA, Technology Sharing Program, Report no. DOT-T-88-21. Washington, D.C.: U.S. Department of Transportation, July 1988.

KOTLER, PHILIP, *Marketing Management: Analysis, Planning, Implementation, and Control* (6th ed.). Englewood Cliffs, N.J.: Prentice Hall, 1988.

LOVELOCK, C. H., *Consumer Oriented Approaches to Marketing Urban Transit*, Research Report no. 3, prepared for UMTA. Stanford, Calif.: Stanford University Graduate School of Business, March 1973. Now available as PB 220 781.

MAZE, T. H., ALLEN R. COOK, AND UTPAL DUTTA, *Bus Fleet Management Techniques Guide*, Final Report, prepared by the Oklahoma Highway and Transportation Engineering Center, University of Oklahoma, for UMTA, Technology Sharing Program. Washington, D.C.: Urban Mass Transportation Administration, August 1985. Now available through NTIS.

PERRY, JAMES L., *Organizational Form and Transit Performance: A Research Review and Empirical Analysis*, Final Report, prepared by the Institute of Transportation Studies, University of California, Irvine, for UMTA. Irvine, Calif.: University of California, Irvine, 1984. Now available through NTIS.

PIKARSKY, MILTON, AND DAPHNE CHRISTENSEN, *Urban Transportation Policy and Management*. Lexington, Mass.: Lexington Books, 1976.

SMERK, G. M., AND OTHERS, *Mass Transit Management: A Handbook for Small Cities; Part 1: Goals, Support and Finance; Part 2: Management and Control; Part 3: Operations; Part 4: Marketing* (3rd ed., rev.), prepared by Indiana University Institute for Urban Transportation, Center for Transit Research and Management Development, for UMTA, Technology Sharing Program, Report no. DOT-T-88-12. Washington, D.C.: U.S. Government Printing Office, February 1988.

SMITH, JAY A., KENNETH M. JENNINGS, AND EARLE C. TRAYNHAM, *Cooperative Initiatives in Transit Labor–Management Relationships*, prepared by the University of North Florida, University Research and Training Program. Washington, D.C.: Urban Mass Transportation Administration, 1985.

EXERCISES

16-1   What major difference in ownership is faced by transit management today that was not true in the first half of the twentieth century?

16-2   Why do transportation firms in general tend to be operations oriented? Why do transit properties tend to be operations oriented?

16-3   What is meant by consumer orientation in the modern business firm?

16-4   What are the roles of strategies, goals, and objectives in transit management?

16-5   What is the role of the governing board in transit management?

16-6   Why is it important for transit managers to understand consumer behavior?

16-7   What environments are faced by the transit manager?

16-8   Why is market segmentation a reasonable marketing strategy for transit?

16-9   What is the marketing mix in transit?

16-10   Why are personnel management and maintenance management critical in transit?

Chapter 17

PUBLIC TRANSPORTATION MARKETING

FRANK W. DAVIS, JR., AND RAY A. MUNDY

Marketing is a word used quite extensively in public transportation, but typically in a micro rather than macro context. Micro-marketing describes the activity of the individual firm as it plans, advertises, and sells. Macro-marketing, on the other hand, is the process by which a community allocates resources for the benefit of its citizens. Too often, public transportation authorities use micro-marketing principles when they should be serving a macro-marketing role.

MARKETING AND RESOURCE ALLOCATION FOR CONSUMERS

The terms macro-marketing and micro-marketing are often confused. Micro-marketing is the process by which a single organization understands and interacts with its customers. Macro-marketing, on the other hand, is the process by which communities assure that individual organizations provide the benefits needed by their citizens. In command economies, resources are allocated by central planning groups who develop long- and short-range plans that individual organizations are required to follow. In market economies, macro-marketing consists of policies that inhibit monopolies and give customers the ability to patronize the organizations that best meet their needs.

Typically, macro-marketing is a regulatory function, whereas micro-marketing is performed in each individual firm. Public transit authorities are unique in that they have to function as both macro-marketer and micro-marketer. This unique situation occurred when government assumed operating or funding responsibility for bus companies that had previously been operated as regulated public utilities. When authorities were created, they received both operating responsibility and regulatory responsibility. Unfortunately, marketing as a discipline is based on micro-marketing, whereas macro-marketing has typically been addressed by economics and regulatory legal precedent.

But how does an authority address this dual responsibility without falling in the trap of assuming that what is good for the transit company is good for the public? How can conflicts of interest be avoided? This conflict can arise whether the authority provides traditional transit service as an employer or as a contractor of service from a private provider. This chapter will discuss some of the issues involved with macro-marketing.

An agency or organization, whether public or private, has specific resources at its disposal. These include financial resources, which may be budgeted, endowed, or received as a result of sales or taxes; people with various skills and training; and existing facilities, including vehicles, buildings, and equipment. The purpose of the organization is to use its resources to generate benefits to society and to the holders of the resources (employees, stockholders, foundations, and funders).

In a free-market economy, customers are given a choice in the marketplace so that if they do not like the benefits that one organization provides they do not have to buy them. This stops the flow of resources to the unresponsive organization and directs funds to the organization that is more responsive to individual needs. As an alternative, organizations may receive their funds from the political budgeting process instead of the marketplace. In this case, the public has the ballot process to vote its approval or disapproval of the way funds are budgeted.

Macro-marketing problems occur when customer choices are restricted in the marketplace or when the citizen's vote is ineffective in redirecting the allocation of resources by the political process. Examples of restrictions include policies that limit innovation, lack of consumer information, seller dishonesty, and large bureaucracies that do not change in response to free elections. Long-term commitments of funds that are not responsive to changing voter mandates and the development of one-sided lobbying efforts also create restrictions. In the long run, the ability of society to use its resources to meet its changing needs is determined by the responsiveness of the resource allocation process to the voice of the consumer.

The major failing of any individual organization is to become so enamored with its current product or internal operations that it no longer considers the evolving needs of customers. The product or service then loses market share because it does not meet society's needs as well as a competitive product or service. Instead of "receiving the consumer's message," the product-oriented company often rationalizes that the product is not at fault but that the consumer is becoming increasingly irrational.

The market-oriented firm has two perspectives. On one hand, it realizes that the existing product or service delivery is not ideal, but it is the only way the firm has to maintain revenue flow. On the other hand, the firm recognizes that it must continually improve the fit between what the customer wants and what the organization delivers. The changing needs of the customer must be the focal point of the organization's activities. Only by selling what is available today can the organization generate the funds that they need to better provide what customers want tomorrow. Tomorrow the product will change as consumer needs change, as the marketing department better understands these needs, and as the agency develops greater flexibility in deploying its resources.

When organizations become enamored with today's responses to customer needs, they do not continue to promote and encourage innovative new solutions. Once the organization loses the ability to dynamically change with customer preferences, it loses the cash flow necessary to make change possible. Equally as devastating is for an organization to become so operationally bound that it is unable to modify responses to customers. Thus the ability to respond to changing customer needs must be built into the organization.

Where transportation authorities are responsible for both operations and policy they must make sure that they do not shelter the operational side from the need to evolve in response to changing customer needs. Unfortunately, it is easy for transportation authorities faced with budget pressures to focus on cost control rather than responsiveness to customers. Once the service is no longer responsive to individual customer needs, however, it is hard to win customers back.

MICRO-MARKETING MANAGEMENT

Micro-marketing consists of two major components: (1) selling the agency's existing products or services in the short run so that it can obtain the funds needed to keep the agency viable, and (2) *market research*, which guides the agency's resources in developing new, more responsive products and services. The selling component includes advertising, order taking, financing, and promotional and distribution programs. Also included are activities that better inform the consumer about the existing product or service, make it easier for the consumer to obtain and use the product or service, and persuade the consumer to try it. Market research, on the other hand, determines what future products or services consumers will want and the options for delivering these benefits.

Generally, the generic sales function is well defined and understood by public transportation companies who regularly advertise, print schedules, experiment with fares, and engage in other promotional programs. (For a description of transit company marketing activities, see Chap. 16.) Therefore, the remainder of this chapter will emphasize macro-research and planning activities. Consequently, the emphasis will not be on how to get more people to ride the existing bus or subway, but rather on how to use public transportation to accomplish community objectives.

PUBLIC TRANSPORTATION MACRO-MARKETING

An effective public transportation macro-marketing effort must address five basic questions.

1. What is the community trying to do?
2. Who must be served to accomplish the community's objectives?
3. What combination of service, vehicles, price, and promotion will have to be offered to win the acceptance of those who must be served to accomplish the community's objectives?
4. When should a specific service be initiated, expanded, revised, reduced, or terminated?
5. How should the community's public transportation authority be organized to ensure that its objectives are accomplished?

When these questions are answered, the public transportation authority can develop and implement a strategy to accomplish these objectives. Unless these questions are asked, the authority is simply operating a transportation company, not protecting the public interest.

WHAT IS THE COMMUNITY TRYING TO DO?

Goals and objectives are given frequent lip service, but are seldom accomplished operationally. In many public transportation agencies, stated goals are so broad that no one could possibly disagree with them; but in daily operations the mandate is so restrictive that there is virtually no flexibility for change. For example, the goals of the urban transportation plan may be "to provide the highest degree of mobility possible to stimulate economic prosperity or the development of human resources and more efficient land use." In practice, however, the regional transit authority may view its mandate to be the preservation of the current fixed-route, fixed-schedule bus company.

Whether the operational goals are limited by public mandate, by the perspective of the operators, or by the regulatory body's vision, there is little probability that product planning will suggest alternative forms of service much different from the narrow range of services currently in operation. If the giant organizations of today had had such a restrictive mandate, IBM would process only punched cards for the Census Bureau, Standard Oil would sell only kerosene for lamps, Sears would be a mail-order house for farm supplies, and the March of Dimes would accept funds only for polio research. The reason these giant endeavors have had room to grow is that they utilized broad operational goals that allowed them to use their resources to change with their consumer's needs. The public transportation authority must likewise seek to broaden its vision of public transportation. An alternative goal may be "to accomplish transportation-dependent urban goals in the most cost-effective manner." The term effective implies two concepts. *Delivery effectiveness* is a measure of how well the service actually meets individual customer needs. *Cost efficiency* is a measure of how efficiently it delivers the desired service.

Some of these transportation-dependent urban goals include:

1. *Increase the efficiency and effectiveness of public investment in transportation facilities and services.* For example, the life of specific facilities may be extended without expending large sums of money for new construction (for instance, people may be channeled into carpools or buses to postpone or substitute for the construction of new bridges or highways). Another example would be to eliminate the need to make long-term capital commitments in areas with rapidly changing land-use patterns that would soon make the expensive infrastructure obsolete (for instance, the use of buses, vans, and carpools to eliminate the need for new highways or rail extensions).

2. *Improve environmental quality and promote efficient energy use, stimulate tourism, and develop human and other resources.* Public transportation can make a major contribution to resolving these issues.

3. *Provide desired mobility to those who are public transportation dependent.* Most communities feel a social obligation to provide transportation to specific groups, such as the elderly, the handicapped, school children, the young, non-automobile owners, nondrivers, low-income groups, and other special groups.

4. *Support and promote desirable land-use development patterns.* The promotion of central business district activity, the control of night or daytime traffic densities in specific areas, or the development of regional activity centers (objectives may vary among communities) are a few examples.

5. *Accommodate individuals who desire public transportation services.* Most communities are willing to provide transportation services to those who desire it or have a need for it, as long as it can be provided economically or can satisfy one of the previously stated goals or objectives.

In each case, these operational goals necessitate the identification of a specific clientele that must be transported between specific origins and destinations at specific times if the goals are to be accomplished. Thus, product planning activities can be directed to the level of services required by these specific individuals, and sales can concentrate on selling new service to the specific groups identified.

WHO MUST BE SERVED TO ACCOMPLISH THE COMMUNITY'S OBJECTIVE?

Market segments are groups of individuals who have common identifiable transportation needs. If a transportation agency does not have specific goals, there is a tendency to operate a system to "serve" all people (the general public) without consciously realizing that each of the many diverse market segments has different transportation needs. Examples of market segments include suburban commuters going to a downtown office complex at 8:30 a.m., blue-collar workers going from the older residential areas to a suburban industrial park, suburban school children going to swim meets and ball games, senior citizens on shopping excursions, or tourists traveling between airport, motels, restaurants, and gift shops. An effort to serve all markets with the same type of service ensures that no market is served well.

Once the public transportation authority has identified its goals, it can identify the market segment that must be served to accomplish these goals. For example, if the goal is to relieve congestion on the Golden Gate Bridge between the hours of 7 a.m. and 9 a.m., the dominant market segment that must be served to accomplish the agency's goals are morning commuters who live in Marin and Sonoma counties and travel to San Francisco. If, on the other hand, the community is concerned about meeting its perceived social and legal obligations to the handicapped, the product planning activity must locate the handicapped who need service and determine when and where they want and/or need to travel. The results of this step may be a list of individuals, complete with trip origins, trip destinations, and trip times. In many cases, the list will include names, addresses, and phone numbers.

Macro-marketers realize that users have widely varying needs and that each need is time and route specific. The more diverse the needs are, the smaller the market segments that can be served with a single service. Now that suburbs are expanding not only for housing but also for employment and shopping, travel segments with common needs continually get smaller. This is not a problem for highway planning since highway networks allow the individual travelers to personalize use in many ways. Travelers can use a variety of vehicles, including trucks, motorcycles, motor homes, pickup trucks, and a large selection of automobiles, to travel personalized routes on personalized schedules to meet their individual travel needs. Frustration occurs when congestion or detours restrict the ability of the individual to customize travel to their personal needs. There is little difference between waiting 30 min for a bus and waiting 30 min in a traffic jam or between having to take a bus on an indirect route and having to drive over an indirect detour route.

In the case of highways, it is the individual user who customizes the service to make it effective. Public transportation service, on the other hand, only allows the customer either to ride or not to ride. Vehicles, schedules, and routes are already predetermined and not adaptable to modification by individual users. Unless the service can be customized to individual user needs, it must be planned on a disaggregate basis.

In general, there are three approaches to making sure that services are responsive to individual customer needs.

1. If needs are uniform among all users, large service systems may be developed. Examples include subways and fixed-route bus systems.
2. If needs are diverse, a network of facilities can be developed so that users can customize the way the network is used. Examples include highways, airports, and car rental agencies.
3. If needs are diverse and the customer cannot customize usage, then it is better to have many small operators who are "close to their customers" and can be responsive to individual needs. Examples include taxicabs, carpools, jitneys, and charter buses for tours.

In short, the key components of public transportation planning are identifying potential market segments, determining the uniformity of travel needs for each segment, and developing strategies for serving each segment's special needs. This is a continual, ongoing process. Unfortunately, too many operators and planners minimize the importance of understanding individual customer needs. Some even suggest that the primary planning role is determining equipment specifications, mapping out routes, and establishing schedules. This operational, as opposed to customer, orientation virtually assures failure since the service will not effectively meet the needs of individual customers. The heart of macro-marketing is that the service must change to meet the changing needs of customers. Market research is the process of determining what changes are desired by the customers. Sales is trying to get people to use what the operators already provide.

WHAT COMBINATIONS OF SERVICES WILL WIN ACCEPTANCE OF THOSE WHO MUST BE SERVED TO ACCOMPLISH COMMUNITY OBJECTIVES?

The private firm whose major goals are improving wages and stabilizing employment opportunities for its workers and increasing rates of return for investors is generally free to offer any type of product or service that is legal, acceptable to the public, and within the firm's financial, technical, and managerial capacities. Thus, rail companies have diversified into fields such as real estate, trucking, bus lines, pipelines, communications, snack foods, and hotels to better accomplish the firm's goals.

Public agencies, however, are expected to accomplish community goals within their mandate at the lowest possible costs. Therefore, the public authority should limit activities to solving community goals through various transportation schemes. Although this implies that the authority should not enter oblique fields such as hotels and food catering, it does require that the authority pursue whatever strategies meet individual user needs so that urban goals might be achieved.

The authority's success in accomplishing its objectives will be determined by how well it provides the consumer with a product or service the consumer wants. Since the customer does not care which firm actually produces, transports, stores, and finances the product, most organizations will make extensive use of many other firms. Sears once tried to manufacture as well as sell its products, but now buys virtually all its products from independent companies. Likewise, Nike relies on independent companies both to produce and to sell all their products. Taxi and trucking companies are increasingly relying on private owner–operators to provide the actual transportation, while the firm handles the dispatching, sales, and product planning functions. This increased reliance on other firms is called *networking*.

Likewise, the public transportation authority has many options available for the actual delivery of service, and its success will depend upon how well it utilizes all the options available to it. For example:

- The authority can own the equipment and use employees to operate all phases of the service.

- The authority can own the equipment and hire one or more contract management firms to provide any or all parts of the service.
- The authority can contract with private companies to provide a wide variety of services on a contractual or fee for service basis.
- The authority can encourage private operators to enter the marketplace by withdrawing from the market and regulating the private carrier as deemed necessary for the specific situation.

Accordingly, it should be recognized that the primary role of the public transportation authority is not to provide one type of transportation service, but rather to provide options that will be used so that community goals are achieved. To do this, the authority must understand the needs of various market segments and develop a mix of service strategies that are responsive to them. It is only when services are used that community goals are accomplished. If the community goals can be accomplished in several ways, the lowest-cost method should be chosen. That is cost-effective management. Specifically, the macro-marketer should:

- Determine whether individuals within the target market are currently making the trip.
- Determine the level of service to which the target market has become accustomed.
- Predict the level of service necessary to induce the target market to shift from the current mode to one that will better accomplish particular urban objectives.
- Develop schemes and strategies to effect this modal shift by utilizing appropriate combinations of vehicles, contractors, private operators, public systems, and the necessary regulatory policies.
- Select the lowest-cost scheme available if several alternatives can accomplish the modal shift necessary to accomplish urban objectives.

Once the macro-marketer has located the target market and developed a strategy for effecting the modal shift necessary to accomplish the urban objectives, it must decide on the most cost-effective method of promoting the service. In general, the publicity should focus on the target group, with as little promotion wasted on nonpotential buyers as possible. Presentations to neighborhood groups, in-plant posters, handbills, or billboards on highly traveled corridors may be effective for commuters; but notices in community clubs or health facilities may be more effective for senior citizens. Promotions in schools, YMCAs, and sports areas may better reach school-age children. In essence, specialized services should be promoted to the special groups that will use them.

The fare charged for the service should be low enough to ensure that goals are met, but high enough to recover costs. The degree of cost recovery will depend upon authority goals. Low price alone will not attract riders to a service that is unresponsive to their needs. Payment methods are also an integral part of the macro-marketing package. For instance, exact-fare programs simplify the collection of fares, expedite loading, and reduce robbery potential. Subscription fares and monthly passes provide the same benefit and encourage the rider to make a one-time commitment to continue riding. Use of credit cards, as is being demonstrated in the lower Naugatuck Valley of Connecticut, has benefits in data collection and elimination of coin collection, allows pricing flexibility, and reduces out-of-pocket payment bias. Payroll deduction programs offer the additional advantage of making the purchase of tickets easier to budget. Employer sales of tickets, especially when accompanied by an employer's strong promotional program and partial subsidy, greatly strengthen the incentive for the worker to ride on a regular basis. Other groups who have similar goals may want to participate. Shopping centers, for example, may be willing either to subsidize a shopper's fare or to supply a vehicle and driver to provide service, if encouraged by the public authority.

Once a service is offered to a specific market segment, it is important to monitor the success of that service to ensure not only that the urban goals are achieved, but also that the service changes to meet the evolving needs of the user. This feedback can best be obtained from someone who is in close contact with the target market. Vanpool programs usually rely on the driver to maintain rider enthusiasm. Company commuter programs may rely on a plant coordinator. Subscription buspool programs often rely on a "busmeister." It does not matter who provides the feedback as long as someone has the responsibility, motivation, and authority to make changes to keep the consumers satisfied and to relay complaints, problems, and observations to those responsible for the service provided. As a general rule, the closer the coordinator can be to the customer the more responsive the service to individual customer needs.

When Should the Service Be Reduced, Revised, or Possibly Terminated?

Public transportation, like all products or services, has a definite product life-cycle. The product life-cycle concept is a recognition that any new service or product when first introduced into the marketplace requires a period of time before it is widely accepted by consumers. During this period, sales increase, slowly at first and then more rapidly, as consumers become aware of the product's benefits. Then the sales of the product level off as it saturates its intended market segment and ceases to attract new users. Soon the service may begin to lose market share to a new product that better meets the new needs of the target market. If the service offering is not modified to keep pace with the changing needs of the consumer, sales will diminish until at some point the authority must decide that it is time to discontinue the product or service. Likewise, transportation authorities should continue to monitor ridership for each individual service offering to determine where it is in the product life-cycle. They should have firm guidelines showing when to promote and expand and also when to discontinue service.

Unlike private firms, public agencies have a political and social obligation to continue a service whose absence would produce a severe social consequence, even though demand is very low. This political pressure to continue sparsely used runs is at the root of much of the criticism of traditional public transportation. The operating company is criticized if it does not provide the service, but if it does provide the service, it is criticized for operating empty vehicles and incurring large deficits. Thus, it is imperative for the politically astute authority to develop alternatives that allow lower-cost ways of continuing to service this segment. The authority should avoid the "all-or-nothing" dilemma, which generates such strong criticism regardless of the decision to continue or discontinue service.

For example, a declining market strategy could consist of continuing traditional bus service as long as the route generates two to four passengers per mile of operation. The second stage might be contractual service with a limousine or van operator to provide service if ridership is slightly below this level. A third stage may be a contractual taxi service, with the fourth stage being a voucher system subsidizing dependent riders who are free to use any mode they desire and can obtain—including the use of casual carriers, such as neighbors, friends, and relatives.

The key to effective product planning and management is to remember that there are individuals who must be served to accomplish urban objectives and that the role of the macro-marketing group is to manage community resources to ensure that the market is served in the most efficient way. Public criticism of public transportation is not typically aimed at the efficiency of the system, but rather at the ineffectiveness of traditional services in meeting the evolving needs of customers and in meeting community goals.

How Should Macro-Marketing Be Organized?

Macro-marketing must be located at a level high enough so that it will not be biased by individual organizational loyalties. For example, if all product and financial planning for Ford Motor Company were done by the Lincoln–Mercury Division, it is highly unlikely that Ford would ever consider the development of farm machinery, industrial equipment, lawn and garden supplies, home appliances, and computers. Likewise, the macro-marketing function in public transportation must be performed at a high enough level so that it considers all transportation alternatives, rather than merely perpetuating existing operations.

Considering the traditional orientation of regional transportation authorities (RTAs) and the public takeover of existing providers, the organization illustrated in Fig. 17-1 is suggested. Under this organization, the public transportation authority would completely divorce itself from any one form of public transportation, but would be responsible for promoting whichever combination of services that would best meet public needs. This is extremely important now, as public expectations for service, especially in the low-density suburban areas and during the peak-hour commuter periods, are simply beyond the ability of traditional bus and rail companies to serve at a reasonable cost. Unless alternatives are developed to meet these needs, the growing taxpayer rebellion may greatly reduce financial support for the transportation agencies.

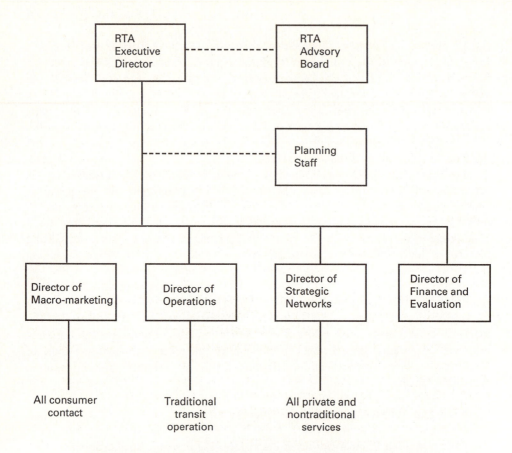

Figure 17-1 *Suggested organizational structure for a market-oriented public transportation agency. This organizational chart is actually a transitional organization that is necessary because of the heavy operational orientation of existing RTAs. Once the potential of the full family of services becomes reality, the director of operations and the director of strategic networks could be merged to become the manager of services. While the RTAs are so extremely oriented toward operations, the director of strategic networks is needed to serve as an advocate for the other options. Once the RTA can become user oriented, then an advocate for other options is no longer needed since the director of services will promote that combination of services that best meets community needs.*

By publicly acknowledging what traditional systems can and cannot realistically do and by developing the multimodal coordinating role of the authority, unrealistic expectations of the traditional systems can be diffused and new types of services to serve suburban residents and commuters can develop. Under this organization, the authority could have the same relationship with the traditional transit systems as they would with private carriers, vanpools, taxicabs, school buses, church buses, human services agencies, commuter bus clubs, and any other evolving services. The director of macro-marketing would become the focal point of citizen input, research into service-level requirements, and all the other activities suggested in this chapter.

The director of operations would be responsible for ensuring that required service levels are met by the traditional transportation system. The director of strategic networks would be responsible for contracting with private operators to provide service to the authority and for overseeing the regulation and promotion of the private sector. The director of finance and evaluation would be responsible for evaluating the cost effectiveness of all the alternatives currently in operation, for coordinating funding, and for billing and paying the users and suppliers of transportation.

In essence, macro-marketing provides the intelligence required to determine what is needed and develops service strategies to meet those needs. Operations provides traditional services; strategic networks develops and promotes new options; and finance evaluates operations and makes sure the community gets the best value for the expenditure. Jointly, a committee composed of the four directors reporting to and including the executive director is responsible for handling the coordination, budgeting, and planning of all transportation services with the support of the planning staff. The regional transportation board is responsible for setting policy and overseeing the directors.

Once a strategy for each problem area is developed by the executive committee, each director carries out his or her responsibility. Marketing sells the program, operations ensures that traditional service is available if appropriate, strategic networks ensures that new options are developed, and finance makes sure that the region is receiving the most cost-effective service. The organization can fully expect that over time traditional operations will probably decline and the nontraditional options will become dominant. This is as predictable as the shift from vacuum tube to transistor to integrated circuits or the shift from stagecoach to air travel.

This organization will sound unusual to those who view government's role in transportation from the highway perspective, where government's role has been limited to the planning, designing, and construction of fixed-facility networks. The only function of government was to plan alternative construction projects and to hold public meetings (1) to eliminate duplication of projects, (2) to ensure the proper interface between completed facilities, and (3) to rank the proposed projects according to community desires. Now, with the continually growing number of vehicles on already congested highways, the completeness of the interstate system, and growing resistance to new highway construction, especially in urban areas, transportation efforts are shifting from a planning role to a macro-marketing–management role. The macro-marketing–management role will consist of increasing vehicle throughput on the highways and increasing the number of people carried in each vehicle. Therefore, the organization needs to be restructured to reflect the new role.

MARKETING STRUCTURE

Fundamental to understanding the potential for using various combinations of service delivery mechanisms is understanding the smallness of market segments. The popular book *Service America!* stresses the need for the upside down organizational structure rather than the traditional military (authoritarian) model used for production and planning activities.[1] According to this model, service success depends upon the "moments of truth" when each individual "customer contact person responds to individual requests made by the customer. To the customer, the customer contact person is the company. If the customer contact person is responsive, the company is responsive. Since success depends upon the responsiveness of the individual customer contact person, he or she should be given the greatest possible flexibility to respond to diverse customer needs. Service blueprints may be used to better understand the diversity of customer needs. This technique uses flow charts to describe the interaction between the customer and the service provider to help the organization see itself from the customer's perspective.[2]

The upside-down organizational chart suggests that the customer contact person should be at the top of the organizational chart and that the role of management is to facilitate the ability of the customer contact person to respond to the customer. This approach is part of the restructuring efforts undertaken by many organizations as they reduce the number of management levels in the organization. The concept is "the organization exists to serve the needs of the people who are serving the customer."[3]

Another finding is that small organizations are much more cost effective in developing new markets. Small organizations can stay "close to the customer."[4] If these small development groups are part of a larger organization, they must be protected from all the administrative and bureaucratic requirements that so often restrict a group's ability to respond to changing customer needs. These small groups have been called "skunkworks."[5] One study has suggested small groups provide 24 times the innovation per dollar of expenditure as large organizations.[6] The small organizations can respond to individual needs by developing and testing prototype services. Once the prototypes are developed, they can be discontinued, modified, or changed any way that will improve customer acceptance.

A champion is typically necessary to force change through the organization. Peters and Austin quote Brian Quinn of Dartmouth's Tuck School who said, "It was difficult to find any successful major innovation derived from formal product planning rather than the championship process." A Bell Labs vice-president echoed the sentiment when he said, "I can't think of anything that ever came directly from the new product planning process."[7] Customer-oriented innovation often comes from small, responsive groups of dedicated champions.

Even the Urban Mass Transportation Administration blames the lack of public transportation success on overcentralization and control. Two factors are identified: (1) the use of a single organization to provide public transportation, and (2) the commingling of policy making and operating responsibility under the same authority.[8] Under this model, policy makers tend to be more interested in protecting traditional operating systems (micro-marketing) than in serving diverse, changing customer needs (macro-marketing). Thus, the environment for new product champions is nonexistent. A body of literature is beginning to develop in strategic network management that could also assist public transportation market planners.[9] Network management is concerned with managing relationships between independent organizations and between departments within the same organization.[10] Jarillo suggests that the study of organizational interaction has typically been limited to understanding bureaucratic relationships and marketplace relationships. Each of these relationships is based upon zero-sum game concepts. That is, the seller must lose for the buyer to win. Network management, on the other hand, is a non-zero-sum game approach to relationships. It looks at the relationship as a total system. For example, in business logistics it is well recognized that the producer does not win by forcing the retailer to overbuy or the carrier to pay for extensive damaged freight. The network manager looks at the entire system and may develop electronic data interchange techniques to ensure high turnover of his or her products on the retailers shelves or improved packaging to reduce freight claims. Thus everyone wins.

It is unfortunate when public transportation agencies use a systems approach to operations planning but cannot visualize the solution of community goals from a network perspective. Once the public transit agency can see beyond operating their own service or contracting for specified services, they will realize that many cost-effective options are available.

A 1989 study examined strategic networking of public transportation and found many options for providing public transportation services.[11] In fact, it is probably more cost effective to develop many small independent providers who serve a limited geographical or customer base but can provide a diversity of services than to operate many single-purpose systems that cover a large geographical area. For example, communities now have areawide rail systems, transit systems, school bus systems, elderly and handicapped (E&H) systems, tour systems, charter systems, and so on. Since most trips are over limited geographical areas, would it not be more cost effective to encourage the development of local neighborhood carriers who were close to their customers and could serve diverse local needs to school, shopping, meals, and sports and even for weekend charters? Carriers must provide a high level of service to be successful. To provide a high level of service, they must solve individual travel needs. This is a role for small organizations that enable and empower their employees to respond to individual travel needs. Large, inflexible, bureaucratic organizations cannot do this.

SUMMARY

If government is going to assume the role of ensuring that public transportation is available to accomplish urban goals, it must develop cost-effective delivery methods. It is not enough to simply lobby for funds to preserve traditional delivery systems. Individuals chose their travel methods as solutions to their specific travel needs. Each selection is situation specific. Unless the public authority has developed a delivery system that is responsive to diverse individual needs, individuals will opt for solutions that may not meet public goals. For example, if the hassle of using public transportation to find a job is too great, individuals may elect to rely on public assistance instead. If the hassle of making bus transfers is too great, commuters may elect to drive instead. If the hassle over van- or carpool insurance is too great, drivers may elect to drive alone instead of pooling.

Operating in a competitive environment where the public is free to choose presents a great challenge. Many firms fail each year and cease to exist, and the cost of their failure is also great. Organizations that succeed must develop customer-oriented delivery systems rather than focusing on operating systems. This is more difficult.

It is much easier to design systems when the design is not complicated by individual customer needs. Customers can be fickle. Individual needs are diverse and may change rapidly. Customer needs are not standard. It is much easier to treat customers as standardized clones with standardized needs. Based on these standardized needs, an "optimum" system can be designed. Macro-marketing, however, recognizes that unless the more difficult human needs are served the system is not successful.

If public transportation is to be successful in accomplishing urban goals, it must be allowed to change to match changing conditions. Where restrictive regulation inhibits change, where contracts and franchises eliminate innovative competition, where governing boards stifle services, where narrowly defined operating mandates merely protect and preserve the traditional over long periods of time, there is no role for marketing since the service offering cannot change to keep pace with evolving consumer needs. If, on the other hand, urban goals and citizens' needs become the focus of public transportation, then macro-marketing will become a key function in the authority's effort to serve the community.

REFERENCES

Some citations are no longer available from their original source. These citations are often available from the National Technical Information Service, U.S. Department of Commerce, 5285 Port Royal Road, Springfield, VA 22161. We have verified the order numbers for many of these citations, and they are found at the end of the citation. Prices are available through NTIS at the address above.

1   KARL ALBRECHT AND RON ZEMKE, *Service America!: Doing Business in the New Economy* (Homewood, Ill.: Dow Jones-Irwin, 1985).

2   See *Service Excellence: Marketing's Impact on Performance*, Proceedings of 8th Annual Services Conference (Chicago: American Marketing Association, 1989) for an entire section on service blueprinting.

3   ALBRECHT AND ZEMKE, *Service America*, p. 40.

4   THOMAS J. PETERS AND ROBERT H. WATERMAN, JR., *In Search of Excellence: Lessons from America's Best-Run Companies* (New York: Harper & Row, Publishers, 1982), Chap. 6.

5   TOM PETERS AND NANCY AUSTIN, *A Passion for Excellence: The Leadership Difference* (New York: Random House, 1985), Part III, pp. 113-96.

6   1981 National Science Foundation report cited by JAMES MARTIN, *An Information Systems Manifesto* (Englewood Cliffs, N.J.: Prentice-Hall, 1984).

7   PETERS AND AUSTIN, *A Passion*, p. 118.

8   URBAN MASS TRANSPORTATION ADMINISTRATION, *The Status of the Nation's Local Mass Transportation: Performance and Conditions*, Report of the Secretary of Transportation to the United States Congress, Pursuant to 49 USC 308, prepared by UMTA (Washington, D.C.: U.S. Government Printing Office, June 1988).

9   J. CARLOS JARILLO, "On Strategic Networks," *Strategic Management Journal*, 9, no. 1 (January-February 1988), 31-41.

10   For an excellent discussion of network management see NORMAN JONAS, "The Hollow Corporation," *Business Week*, no. 2935 (March 3, 1986), pp. 56-59, and accompanying stories.

11   FRANK W. DAVIS, JR., AND OTHERS, *Development of a Public Service Providing Strategy: Agency Provided vs. Privatization; Single Provider vs. Strategic Network*, prepared by the University of Tennessee, Department of Marketing, Logistics, and Transportation, for UMTA, Report no. TN-11-0008 (Washington, D.C.: Urban Mass Transportation Administration, 1989). Now available through NTIS.

FURTHER READING

CRAVENS, DAVID W., RAY A. MUNDY, AND ROBERT B. WOODRUFF, "Potential for Marketing Management Application in Public Transportation Planning," in *New Marketing for Social and Economic Progress and Marketing Contribution to the Firm and to the Society*, the Combined Proceedings of the American Marketing Association, Series no. 36, ed. Ronald C. Curhan. Portland, Ore.: American Marketing Association, 1974.

DAVIS, FRANK W., JR., "Effective Transit Policy-Making at the Local Level," in *Research Needs for Evaluating Urban Public Transportation*, Special Report 155, pp. 9-13. Washington, D.C.: Transportation Research Board, 1975.

——, "Regulatory Barriers to Innovation and the Knoxville Experience," in *Economic Regulation of Urban Public Transportation*, review draft of conference held September 19-22, at Annapolis, Md., sponsored by U.S. DOT, Office of the Secretary, FHWA, UMTA, FEO, and EPA. Washington, D.C.: Transportation Research Board, 1976.

——, AND KRISTEN OEN. *Solving Public Passenger Transportation Problems: A Need for Policy Reorientation*. Washington, D.C.: U.S. Department of Transportation, 1977. Now available through NTIS.

——, AND OTHERS, "Comparison of Privately and Publicly Owned Demand-Responsive Systems," in *Transit Planning*, Transportation Research Record 559, pp. 11-20. Washington, D.C.: Transportation Research Board, 1976.

——, AND OTHERS, *Increased Transportation Efficiency Through Ridesharing: The Brokerage Approach*. Washington, D.C.: U.S. Department of Transportation, 1977. Now available through NTIS.

LEVITT, THEORDORE, "Marketing Myopia," *Harvard Business Review*, 38, no. 4 (July-August 1960), 45-56.

LOVELOCK, CHRISTOPHER H., *Consumer Oriented Approaches to Marketing Urban Transit*, Research Report no. 3, prepared for UMTA. Stanford, Calif.: Stanford University Graduate School of Business, March 1973. Now available as PB 220 781.

MUNDY, RAY A., *Marketing Urban Mass Transit—1973*, prepared for UMTA. University Park, Pa.: Pennsylvania State University Transportation and Traffic Center, January 1974. Now available as PB 231 310.

SCHNEIDER, LEWIS M., *Marketing Urban Mass Transit: A Comparative Study of Management Strategies*. Boston: Harvard University, Graduate School of Business Administration, Division of Research, 1965.

——, "Marketing Urban Transit," in *Mass Transportation*, Highway Research Record 318, pp. 16-19. Washington, D.C.: Highway Research Board, 1970.

STEIN, MARIN M., "Application of Attitude Surveys in Transportation Planning and Impact Studies: A Case Study of Southwest Washington, D.C.," *Traffic Quarterly*, 29, no. 1 (January 1975), 51-63.

WACHS, MARTIN, "Consumer Attitudes Toward Transit Service: An Interpretive Review," *Journal of the American Institute of Planners*, 42, no. 1 (January 1976), 96-104.

EXERCISES

17-1   Why did UMTA point to single providers and commingling of operations and policy making as the major cause for public transportation's lack of success?

17-2   What is the product life-cycle concept and how can it be applied to public transportation?

17-3   What is the difference between macro-marketing, micro-marketing, and selling?

17-4   Contrast and compare the customer-oriented versus operations-oriented delivery system.

17-5   Why are small "skunkworks" organizations able to be more responsive to customer needs?

17-6   What is strategic network management?

17-7   What are some of the alternative delivery systems that a public authority might pursue?

17-8   For most transit authorities the director of operations manages the bulk of the authority's activities. Can you imagine a scenario where this might change? Explain.

Chapter 18

PUBLIC TRANSPORTATION SECURITY

Lester A. Hoel

The occurrence of crime and vandalism on public transportation systems is a subset of the larger problem of violence against citizens and destruction of property in urban areas. Fear for personal safety and the evidence of vandalism to buildings and property may cause changes in habits and life-styles. People may stay away from high-crime areas, move to other neighborhoods, or avoid walking alone at night if there is the perception of danger. Since public transportation systems, both bus and rail, are located within cities and serve all residents, the possibility exists that crime will occur as people travel. Walking to a bus or rail station, waiting for the vehicle to arrive, and traveling on the system are all situations where a person could be assaulted.

Public transportation planners consider attributes such as travel time, cost, comfort, convenience, and availability when evaluating and designing alternatives, but usually underestimate the safety aspect. Transit patrons, however, are becoming more sensitive to their personal safety, and their beliefs will influence decisions to use public transportation. If the system is viewed as dangerous, it is likely that a person will select another mode or defer the trip. In a recent study of the influence of personal security fears on women's travel patterns it was concluded that these concerns should be given a higher profile in transportation planning. Many women, the study noted, avoid placing themselves in vulnerable positions, sometimes not traveling at all.[1] Accordingly, public transportation systems, in addition to being designed on the criteria of economy and efficiency, must include planning procedures that address passenger security. This chapter describes the extent of crime occurrences in public transportation, the options (or countermeasures) available for mitigating the likelihood of crime, and procedures for developing a security program when planning or operating public transportation.

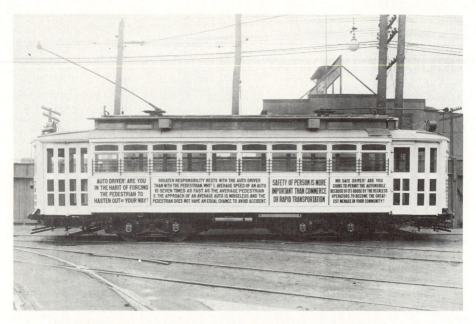

Figure 18-1 *"Transit carries people—there is no more precious cargo."*
—B. R. Stokes, "A Record of Transit Safety," *Transit Journal*, 2, no. 3 (August 1976), 12.
(photo courtesy of American Public Transit Association)

EXTENT OF CRIME ON PUBLIC TRANSPORTATION

One of the earliest attempts to measure the number of crimes on public transit was done by Thrasher and Schnell in 1971. The study included 37 U.S. and 4 Canadian systems accounting for 60% of the total vehicle-miles and passenger revenues for all transit authorities in the United States. The study concluded that the risk of being involved in a criminal incident is at least 2 times greater when riding in most major transit systems than in nontransit circumstances.[2] Of 20,899 crimes recorded on the U.S. systems studied, 1623 (or 7.6%) were violent crimes. Data were not reported for bus and rail separately. The extrapolated data indicated that between 33,000 and 39,000 crimes occurred annually on U.S. transit systems. The cost of vandalism was estimated to range between $7.7 and $9.9 million of the nation's transit bill for 1971. While vandalism costs were usually less than 0.5% of operating costs, this expense did not reflect indirect costs, including lost revenue while vehicles are being repaired, loss of ridership, insurance and legal fees, and intangibles, such as passenger and employee welfare, customer ill will, and injuries caused by acts of vandalism (for example, throwing stones).

A study of transit crimes in Chicago during 1971 and the first 6 months in 1972 indicated that crimes on rail rapid transit accounted for 84% of all Chicago Transit Authority (CTA) robberies, 92% of all transit crimes against persons, and 53% of all transit battery incidents.[3] Of all transit crimes on the CTA system, 75% occurred on rail rapid transit. When measured against ridership, rail rapid transit crimes were 7.2 crimes per million persons, whereas bus crimes were 0.7 crimes per million persons, or a ratio of 10 to 1.

The Southeast Michigan Council of Governments (SEMCOG) conducted surveys in 1979 and 1981 to determine the extent of crimes on public transportation in the United States and Canada.[4,5] The SEMCOG study divided crimes in two parts. Part 1 included violent crimes, such as murder, robbery, and serious assault, and Part 2, less serious crimes, such as vandalism, drunkenness, and disorderly conduct. When comparing rail and bus, the study data revealed that 29% of crimes on rail rapid transit were Part 1 crimes (serious) compared with only 7% on bus transit. The SEMCOG studies reported that in 1980 there were 31,378 serious incidents (Part 1 crimes), 95,659 less serious incidents (Part 2 crimes), and 155,589 local ordinance violations. The most common types of serious crime were larceny (58%) and robbery (24%). Other serious crimes were motor vehicle theft and burglary (6%). Murder and rape were infrequent, constituting less than 0.4%. The SEMCOG study results indicated that security planning should focus on crimes such as larceny (purse snatching, pickpocketing, and the like), robbery, vandalism, drunkenness, and disorderly conduct.

A survey of transit crime incidence on buses was conducted in 1983 and 1984 for west central Los Angeles by Levine and Wachs.[6] Rather than using crime data as reported by transit authorities, this study, based on a survey drawn from a random sample, interviewed people living in the area. The study also included crimes that occurred when walking and waiting for the bus in addition to crimes on the bus itself. (Many transit authorities resist including crimes outside the system.) The study found that the incidence of bus and bus-related crimes, as reported in the telephone survey, was considerably greater than was reported by the Southern California Rapid Transit District. By extrapolating the incidence rate secured from 1088 households interviewed, it was estimated that between 17,000 and 30,000 bus-related crimes occurred in 1983 within the survey area, compared with only 843 crimes reported for the entire service area. The total number of crimes on the bus ranged from 7000 to 12,000 (46%); at the bus stop, 6000 to 10,000 (32%); and to and from the bus stop, 4000 to 7000 (22%). This study suggested that transit crimes may be significantly underreported for crimes on the system and are a sizable portion of crimes off the system. Sources of bias were underreporting by victims of a crime, an inadequate transit crime recording information system, lack of follow-up by police, and failure to correctly attribute a crime occurrence as transit related. The results suggested that bus transit crime may be a far more serious problem than earlier studies had concluded.

SECURITY MEASURES FOR BUS TRANSIT

Crimes related to bus transit can occur in three separate environments: (1) while traveling on the bus, (2) while waiting at a bus stop, and (3) while walking to or from the bus stop.

SECURITY ON BUSES

The problem of robbery of bus drivers has largely been eliminated by the exact-fare, lock-box system used by most public transportation authorities. The threat of an assault always exists, however, as does the possibility of vandalism and rowdy behavior.

There are three strategies to reduce assaults against bus drivers and passengers: (1) create an environment in which a crime will not be attempted (deterrence), (2) furnish devices to enable the driver to summon help (thwarting), and (3) improve the means for capturing the criminal suspect subsequent to the crime (apprehension).[7] Table 18-1 lists various methods that might be used to reduce such assaults.

TABLE 18-1
Methods for Reducing Robberies and Assaults on Buses

DETERRENCE	Reduce crowding Eliminate or reduce cash availability Isolate driver in separate booth Furnish extra personnel on buses Furnish police or security guards Publicize security measures
THWARTING	Furnish means to isolate the criminal Furnish alarms on buses Use impregnable strongboxes Immobilize criminal with mace Furnish protective clothing for drivers
APPREHENSION	Furnish two-way radios on buses Furnish covert alarms on buses Use bus-locator systems Mark property with identification Mark criminals with dyes or radioactive particles Use closed-circuit television Photograph bus patrons Take voice prints

Source: Adapted from Paul Gray, "Robbery and Assault of Bus Drivers," *Operations Research*, 19, no. 2 (March-April 1971), 261.

Some measures that involve the driver directly, such as being isolated in a booth, carrying firearms or mace, wearing protective clothing, isolating or immobilizing the criminal, and traveling with a security guard, have been found to be unworkable. A more acceptable approach is the use of alarms intended to aid the driver in summoning help. Types of alarms include (1) a flashing light to signal nearby police, (2) two-way radios, and (3) silent alarms sent to police headquarters (similar to devices used in banks). Coupled with the alarm system could be the use of automatic vehicle monitoring (AVM) systems. AVM, which has been used successfully in rerouting of buses, is based on coded identification located on the sides of the vehicle that is "read" electronically by posts located along the route.

There is some doubt that alarm systems can be effective in thwarting a crime in progress, unless police help happens to be nearby, because of the time required to transmit the alarm, process the information, dispatch aid, and proceed to the site of the crime. Even if alarms or two-way communication were effective in thwarting assaults, they would not likely be used because drivers tend to forget to activate the alarm or are instructed by the criminal (who is generally aware of the system) not to move. The possibility that alarms will be accidentally or falsely triggered always exists, further limiting the credibility of the devices. Despite the general ineffectiveness of alarms and vehicle monitoring systems to stop a crime in progress, they do furnish some reassurance to the driver and passengers. For example, the two-way radio is especially useful as a means of communicating with the dispatcher's office, and although not effective as a crime deterrent, it is used to report a crime, to notify the police of disturbances on the bus (vandals, rowdies, sudden illness, and the like), and to report traffic accidents, breakdowns, bottlenecks, and other emergencies.

The use of photography, perhaps during high-crime periods, has been suggested as a means of identifying criminals active on buses. Although every person would be photographed, the film is processed only when a crime occurs. This method would assist in apprehending the criminal and could be a deterrent. Although widely used by banks to record holdups in process, it is not deemed cost effective for transit buses, nor has acceptance by the riding public been determined.

Some cities have resorted to special transit crime task forces during periods when assault on drivers and passengers became a highly visible problem. These crisis periods occur following a highly publicized assault (for example, a murder) or a series of assaults either on a specific bus route or within a high-crime area of the city. The usual response has been to furnish a police detail that is assigned to the problem. For example, following a series of assaults on bus drivers in the Los Angeles area, a special roving unit of the Inglewood (California) Police Department was given the problem. Their approach was to be highly visible to the riding public, to follow buses and board them at random times, and to respond rapidly to calls for help. Similar techniques have been used in other cities when public outcry demanded immediate attention. In the Los Angeles area, the program was discontinued after the problem was "solved." The technique of assigned police protection, highly visible and randomly applied, is extremely effective, because it provides an element of surprise. The uncertainty in the criminal's mind as to the likelihood of capture severely reduces illegal activities, and criminals move elsewhere. This method, however, is costly and has been used primarily when special problems arise and not during periods when relative calm prevails.

SECURITY FOR BUS STOPS

The study by Levine and Wachs examined three bus stop locations where the largest number of crimes had occurred. Factors contributing to crime differed for each stop, which suggests that a site-specific analysis is required to correct security problems.[8] This result is consistent with findings for accident locations at urban intersections. Each location must be examined separately to determine the root cause of the problem and then countermeasures implemented to correct the situation.

The causes reported for the three high-crime bus stops were:

1. Pedestrian crowding. Petty thieves could snatch purses, pick pockets, and easily remove jewelry.
2. Dangerous urban location. The stop was near an area that fostered a criminal element. Activity included prostitution, drug sales, adult book stores, and bars.
3. Elderly residence near a high school. Intense crowding when school closed encouraged rowdyism, and petty thefts.

The following strategies were proposed.

Case 1: Create a bus shelter that separates the waiting passengers from other pedestrians on the sidewalk.

Case 2: Move the bus stop to a safer location several blocks away where lighting was better. Close down the bar near the bus stop that was the center of the drug trade.

Case 3: Furnish a limited police presence at school closing hours, reschedule buses to reduce crowding, and institute an education program at the high school.

An interagency task force, comprised of transit agency personnel, police, and elected officials, was appointed to consider the various options, because coordination and cooperation among interested and responsible groups are essential for success. The only strategy that was implemented was to close down the bar in case 2.

SECURITY WHEN WALKING

Countermeasures for crimes that occur while walking to or from a bus stop are also related to the environment in which the crimes occur. Elderly or transit-dependent riders are most likely to be assaulted because they ride most often and are perceived as vulnerable. People feel most safe in daylight hours and many are fearful to ride transit during the evening. This problem can be addressed by a neighborhood effort to provide more lighting, escort services, police, and sidewalks. A "business watch" similar to neighborhood watches, using private security personnel with local police coordination, would create a safer sidewalk environment.

SECURITY MEASURES FOR RAIL RAPID TRANSIT

Transit security measures for rapid transit systems have been directed primarily at station areas, because these are the locations of highest crime occurrence and greatest passenger vulnerability. The principal objective of station-related security countermeasures is that passengers be visible to transit personnel, police, and other passengers so that criminal acts are prevented or help is summoned quickly and so that passengers have the perception of a safe environment. Accordingly, architectural design of transit station areas should include consideration of the following features:

- Clear lines of sight unobscured by columns and concessions.
- Ticket collection booth centrally located for greatest visibility.
- Straight corridors and passageways, with ample width and good lighting.
- Closed-circuit TV monitors on platform areas and other hidden locations.
- High levels of illumination.
- Clearly defined station and circulation areas no larger than needed for passenger boarding and alighting.
- Provision of variable-size areas for peak and off-peak periods to avoid passenger isolation and feelings of vulnerability.
- Minimum number of exit and entry points.
- Locked and supervised toilet facilities.
- Clearly defined corridors and waiting areas partitioned from storage and nonpublic spaces.
- Fences, one-way gates, and other directional devices to control passenger flow.

Rapid transit stations and vehicles can also be made more secure by the provision of communication aids to summon help if a crime occurs. Two types are available: alarms and closed-circuit television.[9]

A simple warning alarm could be used to attract attention or summon police. Silent alarms, for example, are sometimes used by transit ticket agents to alert police of a problem in the station. As with alarms on buses, these devices suffer from the fact that response time is usually too long, passengers may be fearful of attracting attention and not activate the alarm, little information is transmitted by an alarm, and many calls will prove to be false. Telephones with a direct line to the security office can also act as alarm devices, and these have been installed in some transit systems. Telephones can serve to reassure passengers and furnish information as well as assist in calling for help.

Continuous closed-circuit television monitoring is an effective means of visually inspecting station areas from a central control point. Cameras directed at various places, such as passageways, stairs, platforms, and telephone locations, can be called up on a central monitor, when desired, to furnish information about activity anywhere in the station. These devices may also be used to verify a telephone request for help or information. The benefits of continuous television monitoring of transit station areas could suffer from the effects of boredom or fatigue on the observer's ability to detect and report a crime in progress. The likelihood that a crime will be observed at all further depends on the presence of an active television scan at the time. Accordingly, four features are recommended in a surveillance system:

1. *Movable gates or barriers.* Limit the accessible platform area to the space required by a reduced train length during off-peak hours.
2. *Emergency telephones.* Locate direct-line, push-button-activated telephones in the restricted area. The calls are automatically placed to a central security area.
3. *Closed-circuit TV cameras.* Provide cameras activated by push bars or telephone.
4. *Public address systems.* Provide a system for use by staff observing the television monitors to reassure passengers, call to vandals, or provide information.

FACTORS INFLUENCING TRANSIT SECURITY

A procedure for assessing the adequacy of transit station security was developed for use on the San Francisco Bay Area Rapid Transit (BART) system by the University of California at Berkeley.[10] The procedure was based on station and environmental attributes and expectations regarding impacts on security. The following elements provide the highest levels of security according to this evaluation:

- Aerial and surface stations.
- Fewer station levels.
- Higher passenger volumes.
- Suburban stations in residential areas.
- Lower land-use densities.
- Absence of parking.
- Limited number of exits.
- Short walking distances to station agents, major user paths, or courtesy phones.
- Good lighting.
- Open areas unsuitable for hiding.

It should be noted that some of these elements (for example, the absence of parking and lower densities, especially in suburban areas) may not be conducive to increased patronage.

Transit security can be improved by incorporating various policies, procedures, design features, and technologies into a rapid transit system. These crime counter-measures have been divided into five categories: (1) hardware/device related, (2) station/vehicle design related, (3) personnel/operations related, (4) judicial policy related, and (5) land use related.[11] Examples of each type are shown in Table 18-2.

TABLE 18-2
Crime Countermeasures

HARDWARE/DEVICE RELATED

Alarm-activated 35mm camera at exit
Alarm-activated video tape
Burglar-type alarms (hidden) for movement detection
Chemical detection devices
Closed-circuit TV
Locked fareboxes
Medium-volume traffic flow
Metal detectors
Occupancy detection
Passenger-activated alarms
Prescreened riders
Prevention of fare evasion
Public address systems
Telephone (radio) communication between passengers and security
Voice monitors
X-ray devices

STATION/VEHICLE DESIGN RELATED	PERSONNEL/OPERATIONS RELATED
Adaptive space	Aerial patrols
Attractive, clean transit property	Curfews
Automatically sealed exits	K-9 patrols
Barriers and fences	Nonscheduled train stops
Climate control	Plainclothes detectives
Elevated guideways	Police decoys
Elimination of station restrooms	Presence of transit personnel
Good lighting	Publication of incidents
Nonbreakable windows	Reduction of number of cars during off-peak
Open design	Reduction of operating hours
Single exits	Saturation patrols/random patrols
Translucent doors in restrooms	School and community PR programs
Vandalproof surfaces	Selective/off-peak closing of stations
	Visible, uniformed security force

JUDICIAL POLICY RELATED	LAND USE RELATED
Differential penalties	Landscaping
Mandatory sentencing	Site selection
Rapid processing	Station/use integration

Source: Adapted from I. Jacobson and others, *Automated Guideway Transit System Passenger Security Guidebook*, Final Report, prepared by Dunlap and Associates, Inc., for UMTA, Report no. UMTA-MA-06-0048-79-7 (Washington, D.C.: U.S. Government Printing Office, March 1980), pp. 9-10. Now available through NTIS.

A PLANNING PROCESS FOR TRANSIT SECURITY

A unified set of procedures for incorporating security concerns in the planning or operational aspects of public transportation has been developed.[12] While intended for transit station application, they are appropriate as well for other transit situations. The steps in the planning procedure are illustrated in Table 18-3.

TABLE 18-3
Security Planning Process

Step 1:	Assess current situation
Step 2:	Document or anticipate crime problems
Step 3:	Establish security design goals and select possible countermeasures
Step 4:	Evaluate possible countermeasures
Step 5:	Consider limits and constraints
Step 6:	Consider trade-offs with other factors
Step 7:	Establish design and countermeasure strategy

Although the table implies a linear sequence of steps, the process is actually interactive, involving coordination of information, assessment of realistic options, community input, and field testing. A description of each task follows:

1. *Assess the current situation*. Collect relevant information about the existing or proposed transit project, neighborhood characteristics, and crime statistics and surveys of users. The information should include demographic characteristics, perceptions and experiences with crime in each neighborhood, and special area characteristics.
2. *Document or anticipate crime problems*. Identify probable or actual crime problems. For example, areas with a large teenage population or high unemployment rate are likely to have security problems. Area police can provide valuable information.
3. *Establish security design goals and select possible countermeasures*. Determine goals based on the crime problems anticipated (for example, minimize the exposure time of transit patrons). Various countermeasures that complement each other (for example, good lighting, random patrols, and short waits) and are focused on the specific criminal activity involved should be assembled as a package.
4. *Evaluate possible countermeasures*. Evaluate the strategies considered for each situation in terms of effectiveness, operating and capital cost, design implications, feasibility, and flexibility.
5. *Consider limits and constraints*. Consider such factors as finances, politics, community needs, and system functions.

6. *Consider trade-offs with other factors.* Consider any conflicts that security considerations may have with other transit system goals. For example, single exits are preferred for security purposes but can pose safety hazards. Exact-fare requirements are used to limit robberies but may be an inconvenience. Similarly, some security measures may cause difficulties for handicapped persons.

7. *Establish design and countermeasure strategy.* Design key features into the system to provide a minimum set of countermeasures that provides adequate levels of perceived security. Provide selective treatment for targeted high-crime areas. Focus major security efforts where needed. Rank possible counter-measures for each site, assess economic limits, and select the most cost-effective solution within given constraints.

VANDALISM

Vandalism, the willful destruction of property, is a constant problem for transit agencies. Vandals are usually school-age children, and the crime is viewed as an aspect of juvenile delinquency. The types of destruction to transit property include breaking windows, ripping seats, graffiti, and stoning moving vehicles.

The short-term goals of transit agencies are to protect its patrons, to protect its property, to apprehend and prosecute those who vandalize, and to minimize adverse effects on ridership. The long-term goal is to modify the behavior of vandals in such a manner that they will not choose to destroy transit property. Thus, techniques used by transit agencies to combat vandalism include (1) requiring vandals to do community service removing graffiti, (2) using vandalproof materials for seats and windows, (3) using easy-to-clean surfaces to facilitate removal of graffiti, (4) eliminating or making it difficult to purchase spray paint, (5) using police-alarm systems, (6) using helicopter patrols, (7) establishing education programs in schools, (8) cooperating with judicial and school authorities, and (9) maintaining surveillance, fencing, and locked gates to prevent access to storage yards.

Broken windows on buses comprise the largest single replacement cost item. Some transit systems, where problems are minor, are installing low-cost tempered safety glass. More costly break-resistant materials such as coated acrylic or polycarbonate are often used in higher-crime areas. Damaged seats are the second largest cost item, and transit systems have resorted to fiberglass seats that resist the vandal's knife. Hard seats, while puncture-proof, are less comfortable and furnish inviting surfaces for graffiti.

Graffiti is an act of vandalism that is difficult to counteract. The use of strong cleaning compounds, working with suppliers to withhold sales of spray paint, and the use of surface materials that can be cleaned easily have all been tried, but with little success, especially in larger cities. Much graffiti is acquired while the vehicles are in the storage yard, so secure yards are an important deterrent. The extra expense of yard security can be at least partially offset by lower cleaning costs.

A serious problem is the stoning or derailing of vehicles by youths. These acts cause extensive damage to moving buses and trains and have killed or injured drivers and passengers. The use of helicopters to spot trespassers and vandals on railroad property has been successfully demonstrated. Youths walking on railroad property are in personal danger, and stonings of trains have been costly to the railroads.

Several transit agencies and railroads have worked directly with schools by coupling talks about transit safety with the problems of vandalism. The effectiveness of this approach depends on the ability of the speaker to communicate the seriousness of the problem to the students, the extent of cooperation by school authorities, and the follow-up of the talks with other types of reinforcement. Special programs directed at schools located along rail lines where stonings are a serious problem have contributed to reducing the number of incidents. Football players have been used effectively as role models to make presentations in schools about the problems of vandalism and to explain the students' responsibility as good citizens.

FURNISHING POLICE SERVICES

When transit networks cross political boundaries, the question of police jurisdiction over control of the system can become an issue. The matter is especially relevant for large rapid transit systems because of their physical isolation from the city and the many communities that these systems serve.

The viewpoint of many public transit managers is that crime on transit is but a part of the overall urban crime problem and, therefore, is the responsibility of the local law enforcement agency. They contend further that the existence of a rapid transit line does not create new crime and, in fact, the existence of public transit could assist police on foot in moving about the city. Management is also concerned that the additional burden of a separate police force will further strain its budget, and, with rising deficits, the prospect of additional public transit employees added as civil servants is viewed with great concern. Furthermore, transit management has contended that it is the obligation of local law enforcement agencies to protect citizens in their jurisdiction and that such agencies are better trained and qualified to undertake this mission.

Local law enforcement agencies, on the other hand, often regard large-scale rapid transit as a special problem beyond their means to address. This attitude is not held in small- and medium-size cities where buses are the only form of public transit and where they are handled simply as another vehicle that operates on public streets. Local police in large cities view large transit systems as a separate government agency with the resources and responsibility to furnish their own security forces or to reimburse local police for this protection. Legally, local police agencies have the responsibility for the protection and enforcement of laws within their jurisdiction, but often added personnel are required to adequately protect stations, trains in motion, and transit property.[13]

The major problems created by relying solely on a local police force comprised of officers from various communities are:[14]

1. *Jurisdictional confusion.* Which community takes responsibility for the crime, how to handle crimes on trains, what happens when a crime occurring in one community is reported to police in another?
2. *Reporting of and response to crime.* Lack of centralized control of crime reports and standardized procedures cause delays and inconsistency in response. Lack of coordination, ill-defined chain of command, and lack of accountability lead to a loss of confidence by the riding public.
3. *Police patrol coverage.* The number of police assigned to patrol transit properties could vary considerably, especially between inner cities and suburbs.
4. *Crime recording.* Owing to lack of coordination, methods of recording crimes will vary considerably, and compilation of systemwide data would be extremely difficult.
5. *Specialized training required by transit police.* Policing of public transit systems requires special skills and knowledge, including understanding the characteristics of transit riders and crime types, transit system elements, and special problems. On the other hand, a single police force accountable to one jurisdiction would be more effective by furnishing a central location for reporting crimes, specialized patrol procedures, accurate crime reports, and a police force specially trained for transit problems.

The type of police organization available to serve transit systems will affect the level of security that is furnished to its riders. If their services are scattered and without coordination and leadership, then the effectiveness of other countermeasures, which are intended to secure police help quickly, might be limited. Planning for new transit systems and resolving the problems of crime on older ones may require a comprehensive assessment of the organizational and fiscal responsibilities of the transit agency and the local community for security matters.

SUMMARY

Personal security is an important factor in the decision by many people to use public transportation. While individuals are not attracted to transit simply because it promises a risk-free journey, they are deterred if the system is seen as unsafe, regardless of other positive attributes that the system may possess. People avoid transit at night and during off-peak hours if they perceive themselves as vulnerable.

Transit crime is extensive in most large U.S. cities, and its magnitude may be far greater than is shown by published statistics. While crime rates are probably higher on rapid transit than bus, both show significant occurrences that warrant special attention by planners and operators.

Security measures for bus transit should recognize that crimes can occur while traveling on the bus, while waiting at a stop, or while walking to or from a stop. Each situation requires a separate strategy and consequently must be dealt with on a case-by-case basis.

Rail transit security can be improved by considering five categories of counter-measures: hardware and devices, station and vehicle design, personnel and operations, judicial policy, and land use. A planning process for transit design should include a series of steps that assess the situation; anticipate crime problems; establish goals; select and evaluate countermeasures; consider limits, constraints, and trade-offs; and establish a cost-effective strategy.

REFERENCES

Some citations are no longer available from their original source. These citations are often available from the National Technical Information Service, U.S. Department of Commerce, 5285 Port Royal Road, Springfield, VA 22161. We have verified the order numbers for many of these citations, and they are found at the end of the citation. Prices are available through NTIS at the address above.

1   G. LYNCH AND S. ATKINS, "The Influence of Personal Security Fears on Women's Travel Patterns," *Transportation*, 15, 3 (1988), 257-77.

2   EDWARD J. THRASHER AND JOHN B. SCHNELL, "Scope of Crime and Vandalism on Urban Transit Systems," in *Crime and Vandalism in Public Transportation,* Transportation Research Record 487 (Washington, D.C.: Transportation Research Board, 1974), pp. 34-45.

3   RONALD C. JOHNSON, "Mass Transit Security in Chicago," in *Proceedings—Fifteenth Annual Meeting, Transportation Research Forum*, 15, no. 1 (San Francisco) (Oxford, Ind.: The Richard B. Cross Company, 1974), pp. 225-34.

4   SOUTHEAST MICHIGAN COUNCIL OF GOVERNMENTS, PUBLIC SAFETY DIVISION, *Crime and Security Measures on Public Transportation: A National Overview* (Detroit, Mich.: Southeast Michigan Council of Governments, 1979).

5   SOUTHEAST MICHIGAN COUNCIL OF GOVERNMENTS, PUBLIC SAFETY DIVISION, *Crime and Security Measures on Public Transportation Systems: A National Assessment* (Detroit, Mich.: Southeast Michigan Council of Governments, July 1981).

6   NED LEVINE AND MARTIN WACHS, "Bus Crime in Los Angeles, I: Measuring the Incidence, II: Victims and Public Impact," *Transportation Research*, 20A, no. 4 (July 1986), 273-96.

7   PAUL GRAY, "Robbery and Assault of Bus Drivers," *Operations Research*, 19, no. 2 (March-April 1971), 257-69.

8   NED LEVINE AND MARTIN WACHS, "Tracking Crime on Buses," *TR News*, 127 (November-December

1986), 18-21.

9   ROBERT SHELLOW, JAMES P. ROMUALDI, AND EUGENE W. BARTEL, "Crime in Rapid Transit Systems: An Analysis and a Recommended Security and Surveillance System," in *Crime and Vandalism in Public Transportation,* Transportation Research Record 487 (Washington, D.C.: Transportation Research Board, 1974), pp. 1-12.

10   INSTITUTE OF URBAN AND REGIONAL DEVELOPMENT, UNIVERSITY OF CALIFORNIA, BERKELEY, *BART Traveler Environment: Environmental Assessment Methods for Stations, Lines and Equipment*, Final Report, principal investigator, Donald Appleyard (Berkeley, Calif.: Metropolitan Transportation Commission, 1973).

11   I. JACOBSON AND OTHERS, *Automated Guideway Transit System Passenger Security Guidebook,* Final Report, prepared by Dunlap and Associates, Inc., for UMTA, Report no. UMTA-MA-06-0048-79-7 (Washington, D.C.: U.S. Government Printing Office, March 1980). Now available through NTIS.

12   LARRY G. RICHARDS AND LESTER A. HOEL, "Planning Procedures for Transit Station Security," *Traffic Quarterly*, 34, no. 3 (July 1980), 355-75.

13   KEITH BERNARD, "Planning and Development of the BART Police Services Department," in *Proceedings—Fifteenth Annual Meeting, Transportation Research Forum*, 15, no. 1 (San Francisco) (Oxford, Ind.: The Richard B. Cross Company, 1974), pp. 241-44.

14   P. S. WALLACE AND R. M. BUREN, *Policing Inter-Community Mass Transit Systems: Proposed Legislation for Chicago with a Consideration of Other Cities*, prepared for UMTA (Chicago: University of Illinois at Chicago Circle, March 1974). Now available as PB 235 677.

FURTHER READING

HARGADINE, E. O., *Case Studies of Transit Security on Bus Systems*, Final Report, prepared by MANDEX, Inc., for UMTA. Washington, D.C.: Urban Mass Transportation Administration, Office of Technical Assistance, August 1983. Now available through NTIS.

———, EILEEN, AND GAIL SCOTT, *Documentation and Assessment of Transit Security Data Reporting and Its Utilization*, Final Report, prepared by Mandex, Inc., Engineering Economics System Center for UMTA Technical Assistance Program, Report no. UMTA VA-06-0111-85-1. Washington, D.C.: Urban Mass Transportation Administration, Office of Technical Assistance, 1985. Now available through NTIS.

PEARLSTEIN, ADELE, AND MARTIN WACHS, "Crime in Public Transit Systems: An Environmental Design Perspective," *Transportation*, 11, no. 3 (September 1982), 277-97.

RILEY, NORMAN E., AND DONALD L. DEAN, "Bus Station Security: Crime at Intercity Bus Stations," in *Economic and Regulatory Issues in Intercity Bus and Other Transportation*, Transportation Research Record 1012, pp. 56-64. Washington, D.C.: Transportation Research Board, 1985.

EXERCISES

18-1 Discuss the impact of security in public transportation on ridership. What is the effect on choice and captive riders? Under what circumstances does transit security play a minor role in a person's decision to use transit?

18-2 Contact the transit manager in your community to determine the extent to which transit security is a problem. Find out what data are available on transit crimes. Summarize the results in a report that describes the characteristics of crime occurrences in your city.

18-3 Summarize the extent of crime on public transportation as described in previous studies.

18-4 Explain why crime occurrences on public transportation may be greater than reported in official figures.

18-5 Describe the three strategies to reduce assaults against bus drivers and passengers. Illustrate each with two examples.

18-6 Select a bus stop location in your community that appears to be unsafe. Describe the situation and suggest possible remedies.

18-7 Describe the architectural features that should be included in the design of a transit station to ensure a safe environment.

18-8 List the four features of a surveillance system for public transportation security.

18-9 List the four classes of crime countermeasures and illustrate each by describing three approaches that could be used. Discuss the advantages and disadvantages.

18-10 Select a rail or bus terminal in your city and, using the seven-step planning process, prepare a report that reviews the current situation and recommends a program of improvements.

18-11 As a transit manager you are faced with a wave of vandalism in buses parked in the transit garage. Describe what your options are in this situation and how you would proceed to correct the problem.

PART VI

POLICY

CONSIDERATIONS

Chapter 19

LAND USE

W. L. GARRISON AND ELIZABETH DEAKIN

That urban transportation and urban land use are related is not at issue; observation and common sense confirm that they are. The debate is over the nature and extent of this relationship and how it can and should be incorporated into urban planning and development processes. Management of the transportation–land use relationship is seen as a way to solve social problems. Depending on the eye and values of the beholder, scenarios of the future of the metropolis are set forth. Claims, beliefs, and assertions form a puzzle. The puzzle is an important one, since today's actions may be costly or valuable in ensuing years, depending on what the future holds.

Alternative views of the future reflect, in part, different disciplinary perspectives and different assumptions about what is desirable and feasible in transportation and land use. For example, many transportation analysts and some urban geographers foresee an urban and metropolitan future of continuing decentralization and specialization of places, with the automobile remaining and gaining as the principal mode of travel. In this view, the social and economic forces dispersing activities and travel patterns are so great that there is no hope of redirecting them; there is little hope for increased transit ridership, much less transit-induced changes in land use. The main need for the future, in this perspective, is a cleaned-up and more energy-efficient automobile, plus investments in highways to serve dispersed patterns of development.

In contrast, transit advocates (among them a number of urban planning professionals) imagine a considerably different future: one in which substantial improvements in transit service induce major rearrangements of urban land use. Their vision is that new transit investments will create new land development patterns: residential land uses will be denser, and office and retail activity centers will evolve at interchange points on transit lines. In turn, this changed and neatly arranged pattern of land uses served by transit will decrease the consumption of fuel, farmland, and other resources. It also will decrease travel times on foot and bicycle as well as on transit. The city will be a better place to live and more parsimonious in its use of resources. The federal Urban Mass Transportation Administration and some state and local transit agencies believe so strongly in this scenario that they promote "value capture": using the increases in land value from transit investment to help pay for the transit system.

A third vision of the future is driven by environmental and energy constraints. In this view, often held by environmentalists, air pollution and the threat of global warming, along with increasing costs of energy and concerns over the loss of farmland and other open space, of necessity will force policy changes to reduce auto use and suburban sprawl. As auto travel is restricted and as public policies are reoriented to favor compact growth, denser urban and suburban centers and subcenters will result, and transit use, cycling, and walking will increase. Cars will become cleaner and more energy efficient, though their use will be less frequent; telecommunications will serve as a substitute for an increasing number and variety of trips.

Economists often paint still another scenario. They see a mishmash of dysfunctions: subsidies, cross subsidies, ignored externalities, and inappropriate institutional arrangements and regulatory controls. Eventually, in their view, the biases, costs, and failures of the current system will lead decision makers to opt for market-oriented strategies. Congestion pricing, emissions fees, and other charges that reflect the social costs of transportation and land-use choices will be applied. Price signals then will help restructure the urban and metropolitan landscape to a more efficient one.

Many more scenarios could be created by combining land use, transportation, economic, and environmental factors in different ways; by considering different time frames; or by adding new ingredients. But our task is to enrich the reader's understanding of the possibilities, choices, and consequences, and for this we turn to history, theory, and empirical evidence for guidance.

HISTORY

Historical observation reveals strong ties between transportation and the development of cities throughout the world. Ancient religious, market, and government centers grew and extended their influence through the control of movements through mountain passes and along waterways and land routes. Early roads and ports were developed to facilitate trade, extract resources from the hinterlands, and maintain political and social control. The exchange of goods and ideas in turn fed city growth. Later, technological developments in water, rail, and road transport further aided advantaged cities to grow and prosper, while opening up new opportunities for land development as well as new ways of carrying out social and economic activities.

United States transportation and land development history initially followed the same course. Water transportation technology and water routes dominated the colonial period as well as the early days of the nation; cities grew up first on the ports and then on the rivers. Louisville, Kentucky, at the falls of the Ohio River and Cincinnati on its great north bend are examples of inland cities that drew their comparative advantages from a network of waterways. Numerous cities on the Atlantic seaboard developed at the fall line between the crystalline rock of the Piedmont and the flatter coastal plain with its water access to the Atlantic. Later, the destinies of these places waxed or waned depending on land uses in their hinterlands and their transportation connections to those hinterlands. For example, land-use and trade patterns tied to the Erie Canal helped give New York its early advantage over Boston, Baltimore, and Philadelphia.

In the eastern United States, the development of railroads tended to reinforce, in the main, the fabric of urban development and rural land uses established by waterways, although St. Louis lost its dominance to Chicago. Rail created new opportunities in some instances; Atlanta and Indianapolis owe their locational advantages mainly to rail. The settlement of the semiarid and arid West and the Pacific states was a somewhat different story; but there, too, transportation set the major patterns for urban and rural development.

Looking at the way cities were built during these periods, it is clear that transportation also gave a heavy imprint to urban form. Most cities got started during walking, wagon, and buggy days. Transportation was expensive, and the older parts of today's cities have a dense network of streets reflecting the early need for short transportation routes. Often, the old parts of cities are near waterfronts, for good access to that transportation technology was needed. It is no surprise that the streets in Manhattan providing access to the waterfront are closely spaced relative to those oriented up and down the island, because this grid accommodated the early pattern of movement.

Starting in the latter half of the nineteenth century and continuing through the first decade or so of the twentieth, horse-drawn trams, cable cars, suburban rail passenger service, and streetcars all affected the pattern of urban routes and land uses. These mass transportation modes greatly increased the amount of land within commuting distance of the urban center, and they are widely credited with supporting early suburbanization. Indeed, they were marketing tools of land developers and home builders from coast to coast.

Bicycles also affected the urban route and land-use pattern during this period. Bicycles were the first mode to make personal transportation widely available, providing low-cost mobility to men and women, youths and adults. The bicycle also quite literally paved the way for the automobile, for bicyclists were advocates of improved roads, which they soon had to share with motorcars.

The automobile era began around 1900 or a few years later. This was a time when cities were truly booming; the greatest rate of urban growth in this country occurred around the turn of the century. Immigration, industrialization, and mechanization of farming were in full swing, and the nation was in the throes of vast social and political reorganization stimulated by these changes.

Early in the 1900s several ingredients came together: numbers of automobiles attempted to operate in urban areas; the "city-beautiful" movement (which had begun several decades earlier) was at its peak; and urban-based, public-spirited, "good government" organizations were promoting new forms of governmental organization for the delivery of urban services. American cities began to engage in early forms of transportation planning and traffic engineering, intertwined with the broad goals of the city-beautiful movement. American cities' parkways and large parks stem in the main from this period: Philadelphia developed its parkway from City Hall to Fairmount Park; Chicago and Milwaukee began their lakeside parkways and parks; leaders in Pittsburgh dreamed of emulating hilly Mediterranean towns.

Professional departments of public works or city engineering were established, an outgrowth of efforts to apply scientific management principles and efficiency criteria to government. Arterial and local street hierarchies, capital improvement programs, and methods of finance including infrastructure bonds, assessment districts, and user fees were developed. Provision of good roads increasingly was seen as a government responsibility, though transit generally remained in the private sector.

Land use, in contrast, was mainly a laissez-faire matter. Some government controls did apply: subdivision requirements were established to reduce fraud and keep titles clear, and building codes were put in place to prevent fire hazards and sanitation risks. Gradually, these rules were expanded to control building height and bulk, as well as health and safety matters, and to require subdividers to make on-site dedications of streets, parks, and other sites for public uses. Yet, for the most part, developers decided how land development should proceed, and property owners determined the uses made of their buildings.

The transportation–land use relationship during this period was straightforward: transportation was put into place to serve development. Broad debates did occur about the automobiles and transit, about regional planning, and about arrangements of residential and industrial areas, but for the most part these were just debates.

The exception came over the desirability and constitutionality of zoning, an issue that reached the U.S. Supreme Court in 1926 in a case involving Euclid, a suburb of Cleveland. The court ruled in Euclid's favor, and zoning was quickly adopted in cities across the country, aided by the federal government's promulgation of a model state enabling act. But by the time that land-use control by zoning had come into its own, the Great Depression and World War II severely slowed land development, leaving the zoning instrument with little to do. Typically, existing patterns of land uses were surveyed, and zoning ordinances were adopted to protect these existing land uses from prospective nonconforming ones—not much of a challenge to development practices when so little development was taking place. Existing conflicts, on the other hand, persisted since the zoning instrument addressed existing problems only with difficulty.

THE POST-WORLD WAR II PERIOD

Post-World War II development activities reflected a mood of making up for lost time. Two decades of rapid residential suburbanization occurred; industrial, commercial, and service activities also grew and shifted spatially with the suburbs. Automobile ownership and use recovered their prewar rates of expansion. Local government mechanisms for the provision of local streets and arterials continued to function as suburban development proceeded; transportation was provided to meet emerging growth and land-use needs. Such mechanisms also functioned for the delivery of other infrastructure activities such as water supply and sewage treatment; also, the suburbs were zoned, and generally developers were required to comply with subdivision standards.

But growth and recovery were not evenly shared. In comparison to the suburbs, the inner cities did not fare well; some began to lose population relatively, and some lost absolutely. All faced problems of housing, public health, education, transportation, criminal justice, and finance. Also, pressed by modal competition and market shifts, transit systems—which had enjoyed a boom during World War II following Depression hard times—were gradually driven to the brink of bankruptcy and beyond.

During this period a powerful new element entered the transportation infrastructure: federal funding of freeways. Limited-access highways had been tested in parkways and other early designs, but planning for modern freeways began in earnest soon after World War II, particularly in the states of California and Washington and in the cities of Detroit and Chicago. Eastern states and some states in the South built early models as toll roads, and the debate at the time was not over whether to build high-performance roads, but how to finance them. The debate was resolved in favor of "user fees" (excise taxes), rather than tolls, with the federal interstate legislation and funding in 1956, and the freeway movement leaped ahead.

What was new and what was not new?

Transportation and land use for the most part continued in the framework established in earlier decades of the century: the provision of transportation continued to be steered by development goals. Streets were intimately tuned to land development. The grid of arterials was expanded as land was converted to urban uses, and as this land was developed, local streets were built. The addition of freeways changed the size and scope of transportation, but not its relationship to land use, because the freeways also were planned and built to serve the expected expansion of urban development.

What was new was heavy federal and state government involvement in urban transportation. Although just before World War II some federal aid had become available for the urban extensions of the state highway systems, both the amounts and the level of oversight were minor. The new involvement was not. The urban portions of the Interstate Highway System were eligible for federal funding on a 90% federal–10% state match. Additional federal money came with revised programs for other major and minor urban roads. Federal interest in the planning process was felt through the mandating of procedures, as well as through federal review over those proposed projects where federal money was involved.

The federal interest in urban areas was also manifest in many programs other than transportation. While there had been some Depression-era federal interest in housing, federal interest in the general well-being of urban areas expanded in postwar years. Urban renewal programs were undertaken on a massive scale. Assistance programs for housing expanded. The scope of federal involvement enlarged to cover many other programs for schools, health, welfare, sewage, water quality, air pollution, urban design, and public transport.

In the main, then, the years following World War II were ones in which historical transportation and land development relationships continued, but with an augmented cast of characters, primarily because transportation and land-use planning, financing, and other development processes had increased levels of federal involvement.

An Emerging Debate

Freeway planning procedures during this period estimated the physical expansion of the urban area and then located and sized freeways according to the travel implications of spatially extended land uses. The process was the old process: build facilities to support development. The new roads were to serve the inner cities as well as the suburbs and interregional connections so as to share the new transportation benefit widely. But in urban areas the interstate designs meant significant disruption of the urban fabric, and soon objections started to surface.

By the time that interstate building reached full swing in the 1960s, a great freeway revolt was underway. In retrospect, warning signs had been visible in urban highway controversies in the 1950s and even earlier. But the 1960s were a time of civil rights gains and mass protests; this time the freeway opponents could insist on being heard.

The revolt had a land development ingredient; it was marked by community resistance to construction through established residential neighborhoods and commercial districts. But its roots, to the extent that they can be traced, seem to go much deeper than that immediate issue. The freeway revolt seemed to stem, in part, from the belief that the continued building of freeways tilted the competitive balance against the inner city versus the suburb and was directly or indirectly responsible for a host of urban social problems. The revolt also reflected public concern about converting rural land to urban uses, about air pollution and the environment, and perhaps about the cumbersome and complex transportation planning and decision processes in which citizens had little part. On this latter point the cities won a victory of sorts early in the 1960s: a continuous transportation planning process was required of areas greater than 50,000 in population, and local officials were given the ability to veto state highway proposals by omitting them from the urban-area plans.

With the freeway revolt came the beginnings of a great national debate about urban transportation: transit versus the automobile, transportation's effects on urban form, the use of land resources by transportation, methods of finance, the incidence of cost and benefits. One thrust of the debate was that transportation must somehow be more neutral, more balanced. It was argued that automobiles and highways overly dominated urban movements; a modal balance must be restored. The need of some for other forms of transportation became one argument for the preservation and enhancement of transit and helped bring about the passage, in 1964, of legislation providing for federal capital grants to transit systems, most of which by then were in great financial difficulties.

The balanced-transportation argument also had a land-use content. Transportation policy, according to this view, had not been neutral; it had disadvantaged locations in the central city versus locations in outlying areas. Transportation thus was blamed for the decline of the central city, and in particular central business districts, vis-à-vis other parts of the metropolitan area. Here, too, investments in center-serving transit as well as suburb-serving highways were seen as an apt prescription.

Arguments for balance and neutrality aside, the funding for highways was assured, supported by fuel and other taxes distributed by formula, while transit funds were limited and their award discretionary. Highway spending continued to far outstrip that for the transit modes even in areas where transit was heavily subscribed. Yet, despite the highway investments, capacity problems did not disappear; new roads often were congested practically from the day of opening.

The early expectations that new transit investments would stem the loss of market share to the auto also were soon disappointed. Arguments began to be heard that building more facilities and adding more equipment were not necessarily the answer to either highway or transit problems. Too much attention was being placed on fast and efficient movement, this argument went in part; other concerns, including environmental quality and neighborhood preservation, might sometimes outweigh concerns about transportation per se. Sound decision making in such instances might mean foregoing a transportation project or substantially reducing its scale or design.

Concerns about environmental impacts came to the fore in the late 1960s and early 1970s. The environmental impacts of highways received increasing attention following the passage of the National Environmental Policy Act of 1969 and the Clean Air Act of 1970. In 1972, highway legislation itself mandated greater attention to social, economic, and environmental factors. Initially, transportation agencies resisted both the time and dollar costs of environmental assessment requirements and the implication that mobility values might be traded off against other societal objectives. Highway agencies asserted that projects already far along in planning and development should be excused from the requirements; transit agencies proposed that their projects should be exempt because they surely were good for the environment. But the courts rarely found either argument persuasive, and impact studies gradually came to be accepted.

Major social and economic evaluations of both highway and rail transit programs also were undertaken during this period. Economists questioned whether motorists pay the full cost for their transportation, particularly the cost of externalities such as air pollution, noise, and accidents. Other social scientists focused on who benefited from highway and rail projects, versus the incidence of costs and other negative impacts. Studies suggested that buses could provide service as good as or better than that of rail and that carpools often were even more cost-effective. Other studies investigated the costs of sprawl and the role that infrastructure investment had played in supporting it.

The questioning of capital expenditures reflected a broader mood of the times, to emphasize better management of existing resources rather than investment in new ones. Transportation system management (TSM) was the name given to the collection of low-cost strategies for urban transportation endorsed by both federal highway and transit officials. Revamped transit operations were emphasized in place of or as a precursor to additional capital investment (operating subsidies also became available during this period). Rather than further widen streets and highways, congestion relief was to be sought through actions such as better signal timing, high-occupancy vehicle incentives, and metering of freeway ramps. The energy crises and air-pollution-control requirements of the 1970s added to the emphasis on TSM, and the same list of actions became contingency strategies in energy plans and transportation control measures in air quality efforts. Whatever the name for the measures, they also were used as arguments for not raising fuel taxes or investing in additional freeways.

Though the national attention during this period was on better management of existing investments, at the local level many communities were struggling to keep up with growth. Concerns over the effects of growth were particularly at issue where demands for public infrastructure and services were outpacing the local government's ability to deliver them and straining local government budgets even with tax increases. Some communities simply altered their subdivision requirements and zoning regulations to substantially increase lot size and restrict the number of housing units that could be developed, thereby increasing tax income relative to service requirements. Many other communities were more accommodating to development: rather than clamping down on it, they called upon developers to take increased responsibility for streets, sewers, and parks. A few jurisdictions pioneered regulations that combined capital programming and finance with the timing of development approvals, making development contingent on the availability of needed facilities and services. In some instances, developers were given the choice of waiting for the local government to provide these services (often, in accordance with a 20-year program of expenditures) or providing them themselves.

Concerns about urban sprawl, air pollution, energy profligacy, and loss of natural landscapes and farmlands sometimes brought about changes in land-use controls as well. To encourage compact development and infill and to preserve open space, annexations were restricted and urban limit lines, greenbelts, and agricultural preserves were established. Impact assessments were increasingly used as the basis for more extensive and larger, developer exactions and impact fees. In some communities, debates erupted over the effects of rapid population increases, and caps were established on the number of housing units that could be authorized annually. A few places even established overall population maxima. Growth control measures were initiated both by city and county boards and, in some areas, by citizens directly. Concerns about local finances, along with taxpayer distrust of the local government's management capabilities, fueled many of these actions.

In the 1980s the consequences of the policies of the previous decade began to be visible. The 1980 census revealed that the shift to the suburbs had not been deterred; nearly half the work trips no longer headed downtown. Transit had lost market share in most places, despite both capital and operating subsidies. As the decade proceeded, highway congestion again became an issue, but this time the problem extended to the suburbs as well as the city. The interstate highways also were showing their age in deteriorated bridges and poor pavements, and maintenance required increasing shares of available funds.

On the land-use side, the single-family detached house remained the choice of most American households, but affordability became an issue for many. Suburban developments on the metropolitan fringe were located and designed so that an automobile was needed for most trips. Furthermore, urban residents also increased their auto ownership and use, particularly in small- and mid-size cities where transit services were marginal and nearly all developments had plentiful free parking. One result of this auto-dependent land-use pattern was that air quality standards continued to be violated in most metropolitan areas, despite cleaner cars and tough controls on industry. Also, transportation noise was a widespread problem and automobile accident levels remained high.

By the late 1980s and early 1990s, there was a general sense that a change in direction was needed, manifest in the proliferation of "Year 2000" and "Year 2020" planning efforts. The search for a new direction reflected several factors: the interstate program was due to draw to a close in 1991, a new president was coming into office, and a new Clean Air Act was under consideration. New issues, such as the possibility of global warming fed in substantial part by auto use, had been added to the agenda; several recurring ones, such as the shortage of funds for transportation, were on the list as well. New technologies, including "smart cars" and "smart highways," were being proposed for development by some, while others argued for a reemphasis on transit investment, this time with explicit land-development programs to offer support.

ROLES AND POLICY CHOICES FOR THE TWENTY-FIRST CENTURY

Role reversal perhaps best describes one thrust of the debates about transportation and land use in the 1990s. In previous decades, transportation served land development; given a condition ripe for development, transportation was one of the factors that enabled it to happen (though the way in which transportation was made available shaped the nature of developments). The availability of transportation to the interior of the United States had influenced the growth of port cities; streetcar lines, the pre-automobile street grid, and the subsequent location of arterials and freeways had shaped the fine detail of urban land development. Developers converted land at the margins of the city to urban uses, and the transportation system was put in place to provide service to the new urban fringe.

As we approach the twenty-first century, the notion that transportation should serve land development is no longer accepted on its face. Diagnoses and prescriptions of what society ought to be doing vary widely, but one thing is sure: public investments in transportation ought not to be put into place automatically in response to development desires, but should be a tool or an instrument of explicit social policy choices.

To clarify the ways in which transportation and land development entered into this role reversal, it is useful to identify some of the expectations posed for transportation policy in the 1990s. In addition to providing fast, safe, and efficient mobility and access, transportation decisions are expected to meet a number of additional objectives.

1. *Preserving and enhancing investments made previously.* Transportation facilities and services represent important public investments that should be protected. Urban places and rural land uses also represent sizable investments, and transportation should be deployed to support inner cities, help maintain the viability of medium and small urban centers, and increase agricultural productivity.
2. *Supporting new development or redevelopment.* Transportation should serve new suburban activity centers and foster the redevelopment of inner cities; it should encourage the diversification of rural economies.
3. *Protecting environmental resources that are fragile or unique or both.* Transportation should protect coastal environments and wetlands, preserve endangered species, protect wild and scenic places, and save structures with historical value.
4. *Reversing environmental harm and improving environmental quality.* Transportation should reduce air and noise pollution; it should enhance the design quality of the built environment.
5. *Minimizing the consumption of natural resources believed to be scarce.* Transportation and land-use arrangements should decrease energy consumption and save farmlands.
6. *Redistributing income.* Transportation services should be provided to the poor as a direct surrogate for the redistribution of income and also as an instrumentality that will enable them to engage more fully in economic life.
7. *Supporting participation.* Transportation services should be provided to the elderly, the disabled, and perhaps to youth as a way of facilitating their participation in social and economic activities.
8. *Assuring cost-effective investment.* Transportation investments in capital facilities and services should meet economic efficiency criteria; total benefits should exceed total costs.

The policy proposals for accomplishing these ends include some old ideas as well as some new or revamped ones. Transportation should be managed as a multimodal, coordinated system. A full range of alternatives should be considered, including demand management and low-cost operational improvements. Capital investments in transit and highways should be cost effective. The strategies developed should protect sensitive lands; air quality, energy conservation, and noise abatement should be integral to decision making. The special needs of nondrivers, disabled people, and the elderly should be given attention. Citizens, particularly specially affected interests, should have a say in choosing the forms and amounts of transportation services they will have. Transportation should help to redress income differences, and mobility should be available to all. Prices should reflect social costs and policy intentions. Funding should be found to accomplish these objectives, but excess spending should be avoided; investments in transit and highways should be cost effective. The coordination of transportation and land use is seen as a way to accomplish much of this agenda. Into the 1970s, according to this analysis, land developers and urban planners continued to assume that transportation would be provided to serve development—but there no longer is any assurance that this will occur. In some areas, environmental constraints or other community concerns prevent road expansion. Elsewhere, the amount of development undertaken is outstripping the financial resources for transportation improvements. In still other instances the issue is a mismatch—desires for transit but densities suited only to the auto, or vice versa. Meanwhile, transportation agencies have seen the proliferation of programs each with earmarked, isolated funds, which has led to an irrational project selection process in which projects are selected to capture federal and state "match" even if they are not necessarily the best options or the most needed investments.

The prescribed cure is for mutually consistent land development *and* transportation investment. Requirements or inducements would provide for consistency, compatibility, and concurrent delivery of transportation facilities and services along with new development. For areas already built, programs would assist redevelopment, renewal, or retrofit. Changes in transportation finance would provide flexible funding so that the best project, regardless of mode or other specifics, could be implemented. Along with mandates to assure social equity and environmental protection, development would be implemented, and desirable land use–transportation combinations would evolve.

How feasible is such a scenario? History tells us that urban land use and transportation have been closely linked, and appearances suggest that they remain so, though the relationship may not always be a smooth one. Can policy interventions of the sort discussed improve the situation? Or in observing spatial association, historical or current, might we be observing only that land use and transportation are the outcome of a common cause that could stymie the contemplated intervention? Answers to such questions call for us to consult theory and to take a more rigorous look at the empirical evidence.

THEORY AND EVIDENCE

Land-use theory is as old as economics. Land, labor, and capital are the primary inputs of production, and as observed in the early 1900s by von Thünen[1] and Ricardo,[2] the use of land is determined, in part, by its location. The location of transportation facilities and the technology used specify the relative location of places. Social and economic activities and their use of land are determined by relative locational advantages.

Beginning with patterns of causality that are taken to be elementary, we can think through the nature of land use–transportation relationships. The starting concepts are old, and they are simple. The land supply is finite. Human wants are not finite, so land has value. The values of lands with similar characteristics differ depending upon locational attributes. Land in Iowa City has higher value than land on farms in the tributary area of that city because of its more strategic location; it has a higher location rent.

How are different kinds of land uses allocated and equilibrium among land uses achieved? How does land use reflect an equilibrium between the supply of what land produces and demand? Von Thünen and Dunn,[3] among others, have dealt with agricultural land uses and Isard[4] and Alonso[5] with urban land uses. Dunn's agricultural analysis is instructive; while rural in perspective, it provides an easy route to the urban landscape. Define

$$R_i^C = Y^c P_j^C - Y^c T^c D_{ij} \qquad (20\text{-}1)$$

where R_i^c = rent of a unit of land at i producing commodity c
  Y^c = yield of commodity c per unit of land
  P_j^c = price per unit of commodity c at its market at j
  T^c = transportation cost per unit of commodity c, per unit of distance
  D_{ij} = distance to market; the distance from the production point, i, to the market at j

Now imagine a unit of farmland located at some distance D_{ij} from the market at j. The rent calculation is simple. Take the price at the market and multiply by the yield per unit of land; this yields rent per unit of land. But this gross rent must be discounted by transportation cost, which involves the amount to be transported per unit of land, Y^c, the transportation cost per unit of commodity per unit of distance, T^c, and the distance, D_{ij}. The calculation yields the net rent at place i.

Because different commodities have different yields and transportation costs, as well as different prices, individual rent gradients would intercept at the market differently and slope from the market differently. The rent-gradient explanation for rural land use is that the farmer selects the crop that returns the highest net rent, and this selection depends upon the slopes and intercepts of the functions describing rent gradients for different crops. Equilibrium of production and price is achieved through the interaction of the market price and the quality of land where a commodity is produced.

It is not hard to stretch one's imagination and bring this thinking to the urban area. In the urban area, there are many kinds of land uses, so we must think of there being many rent gradients. Most gradients are thought to decrease outward from the center of the urban area. Downtown business activities typically pay the highest rents in order to locate centrally. Residential land uses typically pay lower rents and tend to be nearer the periphery. In Alonso's treatment of urban land uses, users of urban land have bid rent functions that they use to calculate how much they would be willing to pay to rent a piece of land in a particular location. All actors bid against each other, and an equilibrium of land use and land value is achieved.

The theory postulates a clear causality: accessibility determines the worth of land for different uses at different locations. If transportation costs are changed, the rent gradients change; since land uses and rents for land are tied each to the other by market processes, land-use potentials are changed.

Applying this theory, we would expect to find that investments that lower the cost of transportation to an employment center would simultaneously reduce the value of residential land close to the employment center and increase the value at the periphery. Reduced commuting costs (or times, since time has value) would make it possible for commuters to spend more on housing, to travel farther, or both. If, as is usually the case, out-of-pocket costs of travel are cheap relative to housing and one can buy more house per dollar farther from the center, households will have an incentive to live farther away from their workplaces. All else being equal, then, investments in transportation are likely to decrease residential density and increase the size of the urbanized area.

Business location theory follows a similar line of reasoning. While some businesses are tied to particular sites due to needs for special qualities only available there, many other businesses can choose where to locate within an urban area by considering the relative costs and benefits of doing business at a particular place. Transportation is one such cost, for businesses need access to goods and markets, and their labor costs reflect commuting costs. If transportation costs are reduced at a particular place, businesses there will be more profitable and better able to expand; other businesses also will find the location comparatively advantageous and seek to locate there. Thus, in theory, businesses will tend to congregate at points where transportation costs are low.

Population-serving businesses, which sell frequently purchased goods and services, are a special case, because their competitive edge depends in large part on their convenience to residences. If residences decentralize, these firms follow, decentralizing this portion of the work force as well. The specific location of these businesses still depends on the relative costs of transportation to alternative locations. A general reduction in shopping-trip costs would permit population-serving firms to locate farther from residences and still be convenient to customers.

Overall, theory says that transportation improvements will tend, simultaneously, to increase employment at benefited sites and to decentralize workers' housing. Conversely, worsening transportation services will favor decentralization of jobs but support higher densities of housing.

HISTORIC PATH DEPENDENCE AND OTHER FACTORS

Location-rent theory is simple; the world involves complexities. Historic path dependence is among the processes shaping urban development that are not explicitly incorporated into location-rent theory. Yet its results are visible on just about every urban landscape. Development paths got seeded; subsequent location choices depended on previous choices. Here was where the first railroad decided to put its freight terminal. Slaughter houses were located there, along with a smoky foundry. Fashionable housing developed in one part of town, blue-collar housing in another. Such locations might have resulted from accidental choice or they might have been the best transportation-location or environmental choice for the times. Whatever the reason, early location decisions have left a long-lasting imprint on urban development.

California's Silicon Valley illustrates historic path dependence at work as an attractant for modern, "footloose" industries. Early electronics research and development and production facilities located there, spinning off from research at Stanford and other nearby research universities and finding markets in defense industries already in the area. The early locators helped attract and develop the support services and labor availability that continue to attract the location of similar and related firms. In contrast, the now defunct Chicago stockyards created an environment repelling many types of businesses and setting the tone for the development of that part of the city.

Still other factors surely enter into location decisions. In the Silicon Valley example, the availability of suitable sites for development, a positive business climate, and the high-quality California living environment also helped attract high-technology industries. In many inner city areas, ethnic and racial prejudices, restrictions imposed by lenders and insurance companies, and concerns about crime and the quality of public services have restricted development and redevelopment possibilities.

Given such complexities, can theorized land use and transportation relationships be discerned in the real world? A number of studies have investigated various aspects of the interactions, particularly focusing on the effects of transportation investments on land use, location, and economic development. These studies have used a variety of methodologies, including macroeconomic investigations, econometric analyses, and input–output modeling of national and regional effects. Before–after studies of specific facilities or regions and survey-based research on residential and industrial location choices also have been used. While many of the studies suffer from limitations (correlations, difficulty in distinguishing cause and effect, failure to distinguish economic shifts within a region from investment-induced growth, and double counting of benefits), they nevertheless offer insights. Overall, these studies find that transportation availability and quality are factors in location and development, but investments will do relatively little absent other critical factors.

An extensive record of empirical evidence exists on the impact of highways on land values, land development, and the location of urban activities. The record was particularly stimulated by Section 210 of the Highway Revenue Act of 1956, which required that nonuser benefits from investment in interstate highways be investigated.[6] More recent studies were reviewed by Forkenbrock and others.[7] Many relationships were claimed, but the overall conclusions remained the same: highway investments were but one factor in a larger growth and development equation.

While highway investments have surely shaped urban areas, in most cities the question now is whether transit investments will reshape development. The empirical evidence with respect to transit is not nearly so full as it is for highways, though the record is at least as long. Spengler's classic study, published in 1930, summarized a set of investigations undertaken to clarify debate in New York City with respect to transit and land values.[8] Spengler undertook a section-by-section analysis of the New York transit system and developments in its environs. His conclusion was that transit was only one of a number of development forces that, if in place, would lead to development. He observed that if factors were such that a neighborhood was declining, it continued to decline regardless of transit investment; stagnant neighborhoods remained stagnant and developing areas continued to develop.

Considerable work also has been done over the years on Toronto's experience with transit and land use. Kovach,[9] Libicki,[10] and Heenan,[11] among others, have published separate observations on the Toronto experience subsequent to 1954, when the first leg of the subway was completed. Considerable activity-center and dense residential development occurred along the first leg, which Heenan suggested was a spillover from downtown. Subsequent development impacts were much less sharp. Both Libicki and Kovach pointed out that high-density residential development was characteristic of change in Canadian cities, and they suggested that Toronto seemed to be no different from other cities on that scale.

Some work has analyzed more recent U.S. transit investments. Boyce and others,[12] and Gannon and Dear[13] studied the Lindenwold line rather thoroughly. That line, completed in 1968, extends from Philadelphia into Camden County, New Jersey. Boyce's analysis suggested that major changes in Camden County turned on the availability of land and zoning restrictions. Gannon and Dear judged that the Lindenwold line enhanced the attractiveness of the downtown Philadelphia area, and that several percentage points of the increase in downtown office space might be attributed to its presence; whether this was new growth or simply a shift from other areas of the region was not addressed.

A major study was mounted in the mid-1970s to judge the impacts of the San Francisco Bay Area Rapid Transit (BART) system, which had opened a few years earlier. At the time of the study, it was generally agreed that the impacts of BART on the regional growth and development pattern had been minor. Suburban fringe areas thought to be too remote before BART may have experienced accelerated housing development, and there may have been some inducement of office development in downtown San Francisco.[14] BART only served a limited portion of the region, however, and even within its service area the auto remained a faster way to travel for many trips. Thus large shifts in location probably should not have been expected.

The authors have been observing continuing development changes around BART stations. The downtown San Francisco development boom, stimulated at least in part by BART, may have backfired, as in reaction to years of rapid growth, high-rise opponents in 1988 successfully placed a cap on building size in downtown San Francisco. Increased office and housing development has taken place around the suburban stations, in several cases after protracted struggles with local residents who opposed the higher densities. At the eastern end of the line, a boom in office development occurred at the suburban Concord and Walnut Creek stations in the early 1980s. But surveys in these offices found that few of the workers actually used BART for commuting; the stations primarily serve local residents in-bound for San Francisco, Oakland, or Berkeley. Furthermore, BART has been no assurance that growth would be stimulated. Downtown Oakland, troubled by a number of urban ills, has had only moderate success in attracting new development around its stations.

Findings from studies of the Washington, D.C., Metro and several other heavy and light rail systems have been basically consistent with the findings elsewhere. Relationships between transit investment and land development are not particularly visible unless other market and political factors are supportive of such a relationship. For less capital-intensive or place-oriented transit improvements, such as bus transfer centers, the relationships are even harder to find.[15]

Overall, then, the empirical evidence for highways and transit lead to similar conclusions. Transportation availability and quality affect location and land use, but so do many other factors. By itself, a highway is not likely to stimulate economic development. By itself, transit is not likely to save the central city.

Difficulty in finding relationships does not prove that they are absent. Among other things, one could conjecture the following:

- Transportation impacts on land development take a long time to work themselves out. The land-development process has not been studied over a long enough period of time.
- Transportation impacts on land development were large in the 1800s and into the early 1900s because at that time the new services offered made a big difference in the quantity and quality of transportation available. Nowadays, transportation services are widely available; projects of the size and scope being implemented make only a marginal improvement. Thus small effects are to be expected unless much bigger projects are developed.
- Transit's potential for steering urban land development is substantial, but it is often very small and difficult to discern because public policies undermine its effectiveness.

Today's development debates respond in part to these conjectures: they admit that it may take a while for impacts to appear and argue that bigger projects are needed, as well as public policies supporting desired impacts. This discussion will now turn to these responses, especially the latter, which is a subject receiving considerable attention.

COORDINATED LAND USE AND TRANSPORTATION DEVELOPMENT

The earlier discussion explored the question, If transportation is changed, how will land use change? A new question is worded differently. If land-use-development controls or inducements steering land development *and* coordinated transportation development are implemented, would desirable land use–transportation combinations result?

At the scale of street blocks, stations, and individual activities such as stores and apartment buildings, the answer to this question is surely yes. Ordinary experience or a little imagination tells us that attractive and serviceable designs linking transportation and land use can be drawn and implemented. Such designs might provide for convenience-goods shopping near single-family residences; apartments within easy access to department stores and workplaces; places to meet friends or engage in recreation after work; safe bicycle routes and pedestrian ways linking housing to commercial centers and schools; attractive and convenient transit station entrances and exits; and protection from the weather while waiting for the bus or carpool. Much attention is being given to improving transportation and land-use relations at this scale of urban design, and more surely can be done.

Particular hopes are held for land-use planning coordinated in the vicinity of rail stations and major bus transfer points. In downtowns, these often take the form of transit malls lined with shops and restaurants in a festival atmosphere or station designs that incorporate offices and high-density housing. In the suburbs, lower-density but still transit-oriented housing and commercial activities are proposed for clustering in "pedestrian pocket" subdivisions in one concept.[16]

Better ways to coordinate the design of streets and highways with land uses also are being considered. A rethinking of the residential grid is underway in some areas, narrowed down and designed to restrain speed and through traffic but permitting efficient layouts for transit, bicycles, and pedestrians. Where traffic is to be facilitated, land uses are restricted to ones that can coexist with traffic (or better yet thrive on it), and street designs give attention to turning lanes and signal placement and timing.

Some of these new designs have been implemented by developers looking for a better, more salable product; some have come about through the efforts of city planning staffs. The transit station concepts increasingly involve joint transit agency–developer schemes for finance and development; in some proposals the partnership would extend well beyond the immediate station area.

Closely orchestrated land use and transportation relations at the project scale, or even at the scale of subdivisions and office parks, are one thing; larger-scale regional coordination of transportation and land use is something else. Might the city be improved by plans that coordinate land use and transportation development everywhere?

Such coordination is one of the objectives of new statewide planning initiatives in Florida, New Jersey, and Washington State, as well as of older state and regional efforts in Oregon, Vermont, Minneapolis–St. Paul, and Montgomery County,

Maryland. Similar approaches are being debated in California and a few other areas. Techniques for coordinating land use and transportation at the areawide level include:

- Urban limit lines and urban development reserves.
- Mandatory consistency between local land-use plans and local and regional transportation plans.
- Requirements for the provision of adequate public facilities concurrent with development.
- Minimum as well as maximum development densities and floor-area ratios to ensure adequate development for transit to work.
- Incentives and bonuses for desired land uses and for developments that provide desired transportation and land-use amenities.
- Mandatory balancing of job growth with housing development, priced and located to match the needs and incomes of the work force.

Advocates of these techniques for large-scale coordination of land use and transportation believe quality-of-life advantages would be obtained through their use. Improved positioning of work, shopping, educational, recreational, and other facilities relative to residences would reduce trip lengths and make walking and cycling feasible. Explicit planning for alternatives to the auto would create supportive environments for their operation and use. Advantages to society overall would include decreased requirements for travel, lower energy consumption, and less air pollution; urban sprawl would be reduced, sparing valued agricultural lands and other open space.

Sometimes, the concentration of intensive trip-generating land uses is advocated so that high-capacity transit can be successfully deployed; highway improvements are foregone and parking is restricted to make the auto less attractive. This is using land-use control as a means to an end valued by transit advocates. Theory says that these strategies also would tend to provide an advantage to central locations over others and perhaps raise housing prices in the most accessible locations. Advocates counter that the benefits outweigh the costs, and any equity concerns can best be addressed on their own merits.

Excepting some land developers, advocates of the contrary point of view are not well organized; they speak through their behaviors rather than verbalized arguments. Perhaps their line of argument goes this way. No land-use and transportation coordinator can know what the Jane and John Does of the city want and what they are able and willing to pay for it, so individual choices are the best coordinator of desirable development. Market wisdom is revealed by the Does' choices, and those choices are such that urban populations are shifting from places where public transportation is relatively good to places where service is not so good, as was pointed out by Fulton.[17] The Does, through their actions, are voting for low densities served by autos and highways, this argument goes, and while available evidence suggests that their choices are not much constrained by transportation services, an even less constrained world surely would improve the Does' quality of life.

Arguments have counterarguments. Advocates of greater coordination of transportation and land use counter laissez-faire arguments by pointing out that the Does' choices are made from among the transportation services and land uses now available, which in turn are framed by public policy and action. They assert that if public investments in transit equaled those in highways, the Does' options, and probably their choices, would be considerably different. They argue that if the Does paid for their parking spaces and absorbed the cost of their auto emissions, noise, and other externalities, their choices surely would change, even with today's mix of services. They also make appeals to the broader public interest in resource use generally and energy and environmental issues in particular.

Accepting appeals to social goals and the point that costing might be improved, advocates of the laissez-faire approach rebut: even so, no centralized decision maker can substitute for the wisdom of the market. The Does argue that, whatever the future brings, they can decide for themselves what they want and how to spend their own money.

Each side of the argument is shaped by images held, assumptions made, and the metaphors that color and form reasoning. Images and metaphors follow from experiences and cultural norms, and views are more diverse than those we have sketched. Yet what seems absent in these considerations is a lesson from the sweep of experience: change is certain. The current debate does not respond to that point. The debate assumes that the transportation services of the future are limited to those available today; it also assumes that today's urban activities will persist in their current forms. History says that such assumptions are hardly engraved in granite.

Perhaps the debate will be reshaped as new transportation and information services and new urban activities evolve and provide new opportunities for the organization of urban life in ways consistent with social aspirations and ecological and economic realities.

SUMMARY

This chapter began by posing alternative views of the future of urban transportation and urban land development. Historical relationships between transportation and land use were noted; particular attention was given to highway and transit investments and the associated urban development since the turn of the century.

We then examined more recent societal expectations that transportation and land use should work together to manage social, economic, and environmental issues. The notion that transportation should be both modally neutral and supportive of societal goals is to some extent a contradiction. Certainly, the pursuit of any goal favors some more than it does others, no matter how carefully goals and programs are formulated. Perhaps the dispute is more about responsiveness to claims for rights and the allocation of fair shares than about specific expenditures and programs per se.

The ability of transportation to shape land use and otherwise meet societal expectations was then examined through a look at theory and empirical evidence. Theory explains transportation and land-use relationships through location rent. Empirical studies reveal that the land-development process is a highly complex one and that transportation is just one factor bearing on land development, its patterns, and its impacts.

There nevertheless remains a tendency to propose transportation and land-use "cures" in response to issues such as urban sprawl, loss of agricultural lands, or environmental quality. Yet a closer look at such issues makes it clear that transportation and land use are often not at their core. The basic matters are the ways in which individuals organize and control their activities, make claims on resources, and consume goods and services.

Social, economic, and environmental issues become matters of public debate when they are not being adequately handled. What is missing that thwarts issue resolution? Some of the missing elements may be knowledge, consensus, instruments, and articulation. The knowledge category includes sufficient understanding of relationships so that issues can be stated crisply, as well as sufficient data so that problems can be identified and evaluated. Consensus refers to public agreements on goals and the political or marketplace formats for accomplishing them—laws, regulations, and/or markets that form instruments for problem solving. Instruments include institutions and technologies. Finally, articulation refers to coordination of the various instruments necessary for successful accomplishment.

There thus is a contrast between the way transportation and land-use questions enter into public debates about issues and the political, social, and economic processes that must be handled to manage those issues. Transportation and land use are often seen as problematic and must be considered in issue resolution; yet it is on the broader processes that issue resolution must focus: Reach consensus so that . . . Change funding mechanisms in order to . . . Clarify the nature of investment choices in order to . . . Shift regulation to affect . . . Correct prices so that . . . Develop technology to . . . .

Many expect a great deal of the transportation–land development relationship; they tend to view it as the primary shaper of urban areas and as an instrument for social problem solving. The urban transportation professional should be aware that the situation is much more complex. Transportation and land use themselves are reflections of broader and deeper political, social, and economic processes, and hence the analyst should not rely on transportation and land use by themselves to resolve societal issues. The problems to be solved are complicated, and land development is not a simple function of transportation.

REFERENCES

Some citations are no longer available from their original source. These citations are often available from the National Technical Information Service, U.S. Department of Commerce, 5285 Port Royal Road, Springfield, VA 22161. We have verified the order numbers for many of these citations, and they are found at the end of the citation. Prices are available through NTIS at the address above.

1   JOHANN HEINRICH VON THÜNEN, *Der isolierte Staat in Beziehung auf Landwirtschaft und Nationalokonomie* (Hamburg, Germany: F. Pethes, 1836).

2   DAVID RICARDO, *Principles of Political Economy and Taxation* (London: J.M. Dent and Sons Ltd., 1973).

3   EDGAR S. DUNN, JR., *The Location of Agricultural Production* (Gainesville, Fla.: University of Florida Press, 1954).

4   WALTER ISARD, *Location and Space-Economy* (Cambridge, Mass.: The M.I.T. Press, 1956).

5   WILLIAM ALONSO, *Location and Land Use: Toward a General Theory of Land Rents*, Joint Center for Urban Studies Publication Series (Cambridge, Mass: Harvard University Press, 1964).

6   U.S. CONGRESS, *Progress Report of the Highway Cost Allocation Study*; First—House Document no. 106, 85th Congress, 1st Session, March 4, 1957; Second—House Document no. 344, 85th Congress, 2nd Session, March 3, 1958; Third—House Document no. 91, 86th Congress, 1st Session, 1959; Fourth—House Document no. 355, 86th Congress, 2nd Session, 1960; *Final Report of the Highway Cost Allocation Study*, House Document no. 54, 87th Congress, 1st Session, January 16, 1961; *Final Report of the Highway Cost Allocation Study, Part VI: Studies of the Economic and Social Effects of Highway Improvement*, House Document no. 72, 87th Congress, 1st Session, January 23, 1961 (Washington, D.C.: U.S. Government Printing Office).

7   DAVID J. FORKENBROCK AND OTHERS, *Road Investment to Foster Local Economic Development* (Iowa City, Iowa: University of Iowa, Public Policy Center, May 1990).

8   EDWIN H. SPENGLER, *Land Values in New York in Relation to Transit Facilities* (New York: Columbia University Press, 1930).

9   CAROL KOVACH, "On Conducting an 'Impact' Study of a Rapid Transit Facility—The Case of Toronto" (unpublished paper presented at the Montreal Joint Transportation Engineering Meeting, preprint MTL-23, 1974).

10 MARTIN C. LIBICKI, *Land Use Impacts of Major Transit Improvements*, prepared by the Office of Transportation Planning Analysis for U.S. DOT, Office of the Secretary (Washington, D.C.: U.S. Department of Transportation, March 1975).

11 G. W. HEENAN, "The Economic Effect of Rapid Transit on Real Estate Development," *Appraisal Journal*, 36, no. 2 (April 1968), 213-24.

12 DAVID E. BOYCE AND OTHERS, *Impact of Rapid Transit on Suburban Residential Property Values and Land Development*, prepared for U.S. DOT, Office of the Secretary (Philadelphia: University of Pennsylvania, November 1972). Now available as PB 220 693.

13 COLIN A. GANNON AND MICHAEL J. DEAR, *The Impact of Rail Rapid Transit Systems on Commercial Office Development: The Case of the Philadelphia—Lindenwold Speedline*, prepared for UMTA (Philadelphia: University of Pennsylvania, June 1972). Now available as PB 212 906.

14   MELVIN M. WEBBER, "The BART Experience—What Have We Learned?" reprinted from *The Public Interest*, no. 45 (Fall 1976), pp. 79-108. Copyright © by National Affairs, Inc.

15   JOHN R. MEYER AND JOSÉ A. GOMÉZ-IBÁÑEZ, *Autos, Transit, and Cities*, A Twentieth Century Final Report (Cambridge, Mass.: Harvard University Press, 1981).

16   DOUG KELBAUGH, ed., *The Pedestrian Pocket Book: A New Suburban Design Strategy* (Princeton, N.J.: Princeton Architectural Press, 1989).

17   PHILIP N. FULTON, "Public Transportation: Solving the Commuting Problem?" in *Improving the Quality and Efficiency of Transportation Data*, Transportation Record 928 (Washington, D.C.: Transportation Research Board, 1983), pp. 1-10.

FURTHER READING

AMERICAN PLANNING ASSOCIATION, "Special Issue on Transit and Joint Development," *Planning*, 50, no. 6 (June 1984).

CERVERO, ROBERT, *Suburban Gridlock*. New Brunswick, N.J.: Center for Urban Policy Research, 1986.

DEAKIN, ELIZABETH A., *Suburban Traffic Congestion: Land Use and Transportation Planning Issues: Public Policy Options?* Research Report UCB-ITS-RR-87-9. Berkeley, Calif.: Institute of Transportation Studies, University of California, Berkeley, July 1987.

GARRISON, WILLIAM L., AND OTHERS, *Studies of Highway Development and Geographic Change*, Highway Economic Series. Seattle, Wash.: University of Washington Press, 1959.

GIULIANO, GENEVIEVE, "Land Use Impacts of Transportation Investments: Highways and Transit," in *The Geography of Urban Transportation*, ed. Susan Hanson. New York: The Guilford Press, 1986.

HALL, PETER, *The World Cities* (3rd ed.). London: Weidenfeld and Nicolson, 1984.

———, AND CARMEN HASS-KLAU, *Can Rail Save the City? The Impacts of Rail Rapid Transit and Pedestrianisation on British and German Cities*. Aldershot, Hants, England: Gower Publishing Company, 1988.

JACKSON, KENNETH T., *Crabgrass Frontier: The Suburbanization of America*. New York: Oxford University Press, Inc., 1985.

KNIGHT, ROBERT L., "The Impact of Rail Transit on Land Use: Evidence and a Change of Perspective," *Transportation*, 9, no. 1 (1980), 3-16.

LOWRY, IRA S., "Planning for Urban Sprawl," in *A Look Ahead: Year 2020*, proceedings of a conference on long-range trends and requirements for the nation's highway and public transit systems, Special Report 220. Washington, D.C.: Transportation Research Board, 1988, pp. 275-325.

LUTIN, JEROME M., AND BERNARD P. MARKOWITZ, "Estimating the Effects of Residential Joint-Development Policies on Rail Transit Ridership," in *Transit Terminal Facilities and Urban Rail Planning*, Transportation Research Record 908. Washington, D.C.: Transportation Research Board, 1983, pp. 7-12.

PUSHKAREV, BORIS S., AND JEFFREY M. ZUPAN, *Public Transportation and Land Use Policy*, a Regional Plan Association Book. Bloomington, Ind.: Indiana University Press, 1977.

SCHULTZ, STANLEY K., *Constructing Urban Cultures: American Cities and City Planning, 1800-1920*. Philadelphia, Pa.: Temple University Press, 1989.

THRALL, GRANT IAN., *Land Use and Urban Form: The Consumption Theory of Land Rent*. New York: Methuen, Inc., 1987.

WARNER, SAM BASS, *Streetcar Suburbs: The Process of Growth in Boston (1870-1900)*. Cambridge, Mass.: Harvard University Press, 1962, 1978.

EXERCISES

19-1   Economic rent measures the value of something to a production process. For example, one might analyze the output of a factory and find that a certain machine has a value in the context of annual production; that value is the machine's annual economic rent. The economic rent may or may not be closely related to the accountant's valuation of the machine, because the accountant is concerned with the discounted purchase cost of the machine, replacement cost, and similar topics. Location rent is a variety of economic rent. Location rents are created when transportation is involved in the production process. Changes in transportation costs change relative locations and how valuable locations are in production processes. To help you understand the location-rent concept, consider the journey to and from work from a residence. (a) Suppose the cost of travel from a single family residence to and from work decreases by $1.00 per round trip. This cost decrease changes the relative location of the residence. If there is one worker in the household who makes 250 round trips to work per year, what is the annual savings in transportation cost? (b) The annual transportation cost saving is not a location rent, for location rent is associated with land at a place. The residential lot occupies 10,000 square feet. What is the change in the annual location rent per square foot of land? (c) Now suppose there are two workers in the same household. What is the annual transportation cost savings from a $1.00 decrease in round trip commute cost? What happens to the annual location rent? Discuss the implications of your answer.

19-2   Complexities are introduced into location rents and urban land markets by the myriad working, residential living, and transportation processes in urban areas. (a) To begin to develop a more general picture, graph a cross section of Eq. (19-1). (Note that distance from the center is radial and therefore would produce a three-dimensional figure.) Draw the x axis (horizontal) and label it distance. Locate the y axis (vertical) at about the middle of the x axis, and label the y axis location rent. Now sketch the relationship given by the equation; that is indicate how location rent decreases with distance from the market. (b) Keeping the y axis intercept fixed, suppose transportation cost is reduced. Use a dashed line to indicate the changed rent relationship. (c) It is not sensible to assume that the rent intercept on the y axis would be unchanged if transportation cost is reduced, because less expensive transportation would increase the area where the commodity may be produced. Use a dotted line to indicate the new intercept and rent lines. Note the relative changes in rents with distance from the market. (d) The sketches are for an imaginary, simplified rural situation involving the production of a commodity around a single market. While the concepts apply in urban areas, urban areas contain a great diversity of activities and reference points from which rents may be measured. The central business district is one such point; outlying employment and shopping centers are others. Central business districts have become relatively less important in cities. What does this suggest about changing location rent gradients in cities and about relative changes in transportation services?

19-3 Historic path dependence is seeded by decisions on the location of transportation facilities, as well as by many other types of decisions. Identify and describe the consequences of an early decision about the location of a transportation facility, say, a river terminal or the location of a street car line.

19-4 It was said that transportation and land-use relations can be coordinated by good designs at a fine detail scale, say, at the detail of a transit station. "Good" is in the eyes of the beholder. Critique a design, identifying what is good and what is bad and the reasons for your conclusions. It would be interesting if several students made independent critiques and compared results.

19-5 Why do you live where you do? How important were the transportation services you use to your decision about where you live? How much would transportation services have to change before you would move somewhere else? Think about services improving somewhere else enough to make another place attractive, as well as deteriorating where you are and forcing you to move.

19-6 There are ongoing debates about transportation and land use almost everywhere. Select a debate you read about in the newspapers or hear about elsewhere. Who are actors in the debate? What are the points at issue, and what arguments are put forward to support or refute the points? What information might be needed to resolve the issue, and how might such information be obtained?

Chapter 20

ENVIRONMENTAL IMPACTS

Robert L. Knight and Patricia L. Mokhtarian*

Rationales for the development of rapid transit systems in recent decades have been based largely on reducing the adverse effects of overreliance on the automobile. These adverse effects of the auto and its associated roadway facilities have been substantially environmental. Highest in priority are urban air quality and global upper-atmosphere equilibrium, but other concerns include the destruction of homes, neighborhoods, jobs, and other valued urban places, as well as natural habitats and environments, for the construction of freeways and other large-scale facilities.

Further effects of the auto itself include noise, vibration, visual blight, and intrusion, as well as excessive energy use. Dependence on the automobile has also been a major force in urban sprawl, with freeway construction encouraging scattered low-density residential development in suburban areas.

Transit, in one form or another, has often been seen as a means of minimizing such environmental consequences. It is reasoned to do so by reducing auto traffic (particularly commute traffic) generally and avoiding further construction of urban freeways, at the same time encouraging more intensive activity at transit-oriented nodes. In so doing, it is hoped that transit might particularly help to reduce suburban sprawl and strengthen the centers of older cities, now increasingly congested and difficult to reach by car. Transit is also seen as more energy efficient and less polluting than the automobile on a per trip basis. Implicit in these objectives is a vision of transit as a contributor to the humane city. This ideal is typically seen as small in scale, with

---

*The authors wish to dedicate this updated chapter to the memory of the late Professor Donald Appleyard of the University of California's Institute for Urban and Regional Development. Professor Appleyard was a co-author of the original version as it appeared in the first edition, and much of his unparalleled understanding of this subject is still reflected in this updated chapter.

intensely active, pedestrian-oriented public environments.

These hopes may or may not be justified. However, they have been powerful enough to generate widespread and enthusiastic political backing and even considerable public financial support for new transit systems in many cities. In the 1980s this support was tempered by fiscal constraints, although signs of increased public backing of transit-development taxes began to emerge again as traffic problems and environmental concerns intensified. This chapter's purpose is to look at some of the faces behind those hopes—the nature and scale of environmental impacts, for good and for ill, which seem to occur when a major new transit system or component is provided.

ENVIRONMENTAL IMPACT ASSESSMENT

As proposed transit solutions appeared during the 1960s and 1970s, a methodology of environmental impact assessment emerged to aid in their evaluation. Much of this methodology was developed in response to federal environmental protection legislation, as will be discussed later. Its intent is to assess the environmental benefits and costs of new projects and systems in a systematic, comprehensive way. This chapter will outline some of the issues, problems, and models involved in environmental impact assessment, as well as the empirical evidence and other information currently available on such impacts.

ISSUES IN IMPACT ASSESSMENT

A number of issues that have been raised over the years provide a general indication of the scope of environmental impact concerns. Some of these deal with definitions of the key concepts involved: What is the environment? What is an impact? Which impacts should be considered? What criteria should be used in their evaluation? How do direct or immediate impacts relate to indirect or remote impacts?

Another set of important issues addresses to the nature of impacts and how they occur: What are the relationships among environmental, land-use, political, and economic impacts? How are impacts likely to change with time? What are the primary causes of impacts? How reliably and precisely can impacts and causes be identified?

Finally, other issues focus on the policy implications of environmental impacts: How do the impacts of public transit systems compare and combine with those of other transportation systems and strategies? How can impacts be ameliorated and controlled by policy and planning decisions? How does current knowledge of impacts affect the selection of recommended policies? How might improved accuracy of assessment affect this?

KEY CONCEPTS AND DEFINITIONS

IMPACT GENERATION

Environment is a tricky term. Because of its popularization, it is often loosely and inconsistently used. Perhaps its most popular connotation is also its narrowest and most misleading: that of the wild or natural flora and fauna or, only slightly more broadly, all natural ecological components, including atmospheric and waterway systems. In dealing with the environmental effects of public transit in urban areas, such definitions are especially misleading because most elements of the natural environment tend to be relatively little affected.

A properly relevant definition must center on human survival and advancement. This does not mean that protection of the nearby natural environment is unimportant, but rather that other environmental concerns are at least as relevant, if not more relevant, in an urban system. Our current popular concern with even the natural environment is for the most part based on a belief in its importance in ensuring a healthy continuation of the human species, rather than simply protecting flora and fauna for their own sake. Thus, for purposes of transit system development, the relevant environment must be defined much more broadly. It must include all the physical components of the world, be they natural or man-made, local or global, on which people must depend in their everyday functioning. It is this *human* environment, in all its complexity, that is to be protected and advanced.

Environmental *impact* is simply any change (in this case, induced by transit) in this broadly defined environment. Impacts occur in a complex causal pattern, with initial impacts combining and sometimes jointly leading to others (see Fig. 20-1). An initial change in the environment (for example, introduction of a transit system) creates a set of *emissions*, such as sound, physical mass, movement of vehicles, and the flow of patrons. These emissions lead to some *direct* impacts on various aspects of the physical environment (for example, changes in community noise levels), which may in turn generate *indirect* impacts (for example, changes in traffic levels, activity patterns, demographics, or land use). Emissions also can be *magnified* or *mitigated* by intervening features, such as sound barriers, distance, or elevation, which modify the impacts on surrounding populations.

The impacts of a change can be assessed (either before or after implementation) only by comparison to some base case. This base case may be, for example, the "do-nothing" alternative, or an "all-bus" scenario (to compare against a rail system), or a "transportation system management" (TSM) alternative (implementing more efficient use of existing facilities through minor operational and infrastructural changes). Either the base case scenario or the change scenario is necessarily hypothetical, and in many cases, both are. Impacts are, thus, defined as the specific differences between the two cases. This is especially essential for indirect impacts, which often depend on the estimated difference in land-development rates and patterns between the base case and the proposed change. Transportation–land use mathematical projection models are not

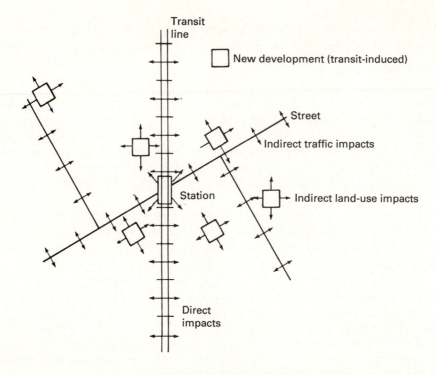

Figure 20-1 *Direct and indirect environmental impacts.*

very satisfactory for this purpose. Whether they or some mechanically less complex approach is used, judgmental adjustments must be applied to the results to ensure consideration of important subjective factors.

Transit systems have *internal* impacts on travelers and *external* impacts on the larger environment. Transit's role as an environment for its users is in many ways as important as its influence on its own external environment and the people who depend on that environment. This chapter will concentrate on external impacts; the traveler's environment is discussed in Chaps. 18 and 22.

An important aspect of environmental impacts is their typically *dynamic* nature. These environmental effects occur not all at once but tend to change as time passes, since a transit system inevitably changes in its impact-causing attributes. Planning and anticipation lead to construction, a substantial period of change that culminates in a start-up phase of operations. Construction, too, may last for several years, with gradual changes until a stable operational condition is reached. Finally, some impacts, such as demographic or land-use changes, may not be visible for many years after operations have stabilized. Each stage has its own environmental impacts, which can differ dramatically in type and consequence.

Impacts can be positive as well as negative. Indeed, if the environmental impacts (broadly defined) are on balance negative, the system should not be built. The introduction to this chapter suggested some positive impacts that can be achieved, including reduced energy consumption, improved air quality, improved accessibility of businesses, improved mobility of residents, and a more structured, compact urban form.

RESPONSE TO IMPACTS

The *perception* and *evaluation* of these impacts and the subsequent behavioral *response* by persons who are affected are the culmination of the environmental impact process. These terms are used in the psychological rather than the colloquial sense to encompass all the reactions of the human organism, including unconscious as well as conscious elements. Thus, an effect on air quality may lead to illness, and noise may cause emotional distress.

Such behavioral responses can lead to further changes in perceptions and evaluations in a cyclical fashion. The degree of behavioral adaptation (such as moving to the back of the house or not allowing the children to play on the street), psychological adaptation (readjusting expectations), environmental modification (building fences or installing soundproof insulation), or public action (participating in political opposition) that the individual finds necessary can profoundly affect perceptions and evaluations of the source of the impacts—in turn possibly leading to other behavioral responses (such as deciding to move).

IMPACT AS A PROCESS

Many of the concepts and definitions just described can be better understood diagrammatically. Figure 20-2 is one form of such a presentation, indicating linkages between the sources of impact, the impacts themselves, their effects on people, and a variety of actions taken in response. Note that the process is continuous, involving substantial feedback, rather than a one-time adjustment of impact. Although the figure emphasizes operational (postimplementation) impacts, those related to the planning (preimplementation) and construction (implementation) phases of a transit system's life fit equally well.

These environmental impacts may fall on several *population groups*. Adjacent residents are usually of greatest concern and may themselves differ in exposure or sensitivity. Others include those who work, play, or travel near the system's facilities and the general population of the region. All must be considered in impact evaluation.

Direct impacts, particularly those occurring only during the stable, full-scale period of the system's operational life, are relatively easily assessed, but may in some cases actually be less important than some of the indirect impacts arising from the system's long-term effects on land use. Likewise, the disruptive impacts of construction may produce lasting effects more serious than any operational impacts, and start-up and shakedown operations may have impacts more severe than those of later stable service. Consequently, the evaluation of impact should be longitudinal (that is, over the life of the system), rather than a cross-sectional "snapshot."

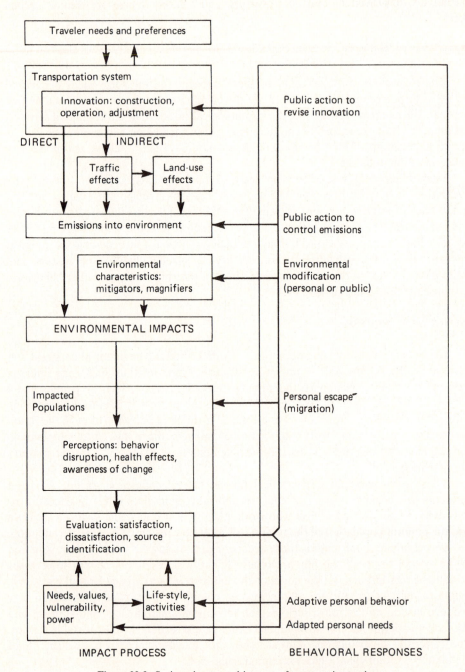

Figure 20-2 *Socioenvironmental impacts of transport innovations.*

THE PRECONSTRUCTION
ENVIRONMENTAL IMPACT EVALUATION PROCESS

An evaluation of environmental impacts can take place during the planning, construction, or operational phases of the transit system. For the latter two phases, the evaluation can be either concurrent (conducted as or shortly after the impacts occur) or retrospective (conducted some time after the impacts occur). During the planning phase, however, an evaluation can only be prospective—that is, conducted before any direct impacts are experienced and therefore based on predictions rather than actual measurements. There can, however, potentially be real *indirect* impacts during the planning phase, for example, on property values near proposed transit stations. The *Metro Rail Before-and-After Study*, conducted for the Southern California Rapid Transit District by its planning consultant, developed regression models to predict property values before a Metro Rail alignment was finalized. These "before" models were then applied to sales taking place after the alignment was adopted. Analysis of the residuals from the application of these models led to the conclusion that proximity to Metro Rail stations contributed modestly to an increase in property values—even though completion of the first segment of the system was still years away.

The prospective nature of a preconstruction environmental evaluation does not make it less significant. In fact, the planning-phase evaluation is arguably the most important one of all, for several reasons:

1. It can allow potentially serious negative environmental impacts of the selected alternative to be identified and mitigation measures to be developed beforehand, rather than after the fact.
2. It can sometimes lead to the selection of an environmentally superior alternative that would not have been identified or selected otherwise, including cases in which environmental considerations are among the reasons a proposed action is ultimately dropped altogether.
3. The public review and comment process associated with the evaluation provides the opportunity for substantive citizen input before committing to an expensive transit system. This input can lead to either of the first two outcomes—that is, implementation of mitigation measures or a different alternative.

An environmental impact evaluation is required by the federal government and most states as a condition for receiving federal or state funding, respectively, for the project. An overview of the federally mandated environmental impact review process is given in this section. To help distinguish between similar but not identical terminology (for example, EIS versus EIR, NOI versus NOP), parallel concepts used in the state-level review process by the state of California are mentioned where appropriate; California is cited because of the adoption of many of its terms and methods by other states. Terminology and process may vary somewhat from state to state, but the general concepts are broadly applicable.

BACKGROUND

The National Environmental Policy Act of 1969 (NEPA) instituted the environmental evaluation process for all new actions (including, for example, water treatment plants and oil drilling operations, not just transportation) involving federal land, funding, or control.[1] Many states passed additional legislation, such as the California Environmental Quality Act of 1970 (CEQA), to cover projects with state or local involvement and major private projects. Subsequently, federal agencies developed regulations and guidelines for the specific application of NEPA to actions under their control. In particular, the U.S. Department of Transportation (DOT) has prepared guidelines that must be followed if a transportation project is to receive federal funding.[2] Both the NEPA and the DOT guidelines are included in the discussion following.

TYPES OF ENVIRONMENTAL STUDIES

As might be expected, different levels of environmental scrutiny are required depending on the size and potential impacts of a proposed project. DOT has defined three classes of transportation projects:

1. Class 1 projects are large-scale transit systems (such as new or extended fixed-guideway construction) that will clearly have environmental impacts. For these projects, an *Environmental Impact Statement (EIS)* must be prepared. (In California and elsewhere, the comparable state-level document is referred to as an *Environmental Impact Report*, or *EIR*; it is permissible, and usually most efficient, to prepare a joint EIS/EIR as long as both sets of requirements are satisfied.)
2. Class 2 transportation projects are those that clearly will *not* have environmental impacts. Examples include operating assistance to transit authorities and maintenance on existing rights-of-way. In these cases, also called *Categorical Exclusions (CEs)*, no environmental review is required.
3. Class 3 projects are those whose environmental impacts are, a priori, uncertain. Examples include transit terminals, park-and-ride facilities, and administrative facilities. For these projects, an *Environmental Assessment (EA)* is required, to determine whether or not the environmental impacts will be important. (In California and elsewhere, the state-mandated comparable report is called an *initial study*; again, it is common to see joint EA/ISs.) EAs are sometimes called *Environmental Impact Assessments (EIAs)*.

If some important environmental impacts are found by the preliminary EA, then an EIS is required for the project. If not, then the lead federal agency issues a *Finding of No Significant Impact*, or *FONSI* (the comparable determination in an Initial Study is called a *Negative Declaration*, or *ND*).

KEY ELEMENTS OF THE ENVIRONMENTAL REVIEW PROCESS

This section describes some key elements of the environmental review process, including some observations drawn from real-world examples. Most of the concepts in the following subsections apply generally to both EAs and EISs, and to a state-level review as well as the federal review.

Selection of Lead Agency

For a proposed action subject to environmental review, the NEPA guidelines require the identification of at least one federal agency to serve as the *lead agency*. The lead agency bears the responsibility for ensuring the adequacy of the environmental documents and process and issues the *Record of Decision (ROD)* regarding the proposed action (the comparable state-level finding in California is called the *Notice of Determination*). In some cases, there is a single logical choice for the lead agency designation. In other cases, the choice is not so clear. For a proposed high-speed rail line connecting San Diego and Los Angeles, California, for example, the Federal Highway Administration (not the Federal Railroad Administration) was named the lead agency, because the rail right-of-way would follow an interstate highway (I-5) for much of its alignment. The California Department of Transportation (Caltrans) was selected as the state lead agency, although the California Coastal Commission (since the route fell partly within the commission's jurisdiction) and the California Public Utilities Commission (because the proposed service would require a *Certificate of Public Convenience and Necessity* from the CPUC) were also logical candidates.[3]

At least one federal agency must be designated the lead agency. Other federal, state, or local entities may be joint lead agencies in certain cases. Any public body that has at least partial jurisdiction over the proposed action and is not a lead agency is considered a *cooperating agency*. The selection of the lead agency is usually determined by mutual consent, but administrative procedures are prescribed for resolving disputes over who should be lead agency or disagreements among lead and cooperative agencies.

Potential Impacts and Potential Alternatives

The proposed action must be evaluated for its impact in a variety of environmental areas, such as noise, traffic, land use, aesthetics, water resources, biological resources, historic properties and park lands, and construction. A list of the 19 specific elements described in the Urban Mass Transportation Administration's (UMTA) *Guidelines for Preparing Environmental Assessments*[4] is provided in Appendix A.

An EA or EIS need not explore each potential environmental impact in depth. Rather, a *scoping process* takes place between the lead agency and the applicant, in consultation with other affected parties, to identify particular issues that are likely to be most important. The environmental review then focuses on these issues. If a proposed alignment does not pass through any wetlands, for example, no study of that element is needed. On the other hand, some topics not specifically cited in the guidelines may be important in some geographical areas. For example, the evaluation of passenger safety for a major transit project in California would likely require an assessment of seismic risks and mitigations.

The environmental process should identify mitigation measures for the objectionable impacts of the project. It should also briefly discuss alternatives to the project, including "alternative locations and designs; alternatives with different characteristics, but that may achieve similar benefits and are preferable from an environmental standpoint; alternatives not within the jurisdiction of UMTA, if appropriate; and the 'do-nothing' alternative."[5] The document should discuss the other alternatives considered and why the proposed action was chosen over the other options.

Public Review and Comment

It is the intent of NEPA that no environmentally significant project be approved without ample opportunity for public review and comment. There are more formal requirements for public input on an EIS than on an EA. The EIS process opens, for example, when the lead agency publishes in the *Federal Register* a Notice of Intent (NOI) to prepare an EIS (for the state-level process in California and elsewhere, a *Notice of Preparation*, or NOP, is circulated). The NOI also sets the time and place for the first scoping meeting and provides contact information. In addition to the *Federal Register*, the NOI should be published in local newspapers and through other appropriate media and sent directly to those individuals and organizations known or expected to have an interest in the proposed action. The same is true of other public notices associated with the environmental review.

When the draft EIS (DEIS) is finished, a notice of publication is placed into the *Federal Register*, and the document is circulated for public review and comment. The final EIS (FEIS) contains the DEIS, the comments received, and the response to those comments (including any new mitigation measures). Notice of publication is also required for the FEIS. The public is allowed at least 45 days to comment on a DEIS. A Record of Decision (ROD) may be signed no sooner then 30 days after the publication of a FEIS or 90 days after the publication of a notice for a DEIS, whichever is later.

Besides allowing the opportunity for written input from the public, UMTA requires that public hearings be held during the scoping process and during the circulation period for a DEIS.

Supplemental EISs

The need for a *Supplemental Environmental Impact Statement (SEIS)* arises if (1) the proposed action is changed in a way that could pose significant environmental impacts that have not already been evaluated or (2) new information is obtained or new circumstances arise relating to potential environmental impacts. A SEIS can be prepared for a DEIS, a FEIS, or a previous SEIS. If more than 3 years pass between publication of a DEIS and an FEIS or between publication of an FEIS and taking major action to advance the project, either an SEIS or a new EIS is required.

For the Los Angeles Metro Rail system, an FEIS was approved in December 1983[6] and construction on the first segment began in September 1986. In March 1985 an explosion and fire occurred near the intersection of Third Street and Fairfax Avenue—an area through which the Metro Rail subway was to pass. The cause of the explosion was determined to be the accidental combustion of naturally occurring underground methane gas. Because of concern about the hazard posed by the gas, the U.S. Congress (in an attachment to Public Law No. 99-1980, December 19, 1985) prohibited tunneling through the areas identified as high risk. This action necessitated consideration of new alignments, including aerial configurations through the high-risk areas and routes that circumvented the areas. These alignments were evaluated in the *Supplemental Environmental Impact Statement/Subsequent Environmental Impact Report*, completed in July 1989.

CONSTRUCTION AND POSTCONSTRUCTION IMPACT EVALUATION: THE BART CASE STUDY

The BART Impact Program was a comprehensive postconstruction study of impacts of the San Francisco Bay Area Rapid Transit system, sponsored by the U.S. Department of Transportation to provide design guidance for future transit systems. Conducted in the mid-1970s, it encompassed impacts on travel patterns and modes, economics, land use, and social groups, as well as a landmark study of environmental impacts. This section will summarize these effects and add observations on impacts since the BART study was completed. A following section will deal with impacts of other transit modes, using the BART data as a point of departure.

BART's size, variations in design, and diversity of surroundings provide a wealth of specific impact conditions, including many similar to those found on other recent transit systems and extensions. At the same time, the BART system overall is not representative of most other conventional rapid rail systems. Its role is primarily that of connecting low-density suburban residential communities in an auto-dependent metropolis to a downtown center, rather than facilitating movement within the densely populated central city.

BART's lines are therefore radial, and they extend much farther into the suburbs than do other systems in cities such as Toronto and Montreal. Its lines and stations are also primarily aboveground (except in the major downtown areas it serves in San Francisco, Oakland, and Berkeley), in contrast to the more subway-dominant configurations of the Toronto and Montreal systems. All these characteristics will be reinforced by the several new radial extensions of the BART system now being planned. These differences have important implications for overall systemwide environmental impact, although the impacts of specific BART segments and stations may be similar to other systems.

THE NO-BART BASELINE

In defining impacts, as already noted, it is essential to have a baseline or "no-build" situation with which to compare. A major environmental benefit, for example, would be the avoidance of construction of additional urban freeways because of the transit system. The difficulty of identifying such a one-for-one substitution, however, should not be underestimated, since the two tend not to serve all the same purposes and also because many other factors are involved in the decision to build a major road.

In BART's case, there was considerable discussion as to whether BART had been instrumental in preventing construction of a very large and potentially environmentally disruptive bridge parallel to the San Francisco–Oakland Bay Bridge. An analysis of the events of that period indicated that the proposed bridge would probably have been stopped for other reasons, so it was not included as a component of the "no-BART" alternative. Clearly, this critically affected the outcome of the BART impact analysis. The "no-BART" scenario against which BART was compared emphasized the use of more express buses on existing roads, which had no discernible environmental effects. As a result, the net environmental impacts attributed to BART, although small, were largely adverse, even though this might not be so elsewhere. Obviously, such a base case must be carefully defined and justified (as it was with BART) to allow a fair and credible impact analysis.

CONSTRUCTION IMPACTS

In an absolute sense, the adverse effects of the rapid transit construction process can be substantial. With BART as well as the Washington, D.C., Metro, the Los Angeles Metro Rail, and other relatively new systems, the most serious effect appears to be that of the disruption of traffic and trade along streets subjected to long periods of open-cut subway construction. In some cases, subway construction on downtown streets was under way for over 5 years, with some indications of large losses in trade for businesses along the right-of-way (see Fig. 20-3). Small businesses were apparently most affected; it has been asserted that many did not survive to enjoy the benefits of the completed subway system, although documentation on this point is sparse. Experiences elsewhere are similar; in Amsterdam, for example, construction of the metro system was responsible for the demolition of a historic neighborhood, causing serious community conflicts.

Housing dislocation is another significant problem. Although the BART system is almost entirely sited along prior transportation rights-of-way such as railroads and freeways, research indicates that over 3000 housing units were taken for the construction of the 71 mi (114 km), 34-station initial system. Many of these were at suburban station parking-lot sites, which are up to 8 acres (32,400 m^2) in size and often in residential areas. Others were concentrated along routes in which the existing right-of-way had to be widened to accommodate the trackway (see Fig. 20-4). Even this large number, however, is small when placed in the perspective of the system's length (an average of well under 50 units/mi or 31/km) and in comparison with urban freeway

Figure 20-3 *Long-term closure of Market Street in downtown San Francisco for BART subway construction. (courtesy of Bay Area Rapid Transit District)*

construction requirements (often 200 to 500 or more units/mi when constructed through existing urban areas).

Construction effects of *aerial and at-grade trackways* are relatively benign, owing to their simplicity and relatively rapid construction. Even this level of activity, however, is at variance with the quiet character of many residential areas and led to many complaints during BART's construction. Construction of *tunneled* subway lines, as in Montreal, is of course least disruptive except at points of access and removal of material. *Open-cut* subway construction, particularly at stations, is most disruptive; other problem areas include suburban station sites, particularly those with parking lots, which tend to be used as staging areas and generate substantial truck traffic and noise.

Major efforts needed to ameliorate such impacts include the use of more rapid subway construction techniques, careful planning of interim traffic and transit reroutings, and an intensive program of public relations (such as BART's) to inform nearby residents and others of impending activity and to respond to complaints. Finally, it must be recognized that minimization of land acquisition and its attendant disloca-

Figure 20-4 *Removal of homes for construction of BART Concord Station and parking lot. (courtesy of Bay Area Rapid Transit District)*

tion, by doing the construction on narrow rights-of-way, necessarily produces the strongest construction impacts (as well as later operational impacts) on the nearby residences and businesses that might otherwise have been taken in right-of-way acquisition. This trade-off must be recognized and carefully assessed in system planning.

EARLY OPERATIONS IMPACTS

The early operations period of some new rail rapid transit systems has been characterized by a variety of difficulties in achieving both reliable system operations and harmony with surroundings. BART's initial problems with the mechanical reliability of its trains and automatic train control system, for example, resulted in a lengthy period of environmental impacts of somewhat less intensity than those that occurred later when the system's trains were running at more frequent intervals and on weekends. Most important among such impacts is train noise along the system's elevated lines; this was at first a moderate problem in the one to two blocks in quiet residential areas nearest the lines, but affected more areas with full operations.

This initial operations period is also characterized by patronage levels substantially lower than those likely to be reached after service is improved. As a result, impacts related to patronage increase. The most important of these are related to traffic, parking, and connecting bus service at the suburban stations. In the case of BART, even in the initial operations period, parking overflowed from many of the station lots onto adjacent streets. Similar patronage-related impacts have been experienced elsewhere, notably on the Toronto and Montreal systems and the Philadelphia area's Lindenwold line.

These change-prone impacts are typically those attributable to the system's *operations*; in contrast, those due to its *facilities* are likely to be relatively stable over time. Included among these are impacts on the visual environment and natural ecology and neighborhood effects such as closing of streets and paths across the right-of-way. These stable effects and other impacts of full operations are discussed in the following section.

IMPACTS UNDER STABLE FULL-SCALE OPERATIONS

The major finding of the BART study of environmental impacts was that the system's effects are generally small and will continue to be so. Despite greatly expanded patronage, more intensive service, and some deterioration of the original level of system maintenance, this conclusion still appeared to hold true more than a decade later. This applies to regional effects, such as reduction of auto air pollution, as well as localized impacts both at the stations and along the lines. Exceptions are noted in the following paragraphs, along with other details that may be applicable to new systems proposed elsewhere.

By 1990, BART patronage had doubled since the completion of the BART Impact Program; parking lot expansions and improved feeder bus service were required during the 1970s and 1980s as patronage increased. In the 1990s, BART is involved in a $90 million parking capacity and station access improvement program, launched by the replacement of a 400-space portion of the surface parking lot at the El Cerrito Del Norte station with a 1300-space multilevel parking structure.[7]

BART's effects on the region's air quality and energy use apparently continue to be very small, primarily because it is estimated to carry only 3% of the region's daily vehicular trips. In addition, much of its patronage is drawn from previous bus users rather than auto drivers or passengers. The system, however, is now a prominent part of the San Francisco Bay area's image. The elevated lines and trains are seen from a number of freeways, arterials, and residential areas, and the system is internationally known (see Fig. 20-5). It has, therefore, become something of a tourist attraction. Older and more closely spaced subway systems, such as those in London, Tokyo, and Paris, have for many become the primary mode of structuring the city's image, since they are simpler and easier to use than the aboveground street networks; BART, however, is much more thinly spread across the region and probably plays a much less significant role in this regard except to help patrons comprehend very large scale spatial relationships (that is, outer suburbs to inner city, rather than the city itself).

BART's effects at stations are mixed. Impacts attributable to the downtown subway stations have been almost entirely positive as a result of the new plazas created around the stations and the street beautification projects that were undertaken by cities in

Figure 20-5 *BART train on typical elevated trackway in residential area, with experimental "linear park." (courtesy of Bay Area Rapid Transit District)*

cooperation with BART (see Fig. 20-6). Many of these environmental improvements have created lively social meeting places. As is true for the entire system, crime has been a minor problem at these downtown stations. On the other hand, the coordinated planning of development around the BART stations has been much more limited than the multilevel pedestrian complexes that have been created around such stations as Place Bonaventure and others in Montreal, Shinjuku in Tokyo, or Insurgentes in Mexico City.

The suburban stations have not been closely integrated with new suburban centers, as at Vallingby near Stockholm or Senri near Osaka, Japan. At suburban BART stations, the large parking lots (some now expanded to over 2000 cars) are often beyond convenient walking distance from adjacent centers (see Fig. 20-7). The opportunity to create suburban pedestrian centers or to reinforce existing ones has, therefore, been largely lost. Many suburban stations could have been located much closer to or even

Figure 20-6 *BART station entrance plaza below street level in downtown San Francisco. (courtesy of Gruen Associates, Inc.)*

within already built suburban shopping centers. Cost, the private nature of these centers, and the fragmentary nature of urban planning around BART, which resulted in BART's inability to plan beyond the right-of-way, precluded such packaging.[8] Although there is still the future option of building on air rights over some BART parking lots, no such development has so far occurred due to the combination of high cost, lack of demand, and local community opposition.

As noted earlier, several parking lots were overfilled shortly after opening; others became so as patronage rose. Terminal stations are most affected. The severity of the problems caused by this overflow and the associated station-area traffic varies widely, depending on the station location and parking-lot access to major streets. In general, it is a significant problem in residential areas—probably the system's largest effect on its surroundings—but not elsewhere. At the same time, solutions, such as either lot expansion or construction of multilevel facilities, are most difficult in existing residential areas. In consequence, the planning of future BART extensions into less-developed suburban areas has included much larger parking lots at most stations to avoid the difficulties of expansion after the initial land acquisition and construction.

The BART Impact Program found few other station-area impacts, and little change has occurred since then. The visual effect of the stations was generally perceived by nearby residents as neutral or positive. Noise was slight. In general, near-by residents were found to be unhappy where there was an overflow parking problem and relatively happy otherwise. They seemed to discount most other effects. Finally, land value or land-use changes appeared to be virtually nonexistent when the BART

Figure 20-7 *BART station and parking lot separated from shopping center by fenced drainage channel. (courtesy of Bay Area Rapid Transit District)*

Impact Study examined them after 5 years of limited operations (apparently no newer efforts have been made to confirm this). For similarly short periods of operation, other recently developed systems have had similar experiences with station-area development, although Toronto is notable for its apparent intensification of land use over a longer period.

Impacts along BART's subway lines are nil where tunneled except around the stations, where large open excavations were necessary. Most cut-and-cover line sections were located in wide arterial streets, causing construction impacts, but limiting the numbers of dwellings taken. In the long run, these are the lines that have had most beneficial impacts, reinforcing and enhancing existing centers, such as Market Street in San Francisco and Shattuck Avenue in Berkeley. BART's 70 mi/h (113-km/h) trains on its aerial lines, however, despite their quietness relative to other systems, were judged in the original BART study to cause some noise problems for many residents living within one or two blocks. A reduction of from 5 to 10 dB(A) is required to eliminate this problem in most places. Sound-barrier baffles on the guideway could do this, although they would increase the presently acceptable visual bulk of the structure as well as its shadow effects and cost. Such barriers were actually built in some especially sensitive areas and have apparently been effective.

Future transit systems may find it necessary to mitigate potential noise impacts through even quieter trains, bulkier structures, wider rights-of-way, underground placement, or line locations outside quiet residential areas. Interestingly, however, even though the BART trains have grown progressively noisier over the years, there has apparently been no public complaint or other indication of increased problems with wayside noise impact, suggesting a higher than expected degree of adaptation by nearby residents and businesses.

The wayside problems identified in the BART Impact Program affect relatively few residents, since most of the BART aboveground trackway shares rights-of-way with other transportation facilities, such as freeways, arterial streets, and railroads (Fig. 20-8). It was found, however, that this is no guarantee of impact-free operation; where the system shares a little-used railway right-of-way, adjacent neighborhoods are not adapted to noise and suffer more than others. A 2-mi (3-km)-long landscaped strip (the "linear park" in Fig. 20-5) beneath the BART aerial structure in one such location was appreciated and actively used by local residents, but apparently did not lessen their unhappiness with the BART train noise. Along the at-grade lines, which are potentially dangerous because of the high-voltage third rail, as well as the high-speed trains themselves, protective cyclone fences now interrupt pedestrian flows, which freely crossed relatively unused railroads in some neighborhoods. This inconvenience has been offset by pedestrian bridges and is apparently only a minor concern. All in all, the use of prior transportation rights-of-way appears to be a useful factor in minimizing environmental impact.

Finally, in consideration of the major Loma Prieta earthquake in October 1989, it is appropriate to comment on the impacts of—and on—rapid transit systems in such events. Despite the 1989 quake's 7.1 Richter magnitude, the highest in Northern California since the 1906 San Francisco disaster, BART suffered virtually no damage. After a brief shutdown for inspection, the system was back in operation within a few hours after the shock. BART's underwater Transbay Tube, supplemented by a fleet of emergency ferries provided the only direct Oakland–San Francisco access during the following month while the seriously damaged Bay Bridge was repaired. Postquake BART ridership ballooned from about 220,000 to a high of 360,000 during this period, but then gradually subsided. About 10% of these new riders stayed with BART; 6 months after the quake, patronage had returned to its former gradually increasing pattern with a net "earthquake dividend" of 10,000 to 15,000 new one-way trips per weekday. This increase was equal to about 1 year's typical patronage growth. It caused no significant environmental effects around BART stations and trackways, but probably led to a small environmental improvement through reduction of rush-hour auto trips and their air pollution effects.

LONG-RANGE EFFECTS

Apart from unexpected increases in the use of the system, which could add to congestion problems at some stations, the major possible long-term environmental effects of a rapid transit system are those on local and regional land-use patterns. Experience with post-World War II transit improvements in the United States and

Figure 20-8 *Low-impact BART right-of-way in freeway median. (courtesy of Bay Area Transit District)*

Canada indicates that such effects are likely to be small unless encouraged by land-use policy and other factors in addition to the transit system itself.[9] Under such encouragement, the most likely effects are an increase in high-rise office development and possibly some strengthening of retail activities in the central business district, plus some focusing of office and apartment construction at some outlying stations. Such effects are probably limited to intraregional transfers of activity, rather than net new growth in a region.

How much the high-rise building boom in San Francisco was caused by BART may never be empirically established. Melvin Webber judged that it "would have happened anyway, but . . . BART . . . made it happen bigger and quicker."[10] The environmental effects of high-rise development in San Francisco have not been very positive. They have been the subject of a separate study, in which increases in noise levels, traffic generation, the blockage of views, shadowing and wind on downtown streets and open space, and their overpowering scale were cited among the negative impacts.[11]

Several Bay Area cities produced ambitious development plans around local stations prior to BART's opening, incorporating high-rise buildings and multilevel commercial and apartment complexes. Many of these were subsequently opposed by the neighboring residents, whose principal response to BART prior to its opening was one of fear about the effects of such development on neighborhood composition and character.[12] In a study of townhouse developments in one of the Bay Area's suburban counties, Dingemans reported that only "some degree of sub-centering (of townhouse developments around BART) has occurred . . . ," and those were more spread out within a mile radius than within the immediate area of the stations.[13] He offered four reasons why more clustering had not happened. First, there were few available building sites and most were too small for the usual 10 acres (40,500 m^2) or more required for such developments. Of the stations studied by Dingemans, most clustering had occurred around the one that had large sites available. Second, the construction of large parking lots (up to 1500 cars or 8 acres) has preempted close-in sites. Third, public opposition to townhouses emerged in the early 1970s partly because they had been allowed to locate in scattered sites. "Residents for Density Control," a local ad hoc group, effectively blocked proposals for townhouses in the vicinity of some stations. The fourth and final reason for little clustering was the willingness of the suburban cities to allow commercial centers to locate away from station sites. Part of this was also due to BART's location policies, which emphasized the use of cheaper sites away from existing centers.

Inner-city neighborhoods have also opposed increasing densities around the stations and have sponsored "down zoning."[14] Environmental change around many stations is, therefore, almost at a standstill, even though it makes "regional" sense to increase densities in those locations. This may, however, only be a slowing down of the process rather than a permanent halt. Here is a case of conflicts among environmental qualities. Increased densities around stations are seen as decreasing comfort conditions for nearby residents, but they improve pedestrian access, encourage transit use, and can create fine urban environments. The need is for more sensitive and participatory planning for densification, identifying particular development sites, utilizing air rights, improving pedestrian access, and so on, while maintaining some continuity of character.

Some observers have noted that low-density residential development has been strong in the BART suburban corridors around and beyond the terminal stations and have offered this as evidence that BART has actually helped to further sprawl in these corridors.[15] Certainly, the rail service's long lines have made the distant suburban areas more attractive for residences of downtown commuters, and the combination of available land, low-density zoning, and large BART parking lots for auto access from such residential areas has encouraged a conventional spread-out form of development. Indeed, it has historically been the case that transportation arteries, whether the original streetcar lines or the later major highways, have had exactly that role.[16] More recently, a study of the Metrorail system in Washington, D.C., suggested that station-area development on the suburban fringes of the system was more likely to be commercial than residential and would attract more auto users (from beyond the end of the rail line) than transit users.[17] These experiences support the contention that careful land-use planning is needed if the desired results are to be achieved.

TRANSIT MODES OTHER THAN RAPID RAIL

The environmental impacts of other transit modes have not been well-documented, in comparison to detailed studies of rail rapid transit systems such as BART.

Nevertheless, the limited evidence available can be used in combination with the rapid rail findings to provide some indicators of how the effects of these other modes compare with those of BART-like rail systems.

Systems of interest in addition to conventional rail rapid transit include commuter rail, light rail, innovative fixed-guideway systems, and regional all-bus operations. Not all of these modes are direct competitors, in that the differences in their service characteristics sometimes lead them to serve quite different markets and purposes. Light rail, for example, is usually not a reasonable substitute for a commuter rail system. Consequently, their environmental impacts should not be interpreted immediately as indications that one system is "better" than another.

COMMUTER RAIL

The environmental impacts of commuter rail systems are likely to be much smaller than even those of rapid rail systems such as BART. Typically, an existing freight rail right-of-way is used, service is infrequent relative to that of rapid rail systems, and suburban station facilities are less obtrusive and their patronage lower in most cases. Construction impacts are likely to be small even if new trackage is laid.

The typical baseline for commuter rail evaluation is an all-highway system. Regional effects on traffic and associated impacts can be estimated quite easily for given patronage levels, as with BART. At a corridor level, effects on parallel freeway traffic and downtown parking can be substantial, although on a regional basis these effects are not substantial except for the largest commuter rail networks. It would appear that other environmental concerns are unlikely to be significant in decisions concerning the inauguration or expansion of commuter rail facilities. Their higher speeds, given the option of express trains, can, however, bring places as far as 60 mi (97 km) from urban centers into commuting range, as has happened in the southern region of London where the commuter rail extensions have resulted in the growth of many small towns, but sprawl has been prevented by green belt controls.

LIGHT RAIL

Light rail systems usually run at moderate speed and on separate at-grade rights-of-way. Attributes of modern light rail systems most relevant to environmental impact include their use of some grade crossings and small, relatively numerous stations or stops. To the degree that these characteristics are rejected in favor of high-speed, mainly grade-separated operation and large, widely spaced stations with parking (as in Edmonton, Canada) impacts will approach those of rapid rail systems. However, with the more standard configuration, impacts should be substantially less because of the lack of concentration of activity. Major concerns are likely to be limited to grade-crossing safety; other impacts, such as noise and visual effects, are less likely to be significant than for rapid rail systems.

Several light rail construction projects have been either undertaken or completed in the United States during the 1980s. These have generally made use of former railroad rights-of-way or freeway medians wherever possible and often resemble full-scale rapid transit systems with station parking lots and grade-separated guideways (for example, Sacramento, California). At the same time, some new light rail systems make heavy use of at-grade mixed-traffic trackage either along or crossing arterial streets, with some attendant problems with traffic accidents (for example, San Jose, California). No other significant environmental problems have been widely reported.

INNOVATIVE FIXED-GUIDEWAY SYSTEMS

Innovative fixed-guideway transit can encompass very different types of systems, such as "personal" (very small cabin) systems with relatively extensive guideway networks, "people-mover" and MRT (medium-density rail transit) systems with small- to medium-capacity vehicles, and very high speed, long-distance systems with advanced propulsion/suspension technologies such as magnetic levitation. Only a few examples of the people-mover variety have been built in the United States; although most are in airports and amusement parks, several small systems have been built for circulation in downtown areas such as Miami and Detroit. All these are very small, low-speed, closed-loop systems with small elevated guideways, simple platforms in lieu of stations, and no parking. As such, they are not comparable to full-scale urban transit systems, although their technologies could be used in larger systems.

The impacts of innovative guideway transit systems will vary substantially, depending on specific system characteristics such as those just noted (for example, size, speed, station patronage, and parking). However, the types of impact and their causes identified as important in the BART study can provide useful indications of the key impact concerns for all systems. Many environmental impacts have little to do with guideway technology. For example, suburban station-area concerns focus on overflow parking and other access-related issues. If used in such commute-oriented applications (and at similar levels of patronage), transit systems usually cannot avoid such problems, no matter what technology is used. Likewise, with any transit technology a system's effects on regional air quality will not be substantial unless the system carries a high proportion of the region's trips.

Innovative guideway systems are most likely to have environmental impacts different from those of BART along the guideway itself. BART has proved that heavy-rail, high-speed rail transit systems can be acceptably quiet; but if an innovative system is only slightly noisier, residents within two or perhaps more blocks will probably have reason to complain. Conversely, a system slightly quieter than BART will cause almost no discernible effect on most acoustic environments. Guideway bulk is another example: Some proposed guideway systems may involve either lighter or bulkier guideways than that of BART. Since the bulk or shadowing effect of BART's guideways is not a cause of significant complaint, lighter guideways are unlikely to produce a significant improvement. Even if such systems require slightly less right-of-way, the resulting closeness of the guideway may offset its smaller size. Bulkier guideways, such as those with side walls for guidance of untracked systems, may cause significant shadow and view-blocking problems. These problems are important when narrow rights-of-way are used in residential areas and are of concern for downtown people-mover systems in congested areas.

REGIONAL ALL-BUS SYSTEMS

As already noted, the BART study defined the system's environmental impacts as the differences between the existing situation (with BART) and a hypothetical "no-BART alternative" scenario that relied on a regional all-bus system large enough to carry about the same number of trips. Some significant environmental impact differences between BART and an all-bus system might be those occurring around the BART stations and guideways, where the alternative bus system would have few or no offsetting effects. However, if the regional bus system were to have terminals or if it were to disperse along arterial streets, its impacts could be more widespread than BART's. Comparative research on the environmental impacts of buses versus automobiles carrying equal numbers of passengers has not been carried out, but buses are known to have substantial negative impacts on residential streets.[18] However, bus systems are necessary even with a rail system, to serve shorter trips and the collector-distributor role. The important issue is whether the increase in total bus operations required by the all-bus alternative to serve the longer trip and express functions (otherwise covered by rail transit) would be enough to have significant environmental effects. In the BART study, it was concluded that it would not.

CONCLUSIONS

ENVIRONMENTAL IMPACT ASSESSMENT PROCEDURES

Several observations can be made concerning how the practice of environmental impact analysis changed in the 1980s.[19] First, the EIS process became more structured. Guidelines from UMTA and other agencies not only provided instructions on what areas to analyze, but indicated, in some cases, how the analysis should be performed, how to deal with certain possibilities, and criteria for acceptability of certain impacts. Such standardization was helpful both to the applicant and to the UMTA reviewer and facilitated an apples-to-apples comparison among competing requests for limited funding.

Second, the treatment of environmental issues, as in urban planning in general, was as much political as technical. A single controversial environmental issue provided an easy target for those who opposed a system on more subtle grounds. When the methane gas explosion, described earlier, occurred in what would be the path of the Los Angeles Metro Rail, extensive technical studies were conducted to assess the dangers of tunneling through the area. While different experts were found to testify on both sides of the question, the preponderance of evidence, including experience with similar conditions elsewhere, indicated that the risks could be reduced to insignificant levels if proper precautions were taken. Yet opponents of the system (who failed to prevail during the EIS process itself and during a subsequent court challenge to the

December 1983 FEIS) succeeded in blocking the original subway alignment.

Third, participation in the EIS process became more sophisticated on the part of both the applicant and the public. In some cases, it seemed that applicants learned how to fulfill the letter of the law and satisfy the funding agency without always adhering to the spirit of the law. Applicants also learned, however, the importance of the public participation process. They became adept at developing and maintaining lists of key special interest groups and individuals, at forming citizens' advisory panels, and at soliciting public input early and throughout the EIS process.

At the same time, the public clearly learned that its actions can make or break a project. Virtually no agency will back a system for funding that has major local opposition. Public values per se did not seem to change much in the 1980s. The most common concern remained: How will this project affect me—my property and its value, my neighborhood, my quality of life, my mobility? The NIMBY (not in my back yard) syndrome continued at least as strong as ever and perhaps became more forcefully and effectively expressed.

Perceived impacts are just as important as real ones in the eyes of the public. For example, the operating noise of a rail transit system is an issue that, technologically, has been largely solved through advances in vehicle, guideway, and sound barrier construction. Yet there is typically a visceral reaction against the expected noise of a proposed system that no amount of scientific measurements and models can reverse.

The prohibition of tunneling through methane gas areas in Los Angeles necessitated the identification of alternatives. Early efforts focused on keeping roughly the same alignment as before, but changing the grade from subway to aboveground. On the other hand, there was vocal opposition by residents to an aerial or at-grade system. In view of this opposition, it was decided to change alignments altogether and head north to Hollywood and the eastern San Fernando Valley rather than west to Santa Monica. Thus, rail service to the Wilshire corridor, containing the densest development in the region outside of downtown Los Angeles, was postponed indefinitely. Also, construction of the second phase of the system was delayed by several years.

Meanwhile, some of the newly proposed alignments were encountering opposition of their own. In particular, the entertainment industry was galvanized into action by a proposed aerial alignment down Sunset Boulevard in proximity to a number of recording studios and sound stages. Again, extensive studies were conducted and, again, the technical evidence and experience elsewhere seemed to indicate that noise and vibration impacts could be mitigated with appropriate measures. Nevertheless, continued industry opposition resulted not only in altering the alignment slightly, but also in changing the grade at that point from aerial to subway. Other noise-reducing measures had already been agreed to because of nearby residential developments.

A final observation on changes in the practice of environmental impact analysis is that postconstruction environmental assessments such as the BART Impact Study, the Washington, D.C., Metrorail Before-and-After Study, and the Transit Impact Monitoring Program for Atlanta's MARTA rail system are seldom conducted.[20] There are several related reasons why postconstruction studies are exceptional. The first is the simple expedient of money. An EIS for a major system can easily cost $1 million. (It is estimated that $3 million was spent on the environmental review process for the Los Angeles Metro Rail). A thorough postconstruction or before-and-after study could cost much more, as did the BART Impact Program. Few agencies can afford such an expense for an impact study, especially one done too late to affect the design and construction of the system in question.

Second, many impacts of interest are long term in nature, making their evaluation more problematic. As indicated earlier, construction impacts alone will be phased over several years (even a decade or more for larger projects or systems), operational impacts will not stabilize for several years after that, and land-use impacts will perhaps not reach equilibrium for decades. In a sense, each of the three postconstruction studies mentioned above took place too soon, did not last long enough, or both. It would be unusual indeed to see a meaningful level of resources committed to studying environmental impacts continuously over a period of 20 years or longer, but that is the order of magnitude of time needed to capture the full spectrum of impacts for a major transit system.

The third reason that few postconstruction studies are seen is the relative efficacy of the EIS process itself. Ideally, the EIS identifies all potentially serious negative impacts, allows for complete airing of all concerns, and develops optimal mitigation measures for reducing or eliminating those impacts. Furthermore, UMTA now requires that these mitigation measures be highlighted in the executive summary of the EIS and writes compliance with those measures into the full funding contract for the project. Therefore, there is less need for an additional study monitoring impacts. On the other hand, it would be a mistake to argue that a postconstruction study is useless. There is still a lot such a study can teach us about how to improve our models of impact prediction and about the effectiveness of certain mitigation strategies.

The environmental impact review process is decidedly a mixed blessing. At its best, it provides the opportunity for crafting a better project (from an environmental standpoint) than would be arrived at otherwise. At its worst, it is either a meaningless formality and a waste of time and money or a tool for obstruction by parties who may not represent the collective best interests of those affected by the project. The challenge here, as in so many other areas of public planning, is to continue to improve the process without unduly impairing its effectiveness.

OBSERVED ENVIRONMENTAL IMPACTS

Overall, our experience to date indicates that the environmental impacts of modern public transit systems are likely to be small in comparison to those of urban freeways. For all types of transit systems, the most important determinant of environmental impacts is the proportion of a region's trips that are captured, because of both their diversion from autos (a local and regional benefit) and their resulting focus on transit stations (with both local benefits and detriments).

Significant regional-scale benefits such as air quality improvement require much larger transit patronage than achieved to date on most existing systems. Similarly, major land-use impacts cannot be anticipated without strong complementary physical, economic, and local public policy factors to support the transit system's potential.[21]

In contrast to the scarcity of regional influence, transit systems can have substantial localized environmental effects. Even moderate patronage levels can cause noticeable adverse impacts, especially at outlying stations in residential areas. At the higher levels of patronage needed to generate desirable regional benefits, these localized adverse effects could become serious problems. Under such conditions, stations should be located away from sensitive environments such as quiet neighborhoods or be planned to combine with regional centers or arterial streets.

Different transit modes do have significant differences in environmental impact. Transit modes may often be more complementary than substitutable; rapid rail systems serve high volumes and long trips; buses are appropriate for station feeder routes and lower-volume, more dispersed corridors; and light rail systems fit best with intermediate conditions. Thus immediate environmental impacts are not likely to be the dominant factor in selecting among transit modes. Once a transit mode is selected, however, its environmental impacts can be controlled in important ways based on the on the experiences reported in this chapter.

Some perspective on this conclusion may be provided through comparison with other transportation strategies. In particular, major regional benefits such as reduction of energy use and air pollution are much more likely through private ridesharing (car- and vanpooling) arrangements; an increase in average peak-period auto occupancy from 1.2 persons per vehicle to 1.4, which is only about one additional person in every sixth car, would do far more toward attainment of most regional environmental objectives than could a rapid transit system such as BART. Improvements in automobile engine combustion efficiency, use of smaller autos with smaller engines, and a shift to electric-powered vehicles could also have larger effects in achieving benefits of this type.

The distribution of impacts can vary for different transit systems. The more transport flows can be concentrated on major channels (such as with rail transit), the fewer the number of persons that are affected, especially since the rail system's typical level of impact is low. The more dispersed the transit system, as with a regional bus system, the more it approaches the pervasive impact of the automobile. No one has yet calculated, to our knowledge, the relative distributions of impacts of different transit systems. Nevertheless, there are some clues. A Bay Area study of noise, for instance, found that 40% of a randomly selected population complained of local street traffic, whereas those disturbed by freeway noise amounted to only 24%. Bus transit systems that use local streets may, therefore, cause more widespread environmental problems than regional rail systems. At the same time, the concentration of transit and other traffic on arterial streets rather than neighborhood streets and the introduction of quieter and less polluting street transit vehicles may pay even greater environmental dividends.

A major issue outstanding in the evaluation of the environmental impacts of transit options is that of long-term effects on urban form and function. Some transit modes, notably high-capacity fixed-guideway systems, may be instrumental in the achievement of a more land-efficient, multicentered urban configuration with major benefits in internal protection of the surrounding natural environment. Studies indicate that such transit systems may have encouraged progress in this direction. At the same time, provision of rapid transit is but one ingredient, albeit a key one, in a necessary blend of closely related physical and policy inducements if cities are to be restructured to any significant degree. Given such interdependence of causal forces, rapid transit alone cannot be credited with long-range benefits of this nature.

Once a local commitment is made to mobilize such complementary forces to change the course of a city's future development, a new (or extended or improved) fixed-guideway form of public transit must be given serious consideration as an element in the overall strategy. At this point the relative environmental merits of alternative systems must be considered, as outlined in earlier sections. Nonguideway systems appear to be much less likely to contribute to urban growth-focusing objectives than do either conventional or innovative fixed-guideway systems.

Where a guideway form of transit is adopted, the evidence indicates that effective steps can be taken to mitigate adverse guideway impacts. The major approaches include thoughtful location of stations, careful planning of their surrounding development, and the selection of trackway configuration in keeping with the sensitivity of the urban environments to be traversed. This sensitivity is largely determined by factors such as ambient sound levels, local traffic intensity and capacity, right-of-way width, and the presence of residential or similarly sensitive land uses. Other efforts to optimize impact may include rapid construction, high-quality architectural design, transit vehicle sound control, provision of adequate parking, extensive feeder bus service, landscaping, and other compensatory measures. With such efforts, rapid transit's environmental impact need not be a major problem and indeed can offer some significant improvements in the quality and structure of urban environments.

APPENDIX A

Typical Areas of Environmental Analysis

For each of these areas, the UMTA *Guidelines* found in Circular 5620.1 provide criteria for judging whether or not a proposed action will have a significant impact.

1. *Land acquisition and displacements:* including displacements of residences and businesses.
2. *Land use and zoning:* compatibility with surrounding uses and conformance to zoning requirements.
3. *Air quality:* due to changes in auto and/or bus traffic, and especially as sensitive areas such as parks, schools, and hospitals are affected.
4. *Noise:* including noise from fixed transit facilities, diverted traffic, or the operation of transit vehicles.
5. *Water quality:* including impacts on surface bodies of water nearby and storm and sanitary sewers.
6. *Wetlands:* that is, "a lowland covered with shallow and sometimes temporary or intermittent waters," and including impacts on associated wildlife.

7. *Flooding:* including "flooding of the proposed project site and flooding induced by the proposed project."

8. *Navigable waterways and coastal zones:* including land near the coast as well as waterways near the proposed project.

9. *Ecologically sensitive areas:* that is, areas containing "natural features that require protection," such as "woodlands, prairies, marshes, bogs, lakes, streams, scenic areas, landforms and geological formations, and pristine natural areas."

10. *Endangered species:* including flora and fauna.

11. *Traffic and parking:* including traffic generated by the project as well changes in traffic patterns.

12. *Energy requirements and potential for conservation:* that is, the energy needed to construct and operate the project; and the potential to reduce energy consumption through increased energy efficiency, increased vehicle occupancy, a shift to energy-efficient modes, reduction of demand for vehicular travel, and/or development of more efficient routes or travel patterns.

13. *Historic properties and parklands:* that is, those properties subject to Section 106 of the National Historic Preservation Act of 1966 (historic sites) and/or Section 4(f) of the Department of Transportation Act of 1966 (parks, recreation areas, wildlife refuges, and historic sites).

14. *Construction:* impacts to be analyzed include noise, disruption of utilities, disposal of debris and spoil, water quality and runoff, access and distribution of traffic, air quality and dust control, safety and security, and disruption of businesses.

15. *Aesthetics:* visual impacts of the proposed action.

16. *Community disruption:* the potential for isolation, disruption, or displacement of physical sectors or activities of the community.

17. *Safety and security:* measures taken to prevent accidents or criminal activity associated with the project.

18. *Secondary development:* land-use changes stimulated by the proximity of a transit facility or service.

19. *Consistency with local plans:* including comprehensive or general plans, specific plans, and transportation plans for the area affected by the project.

REFERENCES

Some citations are no longer available from their original source. These citations are often available from the National Technical Information Service, U.S. Department of Commerce, 5285 Port Royal Road, Springfield, VA 22161. We have verified the order numbers for many of these citations, and they are found at the end of the citation. Prices are available through NTIS at the address above.

1   COUNCIL ON ENVIRONMENTAL QUALITY, "Regulations for Implementing the Procedural Provisions of the National Environmental Policy Act," Reprint, 40 CFR Parts 1500-1508 (Washington, D.C.: U.S. Government Printing Office), November 29, 1978.

2   FEDERAL HIGHWAY ADMINISTRATION, "Environmental Impact and Related Procedures," 23 CFR Part 771, *Federal Register,* 45, no. 212 (October 30, 1980), pp. 71968-87.

3   GEORGE C. SMITH AND EARL SHIRLEY, "High-Speed Rail in California: The Dream, the Process, and the Reality," in *Environmental Issues: Noise, Rail Noise, and High-Speed Rail,* Transportation Research Record 1143 (Washington, D.C.: Transportation Research Board, 1987), pp. 36-43.

4   URBAN MASS TRANSPORTATION ADMINISTRATION, "Guidelines for Preparing Environmental Assessments," Circular # UMTA C 5620.1, October 16, 1979.

5   Ibid., p. 11.

6   URBAN MASS TRANSPORTATION ADMINISTRATION AND SOUTHERN CALIFORNIA RAPID TRANSIT DISTRICT, *Final Environmental Impact Statement (FEIS), Los Angeles Rail Rapid Transit Project: Metro Rail*, (Los Angeles: Southern California Rapid Transit District, December 1983).

7   "BART Breaks Ground for Four-Level Parking Structure," *Passenger Transport*, 48, no. 5 (January 29, 1990), 7.

8   R. BETTS, "Design of Bay Area Rapid Transit Stations" (unpublished Master's thesis in city planning, University of California, Berkeley, 1972).

9   ROBERT L. KNIGHT AND LISA L. TRYGG, *Land Use Impacts of Rapid Transit: Implications of Recent Experience*, prepared for U.S. DOT, Office of the Secretary, Report no. DOT-TPI-10-77-29 (Washington, D.C.: U.S. Department of Transportation, 1977).

10 MELVIN M. WEBBER, *The BART Experience—What Have We Learned?* reprinted from *The Public Interest*, no. 45 (Fall 1976), pp. 79-108. Copyright © by National Affairs, Inc.

11 SAN FRANCISCO PLANNING AND URBAN RENEWAL ASSOCIATION, *Detailed Findings: Impact of Intensive High-Rise Development on San Francisco, Sec. 3: Environment*, prepared for HUD, San Francisco Foundation, and Mary A. Crocker Trust (San Francisco: San Francisco Planning and Urban Renewal Association, June 1975), Chap. 6. Now available as PB 245 577.

12 DONALD APPLEYARD AND OTHERS, *BART Impact Studies, BART-II: Pre-BART Studies of Environment, Land Use, Retail Sales, Part II: Residential Environment Impact Study, Volume III: Residential Quality Prior to the Opening of BART* and *Volume VI: Rationale and Procedures for Collection of Behavioral and Environmental Data*, Final Report, prepared for Metropolitan Transportation Commission, U.S. DOT and HUD (Berkeley, Calif.: University of California, Institute of Urban and Regional Development, 1973). Now available as PB 236 730 and 236 733.

13 D. Dingemans, *Residential Subcentering and Urban Sprawl: The Location of Higher-Density, Owner-Occupied Housing Around the Concord Line BART Stations*, Working Paper no. 275 (Berkeley, Calif.: University of California, Institute of Urban and Regional Development, 1977).

14 ANDREJS SKABURSKIS, "An Economic and Political Analysis of BART Land-Use Impacts: A Planning Study of the Rockridge Conflict" (unpublished Ph.D. dissertation, University of California, Berkeley, College of Environmental Design, 1976).

15 WEBBER, *The BART Experience*.

16 See, for example, PETER O. MULLER, "Transportation and Urban Form: Stages in the Spatial Evolution of the American Metropolis," in *The Geography of Urban Transportation*, ed. Susan Hanson (New York: The Guilford Press, 1986), pp. 24-49.

17 From the Further Reading, see p. *iv* of the Metropolitan Washington Council of Governments, Chap. 6 of Dunphy and Griffiths, and Giuliano.

18 DONALD APPLEYARD, M. SUE GERSON, AND MARK LINTELL, *Liveable Urban Streets: Managing Auto Traffic in Neighborhoods*, Final report, prepared for the FHWA, Report no. DOT-FH-11-8026 (Washington, D.C.: U.S. Government Printing Office, January 1976).

19 Conversations with Mr. Nadeem Tahir, Project Engineer (Metro Rail), Southern California Rapid Transit District, March 22, 1990; and Mr. Steve Beard, Vice President, ICF Kaiser Engineers, March 23, 1990.

20 See examples in the Further Reading.

21 KNIGHT AND TRYGG, *Land Use Impacts*.

FURTHER READING

ALAN M. VOORHEES & ASSOCIATES, INC., AND OTHERS, *HUD's Areas of Environmental Concern*, prepared for HUD, Office of Policy Development and Research. Washington, D.C.: Department of Housing and Urban Development, 1974.

APPLEYARD, DONALD, "Evaluating the Social and Environmental Impacts of Transport Investments," in *Conference Proceedings, Third International Conference on Behavioral Travel Modelling*, Tanunda, Australia, 1977, eds. D. A. Hensher and P. R. Stopher. London: Pergamon Press, 1978.

DUNPHY, ROBERT T., AND ROBERT E. GRIFFITHS, *The First Four Years of Metrorail: Travel Changes: A Metrorail Before-and-After Study Report*, Interim Report, prepared for UMTA, Technology Sharing Program, Report no. DOT-I-82-5. Washington, D.C.: U.S. Department of Transportation, September 1981.

GIULIANO, GENEVIEVE, "Land Use Impacts of Transportation Investments: Highway and Transit," in *The Geography of Urban Transportation*, ed. Susan Hanson (New York: The Guilford Press, 1986), pp. 247-79.

GRUEN ASSOCIATES, INC., AND DE LEUW, CATHER & COMPANY, *Environmental Impacts of BART: Final Report*, prepared for Metropolitan Transportation Commission, U.S. DOT and HUD. Berkeley, Calif.: Metropolitan Transportation Commission, 1978.

LANE, JONATHAN S., AND OTHERS, *The No-Build Alternative: Social, Economic, and Environmental Consequences of Not Constructing Transportation Facilities*, in 2 vols., prepared for NCHRP By David A. Crane & Partners/DACP, Inc., Economics Research Associates, Inc., and Alan M. Voorhees & Associates, Inc. Washington, D.C.: Transportation Research Board, December 1975.

METROPOLITAN WASHINGTON COUNCIL OF GOVERNMENTS, *Metrorail Station Area Planning: A Metrorail Before-and-After Study Report*, Final Report, prepared for UMTA, Technology Sharing Program, Report no. DOT-I-83-50. Washington, D.C.: U.S. Department of Transportation, August 1983.

National Environmental Policy Act of 1969, as amended (42 U.S.C. 4321-4347 *et seq.*).

National Historic Preservation Act of 1966, as amended, Section 106 (16 U.S.C. 470).

SKIDMORE, OWINGS & MERRILL, AND OTHERS, *Environmental Assessment Notebook Series*, Summary and vols. I-VI, prepared for U.S. DOT. Washington, D.C.: U.S. Government Printing Office, 1975.

Urban Mass Transportation Act of 1964, as amended, Secs. 3, 5, 14 (42 U.S.C. 1602, 1604, 1610).

URBAN MASS TRANSPORTATION ADMINISTRATION AND SOUTHERN CALIFORNIA RAPID TRANSIT DISTRICT, *Final Supplemental Environmental Impact Statement/Subsequent Environmental Impact Report (FSEIS/SEIR), Los Angeles Rail Rapid Transit Project, Metro Rail*. Los Angeles: Southern California Rapid Transit District, July, 1989.

EXERCISES

20-1 Define and relate the following terms to build a conceptual description of the environmental impact process: environment, emission, impact, perception, evaluation, and response.

20-2 What two things must be compared to be able to measure impacts? How precisely are these things known, and why? In this context, what is an impact?

20-3 Using the UMTA impact categories, describe five potentially positive and five potentially negative environmental impacts of transit systems.

20-4 Give specific examples of the following: direct and indirect impacts; internal and external impacts; magnifying and mitigating features; planning, construction, start-up, stable-operation, and long-term impacts.

20-5 List four forms of adaptation or response to transit system impacts together with specific examples of each.

20-6 What is the difference between an EIS, an EA, and an EIR? What is a categorical exclusion? What is a FONSI?

20-7 Using BART or another situation as an example, explain why selection of the "no-build" or baseline alternative is not always straightforward.

20-8 What were some of the construction impacts experienced with BART? How and to what extent can these be mitigated in future system construction?

20-9 What are the major impacts of BART under stable, full-scale operations? How might these impacts be mitigated in future systems? What impacts appear to be relatively minor?

20-10 Briefly describe the pros and cons of the environmental impact review process.

20-11 Explain some ways—both desirable and undesirable—in which a major urban rail system might affect land use. How does transit interact with other factors to create land-use impacts?

Chapter 21

THE TRANSPORTATION DISADVANTAGED

SANDRA ROSENBLOOM

Many people in society have difficulty in using public transportation for reasons that range from emotional to financial. But the largest groups of the transportation disadvantaged are those over 65 and those with a physical or mental handicap. Because the elderly and handicapped are not monolithic groups with identical travel patterns and because their travel needs are still far from clear, national, state, and local efforts to provide them with public transportation services have been less than successful and clouded with controversy. In July 1990, Congress put an end to a long-standing debate over equipping transit vehicles with wheelchair lifts: all public and private transit operators in the United States must now equip all newly purchased vehicles with lifts. It is important to note, however, that during the 20 years over which this debate raged, less than 15% of the elderly and fewer than 1% of the nonelderly handicapped ever used any of the transportation services provided or subsidized by government agencies. Clearly, the accessibility issue has obscured both the larger problem of providing transportation to the majority of the elderly and handicapped who are *not* in wheelchairs and the need for transit systems to provide many other improvements and services for handicapped and elderly travelers, from specially routed buses to travel training programs for the blind and developmentally disabled.

Public policy debates have also tended to ignore the crucial role of other social and economic policies in determining the travel needs of elderly and handicapped citizens. Providing transportation services for both the able-bodied elderly and the handicapped of all ages poses a difficult challenge not just to transit operators and transportation planners, but to land-use, housing, medical, and social planners. Communities will have to develop a number of options, including both transportation and nontransportation responses, to meet the diverse needs of the growing number of elderly and handicapped travelers.

This chapter discusses these issues in four major sections. The first examines the characteristics of the elderly and the handicapped and considers the implications of changing demographic patterns on their travel needs. The second section focuses on federal programs and policies that directly or indirectly provide transportation services to elderly and handicapped travelers. The third section examines the cost and operational characteristics of services designed for disabled or elderly citizens. The last section examines ways that society can be more responsive to the transportation needs of the growing number of elderly and disabled citizens living in suburban and rural places.

DEMOGRAPHY

The two major subsections that follow treat demographic trends among the elderly and disabled separately. The first subsection focuses on the largely ablebodied elderly, those who suffer from no major handicapping condition or disability, who could use traditional transit services with little or no system modification. The second subsection focuses on the disabled, including the elderly, whose handicaps might limit their use of traditional transit.

THE ELDERLY

In 1986 approximately 11% of the U.S. population, or over 25 million Americans, were 65 or older. The U.S. Bureau of the Census estimates that between 1985 and 2010 the elderly population will increase 77%, compared to a 32% increase for the population as a whole; the population over 75 years old is expected to more than double in the same period. Such massive changes will cause the median age of the entire society to increase by a decade, from 29.6 years in 1990 to just under 40 years by 2010.

The majority of the elderly do not have significant disabilities but even those who are not handicapped may face problems in using public transportation. For example, the poor elderly require reduced fares; others need help in determining appropriate routes and schedules. Other elderly have heightened security and safety concerns that transit operators must address. Still other older people, while able to board traditional coaches, require additional time to do so or cannot ride standing. Moreover, even the able-bodied elderly occasionally need specialized transportation services—at night or in bad weather—even if they can generally use conventional transit or drive themselves.

Can We Determine the Mobility Losses of the Elderly?

Two major questions still face society, although planners have been discussing the transportation problems of the elderly for decades. First, we have not resolved how much the elderly, who travel significantly less than younger travelers, are foregoing trip making because of their age or because they lack travel options. Second, we do not know the severity of the mobility loss caused by declining driving skills among those who continue to drive.

To begin, the data are clear; those currently elderly travel fewer miles and make fewer trips than those under 65. Figure 21-1 shows that differences are greatest among women under and over 65. Older women make almost 50% fewer trips per capita than younger women, traveling 59% fewer miles. Men over 65 make 25% fewer trips per capita than men between 36 and 65, traveling 56% fewer miles.

Unfortunately, we cannot assume that all or even a significant part of the travel differences between those under and over 65 is due to limited or expensive transportation options or declining transit or driving skills. Observed travel differences may result from diverse preferences for activities outside the home, variations in the ability to pay for the activities themselves, or predictable changes in life-style. For example, a major difference in the number of trips made by those over and under 65 is the work trip missing from the pattern of older travelers.

Another unanswered question is the implication of *declining* driving skills among those who still continue to drive for some or all of their needs. Some of the travel disparity between those over and under 65 seen in Fig. 21-1 is due to voluntary reductions in driving by the able-bodied elderly who either have some difficulties driving, although not handicapped, or cannot afford to fully maintain a car, although not poor.[1]

These patterns can be seen clearly in travel data. First, studies show that the elderly significantly reduce driving to avoid high-risk situations: peak-period traffic, nighttime, and poor weather.[2] This avoidance behavior, which begins at 60, largely explains why elderly drivers have far lower per capita accident rates than younger drivers, although they have higher per-exposure rates.[3,4,5] Unfortunately, the mobility implications of these self-limitations are not always recognized since not all trips can be moved from night or peak period to midday, nor from bad weather to good.

Second, many studies show that the elderly hold on to their licenses and cars as long as possible because they associate significantly higher independence and well-being with remaining car drivers.[6,7] (A Dutch study found that the elderly with driver's licenses *never* sold their cars regardless of age or disability.)[8] Gonda notes that "Driving may be one of the few areas in an older person's life where they can still 'call their own shots'" especially when other supports have been lost.[9]

Can We Meet the Needs of the "Modern" Elderly?

A number of drastic demographic changes have combined to make it difficult to provide transportation to the elderly suffering mobility losses for any reason. Table 21-1 shows how the distribution of the elderly in the United States has changed since 1970, not because the elderly have moved to the suburbs but because the entire U.S. population is aging in place.[10,11] In 1970 the largest number of the elderly not only lived

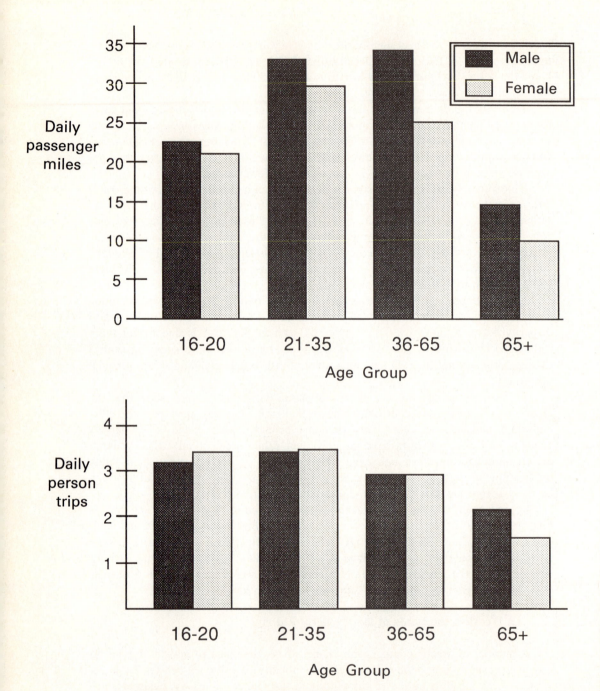

Figure 21-1   *Daily passenger-miles and daily person-trips by age and sex.*
Source: Calculated from Tables 28 and 29, U.S. Department of Transportation, 1983–1984 NPTS: Survey Data Tabulations, pp. 49, 51.

in urban areas, they lived in the central cities of those urban areas. But by 1980 the urban population balance had changed remarkably, with the largest number of elderly residing in the suburbs.

TABLE 21-1
Distribution of the Elderly by Location

	1970	1980	2000 Projections[a]
Urban	72.7%	71.4%	65.8%
Central city	60.4%	42.7%	36.4%
Suburb[b]	39.6%	57.3%	63.6%
Rural	27.3%	28.6%	34.2%

[a]Assuming 1970-1980 rate of change in residential location.
[b]In 1970, "urban fringe" = suburb; in 1980, in the urbanized area, but not in the central city = suburb.
    Source: Derived from 1970 and 1980 data in the U.S. Census of Population, General Social and Economic Characteristics, U.S. Summary. 2000 total population projections from U.S. Census, Series P-25, No. 952.

If current trends were to continue to 2000, as Table 21-1 shows, almost two-thirds of all elderly urban dwellers will live in the suburbs. Just as significantly, rural areas will be the home of a growing concentration of elderly citizens whose travel patterns will be severely circumscribed. In short, by the end of the 1990s, if present patterns persist, over 75% of the entire elderly population will be living in low-density suburban or rural places that are extremely difficult to serve with traditional transit.[12, 13]

Table 21-2 shows the other major demographic change that creates special problems for transit operators: most elderly drive and most are not transit users. Table 21-2, which reports on data from a special survey undertaken by the National Center for Health Statistics in 1977, shows that well over half of the elderly drive, with over two-thirds of the younger elderly doing so. These findings are consistent with 1983 Nationwide Personal Transportation Study (NPTS) data, which show that over 80% of the trips of the elderly are taken in a car, regardless of where they live or whether they drive.

Table 21-2 also demonstrates the other side of the coin: over half of the elderly are not transit users. Transit ridership is highest among the oldest of the elderly, not because, as planners have traditionally assumed,[14] they begin to use transit as they age. Rather the oldest citizens are traditional transit users from the past, while the younger elderly are not. Data from the 1983 NPTS show that transit ridership has been dropping among those over 65 since 1977 as more younger, nontransit users join the growing group of seniors.[15]

Table 21-2 also suggests how difficult it may be for transportation planners to respond to the needs of elderly travelers in traditional ways or by marginal changes in

TABLE 21-2
Transit and Auto Use by Elderly Travelers

Age	Drivers	Transit Use	
		Transit Users	Prevented from Using Transit by Health or Disability
60 plus	60.5%	43.4%	5.1%
60–69	71.9%	39.7%	2.4%
70–79	54.0%	45.6%	6.2%
80 plus	25.6%	54.4%	17.8%

Source: Calculated by author from unpublished data from the 1977 Special National Health Interview Survey, U.S. National Center for Health Statistics.

traditional services. Few of the elderly explain their failure to use transit in terms of their health problems or disability, issues which transit systems might address through vehicle or system modifications. Rather, the elderly do not use traditional transit because it is not responsive to their needs.[16, 17] A study for the National Research Council (NRC), recognizing that the majority of the *urban* elderly lived in suburban communities, concluded that declining transit use among the elderly was the function of major environmental and land-use barriers to both travel and transit use.

The NRC study showed that the problem was not simply lack of transit service (which could be addressed, presumably, by adding additional traditional services), but by the inherent inability of traditional services to serve the far-flung travel patterns of the largely suburban elderly. The NRC study calculated that fewer than half of all trips currently made by the elderly in a car in the United States could be made using almost perfect transit in under one-half hour (that is, assuming affordable, accessible buses routed within two blocks of all origins and destinations, with frequent headways and continuous service availability).[18] Obviously, few cities provide such services, nor could they with even major budget increases.

A 1989 study using actual data showed that, although current service coverage was often poor in suburban areas, improving traditional fixed-route services to near perfect conditions did not bring major mobility gains to most elderly. The study first matched *actual* origins and destinations in six cities to *actual* transit system schedules and routes and found that an average of 50% of the suburban elderly in the six cities simply had no conventional transit available at all. Even among the half of the elderly population who did have access to current services, a large percentage of actual trips could not be made by transit in under one hour.[19] But as the NRC findings suggest, simply improving service coverage did not improve the situation for most citizens because suburban trips were so long and varied; when the study assumed ubiquitous transit services (matched to actual origins and destinations), it found that between 30% and 60% of the suburban elderly could not make desired one-way trips in under 30 min even with almost perfect service![20] Thus, even if transit systems had the funds to dramatically increase route coverage and service schedules, they would meet only some of the needs of some of the elderly.

THE DISABLED

In 1988 the National Institute on Disability and Rehabilitation Research reported that roughly 5% of young people under 17 and 14% of those 16 to 64 had one or more conditions, illnesses, or diseases that limited them in some way in the conduct of their activities. The number of elderly with some activity limitations was much higher: roughly 40% of those over 65 had some form of limitation.[21] All studies show that disabled people make far fewer trips per capita than comparable nondisabled people, but, as with the elderly, the causes of these travel differences and the role played by inadequate transportation services are far from clear.

How Many Handicapped Travelers Are There?

Early estimates calculated that from 5 to 14% of the U.S. population, or between 7 million and 26 million Americans, had impairments that would create transportation barriers, including between 30 and 55% of the elderly.[22] None of the estimates clearly included the 6.5 million Americans with developmental disabilities (unless they also had sharply defined physical handicaps as well).[23]

These estimates were based on a combination of number-crunching and guess-work. Many early studies simply identified the extent of handicapping conditions in the population and then inferred or estimated how these conditions would affect travel behavior and needs. Unfortunately, research later found that many people with significant disabilities actually used transit or reported that they could use transit if they desired. A major Congressional Budget Office study, for example, using unpublished data from the National Center for Health Statistics, found that only 41% of the 3.7 million Americans who used a wheelchair, walker, or cane reported needing assistance to use transit.[24]

In 1977 the Urban Mass Transportation Administration (UMTA) undertook a major study, conducted by Grey Advertising, to identify the number of people with *functional* problems in using public transit. Rather than counting or cataloging physical or mental problems, the study attempted to evaluate which infirmities and conditions would actually prevent people from traveling to or getting on a transit vehicle or riding in that vehicle. The UMTA survey of transportation handicapped people concluded that roughly 5% of the U.S. population over the age of 5, or 7.4 million Americans, had a physical handicap that interfered with or prevented their use of public transit. Again, the developmentally disabled were not clearly included in that estimate.

What's the Relationship Between Disability and Transit Problems?

To this date, the best information we have on the actual relationship between disability and transit use comes from two old and controversial sources: the first is the transit disability question asked on the 1980 census (but not reasked in the 1990 census); the second is the 1977 Special Survey of the population taken with the 1977 National Health Institute Survey (NHIS).

The 1980 census. During the 1980 census, the U.S. Bureau of the Census asked a 19% sample of all noninstitutionalized Americans to answer the following three-part question:

> Do you have a physical, mental, or other health condition which has lasted for 6 or more months and which a) limits the kind or amount of work you can do at a job, b) prevents you from working at a job, or c) prevents you from using public transit? [25]

This particular question and the information it generated have been severely criticized. The Census Bureau did not want to include it at all after pretests showed that (1) two-thirds of the respondents gave totally different answers to this same question in two separate applications and (2) many clearly handicapped people did not respond appropriately to the question.[26] The question was included partially in response to pressure from advocacy groups and partially because the demand for location-specific data on the handicapped was so great.[27] Recent analyses suggest, however, that the census data are far more reliable than originally thought[28] and they coincide very well with other data sources, as shown below.

Table 21-3 shows that in 1985 about 3.5 million elderly reported a transit disability, or roughly 15% of all older Americans; about 8.5% of traditional working age (16 to 64) Americans reported a work disability, but only 1.8% or 2.6 million Americans reported a transit disability. Almost all younger people who reported a transit disability also reported a work disability. Transit disabilities were far more likely to be reported by women, the very old (over 80), those living alone, blacks, and those with low incomes.[29]

The census data also show that, although the single largest block of those with either work or transit disabilities lived in the central cities of American metropolitan areas, the overwhelming majority of both the elderly and those under 65 with disabilities lived in low-density places. While roughly one-third of the handicapped in both population groups lived in central cities, almost two-thirds of all Americans with disabilities did not. In short, the census shows us similar patterns for both the able-bodied elderly and the handicapped of all ages: they are currently concentrated in suburban and rural areas that traditional transit, whether or not accessible, is unable to effectively serve.

The Special National Health Institute Survey. In 1977 the National Center for Health Statistics undertook a special survey of the auto and transit use of Americans with and without activity limitations. The relatively small incidence of transit disability found by the census is also seen in the NHIS data; as Fig. 21-2 suggests, roughly 4% of the U.S. population over 20 reported that a physical handicap interfered with their use of public transit. Approximately 1.6% of those age 20 to 59 and 12.5% of those over 60 reported a public transit disability; this tracks remarkably well with census data.

TABLE 21-3
Disabled Living in Various Locations

	Elderly (as a % of all elderly)	Persons Aged 16-64 (as a % of total 16-64 population)		
	With transit disability	With work disability	With transit disability	With both transit and work disability
Central city	16.4%	9.0%	2.2%	2.0%
Suburb[a]	14.3%	7.0%	1.5%	1.3%
Small towns[b]	13.6%	9.6%	1.7%	1.6%
Rural	14.3%	9.6%	1.8%	1.7%
Total U.S.	14.9%	8.5%	1.8%	1.7%
Total number	3,588,536	12,320,912	2,597,631	2,393,482

[a]Suburban = urban fringe.
[b]Small towns = places of 2500–10,000 plus places 10,000+ (not urbanized).
Source: Derived from Table 106, U.S. Census, General Social and Economic Characteristics, PC80-1-CL, 1-77.

Several other trends found in the NHIS data are shown in Table 21-4. First, although the majority of both those over and under 60 did not use transit, very few people of any age reported that their disability or the requirement for assistance prevented them from doing so. No more than 2% of the entire population had problems that required transit assistance. Even those with the most severe disabilities rarely reported transit problems; less than 15% of the severely disabled elderly and just under 10% of those 20 to 59—with the most severe disability—said that their handicap or the need for assistance explained their lack of transit ridership.

Table 21-4 also suggests why physical handicaps explain so little of the failure to use transit; most disabled people drove their own cars. Clearly, auto use either overcomes more physical barriers than does transit or it is simply more responsive to the environmental and land-use barriers facing the disabled elderly and nonelderly living in suburban and rural places.

Do the Disabled Need Additional Trip Making?

Like the able-bodied elderly, the handicapped as a group make fewer trips per capita than comparable nondisabled people. But do the differences reflect a loss of mobility, and, if so, what is the magnitude of that loss? A number of methods have been used to quantify the trips lost by the handicapped who cannot use traditional transit or have trouble driving. The most straightforward method is to ask handicapped

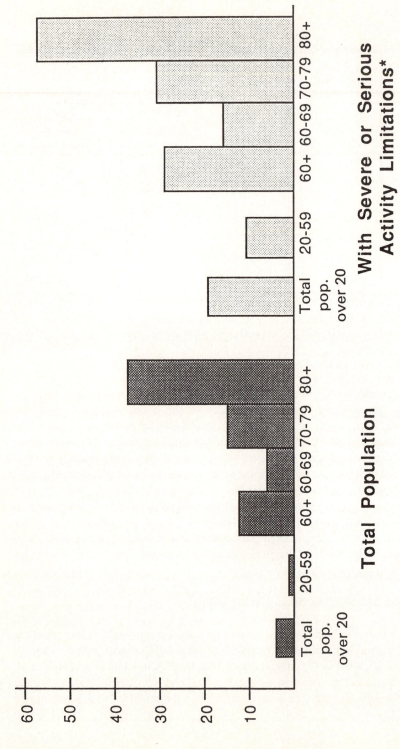

Figure 21-2 *Percentage of the population who have a transit handicap by age and activity limitation.*
* Severe or serious activity limitation is defined as those who are limited in the amount or kind of their major activity or unable to carry out their major activity. [Source: Calculated by the author from unpublished data from the tapes of 1977 Special NHIS Survey.

TABLE 21-4
Transportation Use and Activity Limitation

Transportation Use	Total Pop.	Activity Limitation					
		Unable to carry out major activity[a]		Limited in amount or kind of major activity		Limited in nonmajor activity	
	over 20	20–59	60+	20–59	60+	20–59	60+
No transit use	63.9%	56.9%	50.8%	63.5%	54.8%	61.2%	56.2%
Would need help to use	1.6%	9.6%	14.3%	2.2%	9.6%	1.1%	6.7%
Uses transit	36.1%	43.2%	49.2%	36.5%	45.2%	38.8%	43.9%
But needs help to use	8.5%	41.0%	58.0%	12.6%	36.1%	5.6%	24.4%
Drives a car	82.8%	62.3%	49.0%	77.9%	48.8%	86.5%	54.1%
But unable to use transit	1.9%	23.0%	11.1%	28.3%	10.5%	27.6%	6.0%

[a]Major activity varies with the age of the respondent.
Source: Unpublished data from the tapes of the 1977 Special Survey, NHIS.

or elderly travelers or their advocates whether they have mobility losses. But this approach has serious problems in practice, although it still has widespread popular appeal. First, advocates are far more likely to attribute transportation problems to these citizens than are the handicapped themselves—whom should we believe?[30] Second, the elderly and handicapped may be so constrained by their existing lack of transportation that they cannot conceive of an improvement in their situation; in many studies handicapped respondents reported *no unmet needs,* while others reported the desire for more travel without being able to give examples of where they wanted to go or how frequently.[31] Because of the uncertainty this approach created, it has been largely discredited as an analytical tool[32] unless used in conjunction with other more systematic approaches.

A more quantitative, but no more satisfactory, approach to understanding the magnitude of the mobility losses of the handicapped is often called *gap analysis.* This method simply measures differences in trip rates between those with and without disabilities (or those over and under 65). Nonworkers, however, make fewer trips than those in the paid labor force, and the physical or financial difficulties faced by the handicapped might lower their ability or desire to take part in out-of-home activities. These facts require analysts to separate trips voluntarily given up from those involuntarily foregone by the elderly or disabled, which, of course, is exactly the question the analysis begins with.[33]

A third approach has been to estimate *latent demand,* or the desire for additional travel created or released among the handicapped when they are actually offered accessible or affordable transportation services. This method measures the *before* and *after* travel patterns of the handicapped supplied with new transportation options. Unfortunately, using this method indicates that there is very little latent demand or lost mobility among the handicapped; very few handicapped or elderly people use alternative services. Among those who do use either accessible or special services, many are simply changing from their existing travel mode for a trip they are already making to the subsidized or special service. Several detailed analyses have failed to find evidence of new trip making, representing latent demand or previously unmet transportation needs, among those offered special services.[34, 35]

Not surprisingly, there has been controversy over the low level of latent demand found by these studies. First, since existing alternatives are very limited, they may not be a good test of what the handicapped would do if provided with reasonably high quality special transportation or accessible fixed-route services. Second, these findings do not square with more qualitative assessments of the travel problems of the handicapped. For example, a 1989 study done for the U.S. Department of Transportation conducted comprehensive interviews with six disabled travelers who did not own a car. The study found that, when special service became available, each of the travelers both mode-shifted trips from an existing option to the special service *and* made new trips. However, new trips outnumbered shifted trips by over three to one. In fact, as a group, the handicapped respondents increased their trip making over 56% because of their use of special transit services.[36]

A third complaint about latent demand analyses is that environmental or nonsystem barriers to transit use by the handicapped may explain as much of the inability or unwillingness to travel as does the lack of travel options. The use of fixed-route service may be limited by the inaccessibility of the city, its streets and buildings, whether caused by design, maintenance, or climatic problems. The use of special services may be constrained by service and scheduling restrictions. Unfortunately, this complaint requires the analyst to estimate the number of trips involuntarily given up by the handicapped because of environmental and infrastructure barriers, which is, again, the question the analyst began with.

In summary, we still do not know the extent of unmet travel demand generated by the handicapped nor how much of it could be met by unconstrained special services or fully accessible bus systems. We do not understand if the handicapped do not travel more frequently because they simply don't want to, or because available transportation options do not meet their needs, or because other environmental barriers must first be overcome.

POLICIES AND LAWS TO MEET NEEDS OF THE
ELDERLY AND HANDICAPPED

OVERVIEW OF DOT AND DHHS ROLES

Two U.S. cabinet-level departments have significant responsibility for financing or providing transportation services to the elderly and handicapped: the U.S. Department of Transportation (DOT) and the U.S. Department of Health and Human Services (DHHS). Each of these departments has constituent units that deal with various aspects of transportation service delivery; the major DOT agency charged with responsibility for elderly and handicapped services is the Urban Mass Transportation Administration (UMTA). While there are over two dozen constituent agencies within the DHHS with responsibilities for these citizens, the most notable is the Administration on Aging (AOA).

UMTA and the local transit systems it helps to fund have substantial obligations to the elderly and handicapped. Ironically, they spend far less and provide far fewer direct services to these citizens than do the constituent agencies in the DHHS. Although most congressional mandates to serve the elderly and handicapped have focused on DOT, UMTA actually has only one program designed specifically for the elderly and handicapped. Conversely, the agencies of the DHHS have a multitude of programs designed specifically to provide transportation services to various elderly and handicapped citizens in a wide variety of ways.

OBLIGATIONS OF DOT

DOT's role in serving the elderly and handicapped has developed not from programs directed at these citizens but from congressional mandates about how local transit systems receiving federal aid are to behave. UMTA has three programs that provide financial assistance to local transit operators to help meet their operating deficits and to buy capital equipment. None of these programs is focused on the needs of elderly or disabled citizens. UMTA/DOT has only one relevant program, Section 16(b)2 of the Urban Mass Transportation Act of 1964, as amended, which provides capital equipment to private nonprofit agencies serving disabled or elderly citizens. The UMTA Section 18 program is designed to provide operating and capital assistance to rural transit operators, although the ridership of rural systems is composed largely of elderly citizens. Unfortunately, Congress has not always been clear or consistent about the obligations of transit systems receiving funds from these programs; for example, some requirements apply to both elderly and handicapped citizens, while others apply only to those with handicaps.[37]

Congress has attached requirements to all these programs for years, although the earliest ones were relatively minor. In 1970 the Biaggi Amendments to the Urban Mass Transportation Act of 1964 first spoke to the need for transit systems to pay special attention to the distinctive requirements of the elderly and handicapped. The act required federally aided transit systems to make "special efforts" for the elderly and handicapped, including both involving them in planning efforts and providing special services. Six years later, in April 1976, UMTA first issued regulations specifying what transit systems were actually required to do to pursue these special efforts. Although the 1976 regulations provided only guidelines on what constituted an acceptable special service, the most widely accepted definition of compliance was that transit operators must spend on special services an amount equal to 5% of the federal funds received under the major operating assistance programs. Transit systems could also achieve compliance by equipping 50% of their bus fleet with wheelchair lifts instead of providing special services.

There was a range of local responses to the special efforts requirements.

> A wide variety of special services models were adopted at the local level. Some transit systems provided specialized demand responsive paratransit services in system owned vehicles, some gave eligible citizens coupons or pre-paid taxi rides, others contracted for paratransit services with existing social service providers or with profit making firms. The overwhelming number of systems allowed any elderly person to ride although some required the presence of a handicap.[38]

Some systems chose to put wheelchairs on buses as their preferred response; the first accessible buses in the United States were put into service in 1977 in San Diego and St. Louis in response to these regulations.[39] Some cities only provided special or accessible services after handicapped groups successfully sued them in court; many large cities, like New York, delayed initiation of either type of service for over a decade.

On May 31, 1979, UMTA put more definitive restrictions on its grant recipients. In pursuance of its obligations under Section 504 of the Rehabilitation Act of 1973, UMTA issued regulations requiring that all regular transit coaches bought after July 1979 be accessible to the handicapped, including wheelchair users. Rail system vehicle and station modifications were also required. Shortly after the regulations were issued, the American Public Transit Association (APTA), in conjunction with a number of large transit systems, filed suit to prevent the enforcement of the regulations. On May 26, 1981, a federal appeals court found that UMTA had exceeded its authority in requiring wheelchair lifts on buses.

In July 1981 UMTA issued an "interim final rule," which summarized what transit systems were compelled to do under both the special efforts and the 504 requirements. That rule permitted communities to select their own response to the needs of the handicapped, allowing so-called "local option." It did require, however, that communities spend a maximum of 3.5% of their federal operating assistance on their services for the handicapped. In 1982, in response to an ongoing debate between the transit community and advocacy groups about what constituted acceptable local service, Congress amended the Surface Transportation Assistance Act to specifically require that UMTA develop minimum service criteria for local transit systems to follow when choosing among the options available to meet the needs of the handicapped.

Because of the controversy over both the costs and the effectiveness of the available options, UMTA spent over 5 years developing a final rule that specified specific service criteria that met both the 504 and special efforts mandates. The 1986 "final rule" required that transit operators must spend 3% of their total operating budget in providing either fixed-route accessible buses or demand-responsive service comparable to traditional bus services. There was an escape clause in the final rule, however. If the transit agency could not meet all these service requirements by spending 3% of its total operating budget and was not willing to exceed that maximum cap, the system could negotiate with the disabled community for a reduction in one or more service criteria.

This issue returned to the federal courts in May 1986 when an advocacy group filed suit against DOT. A district court upheld the local option element, ruling that local communities could chose between fixed-route accessible and special transit systems. The court also ruled, however, that the 3% cost cap was arbitrary and capricious. Both UMTA and the advocacy groups were unhappy with this ruling and appealed it. In February 1989 a federal appeals court upheld the district court's ruling overturning the 3% spending cap. To the dismay of the transit industry, however, the appeals court went further, saying that Congress had indeed intended for transit systems to provide *both* special services *and* accessible fixed-route transit.

In July 1990, Congress made clear its agreement with the court's opinion of its intention; it overwhelmingly passed the Americans with Disabilities Act (ADA). That act requires all transportation providers, both public and private, to equip all new vehicles with wheelchair lifts *and* to provide special services for those unable to use accessible fixed-route services. There is an escape clause, however, that will probably be the focus of further litigation: transit systems are allowed to reduce special services, but not accessible traditional transit, if they can prove "undue financial burden."

Transit operators are understandably unhappy with the requirements of the ADA. It is likely that they will try to prove that these requirements cause undue financial burden, allowing them to reduce their special service offerings. So, while all transit systems will be partially or fully accessible in the near future, the majority of handicapped people will face severely restricted travel options as transit systems cut back on special services.

SOCIAL SERVICE PROGRAMS

Between 1960 and 1980 the number of federal (and state) programs providing transportation services for a wide group of transportation handicapped clients grew exponentially. The majority of the federal programs were housed in the U.S. Department of Health and Human Services (DHHS), although there were relevant programs in the Departments of Agriculture, Labor, Education, and Housing and Urban Development, as well as the Veterans Administration. In 1977 the U.S. General Accounting Office estimated that 114 separate federal programs expended money on transportation services for the disadvantaged and elderly, over half of which were located in the DHHS. The impact of so many funding programs was staggering: a study by the Administration on Aging (AOA) found that the number of transportation systems that it sponsored grew from 1000 to 3200 between 1974 and 1980, or over 300%![40] A 1989 study identified 31 major programs in the DHHS alone (each with subcomponent programs) that funded transportation services at the local level.

Because program structures at the state and local level are so complex, it is not possible to determine how much money is actually being spent for transportation services for the elderly or handicapped through these agencies and programs![41] In 1985 a DHHS administrator estimated that the department spent $800 million on transportation services alone,[42] or roughly eight times the combined 1989–1990 expenditures of DOT's 16(b)2 and Section 18 programs. This figure, however, is probably low since a 1980 study for the AOA concluded that between $500 and $800 million was spent for transportation services for the elderly under Title III of the Older Americans Act alone.[43]

This tangle of providers created both financial and service problems. Most services had very narrow target groups, so it was difficult for people to know what services they were eligible for, and redundancy and inefficiency grew remarkably. Individual services rarely coordinated any aspect of their service delivery with one another, and they had little interaction with public transit systems. As a joint report of the U.S. Departments of Transportation and Health and Human Services noted:

> Transportation services to social service recipients were rather haphazard. Persons transported to an appointment could be dropped off, but not picked up. "Breakdown maintenance" was the rule as transit vehicles were run until they could run no more. Some client groups were left unserved, while others had more service than they needed. "Turf" battles among providers and eligibility disputes were common, and funding was uncertain. It was only a matter of time before Congress would be challenged to bring order out of what had been chaos.[44]

COORDINATION OF FEDERAL EFFORTS

The lack of coordination and the overlap and duplication seen in many of the social service systems continued to proliferate with the creation of new federal programs. There were limited federal efforts to increase coordination in the spending of these funds at the local level; for example, the 1978 Amendments to the Older Americans Act mandated that all services delivered to the elderly, including transportation, be provided in a coordinated and comprehensive manner, although there were no guidelines and no sanctions. Moreover, the AOA amendments spoke only to programs funded through the act and not to coordination with local transit systems or other social agencies.

In 1986, the secretaries of the U.S. Departments of Transportation and Health and Human Services signed an Interagency Agreement for the Coordination of Transportation Services funded through the two departments. The agreement established an interagency working group, the DOT/DHHS Transportation Coordinating Council, whose charge was to develop a way to meet the stated goal of the departments to coordinate related programs at the federal level wherever possible and to promote maximum feasible coordination at the state and local levels.

The two departments were interested in a range of potential activities. Coordination could include one agency buying or selling transportation services to another; agencies purchasing services from existing community providers, both profit and nonprofit, rather than operating individual systems; agencies sharing one or more service functions, from dispatching to bulk purchase of supplies to joint vehicle maintenance; and agencies sharing the use of vehicles when their periods of demand were different.

The interagency council found little evidence of actual prohibitions against coordination at the local level (with the exception of UMTA 16(b)2 vehicles, which were not to go to public agencies). The council, however, did find problems created by federal regulations. A major coordination problem reported by states to the council was the complexity of the governmental laws, regulations, and administrative demands accompanying the three-dozen programs in DHHS and DOT. Their overlapping requirements created uncertainty, ambiguity, and fear of retroactive denial of funding, all of which worked against coordination at the local level.[45]

A 1987 study of coordination obstacles in nine major DHHS programs concluded that there were no active barriers to coordination in federal programs, but some fairly significant passive barriers or disincentives to coordination. The study concluded that most federal programs contained active incentives for recipients to buy vehicles and maintain individual, separate services, even where other social service or private systems were available to provide some or all the transportation required by their clients.

The 1987 study of DHHS programs also found that a major barrier to coordination was the failure of local recipients to understand their own cost patterns. Most DHHS agencies (and their state and regional counterparts) do not require local agencies to actually calculate their expenses in providing client transportation. Without such cost data, recipients are unlikely to recognize the financial advantages of coordination or have any basis on which to compare alternative options. For example, of ten states surveyed, only two required local agencies receiving Title III aging program funds to calculate their costs in providing transportation services, and only half required agencies to calculate the cost involved in providing Medicaid transportation. The study concluded that

> It is imperative that federal and state level DHHS agencies compel local recipients to actively consider the cost-effectiveness of their current mode of provision, whether contract or not. Mandatory contracting requirements are inadequate because so much competitive contracting in the social service network is artificial; the process is set up to ensure that other social service agencies, or subsidiaries of the primary agency, receive the contract award .... Requiring these agencies to publicly display the real costs of maintaining their turf, and allowing other providers to publicly compare their service costs, could have profound impacts [on coordination].[46]

A MAJOR ROLE FOR THE STATE

Overall both the 1987 study of DHHS programs and the interagency council concluded that an active state role, rather than federal action, was required to increase coordination. A 1989 study for the interagency council reported that

> In many cases, the role of State and local government is the key to coordination success . . . . In fact, research confirms that the role of States is so important that barriers to coordination can virtually crumble if there is a commitment at the State level.[47]

Most coordination success stories do come from states with mandatory coordination requirements. For example, Florida, Iowa, Maine, and North Carolina have programs requiring local recipients to use their transportation funds effectively. Although the programs differ from state to state, in general each state has established one regional coordinator or provider in each substate region. All agencies receiving most types of state or federal funds must either (1) purchase their transportation services through the designated provider or coordinator, (2) pay a rate set by the designated provider or coordinator, or (3) justify their need for additional vehicles. The designated regional agency may itself be a provider, or it may contract with other community providers to provide service to the local agencies mandated to purchase transportation from it, acting like a transportation broker. Or the designated agency may both provide service in its own vehicle fleet and contract with community private for- and not-for-profit providers.

In states with mandatory coordination, in order to provide service directly or to be allowed to receive additional vehicles, a local agency must convince the designated regional agency to certify that no current provider is able or willing to provide the transportation services for which the vehicles are sought. Iowa, for example, has been divided into 16 planning regions, each with one administrative agency that functions as the regional transportation coordinator. Every public or private operator must be certified by its regional coordinator before it can receive any state or federal funds, whether from DOT or the DHHS. Before any agency is given funds to directly provide its own services it must prove that its transportation costs would be lower than those experienced by currently certified regional operators.

There are, of course, coordination success stories that do not involve mandatory state action. In Pittsburgh, for example, over three dozen social service agencies buy transportation services for their clients from the special service provider established by the transit authority. In Portland (Oregon), Lancaster (Pennsylvania), San Francisco, Sacramento, and Seattle, many local social service agencies contract for either individual or group services for their clients from their local transit operator or other social providers.

In spite of these limited coordination successes, a maze of DHHS and DOT programs still fund local transportation efforts. These efforts vary considerably in the kind and quality of services provided, in the clients and trip purposes eligible for service, in system cost and productivity patterns, and in the extent to which the transportation disadvantaged are offered meaningful *choices* that respond to their lifestyles and needs. The way in which transportation efforts vary from locality to locality and from one subgroup of the handicapped to another are discussed in the following section.

PROGRAMS AND SERVICES FOR THE
ELDERLY AND HANDICAPPED TRAVELER

As the following studies show, special services and accessible transit respond to different user groups, even if unintentionally. The lift features on fixed-route transit vehicles rarely help ambulatory disabled or elderly travelers, and few special service riders are in wheelchairs. Moreover, whoever the target market, few accessible or special services are actually used by many elderly or handicapped travelers.

ACCESSIBLE FIXED-ROUTE TRANSIT

In 1989 the American Public Transit Association (APTA) reported that 56% of the nation's transit systems met their mandated obligations to the elderly and handicapped with some form of accessible fixed-route service, with about one-third of those (or 18% of all systems) providing only accessible fixed-route services. Although service costs for early lift-equipped vehicles were very high and ridership was generally very low, the current picture is slightly different in some cities.

A 1989 survey undertaken by the Metropolitan Transit Authority (MTA) of Harris County found that, even though wheelchair boardings were still relatively low, they were substantially higher than in the previous decade. In a few cities the costs per boarding, although still high, were close to or less than the costs of specialized transit services. The cities responding to the Houston study had an average of 3108 boardings per month, with Seattle, Denver, and Los Angeles showing over 7000 boardings per month. Not surprisingly these three cities experienced costs under $15 per trip. Other cities, such as Philadelphia and St. Louis, however, reported costs in excess of $700 for each trip by a rider in a wheelchair.

In spite of the very real improvements in costs and ridership experiences, accessible fixed-route transit is obviously still very expensive per rider. The Houston MTA survey found that the additional capital costs of purchasing buses with lifts ranged from $8000 to $15,000 per bus, with the average for 10 large cities being $12,900. Although many systems do not keep maintenance records detailed enough to separate out charges attributable only to lift service, 7 cities reported that they spent just over $1400 per lift per year, on average, for maintenance. Seattle had the lowest costs, $585 per lift, and San Diego experienced the highest annual maintenance cost per lift, $2778.

The MTA estimated that purchasing lift-equipped buses would increase its budget by $2.2 million annually, representing a 36% increase in expenditures on services for the elderly and handicapped. The MTA found that it would need 715 wheelchair boardings per day to equal the amount of paratransit or specialized service the authority could provide to elderly and handicapped people for the same amount of money. To achieve that level of wheelchair use, Houston would have to experience ridership 2 to 3 times higher than the most successful cities in its survey.[48]

Two 1989–1990 studies found similar patterns; the cities surveyed represent roughly 40% of all mid- and large-size American cities. Although all of the cities responding had special transit services, only one-half of the mid-size and one-third of the large cities surveyed had accessible fixed-route service. Table 21-5, presenting findings from these studies, shows that (1) many cities did not have accessible services and (2) those cities with accessible vehicles had very limited services.

TABLE 21-5
Availability and Use of Accessible Transit in the United States

	Nineteen Mid-Size Cities[a] (200,000–700,000 population)			Nine Large Cities[b] (1.2–3.0 million population)		
	Average	Highest	Lowest	Average	Highest	Lowest
Percentage of cities without any accessible service	52.6%	—	—	33.3%	—	—
Of those with any accessible service:						
% of vehicle fleet accessible	49.3%	100%[c]	15.7%	26.1%	70.3%[d]	14.8%
% of routes accessible	79.9%	100%	23.7%	31.5%	75.0%	26.5%
Monthly ridership (boardings)	522	3300[e]	2	n.a.	n.a.	n.a.

[a]Albuquerque, Allentown, Austin, Bakersfield, Baton Rouge, Charlotte, Fresno, Grand Rapids, Greensboro, Harrisburg, Jacksonville, Knoxville, Las Vegas, Little Rock, New Haven, Orlando, Raleigh, Syracuse, Toledo, Tucson, Tulsa, and Youngstown. Albuquerque, Charlotte, and New Haven did not provide sufficient information to be included in most of the analyses reported on; they do not appear in the percentage totals.
[b]Dallas, Ft. Lauderdale, Houston, Miami, Milwaukee, Oklahoma City, Pittsburgh, San Diego, and Seattle.
[c]Raleigh and Austin.
[d]Seattle.
[e]Bakersfield.
    Source: S. Rosenbloom, "Elderly and Handicapped Transit and Paratransit Services Across the U.S.: The Experience of Mid-Sized Cities," CRP Working Paper No. 022, Austin, Texas, 1990, and CRA Inc. and S. Rosenbloom, "National Survey of Paratransit Service Quality, Options, and Resources."

As Table 21-5 illustrates, only ten mid-size (or 52.6% of the sample) and three large cities (or 33.3% of the sample) had any level of accessible bus service, although five of the cities were in states that had mandated wheelchair-accessible bus purchases continuously for over 10 years. Table 21-5 also shows how low ridership was in all mid-size cities except Bakersfield (with 3300 boardings per month). Seattle was the only large city in this sample to have appreciable ridership (over 7000 boardings per month).

The cause of poor ridership is far from clear but probably represents a combination of system and nonsystem factors. Most of the transit operators in the sample did not offer much accessible service nor provide marketing or training programs aimed at handicapped travelers. The reliability of service delivery, which can drastically affect ridership, is open to question, given earlier study findings and the complaints of advocates. A host of environmental factors also could have affected ridership, from ice and snow in northern climates to inaccessible streets, stops, and buildings in all climates. Last, advocates argue that many systems undercount actual and attempted boardings by a factor of 2 or 3 to 1.

Another factor in the low utilization of accessible services in many cities may have been the inherent limitations of traditional transit services—accessible or not—in serving the increasingly suburbanized handicapped traveler. Few of the mid-size cities had more than a dozen routes in their network, suggesting that in low-density areas transit systems fail to offer much service to any patrons. Las Vegas, for example, serving almost 8000 mi^2 (22,000 km^2), had only 11 routes; on the other hand, Syracuse, a city with higher than average wheelchair boardings, had 91 routes in a 600-mi^2 service area.

SPECIAL TRANSIT SERVICES

In 1989 APTA reported that the majority of transit systems with accessible fixed-route services supplemented those efforts with specialized paratransit services; roughly 44% of all cities met their mandated responsibilities to the handicapped with special services alone. APTA also calculated that more than 70 million trips were provided by special transit services in 1987.

Two national studies undertaken separately by Tucson and Tulsa in 1989–1990 show that most special systems reach few of the people eligible for services and those people make few trips, suggesting that severe service limitations and restrictions partially explain the limited utilization by those in need.

Usage Patterns and Target Group Penetration

Accessible fixed-route services and special services are targeting two different groups; the data show that the overwhelming majority of special system riders do not require level-changing devices, although they may need special features such as wider doors and aisles and lower entry steps or floors. On average, almost 60% of special system users in the 28 cities studied by Tucson and Tulsa were elderly; well over two-thirds of users were ambulatory, even in systems that required a handicap among the elderly for service eligibility. In over one-third of the cities, over 90% of users were ambulatory.

Table 21-6 shows that registrants in most cities constituted only a small percentage of those eligible for service. Moreover, these cities provided relatively few rides per eligible or registered population. Registration figures were fairly low; on average, mid-size cities had a little over 3000 registrants or roughly 18% of those eligible for service (with the largest number of systems registering under 10%). Large cities, which tended to have far more restrictive eligibility criteria, registered about one in five eligible citizens. Strikingly, these registration numbers are probably overstated, even though low, because registration counts tend to be cumulative; few cities actively try to remove the names of nonusers or those who die or move. Pittsburgh reported 91,000 registrants, which is every person who registered since service inception in 1977!

TABLE 21-6
Penetration and Usage of Special Systems

	Nineteen Mid-Size Cities[a] (200,000–700,000 population)		Nine Large Cities[b] (1.2–3.0 million population)	
	Average	Most common answer	Average	Most common answer
Registrants as a % of eligible population[c]	17.5%	Under 10%	21.9%	Under 20%
Annual one-way trips per registrant	43.8%	20–30	34.9%	20–30
Active[d] users as a % of eligible population	3.1%	Under 2%	15.8%	Under 10%
Active[d] users as a % of registrants	27.6%	Under 20%	10.0%	Under 2%
Annual one-way trips per active user	204.5	Under 200	293	Under 200
Annual one-way trips per capita (total population)	4.7	Under 3.0	.38	Under 3.1

[a] See Table 21-5.
[b] See Table 21-5.
[c] These figures were calculated based on each city's own eligibility criterion.
[d] Using each city's definition of "active" which could be as little as once per year.
   Source: S. Rosenbloom, "Elderly and Handicapped Transit and Paratransit Services Across the U.S.: The Experience of Mid-Sized Cities," CRP Working Paper No. 022, Austin, Texas, 1990, and CRA Inc. and S. Rosenbloom, "National Survey of Paratransit Service Quality, Options, and Resources."

Given the low registration figures, it is not surprising that these cities provided relatively few trips per registrant or eligible citizen. On average, mid-size cities provided fewer than 3 round trips per year to everyone eligible for service or 20 round trips per registrant.

Table 21-6 shows that most cities did not have many active riders, even using a remarkably lenient definition of "active." (Most cities classified people as active riders if they traveled once a month or more; three systems classified active riders as those that rode once a year.) In general, most mid-size cities had less than 1000 active users, representing, on average, slightly more than one-quarter of those registered for service.

More important, these active users generally represented only 3% (or less) of the total eligible population in the mid-size cities.

Almost all the large cities in the sample had less than 4000 active users, representing, on average, less than 10% of those registered for service (with the largest number of cities reporting that less than 2% of their registrants actively used services). Active users represented a higher percentage of those eligible for service in the larger cities—just under 16% on average—because larger cities had much stricter eligibility criteria. Overall, even active riders were not very active, making, on average, less than two round trips per week.

These findings square with unpublished data from the 1984 National Health Interview Survey, which found that only 19.2% of the seriously or severely handicapped elderly and only 4.6% of comparable younger adults had ever used special transportation services of any type. Moreover, a number of ridership studies in 1980 found that citizens who actually rode special services rarely made more than 40% of all their trips on these systems, with the average closer to 12%.

Service Levels and Ridership

Table 21-7 displays some of the key parameters of service that undoubtedly affect rider response, focusing on the specific restrictions that individual systems impose on users. First, not all the systems allow *all* the elderly to receive service. As the table shows, a little over one-half of the mid-size cities and two-thirds of the large cities require the elderly to have a physical or mental handicap that interferes with their ability to use fixed-route transit. (Seattle also requires low income; San Diego also requires the lack of an auto.) Note that being poor or sporadically disabled or even lacking a car—without a serious physical disability—does not meet minimum eligibility criteria in any of the sampled cities. Although disability requirements tend to be liberally interpreted in many communities, such systems technically offer no options to the elderly or disabled person who cannot use a bus in bad weather, but can otherwise, or who is afraid to travel at night, but not otherwise, or who wishes a respite (financial or emotional) from driving a car. Most systems also provide no option for those who could physically use transit but who live in areas without transit service.

Second, all the sample cities tend to restrict the days and times in which service is available. Over one-third of the mid-size cities and one-fifth of the large cities do not provide Sunday service; most provide only limited Saturday service. The mid-size cities have particularly restrictive weekday service, many providing only normal business-hour service: 7 or 8 a.m. to 5 or 6 p.m. (the study average is raised considerably by Raleigh, which uses taxi operators available 24 hours per day). Third, most cities provide only curb-to-curb service, although even ambulatory people may need assistance to and from the door.

Last, most systems require an advance reservation of at least 24 hours; five mid-size systems volunteered that, in reality, the formal requirement was not sufficient time to actually receive a trip. The city of Tucson requires a 3-day (72-hour) advance reservation.

TABLE 21-7
Special Service Restrictions and Parameters

	Nineteen Mid-Size Cities[a] (200,000–700,000)	Nine Large Cities[b] (1.2–3.0 million)
Eligible for special services		
All elderly plus all disabled[c]	47.3%	33.3%
Disabled only (all ages)	52.7%	44.5%
Disabled only plus other restrictions	—	22.2%
Impose trip or user restrictions or priorities	26.3%	22.2%
Type of service		
Curb-to-curb	52.6%	33.3%
Door-to-door	31.6%	66.7%
Both, varying with user	15.8%	0%
Service availability		
Weekday hours (average)	13.5 hours	18.0 hours
Saturday hours[d]	11.7 hours	19.6 hours
Sunday hours[d]	11.4 hours	19.0 hours
Weekday service only	5.3%	11.1%
No Sunday service	36.8%	22.2%

[a]See Table 21-5.
[b]See Table 21-5.
[c]One mid-size and two large cities define elderly as 70 and over; one large city, as 60 and over.
[d]Of those with service on that day.

Overall these systems impose a number of difficult restrictions on potential riders. The lack of evening and, in some cases, weekend service creates a serious constraint on a variety of social, recreational, and personal business trips. Such schedules also provide no option to the many elderly or disabled drivers who are unable to drive after dark or in poor weather. The limited hours of service, advance reservation requirements, and constrained service availability combine to reduce the usefulness of these systems to most people eligible for and genuinely in need of transportation assistance.

Methods of Service Delivery

Transit systems have chosen a variety of ways to provide special services. While a majority of very small systems directly deliver services themselves,[49] most cities over

200,000 contract with community providers for some or all the services they provide.

Cities that contract generally purchase *dedicated services*; the contractor's drivers and vehicles are fully committed to special transit use during specified periods of the day and week. During the time purchased, the contractor may not serve additional clients or mix public riders with special service users. The system commonly pays the operator by the vehicle-hour, but can also pay by the vehicle-mile (or some combination of mile and hour charges) or by the one-way passenger trip.

A small number of systems have a *user-side subsidy* program, where the user rather than the provider receives the subsidy. Users are given a voucher or coupon with which they pay the participating provider of their choice, most commonly local taxi operators. User-side subsidy programs rarely involve dedicated services; taxi operators serve private clients at times when special service users do not request rides. This permits private operators to utilize their equipment more fully, generally increasing productivity and lowering costs.

The Tucson and Tulsa studies found that three-fourths of the mid-size city respondents contract for some or all special services, while the rest provide all special services themselves. One mid-size city, Raleigh, has a user-side subsidy program with local taxi companies. The majority of those contracting for service do so with private providers, although two mid-size cities contract with other governmental agencies. All of the large cities contract for some or all special services, with three also having user-side subsidy programs (Dallas, San Diego, and Seattle).

Almost two-thirds of the systems contracting for service leased their own vehicles to the contractor to lower costs. Many systems contracting for service delivery retained other aspects of service, generally in an attempt to increase efficiency. For example, most systems certified client eligibility themselves, while about one-third of the cities, in an attempt to redress low productivity, took an active role in scheduling or dispatching contractor vehicles (leased or not).

Low productivity is a common feature of special services. Several studies, including an analysis of a large number of Canadian services, indicate that productivity on special transportation systems (the number of passenger trips carried in an hour or per mile) is very low.[50] The cities surveyed in 1989–1990 show similar patterns when their productivity is computed. The mid-size cities carried between a third of a passenger-trip per vehicle-hour to a high of almost five passenger-trips per hour. The average was less than 1.4 trips per vehicle-hour. Although the large-city average was higher (almost 2.4 trips per hour), it was brought up by just one city. Actually, over half of the large cities carried less than 1.5 passenger-trips per hour. To put this in perspective, only three of the mid-size and two of the large systems achieved productivity equal to or in excess of what an ordinary taxi operator routinely achieves.

Cost Patterns

In 1989, APTA reported that the average cost of a one-way special transit trip was $9.70; a 1986 study reported that the average cost per one-way trip for all Canadian special transit services was $10.05.[51] The U.S. cities sampled in the two 1989–1990

TABLE 21-8
Unit Cost Patterns for Special Services

	Nineteen Mid-Size Cities[a] (200,000–700,000 population)		Nine Large Cities[b] (1.2–3.0 million population)	
	Average	Most common answer	Average	Most common answer
Reported costs				
Per one-way passenger-trip	$8.63	$6–$10	$7.25	$4–$7
Per vehicle-hour	$11.50	$9–$14	n.a.	n.a.
Reconstructed costs[c]				
Per one-way passenger-trip	$10.95	$8–$11	$7.75	$7–$9
Per vehicle-hour	$14.57	$8–$10	n.a.	n.a.

[a] Mid-size city costs were reconstructed using the method described in S. Rosenbloom, "Elderly and Handicapped Transit and Paratransit Services Across the U.S.: The Experience of Mid-Sized Cities," CRP Working paper No. 022, Austin, Texas, 1990.

[b] The cost data for the nine large cities were obtained from CRA Inc. and S. Rosenbloom, "National Survey of Paratransit Service Quality, Options, and Resources."

[c] Not all system reported data could be reconstructed; these are the most common responses for the smaller number of respondents.

studies showed similar averages, with wide variations in individual responses. Table 21-8 presents the limited cost data received from respondents on their special services (over 40% of systems did not know all their costs). The costs obtained directly from the systems are shown as "reported costs." The reported costs per one-way passenger trip for mid-size cities ranged from a just over $3 to a little over $15; the average reported cost was $8.63, with almost half of the respondents falling between $4 and $7 a one-way trip. Reported costs among the large cities ranged from a low of $4.89 to a high of $11.47, with an average of $7.25 per one-way trip.

Since many special transit systems do not report or compute all their costs, Table 21-8 also shows *reconstructed* costs calculated by adding an estimate of "missing" expenses to reported costs. It shows that in mid-size cities reconstructed charges are roughly 27% higher than reported costs. The average cost per one-way trip in the mid-size city jumped to almost $11.00. Since big cities were more likely to report a greater percentage of their actual expenses, reported per-trip costs only increased 7% to $7.75.

Unfortunately, the system-wide cost averages obscure major differences in the cost patterns of different providers, particularly within the larger cities. Many of the larger and several mid-size cities had multiple providers; those providing service to ambulatory clients and taxi operators tended to incur costs far below the average. Operators providing services to those in wheelchairs or those requiring significant driver assistance incurred costs far above the average.

SUMMARY

The elderly and handicapped are a significant and growing segment of the U.S. population, but one with a variety of transportation needs and preferences. Although only a small percentage of both groups currently reports serious mobility problems, the growth of the very old and the increasing numbers of active younger handicapped citizens will create severe mobility problems that transportation planners and transit systems must address. The response must match the actual travel needs and preferences of the elderly and handicapped—in all their diversity. The suburban and rural location of over two-thirds of this population and the overwhelming number of elderly and even handicapped travelers who are licensed drivers suggest that transportation planners will have to respond in the future in new and different ways.

There are a variety of reasons why services are largely unresponsive to the needs of the vast majority of these citizens. The low level of utilization of fixed-route and special systems may result from (1) the constrained way in which alternatives are currently provided, (2) the availability of superior travel options (like the private car), and/or (3) personal preferences and the desire to maintain independence and choice.

Both DOT and the DHHS, and the state and local agencies they fund, have failed to develop coherent or particularly useful responses to the transportation needs of elderly and handicapped travelers. Both agencies are hampered, of course, by lack of funding and the enormity of the problem, but other factors contribute significantly. DOT has been unable to respond successfully because it operates without clear information on the real mobility needs of the transportation handicapped and, as such, has focused on only the role of traditional transit service in serving the needs of these citizens. Without DOT leadership, it is unlikely that local transit systems will actively consider changes in traditional services or more appropriate ways to meet the needs of modern elderly or handicapped citizens. DOT has also been hampered by legislative vagaries. The Americans with Disabilities Act (ADA) will now require transportation operators to provide fully accessible transit—in the limited areas where they provide transit services at all—but this will undoubtedly be accompanied by declining special services for the majority of elderly and handicapped unable to use accessible transit. DOT is also handicapped by the failure of other social, medical, urban planning, and housing actors to take any responsibility for their part in creating transportation difficulties for their clients.

The many funding programs of the DHHS support a maze of individual transport systems instead of supporting the clients needing transportation. Although current federal policies call for the coordination of these resources, these efforts tend to have a narrow focus and limited success for several reasons. First, Congress itself has questioned whether the DHHS and the AOA are making serious efforts to coordinate local transportation services; second, the elderly and subgroups of the handicapped have their own advocates who argue for separate programs at the federal and local level. Few of the human or social agencies whose nontransportation services are funded by the DHHS (or other federal, state, and local programs) accept the need to consider alternatives to current service delivery methods, which increase the need for the elderly and handicapped to travel long distances.

In short, the overwhelming number of elderly and handicapped travelers have few meaningful options if or when they cannot drive, find rides, pay full-fare taxis, or use available transit.

CONCLUSIONS AND POLICY IMPLICATIONS

We must develop a repertoire of transportation and nontransportation alternatives that provide mobility for elderly and disabled individuals in ways that they find acceptable and will use. Among the following suggestions, the first five must involve a range of actors and agencies; the last set of suggestions must be the responsibility of local transit operators.

First, since transportation needs are so linked to land-use patterns, we must involve land-use policy makers in the process of making the city more accessible to all travelers. (See also Chap. 25.) As suburbs become the home of increasing concentrations of disabled and elderly citizens, we have to rethink traditional zoning codes that limit nonresidential uses. These limitations force the elderly and handicapped to travel beyond walking distances to needed services and decrease their mobility as their driving skills decrease. We also have to encourage land-use planners to make suburban areas more responsive to the elderly or disabled pedestrian. Pedestrian improvements will facilitate some additional use of accessible fixed-route transit, slightly reduce the demand for motorized transportation (especially if undertaken with meaningful land-use changes), and meet some of the recreational and exercise needs of all citizens.

Second, since transportation needs are clearly linked to where and how human and social services are made available, social agency planners must recognize the changing demographics of the elderly and handicapped population and locate and program their services accordingly. Social and human service agencies must think carefully about the actual location of their facilities; social planners should not locate inaccessible facilities and then demand that transportation planners deal with the resulting loss of mobility. Moreover, social planners must rethink the ways in which their services are provided. Given the serious transportation problems facing the elderly and handicapped, providers may have to bring the services to the client rather than requiring the client to travel to them. Agencies may have to offer service vouchers or reimbursement allowing clients to use services near their home, rather than having to travel to prescribed and limited locations.

Third, communities must develop a range of transportation options that may not directly involve transit operators. Since so many elderly and handicapped people drive or rely on others to drive them, government and private agencies must develop new programs and strengthen existing programs that keep competent drivers in their cars as long as possible. Communities must offer driver training and retraining courses on a much larger scale, develop—and help finance if necessary—more sophisticated physical modifications to passenger cars or vans to facilitate driving by a wider range of disabled citizens, and offer financial support or incentives to competent drivers with low incomes who require assistance in maintaining or insuring a car.

Allied to programs that enable elderly or handicapped people to begin or continue driving, the government must strengthen ridesharing networks. Many elderly are given rides by other drivers, so paid and unpaid carpooling should be strengthened. In rural areas, programs that develop reasonable ways to pay drivers to carry elderly and handicapped people may have more impact than the limited Section 18 rural transit program.

Fourth, we must develop stronger state-level mandatory coordination requirements for agencies receiving federal or state transportation grants to ensure that the limited funds available for transportation for the elderly and handicapped are spent in the most cost-effective ways. These requirements should, at a minimum, refuse vehicles or operating expenses to individual agencies unless they can prove that existing community operators cannot provide cheaper transportation service to their clients. A more comprehensive coordination strategy would set up regional brokers or coordinators to address the excess capacity of existing systems while preventing the formation of new ones.

Fifth, communities should try to involve existing providers in the delivery of services to elderly and handicapped travelers. For example, communities could work with local private operators to develop reduced-fare traditional taxi programs, since many citizens require the service characteristics of the car but cannot pay full taxi or lift-equipped service fees. Analysts have argued that simply by "block-purchasing" trips a community could reduce taxi fares by at least 20% without any appreciable public subsidy. The community could offer subsidized taxi vouchers to those still unable to afford reduced-fare regular taxis. In the spirit of the mandatory coordination requirements previously suggested, communities could pay for those subsidies by combining transit funds with DHHS and other agency funds. Such user-side subsidy programs should be the responsibility not just of transit operators, who could pay only a small part of the total costs, but of all the agencies in a community receiving funds to meet the travel needs of the elderly and handicapped.

Finally, there is a set of options for which transit systems must accept major responsibility. First, transit systems must make good faith efforts to provide reliable accessible services. The paradox of accessible services is that, although few people use it even when fleets are fully accessible, existing investments will not be used to their full if limited potential until the fleet is substantially lift equipped. Several major cities have achieved thousands of monthly boardings by providing reliable service, by carefully deploying accessible buses to routes of heaviest demand by the handicapped, and by developing marketing and training programs.

Second, transit systems must identify and implement more marginal changes that will facilitate ridership by the elderly and handicapped. The debate over wheelchair lifts has obscured the other travel and service needs of the transportation disadvantaged. The internal configuration of buses and rapid transit vehicles is very important to many travelers: the width of the aisles, the placement of fare collection equipment and poles and straps, the texture of flooring, and so on. Many citizens need different or additional scheduling information such as maps and signs in braille and audible bus stops. Safety and security is very important to many vulnerable travelers; systems may have to inaugurate additional patrols or on-vehicle protection. These changes may not appreciably increase ridership, but they will make transit use easier and less traumatic for elderly and handicapped clients.

Third, transit operators must also recognize the changing demographics of the population. They must reorient and reroute their traditional transit services in and near concentrations of elderly and disabled travelers. Several European countries have pioneered a concept that might have widespread use here. In Sweden and England, *service routes*, offering traditional transit services specifically designed to access the origins and destinations of the elderly, have been enormously successful. The Swedish service routes have been so successful that many communities experienced a 50% drop in special service ridership and are so cost effective that many cities have foregone the federal subsidy currently available only for special services for the elderly and handicapped.

Last, transit systems must continue to offer special services, but only to those who are so handicapped that they cannot use accessible buses, low-fare or subsidized taxis, service routes, or ridesharing options. Even with these limitations, transit operators must be given additional financial assistance to expand and improve these special systems so they can offer reasonable transportation alternatives without the severe operational, scheduling, and trip constraints that special services impose.

Our society can only hope to meet the mobility needs of the elderly and the handicapped if all relevant agencies and actors become involved in the process. We must recognize how interrelated with transportation are all the systems in a community and develop a range of options, each focused on different needs within the increasingly heterogeneous groups of disabled and elderly travelers.

REFERENCES

1   SANDRA ROSENBLOOM, "The Travel Patterns of Elderly Women Alone: A Research Note," *Specialized Transportation Planning and Practice*, 3, no. 3 (1989), 298.

2   H. M. SIMPSON, R. A. WARREN, AND L. PAGE-VALIN, *Medical Conditions and Risk of Collision* (Ottawa, Canada: Traffic Injury Research Foundation, 1977).

3   PATRICIA F. WALLER, "Renewal Licensing of Older Drivers," in *Transportation in an Aging Society: Improving Mobility and Safety for Older Persons*, Special Report 218, vol. 2 (Washington, D.C.: Transportation Research Board, 1988), p. 79.

4   P. A. BRAIN[I]N, *Safety and Mobility Issues in Licensing and Education of Older Drivers*, prepared for the NHSA. Washington, D.C.: National Highway Safety Administration, 1980.

5   A. M. YANIK, "What Accidents Reveal about Elderly Drivers," Paper 851688, Society of Automotive Engineers, September 1985.

6   FRANCES M. CARP, "Significance of Mobility for the Well-Being of the Elderly" in *Transportation in an Aging Society: Improving Mobility and Safety for Older Persons*, Special Report 218, vol. 2 (Washington, D.C.: Transportation Research Board, 1988), p.13.

7   JUDITH GONDA, "Perceived Control and Well-Being in the Elderly," *Specialized Transportation Planning and Practice*, 1, no. 1 (1982), 61-72.

8   CARINA VAN KNIPPENBERG, "Car Ownership and Car Use by the Elderly," in *Proceedings of the Second International Conference on Road Safety*, J. A. Rolhengatter and R. A. de Bruins, eds. (Assen, The Netherlands: Van Gorcum, 1988).

9   GONDA, "Perceived Control."

10 SANDRA ROSENBLOOM, "The Mobility Needs of the Elderly," Working Paper 011, the Graduate Program in Community and Regional Planning, University of Texas at Austin, 1989, p. 6.

11 U.S. DEPARTMENT OF COMMERCE, BUREAU OF THE CENSUS, *Prospective Trends in the Size and Structure of the Elderly Population Impact of Mortality Trends and Some Implications*, by Jacob S. Siegel, Current Population Reports, Series P-23, no. 78 (Washington, D.C.: Government Printing Office, 1978), p. 35.

12 SANDRA ROSENBLOOM, *Developing a Comprehensive Service Strategy to Meet Suburban Travel Needs*, Final Report, prepared by the University of Texas, Austin, School of Architecture, for UMTA, University Research and Training Program (Washington, D.C.: Urban Mass Transportation Administration, March 1990), p. 21.

13 ROBERT CERVERO, *Suburban Gridlock* (New Brunswick, N.J.: Center for Urban Policy Research, 1986), pp. 12-13.

14 MARTIN WACHS, *Transportation for the Elderly: Changing Lifestyles, Changing Needs* (Berkeley, Calif.: University of California Press, 1979), pp. 17, 25.

15 ROSENBLOOM, "The Mobility Needs of the Elderly," p.48.

16 VERN I. BENGSTON AND OTHERS, *Transportation: The Diverse Aged*, Policy Report One, U.S.C. Research Program on Social and Cultural Contexts of Aging, prepared for National Science Foundation, RANN Research Applications Directorate (Washington, D.C.: U.S. Government Printing Office, May 1976).

17 U.S. DEPARTMENT OF HEALTH, EDUCATION, AND WELFARE, ADMINISTRATION ON AGING, *Transportation for the Elderly: The State of the Art*, Report no. HD-75-20081 (Washington, D.C.: U.S. Department of Health, Education and Welfare, 1975).

18 Ibid., p. 46.

19 SANDRA ROSENBLOOM, "The Implications of the Suburbanization of the Elderly: An Empirical Analysis," presentation to the 1990 Annual National Conference of the American Institute on Aging, May 7, 1990, San Francisco.

20 Ibid.

21 All data in this paragraph derived from Table 2 in NATIONAL INSTITUTE ON DISABILITY AND REHABILITATION RESEARCH, *Data on Disability from the NHIS, 1983-85* (Washington, D.C.: National Institute on Disability and Rehabilitation Research, 1988), p. 42.

22 For a discussion of national studies, see NATIONAL RESEARCH COUNCIL, COMMISSION ON SOCIOTECH-NICAL SYSTEMS, *NRC Transbus Study, Part II: Mobility Options for the Transportation Handicapped in Urban Areas* (Washington, D.C.: National Academy of Sciences, August 1979).

23 JANE KAMMERER STARKS, "Mobility Training for the Retarded: An Issue of Public Transit Accessibility," *Mobility and Accessibility to Transportation for the Elderly and the Handicapped*, Transportation Research Record 830 (Washington, D.C.: Transportation Research Board, 1981), p. 21.

24 DAVID LEWIS AND BARBARA A. SMITH, "Special Driving Needs: Definition and Market Size for the United States and Canada," presented at the Tenth National Conference on Specialized Transportation, Florida State University, Tallahassee, Florida, 1985.

25 MATHEMATICA POLICY RESEARCH, INC., *Digest of Data on Persons with Disabilities*, prepared for the Congressional Research Service, Library of Congress, John L. Czajka, principal investigator (Washington, D.C.: U.S. Department of Education, June 1984, p. 132.

26 U.S. DEPARTMENT OF COMMERCE, BUREAU OF THE CENSUS,, "Disability Data from the National Content Test and the National Content Test Reinterview," NCT Results Memo 10, September 9, 1979.

27 BARBARA J. LOGUE, "Public Transportation Disability and the Elderly: An Assessment Based on the 1980 Census Data," *Population Research and Policy Review*, 6 (1987), 177-93.

28 Ibid.

29 Derived from Table 106, "Labor Force Status in 1979 and Disability and Veteran Status, 1980," in U.S. DEPARTMENT OF COMMERCE, BUREAU OF THE CENSUS, *General Social and Economic Characteristics*, PC80-1-1, 1-77.

30 SANDRA ROSENBLOOM, CAROLE SCHLESSINGER, AND HENRY DITTMAR, *The Ridership Patterns of Transportation Services for the Elderly and Handicapped*, prepared for UMTA, Report no. DOT-TX-0011 (Austin, Tex.: The Center for Transportation Research, University of Texas, Austin, September 1981), pp. 101-18.

31 SANDRA ROSENBLOOM, "Transportation Needs and Social Service Utilization: A Reassessment," *Traffic Quarterly*, 32, no. 3 (July 1978), 333-48.

32 EDWIN W. HAUSER AND OTHERS, *The Use of Existing Facilities for Transportation Disadvantaged Residents of Rural Areas*, Vol. II, prepared by the Research Triangle Institute for the FHWA (Washington, D.C.: Federal Highway Administration, October 1974.

33 SANDRA ROSENBLOOM AND ALAN ALTSCHULER, "Equity Issues in Urban Transportation," *Policy Studies Journal*, 6, no. 3 (Autumn 1977), 29-40.

34 ROSENBLOOM, *Ridership Patterns*.

35 ROSENBLOOM, "Transportation Needs."

36 CHARLES RIVER ASSOCIATES, *The Economic Benefits of Providing Transportation for the Disabled*, Final Report, prepared for UMTA (Cambridge, Mass.: Charles River Associates, December 1988), p. 96.

37 SANDRA ROSENBLOOM, "Federal Policies to Increase the Mobility of the Elderly and the Handicapped," *Journal of the American Planning Association*, 48, no. 3 (Summer 1982), 337.

38 Ibid., p. 338.

39 ERSKINE S. WALTHER AND OTHERS, "Section 504 Regulations: History and Future Impacts," a paper presented to the *Third International Conference on Mobility and Transport for Elderly and Handicapped Persons*, Orlando, Florida, October 1984.

40 ROSENBLOOM, "Federal Policies," p. 337.

41 TRANSPORTATION RESEARCH BOARD, *Transportation Requirements for Handicapped, Elderly, and Economically Disadvantaged*, NCHRP Synthesis of Highway Practice 39 (Washington, D.C.: Transportation Research Board, 1979).

42 U.S. Congress, House Committee on Public Works and Transportation, *Rural Transportation: The Role of Public and Non-Profit Providers*, hearings before the Subcommittee on Investigations and Oversight, HR, 99th Congress, 1st sess., May 14-15, 1985 (Washington, D.C.: U.S. Government Printing Office), p. 231.

43 Institute of Public Administration and Ecosometrics Incorporated, *Improving Transportation Services for Older Americans, Vol. I: General Report*, prepared by the Administration on Aging for HEW, Technology Sharing Program (Washington, D.C.: U.S. Department of Transportation, 1980).

44 Center for Systems and Program Development, Incorporated, *Best Practices in Specialized and Human Services Transportation Coordination*, prepared for HUD and U.S. DOT, Technology Sharing Program, Report no. DOT-T-89-21 (Washington, D.C.: U.S. Department of Transportation, July 1989), p. 1.

45 Ibid., p. 5.

46 Sandra Rosenbloom and Sarah Copp, "The Role of Private Providers in Transportation Services Funded by Human Service Agencies," Working Paper 028, rev. ed., the Graduate Program in Community and Regional Planning (Austin, Tex.: University of Texas, 1990), p. 29.

47 Center for Systems, *Best Practices*, p. 3.

48 James Laughlin, "Overview of Public Transportation for the Elderly and Disabled in the United States," presented at the UITP Conference, Budapest, Hungary (Houston, Tex.: Metrolift Services, Houston Metropolitan Transit Authority, June 1989).

49 Roger Teal, "Transit Contracting—The State of the Industry," *PTI Journal*, 1, no. 2 (May/June 1987), 6-9.

50 W. G. Atkinson and Ling Suen, "The Role of Private Enterprise in Elderly and Handicapped Transportation in Canada," in *Ridesharing and Transportation for the Disadvantaged*, Transportation Research Record 1170 (Washington, D.C.: Transportation Research Board, 1988), pp. 29-34.

51 Ibid., p. 33.

EXERCISES

21-1 Are there groups in society, besides the elderly and handicapped, with special transportation needs? Who? How are their needs different from the average traveler?

21-2 Why has the use of special services by eligible elderly and handicapped people been so low? Would you use such services instead of driving or riding with a friend? If so, under what circumstances?

21-3 If you were asked to design a service route for the elderly in your community, how would you go about it? What information would you need? Where do you think you could get that information?

21-4 How do you think the travel patterns of the elderly of the 1950s and the elderly of the 1990s differ? What causes the differences? Do you think that there have been comparable changes over 40 years in the makeup of the disabled population?

21-5   The elderly and the handicapped are often lumped together in the same category, yet they may have very different needs and travel patterns. In what ways do the travel patterns of those under 65 with a disability and those over 65 without disability differ, and what are the implications for transportation planners?

21-6   The elderly use transit systems far more frequently in European countries. Why? What improvements or changes would make traditional fixed-route services more responsive to the needs of the elderly? Consider improvements in all aspects of service.

21-7   What kind of land-use changes would reduce the dependence on the private auto by the elderly or handicapped? Why do you think that such changes have not been made?

21-8   How could social service agencies with disabled and elderly clients provide services in ways that reduced the need of these clients to travel? Would such alternatives be cost effective?

21-9   If you were asked to design a coordination mechanism for your community, bringing together all the transportation systems funded by the DHHS and DOT, how would you structure that strategy? What incentives could you create to encourage small providers to participate? What kind of sanctions could you create if they did not participate?

21-10   How could you set up a ridesharing program for the elderly and handicapped in rural areas? What problems would you have to address? What resources might be available to help you?

Chapter 22

PERCEPTIONS OF PUBLIC TRANSPORTATION

GEORGE E. GRAY

As we approach the twenty-first century, the public appears to be reassessing its use of the automobile and its perceptions of the roles expected of public transit. As late as the 1960s, relatively little public thought was given to the subject, but a number of factors have changed that. It is important that the industry, planners, decision makers, and others involved in public transportation keep abreast of the changes in public attitude that are occurring, which, collectively, may be the single most important determinant of the future roles of such service. For, after all, it is the public's perceptions that result in ballot-box decisions. Reed summarized the opportunities as follows:

> Today is clearly a turning point in the story of the automobile. And public transportation could gain from the new public perceptions of the auto and its consequences. If concern with a continued gasoline shortage or pollution control or the environment remains high, transit could regain patrons and once again become a prominent mover. The energy crisis is real, and transit use could be one of the patterns that result as the country adjusts to costly energy. The alternative, equally likely, is that the auto industry will provide smaller, less obtrusive vehicles and the country will decide to continue the pattern of individualized vehicles as the basic means of transport, the transit industry returning to its role as a welfare organization requiring subsidy to help the disadvantaged.[1]

Reed's writing in 1973 was very prophetic. Yet, he did not identify the middle ground, a third scenario that has since been our course: the auto industry has provided smaller vehicles while some auto disincentives or group-ride incentives have been implemented. The evolution in perceptions is still continuing, however, and the final course is still unresolved.

Although this chapter concentrates on perceptions directed at conventional bus systems, there is no evidence that the attitudes underlying these perceptions cannot be applied to other types of transit service. Some paratransit services, such as car- and vanpooling, better address certain attributes for certain trips, but since there is such a variety of service combinations, the perceptional differences relating to this important transit sector are not examined.

The constantly changing values of modern societies often create conflict as well as opportunity for change. The fundamental facts of the chemistry of air quality and reduced natural resources are affecting existing values to a greater extent than the general public yet completely realizes, but that realization is growing and with it is growing the call for change.

The ability of the transit industry to provide a quality service as an alternative to the automobile is a key element in influencing the reaction to the problems of air pollution, energy restrictions, and congestion. Most transportation authorities agree that these external factors, pressuring for changes in our mobility and our methods of achieving that mobility, are major determinants of the growth and acceptance of public transit. Nevertheless, it is obvious that the industry must continue to improve its service and image in order to overcome the general public's formidable resistance, which inhibits significant increased use of most systems. In 1977, about 95% of the *choice riders*, those who had the option of using an auto or taking transit, always used the auto. Several attitude surveys taken in the mid-1970s and the 1980s indicated that, even if considerable disincentives were established on auto use, most people would continue using that mode.

In this chapter, various groups and their attitudes toward transit will be identified. Based on numerous studies, factors that appear to be significant to the groupings will be assessed. Finally, the major factors that affect our perceptions will be discussed and some strategies that may help in strengthening public acceptance of transit use suggested.

Government at all levels has a tremendous responsibility in addressing the problems of mobility. Those engaged in the energy, environmental, and political tugs of war direct much of their rhetoric to this problem without any prior determination as to the basic need for transportation. In the 1980s there was still no established national policy on the subject, and most state and local government units had little more to offer in this regard. The shotgun approach with categorical emphasis appeared to be the accepted practice, with uncoordinated Band-Aid programs continuing to proliferate. The continued requirements for transportation improvement plans (TIPs) and their transportation systems management elements (TSMEs) as established in 1976 had helped to focus on mobility and increased coordination efforts. Although these requirements have the potential to change the basic planning process considerably and to orient it more toward being an effective programming tool, the changed process has yet to be fully developed. Given the history of past changes in the planning process, years will be necessary to develop an effective process (see Chaps. 3 and 13). The efforts of the U.S. Department of Transportation (U.S. DOT) to establish a national transportation policy may be able to draw the conflicting transportation interests together to develop a policy that will receive the needed legislative and administrative endorsement to become the basis of national commitment. Obviously, changing times force a reappraisal of many aspects of our present society, and transportation is but one of these. Unfortunately, it is so ubiquitous and so influential that even minor changes in the methods of providing transportation have ripple effects in almost all aspects of our lives. These consequences have been largely ignored by our government. Except during times of tremendous highway development, government bodies in the United States have not used transportation, to any great extent, as a major tool to help achieve other goals, such as to control land use, reinforce a national energy program, or reduce air pollution.

Federal emphasis on air quality has impacts on all aspects of transportation, because the potential pollution reductions in the transportation sector are so large. As important and necessary as air pollution reduction is, however, it is unfortunate that mobility needs are not considered more. Mobility needs are the cause, and air pollution is the effect. Assuming that this lack of attention to mobility needs will change as we learn to live at a less polluting pace and consume less of our non-renewable energy resources, it is apparent that it is necessary to learn more about the various groups most affected by public transit so that service can be better adapted to address their concerns. At the same time, we may learn how to attract more choice riders to public transit.

THE CONCERNED GROUPS

One of our needs is to identify the various viewpoints that should be considered in looking at transit service. One early study broke the viewpoints into four groups, but had a stratification resulting in a total of 79 categories.[2] Four major groups are self-evident: the transit users, the nonusers, the providers (operators), and the community as a whole (a classification that will be used to represent the spectrum from a small town to the nation as a whole).

THE USERS

Users can be considered to be composed of *captive users*, who have no alternative method for making a particular trip, and *choice users*, who do have an alternative available. The captive market in this country is much larger than many realize. It is about half of the population at any one time. Included in this group are not only the elderly, the young, and certain of the disabled, but also those without an automobile available, including the stranded homemaker. The choice riders—the rest of the population except for a relatively small number who because of age or health are restricted from using public transit—are those who have an alternative transportation mode readily available.

Although the choice user group presents a large potential market for transit, it is also one that is difficult to attract. Tehan and Wachs propose using psychological considerations in the development and evaluation of new transit services in an attempt to meet the fundamental satisfactions of these possible users.[3] Their paper discusses methods of improving both the image and quality of public transit, with these users' fundamental needs in mind, and draws parallels with the development and marketing of the automobile. Although such psychological considerations have not been ignored, they have not, for the most part, been adequately addressed.

Besides conventional transit, a number of specialized services have been developed to meet the needs of captive users. These special services range from those provided by various human services agencies to meet the particular needs of their clients to those established for a portion of the market, such as the wheelchair user and the elderly. Such services may be provided by transit districts normally dedicated to operating conventional services, a variety of paratransit agencies, or other social and human services organizations.

THE NONUSERS

Nonusers include those who are unable to use transit as well as those, the choice riders, who do not choose to use it for a variety of reasons. No doubt a large number of these reasons are psychological, but many are based on either physical limitations or mobility needs that cannot be readily served by transit. Of course, these deterrents will vary in accord with the particular type of service provided, but there will still always be a large number of nonusers who cannot be adequately accommodated. An example would be television technicians, who must carry their tools and repair parts with them.

THE PROVIDERS (OPERATORS)

Providers have changed their perspective considerably since the 1970s. Until fairly recently, the major concern for too many of them was to provide service at a profit, or at least a minimal loss. As all major and many smaller systems have come under public ownership, transit managers have been increasingly interested in how to provide better service at a reasonable cost, even though operating costs are not recovered in the farebox. The emphasis has changed, but the main constraint—limited resources—still dominates their perceptions and resulting actions since the deficits must somehow always be covered. Increasing socially oriented services, such as reduced fares for selected groups during certain periods, causes conflicting objectives for the providers. Providing such human-services programs distorts the financial picture for the transit organization, and the resulting costs are often not adequately understood by their governing bodies or by the public. For instance, federal law stipulates that senior citizens pay only half-fare for off-peak service. In only a few isolated cases are such human-services costs subsidized by their respective social programs.

Another problem that has surfaced with public ownership is the propensity for the governing board to be more conservative in providing resources for transit when the local roads and streets are judged to be underfunded.

THE COMMUNITY

The perspectives of the community are becoming more and more the major determinants of establishing programs for newly developing public transit. Meanwhile, the perceptions among this group are probably the least stable and are undergoing considerable change.

In most areas of this country, mobility has been dominated—even overwhelmed—by the automobile. Such domination causes severe impacts, such as (1) air and sound pollution; (2) increasing auto congestion, which lowers the efficiency of the auto and all those services that share its delegated space; (3) the high social and economic costs of extending or expanding the highway network; (4) land-use concerns focused on providing for the auto; (5) concern for those not served by the auto except at a very high cost—many of these people, the elderly, disabled, and young, feel that they have a civil right to economical, accessible transportation; and (6) diminished resources, specifically the energy problem, which, coupled with air pollution, is bound to eventually cause severe changes in existing transportation patterns.

CHANGING PERCEPTIONS

Obviously, the attitudes of individuals will differ with their particular circumstances. The transportation requirements of a home-to-work trip are quite different from those felt necessary to attend a society ball. Although both trips can be made in comfort by many of the same modes, the range of "acceptableness" of alternatives is different. Peer-group attitudes, financial resources, and a host of other factors can influence acceptableness. To make it even more complex, attitudes change over time and space. Our involvement in the war in Viet Nam was an obvious example of the former, and one has only to compare the travel habits of residents of San Francisco or New York with the average resident of Los Angeles to exemplify the latter.

The closing of the San Francisco–Oakland Bay Bridge as a result of the 1989 Loma Prieta earthquake was a good example of a reason for public perception change. Overnight it became necessary for the 80,000 workday morning peak-period drivers that had been using the bridge to reassess their travel. The largest portion chose to use the parallel San Francisco Bay Area Rapid Transit System (BART). Several months after the disruption, ridership for the BART transbay peak-hour service was still more than 20% higher than prequake. Evidently, many automobile users tried an alternative public transit service and found it not only viable, but preferred.

It is this propensity toward changed attitudes that offers public transportation the opportunity to perform an increased role in providing mobility, especially urban mobility. If the industry can determine the major service attributes to meet user needs and provide them at a reasonable level of public investment, external pressures such as gasoline prices, congestion, parking fees, and environmental concerns, which will modify attitudes, can be expected to cause significant modal shifting.

A number of studies have been made to identify and rank the factors that the public considers important in using conventional fixed-route transit. A few of these studies will be cited to illustrate the broad coverage of study types and the results obtained. A study by INTERPLAN identified six general attribute categories relative to mobility choice decisions:[4] accessibility, efficiency, reliability, comfort, safety, and cost. This study made no attempt to rank these factors.

A system to measure the effectiveness of the transportation services of local government was developed for the U.S. Department of Housing and Urban Development (HUD) by the Urban Institute.[5] The system was based on the quality of transportation as seen by the citizen–consumer and cited the major objectives of a local transportation system: "ease of access to the places people want to go, convenience, travel time (reasonable speed), comfort, safety, economy, maintenance of a habitable environment, and satisfaction among citizens with the overall adequacy of the system."[6]

One of the most comprehensive studies was research conducted by a University of Maryland team over a 3-year period.[7] It included pilot studies in Baltimore and Philadelphia. These studies ranked variables in order of importance for both work and nonwork trips and found that the differences in relative importance were slight except for the travel-time factor. They concluded that the following list of factors[8] (in order of importance) suggested the basic attributes of a generalized, ideal transit system:

- Reliability of destination achievement (including elements of safety and confidence in the vehicle).
- Convenience and comfort.
- Travel time (but with large trip-purpose differences).
- Cost.
- State of vehicle (with cleanliness overshadowing newness).
- Self-esteem and autonomy (with emphasis on independence rather than pride).
- Traffic and congestion (both in and out of the vehicle).
- Diversions (including nature of travel companions, availability of radio, and scenery).

A national survey of transportation attitudes conducted under the sponsorship of the American Association of State Highway Officials (now the American Association of State Highway and Transportation Officials) and the Bureau of Public Roads (now the Federal Highway Administration) identified many of the same items.[9] This survey, however, besides being somewhat dated, was evidently structured toward the use of the auto. Although it was comprehensive, it is of questionable value for the purposes of determining the relative factors that inhibit transit use. It does include valuable information on the segmented transportation market of the 1950s.

A mail questionnaire in the Twin Cities area by Beier attempted to identify why auto use dominated over bus transit. His study resulted in the following top-ranked factors:[10]

- Quickest travel time.
- Elimination of waiting periods.
- Freedom from schedules.
- Reliability of the car.
- Protection from the weather.

A subsequent study by Lovelock agreed substantially with the earlier investigations and recommended three basic strategies operators could use to stimulate patronage:[11] change the physical attributes of vehicles and stations for comfort and safety, change operational characteristics for better service, and use persuasive communication to change nonuser attitudes and preferences.

Stephenson, in a study of commuter attitudes of graduate students at the University of Minnesota, came up with the following listing of the 10 top factors favoring the auto:[12]

- Reliability.
- Able to leave when you desire.
- Shortest door-to-door time.
- Able to stop when you wish.
- Weather protection.
- Adequate space to carry items.
- Transfer not needed.
- Independence
- Clean vehicle.
- Able to travel at own speed.

A comprehensive study by the Orange County Transit District in California focused on the identification and assessment of the relative importance of the attributes of transit as conceived by the consumer and the determination of the extent to which consumers consider that existing modes satisfy their needs.[13] The results were in general agreement with the earlier studies, but indicated that the public placed much more importance on bus-driver attitude than previously identified. Strong general support for transit was found, with 84% responding that benefits of transit were well worth the cost and 90% feeling that bus transport would make their city more livable. The strongest support for transit was found in the demographic groups least likely to use transit, those with incomes over $25,000 per year or with two or more autos. This study provided a good example of how results can be used for policy guidance and management decisions. For example, interpretation of the study results pointed out that in this country more effort was needed to market transit—an interested but largely uninformed public was identified.

The study also disclosed that attitudes concerning other transportation services are evidently not basically different from those focused on fixed-route transit. As part of a program to increase auto occupancy through the formation of carpools, insight into the reasons for basic modal choice decisions was researched so that proposed actions could address the identified reasons behind transportation mode choice. Each person in the survey was asked to rate attributes of work travel as to importance in the mode selection for work trips. A total of 11 factors was included. The four receiving highest importance were reliability, safety from accidents, convenience, and safety from crime. Costs were not specifically identified as an attribute.

A review by Martin Wachs of various studies indicated that the relevant factors influencing modal choice were travel time, reliability, convenience, comfort, safety, cost, and amenities.[14]

Another survey, this one by Hoey and Levinson, covering a medium-size community, found radical differences between transit users and nonusers regarding acceptable transit service levels.[15] Even with an acceptable level of service, nonusers indicated that external factors would be needed to change their travel habits. The study concluded:

> The survey indicates that existing transit riders have a much lower expectation regarding bus service attributes than car drivers. Thus, radically improved service concepts and levels will be necessary to divert motorists to transit use; and they may be feasible only in selected corridors. *If energy, environmental, or public policy considerations require large scale diversions of commuters to transit, then selected auto disincentives may be necessary. Increased motor fuel taxation appears to be more productive than parking taxes and controls—at least in medium-sized cities.*[16]

The Center for Urban Transportation Research of the University of South Florida in a comprehensive report, *Factors Related to Transit Use*,[17] addressed the consumer preferences of both automobile users and transit users in 17 metropolitan areas across the country who had ready access to public transportation. Among the findings were:

- 22% were "auto captives."
- 30% were "transit dependent."
- Of the transit dependent, only 37% indicated they would drive to work if an automobile were available.
- The four most significant reasons given by the transit users for not using the automobile were (1) cost of parking, (2) availability of parking, (3) travel time, and (4) traffic congestion.
- About half of those driving to work could be considered potential transit riders if flexible and convenient transit service were provided.
- Other factors that would favor increased transit use were nontransfer services, express routes, and increased auto parking fees.
- Traffic congestion was viewed as very serious by 36% of respondents and somewhat serious by 28%.

The results of these various studies were far from identical, or even similar in some cases. That, however, does not detract from their value. Attitudinal surveys similar to these are finding increasing popularity with transit organizations and proving to be valuable in helping to determine the type of service that should be considered in a particular area. They are also frequently used in planning studies in ranking proposed service alternatives for new systems.

THE "SCARCE" AMENITIES

Analysis of the various surveys and readings in the field suggests grouping the factors influencing the use of transit into the acronym **SCARCE**—unfortunately, a most appropriate description of their availability in some transit operations. **SCARCE** stands for:

Safety.
Comfort.
Accessibility.
Reliability.
Cost.
Efficiency.

These attributes cover all the major items listed in the cited studies as well as others not referenced in the previous discussion.

It is important to note that there is no rating of importance implied in this acronym. It is obvious from a review of the numerous studies that ranking is not practical. People just are not consistent. They have different needs for different trips at different times in their life-cycles. Besides, there is lack of uniformity in the terminology used in the various studies or surveys.

A short description of the elements constituting these various attributes follows.

Safety (on vehicles and at stops) includes not only safety from accidents but also passenger safety from theft and physical violence, as well as vehicle safety from vandalism.

Comfort embraces the physical comfort of the passenger within the vehicles and at stops (ride quality, adequate environmental controls, effectual seating, handholds, sufficient entrances and exits with easy fare collection, package accommodations); the aesthetic qualities of the system (clean and pleasingly designed vehicles, attractive stops, terminals, guideways, and other facilities); environmental protection of the community (noise and exhaust emissions); facilities for the handicapped; and pleasant, considerate, and helpful operators.

Accessibility implies adequacy of route distribution over the area served, vehicle capacity, service frequency and operating time span, identification of stops and vehicles, and distribution of information on fares, schedules, and the like, as well as ease of fare paying and well-placed stops and terminals.

Reliability depends on low breakdown rate, with special services provided when breakdowns do occur, adherence to schedules with adequate information about any service changes, and guaranteed availability of transfer.

Cost means reasonable, guaranteed fares with minimum zone fares (if any) and easy transfer mechanisms and possibly cost reductions for passes (weekly, daily, and so on) and special groups (students, children, senior citizens, and others). Cost should be perceived as favorable compared to automobile use for the same trip.

Efficiency includes high average speeds with minimum dwell times and the absence of traffic delays, sufficient stops for minimum walking (but not so many as to increase travel time), coordinated schedules and transfer points with minimum user discomfort, direct routing, and express and special-event service when warranted. Efficiency also requires an easily maintained system with adequate maintenance facilities, an efficient management system, and minimal staff necessary to sustain efficient service.

Again, it should be recognized that the attitude toward transit of the three most interested groups (the user, the provider, and the community) with respect to these factors will vary. Even the interests of subgroups within the three principal groups may not be in complete agreement. For instance, the users' requirements vary, depending upon being a commuter, a new traveler to a system (such as a tourist), or a regular user frequenting certain routes (such as the captive rider going shopping).

In some of the identified attributes, there is obvious conflict between the goals of the various groups. For instance, the user and the provider have difficulty agreeing on the amount of service to satisfy certain elements of accessibility, such as adequacy of route distribution, vehicle capacity, and service frequency and time span. This disparity of interests is an example of why conventional transit often cannot compete favorably in an open market with the automobile, and such disparity also indicates why private conventional transit systems rapidly disappeared from the scene. To attract the choice rider, which is the main market for increased ridership, cost-effective service levels cannot be made the sole determining criterion for establishing routings, headways, and the like.

FACTORS AFFECTING THE SCARCE AMENITIES

Seven factors have been identified as being the major causes of the deficiencies in public transit in this country.[18] A short discussion of these factors follows.

Finances

Over the years, lack of funding has severely restricted the development of transit systems. This deficiency, coupled with inadequate allocation of the funds available, contributes to the too frequently found failure to make investments in maintaining the physical plant and equipment as well as to provide for modernization of systems. In many cases, it has resulted in transit systems that will be inadequate to provide for the increased services that will be needed as the air pollution crisis becomes more pronounced. It must be remembered that 3- to 4-year lead times are often necessary to provide added services and up to 10 years for new services.

The addition of Section 5 funding by the Urban Mass Transportation Administration (UMTA) and similar funding by various states, which provides flexibility for capital additions or operating costs, gave temporary relief in the mid-1970s, but the basic problem of inadequate funds, especially to cover ever-increasing operating costs, remains (see Chap. 15).

Transportation policies

Lack of transportation policies has caused imbalances in providing for competitive modes. With few exceptions, parking policies, highway funding, land-use decisions, integrated services, and rate setting were all developed separately. There is little coordinated effort to develop transportation as a whole; only elements of service are addressed. This fractured approach cannot be allowed to continue. A comprehensive national transportation policy agreed upon by the administration and Congress is long overdue. The American Public Transit Association, the American Association of State Highway and Transportation Officials, and others have developed policies reflecting their organizational positions, but the need for an accepted national policy is only more apparent as these more biased policies proliferate. Some state plans that provide policy guidance have been developed, but without a well-established and accepted national policy, such efforts can, at best, be temporary expedients subject to change as federal programs change.

Local political factors

Local political factors often create a plethora of multiple jurisdictions, legal barriers to coordination, rate constraints, and resistance to cooperation. All too often, local jealousies and the narrow interests of political bodies are allowed to overshadow the long-range public good.

Technology

At present, the development of necessary programs such as vehicle improvement, automated ticket devices, and computerized management systems is hindered by a number of factors. Among these are a lack of development funds, unclear development rights, governmental red tape, and often, apathy on the part of both manufacturers and the general public. The problem of short-range programs based on existing technology versus innovation and the development of new concepts is especially difficult to address in an arena faced with decisions involving major financial commitment for providing transit services.

Labor

In many instances, labor restrictions cause uneconomical operations to continue. There is considerable evidence that, in many cases, increased labor costs, if not counterbalanced by increased productivity, may eventually eliminate much of the existing conventional bus service as a viable alternative. To provide for financially sound transit service, it may become necessary to eliminate, or at least severely restrict, not only the right to strike but some of the more restrictive work rules. A less drastic position would be to provide for required arbitration.

Management

For many years, the industry was in a declining market; now that the demands for increased service are growing, there are complicated managerial problems to overcome. Enlightened management is addressing these, but Smerk (see Chap. 16), among others, makes a strong case that "management has almost always been the weakest link in the mass transit chain."[19]

Lack of integration and coordination

Lack of integration and coordination includes such problems as fragmentation of transit service among different agencies, lack of cooperation among agencies, and uncoordinated services within a single agency.

LEVELS OF SERVICE AND THE SCARCE FACTORS

The SCARCE factors are all related to levels of service to some extent. Therefore, one of the best ways to reduce the adverse effects of the SCARCE factors is to increase the quality and quantity of service in general.

The major constraint to an improved level of service continues to be a lack of adequate funding. There is considerable evidence, however, that public attitudes in the 1990s will support increased levels of funding; therefore, this may not be a continuing problem. Programs to improve transit equipment are covered in Chap. 24 and therefore this element to improved service will not be addressed here.

Besides adequate funding and improved equipment, assured effective management and marketing are the remaining necessary elements in providing a high level of service. To improve capability in the management of transit systems, several tools have been made available. UMTA has developed a package of computer programs to provide for management information needs, including cost accounting (Financial Accounting Reporting Elements or FARE), scheduling (Run Cutting and Vehicle Scheduling or RUCUS), maintenance (Service, Inventory, and Maintenance System or SIMS), and planning (Urban Transportation Planning System or UTPS). The greatest additional needs in this area appear to be increased training for middle management and established forums for the resolution of operational problems caused by institutional barriers. Needed is more effort aimed at increasing the supervisory capability of the industry by using modern techniques. Both improved and expanded training of existing practitioners and university programs to produce graduates oriented toward entering the transit field are also positive steps that help to produce improved and efficient management, but more needs to be accomplished in these areas.

The changing composition of the population of the United States will place increased pressures on management. The reduction in the relative size of the work force, the competition for skilled and unskilled labor, the drift toward an increased mix of social programs with transportation services are all examples of factors leading to more complicated challenges to management.

A variety of actions can be undertaken to improve the public attitude toward public transit and mitigate the adverse aspects of the SCARCE factors. It is important to keep in mind that attitudes are the product of perceptions. You must change the way people perceive a service before you can expect to change their attitudes toward it.

Improved services resulting from increased capital investment, improved management, diversification of types of service, and so on, all have a prominent place. According to L. M. Schneider, however;

> The prospect of new capital is not the transit industry's salvation, for capital can too easily be misallocated through investments in inappropriate facilities or dissipated by poor maintenance. The industry is still caught up in the vicious circle of declining productivity, high operating costs, poor service, increasing fares, and level or declining patronage. A radical approach is needed. It is hoped that new marketing-oriented transit strategies will provide the answer.[20]

Although ridership is increasing in most areas, the basic concept behind this statement is still appropriate. Smerk,[21] Lovelock,[22] and Reed[23] have all given emphasis to this position and agree that focus on market segmentation holds considerable promise.

Lovelock concluded his study with the opinion that, by highlighting the consumer's need for information and the relationship between modal choice behavior and attitudes, relatively inexpensive marketing and communication programs might be extremely effective in encouraging the use of public transit.[24] His study also contained several proposed strategies involving elements of the market. Reed took this last approach considerably further and gave a comprehensive analysis of the value of using a segmented marketing approach for the promotion of transit.[25] (For a close look at macro-marketing, see Chap. 17.)

SUMMARY

Attitude surveys in the public transit sector have the potential of providing needed information leading to improved service at a reasonable cost and over a comparatively short time frame.

A study of the literature on transit attitudes indicates considerable agreement on the major factors that influence the level of transit use of the choice rider, although the priority of importance of the factors is varied. The factors can be represented by the acronym SCARCE, standing for *S*afety, *C*omfort, *A*ccessibility, *R*eliability, *C*ost, and *E*fficiency. These six major factors reflect, all too often, the present deficiencies in public transit service. Strategies to mitigate these six elements and improve the SCARCE amenities include the improvement of service levels, equipment, management techniques, and marketing.

REFERENCES

Some citations are no longer available from their original source. These citations are often available from the National Technical Information Service, U.S. Department of Commerce, 5285 Port Royal Road, Springfield, VA 22161. We have verified the order numbers for many of these citations, and they are found at the end of the citation. Prices are available through NTIS at the address above.

1   RICHARD R. REED, *Market Segmentation Development for Public Transportation*, Research Report no. 8, prepared for UMTA (Stanford, Calif.: Stanford University Department of Industrial Engineering, August 1973), pp. 38-39. Now available as PB 227 178.

2   J. L. SORENSON, "Identification of Social Costs and Benefits in Urban Transportation," in *Systems Analysis of Urban Transportation: Study in New Systems of Urban Transportation, Volume III: Network Flow Analysis*, prepared by the General Research Corporation for HUD (Santa Barbara, Calif.: General Research Corporation, January 1968), pp. 22-25.

3   CLAIRE TEHAN AND MARTIN WACHS, "The Role of Psychological Needs in Mass Transit," *High Speed Ground Transportation Journal*, 9, no. 2 (Summer 1975), 35-50.

4   ROMAN KRZYCZKOWSKI AND OTHERS, *Integration of Transit Systems, Summary*, prepared for UMTA (Santa Barbara, Calif.: INTERPLAN Corporation, October 1973). Now available as PB 241 273.

5   RICHARD E. WINNIE AND HARRY P. HATRY, *Measuring the Effectiveness of Local Government Services: Transportation*, prepared for HUD (Washington, D.C.: The Urban Institute, n.d.).

6   Ibid., p. *v*.

7   ALLAN N. NASH AND STANLEY J. HILLE, "Public Attitudes Toward Transport Modes: A Summary of Two Pilot Studies," in *Public Attitudes Toward Highway Improvements*, Highway Research Record 233 (Washington, D.C.: Highway Research Board, 1968), pp. 33-46.

8   Ibid, p. 43.

9   ROBERT K. McMILLAN AND HENRY ASSAEL, *National Survey of Transportation Attitudes and Behavior, Phase I: Summary Report*, NCHRP Report 49 (Washington, D.C.: Highway Research Board, 1968).

10 FREDERICK J. BEIER, *Attitudes of Drivers Toward Mass-Transit*, prepared for UMTA (Minneapolis, Minn.: University of Minnesota, 1971). Now available as PB 207 131.

11 CHRISTOPHER H. LOVELOCK, *Consumer Oriented Approaches to Marketing Urban Transit*, Research Report no. 3, prepared for UMTA (Stanford, Calif.: Stanford University, March 1973). Now available as PB 220 781.

12 F. J. STEPHENSON, JR., *Commuter Attitudes and Modal Choice in a Twin Cities Submarket* (Minneapolis, Minn.: University of Minnesota Graduate School of Business Administration, 1973).

13 GORDON J. FIELDING, DOUGLAS P. BLANKENSHIP, AND TIMOTHY TARDIFF, "Consumer Attitudes Toward Public Transit," in *Public Transportation Planning*, Transportation Research Record 563 (Washington, D.C.: Transportation Research Board, 1976), pp. 22-28.

14 MARTIN WACHS, "Consumer Attitudes Toward Transit Service: An Interpretive Review," *Journal of the American Institute of Planners*, 42, no. 1 (January 1976), 96-104.

15 WILLIAM F. HOEY AND HERBERT S. LEVINSON, "Attitude Surveys, Transit Planning, and Auto-Use Constraints" (unpublished paper presented at the 56th Annual Meeting, Transportation Research Board, January 1977).

16 Ibid., p. 14.

17 CENTER FOR URBAN TRANSPORTATION RESEARCH, *Factors Related to Transit Use*, prepared for UMTA. (Tampa, Fla.: University of South Florida, October 1989).

18 KRZYCZKOWSKI, *Integration of Transit Systems*.

19 GEORGE M. SMERK, "Mass Transit Management," *Business Horizons*, 14, no. 6 (December 1971), 5.

20 LEWIS M. SCHNEIDER, "Marketing Urban Transit," in *Mass Transportation*, Highway Research Record 318 (Washington, D.C.: Highway Research Board, 1970), p. 19.

21 SMERK, "Mass Transit Management."

22 LOVELOCK, *Consumer Oriented Approaches*.

23 REED, *Market Segmentation Development*.

24 LOVELOCK, *Consumer Oriented Approaches*.

25 REED, *Market Segmentation Development*.

FURTHER READING

BURKHARDT, JON E., AND MARGARET T. SHAFFER, "Social and Psychological Impacts of Transportation Improvements," *Transportation*, 1, no. 2 (August 1972), 207-26.

BYRD, JOSEPH P., "Characteristics, Attitudes, and Perceptions of Transit Nonusers in the Atlanta Region," in *Public Transportation Planning*, Transportation Research Record 563, pp. 29-37. Washington, D.C.: Transportation Research Board, 1976.

CRAIN, JOHN L., "Notes on Factors Affecting Acceptance of Travel Modes" (unpublished paper presented at the 26th Annual California Transportation and Public Works Conference, March 27-29, 1974).

GOLOB, THOMAS F., "The Survey of User Choice of Alternate Transportation Modes," in *Urban and Regional Ground Transportation: Surveys and Readings*, ed. James J. Murray, pp. 175-85. Durham, N.C.: Planning-Transport Associates, Inc., 1973.

——, RICARDO DOBSON, AND JAGDISH N. SHETH, "Perceived Attribute Importance in Public and Private Transportation" (unpublished paper presented at the National American Institute for Decision Sciences Meeting, Boston, Mass., November 14-16, 1973).

——, AND OTHERS, "An Analysis of Consumer Preferences for a Public Transportation System," *Transportation Research*, 6, no. 1 (March 1972), 81-102.

HARTGEN, DAVID T., *Variations in Reference Scale and Perception of Modal Attributes for Different Traveler Groups*, Report no. PRR 55. Albany, N.Y.: New York State Department of Transportation, Planning Division, Planning and Research Bureau, December 1973.

NOTESS, CHARLES, "Life-Style Factors Behind Modal Choice," *Transportation Engineering Journal of ASCE*, 99, no. TE3 (August 1973), 513-20.

PAINE, FRANK T., AND OTHERS, "Consumer Attitudes Toward Auto Versus Public Transport Alternatives," *Journal of Applied Psychology*, 53, no. 6 (1969), 474-80.

TARDIFF, TIMOTHY J., "Comparison of Effectiveness of Various Measures of Socioeconomic Status in Models of Transportation Behavior," in *Travel Behavior and Values*, Transportation Research Record 534, pp. 1-9. Washington, D.C.: Transportation Research Board, 1975.

TRANSPORTATION RESEARCH BOARD, *Behavioral Demand Modeling and Valuation of Travel Time*, Special Report 149. Washington, D.C.: Transportation Research Board, 1974.

WICKSTROM, GEORGE V., "Transportation System Performance Measurement and Application," *Institute of Traffic Engineers: Compendium of Technical Papers, 43rd Annual Meeting*, ed. Walter P. Youngblood, Minneapolis, Minn. (1973), pp. 159-63.

EXERCISES

22-1   List the transportation choices available for your most common trip (for example, to and from work or school).

22-2   Estimate the out-of-pocket cost for each of the alternatives in Exercise 22-1.

22-3   Estimate the total cost per mode for the alternatives in Exercise 22-1 (that is, out-of-pocket cost plus prorated sunk costs such as insurance, capital cost, and subsidy).

22-4   The cost per mile for my automobile use in 1989 was approximately 45 cents, broken down as follows:

Miles	17,136
Lease and insurance	$5469.00 (including depreciation)
Gasoline	$ 859.45
Maintenance and repairs	$1030.42
Parking/tolls	$ 45.05
Registration	$ 390.00

(a) Calculate the cost per mile for your or a friend's automobile travel.
(b) What is the cost per gallon of fuel used in part (a)?
(c) Compare part (a) with the cost of public transit in your area.

22-5   Rank the SCARCE factors in priority order for both a necessary trip (work, school, doctor) and a discretionary trip (recreation, visiting) and explain your reasons for your priority determination.

22-6   What improvements in the SCARCE factors would you suggest for the major public transit system in your area?

22-7   What are your perceptions (using the SCARCE factors) of public transit service in your area?

22-8   Conduct a survey of a minimum of 10 people to determine their priority ranking of the SCARCE factors. What group does your sample most represent?

22-9   Rank the importance of the SCARCE factors for the following trips you might take and explain your major differences in factor rankings:
(a) A foreign air flight.

(b) A domestic air flight of over 500 miles.

(c) A short domestic flight for business.

(d) A short domestic flight for pleasure.

(e) An auto trip of 500 miles for business (time critical).

(f) An auto trip of 500 miles for pleasure (time not critical).

(g) A train trip of 500 miles for business.

(h) A train trip of 500 miles for pleasure.

(i) A bus trip of 500 miles for pleasure.

22-10 You decide to establish a for-hire chauffeured auto service in your community.

(a) What would you do to attract first time and continued use?

(b) What factors would enter into your fee structure?

22-11 Assume your fleet in Exercise 22-10 is composed equally of limousines, maxi-vans, mini-vans, school buses, and intercity buses. List the potential markets for each type of vehicle and how you would address acceptance of your services based on the general public's perceptions.

PART VII

THE FUTURE

Chapter 23

PUBLIC TRANSPORTATION IN THE 21st CENTURY

Michael D. Meyer

As indicated in previous chapters, the status and financial well-being of the public transportation industry depends greatly on factors inherent to the industry itself and on external influences often outside the control of transit managers. For example, the internal workings of a transit agency, labor practices, service policies, and the relationship between the agency and other public and private groups in the service area can greatly affect the position of a transit organization. Political and socioeconomic factors, such as changing levels of federal transit subsidies or suburbanization trends in metropolitan areas, can likewise influence agency success or failure.

This chapter examines the likely characteristics of public transportation in the twenty-first century. In doing so, the chapter risks overgeneralizing the characteristics of such service when, in reality, the type and level of public transportation service will vary greatly by city, state, and region. In addition, predicting the characteristics of any social or technological phenomenon 10 or 20 years in the future must necessarily assume some stability in the general background context of that phenomenon, for example, the state of the economy (unless, of course, there is some evidence to suggest otherwise). With regard to transportation, this context must consist of the socio-economic characteristics of the population that influence transportation decisions, economic growth that determines employment patterns and thus commuting, and alternative technologies (such as telecommunications) that could significantly alter working habits and the characteristics of the workplace. Thus, suggestions of the future state of public transportation must rely on some understanding of past trends and on an understanding of the history of the industry itself. Such information is found in previous chapters and will not be repeated in great detail in this chapter. When important to the discussion, however, some of the key observations or conclusions from earlier chapters will again be made.

PERSPECTIVES ON THE FUTURE OF PUBLIC TRANSPORTATION

Historians of transportation policy will probably look at the period from 1985 to 1995 as a time when national transportation policy in the United States was the subject of intense examination and debate. Motivated mainly by the completion of the interstate highway program and the need to determine what should come next on the national transportation agenda, several leading transportation groups initiated national studies to assess possible "futures" for the transportation program and to recommend governmental action to prepare for these futures (see, for example, References 1 to 5). In addition, the U.S. Department of Transportation issued a statement in 1990 on national transportation policy that outlined several major themes for future government action.[6] The policy directions outlined in this document included maintaining and expanding the nation's transportation system, fostering a sound financial base for transportation, keeping the transportation industry strong and competitive, ensuring that the transportation system supports public safety and national security, protecting the environment and quality of life, and advancing U.S. transportation technology and expertise.

Most of these efforts, in various levels of detail, discussed the potential roles of public transportation in the twenty-first century (in some cases the target year was the year 2000 and in others it was 2020). It thus becomes important as a point of departure for this chapter to look briefly at the major conclusions of the most relevant studies.

APTA's TRANSIT 2000

The American Public Transit Association (APTA), the organization that represents most of the large public transportation agencies in the United States and Canada, undertook a study that examined the trends affecting the future of public transportation and recommended specific actions that might be taken by the public transportation industry, government, and private sector groups to provide a favorable future environment for public transportation. In its report, APTA identified five major forces that were apt to affect public transportation in the coming decades. These forces and APTA's observations and conclusions relating to them are as follows:

Congestion and Auto Dominance

> Auto availability and use will continue to increase, but the cost, convenience and consequences of personal vehicle travel are likely to deteriorate significantly in more and more areas of the country, heightening the need for new options and strategies to enhance mobility. . . . the high rate of suburban growth is expected to continue into the next century . . . emerging development patterns require a broader range of public transportation solutions and related actions focused on capturing "choice" riders and serving the needs of particular consumers, geographic sub-areas and trip purposes.[7]

Threats to the Environment

> Worsening air quality represents a growing crisis for the nation. . . . It appears, therefore, any success in reducing air pollution will require strategies that seek to alter travel behavior, including efforts to increase ridership on transit and other high-occupancy modes.[8]

Threats to Energy Independence

> As a nation, we now risk becoming more dependent on foreign sources of petroleum than at any time since the early 1970s. . . . A coherent long-term energy policy must be put in place. . . . Increasing ridership on transit and high-occupancy services will be an important element of this policy.[9]

Inadequate Infrastructure Investment

> The trend of declining infrastructure investment, particularly in transportation and public transit remains a mounting threat to our economy and quality of life.[10]

Demographic Change

> The number of persons over 65 will grow. . . . the number of women in the work force will increase. . . . minorities will account for nearly 60 percent of the population growth through the year 2000. . . . By virtue of their sheer numbers, these segments of the population will require that increased attention be paid to their varying travel preferences and patterns, and that the availability of both traditional and nontraditional services be expanded.[11]

Not surprisingly, APTA concludes that public transportation has an important role in dealing with the major forces likely to influence the future of transportation. The APTA report acknowledges, however, that the transit industry itself might have to take several initiatives in achieving such a role. Table 23-1 lists six goals that the report argues are important in guiding the actions of the transit industry in future decades. Interestingly, APTA portrays a broadened role for the transit industry as being a manager of mobility in metropolitan areas, including involvement in those services such as ridesharing that have traditionally fallen outside the purview of the transit agency. As noted in the report, "elevating these new roles and the establishment of new relationships between the public and private sectors in managing mobility is a major direction for public transit agencies in the future."[12]

AASHTO'S FUTURE DIRECTIONS AND TRANSPORTATION 2020

The American Association of State Highway and Transportation Officials (AASHTO) is a national organization that represents all state transportation agencies in the United States. As such, AASHTO is concerned with all transportation modes and, in particular, focuses on the substance and magnitude of funding programs that support the transportation system. AASHTO undertook two efforts during the 1980s that examined the future of public transportation and made extensive recommendations

TABLE 23-1
Transit Industry Goals for the Future

GOAL 1	Preserve, protect, and expand current markets and choices available to current public transportation users.
GOAL 2	Pursue new markets, increased ridership, and expanded market share by both traditional and innovative means.
GOAL 3	Seek increased investment in public transportation at all levels.
GOAL 4	Assume new responsibilities and forge new relationships in both the management of mobility as well as in the provision of public transportation services.
GOAL 5	Foster and participate in land-use planning actions that more effectively integrate economic development and infrastructure investment decisions to enhance the use of public transportation in its many forms.
GOAL 6	Enhance public awareness and acceptance of the need for greater investment and new partnerships in preserving and enhancing mobility for all.

Source: Adapted from American Public Transit Association, *Transit 2000* (Washington, D.C.: American Public Transit Association, 1989), p. 20.

for future actions. The importance of these efforts is in great part a reflection of the fact that, during the 1980s, state departments of transportation surpassed the federal government as the major source of outside funding to transit agencies. State transportation agencies, consequently, have and will continue to have a major voice in the overall policies and funding arrangements for public transportation.

A Study on Future Directions

In 1985 AASHTO issued a report entitled *A Study on Future Directions of Public Transportation in the United States*. As noted in the report's introduction, the study represented a national effort on the part of state transportation agencies to identify the important role they could play in supporting public transportation, in cooperation with the federal government, the private sector, and local communities. Importantly, AASHTO, similarly to APTA, considered public transportation as consisting of more than one type of service. The AASHTO definition stated that public transportation was "not a single mode, but a mixture of modes (transit, ridesharing, and paratransit) each complementing the other and interacting to form a system for passenger mobility and a cost-effective group of services."[13]

In looking at the different factors that could influence the future of public transportation, the report concluded that it was possible to envision one future scenario in which development of the public transit industry would likely continue. This future scenario would incorporate the following characteristics:

> *Demographic and land use* changes will present new problems and opportunities for the industry. . . .

639

Less federal funding would create problems for some transit systems. There will be a need to develop more stable funding sources with *state and local governments*, but it is unlikely that funds will be in adequate supply.

Transit managers will experience *less political interference* and have greater flexibility to run their system. Part of the reason for this change will be increased involvement by the *private sector* in the transit industry.

Cost consciousness will be a key aspect of all transit system operations. Failure to control costs will lead to bankruptcy and the demise of various systems.

Professionalism will take on new meaning in the industry as managers and governing boards recognize that survival, and expansion, are functions of better professional performance. . . .

Moderate gains in technology will be of value to the transit industry. Such gains are not likely to be spectacular breakthroughs, but more likely system innovations that develop over time.

Increased industry involvement by all participants, leading to increased political involvement, seems likely to occur. . . .[14]

The report concludes by presenting recommendations to the various groups that would necessarily be involved in the future of public transportation—the federal government, state governments, local governments, public transit operators, labor, private operators, the business community, transit users, and industry associations.

Transportation 2020

Several years after publishing the *Future Directions* report, AASHTO was involved in a major national effort called Transportation 2020, which was organized to lay the groundwork for future transportation programs. As part of this effort, several groups were formed and positions and policies adopted on all aspects of a national transportation program, including future consideration for public transportation. AASHTO focused on several components of possible futures for public transportation, but three areas received the most attention—future technological innovations, institutional structures, and financial needs.

The discussion of technology primarily examined the question of whether one could anticipate any major technological breakthroughs in the technology of public transportation during the next several decades. In a paper written to provide the context for the discussion on technology, Harman[15] outlined the major advances anticipated in the different forms of public transportation. These included:

Buses. There will likely be production of a bus that has two methods of propulsion in one coach, a diesel engine for use on suburban streets and electric power for city streets and in tunnels. [This bus is now in use in Seattle.] Some innovation can be expected in alternative forms of access to the vehicle, in particular for the elderly and handicapped. Although some concepts are currently being developed that would make the bus–road interface much more "intelligent" in terms of navigation and vehicle control, such programs are not likely to see widespread implementation in the early part of the twenty-first century.

Heavy and Light Rail. The major source of innovation will likely come in the means of providing propulsion and in automatic system control.

Commuter and Intercity Rail. There were possible major advances that could be anticipated in the application of magnetic levitation technology and other forms of providing high-speed passenger transportation.

Automated Guideway. The technology for implementing automated guideway transit, group rapid transit, or personal rapid transit systems is already available. The key issue is now to find the appropriate applications.

Harman then suggested that perhaps the greatest technological innovations will come in the areas of transit user information systems, automatic vehicle monitoring, and in "revisiting" already tested applications such as high-occupancy vehicle facilities.

The institutional framework within which public transportation agencies operate will be an important factor for the future of the public transportation industry. In a discussion paper[16] on the institutional environment of transit, AASHTO identified four major factors that could heavily influence the reformulation of institutional roles:

1. The impact of budget deficit on public transportation funding programs.
2. The impact of demands on the provision of public transportation service (for example, specialized services for the elderly).
3. The impact of private sector competition.
4. The impact of federal labor protection rules on the costs of providing service.

Finally, the AASHTO 2020 effort gave considerable attention to the financing needs of the industry.[17] Three scenarios were used to develop the expected capital costs of achieving different policy objectives. The first scenario involved maintaining the existing physical system, retiring the backlog of required investments in fixed facilities, and sustaining the fleet of rail and bus vehicles at its current size and average age. It was estimated in the AASHTO effort that simply continuing existing funding levels ($2.09 billion annually in 1988) would result in the average age of a bus vehicle in areas over 200,000 population increasing from 8.4 years in 1989 to 12 years by the year 2000 (optimum bus life is 6 years). Similarly, rail vehicle average age would reach 22 years, up from 17 years in 1989 (optimum is 12.5 years). By the year 2020, nearly 25% of all rail trackage in U.S. rail transit systems and nearly 60% of the bus maintenance and storage facilities would need repair. Deterioration of the physical plant would be even more dramatic in areas under 200,000 population.

The second scenario represented taking the necessary steps to reduce existing average ages of the fleet to the preferred average age. The immediate consequence to the transit industry, of course, would be to accelerate the replacement of the current fleet as compared to existing policies. By so doing, however, a newer fleet could be expected to produce operating and maintenance savings that could be used to offset this increased cost.

The third scenario assumed that transit travel would retain its current market share relative to highway travel in the future. Given an assumed annual increase of 2.14% (the same magnitude assumed for growth in highway travel), to keep its market share annual transit ridership would have to increase from about 8.8 billion annual riders in 1989 to about 11 billion by 2000 and to over 17 billion by 2020. This increase in demand would first fill up existing capacity reserves, but would then require capacity expansion. AASHTO estimated that over 14,000 new buses and 2375 new rail vehicles would be needed to serve this demand. By 2020, this growth would require nearly doubling the 1989 bus fleet and a 50% increase in the rail fleet.

Table 23-2 presents the average annual costs associated with each scenario. One of the major conclusions from this table is that substantial sums of money, more than is being allocated today, must be found just to keep the condition of the transit fleet at 1989 levels. Of special note is that Table 23-2 only presents capital cost estimates. AASHTO estimated that operating costs to maintain the existing conditions scenario between 1988 and 1991 would result in a $1 billion annual shortfall, given 1988 financing outlays.

TABLE 23-2
Capital Investment Estimates for Alternative Scenarios

Enhancements Urbanized Areas $ million (current)	Time Period				
	1988–1991	1992–2000	2001–2010	2011–2020	Total
Projected total capital funding	8,463	18,283	20,050	20,050	66,846
Estimated total capital costs to maintain status quo condition	15,200	27,041	22,217	22,860	87,318
Estimated total incremental investment to achieve ideal condition	1,792	2,688	——	——	4,480
Estimated total incremental investment to maintain market share	——	4,537	4,703	5,813	15,055

Source: Adapted from Linda M. Wheeler, Joseph Voccia, and William Lenski, "Financial Resource Needs of Public Transportation Systems," *Transportation Quarterly*, 43, no. 4 (October 1989), 537.

NATIONAL COUNCIL ON PUBLIC WORKS IMPROVEMENT

In response to a general public concern on the state of the nation's infrastructure, the U.S. Congress in 1984 created the National Council on Public Works Improvement. As part of its mandate, the council undertook a study of mass transit facilities and services in the United States. In reviewing the history of mass transit, especially during recent years, the study concluded that transit policies and programs had fallen short of their stated objectives and that it was the governmental structure of such policies and programs that was in itself primarily to blame. For example, the report concluded that the large federal discretionary capital element of the federal transit program had distorted local decision making toward capital-intensive transit systems and away from more cost-effective approaches such as preferential bus facilities.

The report makes several conclusions that are important in the context of this chapter in that they provide another set of factors that could influence public transportation in the twenty-first century. These include:

> The monopoly operation of mass transit has led to a rather restricted set of organizational arrangements and service offerings, namely public ownership and operation of fixed route services using large buses and rail lines. The demography of urban areas has been evolving in ways which make it more and more difficult for conventional fixed route bus and rail services to serve the demand for trips. More flexible services using taxis, vans and minibuses could serve many of these new markets more effectively. . . .

> There are great difficulties in achieving rational combinations of mass transit, highway, and land use policies in U.S. cities because of the nature of existing institutional arrangements and because of extensive earmarking in transportation funding programs. . . . the prospects for more integrated approaches to transportation and land use planning in U.S. cities do not look very good at the present time. . . .

> The institutional arrangements for transit in most U.S. cities direct all public financial assistance for transit to a single publicly-owned transit agency. . . . alternative services and providers are often neglected, and many important related policy areas such as land use, roads, and parking, are addressed inadequately if at all. The solution to this problem is to separate transit policy-making from transit operations. . . .

> . . . further reforms of policies and programs are critical to future successes, because many of the advances to date have been gained at a very high financial cost and without addressing major institutional issues . . . .[18]

In discussing the prospective impact of public transportation, the report concluded that "More realism will be needed in defining the aspirations of transit in the future, with the focus on what is achievable within the prevailing land use and transportation policy environment."[19]

These three major efforts—from APTA, AASHTO, and the National Council on Public Works Improvement—provide different perspectives on the future prospects of public transportation. Each identifies key factors that will clearly influence the type and level of public transportation service we will see in the twenty-first century. Probably the most important theme that runs through each study is that the characteristics of the future public transportation system are not so much a reflection of the social and economic environment as they are of the willingness of public officials and the private sector to put in place the financing and complementary public policies (for example, parking management) that will be necessary to develop the public transportation system that is desired.

PUBLIC TRANSPORTATION IN THE 21st CENTURY

What then can we expect of public transportation in the twenty-first century? It is first important to state that there *will* be some form of public transportation. Such service provides an important mobility function in urban areas that is unlikely to be replaced by some other system. Many of our cities, especially the older, denser cities of the Northeast and Midwest, and even newer cities like Atlanta, Denver, San Francisco, and Seattle, depend very heavily on transit service. And although the central cities will presumably continue to show proportionately less growth than the surrounding metropolitan area, the central business district of most cities will continue to be an important regional activity center requiring some form of high-capacity transit service.

On the other hand, some aspects of twenty-first-century public transportation, and especially of the public transportation agency, could be very different from today. There are three factors of those described in the previous section that, in particular, will play a relatively greater role in influencing the future than others.

1. The large costs of maintaining existing levels of transit service, and even larger costs for service expansion.
2. The continuing reliance of the American public on the private automobile for personal transportation.
3. Low-density development continuing to occur throughout our metropolitan areas (although there will also probably be some population and employment trends back toward higher densities in urban centers and suburban activity centers).

These factors suggest that it will be very difficult to provide appreciable levels of effective transit service in the growing suburbs of our metropolitan areas, at least with transit service as traditionally defined. Several authors have reached a similar conclusion and have recommended that the future viability of public transportation depends on the industry itself taking several steps. Jones,[20] for example, argued that the federal support for transit in the 1960s and 1970s helped transit agencies to temporarily reverse ridership declines, but that this support was a response to the symptoms rather than the causes of the problems facing the industry. He argued that successful transit agencies of the future would be pursuing six goals: reestablishing manageability, matching services to markets more effectively and efficiently, restraining cost escalation, achieving sustained productivity improvement, preserving reasonable continuity of service and fares, and preserving the economic welfare of the transit worker. Because these six goals do in fact help a transit agency respond to the important trends previously described, they do seem to be appropriate characteristics of future successful transit agencies. In addition to these goals, Jones described six *structural* changes that were also necessary for future success. These changes are shown in Table 23-3. In concluding, Jones stated that "In the absence of fundamental change, gradual economic attrition will characterize the industry's future—as it has its past. . . . For transit, change is the essence of stabilization."[21]

TABLE 23-3
Recommended Structural Changes for Transit

A new fare structure	One that is differentiated by time of day and distance traveled.
Greater discretion to price in relation to cost	Achievable if a surtax is imposed on all-day service parking.
A new sales-oriented organization structure	One that is decentralized so that planning, routing, and scheduling decisions can be based on an intimate knowledge of the market for locally customized services.
A different fleet mix	One with the capacity necessary to serve the peak but better suited to shuttle, charter, and taxilike operations in the off-peak.
A wider diversity of service offerings	Some sold on a contract or subscription basis, some purchased from private vendors.
A new contract with labor	One that permits wider use of part-time and cross-trained employees while creating a wider range of promotion opportunities for transit workers.

Source: Adapted from David W. Jones, Jr., *Urban Transit Policy: An Economic and Political History*, ©1985), p. 171. Adapted by permission of Prentice Hall, Englewood Cliffs, N.J.

The major thrust of Jones's conclusions is for greater productivity in the transit industry. This theme of improved productivity as the basis of a successful transit future is found in several other references as well. Meyer and Gómez-Ibáñez, for example, conclude that the primary goal in the future will be "reducing routine operating labor requirements, while still maintaining reasonable levels of service . . . . Transit can also be adapted to take better advantage of its market opportunities."[22] Similarly, a 1984 conference on the future of public transportation recommended that the future transit industry had to take several steps: take more global and strategic views, develop flexible services for suburban areas, aggressively work with the private sector to develop better market conditions for transit and more cost-effective service, and better meet cost control and efficiency mandates.[23] Finally, Fielding,[24] in identifying the same problems facing transit, concluded that the truly successful transit agency will have adopted a strategic management approach that relates stated goals to the internal and external resources needed to achieve them.

Even with improved productivity and market-based services being major concerns in future transit agencies, it seems likely that the core of the public transportation system in twenty-first-century U.S. cities will be similar to what we have today. High-capacity, line-haul transit service and local bus systems (where ridership permits) will still be the responsibility of a governmental agency. Cities will continue to explore alternative ways of segregating high-speed transit service from normal road traffic to allow transit to operate more effectively. Houston's regional transitway system and Seattle's regional high-occupancy vehicle (HOV) lane and dual-mode bus corridor program are two examples of how this can be done. Other cities, like Los Angeles and Minneapolis–St. Paul are considering rail alternatives. However, there will be an important difference between past efforts and what will be done in the future. Because most of our metropolitan areas will no longer be dominated by a single downtown, but rather will consist of major activity centers dispersed throughout the region, planning for high-capacity public transportation in the future will focus on (1) how to connect regional commuter markets to all major metropolitan activity centers and (2) how to interconnect the activity centers themselves. This latter issue, the interconnection of activity centers, has received attention in numerous studies throughout the United States (for example, in Atlanta, Boston, Houston, and Seattle).

Future public transportation is also apt to have different institutional/funding arrangements from those that exist today. Obtaining the necessary funds to support transit service and dealing with the suburban market are two major reasons why these arrangements will probably be different. The following sections identify some of the most likely changes.

THE PUBLIC TRANSIT AGENCY OF THE FUTURE WILL BE INVOLVED WITH NOT ONLY WHAT IS CONSIDERED TODAY AS TRADITIONAL TRANSIT SERVICES, BUT ALSO WITH ACTIONS THAT FOCUS ON TRAVEL DEMAND MANAGEMENT (TDM).

Transit agency involvement in travel demand management (for example, ridesharing, flextime, and trip reduction ordinances) will be caused primarily by the changing development patterns of our urban areas. Dispersed employment sites and even more dispersed residential locations will preclude the feasible use of high-capacity transit to serve all major work-trip patterns. In high-growth areas, congestion will doubtlessly continue to be a critical public concern. With major expansion of the road system infeasible or unwanted, many local officials have begun to use other means to assure reasonable levels of service on the road system (in some areas, air quality concerns could be an important factor influencing such consideration). Through local ordinances that require certain levels of trip reduction or through initiatives that encourage the development of employer-based mobility plans, the management of travel demand will be an important concern to twenty-first-century transportation officials. Whether the transit agency itself provides the expertise for analyzing TDM actions and eventually implements the service or whether it simply works closely with employer associations and/or nonprofit commuting organizations, the transit agency of the future will be involved with travel demand management strategies. They are a logical extension of the agency's primary purpose.

MANY TRANSIT AGENCIES WILL BE FUNDING NONTRANSIT (FOR EXAMPLE, ROAD) IMPROVEMENTS AS PART FINANCING, PART CONSTITUENCY-BUILDING EFFORTS.

Securing the funds that are necessary to rehabilitate today's physical plant (for example, railbeds, maintenance facilities, and buses) and also to operate tomorrow's service will create serious pressures on a transit agency to broaden its constituency. It will not be surprising to see transit agencies using "transit" funds to build or improve roads as a means of doing this. Such is the case today in Houston, where 25% of the sales tax receipts dedicated to transit use are used for "general mobility" projects, most often road improvements. Such a strategy is effective in showing the general public the transportation benefits of dedicated tax sources for transit. In other cases, transit agencies will not be directly responsible for road improvements, but dedicated sources of funding for transit (like sales taxes) will more likely be dedicated sources of funding for general transportation or mobility purposes. Transit programs would thus be funded within a much broader financing strategy. In some extreme cases, transit agencies might even disappear as separate agencies but remain as a function of a "super transportation" organization. Such a regional transportation agency is currently being considered in Denver.

NONTRANSIT TRANSPORTATION AGENCIES WILL SPEND AN INCREASING SUM OF MONEY ON RETROFITTING ROADWAYS OR TRANSFER POINTS TO ACCOMMODATE PUBLIC TRANSPORTATION SERVICES.

In many urban areas, highway agencies have been spending significant sums of money on traffic signal coordination and transit signal preemption, preferential transit lanes at key congested locations, and pedestrian amenities at transit terminals. These types of highway-related transit investments will likely continue as the result of a continuing emphasis on a multimodal transportation approach to solving mobility and congestion problems.

For at least some travel patterns in U.S. metropolitan areas, high-capacity transit could provide an appealing alternative to automobile travel. To provide such capacity without spending large sums of money in building a new fixed-guideway transit system, many urban areas will likely examine more closely the transit use of existing roadways. For example, in Houston a regional reconstruction of the urban freeway system has been coordinated with the construction of busways in the freeway medians. In numerous metropolitan areas, high-occupancy vehicle lanes are used today to accommodate large volumes of transit riders.[25] In Atlanta, the design for the reconstructed urban freeway system included access and egress points for future HOV lanes, the only issue yet to be decided being when to put the lanes in operation. If for no other reason than the expensive cost of obtaining new land (right-of-way) for the construction of high-capacity transit facilities, one is likely to see more *highway* corridors in urban areas becoming *transportation* corridors, with some form of high-capacity transit in place near the highway, most probably in the freeway median. (In some cases, these transportation corridors will be transportation–utility corridors that include not only transportation facilities, but also distribution systems linked to such things as telecommunication, power, and water).

BESIDES THE CURRENT REVENUES FOR TRANSIT THAT COME FROM GOVERNMENT GRANTS AND FARES, FUTURE TRANSIT FINANCE WILL INCLUDE A GREATER SHARE FROM THOSE (OTHER THAN RIDERS) WHO BENEFIT FROM TRANSIT SERVICES.

Especially in connection with the construction of new high-capacity facilities, we are apt to see such mechanisms as special assessment districts used to provide financial support for transit. In such a case, a specified geographic area and/or a target group such as businesses are identified as gaining from the initiation of new transit service. A special tax is then assessed to contribute toward the public expense of providing the service. Even though such an approach is likely to be used more frequently in the twenty-first century, the base financing for public transportation will still remain as it is today, dedicated tax sources or government grants (increasingly from state governments).

PUBLIC TRANSIT AGENCIES WILL BE INCREASINGLY INVOLVED WITH THE SERVICE DESIGN, FUNDING, AND FARE POLICY ISSUES ASSOCIATED WITH THE CONNECTION OF NONAGENCY SERVICES TO THE BASE TRANSIT NETWORK.

As metropolitan areas continue to grow, many suburban areas will begin offering their own types of transit service, much more limited yet tailored to their specific needs. As opportunities arise, private providers of public transit services will also enter the market. In addition, some major activity centers will construct automated people-mover systems that will provide internal circulation for that site (such systems are currently in use in Las Colinas near Dallas and in downtown Detroit and Miami). Many of these services, to be effective, will need to be connected to the regional transit network. Such connections will require agreements concerning the use and pricing of the respective services. The public transit agency of the future, through its provision of the regional base transit network and its planning expertise, will thus become an important actor in regional mobility even beyond its service area.

PUBLIC TRANSIT IN THE TWENTY-FIRST CENTURY WILL BE VIEWED IN THE CONTEXT OF THE GENERAL TRANSPORTATION SYSTEM, AND THE INTERMODAL TRANSFER FROM ONE SERVICE (FOR EXAMPLE, TRANSIT) TO ANOTHER (FOR EXAMPLE, AN AIRPORT) WILL BE A CRITICAL SYSTEM DESIGN ISSUE.

Metropolitan areas in the twenty-first century will be tied together by economic and political forces that relate more to the global economy than they do to local political considerations. The economic competitiveness of each metropolitan area will be influenced by numerous factors, the existence of an educated labor force, a good quality of life environment, an established service industry, connection to capital markets, and a working transportation system. An effective transportation system will require good interconnections between the different modes of transportation available in the region. Consequently, the twenty-first-century highway system will be expanded or modified to provide convenient access to ports, rail yards, trucking terminals, airports, and transit facilities. Transit services will be viewed with particular interest in providing convenient interconnection opportunities with the highway system and airports. It is no surprise that new rail transit services have recently opened in Atlanta and Chicago. Such connections will become increasingly important for the twenty-first-century city.

SUMMARY

As noted in the beginning of this chapter, predicting the future of public transportation is full of uncertainty. What type of transit services we will have in the twenty-first century depends on many factors that could dramatically change the type and extent of such services. A significant change in the provision of federal transit funds, for example, something that is very difficult to predict, could substantially influence the direction of public transit in almost every U.S. city. Traffic congestion could reach such levels in some cities that local officials would implement development and parking management strategies that would greatly enhance transit's role in the region. Air quality attainment policies will also likely have significant impacts on future transit services. Assuming some stability in the external factors that influence transit, however, the twenty-first-century public transportation system will most likely look something like that shown in Figure 23-1. The key characteristics of this system include:

1. The public transit agency will be primarily responsible for the line-haul, high-capacity means of public transit and for local bus service where ridership warrants such service.
2. The many activity centers in the metropolitan area, of which the downtown is just one, are connected with some form of high-capacity transit.
3. Employee transportation to and from these major activity centers will be managed by activity center business associations or by the transit agency under contract with such associations.
4. Nontransit agency services, provided by either suburban county or private providers, will interconnect with the mainline transit system at major activity centers or at transfer points.
5. People-mover systems will provide internal circulation in the densest of activity centers and will interconnect with the mainline transit system at transfer points.

6. Major transit service, whether high capacity or some form of individualized service, will be provided to key intermodal transportation terminals such as airports.

In addition to these system characteristics, the transit agency of the twenty-first century will exist in a different institutional–funding environment than that which exists today. In particular, it is likely that agency officials will be concerned with more than just traditional transit service. Such things as demand management techniques, land-use planning, combined transit and road funding, and working with a wide variety of other groups interested in transportation will most likely make the transit agency of the twenty-first century an organization that has much broader interests than today's transit agencies.

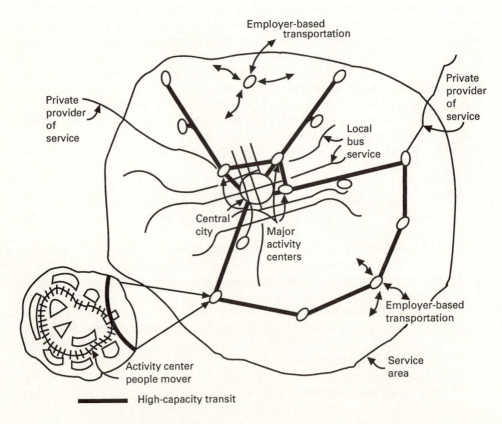

Figure 23-1 *Likely public transportation system in the twenty-first century.*

REFERENCES

1 TRANSPORTATION RESEARCH BOARD, *New Organizational Responses to the Changing Transit Environment*, Special Report 217, proceedings of a conference at Norfolk, Va., December 2-4, 1987, sponsored by UMTA (Washington, D.C.: Transportation Research Board, 1988).

2 HIGHWAY USERS FEDERATION FOR SAFETY AND MOBILITY, *Beyond the Interstate* (Washington, D.C.: Highway Users Federation, n.d.).

3 U.S. DEPARTMENT OF TRANSPORTATION, *Moving America, New Directions, New Opportunities, Volume 1: Building the National Transportation Policy* (Washington, D.C.: U.S. Department of Transportation, July 1989).

4 AMERICAN PUBLIC TRANSIT ASSOCIATION, *Transit 2000* (Washington, D.C.: American Public Transit Association, 1989).

5 AMERICAN ASSOCIATION OF STATE HIGHWAY AND TRANSPORTATION OFFICIALS, *Keep America Moving: New Transportation Concepts for a New Century* (Washington, D.C.: American Association of State Highway and Transportation Officials, October 1989).

6 U.S. DEPARTMENT OF TRANSPORTATION, *Moving America, New Directions, New Opportunities: A Statement of National Transportation Policy, Strategies for Action* (Washington, D.C.: U.S. Department of Transportation, February 1990).

7 APTA, *Transit 2000*, p. 4.

8 Ibid.

9 Ibid., p. 8.

10 Ibid., p. 9.

11 Ibid., p. 10.

12 Ibid., p. 12.

13 AMERICAN ASSOCIATION OF STATE HIGHWAY AND TRANSPORTATION OFFICIALS, *AASHTO Report: A Study on Future Directions of Public Transportation in the United States* (Washington, D.C.: American Association of State Highway and Transportation Officials, February 22, 1985), p. 1.

14 Ibid., pp. 44-45.

15 L. HARMAN, *Technological Change and Public Transportation—Issues for the Year 2020* (draft manuscript, Massachusetts Executive Office of Transportation and Construction, Boston, Mass., 1988).

16 AMERICAN ASSOCIATION OF STATE HIGHWAY AND TRANSPORTATION OFFICIALS, *Transit: Institutional Environment*, a discussion paper (Washington, D.C.: American Association of State Highway and Transportation Officials, 1988).

17 AMERICAN ASSOCIATION OF STATE HIGHWAY AND TRANSPORTATION OFFICIALS, *Keep America Moving: The Bottom Line, A Summary of Surface Transportation Investment Requirements, 1988–2020* (Washington, D.C.: American Association of State Highway and Transportation Officials, September 1988).

18 RONALD F. KIRBY AND ARLEE T. RENO, *Study of Policy Issues in the Public Works Category of Mass Transit*, [cover title] *The Nation's Public Works: Report on Mass Transit*, prepared for the National Council on Public Works Improvement by The Urban Institute, Categories of Public Works Series (Washington, D.C.: National Council on Public Works Improvement, May 1987), pp. 111-13.

19 Ibid., p. 114.

20   DAVID W. JONES, JR., *Urban Transit Policy: An Economic and Political History* (Englewood Cliffs, N.J.: Prentice Hall, 1985).

21   Ibid., p. 178.

22   JOHN R. MEYER AND JOSÉ GÓMEZ-IBÁÑEZ, *Autos, Transit, and Cities: A Twentieth Century Fund Report* (Cambridge, Mass.: Harvard University Press, 1981), pp. 295-96.

23   TRANSPORTATION RESEARCH BOARD, *A Look Ahead: Year 2020*, proceedings of the Conference on Long-Range Trends and Requirements for the Nation's Highway and Public Transit Systems, Special Report 220, (Washington, D.C.: Transportation Research Board, 1988).

24   GORGON J. FIELDING, *Managing Public Transit Strategically: A Comprehensive Approach to Strengthening Service and Monitoring Performance* (San Francisco: Jossey-Bass, Publishers, 1987).

25   INSTITUTE OF TRANSPORTATION ENGINEERS, *A Toolbox for Alleviating Traffic Congestion* (Washington, D.C.: Institute of Transportation Engineers, 1989).

FURTHER READING

ALTSHULER, ALAN, WITH JAMES P. WOMACK AND JOHN R. PUCHER, *The Urban Transportation System: Politics and Policy Innovation*. Cambridge, Mass.: The MIT Press, 1979.

FIELDING, GORDON J., "Transit in American Cities," in *The Geography of Urban Transportation*, ed. Susan Hanson. New York: The Guilford Press, 1986, pp. 229-46.

HAMER, ANDREW MARSHALL, *The Selling of Rail Rapid Transit: A Critical Look at Urban Transportation Planning*. Lexington, Mass.: D.C. Heath and Company, 1976.

HEMILY, B., AND M. MEYER, "The Future of Urban Public Transportation: The Problem and Opportunities of a Changing Federal Role," *Transportation Law Journal*, 12, no. 2, University of Denver, 1982.

PICKRELL, DON H., *The Causes of Rising Transit Operating Deficits*, Final Report, prepared by John F. Kennedy School of Government, Harvard University, for UMTA, Technology Sharing Program, Report no. DOT-I-83-47. Washington, D.C.: U.S. Department of Transportation, July 1983.

SCHOFER, JOSEPH L., "Does This Bus Go to the Future? Some Thoughts on the Future of Urban Public Transit," in *Future Directions of Urban Public Transportation*, proceedings of a conference at Woods Hole, Mass., September 26-29, 1982, Special Report 199, pp. 59-66. Washington, D.C.: Transportation Research Board, 1983.

URBAN MASS TRANSPORTATION ADMINISTRATION, *The Status of the Nation's Mass Public Transportation, Performance and Conditions,* Report of the Secretary of Transportation to the United States Congress, Pursuant to 49 USC 308, prepared by UMTA. Washington, D.C.: U.S. Government Printing Office, June 1988.

ZWERLING, STEPHEN, *Mass Transit and the Politics of Technology: A Study of BART and the San Francisco Bay Area*. New York: Praeger, 1974.

EXERCISES

23-1 Travel behavior is directly tied to the type of development patterns that exist in a metropolitan area. For example, in New York City, dense development patterns have contributed to high levels of transit ridership, whereas in newer, auto-dominated cities, transit ridership is minimal. For the following types of future development patterns for a city with which you are familiar, identify the likely patterns of transit ridership that will result: (a) development occurring mainly in existing major employment sites and activity centers, including the downtown; (b) development occurring mainly in the existing suburban employment sites and activity centers, with disinvestment occurring in the downtown; and (c) development occurring mainly on the current periphery of the urban area, resulting in increased sprawl throughout the region.

23-2 For a city with which you are familiar, identify what you consider to be the key economic, social, demographic, and political characteristics of its future. How will these characteristics influence the future of transit in this city?

23-3 Assume you are an advisor to a secretary of transportation, governor, or mayor who wants to issue a policy statement on the future of transportation. Outline the key components of such a statement that you would recommend. How does your policy relate to public transportation?

23-4 Multimodal transportation planning considers all modes of transportation and their interfaces. Considering transit in the twenty-first century, how should such multimodal transportation planning be undertaken? What are the likely characteristics of such a planning process?

23-5 Previous chapters have outlined the types of improvements that can be made to transit systems, ranging from simple operational changes (like rescheduling) to major capital investments (like subways). For a city with which you are familiar, identify those types of improvements that will likely be made over the next 20 years to improve public transportation. Assume in one scenario that sufficient funds are available to implement whatever improvement is necessary. In another scenario, assume limited funds and thus a serious constraint on what is possible.

23-6 Many people hope that advances in transportation technology will solve all the transportation problems our society currently faces. Think about some of the technological innovations that are likely to occur in the next 20 years (see Chap. 24). How will these technologies affect public transportation?

Chapter 24

NEW PUBLIC TRANSPORTATION TECHNOLOGY

CLARK HENDERSON

The subjects of this chapter are urban public transportation systems that represent significant changes and advances in equipment, facilities, operations, and services, in comparison with conventional rail, bus, taxi, and other street modes. System-level advances, such as automated and remote controls, are the focus of attention, rather than improvements in subsystems or components, such as engines or brakes for existing modes.

The names of advanced systems have not yet been standardized; however, the system classes of main interest are discussed under the following headings:

- Automated guideway transit (AGT).[1]
    Shuttle-loop transit (SLT).
    Group rapid transit (GRT).
    Personal rapid transit (PRT).
- Rent-by-the-trip public automobile service (PAS).
- Dual-controlled AGT (D-AGT).
- Automated mixed-traffic vehicles (AMTV).
- Accelerating moving ways (AMW).
- Fast transit links (FTL).

The term *advanced systems* is used to refer to all such systems.

Four themes are presented. First, an entirely new standard of urban public transportation service is needed, and deserves public financial support, to ensure that transportation-disadvantaged individuals have equal access to opportunities and to provide nonautomobile alternatives for others. This new standard is called *full-service transit* and refers to service of good quality for all urban residents, at all times of day or night and for all trips throughout urban areas. Second, it is technically feasible to develop advanced transit systems that have a variety of valuable new characteristics. Third, a combination of systems, deployed in complementary sets throughout urban areas, can greatly improve the quality, increase the quantity, decrease the unit costs, and ease the accessibility of urban public transportation service. Fourth, the benefits and costs of each proposed system should be assessed in terms of its potential contribution to full-service transit and in comparisons with alternative systems.

EVOLUTION OF INTEREST

Work on advanced systems of some types, such as an accelerating moving way, was done as early as the late nineteenth century. However, the development and use of advanced systems did not attract significant interest and effort until the mid-1960s. Progress has occurred mainly since the passage of the Reuss-Tydings Amendments to the Urban Mass Transportation Act of 1964. The act required the Secretary of Housing and Urban Development to

> undertake a project to study and prepare a program of research, development, and demonstration of new systems of urban transportation that will carry people and goods within metropolitan areas speedily, safely, without polluting the air, and in a manner that will contribute to sound city planning. The program shall (1) concern itself with all aspects of new systems of urban transportation for metropolitan areas of various sizes, including technological, financial, economic, governmental, and social aspects; (2) take into account the most advanced available technologies and materials; and (3) provide national leadership to efforts of States, localities, private industry, universities, and foundations.[2]

The summary report of that project was submitted by President Johnson to the Congress in May 1968.[3] That report and numerous input documents prepared by contractors stimulated interest in the planning of advanced systems in the United States and abroad and provided much of the basis for planning research and development programs by the Urban Mass Transportation Administration (UMTA) from 1968 through the early 1970s. One of the input documents[4] described several conceptual systems of the kinds discussed in this chapter.

Immediate and strong interest was shown by inventors, private sector research and development institutions, transportation planning consultants, government transportation agencies at all levels, industrial firms seeking roles as suppliers, and prospective owners and operators of advanced systems. AGT systems were the main focus of attention, but smaller efforts were applied to several other advanced systems. Industrial firms and government agencies in the United States, Canada, Western Europe, and Japan had spent more than $200 million by the mid-1970s on research, development, prototype fabrication, and testing of advanced systems and on the installation of AGT systems in four U.S. airports, a few recreation parks, a university, a hospital, and two multipurpose real estate developments. During this period, UMTA initiated a program called the Downtown People Mover Project to exploit fully developed, market-ready AGT systems in numerous central business districts. The scope of that program was greatly reduced and, in 1990, included only systems located in Miami and Jacksonville, Florida, and Detroit, Michigan. After the mid-1970s UMTA's appropriations were reduced and their programs to develop AGT systems, dual-mode buses, high-speed transit, and other advanced systems were eventually abandoned. By 1980 the hope that UMTA would provide leadership in the development of advanced systems had ended.

Throughout the 1970s and 1980s, recreation parks and airports were the most important markets for AGT systems in the United States. Many capable United States firms concluded that opportunities for supplying advanced urban public transportation system for profit were lacking and withdrew from the business. Yet several firms did remain active and supplier interest increased in the 1980s. By 1990, systems had been installed for urban public transportation service in Canada, Australia, England, Japan, France, Germany, and the United States, and AGT projects in progress for urban and other settings had a total estimated capital cost of more than $9 billion.[5]

WHY INNOVATE?

Interest in exploiting advanced systems can usually be related to these arguments:

- Important needs of society can be satisfied only by increasing travel via urban public transportation modes.
- Conventional taxi, bus, and rail systems; private autos; bicycles; and so on, cannot provide the quantity and quality of service needed because of inherent physical, cost, and operating characteristics.
- Sets of advanced systems in combinations promise a variety of capabilities needed to provide full-service transit to all travelers, for all trips, at all times, and throughout entire cities and metropolitan areas.

NEEDS OF SOCIETY

The case for improving and expanding urban public transportation service to benefit society is based on two premises. First, there is a need to provide more and better transportation service to certain transportation-disadvantaged individuals who have limited mobility via automobile and transit. Among these are the young, the old, the poor, the handicapped, individuals who lack driving skills, unlicensed drivers, persons who do not have first claim to an auto, and those who do not have access to transit. The transportation disadvantaged need improved mobility to gain equal access to opportunities of all kinds—employment, residences, schools, recreation, cultural resources, professional services, retail stores, and intercity passenger terminals. The proportions of the population who are transportation disadvantaged vary greatly among cities and neighborhoods and also with individual circumstances; but, overall, the transportation disadvantaged may be on the order of 40% of the urban population.

Second, there is a need to shift a great fraction of existing urban travel from the private automobile to public modes to achieve a variety of objectives. Foremost among these are reducing air pollution, saving energy (especially petroleum fuel), controlling urban development patterns, conserving land, reducing the time and effort of travel, and reducing accidents.

Voters frequently indicate support for transit service by approving increased taxes and other uses of public funds to subsidize conventional urban public transportation services even though these systems may provide service of poor quality. If only conventional modes were used to provide full-service transit, the burdens of subsidies would be severe. Subsidies needed for advanced systems may be acceptable, however, if the average cost of subsidies per trip can be greatly reduced or eliminated. This may be achieved through intensive efforts to achieve cost-effective systems and by the economies of scale resulting from increased travel by the transportation disadvantaged plus the diversion of some riders from automobiles. Transit patronage, now roughly 3% of total urban travel, may be increased as much as tenfold.

LIMITATIONS OF CONVENTIONAL TRANSIT MODES

Existing transit modes are limited in hours of operations, frequency of service, and accessibility, especially in areas where demand density is low. Foremost among the limiting factors are high capital costs, high labor costs, and the aesthetic offense of elevated guideways and stations. Other limiting factors are inflexible operations, low utilization of capacity, and inefficient use of energy. Existing modes can be improved, but these disadvantages cannot be eliminated entirely.

Concerns regarding the visual impacts and noise of elevated rail transit systems cause strong opposition by property owners and residents along the routes. Consequently, many elevated rail systems built in the early 1900s have been demolished and replaced with bus service. To avoid such objections, new rail systems have placed parts of their routes underground at costs and with delays so great that completion of the entire project was often endangered.

The capital cost of heavy rail systems is on the order of $100 million/mi (in 1990 dollars) when a mix of underground, at-grade, and elevated guideways is used, as in the Washington, D.C., Metrorail. Such costs limit applications of heavy rail to a few large cities and, within those cities, to a small fraction of the routes that need transit service. Light rail systems can be less costly. For example, the estimated total capital cost of a proposed elevated light rail system in Orange County, California, was about $36 million/mi, at 1982 prices. The cost of constructing guideways, stations, and related structures was estimated to be $24 million/mi, about two-thirds of the total capital cost. The capital costs of light rail systems at grade in street rights-of-way are less than on elevated structures, but much higher than those of the bus systems with which they must compete. Consequently, light rail systems also have limited application.

Most AGT systems in existence use elevated structures, and conceptual designs for urban applications of advanced systems usually assume that elevated structures will be used. The design of advanced systems will reduce, but will not eliminate, the problems of aesthetic offenses and burdensome capital costs of elevated rail structure. Therefore, the extent of the application of advanced systems will depend, in large part, on the ability of designers to minimize aesthetic impacts and to achieve low construction costs. These difficulties suggest that advanced systems capable of operating on nonexclusive guideways at street level also warrant serious attention.

The high cost of labor is a limiting factor in all conventional systems. Labor is, by far, the dominant element in the cost of providing taxi service, so taxi operators tend to concentrate service at times of day and in areas where demand for service is high. From the viewpoint of the taxi operator, this practice minimizes cruising, empty returns, and waiting time. It also provides slow and unresponsive service, or no service, in low-density areas and at times of low demand, although modern dispatching and control systems have alleviated part of this problem in some cities.

Labor also accounts for a major part of bus operating costs, for example, about 80% in a typical large bus system. It is not possible to schedule work shifts and vehicle operations in ways that fully utilize labor. The productivity of bus drivers, in numbers of passengers served per hour of work, is low because of time spent waiting and moving empty buses, and because buses in revenue service cannot utilize their full passenger capacity during periods of slack demand and when traveling in the off-peak direction. Rail systems are also unable to fully utilize labor, but the cost of direct labor per unit of capacity is relatively low, and direct labor costs are less important than in bus systems.

Private automobiles dominate urban travel because of these major advantages: self-service operation makes automobile service available at no direct labor cost; perceived capital costs are low; the capital costs of roads are quite low, on the order of 1 cent/vehicle-mi; and automobiles provide door-to-door, personal service superior to transit modes for most urban trips. Automobiles also have serious limitations. Service is not available to many because of prohibitive costs and the inability to acquire driving skills and a license. Enormous commitments of land and capital are made for traffic lanes in streets and roads, curb-side parking, driveways and garages at residences, parking at businesses and public buildings, and public parking lots and garages. These facilities must be supplied in relative abundance to provide access to all addresses and to avoid congestion, excessive travel times, and high operating costs. Although some streets are heavily traveled, most city streets have unused capacity that could accommodate advanced street modes. Dependence on the automobile encourages the exploitation of low-cost land and the development of low-density, sprawling communities. Automobiles are major contributors to air pollution, although emissions have been reduced by changes in automobile design and maintenance requirements, and further improvements can be made. The depletion of nonrenewable petroleum resources and dependence on foreign petroleum also influence automobile design and in the future will cause shifts to other energy types and sources, as well as major reduction in vehicle size, weight, performance, and operation. Fatalities, injuries, and property damage from automobiles are tolerated by the public and may not limit travel; however, improved safety is highly desirable. Substituting transit for automobiles in cities will help to overcome these problems.

PROSPECTIVE ADVANTAGES OF ADVANCED SYSTEMS

Each of the advanced systems discussed here promises one or more important advantages over conventional modes; however, no single system combines all the desired features. Therefore, sets of complementary systems will be required to provide full-transit service for entire cities. The main avenues for improvement are:

1.   Automatic controls, remote controls, self-service controls, and continuous or process-type operations promise low labor costs and, consequently, a capability to provide service on low-demand routes not presently served and frequent scheduled service or service on demand at all times, 24 h/day and every day. Automation and remote control also promise low labor cost for vehicle movements in stations, yards, and shops.
2.   Small vehicles, structures, and stations of some AGT systems promise relatively low capital costs per lane-mile. Aesthetically pleasing vehicles, guideways, and stations also promise to reduce opposition to elevated structures.
3.   Advanced street systems such as AMTV and PAS promise very low capital costs per lane-mile by avoiding the construction of guideways and stations. Low costs will permit the installation of advanced systems in fine-mesh networks and in areas of relatively low population density and transit demand. The appearance of advanced street vehicles on nonexclusive guideways at grade will be much less offensive than elevated structures and will more likely be accepted.
4.   Fine-mesh networks promise short walking distances and easy access to transit service.
5.   Advanced street modes promise easy access and acceptable speeds for short trips.
6.   Advanced systems promise direct routes, short delays to board vehicles, off-line stations to avoid stops at en route stations, coupled links at the nodes to eliminate transfers, short travel times, and reduced travel effort.
7.   Mechanized stations and platforms at grade promise easy access to vehicles and savings of time, effort, and inconvenience of travel.

8. Electric propulsion promises savings of petroleum fuel, low noise, and low air pollution by vehicles.
9. Accelerating moving ways (AMW) promise attractive speed for very short trips and large capacities without using large amounts of space to accommodate vehicles.
10. Fast transit link (FTL) systems promise acceptable travel times for very long trips of up to 100 miles.

This chapter focuses on the characteristics that aid in defining the capabilities and roles of actual and conceptual systems in a full-service transit program. Space does not permit full descriptions. Detailed factual data and illustrations will be found in the *International Transit Compendium*,[6] assessment reports sponsored by UMTA and usually obtainable from the U.S. Department of Commerce National Technical Information Service, proceedings of professional society conferences,[7, 8] the *Transit Pulse* newsletter,[9] and trade literature. Life-cycle cost estimates for several systems will be found in *Cost Experience of Automated Guideway Systems*.[10] Estimates of life-cycle direct and indirect energy demands for several systems will be found in *Energy Study for Automated Guideway Transit Systems*.[11]

AUTOMATED GUIDEWAY TRANSIT (AGT)

Automated guideway transit (AGT) systems are characterized by the use of exclusive guideways and vehicles operated without a driver on board. In a full-service transit program, AGT networks would extend throughout urban areas and provide a large fraction of all needed services.

AGT systems are attractive for several reasons. They have low direct labor costs for the operation of vehicles in revenue service and for vehicle movements in yards and shops. Exclusive guideways eliminate interference from pedestrians and vehicles of other types and permit vehicles to travel at average speeds higher than those usually attained by vehicles in mixed traffic. AGT systems have demonstrated excellent safety and reliability and can be safer and more reliable than driver-controlled buses, automobiles, and taxis. They use electric propulsion, conserve petroleum fuels, and are quiet and nonpolluting.

In the 1970s and 1980s more than a dozen companies developed and placed in service some 50 AGT systems. Systems of many kinds not yet developed could be conceived. Discussion of AGT systems is aided by using names for three subclasses: *shuttle-loop transit* (SLT), *group rapid transit* (GRT), and *personal rapid transit* (PRT). The main attributes of each class are summarized in Table 24-1.

Technical and scientific knowledge at hand or attainable gives designers of AGT systems freedom to tailor system performance and capacities to match expected loads

TABLE 24-1

CHARACTERISTICS OF AGT SYSTEMS

Category	SLT	GRT	PRT
Vehicles	Any desired capacity. Single units or trains of any desired length.	Intermediate capacity (e.g., 12-40 passengers). Single units or short trains.	Small capacity (e.g., 1-6 passengers). Single units (in most concepts).
System configurations	Lines are independent shuttles and loops. Stations are on-line. Switches are usually not required.	Lines branch and merge. Stations are usually off-line. Switches are required.	Lines cross, branch, and merge at interchanges. Stations are usually off-line. Switches are required.
Areawide networks	Use many interfacing and intersecting shuttles and loops.	Use multiple interfacing and intersecting GRT systems.	Use a single interconnected or coupled network.
Standardization	The design, capacity, performance, and supplier of each SLT element of a network may differ from all others.	The design, capacity, performance, and supplier of each GRT element of a network may differ from all others.	A single design must be used for the entire network, although capacity and performance may differ among links.
Operations	Vehicles follow single routes. No switching or repetitive switching pattern.	Vehicles follow multiple routes. Repetitive switching under normal loads; may be demand responsive in slack periods. Switching is responsive to the identity of each vehicle.	Unlimited route variations. Nonrepetitive switching. Demand responsive at all times. Switching is responsive to requirements of each vehicle.
Passengers	Board first available vehicle. Stop at all intermediate stations. Share vehicles. Make numerous transfers in networks.	Wait to board the particular vehicle that will stop at the desired location. Stop at some intermediate stations. Share vehicles. Make some transfers in networks.	Board first available vehicle. No stops at intermediate stations. Individuals or small travel parties have private use of vehicle. Make transfers.

and a broad range of performance and operational requirements. AGT systems can have lower capacities, lower performance, and lower capital costs per lane-mile than rail transit, although capital costs per lane-mile would be higher than buses. AGT systems can have operating costs lower than rail transit and much lower than bus transit or taxis. The indirect labor costs of maintenance and of monitoring automated operations vary greatly among existing AGT systems and, for many systems, are high enough to limit applications.

SHUTTLE-LOOP TRANSIT (SLT)

SLT systems are the simplest, best understood, and most widely used of the three classes of AGT systems. Shuttle vehicles are bidirectional and operate between pairs of terminals. Loop vehicles travel around closed loops and may be either unidirectional or bidirectional. All such AGT systems are called shuttle-loop transit (SLT). They are also called *automated people movers* (APM), *people movers* (PM), *downtown people movers* (DPM), and intermediate-capacity rapid transit (ICRT). For a discussion of intermediate-capacity systems using standard-gauge railway track guideways, see Chap. 5. Diagrams representing alternative shuttle and loop layouts appear in Figs. 24-1 and 24-2.

Designers of SLT systems can choose characteristics to provide a great range of capacities, speeds, and frequencies of service. The *theoretical capacity* of a transit lane is based on the assumption that each vehicle is fully loaded for every trip. The capacity actually attainable in practice is significantly lower. *Route capacity* in passengers per hour per direction (p/h/d) varies with the passenger loads of individual vehicles, the number of vehicles in trains, the number of round trips per hour, and the number of parallel paths on a route. The number of round trips per hour varies with the length of the shuttle line, the average travel speed, and the average dwell time at the stations. Vehicle cruise speed is also subject to wide variation. *Average speed* is lower than cruise speed, depending on acceleration and deceleration rates, reduction of speeds at curves, and distances between stations. Frequency of service and lane capacity vary with the length of shuttles.

A single shuttle guideway [see diagram (a) of Fig. 24-1] carries one vehicle or train traveling back and forth between two terminals. It provides service to the terminal stations and to intermediate stations if desired. Addition of a bypass [diagram (b)] allows two vehicles or trains to operate simultaneously, thereby increasing capacity 100% and reducing waiting time 50%. The use of dual-shuttle guideways [diagram (c)] has the same result. A dual shuttle with switches at the terminals [diagram (d)] allows vehicles to change guideways for return trips (also called a *pinched loop*).

A single loop with parallel guideways [diagram (e)] provides two-way service among two or more stations. A single loop with an open guideway pattern [diagram (f)] can provide one-way service through an area and is often used in recreation parks. Open loops require those travelers making round trips to follow circuitous paths and usually require extra travel time. Dual loops with parallel guideways [diagram (g)] provide two-way service, can have greater capacity, avoid the need for circuitous travel,

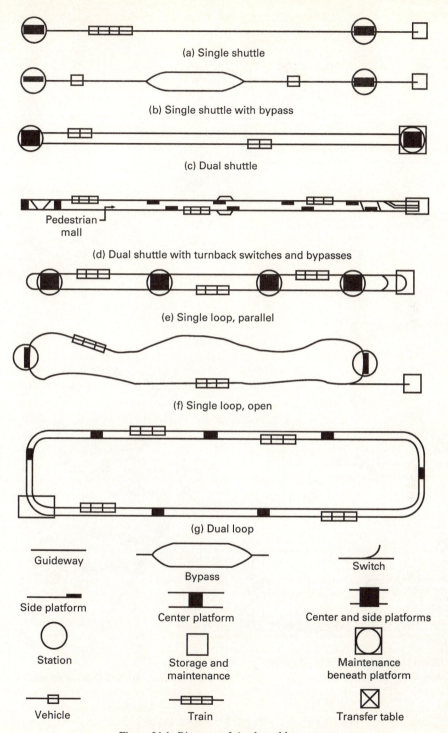

Figure 24-1 *Diagrams of shuttle and loop systems.*

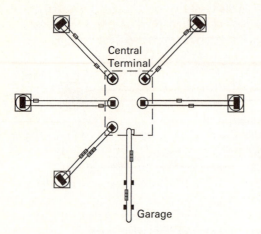

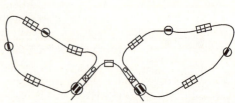

(a) Tampa Airport, dual shuttles and loop

(b) Seattle - Tacoma Airport, single shuttle and single loops, open

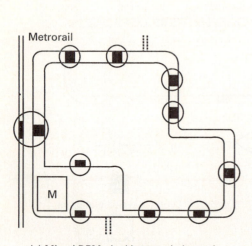

(c) Miami DPM: dual loop and planned dual-shuttle extensions

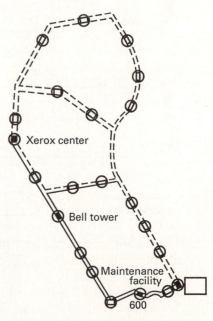

(d) Las Colinas, multiple loops

Figure 24-2 *SLT networks.* (See legend on Fig. 24-1.)

and provide useful service when one loop is shut down. Loop guideways and dual-shuttle guideways with turn-back switches can carry three or more vehicles or trains up to line capacity and can provide high capacity and frequent service on long routes.

The average time passengers must wait to board a vehicle will usually be one-half of the interval between departures. (Average waits of more than 35 s for elevator service are considered objectionable in office buildings, hotels, and the like, and may be regarded as a goal for AGT services.)[12] Consequently, single shuttles are attractive only for relatively short links.

Effective speed depends on the average waiting time as well as travel time. If a shuttle makes one round trip every 3 min, average waiting time is 90 s. If average speed is 10 mi/h (16 km/h), travel time for a 1000-ft trip (305 m) is about 68 s. Total trip time is 158 s and effective speed is 4.3 mi/h. Waiting time can be reduced 50% by employing a bypass and two vehicles. The effective speed would then be 6.0 mi/h. These effective speeds are greater than normal walking speed and would be attractive in many circumstances. Higher effective speeds are usually desirable, however, and are readily attainable.

Examples of SLT Systems

Single SLT systems can serve small areas, but networks made of independent, interfacing modules and transfer stations will be needed to serve large areas or entire cities. By 1990, about a dozen SLT systems provided urban public transportation service (not counting installations in special settings such as airports, recreation parks, shopping centers, and medical facilities). Networks were beginning to be used, and experience had clearly demonstrated the technical feasibility, safety, and reliability of SLT systems, and their suitability for use in networks was not in doubt. Examples of systems and technologies illustrate significant points.

Pearlridge

One of the earliest and simplest single-shuttle systems began operations in 1977 at a shopping complex at Pearlridge, Honolulu, Hawaii (Fig. 24-3). The original supplier, Rohr Industries, is no longer active in the AGT business, but Westinghouse Electric Corporation has acquired the product and replaced the original train with a four-car train of updated design called the C-10. Similar systems have been supplied by Transportation Group, Inc., successor to Universal Mobility, Inc., and by Von Roll Transport Systems, Inc.

SLT systems of this general type are relatively inexpensive and are widely used in recreation parks. Guideways are often fabricated steel beams having small cross sections (for example, 30 in × 30 in or 76 cm × 76 cm). Running surfaces for main vehicle wheels are on top and for guide are wheels on the sides. Secondary suspensions are not provided and are not needed for speeds less than about 15 mi/h (24 km/h). Propulsion is by electric motors. Vehicles are bidirectional.

The Pearlridge shuttle includes a single four-car train, two terminal stations, an elevated guideway about 1000 ft long, and a guideway extension for vehicle storage and maintenance. There are no switches. Each train carries up to 48 passengers, 24 seated and 24 standing. Speed is about 10 mi/h. The trains make about 15 round trips per hour. Average waiting time is about 2 min; theoretical capacity is about 720 p/h/d.

This pioneer installation demonstrated that a simple SLT system can provide capacity equal to that of a high-capacity urban bus route (that is, a route using 40-ft vehicles on 5-min schedule intervals or 12 buses/h).

Figure 24-3 *Rohr Monotrain. (courtesy of LEA TRANSIT COMPENDIUM)*

Tampa Airport

The earliest application of SLT systems to form a network was made at the Tampa, Florida, airport in 1971 by Westinghouse Electric Corporation. It embodied innovations of great value for urban applications. The network was formed by independent shuttles that interface at a transfer station. Passengers transfer on foot from one route to another at the interface, but vehicles cannot move from one route to another. Such networks are said to be *uncoupled* (Fig. 24-2a).

The terminal complex originally included a single multistory "land-side" central terminal with highway access and parking and four "air-side" satellite terminals. A fifth satellite terminal and a separate parking garage were added in 1987 and 1991. The land-side terminal (the common station) and each air-side terminal are linked by a dual elevated shuttle (about 1000 ft long), which also includes a median pedestrian walkway for emergency use. In 1990 the shuttle system included almost 1 mi of dual-shuttle guideway and 12 vehicles. The land-side terminal and parking garage are linked by a pinched loop system, using technology similar to Pearlridge, supplied by The Transportation Group, Inc. (TGI), a subsidiary of Bombardier Corp. All originating and terminating air passengers ride one shuttle; some also ride the loop to or from the garage. Passengers changing planes at Tampa usually use two shuttles.

Plans allow for future construction of a sixth air-side terminal, additional parking garages, and a complete duplicate terminal complex. All future facilities will be served by an enlarged SLT network which, ultimately, may include as many as 15 shuttles and loops.

A major objective of the designers of the terminal was to limit total walking distance to about 700 ft or about 2.7 min between ground transportation and aircraft doors. Specifications for the airport called for each route to have a capacity of 840 passengers/10 min/direction to meet surge demands when large planes unload, or about 5000 p/h/d. Vehicles designed to meet these specifications carry up to 100 standing passengers normally. The vehicles have no seats. The vehicle used in the most recent expansion is the C-100. Vehicles accelerate or decelerate during almost all of each trip. Maximum speed is about 35 mi/h (56 km/h). Each vehicle makes 25 round trips/h and has a capacity of up to 2500 p/h/d with normal loading, and two shuttles have a total theoretical capacity of 5000 p/h/d. The fifth shuttle route employs two-vehicle trains and has a theoretical capacity of 10,000 p/h/d. The average time needed for a passenger to make a 1000-ft trip is 75 s, an effective speed of about 9 mi/h.

Shuttle vehicles are maintained in shops located below the guideways and station platforms. There are no switches. A central control facility is located in the communication center of the air terminal and is monitored, as an extra duty, by communication workers rather than by full-time control staff. Vehicle movements are scheduled during most of the day, but service can be provided on demand (in response to a push button) during slack periods.

The airport terminal and shuttle network are an outstanding success. The Tampa airport network carried about 200 million passengers during the first two decades of operation. It is highly reliable and provides service on each route almost constantly, 99.9% of the time. The stoppage of one vehicle does not impede the vehicle on the parallel path, and passengers can usually board the second vehicle with less than a 2-min delay. In the rare case when both vehicles on a route are out of service, travelers may simply leave the platform or the stopped car, which is always possible, and finish the trip on the walkway. The walk requires less than 4 min.

Seattle–Tacoma Airport

The Seattle-Tacoma (Sea-Tac) airport network began service in mid-1973. It employs equipment similar to that of the Tampa network and has also achieved a high degree of success. The network has three underground routes: one single shuttle about 1000 ft long and two single loops about 4000 ft long (Fig. 24-2b). Passengers are always able to utilize a walkway to evacuate stalled vehicles and walk to emergency exits. The shuttle contains two stations. Each of the two loops shares a platform with the shuttle. Passengers transfer on foot at the interfacing stations. The system employs 24 vehicles and has capacities of about 14,400 p/h/d on each loop and 1800 p/h/d on the shuttle.

Centralized maintenance and storage facilities are located between the shuttle and the loops. Transfer tables, rather than switches, are used to move out-of-service vehicles between guideways. Transfer tables are sections of guideway that can be moved laterally from one guideway to another while carrying a vehicle. They are slow but simple, relatively inexpensive, and require less space than switches.

Duke University

A system installed at Duke University Medical Center, Durham, North Carolina, by Otis Elevator Co. began service in 1980. Dual guideways, about 1200 ft long, link two large medical facilities and then merge in a single guideway extension, about 560 ft long, to a parking garage. Vehicles carry 4 passengers seated and 18 standing and also carry cargo. Air cushions, rather than wheels, provide vehicle suspension. Linear induction motors (LIMs), rather than conventional rotary motors, provide propulsion and service brakes. The use of LIMs and air cushions greatly simplifies the mechanical design of the vehicle. Vehicles are guided by pneumatic tires and guide surfaces (curbs) at the sides of the guideway.

Air cushions make it possible to move vehicles laterally, a capability that may be exploited in three ways. At stations, vehicles may be moved between the main guideway and an off-line passenger loading and unloading dock. At the end of the dual shuttle guideway, vehicles may be transferred between guideways for return trips. At cargo facilities, vehicles may be moved between the main guideway and an elevator, which operates to a loading and unloading position on another floor of the building. These capabilities could be used in urban applications to replace elevated station platforms with smaller, simpler, and less costly facilities at sidewalk level.

Harbor Island

A single shuttle with bypass, installed at Harbor Island, Tampa, Florida, by Otis Elevator Co. in 1985, links a retail complex in a multipurpose land development on an island and a multistory parking garage at the edge of the central business district (CBD) of the city (Fig. 24-1b). The system was installed and is operated by a private development company; however, ownership will pass to a public transit authority after 15 years. A fare is charged.

The route is elevated and is about 2200 ft long. A bypass at the midpoint of the line allows two shuttle vehicles or trains to share a single guideway on about 90% of the route and, thereby, avoids a large fraction of the guideway construction costs that would be needed for a dual-shuttle system having the same capacity.

Each vehicle is propelled by a cable and a direct-current drive machine similar to those used in elevators. Vehicles have air cushion suspension and are guided by pneumatic tires and steel curbs at the sides of the guideway.

The vehicles cruise at 25 mi/h (40 km/h). Normal capacity is 100 standing passengers. Two vehicles make about 30 round trips per hour; theoretical capacity is 3000 p/h/d. Waiting and riding times average about 2.5 min per trip or an effective speed of 10 mi/h.

Shuttle/bypass systems that employ cable propulsion and steel wheels have long been available. A system with rubber-wheel suspension is supplied by VSL Corp. It is not known how the use of wheels rather than air cushions affects capital and operating cost, reliability, safety, and other characteristics, although it does not seem disadvantageous if lateral movement of vehicles is not required.

Atlanta Airport

A dual-shuttle system with turn-back switches and bypasses installed at Hartsfield Atlanta International Airport by Westinghouse Electric Corporation began operations in 1980 (see Fig. 24-1d). The system was designed as an integral and essential part of a new terminal complex, approximately 1 mi long and 0.5 mi wide. It serves a land-side terminal and four air-side terminals, with provisions for future extensions to additional air-side terminals. The system occupies a tunnel some 50 ft underground. A pedestrian mall is located between the guideways. The mall and guideways are separated by walls and access to vehicles is through elevator-type doors. Emergency walkways and exits beside the guideways allow evacuation to the mall in an emergency.

Multiple turn-back switches are employed at each end of the line to provide redundant paths and, thereby, to ensure continuity of service in the event of a major switch failure. Bypasses are provided at the midpoints of each shuttle to ensure continuity of service, at reduced capacity and frequency, in the event of a major failure on the other guideway and to allow shutdown of a guideway for maintenance during slack periods.

The C-100 vehicle is used in trains of up to four vehicles. Trains operate on 100-s headways (36 trains/h) and theoretical capacity is 14,400 p/h/d. Vehicles are guided by an I-beam mounted between the two running surfaces and 8 guide wheels (in sets of 4) attached to the vehicle bogies, which would retain the vehicle on the guideway in an accident. This is the first Westinghouse Electric system to use switches in passenger-carrying operations. The switches are complex and costly to install and maintain. It is not clear whether the safety advantage of the retention feature warrants the penalties associated with the guidance and switch subsystems.

Houston Airport

The Houston Intercontinental Airport employs an underground loop guideway between three terminal buildings, a hotel, and a parking area. Three advanced systems have been employed for this service. The first used battery-powered vehicles in trains. The guidance system employed a signal wire buried in the pathway, sensors on the vehicle to generate a steering signal, and power steering. The vehicles and controls were adapted from systems widely used in factories and warehouses. The passenger vehicles, however, were designed to operate at speeds about 6 or 8 times as fast as industrial models. The system proved unsatisfactory, possibly because of insufficient technical development rather than fundamental flaws, and was replaced. Wire-following guidance technology, however, is of considerable interest both for AGT and AMTV systems. The second system used vehicles and controls similar to those employed at Pearlridge. It also was judged to be unsatisfactory and was replaced.

The third and current system, in service since 1981, was developed and supplied by WED Transportation Systems, Inc., a subsidiary of Walt Disney Productions, and is highly innovative. The product has since been acquired by TGI. Vehicles are passive; propulsion and service braking are by LIMs. Reaction plates are mounted on the underside of the vehicles and motor windings, also called stators, are mounted in the guideway at about 10-ft intervals. Sensors in the guideway and central control apparatus determine the locations, speeds, and separations of vehicles. The central controls adjust the power levels of individual stators to ensure that each vehicle maintains proper speeds and separations. Vehicles employ small-diameter solid tires and have no secondary suspension. Guideways are steel rails fabricated of welded steel tube.

The costs of the vehicles and tracks are relatively low, but the advantages tend to be offset by the relatively high costs of stators and sophisticated controls. These cost characteristics are most attractive when many vehicles operate at short headways on heavily traveled routes rather than on low-volume routes.

The system has attractive maintenance characteristics. The cost of maintaining vehicles and guideways is low. The failure of one or a few stators does not stop operations, and failed units are easily replaced during overnight maintenance periods.

The route includes ten station stops—five stations, each serving two-way traffic. The route is 3680 ft (1121 m) long and will be extended to serve future terminal expansions. A maintenance facility at one end of the loop is connected to the passenger route by switches. The system uses 3-car trains, each with a design capacity of 36 passengers, 18 seated and 18 standing. Maximum speed is 15 mi/h. Theoretical capacity is 1440 p/h/d at 90-s headway.

Vancouver

The Vancouver, British Columbia, SkyTrain system, in service since 1986, was installed by UTDC, Inc., a member of the Lavalin Group. The system is also called Advanced Light Rapid Transit (ALRT). This is the first line-haul AGT system in North America, that is, a system large enough to make a major contribution to the urban transportation needs of a city. The length of the initial route, plus an extension, is 15.2 mi (24.5 km). About 75% of the route is on an elevated structure, 3% is on a purpose-built bridge, 15% is at grade, and 7% is underground in a former railway tunnel beneath the CBD. It employs a dual shuttle guideway with turn-back switches. The route, previously served by buses, is a radial line extending from the CBD to an outlying suburb. The system employs 114 vehicles in married pairs and can operate 2-, 4-, or 6-vehicle trains. Vehicles carry 40 seated passengers and up to 112 passengers (at 8 passengers/m^2). Peak-hour capacity is said to be 25,000 p/h/d.

The system includes three significant innovations. First, guidance and suspension are provided by standard-gauge steel rails and flanged steel wheels with steerable trucks, which allow shorter-radius turns than standard trucks without severe friction and noise. Second, vehicle propulsion and service braking are provided by LIMs, with stators mounted on the vehicles and reaction plates mounted between the guideway rails. Third, the automatic control system employs moving blocks, rather than fixed blocks. Claimed advantages are that the use of LIMs eliminates dependence on the low and unpredictable friction between steel wheels and steel rails for acceleration and primary braking and is an improvement over rubber tires on snow and ice, that the combination of LIM propulsion and unpowered wheels provides significant cost savings, and that moving blocks can provide relatively short headways with safety.

Detroit DPM

The Detroit Downtown People Mover (DPM) was installed by UTDC Corp. and began service in 1987. It is one of three UMTA-sponsored DPM systems constructed for urban public transportation service and organized as an integral part of the local transit agency. It uses technology similar to the system in Vancouver. The route is an elevated, single-guideway, open loop 2.9 mi (4.7 km) long and includes 13 stations.

Miami DPM

The Miami DPM (see Fig. 24-4) was the first of the UMTA-sponsored DPMs. It was installed by Westinghouse Electric Corporation and began service in 1986. The C-100 vehicle is employed. Phase 1 is an elevated double-loop guideway 1.9 mi (3.0 km) long located within the CBD and in adjacent land where the CBD is likely to expand. By 1994, phase 2 will provide two extensions of dual guideways to high-density, multiple-use areas at a cost of about $100 million/mi. Total length will then be 4.4 mi. The counterclockwise loop of the original system will be connected to the extensions. Several operating patterns are possible (see Fig. 24-2c).

The Miami DPM and heavy rail system were planned to complement one another and provide an example of a network using both conventional and advanced transit modes (see Chap. 5).

Las Colinas

The Las Colinas Urban Center is a 12,000-acre private real estate development near Dallas, Texas. An SLT network will be installed and operated by the developer and with private funds. Plans call for the eventual construction of 6 mi (9 km) of dual guideway in a network of 4 loops to serve the 130-acre core area. One long loop will operate counterclockwise around the periphery of the core area and 3 short loops will operate within the core area, as shown in Fig. 24-2d.

The initial phase started service in 1989 and includes two shuttle routes and 3 mi of guideway. It was installed by Westinghouse Electric Corporation and employs, for the first time, a 45-passenger (C-45) vehicle. The vehicle is similar to the C-100 model, except for size. A new switch is employed to invert a section of guideway, along a longitudinal axis, to present tangent, turnout, or wye paths.

Japan

Several urban SLT installations have been made in Japan. The first of these are systems at Kobe by Kawasaki and at Osaka by Niigata, which began service in 1981. Both systems serve new towns on artificial islands and provide links from the island to the public transportation systems of the city. The system at Osaka is notable because

Figure 24-4 *Miami Metromover (courtesy of AEG Westinghouse Transportation Systems, Inc.)*

the new town includes an attractive residential area with high-rise buildings and abundant open space from which automobiles are excluded. Owners of the systems expect to pay both operating and capital costs from fare revenue.

France

A line-haul system at Lille, France, by MATRA, began service in 1983. It was initially planned on a relatively modest scale as an elevated dual-guideway shuttle to link a new-town complex with the central city. The system gained broad community and government support and was greatly enlarged. It has 40 mi (64 km) of dual guideway and 45 stations in two main transit routes crossing the entire city.

A large fraction of the route is underground. The system employs unusually narrow cars to reduce the construction costs of underground facilities. The low capacity associated with narrow cars is offset by short headway intervals gained by the use of automatic controls. Thus, advances in control technology were exploited to reduce construction costs.

The vehicle is steered by guide wheels bearing against curb rails beside the guideway. The rails also serve as power conductors. Switching at branch and merge points employs a double-flanged steel wheel mounted on the center line of each truck and a guideway-mounted switch derived from railroad technology. This is a fast operating, mechanically simple switch and requires no extra space.

MATRA systems of this type have been installed in the United States at the Chicago O'Hare airport and in downtown Jacksonville, Florida, and in other cities in France.

Urban Networks

SLT networks could be developed to serve densely developed major activity centers, such as the central business districts of large cities and multipurpose real estate developments. For example, a grid using 40 shuttle links of 1000-ft length could serve an area as large as the Chicago Loop district [about 1 mi^2 (2.6 km^2)]. Trips of three or four links might be typical. Passengers would transfer between vehicles at every node, and effective speed would be about 6.8 mi/h. Travel time for such a trip would be about 6 min. Maximum walks between stations and points in the area would be about 500 ft or less than 2 min.

Installing a fine-mesh network throughout an existing CBD may be impossible because of the difficulties in obtaining rights-of-way and the high costs of construction. On the other hand, installations made in a newly developing suburban activity center during construction would entail relatively low costs and few difficulties and would permit greater densities than are now observed.

It is technically feasible to design fine-mesh SLT networks to serve entire cities. However, it will be difficult to obtain rights-of-way and to finance construction. These difficulties are discussed at greater length under PRT.

GROUP RAPID TRANSIT

GRT systems are characterized by the use of switches or other means of steering to allow vehicles to follow branching and merging paths for two purposes. First, GRT station platforms are off-line (that is, located on sidings off the main guideway) to allow vehicles stopping at the station to stand clear of the main line while other vehicles pass without stopping. Second, GRT systems employ multiple, partly overlapping loops, with each vehicle programmed to follow a particular loop and to stop at certain stations and bypass all others. Passengers must board the correct GRT vehicle to reach a specific destination and will often have to wait while other vehicles stop or pass the station.

GRT systems represent a level of technical sophistication and may provide a quality of service intermediate between SLT and PRT systems. In a full-service transit program, multiple GRT elements and transfer facilities could be used to form networks serving large urban areas. The main advantages of GRT, versus an SLT network, are that GRT riders would need to make fewer en route station stops and fewer transfers. These advantages are offset, to some extent, by the need for extra waiting time to board vehicles and, in some cases, more circuitous routings. Comparisons of the services and costs of GRT versus SLT networks would have to be made for each application.

GRT systems were installed during the early 1970s at West Virginia University, Morgantown, West Virginia, and at the Dallas–Ft. Worth Regional Airport. Both systems represented major technical advances over existing SLT systems. Both were undertaken without adequate preliminary analysis and on tight schedules. Both experienced severe and costly development problems and delays in starting service. In retrospect, it can be argued, in both cases, that an SLT network could have provided superior passenger service for most travelers and could have been developed, installed, and operated with lower risk and at lower cost. No additional GRT installations had been made by 1990.

Morgantown

The Morgantown GRT system was jointly planned by the university and UMTA as a research, development, and demonstration project with the intention that it would continue in revenue service. The system started service in 1975, after major delays for reorganization and redesign. It was installed by a team headed by Boeing Aerospace Company. The system includes 3.3 mi (5.3 km) of double guideway, two terminals and three intermediate stations, 45 cars, and a maintenance and operations center. The intermediate stations have off-line guideway paths and platform positions that allow vehicles to bypass without stopping, to stop and then continue in the same direction, or to stop and turn back in the opposite direction. The turn-back feature can reduce capacity on routes having low demand and thereby increase vehicle productivity and lower operating costs and energy consumption. The stations, however, are costly to construct and occupy a considerable amount of space, which would often be difficult to obtain and costly in an urban application.

The conceptual roots of the system was a dual-mode PRT system called StaRRcar that would have employed automotive-type running gear and steering. The Morgantown system employs similar technology. Articulated mechanical arms and wheels on each side of the vehicle follow either the right or left curb on command. The movements of the arm generate steering signals, and a power steering subsystem guides the vehicle. This method allows short-radius turns and, like the wire-following guidance previously discussed, eliminates the need for mechanical switches in the guideway. Eliminating mechanical switches would allow significant cost savings in a major urban network, since switches would be needed in vast numbers.

The Morgantown system can operate in both scheduled and demand-responsive modes. Vehicles operate only as single units, are unidirectional, and can carry up to 21 passengers, 8 seated and 13 standing (see Fig. 24-5). The maximum vehicle speed is 30 mi/h (48 km/h). Average speed is about 19 mi/h. Waiting time varies from 2 min at peak periods to 5 min in slack periods; the minimum headway is 15 s. The maximum theoretical capacity is about 5000 p/h/d. In practice, the capacity is about 3500 p/h/d. The system operates well and provides a valuable service.

Boeing has withdrawn from the AGT business, and some purpose-built technical hardware is no longer available from original suppliers. The lack of continuing support from suppliers has been burdensome and costly to the owner.

Figure 24-5 *Morgantown vehicle. (courtesy of Boeing Aerospace Company)*

Dallas–Ft. Worth Regional Airport

The Airtrans GRT system at the Dallas–Ft. Worth Regional Airport was installed by Vought Aeronautics and has been in service since January 1974. The system is far more complex and versatile than any other AGT system constructed through the 1980s (see Fig. 24-6). Originally, it contained the following major elements:

- 13 mi (21 km) of one-way guideway.
- 55 station stops: 14 for passengers and visitors, 14 for airline employees, and 27 for mail, baggage, supplies, and solid waste.
- 68 vehicles: 51 for passengers and 17 for material.
- 74 switches.

Routes were designed to allow vehicles to operate in a scheduled mode over 17 distinctly different service loops as follows:

- Five loops for passengers and visitors, including two between remote parking and terminals and three among terminals.
- Two loops for airline employees between remote parking lots and terminals.
- Two loops for mail between terminals and the air mail facility.
- Four loops for interline baggage and mail transfer.
- Four loops for solid waste and supplies.

The baggage service was abandoned because it was not fast enough to make interline transfers of baggage while passengers changed planes. The mail and solid waste services were also abandoned; however, supplies are still transported.

Passenger transportation services of some kind must always be provided for satisfactory operation of the airport. When Airtrans is out of service for more than about 15 min, buses are used. Although seldom needed, buses and drivers (who also serve as station attendants) are kept on standby at considerable capital and operating cost.

Vehicles are bidirectional. Wheels in contact with both curbs guide vehicles except at switches. Switching is accomplished by vehicle-mounted wheels and guideway-mounted, movable guide rails under central control. Vehicles carry up to 40 passengers (16 seated, 24 standing) and can be operated singly or in two-vehicle trains.

Maximum speed is 17 mi/h (27 km/h). Average trip times between certain station pairs may be as high as 20 min, and maximum trip times may be as high as 30 min, depending upon the origin and destination of the trip. Effective speeds for straight-line distances traveled vary greatly but can be extremely low.

All Airtrans routes are one-way loops; consequently, circuitous travel is usually necessary. Trip lengths could have been shortened and travel time reduced by providing two-way traffic on each link, but at considerably greater cost. Later about 1 mi of one-way route was added to provide a shorter loop. Alternatively, an SLT network could have reduced trip lengths and travel times by even greater amounts and would have reduced development risks and costs.

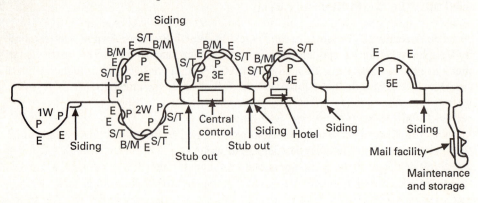

S/T   Supplies and trash station
P   Passenger station
E   Employee station
B/M   Baggage and mail station

Figure 24-6 *Dallas–Fort Worth Airport GRT system.*

Urban GRT Networks

Many different GRT systems could be developed to provide a variety of capacities, physical and performance characteristics, and costs. Networks could be formed with multiple independent GRT elements. Also, SLT and GRT modules could be combined in a network.

PERSONAL RAPID TRANSIT (PRT)

Personal transportation systems serve individuals traveling alone or small groups traveling together by choice in small-capacity vehicles routed directly from origin to destination. Conventional personal transportation systems include private automobiles, taxis, bicycles, motorcycles, and wheelchairs. PRT systems are distinguished by the use of automated vehicles and exclusive guideways to provide prompt, nonstop, transfer-free personal transportation service among all the stations of a network, which might be large enough to serve an entire city or metropolitan area. Automated control of empty vehicle redistribution and storage and of vehicle movements in maintenance and service facilities would facilitate intensive utilization of vehicles and lower capital and operation costs.

The term PRT was first used in 1968 in *Tomorrow's Transportation*[13] and is well suited as the name for AGT systems that would have many of the comfort, convenience, and performance characteristics of private automobiles and taxis. Many conceptual designs have been described. Among these are a design prepared and published by Fichter in 1964. It would use a one-passenger vehicle. Vehicles would operate in short trains to accommodate small travel parties. Maximum speed would be 30 mi/h. Size would be about 32 in wide, 78 in long, and 64 in high (81 cm × 198 cm × 163 cm), with a guideway about 36 in wide and 18 in deep. The characteristics of that system are now called PRT.[14]

Stanford Research Institute described a PRT system concept in 1968[15] (together with several other conceptual designs for advanced systems). Haikalis described a PRT system called Supra-Car in which vehicles and guideway columns would be equipped to lower vehicles to platforms at ground level.[16] Avery described a PRT system based on cable propulsion.[17] Several test vehicles have been developed by others. The Romag system (Rohr Industries, U.S.) used vehicles suspended below the guideway and a sophisticated electromagnetic subsystem for suspension, propulsion, braking, and guidance, thereby achieving a much simpler mechanical design than that of other AGT systems. Aramis (MATRA, France) used an optical subsystem that allowed groups of vehicles to operate with 30-in (0.75-m) spacings. Cabintaxi (MBB, Germany) used a guideway with supported vehicles on the upper surface and suspended vehicles attached below the guideway.

CVS

A PRT prototype system called the Computer Controlled Vehicle System (CVS) was developed in Japan in a program started in 1968.[18] The CVS program was sponsored by the Ministry of International Trade and Industry and had numerous participants, including Tokyo University and eight industrial firms. A 2.9-mi (4.7-km) network of guideways was constructed near Tokyo, and 84 passenger and cargo vehicles were fabricated. Passenger vehicles carried four seated passengers and no standees. Cargo vehicles carried payloads of 660 to 880 lb (300 to 400 kg). Speeds ranged from 24 to 48 mi/h (39 to 77 km/h). The goal was to achieve theoretical capacities of 3600 vehicles/h. Headways of 1 s were achieved in tests with three vehicles at speeds up to 18 mi/h. The CVS test program was the largest and most extensive that has been conducted for PRT systems. The project was abandoned, however, and the extensive test facility was dismantled.

TAXI 2000

In 1989 a technical committee of the Advanced Transit Association (ATRA) found only one active PRT development program.[19] The program was conducted by the TAXI 2000 Corporation, but has a 20-year history under the leadership of Dr. J. Edward Anderson, former Professor of Mechanical Engineering, University of Minnesota. The program is privately funded and proprietary.

The TAXI 2000 vehicle design is illustrated in the ATRA report. The guideway cross section is 36 in (0.9 m) square. It is made of prefabricated steel girders and has a slot in the top surface. The vehicle bogie is enclosed within the guideway and includes a total of 16 wheels for suspension, guidance, and switching. The bogie also carries dual solid-state power conditioning equipment and a pair of LIM stators. The body is entirely above the guideway and is structurally connected to the bogie through a narrow slot in the top of the guideway. This arrangement would exclude snow and ice, which has been a major problem at Morgantown and Dallas–Ft. Worth, where guideways are unsheltered. It would also help to minimize the bulk and visual impact of the vehicles. It appears, however, that the design would complicate the maintenance of the guideway and repair of vehicles that fail while on the guideway.

Dependable estimates of the costs of a TAXI 2000 system (or any other advanced system) cannot be made until detailed technical data are available on the equipment and facilities to be used for a particular system and installation. Sales literature indicates that the system will cost $10 million/lane-mi, but detailed data were not provided.

Vehicle Capacities

Conceptual PRT vehicles vary in passenger capacity, and the optimum size has not been determined. The average number of passengers per loaded vehicle would likely be in a range of 1.2 to 1.5 persons, depending on the purpose of the trip, as in automobiles. Fichter proposed a 1-passenger vehicle. A vehicle of the same width but longer could carry 2 passengers. Stanford Research Institute proposed a 4-passenger vehicle with 2-abreast seating.[20] The TAXI 2000 vehicle is 5 ft 4 in (1.63 m) wide and 4 ft 6 in (1.37 m) high and would carry 3 passengers on a single, forward-facing seat. It should be noted that the choice of vehicle width and passenger capacity will affect the size, visual impact, and cost of elevated structures and the size and capital cost of the vehicle fleet.

Link Capacities

PRT system concepts call for vehicles to follow one another with short time intervals or headways. Experience with automobiles on typical freeway lanes can be used to place this characteristic in perspective. Freeway lanes can carry up to about 1800 automobiles/h under peak load conditions; the average headway is 2 s. At 40 mi/h (53 km/h), the average headway distance is about 117 ft (37 m), and the actual clearance between automobiles is about 100 ft. With average loads of 1.33 persons per automobile, such freeway lanes carry up to 2400 travelers/h. Some PRT conceptual designs call for average headways much lower than 2 s and lane capacities higher than those observed for automobiles in highway lanes.

Short headways have not been achieved on guideway systems in revenue service. Existing rail rapid transit systems seldom operate with headways below 100 s. The two GRT systems were designed to achieve minimum headways of only 15 to 18 s; however, average headways are significantly longer in practice. A major research and development effort would be needed to achieve minimum headways of 2 s or less with safety, reliability, comfort, and acceptable cost if, indeed, such headways are attainable. Only a limited amount of work has been done on these problems, and much of that may have been lost when various program and research projects were terminated.

Important questions remain to be resolved about the headways actually needed in PRT systems. The headways required would vary greatly among links of a PRT network and, on most links, will be much longer than 2 s. Traffic on those routes that appear to require large capacities can be accommodated without extremely short headways by (1) dividing the loads among links of a finer-mesh grid or (2) employing rail transit or larger-capacity AGT systems, rather than PRT, on heavily traveled routes.

Stations

The complexity of PRT stations would vary with the capacity required. Some PRT stations may need the capacity to unload or load up to 1000 vehicles/h, or at average rates of 1 vehicle/3.6 s. The standing time required to unload or load a PRT vehicle is likely to be 10 s or longer. Therefore, a simple siding would not have sufficient capacity. Several ways to increase capacity have been suggested. Among these are parallel platforms, dynamic platforms, and transfer tables and elevators. On-line stations can be used on low-volume links.

Urban PRT Networks

A single, fully coupled PRT network could serve all or a large part of a city or metropolitan area. Lines could be arranged in a gridlike pattern along city streets or in any other pattern to suit particular sites.

Several PRT conceptual designs have proposed fine-mesh networks with spacings of 0.25 mi (0.4 km) between parallel lines and 0.25 mi between stations, which would be most effective if located about midway between nodes (interchanges). In such networks, maximum walking distances for access to stations would be about 0.125 mi or 660 ft (201 m) and would require about 2.5 min at normal walking speed. Most travelers would find these walking distances tolerable or even attractive except in inclement weather and in areas where personal security is of concern. On the other hand, travelers who are physically handicapped or encumbered with small children, groceries, parcels, or luggage would consider the walks burdensome or impossible. Very fine mesh PRT networks are not likely to be economically feasible because the cost of a PRT system would increase as the spacings between lines and stations decrease. It is important to note that the need to walk to and from stations is an important limitation on the usefulness of all fixed-route transit systems. Means to supplement PRT service are discussed under PAS, D-AGT, and AMTV.

The use of 0.5 mi spacings, rather than 0.25 mi spacings, would reduce capital costs and the difficulties of obtaining rights-of-way, but would double walking distances. Without supplemental services of street transit systems for station access, such spacings would effectively deny service to many travelers.

Some PRT concepts envision networks with two-way guideways, two-way stations, and full twelve-way interchanges at nodes. Others would achieve significant reductions in capital costs and visual impacts by using one-way guideways and stations and four-way interchanges (two crossing lanes to accommodate through traffic and two turning lanes). A major disadvantage of one-way networks is that routings of vehicles would be circuitous. An average of four grid intervals (for example, 1 mi in 0.25-mi mesh) would be added to each round trip. The median trip length in many cities is quite short. An average increase of 0.5 mi per one-way trip might be as much as a 20% penalty in travel distance, and would increase operating costs and travel times by significant amounts.

Additional measures that address the need to achieve low capital costs and to minimize the offensive visual impacts of elevated guideways and stations installed in street rights-of-way are:

1. Reduce guideway radii and lengths of guideway structures for left and right turns.
2. Locate stations at grade on space taken from parking strips and sidewalks or on land acquired for the purpose.
3. Use on-line stations on links that have low traffic flows to eliminate off-line guideway structures.
4. Use elevators to transport vehicles between elevated guideways and platforms at ground level to eliminate elevated stations.

San Francisco Example

Although the cost of a PRT network cannot be estimated definitely until detailed designs are prepared, it is likely that a PRT network for a city of moderate physical size would entail multibillion-dollar outlays. To gain some perspective of the problem, a sketch planning exercise was conducted for the city and county of San Francisco. San Francisco has a resident population of about 740,000 in the 1990 census and a total area of nearly 50 mi^2. Some areas would not require PRT service, so a service area of 40 mi^2 was assumed. It was assumed that one-way guideways would be used in a fine-mesh (0.25-mi) grid. Eight miles of guideway and 32 stations would be needed per square mile or a total of 320 mi of guideway and 1280 stations. It was assumed that the capital cost of the entire system would average $10 million/mi. The total capital cost would be $3.2 billion and the average capital cost per resident would be about $4300. Financing a project of this magnitude would establish a new record for the city, but might be acceptable to voters, since it could increase individual mobility, reduce existing congestion, and reduce air pollution.

San Francisco provides more fertile ground for advanced systems than most other U.S. cities. It has high demand density because the population density is high, the fraction of households without automobiles is also high (about one-third), and there are no low-density fringe suburbs. The capital cost of PRT systems per resident in most low-density cities would be much greater than in San Francisco. If the costs of PRT in San Francisco were found acceptable, it would not necessarily mean that networks covering large fractions of other U.S. cities would be acceptable.

Major efforts to achieve low costs would make extensive use of PRT more likely. Even so, in areas of low demand density, it will be necessary to consider networks that use widely spaced routes and stations or the elimination of PRT service entirely in areas of low demand density.

Chicago

The Regional Transportation Authority (RTA), Chicago, Illinois, is the first public transit agency in the United States to make a major commitment to the evaluation of PRT. In April 1990, the authority announced the start of a three-phase program to test and evaluate a PRT system in an urban setting. The first phase will include preliminary engineering studies by two contractor teams, in parallel, each with $1.5 million contracts and 1-year schedules. The second phase will involve one team of suppliers. It will include fabrication of equipment, development of software, construction of a test track of sufficient size to evaluate the system, and conduct of tests. The second phase will be jointly funded by RTA and the suppliers. If the test results of phase 2 are satisfactory, phase 3 will be undertaken. The supplier will fabricate, construct, and operate a prototype PRT system in revenue service at a suburban demonstration site. Phase 3 will be funded by RTA. If PRT is not feasible, RTA will continue to seek improvements in transit service with advanced systems of other kinds.

PUBLIC AUTOMOBILE SERVICE (PAS)

PAS systems would supply small automobiles for rent by the trip to accredited drivers. In a full-service transit program, the principal role of PAS would be to provide service between stands located near transit stations and stands located within easy walking distances of actual origins and destinations of trips. PAS would also provide service for relatively short trips where the use of other transit modes would not be practical. PAS would not be a substitute for the automobile, taxi, or transit for trips longer than perhaps 1 to 2 mi.

Several rent-by-the-trip systems employing ordinary automobiles have been developed and demonstrated in limited applications, such as service for residents in a San Francisco apartment complex. The Witkar system was developed and deployed on a limited scale to provide public transportation service in downtown Amsterdam, the Netherlands. It employed simple, lightweight, battery-powered vehicles, curb-side stands, and access-control and fare-collecting subsystems. These systems were underfunded and, therefore, not able to maintain their operations long enough for evaluation of viability. The following discussion is based on a conceptual system called Public Automobile Service (PAS) developed and described in 1968.[21]

Purpose-built vehicles and equipment would be developed for the specific needs of the service. Vehicles would be battery powered and would be recharged while parked at stands. Speed would be quite low in comparison with automobiles. Maximum speed would be limited to, perhaps, 20 mi/h for fully qualified drivers and 10 mi/h for those with special licenses. Vehicles would be designed for efficient redistribution in trains of empty cars. Purpose-built vehicles have high unit costs when produced in small quantities; however, the cost of lightweight, low-performance PAS vehicles in quantity production could be less than the cost of small conventional automobiles.

Access to PRT vehicles would be limited to licensed and accredited clients. Operating PAS vehicles would present no problems for licensed drivers, and it is likely that many who do not have drivers licenses could be trained to operate PAS vehicles safely on local streets at low speeds and be given special licenses. To satisfy the full-service transit standard, travelers who did not qualify for access to PAS vehicles could be served by dial-a-ride systems or by AMTV systems.

The number of vehicles on hand at each stand would be monitored from a central control facility, and empty vehicles would be redistributed from time to time in anticipation of shifting demands. Movements of empty vehicles could be done in two ways: in trains controlled by a driver or by employing the AMTV techniques discussed later.

PAS vehicles and stands would be vulnerable to vandalism and might become attractive targets, especially to individuals who were denied access to vehicles. This risk is difficult to assess in the absence of experience, but is likely to make it impractical to use PAS vehicles in certain areas.

DUAL-CONTROL AGT SYSTEMS (D-AGT)

In a full-service transit program, dual-controlled AGT systems address the same needs as a combination of an AGT network and a PAS system. D-AGT systems of many kinds can be envisioned. The common characteristics are capabilities to operate vehicles both under automated controls on exclusive guideways and under manual controls on city streets. These concepts are being considered as part of the "smart highway" research. Most D-AGT systems would also require dual-power systems (for example, power from wayside electric conductors while on guideways and from engines, batteries, or fly-wheels while on city streets).[22]

Dual-mode bus systems have been developed and have had limited use in Europe, Japan, and Australia and appear to promise three main advantages over separate AGT and conventional bus systems. First, drivers are not needed to control the vehicle while traveling on the guideway. Yet, this does not necessarily mean that labor costs would be reduced. Ideally, the driver who delivers a bus from the street to a guideway on-ramp would be assigned immediately to another vehicle leaving an off-ramp for travel via street. In fact, it is likely that such close coordination would not be possible. Probably only a small fraction of the labor could actually be utilized, so the labor cost savings may be small. Second, travelers would not have to transfer on foot between street vehicles and guideway vehicles. This would benefit the traveler, but it may be difficult for the system owner to convert the benefit to revenue to pay extra costs. Third, dual-mode buses may operate on close headways to more effectively utilize heavily traveled traffic lanes on bridges, in tunnels, and in similar lanes that are exceptionally valuable and costly to replicate. The ability of dual-mode buses to operate safely at headways shorter than those achieved by driver-controlled buses has not been demonstrated. Also, the length of such links comprise only a minor fraction of bus route networks.

The apparent advantages and disadvantages of dual-mode AGT systems using vehicles with GRT or PRT passenger capacities are similar, in some respects, to those of dual-mode buses. Travelers would be relieved of transfers. There would be little or no savings of driver costs. Areawide use of D-AGT, as an alternative to an AGT network plus conventional buses and other street vehicles, appears to have numerous disadvantages. Foremost among these are additional cost. The essential characteristic of street and AGT vehicles would have to be combined in heavier, more complex, and more costly D-AGT vehicles. On-and-off ramps would have to be added to guideways. Automated test equipment would have to be developed, produced, installed, and maintained, and each vehicle about to enter a guideway would have to be tested to determine that it is functioning properly. Dual-mode systems must use vehicles with automotive-type suspension, propulsion, braking, and steering. Subsystems such as air cushions, magnetic levitation, LIMs, and suspended vehicles would be excluded even though they may offer major advantages when used in AGT systems.

It is also important to note that while on the streets dual-mode PRT would only be usable by accredited drivers and their traveling companions. Other travelers would continue to walk or depend on other modes.

AUTOMATED-MIXED TRAFFIC VEHICLE SYSTEMS (AMTV)

AMTV systems would employ vehicles using a combination of automated, remote, and passenger-activated controls and nonexclusive guideways shared, in varying degrees, with pedestrians and other vehicles. The objective would be to avoid the cost of paid drivers and the cost of guideways and station structures.

In a full-service transit program, AMTV vehicles would provide service to and from transit stations and for other relatively short trips. AMTV systems could address the same needs as PAS and dial-a-ride and might make those systems unnecessary. AMTV systems would also provide low-cost alternatives to AGT systems on low-volume routes. If AGT systems cannot be widely used because of excessive costs, visual impacts, or other reasons, AMTV systems may be the last best hope for full-service transit.

The technology of very low speed AMTV systems is well established. Many systems are used for materials handling in factories, warehouses, office buildings, and hospitals. These vehicles travel about 1 mi/h and are too slow to have much value for passenger service. Higher speeds are presently considered unsafe. The vehicles rely on sensitive bumpers to disconnect power and apply brakes when the vehicle contacts anything in its path. The time available to stop the vehicle before striking the obstacle depends on the reach of the sensitive bumper and the cruise speed of the vehicle. Techniques are needed to achieve higher speeds with safety. Among these are sensors and other devices to give vehicles greater warning of possible collisions and means to limit random access to the guideways.

Several low-speed AMTV prototypes have been developed for passenger service, but none has reached revenue service.[23] In 1974-1976, General Motors Corporation developed and demonstrated an AMTV vehicle operating among pedestrians in a shopping mall at about one-third walking speed. In 1974, Otis Elevator Company developed a similar prototype and conducted tests in an airport terminal. In the mid-1970s, Jet Propulsion Laboratories developed and installed a prototype AMTV system within its laboratory grounds. The vehicle shared rights-of-way with motor vehicles and pedestrians. It employed both an elongated sensitive bumper and a forward-looking optical sensor. The aim was to detect obstacles soon enough to allow safe stops from a speed of about 7 mi/h (11 km/h), more than double normal walking speed and sufficient to be highly attractive in urban service. However, the detection subsystems were not adequate under some circumstances, and it was necessary to carry a standby operator aboard the vehicle to take control when the automatic equipment failed. None of these systems reached regular passenger service. One major factor was concern over safety and public liability in AMTV systems designed to operate at speeds high enough to make the service attractive.

Eliminating drivers would avoid high labor costs. Operating vehicles on nonexclusive guideways, mostly at grade, and rarely with elevated guideways and stations would avoid most construction costs. Most rights-of-way for AMTV networks would be obtained at low cost from traffic lanes of existing streets and curb-side parking strips, as is often done for bike paths; by sharing rights-of-way with pedestrians on sidewalks, in parks, and in shopping malls and multipurpose activity centers; and by using other expedient rights-of-way. Some new rights-of-way would have to be acquired for AMTV stations and vehicle storage. Most of the aesthetic offenses of AGT guideways and stations would be avoided. Together, these features would reduce the most serious disadvantages of conventional and other advanced systems in a full-service transit program. Consequently, the incentives to develop safe and effective AMTV systems are very great. There are two main challenges for AMTV designers. For safe operations, AMTV need sensors and braking systems that can reliably detect fixed obstacles or possible intercepts with moving objects and bring vehicles to a full stop in time to avoid a collision.

To be attractive, they probably need to achieve *average* speeds of 6 mi/h or more. Sensitive bumpers may be improved to permit safe operation at speeds of about 2 mi/h. An AMTV system will need the capability to operate at several higher speed levels (say 2, 4, 8, and 16 mi/h) and to change speed according to the degree of protection and assurance that can be provided against intrusions of the guideway by cross traffic. The AMTV guideway can be divided into sections, and each section can have a specified normal cruise speed level determined by the degree of protection normally obtained from measures used to limit access to the guideway and to increase warning times. Among these measures are physical barriers at the sides of guideways, sensors on the vehicles, in the vehicle path, and on the wayside to detect obstacles on or near the path, sensors on the wayside to detect movements of pedestrians and vehicles toward the path, pedestrian lanes to limit crossings to certain guideway sections, markers and warning signs at crossing points, pedestrian stop and go signals, control gates for pedestrians and vehicles at crossings, and coordinated automobile and AMTV traffic signals at street crossings. When a possible collision is detected, a vehicle would stop until the risk of collision ends or reduce speed to 2 mi/h and rely on sensitive bumpers. When obstacles are not sensed, vehicles would travel through the section at the designated cruise speed. A considerable effort will be needed to develop, test, and evaluate such techniques.

The technical problems of developing AMTV systems are challenging, but are probably no more severe than for PRT or other fine-mesh AGT networks. The nontechnical problem to be solved before AMTV systems are operational and acceptable in urban settings are more complex and present greater risks. It will be necessary to take (or share) rights-of-way for AMTV routes and stands from other uses; to devise protective measures to limit, to some degree, freedom of movement by pedestrians and other vehicles; to establish and enforce new traffic rules designed to accommodate and protect AMTVs from collisions with automobiles; to educate the public regarding the operation, services, hazards, and limitations of AMTVs; to develop effective and economical ways to handle private and public liability responsibilities; and to develop systems and procedures for vehicle management. A method of fare collection will have to be conceived and developed, if possible. Otherwise, the possibility of providing AMTV service free will have to be considered.

It will be desirable to introduce AMTV systems in special settings providing favorable conditions, such as university campuses, retirement communities, industrial parks, multipurpose commercial facilities, and resorts, before attempting their use in urban transit service.

ACCELERATING MOVING WAYS (AMW)

Accelerating moving ways transport passengers on foot or in small captive vehicles. In a full-service transit program, AMWs would be used in densely populated activity centers and would encourage the preservation and development of such areas.

Each AMW element has three speed stages: (1) accelerate from a low boarding speed to cruise speed (for example, one-third walking speed to 5 times walking speed), (2) maintain cruise speed, and (3) decelerate to the initial low speed. In a full-service transit program, accelerating moving ways would be used in densely populated activity centers, such as central business districts and airports, and would be especially attractive in major activity centers because they have large capacities but require small amounts of space.

The SK system by Soulé, S.A., France, is an example of a vehicle AMW. It employs 12-passenger vehicles (6 seated and 6 standing) on a parallel-loop guideway about 13 ft (4 m) wide. Vehicles are drawn by a continuous cable loop at a cruise speed of 12.4 mi/h (20 km/h). Vehicles do not stop at station platforms, but decelerate to a low speed to allow passengers to unload and load. Peak capacity is said to be 3000 p/h/d, which implies 250 v/h/d and about 14-s headways.

Conventional pedestrian conveyors and handrails operate at a constant speed of about 1.5 mi/h or one-half walking speed. Travelers may walk on the conveyor surface to achieve speeds of 4.5 mi/h, a significant improvement. Conventional conveyors are especially useful to travelers encumbered with luggage, parcels, and small children; however, limited speed and high cost deny them a major role in urban public transportation. AMWs with speeds of, say, 7.5 mi/h (two and a half times walking speed) would give more attractive service.

A prototype AMW system without handrails was developed by Applied Physics Laboratory, Johns Hopkins University. Passengers step from a station platform to a conveyor surface moving at one-third walking speed. The surface elongates as it advances until it reaches a speed several times the boarding speed. Near the end of the conveyor the surface contracts and decelerates to the original low speed, and passengers step off the conveyor to a stationary platform.

Prototype acceleration pedestrian conveyors were also developed in Switzerland by Battelle Memorial Institute and by Pierre Petan of the Paris Public Transit Authority (RATP). Prototype versions of these systems have been fabricated, but no AMW system is on the market or in regular passenger service. Rights-of-way for AMWs can be easily provided in new activity centers, but may be quite difficult to obtain in established ones.

FAST TRANSIT LINK SYSTEMS (FTL)

Fast transit link (FTL) systems would provide service at cruise speeds much greater than those of automobiles, buses, and trains, perhaps in the range of 150 to 300 mi/h (240 to 480 km/h). An example was UMTA's Urban Tracked Air Cushion Vehicle (UTACV) system. The vehicle and a short track were developed to the prototype stage by Rohr Industries in the early 1970s, but a full test track was not constructed. The vehicle used air cushions for suspension and guidance and LIMs for propulsion and normal braking. Top speed would have been about 150 mi/h (240 km/h). It would have operated on a elevated guideway with on-line stations. The prototype vehicle would have carried an operator, but revenue vehicles could have been fully automated. The program ended after the LIM and part of the reaction rail were damaged by accidental overheating. In a more fundamental sense, the program was abandoned as UMTA gave up its role as a sponsor of advanced system developments of all types. A similar system was developed in France, but was not placed in revenue service. Systems developed in Germany and Japan for intercity passenger service would exploit magnetic suspension and propulsion systems and are being considered in several applications.

Opportunities to utilize urban FTL systems would only be found in a few areas under certain narrow conditions. Especially long routes are needed (50 to 100 miles). Acceleration and deceleration require considerable travel distances; therefore, long intervals between stations are needed to realize significant time savings from the high cruise speeds. The radii of curves must be great to avoid speed reductions. Large passenger loads are needed to justify the capital costs of rights-of-way, facilities, and equipment. These conditions may be satisfied on a few urban routes, such as links to distant airports, but, in the foreseeable future, the need for FTL routes for urban service is very small. Systems developed for high-speed intercity transit systems could be used in those cases.

CONDITIONS FOR SUCCESSFUL INNOVATIONS

If it is determined, as a matter of public policy, that a proper objective of society is to provide full-service transit, certain basic conditions need to be met. Conventional transit modes will not necessarily be displaced, but complementary sets of advanced systems based on existing and readily attainable technologies will have to be developed and deployed. The development of an advanced system should not be undertaken merely because technology is available. The usefulness of advanced systems will often depend on nontechnical conditions that should either exist or appear attainable before large development and planning efforts are undertaken. These nontechnical requirements can be overlooked or neglected in the early stages of programs, but will have to be faced eventually.

Before developing an advanced system there is need for evidence that its use will supply services that satisfy genuine needs, that are not available, that are available but are inadequate in quality or quantity, that require excessive costs, or that entail other penalties such as environmental impacts or the excessive use of critical resources. Analysis of the demands for advanced transit services is needed.

To select the most appropriate sets of systems, it will be necessary to compare conventional systems, allowing for possible future improvements, with possible future advanced systems, and to compare various advanced systems with one another. Evaluations and comparisons of alternative systems require the use of several techniques including but not limited to the following. Engineering economy is a method of identifying and comparing alternatives.[24] Life-cycle cost comparisons recognize both capital and operating costs over the life of a system and use equivalence calculations at appropriate interest or discount rates and inflation adjustments to make the amounts of money expended at different future times commensurate (that is, comparable at common dates).[25] Value engineering is an aggressive and disciplined method of designing equipment and systems to provide essential services without waste of resources.[26, 27] Energy economy studies estimate total indirect and direct energy demands over the life-cycle of the system and compare alternatives.[28] Cost-benefit analysis evaluates both the benefits and the costs of proposed public works, recognizing the interests of all affected parties.[29] Simulation analysis uses computer models to describe, compare, and evaluate the operation of systems.

Capable institutions, both private and public, will be needed to plan and manage programs. Private firms will be needed to conduct research, development, testing, and evaluation projects on prototype advanced systems with private funds if there is a reasonable hope of profit or, otherwise, with funds from public sources. Manufacturing firms with long-term commitments to the business will be needed to fabricate and install equipment and to provide technical support, replacement equipment, and equipment for future expansion. Appropriate agencies will be needed to set standards for facilities, equipment, operations, and safety. Consultants and construction firms will be needed to design and construct facilities. Organizations will be needed to operate and maintain the systems. Existing public institutions will need to add staff and develop competence to deal with advanced systems, and many will need broader charters. Some new public institutions will have to be established. The development of public institutions is a complex process and often requires considerable experimentation and time. Business firms, by way of contrast, are highly adaptable and will respond quickly to new challenges when and if a reasonable chance for profit is perceived.

Financing on the order of hundreds of billions of dollars will be needed for the capital costs of major deployments of advanced systems in all urban areas. Conventional transit depends on public funds for all or major fractions of operating and capital costs. By contract, advanced systems designs and applications should aim to limit the need for public funds per unit of service, first, by low-cost designs and, second, by increasing patronage and revenue, in comparison with conventional modes. Still, the total requirement for capital for a full-service transit program will be very great. Innovative programs, however attractive, should not be undertaken until the approximate magnitude of capital and operating costs can be estimated and until there is reason to believe that needed funds can be obtained.

Rights-of-way will have to be obtained. If rights-of-way for elevated or underground facilities are in the public domain, they might be obtained at no cost, with approval of city governments or by special legislation. If rights-of-way in the public domain cannot be used, private land will have to be purchased or taken by court action—a long, costly process. Some rights-of-way on private land might be obtained with relative ease (for example, abandoned rail lines and within new land development projects). Underground structures are very costly, and their construction often disrupts surface activities for months or years; therefore, use of underground rights-of-way should be severely limited. To make elevated facilities more acceptable, considerable effort and expense will be warranted to minimize aesthetic offenses and noise. The problem will be less acute where guideways can be widely separated from buildings, as in the medians of wide streets, and in newly developed areas where rights-of-way can be reserved. Experience with elevated rail lines and early AGT systems suggests that elevated structures are often strongly opposed by citizens, and, consequently, the challenge of obtaining rights-of-way for hundreds of miles of elevated guideway for large networks will be daunting. The difficulties and delays of gaining rights-of-way and the costs of construction should be considered carefully in choosing between systems that require guideways and those that depend mainly on street vehicles, such as taxis, dial-a-ride, public automobile service, and automated mixed-traffic vehicles systems.

The adoption of a full-service transit standard represents a major change in public policy. Approvals will be needed from legislative bodies; federal, state, regional and local agencies responsible for regional transportation planning; environmental protection agencies; and safety and security agencies. Complex compromises and agreements will be needed among neighborhoods, municipalities, counties, regional authorities, states, and the federal government. These are time-consuming activities. Change of plans will cause delays and increase costs and should be minimized.

The complex issue of proprietary versus standard designs for advanced systems must be resolved in a way that protects the interests of buyers and suppliers. Buyers of advanced systems will be reluctant and, perhaps, unable under law to purchase a major system, such as a PRT network, from a sole source. Suppliers will be reluctant and, perhaps, unable to finance the development of a nonproprietary system but may be willing and able to develop proprietary systems and then to license the designs to other firms to produce them.

Proposals for major installations of advanced systems will usually require voter approval in an election or approval by elected representatives. The public will not have an easy way to become familiar with advanced systems until examples are prominently displayed. In the meantime, a public information program will be needed in each urban area to describe the proposed systems and services and to explain the benefits and costs.

All these conditions and others, no doubt, will have to be satisfied before proposals for major installations of advanced systems can be completed successfully. The difficulty of satisfying the conditions will vary among system types and settings for applications. In the near future, priority should be given to application settings and systems with features that offer a reasonable chance of ready acceptance and early success.

CONCLUSION

The inability of conventional modes to provide full-service transit throughout urban areas, the need for innovations to achieve that end, and the main avenues for the development of advanced urban public transportation systems are clear if not widely recognized. Progress on advanced system development has been slow and ill-balanced, and many programs may have been prematurely aborted. The problems of planning, developing, producing, installing, and operating advanced systems have proved to be far more complex than expected.

The benefits that appear to be available through the exploitation of advanced systems have not been accepted by many established transit experts, are poorly understood by many of the institutions that would have to install and operate them, and are unknown to most of the potential beneficiaries. Consequently, there is no powerful constituency or political force pressing for the application of advanced systems. In the United States it has seldom been politically feasible for federal, state, regional, and local agencies to exercise leadership or develop aggressive innovative programs.

Potential suppliers of advanced systems demonstrated an enormous capability to develop and produce systems in the early 1970s, but many became discouraged by the lack of market opportunities and, later, government interest. The number of major firms with active programs in advanced systems declined substantially during the mid-1970s, but slowly increased during the 1980s. Although numerous capable suppliers exist, it is unreasonable to expect industry to show strong interest in advanced systems until attractive markets are an early prospect.

Perhaps the most serious need is for competent and innovative planning of advanced systems at the regional and local levels. For this planning to be effective, there must be active cooperation among the national professional organizations and agencies concerned with urban transportation and related environmental, resource, and land-use problems.

REFERENCES

Some citations are no longer available from their original source. These citations are often available from the National Technical Information Service, U.S. Department of Commerce, 5285 Port Royal Road, Springfield, VA 22161. We have verified the order numbers for many of these citations, and they are found at the end of the citation. Prices are available through NTIS at the address above.

1   U.S. CONGRESS, OFFICE OF TECHNOLOGY ASSESSMENT, *Automated Guideway Transit: An Assessment of PRT and Other New Systems*, including supporting panel reports, prepared for Senate Committee on Appropriations, Transportation Subcommittee (Washington, D.C.: U.S. Government Printing Office, 1975). Now available as PB 224 854. The terminology and acronyms used in Chap. 24 for AGT systems were established by this report. For other systems of classification based on different criteria, see Chap. 4.

2   URBAN MASS TRANSPORTATION ADMINISTRATION, *Urban Mass Transportation Act of 1964 and Related Laws*, as amended through February 5, 1976 (Washington, D.C.: U.S. Government Printing Office, 1976), Section 6(b), p. 16.

3   LEON MONROE COLE, ed., *Tomorrow's Transportation: New Systems for the Urban Future*, prepared by U.S. Department of Housing and Urban Development (Washington, D.C.: U.S. Government Printing Office, 1968).

4   CLARK HENDERSON AND OTHERS, *Future Urban Transportation Systems: Description, Evaluations and Programs, Final Report I*, prepared for HUD (Menlo Park, Calif.: Stanford Research Institute, March 1968).

5   *Transit Pulse*, 8, no. 4 (November/December 1990).

6   *International Transit Compendium, Automated Guideway Transit*, vol. IV, no. 1 (Washington, D.C.: N. D. Lea Transportation Research Corporation, 1983).

7   AMERICAN SOCIETY OF CIVIL ENGINEERS, *Automated People Movers: Engineering and Management in Major Activity Centers*, proceedings of a conference sponsored by ASCE, eds. Edward S. Neumann and Murthy V. A. Bondata (New York: American Society of Civil Engineers, 1985).

8   AMERICAN SOCIETY OF CIVIL ENGINEERS, *Automated People Movers II: New Links for Land Use—Automated People Mover Opportunities for Major Activity Centers*, proceedings of the 2nd international conference, Miami, Fla., March 13-15, 1989, eds. Murthy V. A. Bondata, William J. Sproule, and Edward S. Neumann (New York: American Society of Civil Engineers, 1989).

9   *Transit Pulse*, P.O. Box 249, Fields Corner Station, Boston, MA 02122.

10   TRANSPORTATION SYSTEMS CENTER, *Cost Experience of Automated Guideway Transit Systems, Supplement IV* (Cambridge, Mass.: U.S. Department of Transportation, 1982).

11   CLARK HENDERSON, ROBERT H. CRONIN, AND HAZEL T. ELLIS, *Energy Study of Automated Guideway Transit (AGT) Systems*, prepared for Energy Research and Development Administration (Menlo Park, Calif.: SRI International, February 1978).

12   GEORGE R. STRAKOSCH, *Vertical Transportation: Elevators and Escalators*, 2nd ed. (New York: J. Wiley, 1983).

13   COLE, *Tomorrow's Transportation*.

14   DONN FICHTER, *Individualized Automatic Transit and the City* (Providence, R.I.: published privately, 1964).

15   HENDERSON, *Future Urban Transportation Systems*.

16   GEORGE HAIKALIS, *Supra-Car*, in *Urban Mass Transportation Planning*, Highway Research Record 251 (Washington, D.C.: Highway Research Board, 1968), pp. 63-68.

17   WILLIAM H. AVERY, "The Potential Role of Mechanically Linked Systems in Urban Transportation," *Personal Rapid Transit*, (Minneapolis, Minn.: Institute of Technology, University of Minnesota, 1972).

18   *CVS Technical Report* (Tokyo: Japan Society for the Promotion of Machine Industry, 1977).

19   ADVANCED TRANSIT ASSOCIATION, INC., TECHNICAL COMMITTEE ON PERSONAL RAPID TRANSIT,

"Personal Rapid Transit (PRT), Another Option for Urban Transit?, in *Journal of Advanced Transportation*, 22, no. 3 (1988).

20   AVERY, "The Potential Role."

21   HENDERSON, *Future Urban Transportation Systems*.

22   TRANSPORTATION RESEARCH BOARD, *Dual-Mode Transportation*, Special Report 170 (Washington, D.C.: Transportation Research Board, 1976).

23   THE MITRE CORPORATION AND SRI INTERNATIONAL, *Automated Mixed Traffic Transit (AMTT) Market Analysis*, prepared for UMTA (Washington D.C.: Urban Mass Transportation Administration, August 1980). Now available through NTIS.

24   EUGENE L. GRANT AND W. GRANT IRESON, *Principles of Engineering Economy*, 5th ed. (New York: Ronald Press Co., 1970).

25   ALPHONSE J. DELL'ISOLA AND STEVEN J. KIRK, *Life-Cycle Costing for Design Professionals* (New York: McGraw-Hill Book Co., 1981).

26   LAWRENCE D. MILES, *Techniques of Value Analysis and Engineering*, 2nd ed. (New York: McGraw-Hill Book Co., 1972).

27   T. J. McGEAN AND OTHERS, *Value Engineering Methods and Case Studies for the OCTD Guideway Transit System*, prepared for Orange County Transit District (Washington, D.C.: Lea, Elliott, McGean & Co., March 1984).

28   CLARK HENDERSON AND HAZEL T. ELLIS, *Energy Economy Study Methods and Transit Cases*, Final Report, prepared for U.S. Department of Energy (Menlo Park, Calif.: SRI International, July 1981).

29   *Evaluation of Costs and/or Benefits of Programs and Projects*, Circular no. A-94 (Washington, D.C.: U.S. Office of Management and Budget, 1972).

EXERCISES

24-1   What are the limitations on more extensive use of rail and bus transit? What characteristics of advanced systems promise to overcome these limitations?

24-2   What are the advantages promised by AMTV systems? What problems need to be solved to make AMTV systems safe and effective?

24-3   Why will fast transit links have limited roles in urban transportation?

24-4   What are the service characteristics of PRT systems? Why are supplemental street systems required?

24-5   What are the major technical and financial problems in implementing fine-mesh AGT systems in large urban areas?

24-6   What are the major institutional and environmental problems in implementing fine-mesh AGT systems in large urban areas?

24-7   Outline the conditions for successful implementation of a full-service transit system in your area or a nearby urban area.

24-8   As a group project, show how advanced systems could be used to provide full service on your campus and in the surrounding neighborhoods. Consider existing and advanced systems. Identify routes and stations. Describe services.

Chapter 25

A LOOK AHEAD IN PUBLIC TRANSPORTATION

WILFRED OWEN

When the twentieth century comes to a close, historians will be writing end-of-the-century reports on the changes in transportation that took place during the hundred momentous years just passed. Compared to the automotive revolution and the age of flight, the ups and downs of urban transit are not likely to get top billing. Yet the 1990s promise a turnaround in the fortunes of public transportation that will play a major role in upgrading the livability of city and suburb, in bringing relief to the long-suffering commuter, and in releasing the millions of carless trapped in a society that builds on the assumption that everyone drives.

There are many reasons to anticipate more patronage for urban transit in the 1990s and beyond. They include demographic changes, concerns over energy and the environment, mounting traffic congestion, innovations in technology, better management of public transport, more emphasis on multimodal systems, and new approaches to urban design and regional development.

CHANGING PATTERNS OF TRAVEL

Consumers in the late 1980s were spending about 13 cents out of every dollar for transportation. It appears that passenger travel outlays may not rise much above 13% of household expenditures in the future due to the cost of other consumer needs such as housing, clothing, and food. If that should be the case, the traveling public may decide to rearrange its transportation budget in order to accommodate an almost certain increase in the desire for long-distance rather than local travel. People will want to travel to other countries and to take more vacation trips. Intercity air travel may also be favorably affected by an increase in leisure-time activities and tourism. This may put the squeeze on spending for local transportation since there are other alternatives such as moving closer to the job, doing more work at home, or occupying an office closer to home, such as a neighborhood work station or a branch office of the company. Reducing expenditures for local travel might also be made by giving up a second car and riding the bus.

More patronage for local public transportation is also suggested by demographic trends. The rising proportion of people over 65 may be a factor favoring public transit and making driving less attractive. In addition, minorities will constitute some 55% of new entries into the work force. Historically, new minority groups have had a lower than average income as they become assimilated into the work force, and they may desire to save on local transportation by avoiding car ownership altogether, especially if home and work are both in the center city.

It is also possible that local public transit patronage will be increased by new technology. Magnetic levitation and automated rapid transit are possibilities, but their effect may be more on longer-distance commuting and in the category of intercity rather than local urban transport. The dividing line between what is local and what is intercity is already blurred and will become more so with the expanding radius of the multicentered regional city.

The squeeze on household budgets may be paralleled by shortages of public funds for both highways and transit. At the federal level, budget balancing and urgent needs in nontransportation sectors may combine to impose stricter limits on what can be afforded. About 75% of the federal budget is spoken for by three items: defense, payments to senior citizens, and interest on the debt. Competition for the remaining funds is intensifying with the rising demand for housing, education, bailouts, the war on drugs, and environmental programs. If general tax increases continue to be minimal, reduced military spending may help to finance more domestic programs, but a share in any "peace dividend" will not be easy to come by.

Public transit will hurt the most from a decline in federal support as state and local governments are forced to assume the total burden of transit operating deficits. In many communities, the importance of federal operating subsidies had already diminished during the late 1980s. By 1988, according to the American Public Transit Association, only 5% of U.S. transit operating expenditures were covered by federal grants, while state aid was 17% of the total and localities accounted for 25%. The remaining 33% was revenue from fares. Yet in some cities the amount of federal assistance comprised 20 to 30% of total operating funds, and loss of that support would pose a serious problem.

Additional highway funding from the national government is more likely, in part because the federal fuel tax dedicated to building roads is more properly viewed as a price paid for a service and should not be included in the public's opposition to higher taxes. In addition, private capital can be supplied for highway projects by levying tolls and issuing revenue bonds, an alternative made more attractive by electronic billing rather than cash payments at a toll barrier. Private funding may also be possible for the extension of paratransit services supplied by taxi companies and other private entrepreneurs.

MORE ACCURATE PRICING

The bargain prices paid by motorists for the use of high-cost urban roadways has long been a factor in the choice of the automobile over transit. User charges levied by state and federal governments, averaging about 25 cents/gal, are paid by all motorists without regard to where or when their driving takes place. Yet the 1 or 2 cents/mi that such taxes imply are generally far from enough to cover the construction, maintenance, and reconstruction costs associated with multilane expressways in urban areas, to which must be added the social costs of air pollution, accidents, traffic congestion, and the disruption of neighborhoods.

Higher payments need to be charged in order to come closer to covering the costs. Acceptance of much higher charges for needed service is suggested by the fact that an urban toll road in Virginia collects as much as 15 cents/mi, equivalent to a $3.00/gal gasoline tax. Motorists not only have willingly paid the toll but have promptly overloaded the new road, which had to be widened. Full charges thus failed to dampen the demand. On the other hand, when Singapore levied a price of $1.00/day on motorists entering the city without the required minimum of four occupants, this charge was sufficient to cut peak-hour auto travel 70% and shift traffic to buses.

In the United States, making urban driving expensive enough to cover its economic and social costs, if politically acceptable, might not reduce congestion, just as making transit free might not encourage its use. A more positive solution to the conflict between cities and cars would be to impose travel restrictions in high-density areas to prohibit cars from entering specified areas at designated hours. The creation of traffic-free zones, pedestrian streets, and bus-only streets has been favorably received as a means of reducing automobile use in European centers. The idea is replicated in American suburbs, where the shopping mall is the vehicle-free zone and cars are restricted to peripheral parking. But the choice of shopping in the suburbs by public transit is generally impractical, except, for example, when a mall such as Pentagon City is served by underground transit, as in Arlington, Virginia.

SERVING THE CARLESS

The opening of Eastern Europe revealed that freedom for humanity is closely tied to freedom of movement. Millions of Americans saw on television how strongly people objected to being cooped up, unable to travel or make contact with their surroundings and neighbors. The great numbers of East Berliners pouring through the Wall were reminders of how many of our own people are also cooped up for lack of transportation. America's Berlin Wall is the absence of public transit that prevents so many of the carless from finding jobs and benefiting from many of the services available in the city. These conditions have made it increasingly urgent that this wall should come down.

More and better public carrier services may be necessary to serve the growing numbers of persons unable to afford a car or unable to drive. An added factor may be the shortage of workers available to business firms as a result of suburbanization and the separation of affordable housing from available jobs. Inner-city workers dependent on public transportation are already finding the reverse commute to outlying shopping malls and office complexes either too costly or too inconvenient. Their plight will not go unnoticed as the shortage of workers necessitates steps to provide affordable housing in the suburbs or more convenient public transportation. The latter is cheaper and quicker and avoids the more basic problems of racial discrimination in housing.

THE SYSTEM CONCEPT

Much of the urban transportation debate between auto and transit priorities has been a discussion of alternatives. But for many commuters the problem is not choosing one or the other but making it possible to combine the two for best results. In a dispersed urban region, the most efficient means of travel between suburb and city is often a drive to public transportation and completion of the trip by rail or other transit facilities. Intermodal transportation, however, requires conveniently located parking at the rail or bus stop, and the absence of such facilities often prevents the intermodal travel that might otherwise take place. (Commuting from suburb to suburb rather than into the city offers less opportunity for intermodal trips.)

The importance of total systems of passenger service is illustrated by commuting between Washington, D.C., and New York. The choice between express rail and air shuttle hinges on what happens at either end of the journey, including parking facilities at the Washington end (at Union Station or National Airport) and taxi or transit service at the New York end. Getting to a 10-o'clock meeting depends not so much on the relative speed of railway and airplane but on the chances of parking, getting a taxi, or using transit.

In the freight business, fast delivery of documents and small parcels by integrated systems of air and truck transport was a multibillion dollar success story in the 1980s. In the 1990s, getting passengers all the way by a combination of public, private, urban, and interurban transportation will be the passenger travel success story of the decade. Symbolic of that achievement will be the joining of Washington's National Airport to Washington's Metrorail system, which until the 1990s left the traveler stranded a hundred yards and four traffic lanes short of the check-in counter. The integration of the two methods of transportation will be achieved by extending the airport terminal building to meet the trains.

Other intermodal alliances will include ample parking and bus connections at rail stations and the integration of bus and rail schedules. Multimodal movement in urban areas will also be aided by the use of communications to activate electronic bulletin boards that tell the passenger what bus is going where, over what route, and when. People deserve the same consideration accorded packages.

Integrated intermodal travel in the metropolis also presents jurisdictional problems that call for regional organizations capable of promoting areawide transportation management. At the same time the concept of a physically integrated transportation system suggests the merits of a financially integrated system, with all revenues pooled to create the most workable as well as the most socially and environmentally acceptable system. Motorists would end up helping to finance better public transit, but the overall service benefits for all users, including automobile drivers, might make such a solution worthwhile.

CONSERVING TRANSPORTATION

The future of urban public transportation, as well as that of automobile use, will be affected by growing attention to the demand side of transportation and the influences that can be brought to bear on the factors generating the traffic. To what extent is it possible to accomplish the goals normally achieved through travel by means other than travel?

A possibility is to substitute the transportation of information and of information-processing workers by transmitting information electronically. In earlier times, almost all communication required transportation, either in the form of a written message or through the travel of a messenger. The ability to move information by telephone began the process of separating the two fields. Although the overall effect was to generate much more movement of information and add to our radius of activity, in many cases use of the telephone made it possible to forego a trip. Communications became a potential or actual substitute for transportation.

Developments in fiber optics and computers have added new dimensions to communicating that further the possibilities of taking over some of the functions previously performed by transportation. With an increasing percentage of work functions involving information processing, many tasks can be performed wherever there is a computer terminal and a telephone connection.

Some professionals find it convenient to do part of their work at home or in a nearby office, and many businesses looking for ways to reduce costs are dispersing activities to save on rent and parking and on wage rates that reflect commuting costs. The incentive to substitute communications for travel will be supported as more homes and businesses are connected to global fiber-optic networks, permitting major advances in the use of voice, data, and picture transmission.

Working at home or in work stations close to home reduces the demand for both automobile travel and public transit services, but transit riding may be more vulnerable.

The shorter trips made possible by having offices dispersed in locations closer to residences may favor the automobile, especially if a by-product is more flexible work schedules. Serving flexible travel needs is a special attribute of the private car.

Another means of transportation conservation is to be found in the design of whole communities that include housing and jobs as well as services and that reduce the length and frequency of trip taking for a substantial number of families. Urban development and redevelopment trends are moving in this direction.

URBAN REDEVELOPMENT

The desire for more livable cities can be expected to promote efforts to overcome blighted neighborhoods and to introduce more open space and amenities into uninviting center-city environments. In many obsolete urbanized areas, the rehabilitation of run-down housing and the introduction of green space and play space will depend to a considerable degree on making changes in the street system. Streets often comprise one-third to one-half of the public space available in cities, and some can be vacated or converted to other uses. Traffic that disrupts the quiet and safety of neighborhoods needs to be diverted to major commercial streets, while curbsides in residential areas need to be made off limits to all-day parkers. Many streets could be narrowed to make room for wider sidewalks and for planting strips for grass and trees.

Redevelopment may also suggest the abandonment of some street mileage in order to make possible the creation of inner-city shopping centers and campus-type housing estates only accessible to pedestrians. It may also be feasible to convert some streets to pedestrian ways or to linear parks or neighborhood playgrounds. The street may well turn out to be the key to redesigning urban areas and creating more livable and attractive community environments.

Disruption of the street patterns dedicated to the movement of motor vehicles would require an adjustment in the way people move around in cities. Local use of the automobile would be reduced by supplying more convenient substitute forms of collective circulation. This would call for various types of short-haul people movers, including vans or other paratransit, connecting peripheral off-street parking facilities with worker and shopper destinations.

Many communities are already focusing on the need for mixed use urban areas that afford an opportunity to live and work or shop within short distances covered easily on foot or by van shuttle service. Curb parking is being restricted to vehicles owned by adjacent property owners or their visitors, and the designation of one-way streets and other traffic regulations often suffice to protect housing and residential areas from the unwanted encroachments of traffic. Parallel measures aimed at designating exclusive bus lanes or all-transit streets can help to revitalize the community and make possible a quality of life impossible to realize in high-density areas dominated by the automobile.

In the suburbs the automobile will continue to prevail, aided by demand-responsive bus or van services. But suburbs striving to become total communities in the years ahead could be combining transportation management strategies with free bus services and convenient parking to make public or collective transportation an important adjunct to the use of private cars. Redesign and rearrangement of the suburbs plus growth management policies could also help to delineate rapid transit corridors and make it easier to provide better public transit networks throughout the urban region.

Figure 25-1 *Bangladesh—the need for better public transportation—a global problem. (courtesy of World Bank)*

THE REGIONAL CITY

Predictions of a possible doubling of urban traffic by 2010 measure the importance of finding ways to reverse the trends. In most urban areas there is no room to build more roads and, in any case, new highways intended to bring traffic relief are often overloaded almost as soon as they are opened. Building new rapid transit also has limitations, since it encourages high-density development and generates still higher levels of congestion.

There is plenty of evidence that supplying more capacity may fail to solve the problems of moving in the metropolis. Try driving in rush hours in Los Angeles or commuting by subway or train in Tokyo. But there are moderate-size communities around the globe where public and private transportation succeed in serving the community's needs fairly well. Given the fact that major urban concentrations are getting still bigger, why not begin a process of dividing up the megacity into partially self-sufficient smaller communities to create a series of moderate-size communities instead of one amorphous mass? Transportation and communications could then be used to connect the multiple centers along well-defined travel corridors. What is needed is a partnership of regional developers, city builders, and the transportation and communication industries to help carry out a new growth strategy. Such a strategy would avoid the built-in transportation difficulties of planless urbanization.

The process of dispersal is already under way, but the trend needs to be redirected to create whole communities offering a mix of activities that, at a certain scale, create a more manageable urban environment. A total community context allows a certain percentage of the population to live and work in closer proximity. The noncommunities of the sprawling metropolis have imposed a kind of perpetual motion on residents. Efforts to avoid this are already under way throughout the world, and the role of public transportation has proved to be critical.

SWEDEN

In Sweden five major rail and rapid transit lines reach out from Stockholm into the surrounding region to supply fast, convenient travel to the planned suburban towns ringing the capital. Following the end of World War II, the regional plan for the Stockholm metropolis led to the construction of housing, shopping centers, and community facilities in multiple town centers removed from the crowded city. Good public transportation was part of the design, to assure easy access to locations 10 mi or more from downtown Stockholm. A network of modern highways was also constructed to serve those who opted for private transport, especially to destinations outside the old city.

Suburban towns such as Farsta, Kista, and Solna are among the many mixed-use communities that provide attractive residential areas, town centers for offices and shopping, good pedestrian walkways to nearby housing, and plentiful open space and recreation. Outmigration from the old city has reduced densities and made it possible to redesign and rebuild the historic downtown. Sweden ranks in the top half-dozen countries of the world with respect to per capita income and is one of the most highly motorized countries, with one vehicle for every 2.5 persons. It could thus afford both modern expressway and rapid transit systems. It also had the planning tools needed to combine transportation and urban development in a skillfully executed model of how a transit-friendly metropolitan growth strategy can work. Being able to reserve open space and low-density land uses surrounding the separate suburban towns helped delineate transit routes and assure convenient commuting.

SINGAPORE

Another version of much the same regional strategy was begun in Singapore soon after that small island republic gained its independence in 1959. At the time, one-third of Singapore's population was living in slums and squatter settlements, and its per capita income of some $550 (U.S.) per year posed the question whether the country could pay for rapid transit to reduce the traffic congestion of the old city. The decision was reached to make housing the number one priority and to move people out of the congestion rather than trying to accommodate the congestion. The necessary transportation connections would be provided at first by buses and new roadways.

Figure 25-2 *Singapore—downtown redevelopment. (courtesy of the Government of Singapore)*

Today Singapore, like Stockholm, is surrounded by some 20 large suburban new towns, and reduction of center-city densities has permitted the redevelopment of downtown to the most modern standards. Suburban new towns such as Woodlands, Ang Mo Kio, and Jurong have become important residential and employment centers, equipped with modern apartments, schools, markets, and recreation. In the process of training the unemployed to enter the building trades, income per capita was increased more than twelvefold in two decades, and families were able to use their earnings and to borrow on their social security accounts to buy their own flats. After two decades the increase in national product made it possible to launch a rail rapid transit system to link major parts of the regional city. The leasing of public lands adjacent to the Metro helped to pay for the construction of the new transportation system to achieve a more close-knit regional metropolis.

Both Stockholm and Singapore are models of how the arrangement of a city for greater convenience can reduce travel needs, organize transportation flows, and at the same time provide a superior urban living environment. They are exceptions, however, not only because they have different political systems, but because they are relatively small (2.5 million population) and because they do not have to anticipate any substantial amount of population growth.

JAPAN

More relevant to the problems of large American cities, perhaps, is Japan's experience with public transit and suburban settlements outside Tokyo, Osaka, Kobe, and other urban concentrations. Tama, for example, some 20 mi (32 km) from Tokyo, is a planned suburban community of some 300,000 persons that is served by two private rail lines that make the trip to Tokyo in 35 min. The railways were constructed as an integral part of the new town project. Transportation within the town is mainly by private car and taxi, with excellent pedestrian and bicycle circulation among attractive greenways that connect with schools, shopping areas, and playing fields. Compared to the crowding of conventional Japanese cities and their lack of open space, the new suburban mixed-use towns and their accessibility provide a welcome alternative to old-style urban living. Magnetic levitation for high-speed trains and the completion of a national fiber-optic communication network should accelerate the planned dispersal of the Japanese population.

UNITED STATES

The feasibility of rearranging urban areas in the United States and of making suburban growth more workable has been demonstrated by new cities such as Reston, Virginia, and Columbia, Maryland. These very large undertakings are now being followed by a variety of efforts to redevelop sections of older cities and to create smaller multipurpose suburbs. New York's Roosevelt Island in the East River illustrates what might be accomplished elsewhere. It is a residential development 2 mi long for 5000 people, where living, shopping, and recreation are available in a pedestrian environment. Public transportation plays an important role in this planned community, with its one main street served by a free minibus service connecting the automobile storage area with the rest of the community. Buses and an aerial tramway provide public transit to Brooklyn and Manhattan. This pedestrian community is a reminder that the college campus, with adequate parking on the periphery, provides a useful prototype for the kinds of neighborhoods that could be achieved in central cities.

Another model is New York's Battery Park City, housing some 6000 people along the Hudson River adjacent to the Trade Center. Here again a pedestrian-oriented enclave of housing, shopping, and recreation is located where residents can walk to jobs in lower Manhattan or commute by bus, rail, or ferry to more distant locations. In both these examples, nearby employment opportunities minimize commuting for many residents.

The same type of moderate-size, mixed-use community is being introduced in suburban areas. In Arlington, Virginia, for example, developments at the stations of the Metrorail line balance residential and commercial land uses and include recreational facilities and a variety of services. At the Ballston station, apartments, town houses, and single-family dwellings are located within walking distance of offices and shopping, in an area zoned to permit no more than 50% of the land to be used for commercial purposes. Ballston aims not only to be an attractive community day and night, but also to afford good access to alternative destinations in Washington, D.C., and outlying suburbs. The Washington, D.C., metropolitan area has 15 to 20 large mixed-use developments dependent to a considerable degree on rail transit to bind together a series of separate but related communities.

The future role of public transportation in the regional metropolis appears to be twofold. At the local level, traffic management strategies will favor public conveyances plus a combination of automated people movers, moving beltways for pedestrians, and other aids to walking in vehicle-free pedestrian enclaves and shopping malls. At the regional level, the longer hauls to connect with the many separate centers of the region will be supplied by automated roadways for buses and by guideways for high-speed magnetically levitated vehicles. The latter can be expected to expand the radius of the urban region yet make it feasible for many common services to be shared.

There are obviously opposite factors that will continue to influence the future of urban transportation and public transit. For the majority of Americans, the desirability of having one's own automobile will continue to be a dominant factor, given the necessary shift to nonpolluting energy sources. Electric cars, electronic guides to driving, and other technologies may increase the attractions of private travel. At the same time there will be a greater need for public carriers as urban growth, the aging of the population, and other demographic changes combine with congestion, pollution control, and energy conservation to favor substitutes for driving. There will also be a growing sentiment in support of more equitable treatment for low-income families and for those who are carless for many other reasons. The city will also be the main focal point in a global economy of expanding international investment, business travel, and tourism. Competition among cities for a share in global economic activity will compel greater attention to assuring visitors ready access to the community by internationally acceptable standards of public conveyance. This will include the need to serve widely dispersed metropolitan regions with the high-speed, congestion-free transportation not possible by private car.

CONCLUDING OBSERVATIONS

There are promising alternatives to today's perpetual motion. We are learning that the urban transportation task is not simply to supply more capacity, but to solve the problems of mobility and accessibility that often arise from the nature of cities themselves. This means influencing the factors that generate the demand for travel. Some of our daily chores now requiring transportation might be accomplished without traveling and in ways that are easier and less expensive. Two possibilities on the demand side offer the greatest promise. One is the growing ability to move information to people instead of moving people to information, heralding an era of telecommuting, teleconferencing, telemarketing, and other trip-saving communications. The other is the design and redesign of city and suburb to substitute convenient location of urban activities for the travel that inconvenient land-use arrangements have imposed on urban residents.

With improved communications and more convenient communities, transportation would stand a better chance of operating more effectively. Transit, taxis, and automobiles, viewed as a total transportation resource, could play complementary roles in furthering mobility and enhancing urban environments.

In the dispersed regional city of the future, public transportation will be needed to carry out five essential functions:

1. To guarantee citywide mobility for the growing number of people who are nondrivers by choice or necessity.
2. To supply the exclusive means of travel in high-density areas where private cars are prohibited.
3. To complement the services rendered by the automobile on trips that require both methods.
4. To provide local extensions of the intercity and global public transportation networks.
5. To help create a more satisfying, manageable, and pollution-free urban environment that maximizes the ability to move while minimizing the necessity for movement.

FURTHER READING

AMERICAN PUBLIC TRANSIT ASSOCIATION, *APTA Rail Transit Report*. Washington, D.C.: American Public Transit Association, 1989.

———, *Building Better Communities: Coordinating Land Use and Transit Planning*. Washington, D.C.: American Public Transit Association, September 1989.

———, *Transit Fact Book* (1989 ed.). Washington, D.C.: American Public Transit Association, 1989.

———, TRANSIT 2000 TASK FORCE, *Managing Mobility: A New Generation of National Policies for the 21st Century*. Washington, D.C.: American Public Transit Association, November 1989.

————, *Transitways*. Washington, D.C.: American Public Transit Association, October 1987.

ANDERSON, JOYCE M., "Mass Transit and the Poor," *America*, 161, no. 17 (December 2, 1989), 399-402.

BOSSARD, EARL G., "Japan's Notable New Towns," *Planning*, 55, no. 11 (November 1989), 16-19.

DILLON, DAVID, "Las Colinas Revisited: Real Estate Development in Irving, Texas," *Planning*, 55, no. 12 (December 1989), 6-11.

OWEN, WILFRED, "Cities in the Global Network," in *Transportation and World Development*, Chap. 4, pp. 53-84. Baltimore, Md.: The Johns Hopkins University Press, 1987.

————, WITH INAI BRADFELD, *The Accessible City*. Washington, D.C.: The Brookings Institution, 1972.

RUTHERFORD, G. SCOTT, AND JACK LATTEMANN, "Use of Future Scenarios in Long-Range Public Transportation Planning," in *Transit Issues and Recent Advances in Planning and Operations Techniques*, Transportation Research Record 1202, pp. 32-43. Washington, D.C.: Transportation Research Board, 1988.

SCHWAGER, DIANNE S., DANIEL LYSY, AND ELLEN KRETT, "Regional Public Transportation Organizations," in *Transportation Organization and Systems Planning*, Transportation Research Record 1206, pp. 1-9. Washington, D.C.: Transportation Research Board, 1988.

U.S. DEPARTMENT OF COMMERCE, BUREAU OF ECONOMIC ANALYSIS, *Survey of Current Business*, July issues (for annual consumer spending for transportation).

U.S. DEPARTMENT OF TRANSPORTATION, *Moving America, Vol. 1: Building the National Transportation Policy*. Washington, D.C.: U.S. Department of Transportation, July 1989.

EXERCISES

25-1   What are some of the inequities experienced by the carless living in urban areas poorly served by public transportation?

25-2   Who pays for urban transit and urban highways, and what changes in current policies would you suggest?

25-3   How could the transportation sector contribute to upgrading the urban environment?

25-4   What are some of the factors that can be expected to increase the role of public transit in American cities over the next decade?

25-5   Describe the supply side of transportation and some of the elements governing the demand side. How can communications help reduce the need for mobility?

25-6   What transportation technologies and what technologies outside the transportation field may alleviate the problems of moving in urban areas?

25-7   How will the global economy influence the quality and availability of public transportation in American cities?

25-8   What is meant by transportation systems, and what system approaches could make it easier to move around in urban areas?

25-9   Suggest the various elements of an urban transportation strategy that you would recommend to improve the mobility and livability of cities in America.

INDEX